The Roman Eastern Frontier and the Persian Wars (AD 226–)

Schaumburg Township District Library

32 West Library Lane

Schaumburg, Illinois   60194

GAYLORD

The Roman Eastern Frontier and the Persian Wars (AD 226–363)

A Documentary History

Compiled and edited by

Michael H. Dodgeon
and
Samuel N.C. Lieu

London and New York

First published 1991
Paperback edition first published 1994
by Routledge
11 New Fetter Lane, London EC4P 4EE

Simultaneously published in the USA and Canada
by Routledge
29 West 35th Street, New York, NY 10001

© 1991, 1994 Michael H. Dodgeon and Samuel N.C. Lieu

Typeset in 11/12pt Times Autologic by Times Graphics, Singapore
Printed and bound in Great Britain by
Biddles Ltd, Guildford and King's Lynn

British Library Cataloguing in Publication Data
The Roman Eastern Frontier and the Persian Wars
  (AD 226–363): a documentary history.
  1. Roman Empire 284–395
  I. Dodgeon, Michael H.   II. Lieu, Samuel N.C.
  937' .08

Library of Congress Cataloging in Publication Data
The Roman Eastern Frontier and the Persian Wars
  (AD 226–363): a documentary history / compiled and
  edited by Michael H. Dodgeon and Samuel N.C. Lieu.
      p.   cm.
  Bibliography: p.
  Includes indexes.
  1. Rome–Military relations–Iran.   2. Iran–Military relations–
Rome.   3. Rome–History–Empire, 30 BC–476 AD   4. Iran–
History–To 640.   I. Dodgeon, Michael H.   II. Lieu,
Samuel N.C.
  DG271.R56   1991
  937' .08--dc20   90-10376
ISBN 0 415 10317 7 (pbk)

Contents

vi *Contents*

Maps

Notes on the sources

(*Sources which are only quoted once or twice are introduced in the notes.*)

Agathangelos. Name given to the author of an Armenian historical work covering the years 226–330. See below pp. 309–14.

Agathias. Greek historian, lawyer and poet. A native of Myrina in Asia Minor, he was the author of a continuation of the Procopius' history, covering the years 552–68. Ed. R. Keydell, CFHB, 1967.

Ammianus Marcellinus. Latin historian but of Greek origin. A native of Antioch, he saw service on the eastern frontier on the staff of Ursicinus (*Mag. Equ.* 349–59 and *Mag. Ped.* 359–60). The surviving portion of his history which covers the years 353–78 is an essential source of eye-witness information on the later Persian wars of Constantius II and the expedition of Julian. Ed. W. Seyfarth, Berlin, 1968–71.

Artemii Passio. A fictionalized account of the life and martyrdom of Artemius (cf. *PLRE*, I, p. 112), a Christian official who was executed under Julian. The work was composed no earlier than the reign of Justinian. Its authorship is attributed in some manuscripts to a certain John of Rhodes and in others to John of Damascus (*c.* 675–*c.*749). Ed. B. Kotter, *Die Schriften des Johannes von Damaskos*, V, Berlin, 1988, pp. 185–245.

Athanasius. (*c.* 296–373) Bishop of Alexandria and foremost opponent of Arianism. His historical-cum-polemical works (in Greek) yield occasional pieces of valuable information on the eastern frontier, especially on the role of Constantius II. Ed. W. Bright, *St Athanasius's Historical Writings*, Oxford, 1881.

Aurelius Victor, Sextus. Latin historian. A native of Africa, he published (*c.* 361) a brief history of the Roman empire down to his own times. Ed. F. Pichlmayr, revised by R. Gruendel, Berlin, 1970.

Cassius Dio Cocceianus. Greek historian and statesman (*consul suffectus c.* 205 and consul with Severus Alexander in 229). His great history of Rome from the foundation of the city to his own time has only partially survived. The extant sections covering the reign of Severus Alexander are derived from the epitome of Xiphilinus (11th C.). Ed. U. P. Boissevain, Berlin, 1895–1931.

Cedrenus, Georgius. Greek monk (?) and annalist. He compiled a chronicle which begins with the Creation and goes down to the year 1057. Ed. I. Bekker, CSHB, 1828.

Chronichon Paschale. Title given to an anonymous compilation of the early seventh century, covering the period from the Creation to AD 629. Ed. L. Dindorf, CSHB, 1832.

Codex Theodosianus. An official collection of imperial constitutions from AD 312 until 438 when the Code was published by Theodosius II. It is extremely valuable for reconstructing and dating imperial movements because the compilers had preserved the date and place of issue of most of the constitutions. Ed. T. Mommsen, Berlin, 1905.

Ephrem Syrus. Syrian poet and theologian. Born in or near Nisibis, he was compelled to leave his native city because of the treaty of 363 which surrendered it to the Persians. He later settled in Edessa where he distinguished himself both as a Christian poet and ascetic. His *Carmina Nisibena* and *Hymni contra Julianum* both include eye-witness material on the events they describe. Ed. E. Beck, CSCO, 1957 and 1961–3.

Epitome de Caesaribus. Title given to an anonymous epitome in Latin of the history of the Roman Empire from Augustus to Theodosius. The work is sometimes wrongly associated with Aurelius Victor. Ed. F. Pichlmayr, rev. R. Gruendel, Leipzig, 1970.

Evagrius. Greek lawyer and ecclesiastical historian. Native of Epiphaneia in Syria, he wrote an ecclesiastical history at the end of the sixth century covering the period 431–594. The work is noted for its attention to secular matters. Eds J. Bidez and L. Parmentier, London, 1898.

Eunapius. Greek sophist. Born near Sardis in Lydia *c.* 345, he wrote a continuation of the history of Dexippus from the pagan view point covering the period AD 270–404. It was the main source of the historian Zosimus for this period but the work has only survived in fragments. Ed. C. Müller, *FHG* IV, 1885, pp. 11–56. See also Blockley, 1983: 2–126. Eunapius was also the author of a collection of lives of famous sophists of the fourth century which contains some important material on political history. Ed. C. Giangrande, Rome, 1956.

Eusebius. Greek ecclesiastical politician, historian and theologian (*c.* AD 260–340). A native of Palestine; his *Ecclesiastical History* covering the period from the Apostolic Age to the reign of Constantine was the model for later church historians. Ed. E. Schwartz, GCS, 1903–9. His *Life of Constantine* is one of the principal sources on the history of the reign of the first Christian emperor despite its panegyrical tone. Ed. F. Winkelmann, GCS, 1975. Among his works is preserved a number of orations by Constantine. Ed. I. A. Heikel, GCS, 1902.

Eutropius. Latin historian. Probably a native of Bordeaux, he accompanied Julian on his expedition. His epitome of Roman history, published before 380, begins with Romulus and finishes with the reign of Jovian. Ed. C. Santini, Leipzig, 1979.

Eutychius (Sa'id b. al-Bitriq). Christian Arab universal historian. See below pp. 295–6.

Faustus Buzandats'i. Armenian historian. See below pp. 300–9.

Firdawsi (Abu 'l-Kasim). Persian epic poet. See below pp. 297–9.

Festus. Latin historian. He was *magister memoriae* when he published his brief summary (Breviarium) of Roman history *c.* 369–70. The work pays considerable attention, unusual for an epitome, on the eastern campaigns of the emperors down to Jovian. Ed. J. W. Eadie, London, 1967.

Georgius Monachus. Greek monk and author of a widely read world chronicle which runs from Adam to AD 842. Ed. C. de Boor, rev. P. Wirth, Stuttgart, 1978.

Herodian(us). Greek historian. His history from the death of Marcus Aurelius (AD 180) to the accession of Gordian III (AD 238) is one of the most important sources for the history of the third century, especially for the period not covered by the surviving parts of the history of Cassius Dio. Ed. C. R. Whittaker, London, 1969–70.

Jerome (Eusebius Hieronymus). Biblical scholar and theologian (*c.* 342–420). Born near Aquileia, he is best known for his translation of the Christian Bible from Hebrew and Greek into Latin. He also translated (into Latin) and continued Eusebius's 'Chronicle'. The work (published *c.* 380/1) is specially useful for the dating of particular events. Ed. R. Helm, GCS, 1956.

John of Antioch (Iohannes Antiochenus). Greek historian of whom nothing is known. His chronicle covers the period from the Creation to 610. Ed. C. Müller, *FHG* IV, 1885, pp. 535–622.

Jordanes. Latin historian who lived *c.* AD 550. He summarized the Gothic histories of Cassiodorus in his *Getica* to which he added a summary of Roman history (*Romana*), which he seems to have derived from the lost history of Aurelius Memmius Symmachus. Ed. T. Mommsen, *MGH*, 1882.

Julian(us Apostata). Roman emperor (AD 361–3) and Greek man of letters. His panegyrics in honour of his cousin, the emperor Constantius II (AD 324–61), are a valuable source on the Persian Wars of the early part of the latter's reign. Ed. J. Bidez, Paris, 1932.

Lactantius. Latin Christian apologist (*c.* 240–*c.* 320), his polemical treatise *De mortibus persecutorum* (On the Manner in which the Persecutors died) published *c.* 314–15, is one of the main sources on the reigns of Diocletian and his colleagues. Ed. J. Creed, Oxford, 1984.

Libanius. Greek sophist and rhetor of Antioch (314–*c.* 393). One of the most influential pagans of the fourth century; his speeches and letters composed during the reigns of Constantius, Julian and Jovian provide a wealth of information on events in the East and he knew personally a considerable number of those who took part in the campaigns. Ed. R. Förster, Leipzig, 1909–27.

Malalas, Ioannes. Greek advocate of Antioch who published sometime after 574 a world chronicle from the Creation to AD 563. It preserves much that is important as well as trivial on Antioch and the province of Syria. Ed. L. Dindorf, CSHB, 1831. See also Stauffenberg, 1931 (Bks IX–XII only).

Michael the Syrian. (1126–1199) Jacobite Patriarch of Antioch and compiler of an important chronicle in Syriac from the Creation to 1194/5. Ed. J. B. Chabot, Paris, 1899–1910.

(Ps.)Moses Khorenats'i. Name given to the author of a work of great importance on Armenian history. See below pp. 314–27.

Notitia dignitatum. Title given to a catalogue of titles of administrative offices in the two halves of the Roman Empire. Ed. O. Seeck, 1876. See below pp. 340–8.

Orosius. (*fl.* early fifth century) Spanish priest and controversialist. In 417, he undertook, at the invitation of Augustine, a *Historia adversus Paganos* – i.e. a history of Rome from the beginning to AD 417 as seen from the Christian viewpoint. The work is of importance to the study of the history of the third century through lack of other more reliable evidence. Ed. C. Zangemeister, Leipzig, 1889.

Panegyrici Latini. A collection of twelve Latin panegyrics given by various authors in honour of specific emperors. All but one (the one being that of Pliny the Younger) of the twelve were composed after the third century and some make occasional mention of imperial achievements in the East. Ed. E. Galletier, Paris, 1949–55.

Petrus Patricius. Greek diplomat and official under Justinian who composed various works on historical matters. These have come down to us only in excerpts but they yield some valuable information on Romano-Persian relations not found elsewhere. Ed. C. Müller, *FHG* IV, pp. 181–91.

Philostorgius. (*c.* 368–*c.* 439) Greek ecclesiastical historian. His principal work, a history of the church from the Arian view point has come down to us mainly in an epitome by Photius and in the historical sections of the *Artemii Passio* (see above). Ed. J. Bidez, rev. F. Winkelmann, GCS, 1981.

Procopius. (*fl.* sixth century) Greek historian and chronicler of the reign of Justinian. A native of Caesarea, he was military secretary to Belisarius and saw service on the eastern frontier. His account of the Persian Wars of his time contains some useful pieces of information on those of the earlier periods. Ed. J. Haury, rev. P. Wirth, Leipzig, 1963–4.

Scriptores Historiae Augustae. Collective title given by Casubon to the author(s) of a collection of Latin biographies of Roman emperors from Hadrian to Numerianus. The work claims to have been composed by six authors in the reign of Diocletian. Most modern scholars subscribe to single authorship and a post 360 date of composition. The biographies down to Opelius Macrinus contain much accurate information but the remaining ones combine reliable facts with outright forgeries and inventions. Ed. E. Hohl, Leipzig, 1927, tr. D. Magie, LCL, 1922–32.

Oracula Sibyllina. Collections of the prophetic utterances of the Sibyls had been in existence in Rome since the time of the Kings. The fourteen miscellaneous books of prophecies in verse which bear the title of the Sibylline Oracles are blatant Judaeo-Christian forgeries. Book 13, composed before the death of Odaenathus, is particularly informative on conditions in Syria during the invasions of Shapur I. Ed. J. Geffcken, GCS, 1902.

Socrates (Scholasticus). Greek lawyer and ecclesiastical historian. He was the author of a continuation of the Church History of Eusebius and extends from 305 to 439. Ed. R. Hussey, Oxford, 1853.

Sozomen(us). Greek ecclesiastical historian and another continuator of Eusebius. His work which covers the period 323–425 is heavily dependent on that of Socrates but contains valuable information on the history of Christianity in Armenia and the Sassanian Empire. Ed. J. Bidez, rev. G. C. Hansen, GCS, 1960.

Suidas (or *Suda*). Name of a Greek encyclopaedic lexicon compiled about the end of the tenth century AD. Ed. A. Adler, Leipzig, 1929–38.

Syncellus, Georgius. Greek chronographer who lived in the latter part of the eighth and the early part of the ninth century. He intended to compile a chronicle down to his own time but the project was cut short by his death and the extant text goes only as far as the accession of Diocletian in 284. He made extensive use of the now lost Greek version of the chronicle of Eusebius. Ed. A. A. Mosshammer, Leipzig, 1984.

al-Tabari. Arab historian, whose principal work contains an important monograph on the history of the Sassanian dynasty in Persia. See below pp. 275–95.

Themistius. (*c.* 317–*c.* 388) Greek philosopher and rhetor whose panegyrics found favour with every emperor from Constantius II to Theodosius. His speeches are also important as sources for the history of his time. Eds H. Schenkl, G. Downey and A. F. Norman, Leipzig, 1965 ff.

Theodoret(us). (*c.* 393–*c.* 466) Greek ecclesiastical politician and historian. A native of Antioch, he later became the Bishop of Cyrrhus and was embroiled in the Christological controversy between Nestorius and Cyril of Alexandria. His *Ecclesiastical History* continues that of Eusebius down to 425. Ed. L. Parmentier, rev. F. Scheidweiler, GCS, 1954. He also wrote a history of the monks of Syria and Mesopotamia (*Historia Religiosa*) which contains the life of Jacob of Nisibis. Eds P. Canivet and A. Leroy-Molinghen, Paris, 1977–9.

Theophanes (Confessor). A Byzantine monk who compiled a chronicle (in Greek) covering the years 284 to 814. Though a major source on the Arab Conquest and the Iconoclast Controversy, its coverage of the events of the third and fourth centuries is very sketchy. Ed. C. De Boor, Leipzig, 1883.

Zonaras, Ioannes. Byzantine historian and canonist of the twelfth century. He was the author of a universal history (in Greek) down to 1118 which is in essence an epitome of the standard histories. For the Severan period he used mainly Dio Cassius and for the period between Severus Alexander and Constantine, probably the lost portions of the histories of Petrus Patricius. Eds M. Pinder and T. Büttner-Wobst, CSHB, 1841–97.

Zosimus. Greek pagan historian and imperial bureaucrat, whose only surviving work, the *Historia Nova*, covers Roman history from 180–410, he is second only in importance to Ammianus as a source for the history of the fourth century. The work contains much material drawn from the now lost history of Eunapius (see above). Ed. F. Paschoud, Paris, 1971 ff.

List of abbreviations

AAS	*Les Annales archéologiues Arabes syriennes* (Damascus, 1951 ff.).
Abh. (Gött.)	*Abhandlungen der (königlichen) Gesellschaft (Akademie) der Wissenschaften zu Göttingen,* Philolog.-hist. Kl., N.F. (Berlin, 1897 ff.).
AE	*L'Année épigraphique,* published in *Revue archéologique* and separately (Paris, 1888 ff.).
Amm.	Ammianus Marcellinus.
AMS	*Acta Martyrum et Sanctorum* ed. P. Bedjan, 7 vols (Paris, 1890–7).
ANCL	Ante-Nicene Christian Library (Edinburgh, 1864 ff.).
ANRW	*Aufstieg und Niedergang der Römischen Welt,* eds H. Temporini *et al.* (Berlin, 1972 ff.).
BAR	*British Archaeological Reports* (Oxford) (S = International Series).
BGU	*Berliner Griechische Urkunden* (Berlin, 1895 ff.).
BMC	*British Museum Catalogue of Coins of the Roman Empire* (London, 1923 ff.).
CAH	*The Cambridge Ancient History* (Cambridge, 1923 ff.).
CHI	*The Cambridge History of Iran* (Cambridge, 1968 ff.).
CIL	*Corpus Inscriptionum Latinarum* (Berlin, 1863 ff.).
CISem.	*Corpus Inscriptionum Semiticarum* (Paris, 1881 ff.).

CJ	*Codex Justinianus*, ed. P. Krüger (*Corpus Iuris Civilis*, Berlin, 1929).
CMC	*Codex Manichaicus Coloniensis*, eds L. Koenen and C. Römer (Opladen, 1988).
Cooke	G. A. Cooke, *A Text-Book of North Semitic Inscriptions* (Oxford, 1903).
CRAI	*Comptes rendus de l'Académie des Inscriptions et Belles-lettres* (Paris, 1857 ff.).
CSCO	Corpus Scriptorum Christianorum Orientalium (Paris, Louvain etc, 1903 ff.).
CSHB	Corpus Scriptorum Historiae Byzantinae, 49 vols (Bonn, 1828–78).
CT	*Codex Theodosianus.*
Dessau	*Inscriptiones Latinae Selectae*, ed. H. Dessau, 3 vols (Berlin, 1892–1916).
Diz. Epig.	*Dizionario epigrafico di antichità romana*, ed. E. de Ruggiero (Rome, 1895 ff.).
EE	*Ephemeris Epigraphica Corporis Inscriptionum Latinarum Supplementum* (Berlin, 1872–1913).
Ephr., HcJul.	Ephrem Syrus, *Hymni contra Julianum.*
FHG	*Fragmenta Historicorum Graecorum*, ed. C. Müller, 5 vols (Paris, 1841–70).
GCS	Die griechischen christlichen Schriftsteller der ersten drei Jahrhunderte (Leipzig 1897–1941; Berlin and Leipzig, 1953; Berlin 1954 ff.).
Gk	Greek
GRP	*Gazeteer of Roman Palestine*, ed. M. Avi-Yonah, QEDEM 5 (Jerusalem, 1976)
hist. eccl. or *h.e.*	*historia ecclesiastica.*
IGLS	*Inscriptions grecques et latins de la Syrie*, eds L. Jalabert *et al.* (Paris, 1929 ff.).

IGR   *Inscriptiones Graecae ad res Romanas pertinentes*, eds R. Cagnat and G. Lafaye (Paris, 1906–27).

ILAl   *Inscriptions latines del'Algérie*, I-II, eds St. Gsell and H.-G. Pflaum (Paris, 1922–57).

Inv.   *Inventaire des inscriptions de Palmyre*, eds J. Cantineau *et al.* fasc. 1-11 (Beirut, 1930–65).

IRT   *The Inscriptions of Roman Tripolitania*, eds J. M. Reynolds and J. B. Ward-Perkins (Rome, 1952).

Itin. Anton.   *Itineraria Antonini Augusti* ed. O. Cuntz, *Itineraria Romana*, I (Berlin, 1929).

Joh. Chrys.   Ioannes Chrysostomus.

JRS   *Journal of Roman Studies* (London, 1911 ff.).

KKZ   (Inscription of Kirdir at the Kaaba of Zoroastre) ed. M. L. Chaumont, 'L'inscription de Kartir à la "Ka-'bah de Zoroastre" (texte, traduction, commentaire)', *Journal Asiatique*, 248 (1960) pp. 339–80.

LCL   Loeb Classical Library (London and Camb., Mass., 1911 ff.)

Lib.   Libanius Sophista.

MGH   Monumentae Germaniae Historica (Berlin, 1877–1919) (*Auct. Ant* = *Auctores Antiquissimi*).

mp.   Middle Persian.

MUSJ   *Mélanges de l'Université Saint-Joseph* (Beirut, 1906 ff.).

Nöldeke   Th. Nöldeke, *Geschichte der Perser und Araber zur Zeit der Sasaniden. Aus der arabischen Chronik des Tabari übersetzt und mit ausfürlichen. Erlaüterungen und Ergänzungen versehn* (Leiden, 1879).

Not. Dig.   *Notitia Dignitatum* (Or. = *in partibus . . . orientis*)

PAES   E. Littmann, D. Magie, and D. R. Stuart, *Syria, Publications of the Princeton University Archaeological Expeditions to Syria in 1904–5 and 1909, Div. III, Greek and Latin Inscriptions: (A) S. Syria; (B) N. Syria* (Leiden, 1921–2).

PECS	*Princeton Encyclopaedia of Classical Sites*, eds R. Stillwell *et al.* (New Jersey, 1976).
PG	*Patrologiae cursus completus, series Graceco-Latina*, eds J. P. Migne *et al.*, 162 vols (Paris, 1857–66).
PIR²	*Prosopographia Imperii Romani Saeculi I, II, III*, 2nd edn by E. Groag and A. Stein (Berlin, 1933 ff.).
PL	*Patrologiae cursus completus, series Latina*, eds J. P. Migne *et al.*, 221 vols (Paris, 1844–64) and 5 Suppl. (1958–74).
PLRE, I	*The Prosopography of the Later Roman Empire*, I, eds A. H. M. Jones, J. Morris and J. R. Martindale, I (Cambridge, 1971).
PO	*Patrologia Orientalis*, eds R. Graffin and F. Nau (Paris, 1907 ff.).
PS	*Patrologia Syriaca*, 3 vols (Paris, 1893–1926).
PDura	*The Excavations at Dura-Europos, Final Report V, Pt. I, The Parchments and Papyri*, eds C. B. Welles, R. O. Fink and J. F. Gilliam (New Haven, 1959).
POxy.	*Oxyrynchus Papyri*, eds B. P. Grenfell, A. S. Hunt *et al.* (London, 1898 ff.).
PThead.	*Papyrus de Théadelphie*, ed. P. Jouguet (Paris, 1911).
pth.	Parthian.
RAC	*Reallexikon für Antike und Christentum*, ed. T. Klauser (Stuttgart, 1950 ff.).
RE	*Real-Encyclopädie der klassischen Altertumswissenschaft*, eds A. Pauly, G. Wissowa *et al.* (Stuttgart, 1893 ff.)
RÉA	*Revue des études arméniennes* (Paris).
RGDS	*Res Gestae Divi Saporis.* See *SKZ*.
RIC	*Roman Imperial Coinage*, eds H. Mattingly, E. A. Sydenham *et al.* (London, 1923 ff.).
Sb. (Bayr.)	*Sitzungsberichte der (königlich) bayerischen Akademie der Wissenschaften (zu München)* (Munich, 1860–

1871, philosoph.-philolog. und hist. Kl., 1871–1930; Philosoph.-hist. Abt., 1930 ff.).

Sb. (Wien) *Situzungsberichte der (kaiserlichen) Akademie der Wissenschaften (in Wien)*, Philosoph.-hist. Kl. (Vienna, 1848 ff.).

SEG *Supplementum Epigraphicum Graecum* (Berlin, 1923 ff.).

SHA *Scriptores Historiae Augustae.*

SKZ (Inscription of Shapur at the Kaaba of Zoroastre), 'Res Gestae Divi Saporis', ed. and trans. A. Maricq, *Syria* 35 (1958) 245–60.

Soc. Socrates (Scholasticus).

Soz. Sozomenus.

TAPA *Transactions of the American Philological Association* (Philadelphia, 1870 ff.).

TAVO *Tübinger Atlas des Vorderen Orients* (Wiesbaden)

Tab. Peut. *Tabula Peutingeriana*, ed. K. Miller, *Itineraria Romana* (Stuttgart, 1916).

Thdt. Theodoretus Cyrrhensis.

Zos. Zosimus Historicus.

Foreword

The compilation and translation of this collection of texts on Romano-Persian relations were begun by Sam Lieu about five years ago for students taking his course on the history of Roman Mesopotamia (and adjacent Syria) at Warwick University. The need for some sort of collection was particularly felt for the period *c.* AD 224–350 because of the diverse nature of the surviving evidence and the lack of a major historical source. Michael Dodgeon joined the task of translating when the collection was already half completed, thus enabling Sam Lieu to extend his search for relevant material and, later, to concentrate on compiling the notes and the appendices. We are both extremely grateful to Richard Stoneman of Routledge for his generous invitation to publish what can only be regarded as a working collection since a great deal of new research remains to be done on Rome's Eastern Frontier and relations with Persia in one of the more tempestuous and less well-studied periods of its history. Richard's personal interest in this collection and his infinite patience have been invaluable assets to the editors. It is fortunate that the first part of the excellent commentary by Wolfgang Felix on the literary sources on Romano-Sassanian relations (*Antike literarische Quellen zur Aussenpolitik des Sasanidenstaates*, Vienna, 1985) became available to us at a time when it was still possible to make additions and alterations to our collection. Our debt to Felix's work is enormous and is amply reflected in the notes to the first five chapters of this collection. It is a cause of some regret that we could not delay the publication of our collection until after the appearance of the second part of his work covering the period from AD 309 onwards.

The diverse origins of the texts in this collection (Greek, Latin, Arabic, Syriac, Hebrew, Palmyrene, Middle Persian, and Armenian) necessitated our turning to friends and colleagues for help at every stage of compilation. We are immeasurably indebted to their willingness to give of their valuable time. Sebastian Brock, always an unfailing source of profound knowledge and learned advice for anyone working on the history of the Near East in this period, undertook the arduous task of revising the translations of all the Syriac texts and Palmyrene inscriptions in this collection. Ahmad al-Issa, Doris Dance, and Sheila Vince have contributed much to the preparation of the translations given in the appendices. James Russell kindly checked Mrs Vince's translation of parts of Renoux's French translation of Ephrem's *Sermones de Nicomedia* against the original Armenian. Paddy Considine generously agreed to translate several chapters from the *History of the Armenians* of Faustus of Buzanda at short notice. Stephen Mitchell read the first draft of the collection and proffered many useful corrections, additions, and suggestions. His fellow Anatolian researcher, Stephen Hill, corrected a number of misidentifications we had made of Cilician place names given in the Great Inscription of Shapur I. David Kennedy gave us much of his valuable time and expert knowledge in checking our attempts to identify the place-names in the sections of the *Notitia Dignitatum* which cover Syria and Arabia and made available to us material which is still in press. Werner Sundermann kindly commented on the first part of the collection from the perspective of an Iranologist and has saved us from a number of factual and chronological errors. Much help and advice on the translations were also received from James Jordan, Charles and Marna Morgan, Judith Lieu, and Ze'ev Rubin. Tim Barnes, Roger Blockley, Han Drijvers, and Michael Speidel generously sent us off-prints of their articles and monographs. Kay Rainsley ungrudgingly undertook the bulk of the word-processing and we owe much to her skill, dedication, and good humour. Michael Dodgeon is deeply indebted to Brian H. Warmington of Bristol University for his critical but kind direction of his earlier research. He would also like to express his gratitude to his wife Jean for her painstaking help with proof-reading. Sam Lieu would like to record a personal word of thanks to Sir Ronald Syme for several stimulating and informative discussions on the extracts from the *Scriptores Historiae Augustae* included in this collection and also to Peter Brown for first introducing him to the history of the fascinating world which existed between the Roman and the Sassanian Empires.

A grant for 'innovative teaching' from the Nuffield Foundation to Sam Lieu enabled work on this collection to be started at Warwick University alongside his other academic and administrative commitments. He is grateful to the Foundation for the award of a further research grant on Urbanism in Mesopotamia in the Parthian and Roman periods which yielded much material that is relevant to this collection. He would also like to thank the Wolfson Foundation for a research grant on Roman foreign policy, and the British Academy for two small research grants, one on Libanius and the other on the *Artemii Passio*. The Research and Innovation Committee and the European Humanities Research Centre, both of Warwick University, have made a number of small grants over the last five years to the project, mainly to cover secretarial, reprographic, and travel costs. Without the generous help from all these grant-giving bodies, the task of compiling a documentary history which draws material from more than a hundred classical, oriental, and medieval sources, as well as collections of inscriptions and papyri, would have been well nigh impossible from local resources. The main part of the research for this collection was carried out at the Joint Library of the Hellenic and Roman Societies in London. The helpfulness of its staff is a delight to record.

Acknowledgements

The editors of this collection are grateful to the following publishers and authors for permission to republish copyright material: to the Loeb Classical Library and the publishers William Heinemann and Harvard University Press for extracts from *Libanius Selected Works,* vol. 1, translated by A. F. Norman (1971); to Harvard University press for extracts from Moses Khorenats'i, *History of the Armenians,* translated by R. W. Thomson (1978); to State University of New York Press for extracts from *Agathangelos, History of the Armenians,* translated by R. W. Thomson, (1976); to University of California Press for extracts from *Herodian of Antioch's History of the Roman Empire,* translated by E. Echols (1961); to Oxford University Press for extracts from *Essays and Hymns of Synesius of Cyrene,* vol. 1, translated by A. Fitzgerald (1930), and *Libanius, Autobiography, Oration I,* translated by A. F. Norman (1965); to Princeton University Press for extracts from *The Theodosian Code,* translated by C. Pharr and others (1952), and *The Gothic History of Jordanes,* translated by C. C. Mierow (1915); to Catholic University of America Press Inc. for extracts from *Paulus Orosius, The Seven Books of History against the Pagans,* translated by R. J. Deferrari, *Fathers of the Church,* vol. 50 (1964); to Yale University Press and the Yale Art Gallery for four documents from *Dura Europos Final Report,* vol. 5, *Parchments and Papyri,* translated by C. B. Welles and others (1957), and three Middle Iranian Inscriptions from Ibid., vol. 6, *The Synagogue,* translated by B. Geiger (1952); to the editor of *Dumbarton Oaks Papers* and Prof. Averil Cameron for extracts from her translation of Agathias, *historiae* (vol. 23/24, 1969–70); to Manchester University Press for the extract from M. Boyce (ed. and trans.), *Textual Sources for the Study of Zoroastrianism* (1984), and Map 1 from S. N. C. Lieu, *Manichaeism in the Later Roman Empire and Medieval China* (1985); to Liverpool

University Press for extracts of J. M. Lieu's translation of Ephrem Syrus, *Hymni contra Julianum* in S. N. C. Lieu (ed.), *The Emperor Julian, Panegyric and Polemics* (1986); to Dr Ludwig Reichert GMBH for an extract from A. Oppenheimer, *Babylonia Judaica in the Talmudic Period* (1983); to the American Philosophical Society at Philadelphia for an extract from G. Downey's translation of *Oration XI* of Libanius published in its *Proceedings* (1959), and for an extract from A. Bandy's translation of *Ioannes Lydus, On Powers or The Magistracies of the Roman State* (1983); to the editors of *Sumer* for the map on Julian's attack against Ctesiphon by M. Fiey (1967); to J.M. Dent for an extract from Sir Walter Lamb's translation of *Heliodorus, Ethiopian Story*, Everyman's Library (1961); and finally to Prof. Michael Speidel for his personal permission to reproduce his translation of two Latin military inscriptions.

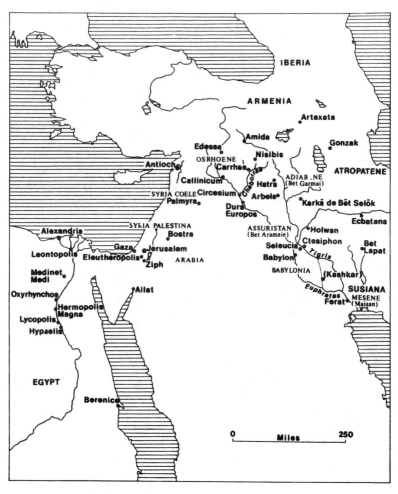

Map 1   The Near East in the third century

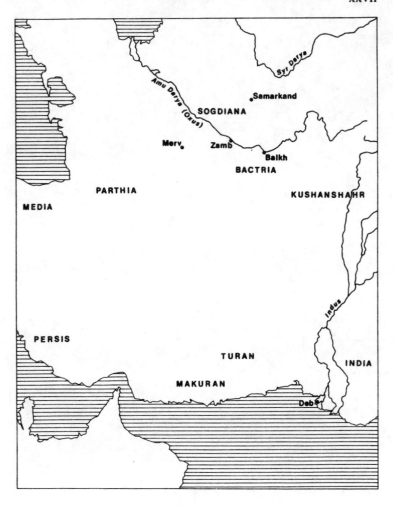

Introduction

(1) Outline of Romano-Persian relations (224–363)

The coming to power of the Sassanian Dynasty in Iran in AD 224 opens a new chapter in the struggle for hegemony in the Near East. Till then, Rome's fortunes had fared reasonably well in its perennial conflict with the Parthians. The ignominy of Crassus' defeat at Carrhae was little more than a schoolboy jingle: 'Carrhas Crassi clade nobiles' (Carrhae whose name was renowned by reason of her defeat of Crassus) and it certainly did not compel commanders like Corbulo to regard the Euphrates as a sacred barrier to ambition and fame. Though Trajan's sweeping conquests at the beginning of the second century in Mesopotamia were mostly abandoned by his immediate successors, Roman power gradually reasserted itself east of the Euphrates as the century progressed. The Parthian Wars of Lucius Verus in 165 saw the formal incorporation of the Euphrates corridor into the Roman sphere of influence with Roman troops garrisoned as far south as Salihiye (Dura Europos), Ana (Anatha), and Kifrin. The oasis city of Palmyra, a Roman colony since the time of Hadrian, contributed to the stability on the southern flanks by acting as policeman of the Syrian Desert. More importantly, Septimius Severus created the new province of Osrhoene c. 197, confining the power of the Abgars, renowned for their political vacillations, to the city of Edessa and its immediate environs. The new network of roads allowed Nisibis and Singara to be more firmly integrated into Rome's eastern defences, giving her valuable access to the Tigris and a choice of invasion routes. Thus, when Opelius Macrinus withdrew the army of the murdered Caracalla, whose Praetorian Prefect he was, from Mesopotamia after an indecisive battle with the Parthian king Artabanus V near Nisibis in 217, few would have predicted any major change in the balance of power. Both sides seemed set for a period of minor wars and the consolidation of their existing frontiers.

Yet, seven years later, Artabanus V was dead on the field of Hormizdagan, victim of a rebellion which began inconspicuously in c. 208. The victor, Ardashir, the scion of an Iranian royal house from Istachr, wasted no time in trying to incorporate client states of the former Parthians like Hatra and Armenia into his new dominion, in flagrant disregard of the status quo which had existed between the Roman Empire and the Parthian kingdom. Rome was not slow to send help to the threatened areas and a three-pronged expedition in 231–3 fought the Persians to a draw, with victory in Media and defeat in Mesopotamia. By 238/9, however, the Persians had recovered sufficiently to resume the attack on Roman Syria and Mesopotamia, capturing a number of cities, and in 240 the crown prince Shapur finally subdued the kingdom of Hatra, thus neutralizing the main threat to Persian expansion into Armenia and Upper Mesopotamia. The Roman response came four years later when the young Gordian III led an expedition which liberated some of the captured cities but suffered a major defeat near the Sassanian twin royal city of Seleucia-Ctesiphon. Gordian perished in mysterious circumstances and his successor Philip signed a pact with Shapur which was detrimental to Roman interests in Armenia. Later attempts to redress this by the Romans were the perfect pretext for Shapur (Shahanshah since 242) to direct a series of raids from 252 onwards against Syria, Commagene, and Cappadocia. The capture of Antioch, the metropolis of Syria, by the Persians would have undoubtedly sent shock waves reverberating through all the eastern parts of the Roman Empire. Against these razzias Rome made no effective reply, thus encouraging Shapur I to launch a full-scale invasion of Roman Mesopotamia via the Tigris route in 260. An attempt by Valerian (emperor 253–60) to oppose this led to his defeat near Edessa and captivity in Persia. The victorious Persians plundered Syria, Cilicia, and Cappadocia at will and were only halted by local resistance by Valerian's officers at Pompeiopolis and the unexpected rise to prominence of Odaenathus, the prince of Palmyra, who seized the opportunity of the power vacuum created by the conflict in the north to raid deeply into Sassanian-held Mesopotamia (Assuristan). His victories kept the Persians at bay but Rome had effectively lost control of territories south of the Anti-Taurus, especially when, under Odaenathus' successor Vaballathus (with his mother Zenobia ruling as regent), Palmyrene power extended into Egypt. The success, however, proved to be short-lived as Rome had now realized the need for stronger men at the helm. Under Aurelian (270–5), the first of a series of soldier-emperors who would restore military discipline and revive Roman fortunes in the face of foreign adversaries, Rome regained control over her Near Eastern possessions from the Palmyrenes after a decisive victory outside Antioch in 272.

The death of Shapur I, *c.* 272, heralded a period of political unrest in Persia as his immediate successors, Hormizd, Bahram I, and Bahram II, all had very short reigns. A struggle for power broke out after 282 between Bahram III, the descendant of a minor queen or concubine of Shapur, and Narses, the king of Armenia, the last of Shapur's sons. The Roman emperor Carus took advantage of this and made a successful raid against Assuristan in 283, penetrating as far as Seleucia-Ctesiphon. His death on campaign compelled the Romans to withdraw and on the mysterious death of his successor Numerianus, the army elected Diocletian, a soldier from Dalmatia, as emperor. He used the years of relative peace to overhaul the defence of Rome's Eastern Frontier, constructing a major line of communication across the Syrian Desert from Sura on the Euphrates to Damascus via Palmyra. The line (*limes*) was interspaced with a series of fortresses and camps for patrolling cavalry units. In 296, Narses, now secure on the throne of Persia, took to the offensive and defeated Diocletian and his junior colleague, the Caesar Galerius, near Carrhae. The fact that he seems to have been unable to exploit his victory is a testimony to the frontier reorganization carried out in the intervening years. With a fresh army Galerius surprised Narses in Armenia and scored a major victory, capturing the harem of the Shahanshah, thus forcing Narses to make major territorial concessions beyond the Tigris (the Transtigritanian *regiones*) to the Romans in the negotiations conducted in 297/8.

The new gains confirmed the upper reaches of the Tigris as Rome's first line of defence and gave the cities of northern Mesopotamia like Amida, Nisibis, Singara, and Bezabde a new defensive role. They also ensured Persian hostility as no self-respecting Shahanshah would allow the matter to rest. The steady growth of the Christian community in the Eranshah introduced a new ingredient to Romano-Persian relations after the persecution of Christians came to an end in the Roman Empire under Constantine, who also actively promoted Christianity as one of the official religions of Rome. Not long before hostility resumed between the two empires in 337, Constantine put himself forward as the advocate of the Christians in Persia, adding a possible religious dimension to the impending conflict. The Diocletianic frontier reforms proved their worth in the long reign of Constantius II (337–62) as Shapur II (309–79) made repeated and fruitless attacks on Nisibis. Though some cities were lost to the Persians in 359/60, the valiant defenders of Amida, Singara, and Bezabde inflicted such heavy casualties on the enemy that Shapur·was unable to follow up or consolidate his gains. However, three years later, the premature death of Constantius' successor, Julian, in the course of his Persian campaign (363) led directly to the loss to the Romans on the negotiating table of three of the five Transtigritanian *regiones* which they had gained through the victory of Galerius, as well as of Nisibis and a number of key fortresses. The citizens of Nisibis, who had proved their loyalty to Rome on so many occasions, were allowed to be evacuated under truce to the west, leaving their city to become a major Persian stronghold on the very doorstep of the Roman Empire.

(2) The problem of the sources

The study of the events outlined in the above section has long been bedevilled by the lack of a coherent and reliable ancient authority. The loss of the first thirteen books of the *Res Gestae* of Ammianus Marcellinus has left a gap in chronological narrative down to 353 which is only partially filled by the history of Herodian, the *Historia Nova* of Zosimus (which itself has gaps, especially on the reign of Diocletian), the highly problematic *Scriptores Historiae Augustae*, and the polemical *Historia adversus Paganos* of Orosius. Though a number of important sources on early Sassanian history exist in oriental languages (especially in Arabic, New Persian, and Armenian), they are relatively late compilations and the political and military relationship between Rome and Persia was rarely the main interest of the compilers. In the case of the Armenian sources, scholars since Whiston and Gibbon have noted that they abound in problems of genealogy and chronology, which means that they cannot be regarded as reliable or independent, or even be used as a check on the more contemporary classical sources. Nevertheless, the period is covered in outline by a number of epitomes of Roman history (especially those of Aurelius Victor, Eutropius, Festus, and the anonymous *Epitome de Caesaribus*) which were all compiled in the fourth century, and also by Byzantine chroniclers like Petrus Patricius, Malalas, John of Antioch, Theophanes, Syncellus, Cedrenus and Zonaras who had access to earlier material now lost to us. Moreover, contemporary documents like the works of the Church Fathers and the Latin Panegyrics make occasional references to the events in the east. And in the thirteenth book of the so-called *Sibylline Oracles* we have the work of an author who was well informed on Romano-Persian wars and particularly their effects on Syria from the reign of Gordian III to the domination of the province by Odaenathus of Palmyra. For the early wars of Constantius, we also possess the poems (in Syriac) of one eyewitness, Ephrem Syrus, and the panegyrics of two contemporaries, Julian and Libanius. Though Libanius himself was not a witness to the fighting, he personally knew a number of the officers who held important military commands in the east and with whom he corresponded regularly.

The dismemberment of the Ottoman Empire by European powers after the Treaty of Versailles opened Syria and Iraq to systematic archaeological surveys and selective excavations. The pioneering work of Poidebard, Mouterde, and Stein in the use of aerial photography has afforded us a better understanding of Rome's frontier defence system, especially of the Syrian and the Arabian *limes*. Though the number of inscriptions from the region remains small, they yield much new information, especially on the history of the Roman army in the frontier regions. As many of them are dated, they also serve as an important correlate to our literary evidence. Those from Palmyra, in both Greek and Palmyrene, have proved particularly valuable to both our understanding and dating of certain important events in the third century, especially those related to the rise and fall of the city as a major political power between the two empires. The excavations at Dura Europos yielded a number of important documents on papyri, especially the files of the Twentieth Cohort of the Palmyrenes, and these go down to within a few years of the capture and destruction of the city in 256. The trilingual Great Inscription of Shapur on the Kaaba of Zoroaster, first discovered in 1936 near Persepolis, gives us a detailed and unique account of the three main wars of Shapur I against the Romans, albeit solely expressing the Persian point of view.

(3) The structure of the book

Modern scholarship on Rome's Eastern Frontier and her relationship with Persia, her chief adversary, in the third and early fourth centuries, then, is based on the critical examination of this very wide range of literary and archaeological evidence. The fact that the relevant texts exist in more than half a dozen ancient languages imposes a considerable burden on the researcher and puts the subject out of the reach of the average undergraduate. Jean Gagé's *La Montée des Sassanides et l'heure de Palmyre* (Paris, 1964) remains the only work known to us which attempts to make some of this diverse material available to the non-specialist. However, its small selection of classical sources makes any critical evaluation of Rome's part in the struggle impossible and the epigraphical material is represented by only three Sassanian royal inscriptions and the famous Tariff of Palmyra which was inscribed in AD 137, almost a century before the rise of the Sassanians. Gagé's collection also stops with the reign of Diocletian, while the historiographical problems which necessitate such a collection continue until the last years of Constantius II. The work of Felix, mentioned in the Foreword, is the only systematic attempt to locate the main classical and Byzantine sources on Romano-Sassanian relations but the work is purely a commentary, containing neither text nor translation.

The present collection is divided into two parts and the division does not represent a natural chronological break but a major difference in the presentation and organization of the material. Part One contains translations of all classical and Byzantine sources on Romano-Sassanian relations from *c.* 224–*c.* 350, i.e. from the coming to power of Ardashir to the end of the early conflict between Shapur II and Constantius II. It includes material on the rise of the Sassanians in order to allow the collection to be used as a corpus of Roman and Byzantine sources on the early history of the Sassanian Dynasty. The only major omissions, necessitated purely by the problem of space, are the Greek version of the Acts of the Persian Martyrs under Shapur II and Sozomen's *Historia Ecclesiastica* account of the same (*hist. eccl.* II, 9–15). The extracts are grouped under headings in chronological sequence; under each heading, the extracts are given chronologically according to the generally accepted date of composition of the source. We are aware that such an arrangement implies a high degree of interpretation, especially when problems of dating surround particular events. It also means taking the relevant material out of its literary and historiographical context, and, in the case of the extracts from the *Augustan History*, running the risk of presenting probable fiction as palpable truth. However, the information we are seeking is often of a specialized and well–defined nature which lends itself to being studied in isolation. Where knowledge of the context of the extract is essential to its evaluation, we have tried to indicate this in the notes. Furthermore, it is only through juxtaposing the extracts from the *Augustan History* with all other known sources on the same topic that we can determine their historical value.

From 353 onwards, we have a superlative and substantial eyewitness source to the main events on the Eastern Frontier in the *Res Gestae* of Ammianus Marcellinus. He was one of the defenders of Amida in 359 who survived the subsequent massacre at the fall of the city to take part in the ill-fated Persian expedition of Julian in 363 (XVIII, 5–XIX, 9 and XXIII, 2–XXV, 8). In view of the different state of the sources, Part Two of our collection follows a very different format. Since an excellent modern English translation of the main parts of Ammianus' historical work including nearly all the relevant material on the Eastern Frontier and the Persian Wars from 353 to 378 is now generally available (Ammianus Marcellinus, *The Later Roman Empire*, translated by W. Hamilton, and introduced and annotated by A. Wallace-Hadrill, London, 1985), the need to include lengthy extracts from it is no longer justifiable in terms of space and cost. The same applies to the other two main literary sources on the Persian Expedition of Julian, namely *Oration* XVIII, 212–75 of Libanius and Book III, 12–34 of the *Historia Nova* of Zosimus, as reliable English translations of these works, by A. F. Norman (LCL, London, and Cambridge, Mass., 1969) and Ridley (Canberra, 1982) respectively, are also readily available. (We have, however, included passages from these three authors in Part One of our collection as the 'flashbacks' from Ammianus and Libanius often provide valuable pin-point information on earlier events. As for Zosimus, his exclusion from Part One would deprive the reader of one of the more coherent narrative sources on third-century history and would make the reconstruction of the events immensely more difficult.) The two chapters in Part Two are each preceded by a chronological analysis of the sources including Ammianus, Libanius, and Zosimus. This is then followed by the translated sources, listed alphabetically, a format well-known to many ancient historians through its adoption by the revisers of G. F. Hill's much-used source collection for the study of the Pentekontaetia (*Sources for Greek History between the Persian and the Peloponnesian Wars*, a new edition by R. Meiggs and A. Andrewes, Oxford, 1951).

Since this is a predominantly literary collection, the selection of epigraphical material has inevitably been difficult, not least because of the signal contribution given to our knowledge of the physical evolution of the Eastern Frontier by the study of inscriptions on a regional basis. The problem of space limits us to a selection of the more often cited, and therefore the more important, inscriptions, especially those which provide information on events described in the literary sources. We have included a number of recently published inscriptions like the dedication to Septimius Odaenathus of 252 published by Gawlikowski and the 'praetensio' inscription from Azraq published by Speidel, in recognition of their significance even though other scholars have not yet had the opportunity to comment on them. A small number of oriental sources are given in the appendices, chosen mainly according to the same criteria as the epigraphical material. Syriac sources, however, are included in the main body of the collection because they are often contemporary or near contemporary with the events they describe.

1 The Rise of the Sassanians

1.1.1. The lineage, parentage, and childhood of Ardashir (r. 226–241/2)

Agathias II, 27, 1–5: It is said that Artaxares' (i.e. Ardashir's) mother was married to a certain Pabak, who was quite obscure, a leather worker by trade, but very learned in astrology and easily able to discern the future. 2. It so happened that a soldier called Sasanus, who was travelling through the land of the Cadusaei,[1] was given hospitality by Pabak and lodged in his house. 3. The latter recognized somehow, in his capacity as a seer, I presume, that the offspring of his guest would be splendid and famous and would reach great good fortune. He was disappointed and upset that he had no daughter or sister or any other close relative. But finally he yielded his own wife to him and gave up his marriage bed, nobly enduring the shame and preferring the future good fortune to the present disgrace and dishonour. 4. And so Artaxares was born, and was reared by Pabak. But when he grew up and boldly seized the throne, a bitter quarrel and dispute immediately broke out between Sasanus and Pabak. Each of them wanted him to be called his son. 5. Finally, and with difficulty, they agreed that he should be called the son of Pabak, though born from the seed of Sasanus. This is the genealogy of Artaxares given by the Persians, and they say it is true since it is actually recorded in the Royal Archives.[2]

(Cameron 1969/70: pp. 87–8.)

Syncellus pp. 440, 11–441, 2 (pp. 677, 11–678, 7 *CSHB*): Alexander, the son of Mamaea (i.e. Alexander Severus), was emperor when Artabanus the Parthian was the king of Persia. After Artabanus, the family of Chosroes (i.e. the Sassanians) began to rule. It began as follows: Artaxerxes (i.e. Ardashir), an unknown and undistinguished Persian, gathered a body of irregular troops, destroyed Artabanus and assumed the crown. And he once more restored the Kingship to the Persians. He was a Magian and through him the Magians have become prestigious in Persia. They say that the mother of Artaxerxes (i.e. Ardashir) lived with a man called Pambecus, who was a shoe-maker by profession, but an astrologer and in this respect versed in the dark arts or stuff and nonsense. And a soldier by the name of Sananus (*sic.*) was marching through the land of the Cadusaei and was entertained in the house of Pambecus, and Pambecus had 'foreknowledge', we suppose, through his astrology, that the offspring of Sananus would be raised to a high level of good fortune. But not having a daughter or a sister or any female relative, he shut in his own wife with Sananus, and she conceived and brought forth Artaxerxes. Chosroes' family, therefore, was descended from this Artaxerxes, also called Artaxares.

(Dodgeon)

al-Tabari, pp. 813–15 (Nöldeke, pp. 2–5): see Appendix 1, pp. 275–6.

1.1.2. The revolt of Ardashir (*c.* 208–224)

Dio Cassius (Reliq.) LXXX, 3, 1–2: Many uprisings were made by many persons, some of which caused serious alarm, but they were all checked. But affairs in Mesopotamia were still more terrifying, and provoked in the hearts of all, not merely the men of Rome but the rest of mankind, a fear that had a truer foundation. 2. Artaxerxes (i.e. Ardashir), a Persian, having conquered the Parthians in three battles[3] and killed their king Artabanus....[4]

(Foster, vi, p. 108)

Herodian VI, 2, 6–7: He (i.e. Ardashir) was the first Persian to dare to launch an attack on the kingdom of the Parthians and the first to succeed to recover the kingdom for the Persians. Indeed, after Darius had been deprived of his kingdom by Alexander of Macedon, the Macedonians and Alexander's successors divided up the territory by countries and ruled the nations of the East and all Asia for many years. 7. When these governors quarrelled and the power of the Macedonians was weakened by continual wars, they say that Arsaces, a Parthian by race, was the first to persuade the barbarians in those regions to revolt from the Macedonians. Invested with the crown with the consent of the Parthians and the neighbouring barbarians, Arsaces ruled as king. For a long time the empire remained in his own family, down to Artabanus in our time; then Artaxerxes killed Artabanus and took possession of his kingdom for the Persians. After easily subduing the neighbouring barbarian nations, the king began to plot against the Roman Empire.

(Echols, 1961: pp. 155–7, revised)

Agathangelos, *History of the Armenians*, 3–9 (Gk version), ed. Lafontaine, pp. 173–7:[5] I shall begin at that point at which the Parthians started to collapse. Artabanus, the son of Valarses, being of Parthian origin, had experience of the teaching of the Chaldaeans. He understood how to measure the course of the stars and their turning points and was educated in divination. While he was sleeping with his wife in his tent, he looked out at the stars on view and made a discovery and he said to the queen, 'I observed the course of a star and I have inferred today the following, that if someone wished to rebel against his own master and to make war upon him, on the present occasion he would win and his master be defeated.' And after saying this he turned back to sleep. Following the usual custom, one of the queen's servant girls was sleeping in the same tent and fulfilled the duties that were ordered by her mistress. She was the daughter of high officials and was a close friend of one of the magnates, who was called Artasiras and whose native country was Assyria. She was in love with him and, after hearing the king's words, she slipped out past the king and queen; she ran to Artasiras (i.e. Ardashir), son of Sasanus, which is the origin of the Sassanian name of the Persian kings descended from him.

4. Therefore she entered his tent (for she could not be prevented by the servants; for the affection of the pair was well understood) and spoke as follows: 'Dear Artasiras, let sleep depart from your eyelids. Start now upon the design which you have had for a long time. Be confident when you look upon the king's prophecy. Now is the time for your suit of armour, now there is need for the advice of the wisest men, now you must gather an army for battle. For the king has seen the course of the stars and said: "Now a slave working against his master gains the victory upon the present occasion." But here, you go upon your design and give me your assurance and upon oath give guarantee of my proposition – that when you have gained the throne of Persia you do not place me outside your bed and authorise me as the partner of your dignity. For this is what you always said to me in your professions when you began the same

design.' These were the words of Artaducta. Artasiras admitted his deep gratitude and, holding the woman's hand in his own right hand, he stretched (their arms) up to heaven and said the following: 'Behold, divine power, sun and fire, air and earth, how today I take counsel with the nobility of Persia and rebel from the King and that presently in my household I shall make you mistress of all.'

5. Upon hearing this, Artaducta said, 'I shall go now to the King's tent. For I must today continue my service of the preceding days. For though we have the status of being free, since we are born of high nobles, nevertheless we must serve the royal needs.' Saying this she proceeded to the King's tent and without being noticed slipped into bed and lay down. Artasiras arose and gathered the magnates of the Persians and Assyrians[6] with whom he took counsel on other days too. Standing in their midst, he said, 'Noblest of the Persians and Assyrians, we know of the boastfulness of the Parthians from a long time ago, as they snatch the produce of other peoples' labours. They take pride in their injustice; they do not cease killing pointlessly; the Parthians loathe the Persians and Assyrians; they stole upon us from a barbarian land. So what will you say? If my words are untrue, let him remain as your unjust king. But if I have not spoken untruthfully, let us start out for battle. For it is better to die than to be slaves of an unjust master.' These were the words of Artasiras.

6. The Persian nobles welcomed what was said; for they prayed to be freed from the Parthians and that the king of Persia should belong to their own race. And they said to Artasiras: 'We have you as our leader in words and deeds, and hold onto the experience of your good judgment and understand that in your person the state is based upon virtue. So take the lead and do whatever you wish while we follow your words to do what is in the interest of both our parties.' When therefore it was daytime and the Persians with their leader Artasiras looked to war, they first sent to King Artabanus the ambassadors Zecas (i.e. Zik)[7] and Carinas (i.e. Karen), the most important clan leaders and generals, who departed and stood before the king of kings. The following was the introduction to their address: 'We are the envoys of the Persians, and if you are possessed of a most calm attitude for receiving the words of the Persians, we shall speak like ambassadors to announce our lengthy message, being outside fear and danger – and the law established by the nobles of old urges this practice when they kept unharmed visiting envoys. If therefore you agree, o king, we shall speak.' And Artabanus granted them leave to speak as they wished.

7. Then they began their speech as follows: 'Your Majesty, among us the Persians it is customary practice to obey kings, inasmuch as the king is master of all; whereas the king himself governs the state with one observance of the law and in justice, conducts the government without barbarian arrogance, appears frightening to his adversaries and kindly to his subjects. For how can he hinder those who are unjust if he himself starts the injustice? How does he punish the perpetrators of dreadful deeds if he himself is quick to trespass? We have experience of your dread deeds and have withdrawn ourselves from your kingdom, not because we hate to obey but in avoidance of a lawless king, not becoming despots but because we do not tolerate a despotic attitude.' These were the words of the Persians. King Artabanus inclined his head for very many hours and looked at the floor. He foresaw the coming fall of his kingdom and facing the envoys he said, 'I am the author of this outrage, having honoured some with offices and positions of authority, and by royal gifts establishing many as owners of fields and property. But you proceed to what you have resolved upon; you will see that I am reformed to your viewpoint. I shall teach you not to stand against your king. But you envoys go forth and no longer be the authors of such words, lest somehow I make you the first examples for insulting me.'

8. When they heard this, Zecas and Carinas proceeded to the council of the Persians and on their arrival they made a full report to Artasiras and the remaining Persian nobles. They added to what was said the madness of the king since he was no longer awaiting a second embassy but was arming against the leaders of the council. Artasiras sent to Artaducta and bore her away and put her with his own property in a very strong fortress, and himself armed with the Persians and Assyrians against Artabanus the King of Kings. When he saw the preparation against him, Artabanus himself also armed with his Parthians. He had a large number of Persians who were not confederates of the council of their fellow countrymen. When the Persians and Parthians warred upon each other in their first clash, very many from each side fell. But Artasiras gained the upper hand, when very many others deserted Artabanus and joined him. When they charged at each other in the second battle, they destroyed a very large number of the Parthians and King Artabanus quickly turned to flight. He once more prepared for war. And so for twelve months they rode against each other, at one moment making war and then taking a rest; finally they looked once more to battle and came to the place of conflict.

9. (Fragmentary) But remember your words when you spoke to the queen, after you saw the course of the stars. We heard (them) on that day ... We set forth on the understanding ... the victory was mine and the destruction (would be) yours.

(Fragmentary) King Artabanus himself said to Artasiras 'I cannot while still alive ... be deprived of my kingdom nor serve you.

(Fragmentary) He charged at the Persians ... and casting his spear at Artasiras.

When he admitted this, he governed with her over the remaining Parthians, Persians and Assyrians. All his actions were reasonable and he rejoiced in respect for the law and most just government. For he was eager to earn praise since he had unexpectedly mounted the throne of Persia. These events were reported to Chosroes the Arsacid ruler of Great Armenia, that Artasiras the son of Sasanus had gained the throne of Persia and had destroyed Artabanus his brother. There was an additional report that the Parthians preferred the kingship of Artasiras to that of their own countryman.

(Dodgeon)

Agathias IV, 24, 1: But my narrative, by a natural progression, has come back to Artaxares. It is time to fulfil the promise I made earlier, to record the kings who came after him. As for Artaxares himself, I have already told in detail his origins and how he assumed the throne. I will add only this about him – that Artaxares seized the throne of Persia 538 years after Alexander the Great of Macedon, in the fourth year of the other Alexander, the son of Mamaea (i.e. 226), in the way that I have already recorded, and held it for fifteen years less two months.

(Cameron, p. 121)

George of Pisidia,[8] *Heraclias* II, 173–7, p. 259, ed. Pertusi: For they say that Artaser (i.e. Ardashir), being a slave by station, with his despotic and arrogant sword removed the Parthians from their former (share of) power to the captive throne which he had seized and is now enthroning Persia again in evil.

(Lieu and C. J. Morgan)

al-Tabari, pp. 816–18 (Nöldeke, pp. 7–14): see Appendix 1, pp. 276–7.

Zonaras XII, 15, p. 572, 7–17 (iii, p. 121, 3–16, Dindorf): Artaxerxes (i.e. Ardashir) however the Persian, who was from an unknown and obscure background, transferred the kingdom of the

Parthians to the Persians and ruled over them. From him Chosroes is said to trace his descent. For after the death of Alexander the Macedonian, his Macedonian successors ruled over Persians and Parthians and the other nations for a long time, but in going against one another they destroyed each other's power. After they had thus become weakened, Arsacides the Parthian was the first to attempt rebellion from them and he gained control over the Parthians; and he left his dominion to his own descendants. Artabanus was the last of these. The afore-mentioned Artaxerxes defeated him in three battles and captured and killed him.

(Dodgeon)

1.1.3. Ardashir's initial (and unsuccessful) attempt to capture Hatra (*c.* 229)

Dio Cassius (Reliq.) LXXX, 3, 2: (After killing Artabanus, Artaxerxes) made a campaign against Hatra which he endeavoured to take as a base for attacking the Romans. He did make a breach in the wall but he lost a number of soldiers through an ambuscade; he transferred his position to Media.[9]

(Foster vi, pp.108–9)

1.1.4. His failure in Armenia[10]

Dio Cassius (Reliq.) LXXX, 3, 3: Of this district (Media), as also of Parthia, he acquired no small portion, partly by force and partly by intimidation, and then marched against Armenia. Here he suffered a reverse at the hands of the natives, some Medes and the children of Medes, and the children of Artabanus, and either fled (as some say) or (as others assert) retired to prepare a larger expedition.

(Foster, vi, p. 109)

Agathangelos, *History of the Armenians* I, 18–23 (Thomson 1976: 35–43): see Appendix 2, pp. 309–311.

Moses Khorenats'i, *Hist. Arm.* II, 71–3 (Thomson pp. 218–20): see Appendix 2, pp. 314–16. Zonaras XII, 15, p. 572,18–19 (iii, p. 121, 16–19, Dindorf): Then when he marched against Armenia, he was defeated by the Armenians and Medes who were joined in an attack upon him by the sons of Artabanus.

(Dodgeon)

1.1.5. Ardashir's invasion of Roman territory and his demand for the restitution of the Achaemenid possessions in Europe

Dio Cassius, (Reliq.) LXXX, 4, 1-2: He accordingly became a source of fear to us; for he was encamped with a large army over against not Mesopotamia only but Syria also and boasted that he would win back everything that the ancient Persians had once held as far as the Grecian Sea. It was, he said, his rightful inheritance from his forefathers. He was of no particular account himself, but our military affairs are in such a condition that some joined his cause and others refused to defend themselves. 2. The troops are so distinguished by wantonness, and arrogance, and freedom from reproof, that those in Mesopotamia dared to kill their commander, Flavius Heracleo. . . .

(Foster vi, p. 109)

Herodian VI, 2, 1-2: And so for thirteen years he (i.e. Alexander Severus) ruled the empire in blameless fashion as far as he personally was concerned. In the tenth (MS: fourteenth)[11] year (AD 222), however, unexpected dispatches from the governors of Syria and Mesopotamia revealed that Artaxerxes (i.e. Ardashir), the King of the Persians, had conquered the Parthians and broken up their Eastern kingdom, killing Artabanus who was formerly called the Great King and wore the double diadem. Artaxerxes then subdued all the barbarians on his borders and forced them to pay tribute. He did not remain quiet, however, or stay on his side of the Tigris River, but, after crossing its banks which were the borders of the Roman empire, he overran Mesopotamia and threatened Syria. 2. The mainland facing Europe, separated from it by the Aegean Sea and the Propontic Gulf, and the region called Asia he wished to recover for the Persian empire. Believing these regions to be his by inheritance, he declared that all the countries in that area, including Ionia and Caria, had been ruled by Persian governors, from the rule of Cyrus, who first made the Median empire Persian, and ending with Darius, the last of the Persian monarchs, whose kingdom Alexander the Macedonian had destroyed. He asserted that it was therefore proper for him to recover for the Persians the kingdom which they formerly possessed.[12]

(Echols, p. 156, revised)

Zonaras XII, 15, p. 572, 20-2 (iii, p. 121,19-22, Dindorf): But he (i.e. Ardashir) once more recovered (i.e. from his failure in Armenia) and, with a greater force, occupied Mesopotamia and

Syria and threatened to recover all the lands that belonged to the Persians, as it were, from their ancestors.

(Dodgeon)

1.2.1. The reply of Alexander Severus to Ardashir

Herodian VI, 2, 3–4: When the Eastern governors revealed these developments in their dispatches, Alexander was greatly disturbed by these unanticipated tidings, particularly since, raised from childhood in an age of peace, he had spent his entire life in urban ease and comfort. Before doing anything else, he thought it best, after consulting his advisers, to send an embassy to the king and by his letters halt the invasion and check his expectations. 4. In these letters he told Artaxerxes that he must remain within his own borders and not initiate any action; let him not, deluded by vain hopes, stir up a great war, but rather let each of them be content with what already was his. Artaxerxes would find fighting against the Romans not the same thing as fighting with his barbarian kinsmen and neighbours. Alexander further reminded the Persian king of the victories won over them by Augustus, Trajan, Verus, and Severus. By writing letters of this kind, Alexander thought that he would persuade the barbarian to remain quiet or frighten him to the same course.

(Echols, pp. 156–7, revised)

1.2.2. Invasion of Mesopotamia and Cappadocia by Ardashir

Herodian VI, 2, 5–6: But Artaxerxes (i.e. Ardashir) ignored Alexander's written messages; believing that the matter would be settled by arms, not by words, he took the field, pillaging and looting all the Roman provinces. He overran and plundered Mesopotamia with both infantry and cavalry. He laid siege to the Roman garrison camps on the banks of the rivers, the camps which defended the empire. Rash by nature and elated by successes beyond his expectations, Artaxerxes was convinced that he could surmount every obstacle in his path. 6. The considerations which led him to wish for an expanded empire were not small.

(Echols, p. 157, revised)

Zonaras XII, 15, pp. 572, 22–573,2 (iii, p. 121, 22–4, Dindorf): Then this Artaxerxes and the Persians overran Cappadocia and put Nisibis under siege.

1.2.3. Alexander Severus' preparation for his campaign and his speech before the troops

Herodian, VI, 3, 1–4, 3: When the bold actions of this Eastern barbarian were disclosed to Alexander while he was passing the time in Rome, he found these affronts unendurable. Though the undertaking distressed him and was contrary to his inclinations, since his governors there were calling for him, he made preparations for departure. He assembled for army service picked men from Italy and from all the Roman provinces, enrolling those whose age and physical condition qualified them for military service. 2. The gathering of an army equal in size to the reported strength of the attacking barbarians caused the greatest upheaval throughout the Roman world. When these troops were gathered in Rome, Alexander ordered them to assemble on the usual plain. There he mounted a platform and addressed them as follows: 3. 'I wished, fellow soldiers, to make the customary speech to you, the speech from which I, speaking to the popular taste, receive approval, and you, when you hear it, receive encouragement.

Since you have now enjoyed many years of peace, you may be startled to hear something unusual or contrary to your anticipations. 4. Brave and intelligent men should pray for things to turn out for the best, but they should also endure whatever befalls. It is true that the enjoyment of things done for pleasure brings gratification, but good repute results from the manliness involved in setting matters straight when necessity demands. To initiate unjust actions is not the way of issuing a fair challenge, but it is a courageous deed to rid oneself of those who are troublesome if it is done with good conscience. Optimism stems not from committing injustice but from preventing injustice from being committed. 5. The Persian Artaxerxes has slain his master Artabanus, and the Parthian empire is now Persian. Despising our arms and contemptuous of the Roman reputation, Artaxerxes is attempting to overrun and destroy our imperial possessions. I first endeavoured by letters and persuasion to check his mad greed and his lust for the property of others. But the king, with barbarian arrogance, is unwilling to remain within his own boundaries, and challenges us to battle. 6. Let us not hesitate to accept his challenge. You veterans remind yourselves of the victories which you often won over the barbarians under the leadership of Severus and my father, Antoninus. You recruits, thirsting for glory and honour, make it clear that you know how to live at peace mildly and with propriety, but make it equally clear that you turn with courage to the tasks of war when necessity demands. 7. The barbarian is bold against the hesitant and the cowardly, but he does not stand up in like fashion to those who fight back; it is not in set-battles that they fight the enemy with hope of success. Rather, they believe that whatever success they win is the result of plundering after a feigned retreat and flight. Discipline and organized battle tactics favour us, together with the fact that we have always learnt to conquer the barbarian.'

4   When Alexander finished speaking, the cheering army promised its wholehearted support for the war. After a lavish distribution of money to the soldiers, the emperor ordered preparations for his departure from the city. He then went before the senate and made a speech similar to the one recorded above; following this, he publicly announced his plans to march out. 2. On the appointed day, after he had performed the sacrifices prescribed for departures, Alexander left Rome, weeping and repeatedly looking back at the city. The senate and all the people escorted him, and everyone wept, for he was held in great affection by the people of Rome, among whom he had been reared and whom he had ruled with moderation for many years.

3. Travelling rapidly, he came to Antioch, after visiting the provinces and the garrison camps in Illyricum; from that region he collected a huge force of troops. On arrival at Antioch he continued his preparations for the war, giving the soldiers military training under field conditions.

(Echols, pp. 157–60, revised)

1.2.4. Renewed attempts at negotiation and their failure

Herodian, VI, 4, 4–6: He thought it best to send another embassy to the Persian king to discuss the possibility of peace and friendship, hoping to persuade him or to intimidate him by his presence. The barbarian, however, sent the envoys back to the emperor unsuccessful. Then Artaxerxes chose four hundred very tall Persians, outfitted them with fine clothes and gold ornaments, and equipped them with horses and bows; He sent these men to Alexander as envoys, thinking that their appearance would dazzle the Romans.

The envoys said that the great king Artaxerxes ordered the Romans and their emperor to withdraw from all Syria and from that part of Asia opposite Europe; they were to permit the Persians to rule as far as Ionia and Caria and to govern all the nations separated by the Aegean Sea and the Propontic Gulf, inasmuch as these were the Persians' by right of inheritance. 6. When the Persian envoys delivered these demands, Alexander ordered the entire four hundred to be arrested; stripping off their finery, he sent the group to Phrygia, where villages and farm land were assigned to them, but he gave orders that they were not to be allowed to return to their native country. He treated them in this fashion because he thought it would violate their sanctity and it would be cowardly to put them to death, since they were not fighting but simply carrying out their master's orders.

(Echols, p. 160, revised)

Zonaras XII, 15, p. 573, 2–14 (iii, pp. 121, 24–122, 7, Dindorf): However Alexander sent envoys to him and requested a peace. But the Persian did not admit the embassy, but he sent to Alexander four hundred grandees, dressing them in expensive clothing and mounting them on horses of the very best and equipping them with splendid arms. He thought that in this way he would overawe the emperor and the Romans. When they arrived and came into Alexander's sight, they said, 'The Great King Artaxerxes orders the Romans to retire from Syria and all of Asia opposite Europe, and to make way for the Persians to govern as far as the sea.' Alexander seized these men and stripped them of their weapons and clothes and took away their horses. He scattered them among a large number of villages and compelled them to till the land. For he judged it impious to kill them.

(Dodgeon)

1.2.5. Suppression of mutinies by Alexander Severus

Herodian VI, 4, 7: This is the way the affair turned out. While Alexander was preparing to cross the Tigris and Euphrates rivers and lead his army into barbarian territory, several mutinies broke out among his troops, especially among the soldiers from Egypt; but revolts occurred also in Syria, where the soldiers attempted to proclaim a new emperor. These defections were quickly discovered and suppressed. At this time Alexander transferred to other stations those field armies which seemed better able to check the barbarian invasions.

(Echols, p. 160)

SHA Severus Alexander 50, 53–4: And so, after showing himself such a great and good emperor at home and abroad, he embarked upon a campaign against the Parthians; and this he conducted with such discipline and amid such respect, that you would have said that senators, not soldiers, were passing that way. 2. Wherever the legions directed their march, the tribunes were orderly, the centurions modest, and the soldiers courteous, and as for Alexander himself, because of these many great acts of consideration, the inhabitants of the provinces looked up to him as a god. 3. And the soldiers too loved their youthful emperor like a brother, or a son, or a father; for they were respectably clad, well shod, even to the point of elegance, excellently armed, and even provided with horses and suitable saddles and bridles, so that all who saw the army of Alexander immediately realized the power of Rome. 4. In short, he made every effort to appear worthy of his name and even to surpass the Macedonian king, and he used to say that there should be a great difference between a Roman and a Macedonian Alexander. 5. Finally, he provided himself with soldiers armed with silver and golden shields, and also a phalanx of thirty thousand men, whom he ordered to be called phalangarii, and with these he won many victories in Persia. This phalanx, as a matter of fact, was formed from six legions, and was armed like the other troops, but after the Persian wars received higher pay. . . .

53 Now, in order to show his strictness, I have thought it right to insert one military harangue, which reveals his methods of dealing with the troops. 2. After his arrival in Antioch the soldiers began to use their leisure in the women's baths and the other pleasures, but when Alexander learned of it he ordered all who did so to be arrested and thrown into chains. 3. When this was made known, a mutiny was attempted by that legion whose members were put in chains. 4. Thereupon, after bringing all those who had been thrown into chains to the tribunal, he mounted the platform, and, with the soldiers standing about him, and that too in arms, he began as follows: 5. 'Fellow-soldiers, if, in spite of all, such acts as have been committed by your comrades are to you displeasing, the discipline of our ancestors still governs the state, and if this is weakened, we shall lose both the name and the empire of the Romans. 6. For never shall such things be done in my reign which were but recently done under that filthy monster. 7. Soldiers of Rome, your companions, my comrades and fellow-soldiers, are whoring and drinking and bathing and, indeed, conducting themselves in the manner of the Greeks. Shall I

tolerate this longer? Shall I not deliver them over to capital punishment?' 8. Thereupon an uproar arose. And again he spoke: 'Will you not silence that shouting, needed indeed against the foe in battle but not against your emperor? 9. Of a certainty, your drill-masters have taught you to use this against Sarmatians, and Germans, and Persians, but not against him who gives you rations presented by the men of the provinces, and who gives you clothing and pay. 10. Therefore cease from this fierce shouting, needed only on the battlefield and in war, lest I discharge you all today with one speech and with a single word, calling you "Citizens". 11. But I know not whether I should even call you Citizens; for you are not worthy to be members even of the populace of Rome, if you do not observe Rome's laws.'

54   And when they clamoured still more loudly and even threatened him with their swords, he continued: 'Put down your hands, which, if you are brave men, you should raise against the foe, for such things do not frighten me. 2. For if you slay me, who am but one man, the state and the senate and the Roman people will not lack someone to take vengeance for me upon you.' 3. And when they clamoured nonetheless at this, he shouted, 'Citizens, withdraw, and lay down your arms.' 4. Then in a most marvellous fashion they laid down their arms and also their military coats, and all withdrew, not to the camp, but to various lodgings. 5. And on that occasion, particularly, it was seen how much could be accomplished by his strictness and discipline. 6. Finally, his attendants and those who stood about his person carried the standards back to the camp, and the populace, gathering up the arms, bore them to the Palace. 7. However, thirty days afterwards, before he set out on the campaign against the Persians, he was prevailed upon to restore the discharged legion to its former status; and it was chiefly through its prowess in the field that he won the victory. Nevertheless, he inflicted capital punishment on his tribunes because it was through their negligence that the soldiers had revelled at Daphne or else with their connivance that the troops had mutinied.

(Magie ii, pp. 279–89)

1.3.1. Visit of Alexander Severus to Palmyra (*c.* 230/1)

CISem. II, 3932 (= *Inv.* III, 22; Greek and Palmyrene): Statue of Julius Zabdilah (Gk: Zenobios who is also (named) Zabdilah), son of Malkho, son of Malkho, son of Nassum, who was strategos of the colony (i.e. Palmyra – the last word is missing in the Gk) at the time of the coming of the divine Emperor Alexander; who assisted Rutilius Crispinus, the general in chief, during his stay here, and when he brought the legions here (Gk: at the time of troubles here) on numerous occasions; who was director of the market and saved large sums of money (Gk: and did not hesitate to spend not inconsiderable sums); who conducted his career so honourably that he received a testimonial from the god Yarhibol, and also from Julius (Priscus), most eminent prefect of the holy praetorium, and who loved his city: it is why the Senate and the People have raised (this statue) to him to honour him, in the year 554 (AD 242/3).[13]

(Vince, revised Brock)

1.3.2. Repair to the Zela–Sebastopolis road as preparation for Alexander Severus' Persian campaign (231)

Wilson, *Anatolian Studies* 10 (1960), p. 133 (Latin milestone found lying inside Zile castle): The Emperor, Caesar, M(arcus) Aure(lius) [S]everu[s] A[lexa]n[der], the Devout, the Fortunate, the Unconquered, Augustus, Pon(tifex) Max(imus), holder of the tribunician power, Consul, Father of the Fatherland, Proconsul through the agency of Q(uintus) Jul(ius) Proculeianus, imperial praetorian legate. One Mile (?). (The district of?) Zelit(is?).

Cumont, *CRAI* 1905, p. 348 (Latin milestone found in a cemetery south of Zile): The Emperor, Caesar, M(arcus) A[ur(elius) Se]v[erus] Alexander, the Devout, the Fortunate, the Unconquered, Aug(ustus), Pont(ifex) Max(imus), holder of the tribunician power ten times, of the consulship three times, proconsul through the agency of Q(uintus) Jul(ius) Proculeianus, imperial praetorian legate of [Cap]pa[docia]. (. . .) seven (miles?).

Cumont, *CRAI* 1905, p. 349 (Latin milestone found at Malumseyit): [The Emperor Caesar Marcus Aurelius] Severus [Alexander], the Devout, the Fortunate, the Unconquered, Augustus, Pont(ifex) Max(imus), holder of the tribunician power ten times, through the agency of Jul(ius) Proclianus (*sic*), imperial praetorian legate. Five miles from Sebastopolis.

(Lieu)

1.3.3. The Persian campaign of Alexander Severus (231–3)

Herodian VI, 5, 1–6, 6: After thus setting matters in order, Alexander, considering that the huge army he had assembled was now nearly equal in power and number to the barbarians, consulted his advisers and then divided his force into three separate armies. One army he ordered to overrun the territory of the Medes and to reconnoitre the northern regions and pass through Armenia, which seemed to favour the Roman cause.[14] 2. He sent the second army to the eastern sector of the barbarian territory, where, it is said, the Tigris and Euphrates rivers at their confluence empty into very dense marshes; these are the only rivers whose mouths cannot be clearly determined.[15] The third and most powerful army he kept himself, promising to lead it against the barbarians in the central sector.[16] He thought that in this way he would attack them from different directions when they were unprepared and not anticipating such strategy, and he believed that the Persian horde, constantly split up to face their attackers on several fronts, would be weaker and less unified for battle. 3. The barbarians, it may be noted, do not have a paid army as the Romans do, nor do they maintain trained standing armies. Rather, all the available men, and sometimes the women too, mobilize at the king's order.[17] At the end of the war each man returns to his regular occupation, taking as his pay whatever falls to his lot from the general booty. 4. They use the bow and the horse in war, as the Romans do, but the barbarians are reared with these from childhood, and live by hunting; they never lay aside their quivers or dismount from their horses, but employ them constantly for war and the chase.

Alexander therefore devised what he believed to be the best possible plan for action, only to have Fortune defeat his design. 5. The army sent through Armenia had an agonizing passage over the high, steep mountains of that country.[18] (As it was still summer, however, they were able to complete the crossing.) Then, plunging down into the land of the Medes, the Roman soldiers devastated the countryside, burning many villages and carrying off much loot. Informed of this, the Persian king put up as strong a resistance as he could, but met with little success in his efforts to halt the Roman advance. 6. This is rough country; while it provided firm footing and easy passage for the infantry, the rugged mountain terrain hampered the movements of the barbarian cavalry and prevented their riding down the Romans or even making contact with them. Then men came and reported to the Persian king that another Roman army had appeared in eastern Parthia and was overrunning the plains there.

7. Fearing that the Romans, after ravaging Parthia unopposed, might advance into Persia, Artaxerxes left behind a force which he

thought strong enough to defend Media, and hurried with his entire army into the eastern sector. The Romans were advancing much too carelessly because they had met no opposition and, in addition, they believed that Alexander and his army, the largest and most formidable of the three, had already attacked the barbarians in the central sector. They thought, too, that their own advance would be easier and less hazardous when the barbarians were constantly being drawn off elsewhere to meet the threat of the emperor's army. 8. All three Roman armies had been ordered to make a flanking assault on the enemy's territory, and a final rendezvous had been selected where they would meet after the regions in between them had been brought under control. But Alexander failed them: he did not bring his army or come himself into barbarian territory, either because he was afraid to risk his life for the Roman empire or because his mother's feminine fears or excessive mother love restrained him. 9. She blocked his efforts to behave bravely by persuading him that he should let others risk their lives for him, but that he should not personally fight in battle. It was this reluctance of his which led to the destruction of the advancing Roman army.[19] The king attacked it unexpectedly with his entire force and trapped the Romans like fish in a net; firing their arrows from all sides at the encircled soldiers, the Persians massacred the whole army. 10. The outnumbered Romans were unable to stem the attack of the Persian horse; they used their shields to protect those parts of their bodies exposed to the Persian arrows. Content merely to protect themselves, they offered no resistance. As a result, all the Romans were driven into the one spot, where they made a wall of their shields and fought like an army under the siege. Hit and wounded from every side, they held out bravely as long as they could, but in the end all were killed. The Romans suffered a staggering disaster; it is not easy to recall another like it, one in which a great army was destroyed, an army inferior in strength and determination to none of the armies of old.[20] The successful outcome of these important events encouraged the Persian king to anticipate better things in the future.

6.   When the disaster was reported to Alexander, who was seriously ill either from despondency or from the lack of acclimatization to the unfamiliar climate, he fell into despair. The rest of the army angrily denounced the emperor because the invading army had been betrayed as a result of his failure to carry out the plans faithfully agreed upon. 2. And now Alexander refused to endure his indisposition and the stifling air any longer. The entire army was

sick and the troops from Illyricum especially were seriously ill and dying, being accustomed to moist, cool air and to more food than they were being issued. 3. Eager to set out for Antioch, Alexander ordered the army in Media to proceed to that city. This army, on its return journey, was almost totally destroyed in the mountains; a great many soldiers suffered mutilation in the wintry condition of the region, and only a handful of the large number of troops who started the march managed to reach Antioch. The emperor led his own large force to that city, and many of them perished too; so the affair brought the greatest discontent to the army and the greatest dishonour to Alexander, who was betrayed by bad luck and bad judgement. Of the three armies into which he had divided his total force, the greater part was lost by various misfortunes – disease, war and cold.

4. In Antioch, Alexander was quickly revived by the cool air and good water of that city after the acrid drought in Mesopotamia, and the soldiers too recovered there. The emperor tried to console them for their sufferings by a lavish distribution of money, in the belief that this was the only way he could regain their good will. He assembled an army and prepared to march against the Persians again if they should give trouble and not remain quiet. 5. But it was reported that the Persian king had disbanded his army and sent each soldier back to his own country. Though the barbarians seemed to have conquered because of their superior strength, they were exhausted by the numerous skirmishes in Media and by the battle in Parthia, where they lost many killed and many wounded. The Romans were not defeated because they were cowards; indeed they did the enemy much damage and lost only because they were outnumbered. 6. Since the total number of troops which fell on both sides was virtually identical, the surviving barbarians appeared to have won, but by superior numbers, not by superior power. It is no little proof of how much the barbarians suffered that for three or four years after this they remained quiet and did not take up arms. All this the emperor learned while he was at Antioch. Relieved of anxiety about the war, he grew more cheerful and less apprehensive and devoted himself to enjoying the pleasures which the city offered.

(Echols, pp. 161–5, revised)

Aurelius Victor, *liber de Caesaribus* 24, 2: Though a young man, (Alexander Severus) exhibited talents beyond his age and immediately waged war against Xerxes (*sic*), the king of the Persians, with vast resources; and after defeating him and putting him to flight, he marched with all haste to Gaul which was disturbed by the incursions of the Germans.

(Dodgeon)

Festus, *breviarium* 22, pp. 63, 17–64, 2: Aurelius Alexander, as if reborn by some sort of fate for the destruction of the Persian race, took up the administration of the Roman Empire while he was still a youth. He most gloriously defeated Xerxes (i.e. Ardashir) the most noble king of the Persians. . . . At Rome he celebrated his triumph over the Persians with a spectacular display.

(Dodgeon)

Eutropius, *breviarium* VIII, 23: To him (i.e. Heliogabalus) succeeded Aurelius Alexander, a very young man, who was named Caesar by the army and Augustus by the senate. Having undertaken a war with the Persians, he defeated their king Xerxes (i.e. Ardashir) with great glory. He enforced military discipline with much severity, and disbanded whole legions that raised a disturbance.

(Watson, p. 516)

Jerome, *chronicon*, s. a. 223, p. 215, 3–7: Alexander (Severus) triumphed gloriously over Xerxes (*sic*), the king of the Persians, and he was a severe reviser of military discipline as he would discharge dishonourably entire legions which were mutinous.

(Dodgeon)

SHA Severus Alexander 55, 1–3: And so, having set out from there against the Persians with a great array, he defeated Artaxerxes, a most powerful king. In this battle he himself commanded the flanks, urged on the soldiers, exposed himself constantly to missiles, performed many brave deeds with his own hand, and by his words encouraged individual soldiers to praiseworthy actions. 2. At last he routed and put to flight this great king, who had come to the war with seven hundred elephants, eighteen hundred scythed chariots, and many thousand horsemen.[21] Thereupon he immediately returned to Antioch and presented to his troops the booty taken from the Persians, commanding the tribunes and generals and even the soldiers to keep for themselves the plunder they had seized in the country. 3. Then for the first time Romans had Persian slaves, but because the kings of the Persians deem it a disgrace that any of their subjects should serve anyone as slaves, ransoms were

offered, and these Alexander accepted and then returned the
men, either giving the ransom-money to those who had taken the
slaves captive, or depositing it in the public treasury.

(Magie, ii, pp. 289–91)

Orosius, *adversus paganos* VII, 18, 7: Now Alexander immediately
made an expedition against the Persians and victoriously overcame
Xerxes (i.e. Ardashir), their king, in a very great battle.

(Deferrari, pp. 313)

Syncellus p. 437, 15–25 (pp. 673, 17–674, 8, CSHB): After him (i.e.
Elagabalus) ruled Alexander the son of Mamaea his cousin, who
was born at Arcae on the sea coast of Phoenicia. He was led on by
the advice of Ulpian the Jurist who was very strongly attached to
good military discipline. Therefore he too was slain by the soldiers
before the emperor's gaze. A certain Uranius was named emperor
at Edessa in Osrhoene and, taking power in opposition to Alexander, he was killed by him when Alexander drove out the Persians
who were raiding Cappadocia and besieging Nisibis. But when he
returned to Rome he was slain with his mother Mamaea in a
military riot. And a certain Maximus, a Mysian by birth, a general
of Celtic troops, was declared Roman emperor by the armies. He
governed the Roman Empire for three years.

(Dodgeon)

Cedrenus, i, p. 450, 3–7: Alexander the son of Mamaea, nephew of
Avitus, was emperor for thirteen years and eight months. In his
reign there was a famine in Rome (of such severity) that the citizens
would even avail themselves of human flesh. He campaigned
against the Persians and was overwhelmed in defeat. And losing his
prestige, he was murdered (by his soldiers) together with his mother.

(Dodgeon)

Zonaras XII, 15, p. 573, 14–22 (iii, pp. 122, 7–16, Dindorf): But
he divided his own armies into three divisions and launched a
three-pronged attack on the Persians. A great number of the
Persians were destroyed, but the Romans also suffered heavy
casualties, not so much by the enemy as in the return through the
mountains of Armenia. For the feet of the marchers and also some
hands got frost-bitten and had to be amputated after turning black
and becoming lifeless. For this reason Alexander was also blamed
by the Romans and consequently he fell gravely ill either from
despondency or from the change of climate.

(Dodgeon)

1.3.4. Road repair in Mesopotamia, near the Tigris (231/2)

Maricq, *Syria* 34 (1957), p. 294 (Milestone found about 5 km SE of Singara, Latin): Imp(erator) Caesar M(arcus) Aurelius Severus Alexander, Devout, Fortunate, Augustus, Pont(ifex) Maxim(us), in his eleventh year of tribunician power, consul for the third time, father of his country, proconsul. Three miles from Sing(ara).[22]

(Lieu)

1.3.5. Appearance of the *dux ripae* at Dura Europos[23] (before 245)

Gilliam, *TAPA* 72 (1941), p. 158 (Graffito found in the house of the *Dux Ripae*, Greek): May Elpidephorus, the tragic-actor from Byzantium, raised as a fosterling (?)[24] by Domitius Pompeianus, the devout and just *dux ripae*,[25] be remembered[26] together with Probus his accompanying actor.[27] May the one remaining here and the reader be remembered.[28]

(Lieu)

1.4.1. Causes of Alexander Severus' withdrawal from the East

Herodian VI, 7, 1–6: 1. Alexander thought that Persian affairs would remain quiet and peaceful for the duration of the truce which would delay and hinder the barbarian king from launching a second campaign. For the barbarian army, once disbanded, was not easily remustered, as it was not organized on a permanent basis. More a mob than a regular army, the soldiers had only those supplies which each man brought for himself when he reported for duty. Moreover, the Persians are reluctant to leave their wives, children, and homeland. 2. Now unexpected messages and dispatches upset Alexander and caused him even greater anxiety: the governors in Illyria reported that the Germans had crossed the Rhine and the Danube rivers, were plundering the Roman empire, and with a huge force were overrunning the garrison camps on the banks of these rivers, as well as the cities and villages there. They reported also that the provinces of Illyricum bordering on and close to Italy were in danger. 3. The governors informed the emperor that it was absolutely necessary that he and his entire army come to them. The revelation of these developments terrified Alexander and aroused great concern among the soldiers from Illyricum, who seemed to have suffered a double disaster; the men who had undergone many hardships in the Persian expedition now learned that their families had been slaughtered by the Germans. They were naturally enraged at this, and blamed Alexander for their misfortunes because he had betrayed affairs in the East by his cowardice and carelessness and was hesitant and dilatory about the situation in the North. 4. Alexander and his advisers, too, feared for the safety of Italy itself. They did not consider the Persian threat at all similar to the German. The fact is that those who live in the East, separated from the West by a great continent and a broad sea, scarcely ever hear of Italy, whereas the provinces of Illyricum, since they are narrow and very little of their territory is under Roman control, make the Germans actually neighbours of the Italians: the two peoples thus share common borders. 5. Although he loathed the idea, Alexander glumly announced his departure for Illyria. Necessity compelled him to go, however; and so, leaving behind a force which he considered strong enough to defend the Roman frontiers, after he had seen that the camps and outposts were given more efficient defences, and had assigned to each camp its normal complement of troops, the emperor marched out against the Germans with the rest of his army. 6. Completing the journey quickly, he encamped on the banks of the Rhine and made preparations for the German campaign. Alexander spanned the river with boats lashed together to form a bridge, thinking that this would provide an easy means of crossing for his soldiers.

(Echols, pp. 165–6, revised)

1.4.2. Eastern troops taken by Alexander Severus to Germany

Herodian VI, 7, 8: Alexander had brought with him many Moorish javelin-men and a huge force of archers from the East and from the region of Osrhoene, together with Parthian deserters who had offered their help; with these he prepared to battle with the Germans.[29]

(Echols, p. 166)

SHA Sev. Alex. 61, 8: But all the military array which Maximinus afterwards led to Germany (in 235) was Alexander's, and it was a very powerful one, too, by reason of the soldiers from Armenia, Osrhoene and Parthia, composed, as it was, of men of every race.

(Magie, ii, p. 303)

1.4.3. The triumphal return to Rome of Alexander Severus and his speech to the Senate (25 September 233)

SHA *Sev. Alex.* 56–57, 3, 58,1: 1. After this, returning to Rome, he conducted a most splendid triumph and then first of all addressed the senate in the following speech: 2. From the transactions of the senate for the seventh day before the Kalends of October: 'Conscript Fathers, we have conquered the Persians. There is no need of lengthy rhetoric; you should know, however, this much, namely, what their arms were, and what their array. 3. First of all, there were seven hundred elephants provided with turrets and archers and great loads of arrows. Of these we captured thirty, we have left two hundred slain upon the field, and we have led eighteen in triumph. 4. Moreover, there were scythed chariots, one thousand eight hundred in number. Of these we could have presented to your eyes two hundred, of which the horses have been slain, but since they could easily be counterfeited we have refrained from so doing. 5. One hundred and twenty thousand of their cavalry we have routed, ten thousand of their horsemen clad in full mail, whom they call cuirassiers, we have slain in battle, and with their armour we have armed our own men. We have captured many of the Persians and have sold them into slavery, 6. and we have re-conquered the lands which lie between the rivers, those of Mesopotamia I mean, abandoned by that filthy monster. 7. Artaxerxes, the most powerful of kings, in fact as well in name, we have routed and driven from the field, so that the land of the Persians saw him in full flight, and where once our ensigns were led away in triumph, there the king himself fled apace leaving his own standards. 8. These are our achievements, Conscript Fathers, and there is no need of rhetoric. Our soldiers have come back enriched, and in victory no one remembers his hardships. 9. It is now your part to decree a general thanksgiving, that we may not seem to the gods to be ungrateful.' Then followed the acclamations of the senate: 'Alexander Augustus, may the gods keep you! Persicus Maximus, may the gods keep you! Parthicus in truth, Persicus in truth.[30] We behold your trophies, we behold your victories too. 10. Hail to the youthful Emperor, the Father of his Country, the Pontifex Maximus! Through you we foresee victory on every hand. He conquers who can rule his soldiers. Rich is the senate, rich the soldiers and rich the Roman people!'
57   Thereupon he dismissed the senate and went up to the Capitolium, and then, after offering sacrifices and dedicating the

tunics of the Persians in the temple, he delivered the following address: 'Fellow-citizens, we have conquered the Persians. We have brought back the soldiers laden with riches. To you we promise a largess, and tomorrow we will give games in the Circus in celebration of our victory over the Persians.'

2. All this we have found both in the annals and in many writers. Some assert, however, that he was betrayed by one of his slaves and did not conquer the king at all, but, on the contrary, was forced to flee in order to escape being conquered. 3. But those who have read most of the writers are sure that this assertion is contrary to the general belief. It is also stated that he lost his army through hunger, cold, and disease, and this is the version given by Herodian, but contrary to the belief of the majority.

58   Other victories were also won – in Mauretania Tingitana by Furius Celsus, in Illyricum by Varius Macrinus, Alexander's kinsman, and in Armenia by Junius Palmatus, and from all these places laurelled letters were sent to Alexander.

(Magie, ii, pp. 291–5)

1.4.4. The Persian attack of 238/9

SEG 7 (1934) 743b, lines 17–19 (Greek graffito from the house of Nebuchelus in Dura Europos): On the thirtieth day of the month of Xandikus of the year 550 (20 April 239), the Persians descended upon us.

AE 1948, 124 (Greek epitaph found in a private house in the north-western part of the Agora complex in Dura Europos): Julius Terentius, tribune of the Twentieth Cohort of Palmyrenes, the brave in campaigns, mighty in wars, dead – a man worthy of memory, Aurelia Arria buried this her beloved husband, whom may the divine spirits receive and the light earth conceal.

SHA Max. et Balb. 13, 5: But when it was now arranged that Maximus (*r.* 235–8) should set out against the Parthians (*sic*) and Balbinus (emperor in 238) against the Germans, while the young Gordian remained at Rome, the soldiers, who were seeking an opportunity of killing the Emperors, and at first could not find (them) because Maximus and Balbinus were even attended by a German guard, grew more menacing every day.

(Magie ii, pp. 473–5)

Syncellus, p. 443, 5–6 (p. 681, 5–9, CSHB): see 2.2.1.

1.4.5. Roman assistance to Hatra

AE 1958, 238 (Latin): (This altar was) presented on the fifth day of June in the consulship of Severus and Quintianus (i.e. 5 June, 235). (Cf. Oates, 1955: 39)

AE 1958, 239 (Latin): To the Unconquered Sun God, Quintus Petronius Quintianus, military tribune of the First Parthian Legion, tribune of the Ninth Gordian Cohort of Moors, set up (this statue) which he had vowed to the cult of the place (i.e. Samas the Sun God).

(Oates, 1955: 39)

AE 1958, 240 (Latin): Consecrated to Hercules for the health of our Lord the Emperor, Petronius Quintianus, a native of Nicomedia (?), (set up this statue) to the patron deity of the cohort.

(Oates, 1955: 40; Maricq, 1957: 289)

1.5.1. The fall of Hatra to the Persians (240)[31]

Codex Manichaicus Coloniensis[32] 18, 1–16, eds Koenen and Römer, pp. 10–12: When I was twenty[-four] years old, in the year in which Dariadaxir[33] (i.e. Ardashir), the king of Persia, subjugated the city of Hatra, and in which Sapores (i.e. Shapur), his son assumed the mighty diadem in the month of Pharmuthi on the [eighth] day according to the moon (i.e. 17/18 April, 240), the most blessed Lord had compassion on me and called me to his grace and [immediately] sent to me [from there] my Syzygos (i.e. divine Twin) [. . .].

al-Tabari, pp. 827–31 (Nöldeke, pp. 33–40): See Appendix 1, pp. 283–5.[34]

2 The Persian Expedition of Gordian III

(the 'first campaign' of Shapur I against the Roman Empire)

2.1.1. Renewal of hostility between Rome and Persia (241)

SHA Gordian⟨i Tres⟩ 23, 5-6: When, however, this trouble in Africa had been ended,[1] a war broke out with the Persians – this being in the first consulship of Pompeianus and the second of Gordian (i.e. 241). 6. But, before setting out for this war, the young Gordian took a wife, the daughter of Timesitheus, a most erudite man, whom Gordian considered worthy of being his relation because of his powers of eloquence, and immediately made him prefect.[2]

(Magie, ii, pp. 423–5)

2.1.2. Shapur's accession to sole rule

Agathias IV, 24, 2: The wicked Shapur of whom I have spoken succeeded him (i.e. Ardashir), and lived on for thirty-one years more,[3] doing great harm to the Romans.

(Cameron, 1969/70 p. 121)

al-Tabari, pp. 822–7 (Nöldeke, pp. 25–31): See Appendix I, pp. 280–3.

2.1.3. Description of his Empire

ŠKZ (Gk = Res Gestae Divi Saporis), lines 1-6: I am the Mazda-worshipping divine Shapur, King of Kings of Aryans (i.e. Iranians) and non-Aryans, of the race of the gods, son of the Mazda-worshipping divine Ardashir, King of Kings of the Aryans, of (2) the race of the gods, grandson of the King Papak, I am the Lord of the Aryan (i.e. Iranian) nation.

And I possess the following places: Persis, Parthia, Susiana, Mesene, Assuristan, Adiabene, Arabia (i.e. Bet Arabaye), Atropa (3)-tene, Armenia, Iberia (i.e. Georgia), Makhelonia, Albania, (Balasa)gan until the foot of the Caucasus and the (Alban)ian Gates and the whole of the Pressouar Mountains (i.e. the Elbourz), Media, Gourgan (i.e. Hyrcania), Marou (i.e. Margiane) (4) Are (i.e. Aria) and all the nations in the upper parts: Kermazene (i.e. Carmania), Segistane (i.e. Sakastan), (Turan, Makuran, Paradan), India and the nations of the Kusene (i.e. Kushan) as far as this side of Pash Kibour and up to the frontier of Kas (i.e. Kashgar), Sodikene (i.e. Sogdiana) and (5) Tsatsene (i.e. Tashkent) and from the other shore of the sea the nation of Mi(. . .) (Pth.: Mzwn = Oman?). And we have given the name Peros-sabour (i.e. Anbar) to a (fief?) and we have given a name to Hormizdartazir (modern Ahwaz).[4] And such nations (6) and the rulers from every nation we have made subject to tribute.

(Lieu)

2.1.4. Restoration of the kingdom of Edessa by Gordian III

Michael the Syrian, *Chron.* V, 5, pp. 77–8 (Syriac): The Edessenes and their kings came under the Roman yoke in the year 477 of the Greeks (AD 166), the seventh year of Lucius, the emperor of the Romans.[5] . . . They were deprived of their king and their kingdom ceased completely to exist in the fifth year of Philip, the emperor of the Romans. In the five hundred and sixtieth year of the Greeks (AD 249) their kingdom was taken away from them during the time of Abgar Severus.[6] In fact the Romans expelled him because he wished to rebel against them. They established Aurelianus, son of Habesai, as governor in place of their king, and imposed on them a tribute of servitude.

(Vince, revised Brock)

2.1.5. The death of Gordian and the Roman withdrawal (244): (a) the Persian view

ŠKZ (Gk) lines 6–9: And when I was first established over the dominion of the nations, the Caesar Gordian (7) from the whole of the Roman Empire and the nations of the Goths and the Germans raised an army and marched against Assyria, against the nation of the Aryans (i.e. Iranians) and against us. A great battle took place between the two sides on the frontiers of (8) Assyria at Meshike.[7]

Caesar Gordian was destroyed[8] and the Roman army was annihilated. The Romans proclaimed Philip (9) Caesar.

(Lieu)

2.2.1. The death of Gordian: (b) the Roman view[9]

Oracula Sibyllina XIII, 13–20:

> Then there will be an uprising of the enterprising Persians,
> together with the Indians, Armenians and Arabs,
> A Roman emperor (i.e. Gordian), insatiable for war, will
> approach them –
> 15   A young Ares (i.e. Mars), he will lead spearmen against the
> Assyrians.
> Unto the Euphrates, deep flowing, silver,
> shall warlike Ares stretch forth his spear
> for the sake of vengeance. Betrayed by his colleague,
> 20   he will fall down in the ranks, smitten by the gleaming iron.[10]

(Lieu)

Aurelius Victor, *liber de Caesaribus* 27, 7–8: 7. In that year (i.e. 242), after having increased and confirmed the quinquennial games which were introduced to Rome by Nero, he marched against the Persians[11] but before that, in accordance with an ancient custom, he opened the temple of Janus, which had been closed by Marcus Aurelius. 8. Then, after a brilliant campaign, he was murdered in the sixth year of his reign (Feb./March 244), the victim of the intrigues of his Praetorian Prefect, Marcus Philippus.

(Dodgeon)

Festus, *breviarium* 22, p. 64, 2–7: Under Gordian, the Parthians (*sic*) encouraged by the youth of the (Roman) prince, rebelled and were crushed in major battles. On his return as victor from Persia, he (i.e. Gordian) was murdered through the treachery of Philip, his Praetorian Prefect. The soldiers erected a memorial to him about twenty miles from the fortress of Circesium which is now still extant and they conducted his remains to Rome with every mark of respect.

(Dodgeon)

Eutropius, *breviarium* IX, 2, 2–3, 1: 2. Gordian, while still very much a youth, married Tranquillina at Rome, opened the twin gates of Janus and, setting out for the east, made war upon the Parthians (*sic*) who were then planning to make an incursion. He conducted the war with success and made havoc of the Persians in great battles. 3. As he was returning, he was killed, not far from the Roman boundaries, by the treachery of Philip who reigned after him. The Roman soldiers raised a monument for him twenty miles from Circesium, which is a fortress of the Romans, overlooking the Euphrates. His remains they brought to Rome, and gave him the title 'the Divine'.

3 When Gordian was killed, the two Philips, father and son, seized the government. After withdrawing the army intact, they set out from Syria to Italy.

(Watson)

Jerome, *Chronicon*, s. aa. 241–4, p. 217, 1–7: Gordian, while still a young man, vanquished the nation of the Parthians and when the victor was on his return to the native land he was killed by the treachery of Philip, the Praetorian Prefect, not far from Roman soil. The soldiers built a mound for Gordian which was near the Euphrates and his bones were conveyed to Rome.

(Lieu)

Ammianus Marcellinus XXIII, 5, 7–8: (AD 363) Leaving Circesium, we (i.e. Julian's expeditionary force) came to Zaitha, the name of the place meaning an olive-tree.[12] Here we saw the tomb of the emperor Gordian, which is visible a long way off. . . . 8. When, in accordance with his innate piety, he (i.e. Julian) made offerings to this deified emperor and was on his way to Dura, a town now deserted. . . .

(Yonge)

Ammianus Marcellinus XXIII, 5, 17: (Gordian's achievements recalled by the Emperor Julian) 'But to leave those ancient times, I will enumerate other exploits of more recent memory. Trajan and Verus have all gained victories and trophies in this country; and the younger Gordian, whose monument we have just been honouring, would have reaped similar glory, having conquered and routed the king of Persia at Rhesaina, if he had not been treacherously murdered by the (criminal) action of Philip,[13] the Praetorian Prefect, with a few other wicked accomplices in this very place where he is buried.'

(Yonge, p. 328, revised)

SHA Gord. 26, 3–30, 9: 3. But after this earthquake was stayed, in the consulship of Praetextatus and Atticus, Gordian opened the twin gates of Janus, which was a sign that war had been declared, and set out against the Persians with so huge an army and so much gold as easily to conquer the Persians with either his regulars or his auxiliaries. 4. He marched into Moesia and there, even while making ready, he destroyed, put to flight, expelled, and drove away whatever forces of the enemy were in Thrace. 5. From there he marched through Syria to Antioch, which was then in the possession of the Persians. There he fought and won repeated battles, and drove out Sapor, the king of the Persians, the successor of Artaxerxes.[14] 6. After this he recovered Antioch, Carrhae, and Nisibis, all of which had been included in the Persian empire. 27 Indeed the king of the Persians became so fearful of the Emperor Gordian that, though he was provided with forces both from his own lands and from ours, he nevertheless evacuated the cities and restored them unharmed to their citizens; nor did he injure their possessions in any way. 2. All this, however, was accomplished by Timesitheus, Gordian's father-in-law and prefect.[15] 3. And in the end Gordian's campaign forced the Persians, who were then dreaded even in Italy, to return to their own kingdom, and the Roman power occupied the whole of the East.

4. There is still in existence an oration of Gordian's to the senate, wherein, while writing of his deeds, he gives boundless thanks to his prefect and father-in-law, Timesitheus. I have set down a part of it, that from this you may learn his actual words: 5. 'After those deeds, Conscript Fathers, which were done while on our march and done everywhere in a manner worthy of as many separate triumphs, we (to compress much into little) removed from the necks of the people of Antioch, which were bent under the Persian yoke, the Persians, the kings of the Persians, and the Persians' law.[16] 6. After this we restored Carrhae and other cities also to the Roman sway. We have penetrated as far as Nisibis,[17] and if it be pleasing to the gods, we shall even get to Ctesiphon.[18] 7. Only may our prefect and father-in-law, Timesitheus prosper, for it was by his leadership and his arrangements that we accomplished these things and shall in the future continue to accomplish them. 8. It is now for you to decree thanksgivings, to commend us to the gods, and to give thanks to Timesitheus.'

9. After this was read to the senate, chariots drawn by four elephants were decreed for Gordian, in order that he might have a Persian triumph inasmuch as he had conquered the Persians, and for Timesitheus a six-horse chariot and a triumphal car and the following inscription: 10. 'To His Excellency Timesitheus, Father of

Emperors, Prefect of the Guard and of the entire City, Guardian of the State, the senate and the Roman people make grateful acknowledgment.'

28 But such felicity could not endure. For, as most say, through the plotting of Philip, who was made prefect of the guard after him, or, as others say, because of a disease, Timesitheus died, leaving the Roman state as his heir. Everything that had been his was added to the city's revenues. 2. So excellent was this man's management of public affairs that there was nowhere a border city of major size, such as could contain an army and emperor of the Roman people, that did not have supplies of cheap wine, grain, bacon, barley, and straw for a year; other smaller cities had supplies for thirty days, some for forty, and not a few for two months, while the very least had supplies for fifteen days. 3. When he was prefect, likewise, he constantly inspected his men's arms. He never let an old man serve and he never let a boy draw rations. He used to go over the camps and their entrenchments, and he even frequently visited the sentries during the night. 4. And because he so loved the emperor and the state, everyone loved him. The tribunes and generals both loved and feared him so much that they were unwilling to do wrong and, for that matter, in no way did wrong. 5. Philip, they say, was mightily in fear of him for many reasons and on this account plotted with the doctors against his life. 6. He did it in this way: Timesitheus, as it happened, was suffering from diarrhoea and was told by the doctors to take a potion to check it. And then, they say, they changed what had been prepared and gave him something which loosened him all the more; and thus he died.

29 When he died, in the consulship of Arrianus and Papus, Philippus Arabs was made prefect of the guard in his place.[19] This Philip was low-born but arrogant, and now could not contain himself in his sudden rise to office and immoderate good fortune, but immediately, through the soldiers, began to plot against Gordian, who had begun to treat him as a father. He did it in the following manner. 2. As we have said, Timesitheus had stored up such a quantity of supplies everywhere, that the Roman administration could not break down. But now Philip intrigued first to have the grain-ships turned away, and then to have the troops moved to stations where they could not get provisions.[20] 3. In this way he speedily got them exasperated against Gordian, for they did not know that the youth had been betrayed through Philip's intriguing. 4. In addition to this, Philip spread talk among the soldiers to the effect that Gordian was young and could not manage the Empire, and that it were better for someone to rule who could command the army and understood public affairs. 5. Besides this, he won over the leaders, and finally brought it about that they openly called him to the throne. 6. Gordian's friends at first opposed him vigorously, but when the soldiers were at last overcome with hunger, Philip was entrusted with the sovereignty, and the soldiers commanded that he and Gordian should rule together with equal rank while Philip acted as a sort of guardian.

30   Now that he had gained the imperial power, Philip began to bear himself very arrogantly towards Gordian and he, knowing himself to be an emperor, an emperor's son, and a scion of a most noble family, could not endure this low-born fellow's insolence. And so, mounting the platform, with his kinsman Maecius Gordianus standing by him as his prefect, he complained bitterly to the officers and soldiers in the hope that Philip's office could be taken from him. 2. But by this complaint – in which he accused Philip of being 'unmindful' of past favours and too little grateful – he accomplished nothing. 3. Next he asked the soldiers to make their choice, after openly canvassing the officers, but as a result of Philip's intriguing he came off second in the general vote. 4. And finally, when he saw that everyone considered him worsted, he asked that their power might at least be equal, but he did not secure this either. 5. After this he asked to be given the position of Caesar, but he did not gain this. 6. He asked also to be Philip's prefect, and this, too, was denied him. 7. His last prayer was that Philip should make him a general and let him live. And to this Philip almost consented – not speaking himself, but acting through his friends, as he had done throughout, with nods and advice. 8. But when he reflected that through the love that the Roman people and senate, the whole of Africa and Syria, and indeed the whole Roman world, felt for Gordian, because he was nobly born and the son and grandson of emperors and had delivered the whole state from grievous wars, it was possible, if the soldiers ever changed their minds, that the throne might be given back to Gordian if he asked for it again, and when he reflected also that the violence of the soldiers' anger against Gordian was due to hunger, he had him carried, shouting protests, out of their sight and then despoiled and slain. 9. At first his orders were delayed, but afterwards it was done as he had bidden. And in this unholy and illegal manner Philip became emperor.

(Magie, ii, pp. 429–39, altered)

SHA Gord. 31, 2-3: And now, that he (i.e. Philip) might not seem to have obtained the imperial office by bloody means, Philip sent a letter to Rome saying that Gordian had died of a disease and that he, Philip, had been chosen emperor by all the soldiers. The senate was naturally deceived in these matters of which it knew nothing, and so it entitled Philip emperor and gave him the name Augustus and then placed the young Gordian among the gods.

(Magie, ii, pp. 439-41)

SHA Gord. 34, 2-5: The soldiers built Gordian a tomb near the camp at Circesium, which is in the territory of Persia, and added an inscription to the following effect in Greek, Latin, Persian, Hebrew and Egyptian letters, so that all might read. 'To the deified Gordian, conqueror of the Persians, conqueror of the Goths, conqueror of the Sarmatians, queller of mutinies at Rome, conqueror of the Germans, but no conqueror of Philippi.' This was added ostensibly because he had been beaten by the Alani in a disorderly battle on the plains of Philippi and forced to retreat, but at the same time it seemed to mean that he had been slain by the two Philips. But Licinius, it is said, destroyed the inscription at the time when he seized imperial power; for he desired to have it appear that he was descended from the two Philips.

(Magie, ii, pp. 445-7)

Epitome de Caesaribus 27, 1-3: Gordian, a grandson of Gordian by his daughter, was born at Rome to a most eminent father and ruled for six years. He was killed by the troops who had been incited to mutiny by the Praetorian Prefect Philip. His body was buried near the frontier between the Roman and Persian Empires at a place which, for this reason, is now called the Tomb of Gordian.

(Dodgeon)

Orosius, *adversus paganos* VII, 19, 5: So Gordian, after successfully waging great battles against the Parthians, was treacherously killed by his own men not far from Circesium on the Euphrates.

(Deferrari, p. 314)

Zosimus I, 17, 2-19, 1: Meanwhile Gordian married the daughter of Timesicles (i.e. Timesitheus), a man highly esteemed for his learning, and appointed him prefect of the court; by which he seemed to compensate for the deficiency of his own youth in the administration of public affairs.

18   Having secured his empire, he expected that the Persians would make an attack on the eastern provinces, as Shapur had assumed control in succession to Ardashir, who had restored the government to the Persians from the Parthians. . . . 2. The Emperor, having made all possible preparations, then marched against the Persians. The Roman army appeared to have the upper hand in the first engagement but the death of Timesicles, the Praetorian Prefect, considerably diminished the emperor's confidence in the certainty of his rule. Philip was chosen Prefect in his place and soon the good will of the troops towards the emperor abated. 3. Philip came from Arabia, a nation in bad repute, and had advanced his fortune by not very honourable means, and once he had assumed office he began to aspire to imperial dignity and endeavoured to seduce all the soldiers who were disposed to revolt. Observing that an abundance of military provisions was supplied, while the emperor was with the army near Carrhae and Nisibis, he ordered the ships that brought those provisions to go further inland, so that the army, oppressed by hunger[21] and want of supplies, might be provoked to mutiny.

19   His plan was successful; for the soldiers, on the pretext of a shortage of necessities, surrounded Gordian in a disorderly manner, killed him as the chief cause of so many of the casualties and, as agreed, they conferred the purple on Philip. He therefore made a sworn peace with Shapur, thus ending the war, and then set out for Rome. He bound the soldiers to him by generous donations and sent messengers ahead to Rome to announce that Gordian had died of a disease.

(Anon., revised Lieu)

Zosimus III, 14, 2: (AD 363) Then, moving forward sixty stades, he (i.e. the Emperor Julian) came to a place called Zautha (i.e. Zaitha), and from there to Dura (i.e. Europos) where there were the ruins of a city which was now deserted; here also was the tomb of the Emperor Gordian.

(Anon., revised Lieu)

Zosimus III, 32, 4: Long afterwards, when the emperor Gordian fought against the Persians, and lost his life in the midst of the enemy's country, the Persians, even after that disaster, were not able to acquire any part of the Roman dominion.

(Anon., revised Lieu)

Jordanes, *Historia Romana* 282, p. 36, 27–31: Gordian, still a boy, was now made emperor and he reigned a mere six years. Then, after opening the twin gates of Janus, he set out for the east and took the offensive against the Parthians (*sic*). While returning in triumph he was killed by the treachery of Philip, the Praetorian Prefect, when he was not far from Roman territory.

(Dodgeon)

John of Antioch, *frag.* 147, *FHG* IV, p. 597: When the common end of life was about to take hold of Gordian (i.e. Gordian II, reigned 238), the governor of Syria sent a message that the king of the Persians had exceeded his own boundaries and was ravaging Roman territory, and that the war required his presence. When the young Gordian learned of this, though exceedingly faint-hearted, he nevertheless announced an expedition against the Persians. After opening the gates (of the temple) of Janus, which were only opened in times of the greatest wars, he set out for the east. When he reached the Euphrates and also the approaches of the Tigris,[22] he engaged the barbarians and through conducting the war in a most brilliant manner, he defeated the Parthian (*sic*) forces in a series of fierce battles. Then, after this accomplishment, in the sixth year of his reign, as he was returning to the frontiers of his own empire, he was murdered by Philip, the successor to his throne, who at that point of time trained the youth of the troops. Philip was duly proclaimed emperor.

(Lieu)

Chronicon Paschale, p. 504, 2–6: This Philip Junior, who was prefect under the Emperor Gordian, who had appointed him, took from Gordian his son as hostage. After the death of Emperor Gordian, Philip killed the son and became emperor.

(Dodgeon)

Malalas, *ap. Synopsis Sathas* (cf. Stauffenberg 1939: 62): He (i.e. Gordian III?) in the battle against the Persians was brought down from his horse and crushed his thigh.[23] On his return to Rome, he died from it (i.e. the wound) in his fiftieth year.

(Lieu)

Syncellus p. 443, 3–9 (p. 681, 5–11, CSHB): Gordian, the twenty-second emperor of the Romans, reigned for six years. He left Italy for Persia and afterwards routed Shapur, the king of the Persians and the son of Ardashir, in battle and brought Nisibis and Carrhae under subjection – cities which had been captured by the Persians from the Romans during the reign of Maximinus the Moesian. But as he was approaching Ctesiphon, he was murdered by his own troops at the instigation of the Prefect Philip, who reigned after him for five, some say seven, years.

(Dodgeon)

Georgius Monachus (Hamartolus), *Chronicon* 32, p. 461, 12–15: Jounorus' (Gordian II?) son Gordian ruled after him for four years. He fell from his horse in battle, broke his thigh and died.

(Lieu)

Cedrenus, i, pp. 450, 23–451, 1, 11–12: But Philip the prefect forbade the corn to be conveyed to the camp. . . . After him (i.e. Gordian Junior?) his son reigned for four years. He died after falling from his horse and crushing his thigh.

(Dodgeon)

Zonaras XII, 17, p. 580, 7–14 (iii, pp. 128, 8–17, Dindorf): There are others who hold that the imperial rule passed to the younger Gordian (II) after the death of his father, the elder Gordian, through illness. They wrote that he campaigned against the Persians and fell in with them. He drove his horse forward in battle, exhorting his men and stirring them to feats of courage. The horse stumbled and fell on him, crushing his thigh. He therefore returned to Rome and died from the fracture after a reign of six years.

(Lieu)

Zonaras XII, 18, pp. 581, 16–582, 14 (iii, pp. 129, 19–130, 13, Dindorf): After the younger Gordian (i.e. Gordian II, reigned 238), another Gordian who, it was said, was a kinsman to the departed Gordians, assumed the purple. He marched against the Persians and joined with them in battle. Shapur, the son of Ardashir, was then their reigning monarch. He (Gordian) vanquished his foes and recaptured Nisibis and Carrhae which had been taken by the Persians during the reign of Maximinus (235–8). Then while on his way to Ctesiphon, he was murdered through the treachery of Philip, the Praetorian Prefect. For when Gordian came to power, he appointed his father-in-law, called Timesocles (*sic*), as Praetorian Prefect. While the latter was alive, matters pertaining to imperial authority fared well and were smoothly executed by him, but after his death, Philip was appointed Prefect. Scheming to provoke the soldiers to revolt, he reduced the food-provisions of the soldiers, giving the impression that this was at the command of the emperor. Some say that he (Philip) withheld the corn which was being conducted to the camp so that the soldiers would be oppressed by shortages and they would then be roused to mutiny. They duly revolted against the emperor, whom they regarded as the source of their famine. They came upon him suddenly and killed him in the sixth year of his reign. Philip immediately made a leap for the empire.

(Lieu)

2.2.2. The participation of the philosopher Plotinus in the expedition of Gordian

Porphyry, *vita Plotini* 3: So great a taste for philosophy did he (i.e. Plotinus) develop, that he made up his mind to study that which was being taught among the Persians and among the Indians. When emperor Gordian was preparing himself for his expedition against the Persians, Plotinus, then thirty-nine years old, went on the expedition. After Gordian was killed in Mesopotamia, Plotinus escaped with difficulty to Antioch.[24]

(Armstrong)

2.2.3. Philip's treaty with Shapur I

ŠKZ (Gk) lines 9–10: And Caesar Philip came to sue for peace, and for their lives he paid a ransom of 500,000 denarii and became tributary to us.[25] (10) For this reason, we have renamed Meshike Peros-Sabour[26] (i.e. the victorious Shapur).

(Lieu)

Evagrius, *Historia Ecclesiastica* V, 7 (ed. Bidez and Parmentier, p. 203, 3–8). . . . what was formerly Greater Armenia but afterwards Persarmenia – not long ago was subject to the Romans but Philip, in succession to Gordian, had betrayed it to Shapur – the part called Lesser Armenia[27] was ruled over by the Romans, but the rest by the Persians.

(Lieu)

Zosimus III, 32, (4): The same applied when Philip was emperor,[28] although he entered into a most dishonourable peace with the Persians.

(Anon. revised by Lieu)

Zonaras XII, 19, p. 583, 1–5 (iii, p. 130, 22–7): On his return, Philip became master of the Roman Empire, and while on his way he elected his son Philip as his colleague. He made a peace with

Shapur, then the king of the Persians, to end the war by ceding Mesopotamia[29] and Armenia.

(Lieu)

2.2.4. The accession of Philip and general political instability in the East

Oracula Sibyllina XIII, 21–45:

> Straightaway then a purple-loving warrior (i.e. Philip) will rule,
> appearing from Syria, terror of Ares, and with his son Caesar
> (Philip) shall oppress all the earth.
> One name is to them both, on the first (i.e. A = Augustus) and
> twentieth (i.e. K = Caesar)
> 25 five hundred (i.e. Φ = Philip) is placed. But when they who will
> gain power in war have become law-givers,
> there will indeed be a little respite from war but not for long.
> For when the wolf pledges oaths to the flock
> against the white-toothed dogs, it will afterwards deceive[30]
> 30 and hunt the woolly sheep, and cast aside the oaths.
> Then there will be an unlawful contest of overbearing kings
> in wars. Syrians will perish terribly.
> Indians, Armenians, Arabs, Persians, and Babylonians
> will destroy one another through fierce battles.[31]
> 35 But when the Roman Ares (i.e. Philip) vanquishes the German
> Ares, conquering the spirit destroying one of the ocean (i.e. Ti.
> Claudius
> Marinus Pacatianus)[32] then indeed for the Persians, overween-
> ing men,
> will be war of many years, but victory will elude them.
> For as a fish does not swim
> 40 on the crest of a high rock with many ridges, windy and high nor
> a tortoise fly, nor an eagle swim in water,
> So also the Persians will be far from victorious
> on that day, in so far as the friendly nurturer of the Italians,
> lying in the plain of the Nile by the oracular water,
> 45 sends an appointed tribute to seven-hilled Rome.

(Lieu)

2.2.5. Attempt by Philip to regain Mesopotamia and Armenia(?)

Zonaras XII, 19, p. 583, 5–9 (iii, pp. 130, 28–131, 3, Dindorf):
However, once he learned that the Romans were distressed by the

loss of these regions (i.e. Mesopotamia and Armenia), he, a little while later, broke the peace and gained possession of Mesopotamia and Armenia. This Shapur was said to be of enormous physical bulk, the like as had yet never before been seen.

(Lieu)

2.3.1. Julius Priscus placed in charge of the East

IGR III 1201 (= Le Bas, P. and Waddington, W.H., 1870. *Inscriptions Grècques et Latines recueillies en Asie Mineure*, Paris, 2077, Prentice 1908: 401a; found at Philippopolis, Arabia, Greek): (This statue of) [. . .], youthful son of Julius Priscus, the most excellent Prefect of Mesopotamia,[33] the city erected, through Julius Malchus, councillor (i.e. decurion), syndic and superintendent, for (his) remembrance.

(Prentice, 1908: 314)

IGR III 1202 (= Le Bas – Waddington, 2078 and Prentice 1908: 401b, also found at Philippopolis, Greek): (This statue of). . ., youthful son of Julius Priscus, the most excellent Prefect of Mesopotamia, Kassios Teimothos, Beneficarius and afterwards Petitor, erected for (his) remembrance.

(Prentice, 1908: 314)

Oracula Sibyllina XIII, 59–63:

    Wretched Antioch, the exacting Ares will not leave you
60 while the Assyrian War is waging around you.
    For a leading man will dwell under your roofs
    who will battle against all the arrow-shooting Persians,
    he himself coming from the royal house of the Romans.[34]

(Lieu)

Zosimus I, 19, 2: When he (i.e. Philip) arrived at Rome, he won over the senatorial order with his fine oratory. However, he believed that the most important offices of the realm should be vested with his closest relatives. He therefore placed Priscus, his brother, in command of the Syrian forces and entrusted the armies in Moesia and Macedonia to Severianus, his brother-in-law.

(Anon., revised Lieu)

2.3.2. Julius Priscus made rector orientis

CIL III, 141495[5] (= Dessau 9005, Prentice 1908, 393): To Julius Priscus, *vir eminentissimus* and uncle of our lords Philippi Augusti, and Praetorian Prefect and Rector of the East (*rector orientis*),[35] Trebonius Sossianus, *primus pilus*, of the Colonia Heliopolis (Ba'albek?), who was devoted to their will and majesty.

(Prentice, 1908: 308)

2.3.3. Dedication by a prefect of a newly formed (or reformed) heavy cavalry unit at Bostra (between 244 and 249)

IGLS 9090 (= *CIL* III, 99 Dessau, 2771): To the excellent (*vir egregius*) Julius Julianus, *ducenarius*[36] prefect of the Legio I Parthica Philippiana, a most devoted general (*dux*): Trebicius Gau(d)inus, prefect of the New (Thousand-strong)[37] Steadfast Armoured Cavalry Philippiana[38] (*alae novae firmae (miliariae) catafractariae Philippianae*), to an outstanding officer.

(Lieu)

2.3.4. Sepulchral inscription of a veteran of Legio VIII Augusta in Syria

IGR III, 1007 (bilingual tomb-inscription, found at Katura on the Jebel Halakah, Latin and Greek): Titus Flavius Julianus, veteran of (the) Eighth Legion, (called) 'Augusta',[39] has dedicated this monument forever to his *manes* (*diis manibus suis*) and (those) of Flavia Titia, his wife and to those in the world below, to his heirs also and to the descendants of these, so that none of them may dispose of this monument in any way. Thou also (farewell).

(Prentice, 1908: 129)

3 The Second and Third Campaigns of Shapur I against the Roman Empire

3.1.1. Khosrov II of Armenia was murdered at the instigation of the Sassanians (after 244)

Agathangelos, *History of the Armenians* (I), 23-35 (Thomson 1976, pp. 41-51): see Appendix 2, pp. 311-13.

Moses Khorenats'i, *History of the Armenians* (II), 76-7 (Thomson 1978, pp. 221-5): see Appendix 2, pp. 314-17.

3.1.2. Nisibis captured by the Persians (252?)[1]

al-Tabari, p. 826 (Nöldeke, pp. 31-2): see Appendix 1, p. 282.

Eutychius, *Annales*, ed. Cheikho, pp. 109, 10-110, 4 (Arabic):[2] see Appendix 1, pp. 295-6.

3.1.3. The murder of Khosrov II of Armenia and flight of Trdat (Tiridates) to the Roman court(?)

Agathangelos, *Hist. Arm.* (I), 36 (Thomson, 1976 pp. 51-3): see Appendix 2, p. 313.

Moses Khorenats'i, *Hist. Arm.* (II), 78 (Thomson, 1978 pp. 225-6): see Appendix 2, pp. 317-18.

Zonaras XII, 21, pp. 589, 24-590, 3 (iii, p. 137, 2-6, Dindorf): At this time[3] the Persians once more began hostile moves and brought Armenia under their control. Tiridates, the king of the Armenians, fled but his uncles[4] hurried over to the Persians.

(Lieu)

3.1.4. Shapur's second campaign against the Roman Empire (252)

ŠKZ (Gk), lines 10–19: And the Caesar (Philip I?) lied again and did injustice to Armenia.[5] We (11) marched against the Roman Empire and annihilated a Roman army of 60,000 men at Barbalissos.[6] The nation of Syria and whatever nations and plains that were above it, we set on fire and devastated (12) and laid waste. And in that campaign ⟨we took⟩ (the following) fortresses and cities from the nation of the Romans:[7] the city of Anatha with its surrounding territory ⟨Parthian only: BYRT'rwpn or BYRT'kwpn with its surrounding territory⟩ Birthan in Asporakos with its surrounding territory, (13) – Sura,[8] – Barbalissos, – Hierapolis, – Beroea, – Chalcis, – Apamea, (14) – Rephaneia,[9] – Zeugma, – Ourima, – Gindaros, – Larmenaz, (15) – Seleucia, – Antiochia,[10] – Cyrrhus,[11] – another city by (the name of) Seleucia,[12] – Alexandretta, (16) – Nicopolis, – Sinzara, – Chamath, – Ariste,[13] – Dikhor, (17) – Doliche,[14] – Doura, – Circesium,[15] – Germanicia,[16] – Batna,[17] – Chanar;[18] (18) and from Cappadocia:[19] the city of Satala with its surrounding territory, – Domana, – Artangil, – Souisa, (19) – Phreata, a total of thirty-seven cities with their surrounding territories.

(Lieu)

Oracula Sibyllina XIII, 108–30: (For lines 89–102, see below, 3.1.5.)

The Syrians will perish frightfully.
For the great wrath of the Most High will come upon them,
110   and immediately a revolt of enterprising Persians.
Syrians, mingling with Persians, will destroy the Romans.
Nevertheless they will not conquer by divine will.
Alas, many natives of the East will flee with all their
possessions to men speaking strange tongues.
115   Alas, the earth will drink the dark blood of many men.
For this will be the time when the living will at some time
bless the dead with their mouths, and will
pronounce death as fair but it will flee from them.
As for you, wretched Syria, I weep for you with great pity.
120   To you too will come a fearful attack by arrow-shooting
men, which you never expected to befall you.
The fugitive of Rome will come, brandishing a great spear,
crossing the Euphrates with many thousands,
who will put you to the torch and maltreat everything.

125 Wretched Antioch, they will never call you a city
after you have fallen under the spears through lack of
judgement.
Having despoiled you and stripped you of everything, he will
leave you roofless and uninhabited. Suddenly anyone who sees
you will weep for you.
To you Hierapolis will be a triumph, and you Beroea.
130 At Chalcis you will weep over newly fallen sons.

(Lieu)

Philostratus (*FGrH* 99F): see under Malalas (XII, p. 297, 10–18),
3.2.2.

Zosimus I, 27, 2: At the same time[20] the Persians invaded Asia,
ravaged Mesopotamia and advanced as far as Antioch. Finally they
took that city which was the metropolis of all the east. They
massacred some of the inhabitants and carried the remainder into
captivity, returning home with immense plunder, after they had
destroyed all the buildings in the city, both public and private,
without encountering any serious resistance. And indeed the
Persians could have easily conquered the whole of Asia, had they
not been so overjoyed at their excessive spoils as to be contented
with keeping and carrying home what they had acquired.

(Anon., revised Lieu)

Zosimus III, 32, 5: see 3.3.1.

Eutychius, *Annales*, p. 110, 4–5, ed. Cheikho (Arabic):[21] see
Appendix 1, pp. 295–6.

3.1.5. Antioch betrayed by Mariades (or Kyriades)[22] to Shapur I (253?)[23]

Oracula Sibyllina XIII, 89–102:

Then when a wily man comes, upon a bier,[24]
90 appearing as a bandit from Syria, an undistinguished Roman,
and will stealthily approach the race of Cappadocians
and will besiege and (suddenly) fall on them, insatiable for
war.
As for you, Tyana and (Caesarea) Mazaka, there will be
captivity.
You will be plundered and your neck will be placed under the
yoke because of him.

95   And Syria will wait for men who had fallen,
    nor will Selenaie, the sacred town, be saved.
    But when a brutal man will flee for protection (?) from Syria
    across the Euphrates' streams, in anticipation of the Romans,
    no longer resembling the Romans, but overweening
100 arrow-shooting Persians, then the leader of the Italians
    will fall in the ranks, struck by gleaming iron,
    abandoning his dignity, and his sons will also perish in
    addition to him.

(Lieu)

SHA triginta tyranni 2: This man (i.e. Cyriades = Myriades), rich and well-born, fled from his father Cyriades when, by his excesses and profligate ways, he had become a burden to the righteous old man, and after robbing him of a great part of his gold and an enormous amount of silver he departed to the Persians. Thereupon he joined King Sapor and became his ally, and after urging him to make war on the Romans, he brought first Odomastes[25] and then Sapor himself into the Roman dominions; and also by capturing Antioch and Caesarea he won for himself the name of Caesar. Then, when he had been hailed Augustus, after he had caused all the Orient to tremble in terror at his strength or his daring, and when, moreover, he had slain his father (which some historians deny), he himself, at the time that Valerian was on his way to the Persian War, was put to death by the treachery of his followers. Nor has anything more that seems worthy of mention been committed to history about this man, who has obtained a place in letters solely by reason of his famous flight, his act of parricide, his cruel tyranny, and his boundless excesses.

(Magie, iii, pp. 67–9)

Malalas XII, ed. Stauffenberg, pp. 64–5 (CSHB pp. 295, 20–296, 10): Under this emperor (i.e. Valerian), one of the magistrates of Antioch the Great by the name of Mariades was expelled from the city council (*boule*) at the contrivance of the entire council and citizen body. He was found wanting in his administration of the chariot races, for whenever he was leader of the faction, he did not purchase horses but kept for his own benefit the public funds destined for the circus. He departed for Persia and offered to betray Antioch the Great, his own native city, to Shapur the king. This Shapur, the king of the Persians, came with a large force through the *limes* of Chalcis[26] and occupied and devastated the whole of Syria. He captured Antioch the Great in the evening and plundered it, tormented it and set it on fire. Antioch then was in her three hundred and fourteenth year (= AD 265/6?).[27] However, he decapitated the magistrate (i.e. Myriades) for his betrayal of his native city.

(Lieu)

Anonymous continuator of Dio Cassius, *frag.* 1, *FHG* IV, p. 192): When the king of the Persians came before Antioch with Mariadnes (i.e. Mariades), he encamped some twenty stadia (from the city). The respectable classes fled the city but the majority of the populace remained: partly because they were well disposed towards Mariadnes and partly because they were glad of any revolution; such as is customary with ignorant people.

(Lieu)

3.2.1. Some incidents related to the fall of Antioch (253? or 260?)

Libanius, *oratio* XI, 158: For one thing, when the Persians came upon them, our ancestors did not think fit to save themselves by flight, but they held their ground, holding fast to their fatherland, more firmly than the Lacedaemonians did to their shields. . . .

(Downey, 1959 p. 669)

Idem, *oratio* XXIV, 38: So let every one of his successors acknowledge the debt he owes him (i.e. Julian). Our womenfolk too would agree that it was due to him that all this region does not belong to Persia. We build no walls, we import no stocks of corn, we do not live with fear to keep us company, nor are we afraid that any such disaster will befall us as occurred in the days of our ancestors, when they were attacked as they sat in the theatre by archers who had occupied the mountain top.

(Norman, i, pp. 519–21.)

Idem, *oratio* XV, 16: We may have no noble buildings – the age-old insolence of the Persians that fired all that stood in its path has seen to that. . . .

(Norman, i, p. 157)

Idem, *oratio* LX, 2–3, pp. 312, 3–313, 2, ed Foerster (*ap.* John Chrysostom, *de Sancto Babyla contra Julianum et gentiles*, ed. Schatkin, XVIII/98 and XIX/106): When the king of the Persians (i.e. Shapur I) the ancestor of the one who is waging war against us (i.e. Shapur II), had taken the city (of Antioch) by treason and set it on fire, he proceeded to Daphne and was about to do the same when Apollo made him change his mind. He threw away his torch and paid homage to Apollo for he (i.e. the god) had so apparently mollified and reconciled him. 3. This general, leading an army against us, nevertheless thought it safer and better for his reputation to preserve the temple and the beauty of the statue quelled his barbaric rage.[28]

(Dodgeon)

Ammianus Marcellinus XX, 11, 11: (AD 360) Therefore on the tenth day from the start of the siege,[29] when the confidence of our men began to fill the town with alarm, it was decided to bring up a vast battering-ram which the Persians, after having used it before to subdue Antioch, had brought back and left at Carrhae.

(Yonge, p. 237, revised)

Idem, XXIII, 5, 3: For it happened one day at Antioch, when the city was in perfect tranquillity, a comic actor being on the stage with his wife, acting some common scene from daily life, while the people were delighted with his acting, his wife suddenly exclaimed: 'Am I dreaming or are the Persians here?' The audience immediately turned round and then fled in every direction while trying to avoid the missiles which were showered upon them. The city was burnt and a number of her citizens killed, who, as is usual in time of peace, were strolling about carelessly, and all the places in the neighbourhood were burnt and laid waste. The enemy, loaded down with plunder, returned without loss to their own country after having burnt Mareades who had wickedly guided the Persians to the destruction of his fellow citizens. This event took place in the time of Gallienus.

(Yonge, p. 325, revised)

Eunapius, *vitae Sophistarum* VI, 5: (AD 358) see Chapter 8, pp. 219–20.

3.2.2. A Persian column defeated at Emesa (?)

Oracula Sibyllina XIII, 147–54:

> And again the ordered world will become disordered with men perishing
> by famine and war. The Persians for the toil of Ares (i.e. war)
> will again make inroads, raging against the Ausonians (i.e. Romans)

150 And then there will be a flight of Romans. Immediately afterwards
    the last priest of all (i.e. Sampsigeramus?) sent by the sun will come,
    appearing out of Syria and will accomplish everything by treachery.
    And then there will be a city of the sun (i.e. Emesa ?) Around it
    the Persians will undergo the fearful threats of the Phoenicians (i.e. Emesenes).

                                            (Lieu)

Malalas, XII, ed. Stauffenberg, pp. 65–6 (pp. 296, 10–297, 20 *CSHB*): (After the capture of Antioch, Shapur) took possession of the eastern part (of the Roman Empire) and subjected it to torment, fire and plunder and killed everyone until he came to Emesa, a city of Phoenice Libanensis. A priest of Aphrodite by the name of Sampsigeramus[30] came out to meet him with a rustic force of slingers. Shapur, the king of the Persians, when he noticed the priestly robe, ordered his army not to shoot at them nor to fall upon them nor to fight with them; and he received the priest as an envoy. He had earlier requested the king to receive him as envoy of his territory. While Shapur the king was seated on a high platform and engaged in discussion with the priest, one of the rustic slingers let fly a stone which hit Shapur in the forehead and he died on the spot. Pandemonium broke out [p. 390] when his army heard that he had died. Thinking that the Romans were coming upon them, they all fled to the *limes*, with the rustic slingers and Sampsigeramus in pursuit.[31] They vanished, leaving behind their booty. They were met while passing through the *limes* by Enathos (i.e. Odaenathus), an ally of the Romans who was the king of the barbarian Saracens and ruled over Arabia, who had a wife called Zenobia, a Saracen queen. Enathos destroyed all of the entire Persian army of Shapur, according to the statement of Domninus, the learned chronographer. However, the most learned Philostratus (*FGrH* 99F) had something different to say about Shapur, the king of the Persians. He said that he seized Syria and put Antioch the Great and many other cities to the torch. He also seized Cilicia and put to the torch Alexandretta, Rhosus, Anazarbus, Aigai, Nicopolis, and many other cities of Cilicia and then returned to Persian territory via Cappadocia, and he (Philostratus) said that Enathos, the king of the Saracens, met him, coming to him as an ally and killed him. Domninus, on the other hand, is more reliable in asserting that Shapur dispatched a satrap by the name of Spates to Armenia with a large army.[32]

(Lieu)

3.2.3. Inscriptions commemorating the victory of Emesenes over Shapur I (?)[33]

IGLS 1799 (p. 277, found in Qal 'at el-Haways, NE of Hamath, Greek): Year 564 (252/253 AD), the men were then exposed to Nemesis (?) (i.e. vengeful justice). But the hero invoked Kronos and victory was given to him. Neither the Barbarians nor anybody in the vicinity suffered injury for they settled (?) that they should suffer a just punishment for their crime those who . . . .

(Lieu)

IGLS 1800 (p. 278, on the same rock, Greek): Read what is written and believe!

(Lieu)

IGLS 1801 (p. 278, on a nearby rock, Greek): The god of all power loves loyalty and wishes (?) that it exist in his presence.

(Lieu)

3.2.4. Repair to the walls of Batnae by a Prefect of Osrhoene (after 256?)

Petersen, *TAPA* 107 (1977), p. 267 (Greek inscription found in a cave formerly used as a shelter on the modern highway between Birecik and Urfa): Aur(elius) Dasius, the most distinguished [. . .] prefect of Osrhoene rebuilt the city wall at Batnae and refurnished in that place a public hostel and a shady shelter so that those who take refuge in it because of the heat might rest and find some relief.

(Lieu & J.C. Morgan)

3.2.5. Transfer of troops to Arabia (259?)

PAES III, A, no. 10, pp. 16–17 (Latin inscription from Qal'at es Zerqa which may have originally been at el-Hadid: The Emperors Augustuses (Valerian and Gallienus?) who had transferred [. . . *name of unit(s)* . . .] from Palestine to Arabia for the protection (of the country?),[34] also constructed a camp from foundation at a suitable site through Aurel[ius Theo], Legate of the Augustuses. . . .[35]

3.2.6. Shapur's third campaign against the Roman Empire (260?): (a) The Persian view

ŠKZ (Gk) lines 19–37: In the third contest, when we marched against Edessa and Carrhae and had the cities laid under siege, (20) Caesar Valerian came upon us. There was with him a force of seventy thousand men from the nations of Germania, Raetia, Noricum, Dacia, Pannonia, (21) Moesia, Istria, Hispania, Mauritania, Thracia, Bithynia, Asia, Pamphylia, Isauria (22) Lycaonia, Galatia, Lycia, Cilicia, Cappadocia, Phrygia, Syria, Phoenicia, (23) Judaea, Arabia, Mauritania, Germania, Lydia and Mesopotamia. (24) A great battle took place beyond Carrhae[36] and Edessa between us and Caesar Valerian and we took him prisoner with our own hands (25) as well as the other commanders of the army, the Praetorian Prefect,[37] senators and officials. All these we took prisoner and deported (26) to Persis. We also burnt, devastated, and pillaged Syria, Cilicia, and Cappadocia.

On this third campaign we also conquered from the Empire of the Romans their city of Samosata[38] with its surrounding territory, the city of Alexandria[39] with its surrounding territory, – Katabolon[40] (28), – Aig (e)ai, – Mopsuestia, – Mallos, – Adana, – Tarsus, [– mp. Augousta (?), –], – Zephyrion,[41] (29), – Sebaste, – Korykos, – Agrippiada,[42] – Kastabala, – Neronias, (30) – Flavias, – Nicopolis, – Kelenderis,[43] – Anemourium, (31) – Selinus, – Myonpolis, – Antiochia, – Seleucia, – Dometioupolis,[44] (32) – Tyana,[45] – Meiakarire, – Comana, – Kybistra, – Sebastia, (33) – Birtha, – Rhakoundia, – Laranda, – Iconium; all these cities (34) together with their surrounding territories are thirty-six (in number).

We led away into captivity men from the Empire of the Romans, non-Iranians, and settled them into our Empire of Iranians, in Persia (35), in Parthia, in Susiana and in Asorestan (= Assuristan) and in every other nation where our own and our fathers' and our forefathers' (36) foundations were.

And we searched out (for combat) many other lands and we acquired great renown for bravery, and many heroic deeds (we performed) which are not engraved here beside the preceding. For this reason we commanded (37) this to be engraved, that whoever comes after us will realize this renown, this courage, and this sovereignty of ours.

(Lieu)

3.3.1. The third campaign of Shapur and the capture of Valerian: (b) The Roman and Byzantine view[46]

Lactantius, *de mortibus persecutorum* 5: Not long afterwards, Valerian also in a state of frenzy lifted his impious hands to assault God, and, even though his time was short, shed much righteous blood. But God punished him in a new and extraordinary manner, that it might be a lesson to future ages that the adversaries of Heaven always receive the just recompense of their iniquities. He was made prisoner by the Persians and lost not only that power which he had exercised without moderation, but also the liberty of which he had deprived others. He squandered the remainder of his days in the abject form of slavery: for whenever Shapur, the king of the Persians, who had made him prisoner, chose to get into the carriage or to mount on horseback, he commanded the Roman to stoop and present his back; then, placing his foot on the shoulders of Valerian, he said, with a smile of reproach, 'This is true, and not what the Romans depicted on their tablets and walls.'[47] Valerian lived for a considerable time under the well-merited insults of his conqueror; so that the Roman name remained long the scoff and derision of the barbarians: and this also was added to the severity of his punishment, that although he had an emperor for his son, he found no one to avenge his captivity and most abject and servile state; neither indeed was he ever demanded back.[48] Afterward, when he had finished this shameful life under so great dishonour, he was flayed, and his skin, stripped from the flesh, was dyed with vermilion, and placed in the temple of the gods of the barbarians, that the remembrance of a triumph so signal might be perpetuated, and that this spectacle might always be exhibited to our ambassadors, as an admonition to the Romans, that, beholding the spoils of their captive emperor in a Persian temple, they should not place too great confidence in their own strength.[49]

(Fletcher, pp. 302–3, revised)

Eusebius, *Historia ecclesiastica.* VII, 13: But not long afterwards, Valerian underwent slavery at the hands of barbarians, and his son (i.e. Gallienus), succeeding to the sole power, conducted the government with more prudence, and immediately by means of edicts put an end to the persecution against us (i.e. Christians).

(Lawlor and Oulton, p. 228)

Eusebius, *vita Constantini* IV, 11, 2: see below, 6.2.5.

Julian (Emperor), *de Caesaribus*, 313C: Next entered Gallienus and his father (i.e. Valerian), the latter still dragging the chains of his captivity, the other with the dress and languishing gait of a woman. Seeing Valerian, Silenus cried, 'Who is this with the white plume that leads the army's war?' Then he greeted Gallienus with, 'He who is all decked with gold and dainty as a maiden.' But Zeus ordered the pair to depart from the feast.

(Wright, ii, p. 361)

Aurelius Victor, *liber de Caesaribus* 32, 5: For when his father (i.e. Valerian) was conducting an indecisive and long war in Mesopotamia, he was ambushed by a trick of the king of the Persians called Shapur and was ignominiously hacked to death in the sixth year of his reign[50] while still vigorous for his old age.

(Lieu)

Festus, *breviarium* 23, p. 64, 8–13: It is painful to recount the fortunes of Valerian, the unlucky monarch. He took power with Gallienus. Since the army made Valerian emperor and the Senate, Gallienus, it was Valerian who joined battle against the Persians in Mesopotamia and was vanquished and captured by Shapur, the king of the Persians. He spent the rest of his old age in ignominious servitude.

(Lieu)

Eutropius, IX, 7: Valerian, while he was occupied in a war in Mesopotamia, was overthrown by Shapur, king of Persia, and being soon after made prisoner, grew old in ignominious servitude among the Parthians (*sic*).

(Watson)

Jerome, *Chronicon*, s. aa. 258–60, p. 220, 12–19: Valerian, immediately after he had incited persecution against the Christians, was captured by Shapur, the king of the Persians, among whom he grew old in miserable servitude. (= Jordanes, *hist. rom.* 287) Shapur, king of the Persians, pillaged Syria, Cilicia and Cappadocia. Valerian was taken to Persia and Gallienus brought peace to us (i.e. Christians).

(Lieu)

SHA Valerian, 1, 1–4, 1 (the beginning is fragmentary):[51] ... to Shapur, Velsolus, king of kings,[52] 'Did I but know for a certainty that the Romans could be wholly defeated, I should congratulate you on the victory of which you boast. 2. But inasmuch as that nation, either through Fate or its own prowess, is all-powerful, look to it lest the fact that you have taken prisoner an aged emperor, and that indeed by guile, may turn out ill for yourself and your descendants. 3. Consider what mighty nations the Romans have made their subjects instead of their enemies after they had often suffered defeat at their hands. 4. We have heard, in fact, how the Gauls conquered them and burned that great city of theirs; 5. it is a fact that the Gauls are now servants to the Romans. What of the Africans? Did they not conquer the Romans? It is a fact that they serve them now. Examples more remote and perhaps less important I will not cite. Mithridates of Pontus held all of Asia; it is a fact that he was vanquished and Asia now belongs to the Romans. 6. If you ask my advice, make use of the opportunity for peace and give back Valerian to his people. I do indeed congratulate you on your good fortune, but only if you know how to use it aright.'[53]

2   Velenus, king of the Cadusii,[54] wrote as follows: 'I have received with gratitude my forces returned to me safe and sound. Yet I cannot wholly congratulate you that Valerian, prince of princes, is captured; I should congratulate you more, were he given back to his people. For the Romans are never more dangerous than when they are defeated. 2. Act, therefore, as becomes a prudent man, and do not let Fortune, which has tricked many, kindle your pride. Valerian has an emperor for a son and a Caesar for a grandson, and what of the whole Roman world, which, to a man, will rise up against you? 3. Give back Valerian, therefore, and make peace with the Romans, a peace which will benefit us as well, because of the tribes of Pontus.'

3   Artavasdes, king of the Armenians,[55] sent the following letter to Shapur: 'I have, indeed, a share in your glory, but I fear that you have not so much conquered as sown the seeds of war. 2. For Valerian is being sought back by his son, his grandson, and the generals of Rome, by all Gaul, all Africa, all Spain, all Italy, and by all the nations of Illyricum, the East, and Pontus, which are leagued with the Romans or subject to them. 3. So, then, you have captured one old man but have made all the nations of the world your bitterest foes, and ours too, perhaps, for we have sent you aid; we are your neighbours, and we always suffer when you fight with each other.'

4   The Bactrians, the Hiberians, the Albanians,[56] and the Tauroscythians refused to receive Shapur's letters and wrote to the Roman commanders, promising aid for the liberation of Valerian from his captivity.

(Magie, iii, pp. 3–7)

Epitome de Caesaribus 32, 5–6: Valerian, while conducting a war in Mesopotamia, was vanquished by Shapur, the king of the Persians. He was captured shortly afterwards and grew old among the Parthians (*sic*) in ignoble servitude. For while he lived, the king of that province was wont to alight from his horse by putting his feet on the neck of Valerian, who was bent double.

(Lieu)

Orosius, *adversus paganos*, VII, 22, 3–4: ... For Valerian, as soon as he had seized the power, ordered the Christians to be forced by tortures into idolatry, the eighth emperor after Nero to do so. When they refused, he ordered them to be killed, and the blood of the saints was shed throughout the length and breadth of the Roman Empire. 4. Valerian, the author of the abominable edict, the emperor of the Roman people, being immediately captured by Shapur, the king of the Persians, grew old among the Persians in the most humiliating slavery, for he was condemned to this menial service for as long as he lived, namely always by bending on the ground to raise the king as he was about to mount his horse, not by his hand but by his back.

(Deferrari, p. 316)

Zosimus I, 30, 1: Valerian, perceiving the empire in danger on every side, associated his son Gallienus with himself in the government and himself went to the east to oppose the Persians. . . .

(Anon., revised Lieu)

Zosimus I, 36, 1–2: Valerian had by this time heard of the disturbances in Bithynia, but he dared not to confide the defence of it to any of his generals through distrust. He therefore sent Felix to Byzantium, and went in person from Antioch into Cappadocia, and he returned after he had done some injury to every city through which he passed. But the plague then attacked his troops, and destroyed most of them, at the time when Shapur made an attempt upon the east, and reduced most of it into subjection. 2. In the meantime, Valerian became so weak that he despaired of ever recovering from the present sad state of affairs, and tried to conclude the war by a gift of money. Shapur, however, sent back empty-handed the envoys who were sent to him with that proposal, and demanded that the emperor come and speak with him in person concerning the affairs he wished to negotiate. Valerian most imprudently consented, and, going incautiously to Shapur with a small retinue to discuss the peace terms, was presently seized by the enemy, and so ended his days in the capacity of a slave among the Persians, to the disgrace of the Roman name in all future times.

(Anon., revised Lieu)

Zosimus III, 32, 5: A short time afterwards, when the Persian fire had set all the east in flames, and the great city of Antioch was taken by the Persian army, which advanced as far as Cilicia, the emperor Valerian made an expedition against them, and though he was taken by them, yet still they did not dare to claim the sovereignty of those countries.

(Anon., revised Lieu)

Jordanes, *Historia Romana* 287 (p. 37, 14–16): = Jerome, *Chronicon*, s. a. 258.

Evagrius, *Historia ecclesiastica* V, 24 (ed Bidez – Parmentier, pp. 218, 31–219, 2): And in (the work of) Nikostratus, the sophist of Trapezus (*FGrH* 98), (the account extends) from Philip, the successor of Gordian, to Odenathus of Palmyra, and the ignominious expedition of Valerian against the Persians.

(Lieu)

Petrus Patricius, *frag.* 9, *FHG* IV, p. 187: Valerian, wary of the Persian attack when his army, particularly the Moors, was afflicted with the plague, amassed an immense amount of gold and sent ambassadors to Shapur, in the hope of bringing an end to the war through lavish gifts. Shapur heard about the plague and was greatly elated by Valerian's request. He kept the ambassadors waiting, then dismissed them without success in their mission and immediately set out in pursuit.

(Lieu)

Petrus Patricius, *frag.* 13: see below, 5.4.2.

Agathias IV, 23, 7: Shapur was very wicked and bloodthirsty, quick to anger and cruelty and slow to mercy and forgiveness. Whether he had made use of this terrible punishment against others previously, I cannot be sure. But that he punished Valerian, the Roman emperor, in this way after taking him alive when he had made war on him and been defeated, many accounts testify. Indeed, the first rulers of Persia after the defeat of the Parthians, Artaxares and Shapur, were both wicked and abominable men, if indeed the one killed his own overlord and set up by force a usurper's rule, while the other initiated such a dreadful punishment and terrible defilement.

(Cameron, 1969/70 p. 121)

Agathias IV, 24, 3: For, after killing their emperor, and thinking that there would now be nothing to stop him, he (Shapur) advanced further, ravaged Mesopotamia and then the land adjoining it, and plundered Cilicia and Syria, and pressing on as far as Cappadocia caused wholesale slaughter. Even the valleys and hollows of the mountain thickets he filled with corpses and levelled the spaces between the hills and flattened their projecting summits; then he rode across them, traversing the mountain ridges as though they were level ground.[57]

(Cameron, 1969/70 p. 121)

Chronicon Paschale, p. 508, 1–2, CSHB: During the consulships of the aforesaid (i.e. Claudius and Paternus), Valerian Augustus was killed by Persians who had risen against him. He was in his sixty-first year.

(Lieu)

Chronicon miscell. ad ... 724 pertinens, CSCO 3, p. 126, 7–11 (Syriac): (Valerian) excited persecution against the Christians and was soon taken away as a slave among the Persians. His son (i.e. Gallienus) accorded peace to the Christians. Shapur, king of the Persians, devastated Syria and Cappadocia.

(Lieu)

Syncellus, p. 466, 8–15 (pp. 715, 16–716, 3, CSHB): During their (i.e. Valerian and Gallienus) reign, Shapur, the king of the Persians, laid waste to Syria and captured Antioch and also ravaged Cappadocia. The Roman army was afflicted by famine in Edessa and as a result was in a mutinous mood. Valerian, thoroughly scared and pretending that he was going into another battle, surrendered himself to Shapur, the king of the Persians, and agreed to betray the main body of his forces. When the Romans got wind of this, they escaped with difficulty and some of them were killed. Shapur pursued them and captured the great Antioch, Tarsus in Cilicia and Caesarea in Cappadocia.

(Lieu)

Cedrenus, i, p. 454, 3–6, CSHB: Valerian and Gallienus reigned for fifteen years. This Valerian made war against Shapur the Persian and was captured in Caesarea with a force of twenty thousand men. He was flayed by Shapur and died. His son Gallienus established the first cavalry cohorts: for the majority of Roman soldiers till then were infantry.

(Lieu)

Zonaras XII, 23, pp. 593, 10–595, 6 (iii, pp. 140, 5–141, 25, Dindorf): Furthermore, the Persians, when Shapur was their king, overran Syria, ravaged Cappadocia, and besieged Edessa. Valerian hesitated to engage with the enemy. But, learning that the soldiers in Edessa were making vigorous sorties against the barbarians, killing many of them and capturing vast quantities of booty, he gained new courage. He went forth with the forces at his disposal and engaged with the Persians. But they, being many times more numerous, surrounded the Romans; the greater number (of the Romans) fell, but some fled, and Valerian and his retinue were seized by the enemy and led away to Shapur. Now that he was master of the emperor, Shapur thought that he was in control of everything; and, cruel as he was before, he became much worse afterwards.

Such was the manner in which Valerian was taken prisoner by the Persians, as recorded by some authors. But there are those who say that Valerian willingly went to the Persians because during his stay in Edessa his soldiers were beset by hunger. They then became seditious and sought to destroy their emperor. And he, in fear of the soldiers' insurrection, fled to Shapur so that he might not be killed by his own people. He surrendered (not only) himself to his enemy but, as far as it was in his power, the Roman army. The soldiers were not destroyed but learnt of his betrayal and fled, and (only) a few were lost. Whether the emperor was captured in war by the Persians or whether he willingly entrusted himself to them, he was treated dishonourably by Shapur.

The Persians attacked the cities in complete freedom from fear, and took Antioch on the Orontes and Tarsus, the most notable of the cities in Cilicia, and Caesarea in Cappadocia. As they led away the multitude of prisoners they did not give them more than the minimum amount of food needed to sustain life, nor did they allow them a sufficient supply of water, but once a day their guards drove them to water like cattle. Caesarea had a large population (for four hundred thousand men are said to dwell in it) and they did not capture it, since the inhabitants nobly resisted the enemy and were commanded by a certain brave and intelligent Demosthenes, until a certain doctor was taken prisoner. He was unable to bear the torture inflicted upon him and revealed a certain site from which during the night the Persians made their entrance and destroyed everyone.[58] But their general Demosthenes, although encircled by many Persians who were under orders to take him alive, mounted his horse and raised aloft an unsheathed sword. He forced his way into the midst of the enemy; and, striking down very many, he escaped successfully from the city.

(Dodgeon)

3.3.2. The Prophet Mani's participation in the campaigns of Shapur I[59]

Alexander Lycopolitanus, *contra Manichaei opiniones disputatio* [60] 2, ed Brinkmann, p. 4, 19–22: Manichaeus himself is said to have lived during the reign of Valerian and to have accompanied Shapur the Persian king during his military campaigns . . . .

(van der Horst and Mansfield, p. 52)

3.3.3. Attempt by Kirder the Mobed to introduce Zoroastrianism to conquered Roman territory

KKZ, lines 11–13, cf. Back 1978: 419–29 (Middle Persian): And from the first, I, Kirder, underwent much toil and trouble for the yazads and the rulers, and for my own soul's sake. And I caused many fires and priestly colleges to flourish in Iran, and also in non-Iranian lands. There were fires and priests in the non-Iranian lands which were reached by the armies of the King of kings. The provincial capital of Antioch and the province of Syria, and Cilicia, and the districts dependent on Cilicia; the provincial capital of Caesarea and the province of Cappadocia, and the districts dependent on Cappadocia, up to Pontus, and the province of Armenia, and Georgia and Albania and Balasagan, up to the 'Gate of the Alans' – these were plundered and burnt and laid waste by Shapur, King of kings, with his armies. There too, at the command of the King of kings, I reduced to order the priests and fires which were in those lands. And I did not allow harm to be done them, or captives made. And whoever had thus been made captive, him indeed I took and sent back to his own land. And I made the Mazda-worshipping religion and its good priests esteemed and honoured in the land.

(Boyce, 1984: 113)

3.3.4. Fulvius Macrianus refused to send help to Valerian

Anonymous Continuator of Dio Cassius, *frag.* 3, *FHG* IV, p. 193: Macrinus (*sic*) then was Count of the (Sacred) Largesse and (Prefect) of the *annona* (i.e. in charge of supplies) and because he was disabled in one foot, he took no part in the battle but was expecting the troops at Samosata and received them. Shapur then sent Cledonius, who was the *ab admissionibus* (i.e. the person who introduced the judges to the emperor) of Valerian, to urge him (i.e. Macrianus) to come to his emperor. However, he declined to go, saying: 'Is anyone so insane that he would willingly become a slave and prisoner of war instead of being a free man? Furthermore, those who are ordering me to go from here are not my masters since one of them is an enemy and the other who is not master of himself (i.e. a prisoner) can in no way be our master.' He also urged Cledonius to remain and not to return. However, he said that he would not betray the trust of one who was his sovereign. On his return he was incarcerated with the prisoners of war.

(Lieu)

3.3.5. Ballista rallied Roman stragglers and inflicted defeats on Persians in Lykaonia

Syncellus, p. 466, 15–23 (p. 716, 3–11, CSHB): The Persians became dispersed here and there by their greed (for booty). They were on the point of capturing Pompeiopolis on the coast, having laid waste much of Lykaonia, when Callistus (= Ballista) came upon them unawares with ships and a Roman force consisting of men who in their flight had chosen him as their leader. He captured the harem of Shapur with much wealth. Returning with his fleet to Sebaste and Corycus, he wiped out a force of three thousand Persians. Shapur was greatly distressed by this and he withdrew in haste and in fear, and Valerian sojourned among the Persians until the end of his life.

(Lieu)

Zonaras XII, 23, pp. 595, 7–596, 9 (iii, pp. 141, 26–142, 25, Dindorf): While the situation so favoured the Persians, they spread out over all the east subject to Rome and plundered it without fear. The Romans, however, in their flight appointed as their general one Callistus, so it is said. He saw that the Persians were spread out and attacking the lands without a thought for anyone facing up to them. He launched a sudden attack on them and completed a very great slaughter of the barbarians, and he captured Shapur's concubines together with great wealth. Shapur was greatly pained by this and hastily turned to home, taking Valerian with him. Valerian ended his life in Persia, being reviled and mocked as a prisoner. But

Callistus was not the only one then to triumph over the Persians, but also a Palmyrene called Odaenathus made an alliance with the Romans and destroyed many of the Persians. As they retreated, he attacked them along the Euphrates. Gallienus, in return for his generalship, appointed him as *dux orientis*.

Amongst those who fell in the Persian army and were being stripped of their arms there are said to have been found women also, dressed and armed like men, and that such women were also taken alive by the Romans. And during his retreat Shapur came to a deep gorge, through which it was impossible for his baggage animals to pass. He ordered the prisoners to be killed and thrown into the gorge, so that when its depth was filled up with the bodies of the corpses, his baggage animals might make their way across. And in this way he is reported to have crossed the gorge.

(Lieu)

3.4.1. Shapur bribed the Roman soldiers at Edessa to facilitate his return journey

Petrus Patricius, *frag.* 11, *FHG* IV, p. 187: Shapur, the Persian king, crossed the Euphrates with his army ... [the soldiers] greeted each other and rejoiced that they had escaped the danger which had been repelled. He sent word to the soldiers in Edessa, promising to give them all the Syrian money he had with him, so that they would allow him to pass undisturbed and not choose a venture which would lead them to be subject to attack on both sides and bring him trouble and loss of speed. He said that he did not offer them these things out of fear but because he was eager to celebrate the festival in his own home and he did not want there to be any delay or any hold-up on his journey. The soldiers chose to take the money without risk and to permit him to pass.

(J. M. Lieu)

3.4.2. The settlement of Roman prisoners by Shapur in Persian territory

Chronicle of Se'ert 2, ed. Scher, *PO* 4, pp. 220–1: see Appendix 1, p. 297.

4 The Rise and Fall of Palmyra

4.1.1. Dedication to Septimius Odaenathus (date uncertain)

Cantineau, *Syria* 12 (1931), p. 138, no. 17 (Palmyrene only): In honour of Odainath[1] (i.e. Odaenathus) son of Hairan (, son of ?) Vaballath, the chief of Tadmor ([rš] ' dy tdmwr), 'Ogeilu son [of Maq]qai Haddudan Hadda, made this [thr]one and brought as offering [the hearth and the bra]zier and the holo[caust . . .].

(Lieu, revised Brock)

4.1.2. Sepulchral inscription of Septimius Odaenathus (date uncertain)[2]

CISem. II, 4202 (= *Inv.* VII B, 55, Greek and Palmyrene): (Greek:) This monument of burial has been built, at his own expense, by Septimius Odaenathus, the most illustrious senator, son of Haeranes, (son of) Vaballathus, son of Nasor, for himself, his sons and the sons of his sons, forever, eternal honour. (Palmyrene:) This sepulchre has been built by Odainath, senator, son of Hairan ('dynt br hyrn), (son of) Vaballath, (son of Nasor), for himself, his sons and the sons of his sons forever.

(Lieu, revised Brock)

4.1.3. Unsuccessful attempt by Septimius Odaenathus to make a treaty with Shapur I

Petrus Patricius, *frag.* 10, *FHG* IV, p. 187: Odaenathus paid [much] court to Shapur as one who had greatly surpassed the Romans. Wanting to lead him on, he sent magnificent gifts and other goods which Persia was not rich in, conveying them by camels. He also sent letters expressing entreaty and saying that he had done nothing against the Persians.[3] Shapur, however, instructed the slaves who received the gifts to throw them into the river and tore up and crushed the letters. 'Who is he', he declared, 'and how has he dared to write to his master? If then he wants to obtain a lighter punishment, let him prostrate himself again with his hands in chains. Otherwise, let him know that I shall destroy him and his people and his land.'

(Lieu)

4.1.4. Dedication to Septimius Haeranes, son of Septimius Odaenathus (251)

CISem. II, 3944 (= *Inv.* III, 16, Palmyrene and Greek): This statue is that of Septimius Hairan (sptmyws hyrn), son of Odainath (br 'dynt), the illustrious senator and chief of Palmyra (rš' tdmwr), which has been set up to him by Aurelius Philinus, son of Marius Philinus (Gk: Heliodorus), (son of) Ra'ai ('wrlys plynws br mry' plyn' r'y), the soldier who was in the (Gk only: Cyrenean) legion of Bostra (Palmyrene: Bosra): to his honour. In the month Tishri of the year 563 (Oct. 251). (Cooke, no. 125, pp. 284–5)

(Cooke, revised Brock)

4.1.5. Dedication to Septimius Odaenathus (April, 252)

Gawlikowski, *Syria* 57 (1985), p. 257, no. 13 (Palmyrene and Greek, found on a column in the Great Colonnade): To (Palmyrene: The statue of) Septimius Odaenathus, son of Haeranes, son of Vaballathus Nasor, the most illustrious exarch[4] of the Palmyrenes (Palmyrene: rš' dy tdmwr = 'Chief of Palmyra'), Julius Aurelius Ate'aqab (Palmyrene: was made by `t'qb) son of 'Ogeilu, son of Zabdibol, son of Moqimu, whose surname is Qora, to his friend, with affection (Palmyrene: to his friend, in his honour, under his presidency). In the month of Nisan, the year 563 (April, 252).[5]

(Lieu, revised Brock)

4.2.1. Dedication to Julius Aurelius Oge, strategos of Palmyra (254)

CISem. II, 3934 (= *Inv.* III, 14, Palmyrene and Greek): The Senate and People to Julius Aurelius Oge, who is called Seleucus, son of 'Azizu, (son of) 'Azizu, (son of) She'ila (ywlys 'wrlys 'g' dy mtqr' slwqws br 'zyzw 'zyzw š' yl'), who served and was well-pleasing to them in his office of strategos; and he presented ten thousand drachmae: to his honour. In the month of Tishri, the year 566 (Oct., 254).

(Cooke, no. 123, pp. 282–3)

4.2.2. Dedication to Septimius Haeranes (257/8)

Seyrig, *AAS* 13 (1963), pp. 161–2 (Greek only, found in the southern portico of the Colonnade near the theatre): (Statue) of Septimius Haeranes, the illustrious son of the illustrious consul (Gk: *hypatikos*) Odaenathus (erected by) the guild of tanners and makers of leather rafts, for its patron, year 569 (257/8).

(Ingholt, 1976: 131)

4.2.3. Statue of Septimius Odaenathus (junior?) raised by the guild of gold and silver workers at Palmyra (258)

CISem. II, 3945 (= *Inv.* III, 17, Greek and Palmyrene): Statue of Septimius Odainath (sptmyws 'dynt), illustrious consul, our lord, which the corporation of gold and silver-smiths have raised in his honour. In the month of Nisan in the year of 569 (April, 258).

(Lieu, revised Brock)

4.2.4. Dedication to Aurelius Vorodes, Knight and senator of Palmyra (258/9)

Ibid., 3937 (= *Inv.* III, 12, Greek and Palmyrene): To Aurelius Vorodes, equestrian (Gk and Palmyrene: *hippikos* = Lat.: *vir egregius*) and senator (Gk: *bouleutes*) of Palmyra, made by (Gk only: his friend) Bel'aqab, son of Harsa, to his honour. The year 570 (258/9).

(Cooke, no. 124, p. 284)

4.2.5. Dedication to Septimius Haeranes by (Septimius?) Vorodes, senator (date unknown)

Seyrig, *op. cit.*, p. 161, n. 134 (Greek only, found in the portico of theatre): (This statue is dedicated) to Septimius Haeranes, the illustrious (son) of Odaenathus, by Vorodes the senator [. . .]

(Lieu, revised Brock)

4.3.1. Sack of Nehardea by Odaenathus (?) (between 259 and 263)

Iggereth Rav Sherira Gaon [6] p. 82, ed. Lewin (Hebrew): And in the year 570 (Sel. = AD 259)[7] Papa ben Natzer (= Odaenathus ?)[8]

came and destroyed Nehardea[9] and Rabba b. Avuha, our ancestor, went to Sechansiv[10] and to Silhe (and) to Mahoza.[11] And Rav Joseph b. Hama, Rava's father, was there. (And the rest of) our sages (went) to Pumbedita,[12] which from the day of the Second Temple was the Chief Exile, as we learned from Rosh ha-Shanah, 'until he sees the Exile before him like a bonfire' (*Midrash Rosh ha-Shanah* II, 4) and Abbaye said the Exile in Pumbedita.

(Oppenheimer, 1983: 290)

4.3.2. The victories of Septimius Odaenathus over the Persians and Roman pretenders (*c.* 262–*c.* 266)

Oracula Sibyllina XIII, 155–71:

155 At which time will reign over the mighty Romans
two men, swift lords of war. One will have
the number seventy (i.e. Valerian) and the other three (i.e. Gallienus).
And then a haughty bull, digging the earth
with its hoofs and lifting the dust with its two horns,
160 will do much harm to a dark-skinned reptile,
dragging its coil by its horny scales. But he will perish with it.
Another well-horned stag (i.e. Macrianus?) will again come after him,
hungering in the mountains, desiring in its belly to feed upon the venomous beasts. Then shall come one who was sent by the sun (i.e. Odaenathus)
165 a mighty and fearful lion, breathing much flame.
Then he with much shameless daring will destroy
the well-horned swift-moving stag (i.e. Quietus, son of Macrianus)
and the greatest beast –
venomous, fearful and emitting a great deal of hisses (i.e. the Persians)
and the sideways walking goat (i.e. Callistus?) and fame will attend him,
170 He himself, entire, unhurt and great,
will rule over the Romans, but the Persians will be weakened.

(Lieu)

Festus, *breviarium* 23, p. 64, 13–18: Under Gallienus the Persians invaded Mesopotamia and would even have begun to lay claim to Syria, except that (it is shameful to relate) Odaenathus, the

Palmyrene decurion, collected a band of Syrian country folk and put up a spirited resistance. On a number of occasions he routed the Persians and not only defended our border but even as the avenger of the Roman empire, marvellous to say, forced his way to Ctesiphon.

(Dodgeon)

Eutropius, IX, 10: But while these events were taking place in Gaul (i.e. the usurpation of Tetricus), the Persians in the East were overthrown by Odaenathus, who, having defended Syria and recovered Mesopotamia, penetrated into (enemy) territory as far as Ctesiphon.

(Watson, p. 520, revised)

Jerome, *Chronicon*, s. a. 266, p. 221, 10–12: Odaenathus, a decurion of Palmyra, with a band of rustics defeated the Persians so heavily that he established camp at Ctesiphon.

(Dodgeon)

SHA Valer. IV, 2–4: Meanwhile, however, while Valerian was growing old in Persia, Odaenathus the Palmyrene gathered together an army and restored the Roman power almost to its pristine condition. 3. He captured the king's treasures and he captured, too, what the Parthian monarchs hold dearer than treasures, namely his concubines. 4. For this reason Sapor was now in greater dread of the Roman generals, and out of fear of Ballista and Odaenathus he withdrew more speedily to his kingdom. And this, for the time being, was the end of the war with the Persians.

(Magie, iii, p. 7)

SHA Gall. 1, 1: When Valerian was captured ... when the commonwealth was tottering, when Odaenathus had seized the rule of the East, and when Gallienus was rejoicing in the news of his father's captivity, the armies began to range about on all sides, the generals in all the provinces to murmur, and great was the grief of all men that Valerian, a Roman emperor, was held as a slave in Persia.

(Magie, iii, p. 17)

SHA Gall. 3, 1–5: Meanwhile, the commonwealth had been thrown into confusion throughout the entire world. Odaenathus, learning that Macrianus and his son had been slain, that Aureolus was ruling, and that Gallienus was administering the state with still greater slackness, hastened forward to seize the other son of Macrianus, together with his army, should Fortune so permit. 2.

But those who were with Macrianus' son – whose name was Quietus[13] – taking sides with Odaenathus, by the instigation of Ballista, Macrianus' prefect, killed the young man,[14] and, casting his body over the wall, they all in large numbers surrendered to Odaenathus. 3. And so Odaenathus was made emperor[15] over almost the whole East, while Aureolus held Illyricum and Gallienus Rome. 4. This same Ballista murdered, in addition to Quietus and the guardian of his treasures, many of the people of Emesa, to whom Macrianus' soldiers had fled, with the result that this city was nearly destroyed. 5. Odaenathus, meanwhile, as if taking the side of Gallienus, caused all that had happened to be announced to him truthfully.

(Magie, iii, pp. 21–3)

SHA Gall. 10, 1–8: In the consulship of Gallienus and Saturninus, Odaenathus, king of the Palmyrenes, held the rule over the entire East – chiefly for the reason that by his brave deeds he had shown himself worthy of the insignia of such great majesty, whereas Gallienus was doing nothing at all or else only what was extravagant, or foolish and deserving of ridicule. 2. Now at once he proclaimed a war on the Persians to exact for Valerian the vengeance neglected by Valerian's son. 3. He immediately occupied Nisibis and Carrhae, the people of which surrendered, reviling Gallienus. 4. Nevertheless, Odaenathus showed no lack of respect toward Gallienus, for he sent him the satraps he captured – though, as it seemed, merely for the purpose of insulting him and displaying his own prowess. 5. After these had been brought to Rome, Gallienus held a triumph because of Odaenathus' victory; but he still made no mention of his father and did not even place him among the gods, when he heard he was dead, until compelled to do so – although in fact Valerian was still alive, for the news of his death was untrue. 6. Odaenathus, besides, besieged an army of Parthians at Ctesiphon and devastated all the country round about, killing men without number. 7. But when all the satraps from all the outlying regions flocked together to Ctesiphon for the purpose of common defence, there were long-lasting battles with varying results, but more long-lasting still was the success of the Romans. 8. Moreover, since Odaenathus' sole purpose was to set Valerian free, he daily pressed onward, but this best of commanders, now on foreign soil, suffered greatly because of the difficult ground.

(Magie, iii, p. 37)

SHA Gall. 12: One excellent deed of his, to be sure, is mentioned with praise. For in the consulship of his brother Valerian and his kinsman Lucillus, when he (Gallienus) learned that Odaenathus had ravaged the Persians, brought Nisibis and Carrhae under the sway of Rome, made all of Mesopotamia ours, and finally arrived at Ctesiphon, put the king to flight, captured the satraps and killed large numbers of Persians, he gave him a share in the imperial power, conferred on him the name Augustus, and ordered coins to be struck in his honour, which showed him hauling the Persians into captivity. This measure the senate, the city, and men of every age received with approval.

(Magie, iii, p. 41)

SHA trig. tyr. 15, 1–5: Had not Odaenathus, prince of the Palmyrenes, seized the imperial power after the capture of Valerian, when the strength of the Roman state was exhausted, all would have been lost in the East. 2. He assumed, therefore, as the first of his line, the title of King, and after gathering together an army he set out against the Persians, having with him his wife Zenobia, his elder son, whose name was Herodes, and his younger sons, Herennianus and Timolaus. 3. First of all, he brought under his power Nisibis and most of the East together with the whole of Mesopotamia, next, he defeated the king himself and compelled him to flee. 4. Finally, he pursued Sapor and his children even as far as Ctesiphon, and captured his concubines and also a great amount of booty; then he turned to the oriental provinces, hoping to be able to crush Macrianus, who had begun to rule in opposition to Gallienus, but he had already set out against Aureolus and Gallienus. After Macrianus was slain, Odaenathus killed his son Quietus also, while Ballista, many assert, usurped the imperial power in order that he, too, might not be slain.

(Magie, iii, p. 105)

SHA trig. tyr. 18, 1–3: As to whether this man (i.e. Ballista) held the imperial power or not, historians do not agree. For many assert that when Quietus was killed by Odaenathus, Ballista was pardoned, but nevertheless took the imperial power, putting no trust in either Gallienus or Aureolus or Odaenathus. 2. Others, again, declare that while still a commoner he was killed on the lands which he had bought for himself near Daphne. 3. Many, indeed, have said that he assumed the purple in order to rule in the Roman fashion, and that he took command of the army and made many promises on his own account, but was killed by those dispatched by Aureolus for the purpose of seizing Quietus, Macrianus' son, who, Aureolus averred, was his own due prey.

(Magie, iii, pp. 109–11)

Libanius, *epistulae* 1006, 2 (*c.* 391): see below 4.11.4.

Orosius, *adversus paganos* VII, 22, 12: But in the east, Odaenathus gathered a band of peasants and overcame and repulsed the Persians, defended Syria, recovered Mesopotamia, and the Syrian peasants with their leader, Odaenathus, went as far as Ctesiphon.

(Deferrari, p. 318)

Zosimus I, 39, 1–2: The Scythians had laid waste to Greece and had even taken Athens by siege, when Gallienus advanced against those who were already in possession of Thrace, and ordered Odaenathus of Palmyra, a person whose ancestors had always been highly respected by the emperors, to assist in the east which was then in a very desperate condition. Accordingly, having joined to the remnants of the legions in the east the maximum number of his own troops, he attacked Shapur with great vigour; and having taken several cities belonging to the Persians, he also retook Nisibis, which Shapur had formerly taken and which favoured the Persian cause, by a first assault and ravaged it. 2. Then advancing not once merely, but a second time, as far as Ctesiphon, he shut the Persians up in their fortifications, and rendered them content to save their wives, their children and themselves, while he restored order as best as he could to the pillaged territory.

(Anon., revised Lieu)

Jordanes, *Historia Romana* 290, p. 37, 29–30: Before him (i.e. Aurelian), Odaenathus the Palmyrene with a band of rustics had expelled the Persians from Mesopotamia and had occupied it.

(Dodgeon)

Agathias IV, 24, 4: When he came home again, far from showing restraint in his use of his ill-won gains, he was puffed up with pride. But it was not long before Odenathus of Palmyra put a stop to his arrogance. Odenathus was at first unknown and obscure, but won great fame as a result of the disasters he inflicted on Shapur, and many earlier historians wrote about him.

(Cameron, p. 121)

Anonymous Continuator of Dio Cassius, ed. Boissevain, iii, p. 744 (= *FHG* IV, p. 197): As soon as Quietus, the son of Macrinus, had established imperial rule at Emesa, Odaenathus came upon him with a barbarian horde and made clear to them that they should either surrender themselves or prepare for battle. However, they replied that they were prepared to endure anything rather than to hand themselves over.

(Lieu)

Anonymous Continuator of Dio Cassius 8, 2 (= *FHG* IV, p. 195): Kyrinus (Quirinus?)[16] was greatly displeased when Odaenathus took over the war of the Romans (against the Persians). When Odaenathus got wind of this, he ordered him to be executed but he lavished upon him many gifts from his own belongings for his funeral and showed them to him while he was still alive. Kyrinus laughed and said that the man was suffused with ignorance and silliness – ignorance, because we normally destroy our enemies and benefit our friends, but he did not know whether to class him as friend or foe; silliness, because he wished to afflict and kill him while he was alive and feeling, but to honour him with gifts once he was dead and unfeeling. Such good fortune (as had befallen him) underwent a rapid change.

(Lieu)

Syncellus, pp. 466, 23–467, 7 (p. 716, 12–22 CSHB): But Odaenathus the Palmyrene, who was a fine general, allied with the Romans, and he destroyed many of the Persians when he attacked them on their retreat across the land of the Euphrates. For this service he was honoured with the title of commander-in-chief (*strategos*) of the East by Gallienus, and also he destroyed some of the Romans who rose in insurrection against him in Phoenicia. Then again the Scyths, also called the Goths in their own language, came through the Black Sea to Bithynia and overran all Asia and Syria. They captured Nicomedia, a great city of Bithynia, and they destroyed the Ionian cities. Some of the cities they captured were unfortified, others were fortified in part. In addition they also set upon Phrygia and laid waste Troy, Cappadocia and Galatia.

(Dodgeon)

Zonaras, XII, 24, pp. 598, 19–600, 9 (iii, pp. 144, 32–145, 9 and 146, 4–15): Another war was undertaken by Gallienus against Macrinus who had two sons, Macrianus and Quintus, and made an attempt for the emperorship. Because he himself was disabled in one leg, he did not assume the purple but endowed it upon his sons. They happily welcomed him in Asia. After spending some time facing the Persians, he began preparations against Gallienus. He appointed Ballista in his place against the Persians, and he himself selected him as his Master of Cavalry. With him he left his son Quintus ... (p. 599, 23) Quintus, indeed, the younger son of Macrinus, was in the Orient with Ballista, having made practically all of it subject to his authority. Gallienus sent Odaenathus, commander of the Palmyrenes, against them. When the news was announced to Quintus and Ballista of the defeat that had occurred to the Macrini in Pannonia, many of the cities subject to them defected. But they delayed in Emesa. Odaenathus came there and joined battle and defeated them. He himself killed Ballista, while Quintus was slain by the people of the city. The emperor rewarded Odaenathus for his courage and appointed him as Commander-in-Chief (*strategos*) of the entire East.

(Dodgeon)

4.3.3. Dedication to Septimius Odaenathus from the Tyrians (date unknown).

Mouterde, *MUSJ* 38 (1962), pp. 19–20 (Greek only, found on a marble base at Tyre): To Septimius Odaenathus, the most illustrious (senator?). The Septimian colony of Tyre.

(Lieu)

4.3.4. Dedication to Septimius Herodianus for victory over the Persians in Syria (date unknown).

IGR III, 1032 (Greek only, found on a block, once the base of a statue which stood on top of the easternmost of the two lateral arches north of the Great Colonnade): (This statue is dedicated) to the King of Kings, [having received?] the royalty near the Orontes, crowned for victory over the Persians, Septimius Herodianus,[17] by Julius Aurelius Septimius Vorodes and [Julius Aurelius... , procurator] of the Queen, *centenarius*, both strategoi of the illustrious colony.

(Lieu)

4.3.5. Peace between Odaenathus and Gallienus (c. 264)

SHA trig. tyr. 21, 5: ... on the other hand, it is generally known that he (i.e. Gallienus) celebrated a decennial festival at Rome, and that after this festival he defeated the Goths, made peace with Odaenathus, entered into friendly relations with Aureolus, warred against Postumus and against Lollianus, and did many things that make a virtuous life, but more that tend to dishonour.

(Magie, iii, p. 63)

4.4.1. Dedications to Septimius Vorodes,[18] *Procurator Augusti ducenarius*

CISem. II, 3938 (= *Inv.* III, 11, Greek and Palmyrene): This statue is that of Septimius Vorodes, (Gk only: the eminent) procurator ducenarius (i.e. procurator second class, of Caesar (qsr), our lord, which has been set up to him by the Senate and People: to his honour. In the month of Nisan of the year 573 (April, 262).

(Cooke, no. 128, p. 288, with different dating)

CISem. II, 3939 (= *Inv.* III, 10, Greek and Palmyrene): Septimius Vorodes, the most excellent procurator ducenarius (this statue) has been set up to his honour by Julius Au[r]elius Nebuzabad, son of So'adu, son of Haire, strategos of the colony, his friend. The year 574 in the month of Kislul (Dec., 262).

(Cooke, no. 127, pp. 287–8)

CISem. II, 3940 (= *Inv.* III, 9, Greek and Palmyrene): Septimius Vorodes, the most excellent procurator ducenarius and commandant, (Gk: *argapetes* = Pers. hargbed, commander of a fort, see below Ch. 5, n. 46), (this statue) has been set up to him by Julius Aurelius Septimius Iade, equestrian (= *vir egregius*), son of Alexander, son of Hairan, (son) of Soraiku, to the honour of his friend and patron. In the month of Sivan of the year 575 (May–June 575, Gk gives April).

(Cooke, no. 128, pp. 288–9)

CISem. II, 3941 (= *Inv.* III, 8, Greek and Palmyrene, both very fragmentary, text reconstructed from Ibid. 3940): Septimius Vorodes, the eminent procurator ducenarius and commandant, (this statue) has been set up to him by [Julius Aurelius Septimi]us Malku, son of Mal[oka, son of Nassum] ([ywlys 'wrlys sptmy]ws ml[kw br mlwk' nšwm), to the honour of his friend and patron. In the month of Nisan, 576 (April, 265).

(Lieu, revised Brock)

CISem. II, 3942 (= *Inv.* III, 7, Greek and Palmyrene, the latter is badly preserved): The Senate and the People have erected this statue to Septimius Vorodes, the eminent imperial procurator ducenarius, administrator of justice of the metro-colonia (i.e. Palmyra), who has brought up the caravans at his own expense, and has (worthy) testimony borne to him by the chiefs of the merchants, who has exercised brilliantly his function as strategos, who has been public notary (Gk: 'being *agoranomos*')[19] of the metro-colonia; who has spent large sums from his own coffers, who has been pleasing to the Senate and the People and who is now the symposiarch, with brilliance, of the priests of the god Zeus-Bel; on account of his integrity and his honour, in the year [577], in the month of Xandikos (April, 266).

(Lieu, revised Brock)

CISem. II, 3943 (= *Inv.* III, 6, Greek and Palmyrene): Septimius Vorodes, the eminent (Gk adds: imperial) procurator ducenarius and commandant, (this statue) has been set up to him by Julius Aurelius Shalme, son of Cassianus, son of Ma'nai, knight (Gk adds: of the Romans), to the honour of his friend and patron. In the month of Nisan, 578 (April, 267).

(Lieu, revised Brock)

4.4.2. The Persian war of Gallienus as told by Malalas

Malalas, XII, p. 298, 3–16: After the reign of Valerian, Gallienus also called Licinianus ruled for fourteen years. . . . He had only just become emperor, when he marched against the Persians and came to avenge the Romans. He was also very generous to those who had survived the Persian raids, and he rebuilt what had been burnt and alleviated taxation for four years and he also founded a large temple in Emesa. When he joined war against the Persians, many fell on both sides and he made a treaty of peace. And he turned back from there into Arabia and made war on Enathus (Odaenathus), King of the barbarian Saracens, and he slew him and took over Arabia. He returned to Rome and died of illness at the age of fifty.

(Dodgeon)

4.4.3. Odaenathus' devotion to his son Herodes

SHA trig. tyr. 16: Herodes, who was the son, not of Zenobia, but of a former wife of Odaenathus, received the imperial power along with his father, though he was the most effeminate of men, wholly oriental and given over to Grecian luxury, for he had embroidered tents and pavilions made out of cloth of gold and everything in the manner of the Persians. 2. In fact Odaenathus, complying with his ways and moved by the promptings of a father's indulgence, gave him all the king's concubines and the riches and jewels that he captured. 3. Zenobia, indeed, treated him in a step-mother's way, and this made him all the more dear to his father. Nothing more remains to be said concerning Herodes.

(Magie, iii, pp. 107-9)

4.4.4. His other two sons, Herrenianus and Timolaus

SHA trig. tyr. 27: Odaenathus, when he died, left two little sons, Herennianus and his brother Timolaus, in whose name Zenobia seized the imperial power, holding the government longer than was meet for a woman. These boys she displayed clad in the purple robe of a Roman emperor and she brought them to public gatherings which she attended in the fashion of a man, holding up, among other examples, Dido and Semiramis, and Cleopatra, the founder of her family.[20] 2. The manner of their death, however, is uncertain; for many maintain that they were killed by Aurelian, and many that they died a natural death, since Zenobia's descendants still remain among the nobles of Rome.

(Magie, iii, p. 131)

SHA trig. tyr. 28: With regard to him (i.e. Timolaus) we consider only those things to be worth knowing which have been told concerning his brother (i.e. Herrenianus). 2. One thing there is, however, which distinguishes him from his brother, that is, that such was his eagerness for Roman studies that in a short time, it is said, he made good the statement of his teacher of letters, who had said that he was in truth able to make him the greatest of Latin rhetoricians.

(Magie, iii, pp. 131-3)

4.5.1. Death of Odaenathus (*c* 266/7)

SHA Gall. 13, 1: About this same time (i.e. as the invasion of the Scythians), Odaenathus was treacherously slain by his cousin, and with him his son Herodes, whom also he had hailed as emperor.

(Magie, iii, p. 43)

SHA trig. tyr. 15, 5-6: Then, after he had for the most part put in order the affairs of the East, he was killed by his cousin Maeonius (who also had seized the imperial power), together with his son Herodes,[21] who, also, after returning from Persia along with his father, had received the title of emperor. 6. Some god, I believe, was angry with the commonwealth, who, after Valerian's death, was unwilling to preserve Odaenathus alive.

(Magie, iii, pp. 105-7)

SHA trig. tyr. 17, 1–3: This man (i.e. Maeonius), the cousin of Odaenathus, murdered that excellent emperor, being moved thereto by nothing else than contemptible envy, for he could bring no charge against him save that Herodes was his son. 2. It is said, however, that previously he had entered into a conspiracy with Zenobia, who could not bear that her stepson Herodes should be called a prince in a higher rank than her own two sons, Herennianus and Timolaus. 3. But Maeonius, too, was a filthy fellow, and so, after being saluted as emperor through some blunder, he was shortly thereafter killed by the soldiers, as his excesses deserved.

(Magie, iii, p. 109)

Zosimus I, 39, (2): Shortly afterwards (i.e. his victory over Shapur), whilst residing at Emesa, he (i.e. Odaenathus) was killed in a conspiracy as he was celebrating the birthday of a friend. Zenobia then took over the reins of government. She was the wife of Odaenathus, but had the courage of a man, and with the assistance of her husband's friends, governed with the same circumspection.

(Anon., revised Lieu)

Anonymous Continuator of Dio Cassius 7, ed. Boissevain, iii, p. 744 (= *FHG* IV, p. 194): As Rufinus had executed the elder Odaenathus for fomenting revolt, the younger Odaenathus[22] accused him of having murdered his father. The Emperor (*sc.* Gallienus) asked Rufinus why he did this. He replied that he was justified in so doing. 'Would that you had entrusted me to kill this Odaenathus, his son, and that I did it immediately.' Rufinus was suffering from gout in his hands and feet and was unable to move at all. The Emperor said to him, 'By what strength and by what person do you have confidence in what you are saying?' But he replied, 'Not even if I was healthy, more so than in my youth, was I able to do anything against him. But by giving orders and making dispositions by your authority, I managed all the affairs well. And you, your Majesty, do not personally carry out what you undertake but give orders to your soldiers.' Gallienus praised him for this reply.

(Lieu)

John of Antioch, *frag.* 152, 2, *FHG* IV, p. 599: Odaenathus was killed in a conspiracy of Gallienus; and Zenobia, who was his wife, took over the affairs there. She had a man's courage and avenged her husband's death with his friends.

(Lieu)

Syncellus, p. 467, 4–14 (pp. 716, 22–717, 8 CSHB): But once more Odaenathus, who had gained distinction over the Persians and had subdued Ctesiphon by siege, heard of the disasters of Asia and hurriedly came with his forces through Cappadocia to Heraclea in Pontus. When he was about to fulfil his intention of falling upon the Goths, he was treacherously slain by an individual called Odaenathus like himself. Before his arrival, the Goths returned to their homeland through the same Pontus and the bodyguard killed Odaenathus, the murderer of (their king) Odaenathus; they entrusted the government of the Orient to his wife Zenobia.

(Dodgeon)

Zonaras XII, 24, p. 600, 10–23 (iii, pp. 146, 16–147, 3, Dindorf): This Odaenathus became a great man and loyal to the Romans, and was victorious in many wars against different nations and against the Persians themselves. But in the end he was killed by his own nephew. For that man joined this uncle in a hunt, and when the animal leapt out, he made the first attack and threw and killed the beast. Odaenathus was angry and threatened his relative. But the nephew did not desist, but did this two or three times. Odaenathus flew into a rage and took away his horse. This is considered a great insult among the barbarians. So the young man angrily threatened his uncle. For this reason, he put him in chains. Later the elder of Odaenathus' sons requested his father that the prisoner be freed. And when the young man was released, while Odaenathus was drinking, he came at him with a sword and killed him and his son by whom the release had been obtained. But the young man was slain when some of them attacked him.

(Dodgeon)

4.5.2. The character and achievements of Odaenathus

SHA trig. tyr. 15, 7–8: For of a surety he, with his wife Zenobia, would have restored not only the East, which he had already brought back to its ancient condition, but also all parts of the whole world everywhere, since he was fierce in warfare and, as most writers relate, ever famous for his memorable hunts; for from his earliest years he expended his sweat, as is the duty of a man, in taking lions and panthers and bears and other beasts of the forest, and always lived in the woods and the mountains, enduring heat and rain and all other hardships which pleasures of hunting entail.

8. Hardened by these, he was able to bear the sun and the dust in the wars with the Persians; and his wife, too, was inured to hardship and in the opinion of many was held to be more brave than her husband, being, indeed, the noblest of all the women of the East, and, as Cornelius Capitolinus declares, the most beautiful.

(Magie, iii, p. 107)

4.5.3. The character and ambition of Zenobia

SHA trig. tyr. 30, 1–3 and 12–22: Now all the shame is exhausted, for in the weakened state of the commonwealth things came to such a pass that, while Gallienus conducted himself in the most evil fashion, even women ruled most excellently. 2. For, in fact, even a foreigner, Zenobia by name, about whom much has already been said, boasting herself to be of the family of the Cleopatras and the Ptolemies, proceeded upon the death of her husband Odaenathus to cast about her shoulders the imperial mantle; and arrayed in the robes of Dido and even assuming the diadem, she held the imperial power in the name of her sons Herennianus and Timolaus, ruling longer than could be endured from one of the female sex. 3. For this proud woman performed the functions of a monarch, both while Gallienus was ruling and afterwards when Claudius was busied with the war against the Goths, and in the end could scarcely be conquered by Aurelian himself, under whom she was led in triumph and submitted to the sway of Rome. ...

12. Such was her continence, it is said, that she would not know even her own husband, save for the purpose of conception. For when once she had lain with him, she would refrain until the time of menstruation to see if she were pregnant; if not, she would again grant him an opportunity of begetting children. 13. She lived in regal pomp. It was rather in the manner of the Persians that she received worship and in the manner of the Persian kings that she banqueted; 14. but it was in the manner of a Roman emperor that she came forth to public assemblies, wearing a helmet and girt with a purple fillet, which had gems hanging from the lower edge, while its centre was fastened with the jewel called cochlis, used instead of the brooch worn by women, and her arms were frequently bare. 15. Her face was dark and of a swarthy hue, her eyes were black and powerful beyond the usual wont, her spirit divinely great, and her beauty incredible. So white were her teeth that many thought that she had pearls in place of teeth. 16. Her voice was clear and like that of a man. Her sternness, when necessity demanded, was that of

a tyrant, her clemency, when her sense of right called for it, that of a good emperor. Generous with prudence, she conserved her treasures beyond the wont of women. 17. She made use of a carriage, and rarely of a woman's coach, but more often she rode a horse; it is said, moreover, that frequently she walked with her foot-soldiers for three or four miles. 18. She hunted with the eagerness of a Spaniard. She often drank with her generals, though at other times she refrained, and she drank, too, with the Persians and the Armenians, but only for the purpose of getting the better of them. 19. At her banquets she used vessels of gold and jewels, and she even used those that had been Cleopatra's. As servants she had eunuchs of advanced age but very few maidens. 20. She ordered her sons to talk Latin, so that, in fact, they spoke Greek but rarely and with difficulty. 21. She herself was not wholly conversant with the Latin tongue, but nevertheless, mastering her timidity, she would speak it; Egyptian, on the other hand, she spoke very well. 22. In the history of Alexandria and the Orient she was so well versed that she even composed an epitome, so it is said; Roman history, however, she read in Greek.

(Magie, iii, pp. 135–41)

4.5.4. Zenobia held power in the name of her sons after the death of Odaenathus

SHA Gall. 13, 2–3: Then Zenobia, his wife, since the sons who remained, Herennianus and Timolaus, were still very young assumed the power herself and ruled for a long time, not in feminine fashion or with the ways of a woman, 3. but surpassing in courage and skill not merely Gallienus, than whom any girl could have ruled more successfully, but also many an emperor.

(Magie, iii, p. 43)

SHA Aurel. 38, 1: . . . it was in the name of her son Vaballathus and not in that of Timolaus or Herennianus, that Zenobia held the imperial power, which she did really hold.

(Magie, iii, p. 269)

4.5.5. Dedication to Zenobia and her son Vaballathus Athenodorus (c 268/70)

CISem. II, 3971 (Milestone found west of Palmyra, Greek and Palmyrene): (Gk): . . . and [for the sa]fety of Septimia Zenobia, the most illustrious queen, the mother of the Emperor Septi[mius] Athen[odorus]... (Palmyrene): For the life and [victory] of Septimius Vaballathus Athenodo[rus] (sptymyws whblt 'tndr[ws], the most illustrious King of Kings and Corrector (w' pnrtt' = Gk ἐπανορθωτής) of the entire Orient, son of Septimius [Odainath, King] of Kings; and for the life of Septimia Bathzabbai (sptymy' btzby, i.e. Zenobia), the most illustrious queen, mother of the King of Kings, daughter of Antiochus ('ntywkws). Fourteen miles.

(Vince, revised Brock)

4.6.1. Predominance of Palmyrene power in the East – defeat of Heraclianus (*c.* 268)

Aurelius Victor, *liber de Caesaribus* 33, 3: He (Gallienus), together with his son Saloninus on whom he had conferred the rank of Caesar, had left the Roman commonwealth to sink to such a point that the Goths, traversing Thrace without hindrance, had occupied Macedonia, Achaea and the confines of Asia, that the Parthians (*sic*) had had possession of Mesopotamia and that the East had fallen under the dominations of brigands and a woman (i.e. Zenobia); ...

(Dodgeon)

SHA Gall. 13, 4–5: As for Gallienus, indeed, when he learned that Odaenathus was murdered, he made ready for war with the Persians – an over tardy vengeance for his father – and, gathering an army with the help of Heraclianus, he played the part of a skilful prince. 5. This Heraclianus, however, on setting out against the Persians, was defeated by the Palmyrenes and lost all the troops he had gathered, for Zenobia was ruling Palmyra and most of the East with the vigour of a man.

(Magie, iii, pp. 43–5)

4.6.2. Zenobia founded a city/fortress on the Euphrates (date uncertain)

Procopius, *de bello Persico* II, 5, 4–6: (AD 540) Chosroes, therefore, not wishing to make trial of so strong a fortress (i.e. Circesium) and not having in mind to cross the River Euphrates, but rather to go against the Syrians and Cilicians, without any hesitation led his army forward, and after advancing for what, to an unencumbered traveller, is about a three days' journey along the bank of the Euphrates, he came upon the city of Zenobia; this place Zenobia had built in former times, and, as was natural, she gave her name to the city. 5. Now Zenobia was the wife of Odaenathus, the ruler of the Saracens of that region, who had been on terms of peace with the Romans from of old. 6. This Odaenathus rescued for the Romans the Eastern Empire when it had come under the power of the Medes (i.e. Persians); but this took place in former times.

(Dewing, i, pp. 295–7)

4.6.3. Alleged support for Paul of Samosata, heretical bishop of Antioch (*c.* 260–89), by Zenobia

Athanasius, *historia Arianorum* 71, ed. Bright, p. 233: Zenobia was a Jewess,[23] and a supporter of Paul of Samosata; but she did not give up the churches to the Jews for synagogues.

(Atkinson *ap.* Robertson, p. 296)

4.6.4. The invasion of Arabia by Zenobia

IGLS 9107 (= AE 1947, 165, inscription of the lintel over the entrance to the temple of Iuppiter Hammon at Bostra in Arabia, Latin): ... the temple of Iuppiter Hammon, destroyed by the Palmyrene enemies, which ... rebuilt, with a silver statue and iron doors (?).[24]

(Speidel, 1977: 723)

Malalas, XII, p. 299, 3–10: At the same time Zenobia the Saracen, the wife of Enathus (i.e. Odaenathus), exacting revenge for the death of her own husband, gathered his kinsmen and took over Arabia, then held by the Romans. She also slew the Dux Trassus of the Romans and all the force with him during the reign of Apollianus himself (also called Claudius) (268–270). The same Claudius was in Sirmium, waging war, and there he died at the age of fifty-six.

(Dodgeon)

4.6.5. Expansion of Palmyrene power into Egypt (*c.* 270)[25]

SHA Divus Claudius 11, 1–2: While these things were being done by the Deified Claudius, the Palmyrenes, under the generals Saba and Timagenes, made war against the Egyptians, who defeated them with true Egyptian pertinacity and unwearied continuance in fighting. 2. Probatus, nevertheless, the leader (dux) of the Egyptians, was killed by a trick of Timagenes'. All the Egyptians, however, submitted to the Roman emperor, swearing allegiance to Claudius, although he was absent.

(Magie, iii, p. 173)

SHA Probus 9, 5: He (i.e. Probus) fought also against the Palmyrenes, who held Egypt for the party of Odaenathus and Cleopatra (i.e. Zenobia), fighting at first with success, but later so recklessly that he nearly was captured; later, however, when his forces were strengthened, he brought Egypt and the greater part of the Orient under the sway of Aurelian.

(Magie, iii, p. 353)

Zosimus I, 44, 1–2: The Scythians were thus dispersed, with the loss of a great part of their troops. Zenobia now began to conceive of more ambitious projects and sent Zabdas into Egypt, because Timagenes, an Egyptian, attempted to place Egypt under the government of the Palmyrenes.[26] He had for this purpose raised an army of Palmyrenes, Syrians and barbarians, to the number of seventy thousand, which was opposed by fifty thousand Egyptians. A sharp engagement ensued between them, in which the Palmyrenes had the greater advantage. He then departed, leaving them a garrison of five thousand men. 2. Probus, who had been appointed by the emperor to clear the sea of pirates, when hearing of the subjugation of Egypt by the Palmyrenes, marched against them with his own forces, and with as many of the Egyptians as were opposed to the Palmyrenes, and drove out their garrison. The Palmyrenes rallied with fresh forces but Probus, who also levied a body of Egyptians and Africans, gained another victory, and drove the Palmyrenes out of Egypt. When Probus was encamped on a mountain near Babylon,[27] thereby cutting off the passage of the enemy into Syria, Timagenes, who was well acquainted with the country, gained the summit of the mountain with two thousand men and attacked the Egyptians by surprise. Probus was among those taken prisoner but he killed himself.[28]

(Anon., revised Lieu)

Syncellus, p. 470, 1–2 (p. 721, 4–9, CSHB): Aurelian subjugated the Palmyrenes and brought Gaul under subjection. It is said that Philostratus, the Athenian historian (*FGrH* 99T), and Longinus flourished in his reign.

Then Zenobia revolted against the Romans, and assembling a

large army, took control of Egypt and defeated Probus the Roman general there.

(Dodgeon)

4.7.1. Epitaph of a soldier who fell in the Egyptian campaign

Seyrig, *Syria* 31 (1954) p. 215 (Greek funerary epitaph of uncertain provenance, probably from the Hauran in Arabia): Odious Egypt snatched away the souls of many, including that of yours. While your uncle and your illustrious mother have buried you with the appropriate rites, the others had become food for birds of prey. Courage . . .

(Speidel 1977: 724)

4.7.2. Statues to Septimius Odaenathus and Zenobia raised on adjacent columns at Palmyra (271)

CISem. II, 3946 (= *Inv.* III, 19, Palmyrene only, the Greek text has disappeared, probably erased): Statue of Septimius Odainath (spt-myws 'dy[nt]), King of Kings and Restitutor of all the Orient (mtqnn' dy mdnh' klh);[29] Septimius Zabda, commander in chief, and Septimius Zabbai, commander of Palmyra, (both) eminent men raised it to their Lord, in the month of Ab in the year 582 (Aug., 271).

(Lieu, revised Brock)

CISem. II, 3947 (= *Inv.* III, 20, Greek and Palmyrene): Statue of Septimia Zenobia (Gk; Palmyrene gives her name as sptymy ' btzby: Septimia Bathzabbai), most illustrious and pious queen; Septimius Zabda, commander in chief and Septimius Zabbai, commander of Palmyra, (both) eminent (men) raised it to their sovereign lady, in the month of Ab in the year 582 (Aug., 271).

(Brock)

4.7.3. Dedications to Vaballathus Athenodorus found on milestones near Bostra

AE 1904, 60 (= Dessau, 8924, Latin): To the Imperator Caesar L. Julius Aurelius Septimius Vaballathus Athenodorus, Persicus Maximus, Arabicus Maximus, Adiabenicus Maximus, the Devout, the Fortunate, the Unconquered, Augustus, [. . .]

Bauzou, 1986: 2 (Latin milestones found at the 15th and 20th mile stations on the *Via Nova* from Bostra): [Lu(cius) Juli]us

Aurelius Septimius Vaballathus Athenodorus, King, Consul, Imperator, *dux* of the Romans. Fifteen miles.

Ibid. p. 3 (Latin): L(ucius) Julius Aurel[ius Septimius] Baballa[thus Athenodorus], King, Co(n)[s(ul) Imperator, *dux* of the Ro]mans . . .

(Lieu)

4.7.4. Aurelian marched against Zenobia, the recovery of Tyana (271/2)

SHA Aurel. 22, 1–24, 9: And so, having arranged for all that had to do with the fortifications and the general state of the city and with city affairs as a whole, he directed his march against the Palmyrenes, or rather against Zenobia, who, in the name of her sons, was wielding the imperial power in the East. 2. On this march he ended many great wars of various kinds. For in Thrace and Illyricum he defeated the barbarians who came against him, and on the other side of the Danube he even slew the leader of the Goths, Cannabas, or Cannabaudes as he is also called, and with him five thousand men. 3. From there he crossed over by way of Byzantium into Bithynia, and took possession of it without a struggle. 4. Many were the great and famous things that he said and did, but we cannot include them all in our book without causing a surfeit, nor, indeed, do we wish to do so, but for the better understanding of his character and valour a few of them must be selected. 5. For instance, when he came to Tyana and found its gates closed against him, he became enraged and exclaimed, it is said: 'In this town I will not leave even a dog alive.'

6. Then, indeed, the soldiers, in the hope of plunder, pressed on with greater vigour, but a certain Heraclammon, fearing that he would be killed along with the rest, betrayed his native-place, and so the city was captured.

23 Aurelian, however, with the true spirit of an emperor, at once performed two notable deeds, one of which showed his severity, the other his leniency. 2. For, like a wise victor, he put to death Heraclammon, the betrayer of his native-place, and when the soldiers clamoured for the destruction of the city in accordance with the words in which he had declared that he would not leave a dog alive in Tyana, he answered them, saying: 'I did, indeed, declare that I would not leave a dog alive in this city; well, then, kill all the dogs.' 3. Notable, indeed, were the prince's words, but more notable still was the deed of the soldiers; for the entire army, just as though

it were gaining riches thereby, took up the prince's jest, by which both booty was denied them and the city preserved intact.

4. The letter concerning Heraclammon: 'From Aurelian Augustus to Mallius Chilo. I have suffered the man to be put to death by whose kindness, as it were, I recovered Tyana. But never have I been able to love a traitor and I was pleased that the soldiers killed him; for he who spared not his native city would not have been able to keep faith with me. 5. He, indeed, is the only one of all who opposed me that the earth now holds. The fellow was rich, I cannot deny it, but the property I have restored to the children to whom it belonged, that no one may charge me with having permitted a man who was rich to be slain, for the sake of his money.'

24   The city, moreover, was captured in a wonderful way. For after Heraclammon had shown Aurelian a place where the ground sloped upward by nature in the form of a siege-mound, up which he could climb in full attire, the emperor ascended there, and, holding aloft his purple cloak he showed himself to the townsfolk within and the soldiers without, and so the city was captured, just as though Aurelian's entire army had been within the walls.

2. We must not omit one event which enhances the fame of a venerated man. 3. For, it is said, Aurelian did indeed truly speak and truly think of destroying the city of Tyana; but Apollonius of Tyana, a sage of the greatest renown and authority, a philosopher of former days, the true friend of the gods, and himself even to be regarded as a supernatural being, as Aurelian was withdrawing to his tent, suddenly appeared to him in the form in which he is usually portrayed, and spoke to him as follows, using Latin in order that he might be understood by a man from Pannonia: 4. 'Aurelian, if you wish to conquer, there is no reason why you should plan the death of my fellow-citizens. Aurelian, if you wish to rule, abstain from the blood of the innocent. Aurelian, act with mercy, if you wish to live long.' 5. Aurelian recognized the countenance of the venerated philosopher, and, in fact, he had seen his portrait in many a temple. 6. And so, at once stricken with terror, he promised him a portrait and statues and a temple, and returned to his better self. 7. This incident I have learned from trustworthy men and read over again in the books in the Ulpian Library, and I have been the more ready to believe it because of the reverence in which Apollonius is held. 8. For who among men has ever been more venerated, more revered, more renowned, or more holy than that very man? He brought back the dead to life, he said and did many things beyond the power of man. If any one should wish to learn

these, let him read the Greek books which have been composed concerning his life. 9. I myself, moreover, if the length of my life shall permit and the plan shall continue to meet with his favour, will put into writing the deeds of this great man, even though it be briefly, not because his achievements need the tribute of my discourse, but in order that these wondrous things may be proclaimed by the voice of every man.

(Magie, iii, pp. 237–43)

Zosimus I, 50, 1: After the problems in Italy and Pannonia had been solved, the emperor prepared to march against the Palmyrenes, who had already become master of all Egypt and the East, as far as Ancyra in Galatia, and would have acquired Bithynia even as far as Chalcedon, if the Bithynians had not learned that Aurelian had been made emperor, and so shook off the Palmyrene yoke.

(Anon., revised Lieu)

Anonymous Continuator of Dio Cassius, 10, 4, ed. Boissevain, iii, p. 746 (= *FHG*, IV, p. 197): In the course of the siege of Tyana, Aurelian said to his troops: 'If we should enter the city, no dog should be left alive.' However, after the city had been captured, he forbade the soldiers to kill or plunder. The enraged soldiers said to him: 'You should now permit us to do what you have promised.' But he replied to them saying: 'You have correctly repeated what I have said. Go now, therefore, and kill all the dogs, so that none of them may be found alive in the city.' Thereupon he dispatched the tribunes and the soldiers and exterminated the dogs, so that the anger of the army dissolved into jest. Afterwards he called the soldiers together and addressed them as follows: 'We are fighting to liberate the cities and if we prefer to pillage them, they will have no more faith in us. Let us rather seek plunder from the barbarians and we will spare those whom (we regard) as our own.'

(Lieu)

4.7.5. Egyptian documents (in Greek) dated by the joint regnal year of Aurelian and Vaballathus Athenodorus (272)

P. Oxy. 1264, 20–27:[30] . . . The second year of the Emperor Caesar Lucius Domitius Aurelianus Pius Felix Augustus and the fifth year of Julius Aurelius Septimius Vaballathus Athenodorus, most illustrious king, consul, Emperor, general of the Romans, Phamenoth 8 (14 March, 272).

(Grenfell and Hunt)

BGU 946: (The main text is lost.) The second year of our Lord Lucius Domitius Aurelianus Augustus and the fifth year of our Lord Septimius Vabalathus (*sic*) Athenodorus, the most illustrious king, consul, Emperor, general of the Romans, Phamenoth 15 (21 March, 272) . . .

(Lieu)

4.8.1. Accession of Hormizd as Shahanshah of Persia (272). His succession by Bahram I (273–276).

Agathias IV, 24, 5: On Shapur's death, his son Hormizd took over the throne, but held it only for a very short time. He enjoyed his good fortune for a year and ten days, without doing anything that has ever been recorded. The next king, Varanes (i.e. Bahram), who reigned for three years, was the same.

(Cameron, p. 123)

4.8.2. Aurelian defeated the Palmyrenes at Immae and recovered Antioch (272).

Festus, *brev.* 24, p. 65, 1–6: Zenobia, the wife of Odaenathus, was an addition to the glory of the emperor Aurelian. For after her husband's death she held the Eastern empire within her female control. Although she relied on many thousands of heavy cavalry and archers, Aurelian defeated her at Immae not far from Antioch and captured her . . .

(Dodgeon)

Eutropius IX, 13, 2: He (i.e. Aurelian) also took prisoner Zenobia, who, having killed her husband Odaenathus, was mistress of the east, in a battle of no great importance not far from Antioch, . . .

(Watson)

Jerome, *Chronicon*, s. a. 273, p. 222, 15–22: Zenobia was defeated in battle at Immae, not far from Antioch. She had ruled over the East after the death of her husband Odaenathus. In that battle, the dux Pompeianus, surnamed Francus, fought most bravely against her. His family is still surviving today in Antioch and from his line, Evagrius the presbyter, dearest to me, is descended.

(Dodgeon)

SHA Aurel. 25, 1–6: After thus recovering Tyana, Aurelian, by means of a brief engagement near Daphne, gained possession of Antioch, having promised forgiveness to all; and thereupon, obeying, as far as is known, the injunctions of that venerated man,

Apollonius, he acted with greater kindness and mercy. After this, the whole issue of the war was decided near Emesa in a mighty battle fought against Zenobia and Zaba, her ally. 3. When Aurelian's horsemen, now exhausted, were on the point of breaking their ranks and turning their backs, suddenly by the power of a supernatural agency, as was afterwards made known, a divine form spread encouragement throughout the foot-soldiers and rallied even the horsemen. Zenobia and Zaba were put to flight, and a victory was won in full. 4. And so, having reduced the East to its former state, Aurelian entered Emesa as a conqueror, and at once made his way to the Temple of Elagabalus, to pay his vows as if by a duty common to all. 5. But there he beheld that same divine form which he had seen supporting his cause in the battle. 6. Wherefore he not only established temples there, dedicating gifts of great value, but he also built a temple to the Sun at Rome, which he consecrated with still greater pomp, as we shall relate in the proper place.

(Magie, iii, pp. 243–5)

Zosimus I, 50, 2–54, 2: Ancyra submitted to the Romans as soon as the emperor arrived there, and afterwards Tyana, and all the cities between that and Antioch. There finding Zenobia with a large army ready to engage, as he himself also was, he marched into battle as honour obliged him. 3. But observing that the Palmyrene cavalry placed great confidence in their armour, which was very strong and heavy, and that they were very much better horsemen than his soldiers, he placed his infantry by themselves somewhere on the other side of the Orontes. He ordered his cavalry not to engage immediately with the fresh cavalry of the Palmyrenes, but to wait for their attack, and then pretend to flee and to continue so doing until excessive heat and the weight of their armour had so wearied both the men and their horses that they had to give up the chase. 4. This stratagem worked as the cavalry adhered to the order of the emperor. When they saw their enemy tired, and that their horses were scarcely able to stand under them, or themselves to move, they drew up the reins of their horses, and, wheeling round, charged them, trampling them as they fell from their horses. A confused slaughter ensued, some falling by the sword, and others by their own and the enemies' horses.

51 After this defeat, the survivors fled into Antioch, and Zabdas, the general of Zenobia, fearing that the Antiochenes, on hearing of the defeat, should rebel, chose a bearded man who bore some resemblance to the emperor in silhouette, and clothing him in

a dress such as Aurelian was accustomed to wear, led him through the city as if he had taken the emperor prisoner. 2. After deceiving the Antiochenes by this ploy, he stole out of the city by night, and took with him Zenobia together with the remainder of the army to Emesa. As soon as it was day, the emperor called together the infantry, intending to attack the defeated enemy on both sides; but, hearing of the escape of Zenobia, he entered Antioch, where he was joyfully received by the citizens. 3. Finding that many had left the city, under apprehensions that they should suffer for having espoused the party of Zenobia; he published edicts in every place to recall them and told them that such events had happened more through necessity than of his own inclination.

52   When this was known to the exiles, they flocked back to share in the emperor's magnanimity; who having settled the affairs of that city proceeded to Emesa. There he found a contingent of Palmyrenes had got possession of a hill above the suburbs of Daphne, thinking that its steepness would enable them to obstruct the enemy's passage. He therefore commanded his soldiers to march with their shields close to each other, and in compact formation, to keep off any missiles and stones that might be thrown at them. 2. The soldiers followed the order with vigour and as soon as they had ascended the hill, and could engage their adversaries on equal terms, they put them to flight in such disorder, that some of them were dashed in pieces from the precipices, and others slaughtered in the pursuit by those who were on the hill, and those who were still making their ascent. Having gained the victory, they made the crossing, marched on unopposed [. . .], the emperor making his way through these regions. 3. He was liberally entertained at Apamea, Larissa, and Arethusa. Finding the Palmyrene army drawn up before Emesa, numbering seventy thousand men, consisting of Palmyrenes and their allies, he arrayed against them the Dalmatian cavalry, the Moesians and Pannonians, and the Gothic legions of Noricum and Rhaetia, 4. and besides these the praetorians, chosen by merit from all and the most distinguished, the Mauritanian horse, and from Asia came contingents of Tyaneans, as well as Mesopotamians, Syrians, Phoenicians, and Palestinians, all known for their bravery. The Palestinians wielded clubs and staves, besides other weapons.

53   At the commencement of the engagement, the Roman cavalry made a partial withdrawal, in case the Palmyrenes, who outnumbered them, and were better horsemen, should surround the Roman army unawares. But the Palmyrene cavalry pursued them so fiercely, though their ranks were broken, that the outcome was quite contrary to the expectation of the Roman cavalry. For they were pursued by an enemy much their superior in strength, 2. and therefore most of them fell. The infantry had to bear the brunt of the action. Observing that the Palmyrenes had broken their ranks when the cavalry commenced their pursuit, they wheeled about, and attacked them while they were scattered and in disarray. An immense slaughter ensued, because while some fought with the usual weapons, those of Palestine brought clubs and staves against coats of mail made of iron and brass. 3. This was perhaps a contributory factor to the victory, as the enemies were paralysed by the unexpectedness of being attacked by staves. The Palmyrenes therefore ran away with the utmost haste and in their flight trod each other to pieces and were slaughtered by the enemy. The field was filled with dead men and horses, whilst those who could escape took refuge in the city.

54 Zenobia was naturally much disturbed by this defeat, and therefore deliberated on what measures to adopt. It was the common opinion that it would be prudent to relinquish all pretensions to Emesa, because the Emesenes were ill-disposed towards her and friendly to the Romans. They advised her to remain within Palmyra, and when they were safe in that strong city, they would deliberate at leisure on their important affairs. This was no sooner proposed than done, as there was no disagreement. 2. Aurelian, upon hearing of the flight of Zenobia, entered Emesa, where he was enthusiastically welcomed by the citizens, and found the treasure which Zenobia could not carry along with her.

(Anon., revised Lieu)

Jordanes, *Historia Romana* 291, p. 37, 30–2: After his (i.e. Odaenathus') murder, Zenobia had control of the East: Aurelian undertook an expedition against her and defeated her at Immae in the vicinity of Antioch . . .

(Dodgeon)

Syncellus, p. 470, 3–5 (p. 721, 9–12, CSHB): Aurelian, unable to bear what he had heard (about the Palmyrene occupation of Egypt), departed with an army and near Antioch in Syria, at a place called Immae, he destroyed the Palmyrene forces, . . .

(Dodgeon)

4.8.3. Aurelian marched on Palmyra, attempts at negotiation (Spring, 272)

SHA Aurel. 26, 1–27, 6: After this, he directed his march toward Palmyra, in order that, by storming it, he might put an end to his labours. But frequently on the march his army met with a hostile reception from the brigands of Syria, and after suffering many mishaps he incurred great danger during the siege, being even wounded by an arrow.

2. A letter of his is still in existence, addressed to Mucapor, in which, without the wonted reserve of an emperor, he confesses the difficulty of this war: 3. 'The Romans are saying that I am merely waging a war with a woman, just as if Zenobia alone and with her own forces only were fighting against me, and yet, as a matter of fact, there is as great a force of the enemy as if I had to make war against a man, while she, because of her fear and her sense of guilt, is a much baser foe. 4. It cannot be told what a store of arrows is here, what great preparations for war, what a store of spears and of stones; there is no section of the wall that is not held by two or three engines of war, and their machines can even hurl fire. Why say more? 5. She fears like a woman, and fights as one who fears punishment. I believe, however, that the gods will truly bring aid to the Roman commonwealth, for they have never failed our endeavours.'

6. Finally, exhausted and worn out by reason of ill-success, he dispatched a letter to Zenobia, asking her to surrender and promising to spare her life; of this letter I have inserted a copy:

7. 'From Aurelian, Emperor of the Roman world and recoverer of the East, to Zenobia and all others who are bound to her by alliance in war. 8. You should have done of your own free will what I now command in my letter. For I bid you surrender, promising that your lives shall be spared, and with the condition that you, Zenobia, together with your children, shall dwell wherever I, acting in accordance with the wish of the most noble senate, shall appoint a place. 9. Your jewels, your gold, your silver, your silks, your horses, your camels, you shall all hand over to the Roman treasury. As for the people of Palmyra, their rights shall be preserved.'

27   On receiving this letter, Zenobia responded with more pride and insolence than befitted her fortunes, I suppose with a view to inspiring fear; for a copy of her letter, too, I have inserted:

2. 'From Zenobia, Queen of the East, to Aurelian Augustus. None save yourself has ever demanded by letter what you now demand. Whatever must be accomplished in matters of war must be done by

valour alone. 3. You demand my surrender as though you were not aware that Cleopatra preferred to die a Queen rather than remain alive, however high her rank. 4. We shall not lack reinforcements from Persia, which we are even now expecting. On our side are the Saracens,[31] on our side, too, the Armenians. 5. The brigands of Syria have defeated your army, Aurelian. What more need be said? If those forces, then, which we are expecting from every side, shall arrive, you will, of a surety, lay aside that arrogance with which you now command my surrender, as though victorious on every side.'[32] 6. This letter, Nicomachus says (*FGrH* 215F), was dictated by Zenobia herself and translated by him into Greek from the Syrian tongue. For that earlier letter of Aurelian's was written in Greek.

(Magie, iii, pp. 245–9)

Anonymous Continuator of Dio Cassius 10, 5, ed. Boissevain, iii, pp. 746–7 (= *FHG* IV, p. 197): Aurelian sent envoys to Zenobia, urging her finally to surrender to him. She replied, saying: 'I have hardly sustained any serious losses. For of those who had fallen, the majority were Romans.'

(Lieu)

4.8.4. The siege of Palmyra, the escape and capture of Zenobia

SHA Aurel. 28, 1–5: On receiving this letter, Aurelian felt no shame, but rather was angered, and at once he gathered together from every side his soldiers and leaders and laid siege to Palmyra; and that brave man gave his attention to everything that seemed incomplete or neglected. 2. For he cut off the reinforcements which the Persians had sent, and he tampered with the squadrons of Saracens and Armenians, bringing them over to his own side, some by forcible means and some by cunning. 3. Finally, by a mighty effort he conquered that most powerful woman. Zenobia, then, conquered, fled away on camels (which they call dromedaries), but while seeking to reach the Persians she was captured by the horsemen sent after her, and thus she was brought into the power of Aurelian.

4. And so Aurelian, victorious and in possession of the entire East, more proud and insolent now that he held Zenobia in chains, dealt with the Persians, Armenians, and Saracens as the needs of the occasion demanded. 5. Then were brought in those garments, encrusted with jewels, which we now see in the Temple of the Sun, then, too, the Persian dragon-flags and head-dresses, and a species of

purple such as no nation ever afterward offered or the Roman world beheld.

29   Concerning this, I desire to say at least a few words. For you remember that there was in the Temple of Jupiter Best and Greatest on the Capitolium a short woollen cloak of a purple hue, by the side of which all other purple garments, brought by the matrons and by Aurelian himself, seemed to fade to the colour of ashes in comparison with its divine brilliance. 2. This cloak, brought from the farthest Indies, the King of the Persians is said to have presented as a gift to Aurelian, writing as follows: 'Accept a purple robe, such as we ourselves use.' 3. But this was untrue. For later both Aurelian and Probus and, most recently, Diocletian made most diligent search for this species of purple, sending out their most diligent agents, but even so it could not be found. But indeed it is said that the Indian sandyx yields this kind of purple if properly prepared.

(Magie, iii, pp. 249–53)

Orosius, *adversus paganos* VII, 23, 4: Then turning to the East, he (i.e. Aurelian) reduced Zenobia, who, when her husband, Odaenathus, was slain, was taking the recovered province of Syria to herself, under his power by fear of battle rather than by battle.

(Deferrari, p. 319)

Zosimus I, 54, (2)–56, 2: He (i.e. Aurelian) then immediately set off with his army to Palmyra, which on arrival he invested on every side, while every kind of provision was levied for his troops from the neighbouring countryside. Meanwhile, the Palmyrenes derided the Romans, as if they thought it impossible for them to take the city; and one man in particular made obscene remarks about the emperor's own person. At this, a Persian who stood by the emperor said, 'If you will allow me, sir, you shall see that insolent fellow dead.' 3. The emperor consented to this, and the Persian, concealing himself behind some other men, shot at the man while he was looking over the battlements, and hit him whilst still uttering his insulting language, so that he fell down from the wall before the emperor and the army.

55   The besieged, however, held out in the hope that the enemy would withdraw for want of provisions. When they saw the Romans persisting in their resolution, and that they were themselves without essentials, they made the decision to flee to the Euphrates and from there request aid of the Persians and to cause new difficulties for the Romans. 2. Having made the plan, they set Zenobia on a female camel, . . . which is the swiftest of that kind of animal, and much more swift than horses, and conveyed her out of the city. 3. Aurelian was annoyed by the escape of Zenobia; but naturally did not give way to the audacious deed and immediately sent out horsemen in pursuit. They succeeded in capturing her, as she was about to cross the Euphrates and took her off the boat to Aurelian. Though much pleased at this unexpected sight, yet being ambitious for honour, he became uneasy at the thought that the conquest of a woman would not stand to his credit among future generations. 56 Meanwhile, opinions came to be divided among Palmyrenes, who were shut up in the city, some resolved to risk themselves in defence of their city and to take on the full strength of the Roman army. While others, on the contrary, employed humble and submissive gestures from the walls, and begged pardon for what they had done. The emperor accepted their supplication, and beseeched them to take courage. They poured out of the city, bearing gifts and sacrifices. 2. Aurelian paid due respect to the victims, received the gifts, and sent the bearers away unpunished.

(Anon., revised by Lieu)

Zonaras XII, 27, p. 607, 1–6 (iii, pp. 152, 19–25, Dindorf): But we have not yet completed the story of his (i.e. Aurelian's) end, but must narrate what he accomplished in his period of supreme command. Being an excellent general, he defeated many enemies. For he overwhelmed the Palmyrenes; their queen Zenobia had gained control of Egypt and captured Probus, the military commander there at that time. He himself campaigned against her, wearing her down in war and bringing her under his authority.

(Dodgeon)

4.8.5. Dialogue between Aurelian and Zenobia after her capture

SHA trig. tyr. 30, 23: When Aurelian had taken her prisoner, he caused her to be led into his presence and then addressed her thus: 'Why is it, Zenobia, that you dared to show insolence to the emperors of Rome?' To this she replied, it is said: 'You, I know, are an emperor indeed, for you win victories, but Gallienus and Aureolus and the others I never regarded as emperors. Believing Victoria to be a woman like me, I desired to become a partner in the royal power, should the supply of lands permit.'

(Magie, iii, p. 141)

4.9.1. Execution of the supporters of Zenobia

SHA Aurel. 30, 1–3: But to return to my undertaking: despite all this, there arose a terrible uproar among all the soldiers, who demanded Zenobia for punishment. 2. Aurelian, however, deeming it improper that a woman should be put to death, killed many who had advised her to begin and prepare and wage the war, but the woman he saved for his triumph, wishing to show her to the eyes of the Roman people. 3. It was regarded as a cruel thing that Longinus the philosopher should have been among those who were killed. He, it is said, was employed by Zenobia as her teacher in Greek letters, and Aurelian is said to have slain him because he was told that the over-proud letter of hers had been dictated in accord with his counsel, although, in fact, it was composed in the Syrian tongue.

(Magie, iii, p. 253)

Zosimus I, 56, (2)–3: Having made himself master of this city (i.e. Palmyra), with all the wealth it contained, as well as other provisions and offerings, he returned to Emesa, where he brought Zenobia and her accomplices to trial. Zenobia claimed to be innocent and openly implicated many persons, who had led her astray as she was a simple woman. Among them was Longinus, whose writings are highly beneficial to all those interested in learning. 3. Upon finding him guilty of the crimes of which he was accused, the emperor immediately sentenced him to death. He bore the sentence with such fortitude that he was a comfort to those who were indignant at his suffering. Others besides Longinus suffered punishment on being denounced by Zenobia.

(Anon., revised Lieu)

John of Antioch, *frag.* 155, *FHG* IV, p. 599: The Emperor Aurelian was extremely proficient in matters of war, but undisciplined in mind and was much inclined towards cruelty. He inflicted the death penalty on many distinguished men in each city who were accused by Zenobia. He was a brutal sort of person and bloodthirsty – more of a general necessary for the time than an amiable emperor. Always ill-tempered and inaccessible, he did not remain free from the blood of his own household for he put to death the innocent wife of his son. However he was to a large extent a genuine restorer of military discipline and a rejuvenator of faded custom and reformer of dissolute morals.

(Lieu)

4.9.2. The defeat and capture of Zenobia as told by Malalas

Malalas, XII, p. 300, 3–23: Immediately after he had received a dispatch, the same Aurelian mounted an expedition against Zenobia, the queen of the Saracens, and departed for the East. For concerning her he was informed (by the dispatch) that she had plundered and burnt the regions of the Orient as far as the borders of Antioch the Great and that she had encamped near the river Orontes. No sooner had the same emperor Aurelian arrived in Antioch than he immediately set out, just as he was, and went against her. When the battle was joined, he annihilated her forces. He seized Zenobia herself and sat her on a dromedary, and he put her on parade and led her through all the lands of the Orient and into Antioch the Great. After he had watched the chariot-races there, he brought her into the ring on a dromedary. He also set up a stage in Antioch itself, and chained her up and placed her on top of it for three days. He called the stage he set up a 'Triumph'. Taking her away from there, he led her to Rome as 'Queen of the barbarian Saracens'. After he had paraded her in Rome in triumph in the accustomed fashion, he beheaded her. The same emperor Aurelian also made Arabia subject to the Romans by killing all the Saracens, relatives of Enathus, who were holding it.

(Dodgeon)

4.9.3. The victory salutations of Aurelian

SHA Aurel. 30, 4–5: And so, having subdued the East, Aurelian returned as a victor to Europe, and there he defeated the forces of the Carpi; and when the senate gave him in his absence the surname Carpicus, he sent them this message, it is said, as a jest: 'It now only remains for you, Conscript Fathers, to call me Carpisculus also' – 5. for it is well known that carpisculum is a kind of boot. This surname appeared to him as ignoble, since he was already called both Gothicus and Sarmaticus and Armeniacus and Parthicus and Adiabenicus.[33]

(Magie, iii, pp. 253–5)

4.9.4. The revolt of Palmyra under Septimius Apsaeus and its final destruction by Aurelian (*c.* 272)

SHA Aurel. 31, 1–10: It is a rare thing, or rather, a difficult thing, for the Syrians to keep faith. For the Palmyrenes, who had once been defeated and crushed, now that Aurelian was busied with matters in Europe, began a rebellion of no small size. 2. For they killed Sandario, whom Aurelian had put in command of the garrison there, and with him six hundred bowmen, thus getting the rule for a certain Achilleus, a kinsman of Zenobia's. 3. But Aurelian, indeed, prepared as he always was, came back from Rhodope and, because it deserved it, destroyed the city. 4. In fact, Aurelian's cruelty, or, as some say, his sternness, is so widely known that they even quote a letter of his, revealing a confession of most savage fury; of this the following is a copy:

5. 'From Aurelian Augustus to Cerronius Bassus. The swords of the soldiers should not proceed further. Already enough Palmyrenes have been killed and slaughtered. We have not spared the women, we have slain the children, we have butchered the old men, we have destroyed the peasants. 6. To whom, at this rate, shall we leave the land or the city? Those who still remain must be spared. For it is our belief that the few have been chastened by the punishment of the many. 7. Now as to the Temple of the Sun at Palmyra, which has been pillaged by the eagle-bearers of the Third Legion,[34] along with the standard-bearers, the dragon-bearer, and the buglers and trumpeters, I wish it restored to the condition in which it formerly was. 8. You have three hundred pounds of gold from Zenobia's coffers, you have eighteen hundred pounds of silver from the property of the Palmyrenes, and you have the royal jewels. 9. Use all these to embellish the temple; thus both to me and to the immortal gods you will do a most pleasing service. I will write to the senate and request it to send one of the pontiffs to dedicate the temple.' 10. This letter, as we can see, shows that the savagery of the hard-hearted prince had been glutted.

(Magie, iii, pp. 255-7)

Zosimus I, 59, 1–61, 1: ... Aurelian marched towards Europe, taking with him Zenobia, her son, and those who were accomplices in the rebellion. Zenobia is said to have died, either of disease, or of her refusal of food, and all the rest, except for the son of Zenobia, were drowned in the strait between Chalcedon and Byzantium.

60   As Aurelian continued his journey into Europe, he received the news that some of those he had left at Palmyra, having won over Apsaeus, who was responsible for the earlier events, were tempting Marcellinus, whom the emperor had appointed prefect of Mesopotamia and Rector of the East, to assume the purple. 2. Under pretence of taking time to decide on the right course of action, he delayed them so long, that they had to pester him repeatedly. He therefore framed ambiguous answers to their demands, while he notified Aurelian of their design. In the meantime, the Palmyrenes, having clothed Antiochus in purple, shut themselves in at Palmyra. **61** On hearing this news, Aurelian immediately set off for the east with only the troops at his disposal. On reaching Antioch, he surprised the people, who were then attending a horse-race, by his sudden appearance and carried on to Palmyra, which he took and razed without a contest, but, not thinking Antiochus worthy of being punished on account of his obscure origins, he dismissed him.

(Anon., revised Lieu)

4.9.5. Dedication to Septimius Apsaeus (date uncertain)

Inv. III, 18 (= *IGR* III, 1049, Greek): The City (i.e. Palmyra) to Septimius Apsaios, citizen and protector.

4.10.1. Support given to Aurelian by the priests of Bel (273–4)

Gawlikowski, *Syria* 47 (1971), p. 420 (*Inv.* IX, 40, commemorative inscription in Palmyrene found *in situ* outside the main entrance of the Temple of Bel): During the presidency of the cofraternity of the priesthood (mrzhwt = Gk: θίασος) of Se[p]tim[ius] Haddudan, illustrious [senator,] son of Septimius 'Ogeilu Maqqai, who had aided [the army of Au]relian Caesar (['w]rlynws qsr), [our master], and who had custody together with the progeniture of the [cofraternity and who had been] with those in [the temple in the month] of Ab of the year 5[83 (= AD 273) in the month] of Adar of [the year 584 (= AD 274), are commemorated and blessed]: W[ahbai] son of [Sa.'a] son of Ate'aqab [in charge of . . .; and So-and-so son of So-and-So] in charge of [. . .; and So-and-So, son of Ate']aqab Yar[hai] in charge of the chamber; and 'Og[eilu son of So-and-So, in charge of the porticos; and So-and-so son of 'Ogeilu, in charge of the pages . . .; and] Yarhib[ola son of 'O]gei[lu], in [charge of the ho]use [of guardians. Well] remembered.[35]

(Brock)

4.10.2. Firmus, friend and ally of Zenobia, seized Egypt after her defeat (*c.* 272)

SHA Aurel. 32, 1–3: At length, now more secure, he returned again to Europe, and there, with his well-known valour, he crushed all the enemies who were roving about. 2. Meanwhile, when Aurelian was performing great deeds in the provinces of Thrace as well as in all Europe, there rose up a certain Firmus, who laid claim to Egypt, but without the imperial insignia and as though he purposed to make it into a free state. 3. Without delay Aurelian turned back against him, and there also his wonted good-fortune did not abandon him. For he recovered Egypt at once and took vengeance on the enterprise – violent in temper, as he always was; ...

(Magie, iii, p. 257)

SHA Firmus 3, 1–6 and 5, 1–6: Now Firmus was a native of Seleucia, though many of the Greeks write otherwise, not knowing that at that same time there were three men called Firmus, one of them prefect of Egypt, another commander of the African frontier and also proconsul, and the third this friend and ally of Zenobia's, who, incited by the madness of the Egyptians, seized Alexandria and was crushed by Aurelian with the good fortune that was wont to attend his valour.

2. Concerning the wealth of this last-named Firmus, much is related. For example, it is said that he fitted his house with square panes of glass set in with pitch and other such substances and that he owned so many books that he often used to say in public that he could support an army on the paper and glue. 3. He kept up, moreover, the closest relations with the Blemmyae and Saracens, and he often sent merchant-vessels to the Indians also. 4. He even owned, it is said, two elephant-tusks, ten feet in length, to which Aurelian planned to add two more and make of them a throne on which he would place a statue of Jupiter, made of gold and decked with jewels and clad in a sort of bordered toga, to be set up in the Temple of the Sun; and after asking advice of the oracle in the Apennines, he purposed to call him Jupiter the Consul or the Consulting. 5. These tusks, however, were later presented by Carinus to a certain woman, who is said to have made them into a couch; her name, both because it is known now and because future generations will have no profit from knowing it, I will leave unmentioned. 6. So under a most evil prince the gift of the Indians, consecrated to Jupiter Best and Greatest, seems to have become both the instrument and the reward of lust ...

5   He, then, seized the imperial power in opposition to Aurelian with the purpose of defending the remainder of Zenobia's party. Aurelian, however, returning from Thrace, defeated him. 2. Many relate that he put an end to his life by strangling, but Aurelian himself in his proclamations says otherwise; for when he had

conquered him he gave orders to issue the following proclamation in Rome: 3. 'From Aurelian Augustus to his most devoted Roman people, greeting. We have established peace everywhere throughout the whole world in its widest extent, and also Firmus, that brigand in Egypt, who rose in revolt with barbarians and gathered together the remaining adherents of a shameless woman – not to speak at too great length – we have routed and seized and tortured and slain. 4. There is nothing now, fellow-citizens, sons of Romulus, which you need fear. The grain-supply from Egypt, which has been interrupted by that evil brigand, will now arrive undiminished. 5. Do you only maintain harmony with the senate, friendship with the equestrian order, and good will toward the praetorian guard. I will see to it that there is no anxiety in Rome. 6. Do you devote your leisure to games and to races in the circus. Let me be concerned with the needs of the state, and do not busy yourselves with your pleasures. Wherefore, most revered fellow-citizens,' and so forth.

(Magie, iii, pp. 391–5)

Zosimus I, 61, 1: After this action (i.e. the final subjection of Palmyra), he quickly won over the Alexandrians who were on the point of revolt, being already divided among themselves.

(Anon., revised Lieu)

4.10.3. Zenobia was paraded in Aurelian's triumph in Rome (274)

Festus, *brev.* 24, p. 65, 5–6: . . . and (Aurelian) led her (i.e. Zenobia) in triumph before his chariot in Rome.

(Lieu)

Eutropius IX, 13, 2: . . . and entering Rome, (Aurelian) celebrated a magnificent triumph as restorer of the East and West, Tetricus (a usurper) and Zenobia going before his chariot.

(Watson, altered)

Jerome, *chron.*, s. a. 274, pp. 222, 25–6: Tetricus and Zenobia were paraded before a triumphant Aurelian in Rome.

(Lieu)

SHA trig. tyr. 30, 24–6: And so she was led in triumph with such magnificence that the Roman people had never seen a more splendid parade. For, in the first place, she was adorned with gems so huge that she laboured under the weight of her adornments; 25. For it is said that this woman, courageous though she was, halted very frequently, saying that she could not endure the load of her gems. 26. Furthermore, her feet were bound with shackles of gold and her hands with golden fetters, and even on her neck she wore a chain of gold, the weight of which was borne by a Persian buffoon.

(Magie, iii, p. 141)

SHA Aurel. 33, 1–34, 6: It is not without advantage to know what manner of triumph Aurelian had, for it was a most brilliant spectacle. 2. There were three royal chariots, of which the first, carefully wrought and adorned with silver and gold and jewels, had belonged to Odaenathus, the second, also wrought with similar care, had been given to Aurelian by the king of the Persians, and the third Zenobia had made for herself, hoping in it to visit the city of Rome. And this hope was not unfulfilled; for she did, indeed, enter the city in it, but vanquished and led in triumph. 3. There was also another chariot, drawn by four stags and said to have once belonged to the king of the Goths. In this – so many have handed down to memory – Aurelian rode up to the Capitol, purposing there to slay the stags, which he had captured along with this chariot and then vowed, it was said, to Jupiter Best and Greatest. 4. There advanced, moreover, twenty elephants, and two hundred tamed beasts of diverse kinds from Libya and Palestine, which Aurelian at once presented to private citizens, that the privy-purse might not be burdened with the cost of their food; furthermore, there were led along in order four tigers and also giraffes and elks and other such animals, also eight hundred pairs of gladiators, besides the captives from the barbarian tribes. There were Blemmyes, Axomitae, Arabs from Arabia Felix, Indians, Bactrians, Iberians, Saracens and Persians, all bearing their gifts; there were Goths, Alans, Roxolani, Sarmatians, Franks, Suebians, Vandals and Germans – all captive, with their hands bound fast.

5   There also advanced among them certain men of Palmyra, who had survived its fall, the foremost of the State and Egyptians, too, because of their rebellion. 34 There were led along also ten women, who, fighting in male attire, had been captured among the Goths after many others had fallen; these a placard declared to be of the race of the Amazons – for placards were borne before all, displaying the names of their nations. 2. In the procession was Tetricus also, arrayed in scarlet cloak, a yellow tunic, and Gallic trousers, and with him his son, whom he had proclaimed in Gaul as emperor. 3. And there came Zenobia, too, decked with jewels and in golden chains, the weight of which was borne by others. There were carried aloft golden crowns presented by all the cities, made known by placards carried aloft.

4. Then came the Roman people itself, the flags of the guilds and the camps, the mailed cuirassiers, the wealth of the kings, the entire army, and, lastly, the senate (albeit somewhat sadly, since they saw senators, too, being led in triumph) – all adding much to the splendour of the procession. 5. Scarce did they reach the Capitol by the ninth hour of the day, and when they arrived at the Palace it was late indeed. 6. On the following days amusements were given to the populace, plays in the theatres, races in the Circus, wild-beast hunts, gladiatorial fights and also a naval battle.

(Magie, iii, pp. 259–63)

Zosimus I, 61, (1)–2: He then entered Rome in triumph, where he was most enthusiastically received by the senate and people. 2. At this period also he erected that magnificent temple of the Sun, which he ornamented with all the votive offerings that he brought from Palmyra; placing in it the statues of the Sun and Bel.

(Anon., revised Lieu)

Jordanes, *Historia Romana* 291, p. 37, 32: . . . he (i.e. Aurelian) led her alive in triumph in Rome.

4.10.4. Aurelian's high regard for Zenobia

SHA trig. tyr. 30, 4–12: There is still in existence a letter of Aurelian's which bears testimony concerning this woman, then in captivity. For when some found fault with him, because he, the bravest of men, had led a woman in triumph, as though she were a general, he sent a letter to the senate and the Roman people, defending himself by the following justification: 5. 'I have heard, Conscript Fathers, that men are reproaching me for having performed an unmanly deed in leading Zenobia in triumph. But in truth those very persons who find fault with me now would accord me praise in abundance, did they but know what manner of woman she is, how wise in counsels, how steadfast in plans, how firm towards the soldiers, and how generous when necessity calls, and how stern when discipline demands. 6. I might even say that it was her doing that Odaenathus defeated the Persians and, after putting Sapor to flight, advanced all the way to Ctesiphon. 7. I might add thereto that such was the fear that this woman inspired in the peoples of the East and also the Egyptians that neither Arabs nor Saracens nor Armenians ever moved against her. 8. Nor would I have spared her life, had I not known that she did a great service to the Roman state when she preserved the imperial power in the East for herself, or for her children. 9. Therefore let those whom nothing pleases keep the venom of their own tongues to themselves. 10. For if it is not meet to vanquish a woman and lead her in triumph, what are they saying of Gallienus, in contempt of whom she ruled the empire well? 11. What of the Deified Claudius, that revered and honoured leader? For he, because he was busied with his campaigns against the Goths, suffered her, or so it is said, to hold the imperial power, doing it of purpose and wisely, in order that he himself, while she kept guard over the eastern frontier of the empire, might the more safely complete what he had taken in hand.' This speech shows what opinion Aurelian held concerning Zenobia.

(Magie, iii, pp. 135–7)

4.10.5. Aurelian's declaration of war on the Persians and his murder (275)

SHA Aurel. 35, 4–5: After doing these things, he set out for the regions of Gaul and delivered the Vindelici from a barbarian inroad; then he returned to Illyricum and having made ready an army, which was large, though not of inordinate size, he declared war on the Persians, whom he had already defeated with the greatest glory at the time that he conquered Zenobia. 5. While on his way thither, however, he was murdered at Caenophrurium, a station between Heraclea and Byzantium, through the hatred of his clerk but by the hand of Mucapor.

(Magie, iii, p. 265)

4.11.1. Zenobia's subsequent life in Rome and her descendants

Eutropius, IX, 13, 2: Zenobia left descendants, who still live at Rome.

Jerome, *chron.*, s. a. 274, p. 223, 1–3: Zenobia spent the rest of her days in the city (of Rome) and was accorded the highest respect. It is after her that the family of Zenobia in Rome is named.

(Dodgeon)

SHA trig. tyr. 30, 27: Her life was granted her by Aurelian, and they say that thereafter she lived with her children in the manner of a Roman matron on an estate that had been presented to her at Tibur, which even to this day is still called Zenobia, not far from the palace of Hadrian or from that place which bears the name of Concha.[36]

(Magie, iii, pp. 141-3)

Syncellus, p. 470, 5-7 (p. 721, 12-14, CSHB): ... having taken Zenobia prisoner, he (i.e. Aurelian) led her to Rome and treated her with great magnanimity. He joined her in marriage to a distinguished senator.

(Dodgeon)

Zonaras XII, 27, p. 607, 6-11 (iii, pp. 152, 25-153, 4, Dindorf): Some sources say that she (i.e. Zenobia) was led away to Rome and married off to a husband from the more distinguished classes, but others say that she died on the journey from excessive grief about the change in her fortunes; that Aurelian took one of her daughters to wife, and that he married off the rest to notable Romans.

(Dodgeon)

4.11.2. Peace between Rome and Persia after the death of Aurelian

SHA Tac. 3, 5: (Speech of the consul Velius Cornificius Gordianus, 25 Sept., 275): And even if we hear nothing now of any movement among the Persians, reflect that the Syrians are so light-minded that, rather than submit to our righteous rule, they desire even a woman to reign over them.

(Magie, iii, p. 301)

4.11.3. Attempt by Florianus (Augustus, April–June 276) to attack Persia was foiled by his assassination

Malalas, XII, pp. 301, 21-302, 2: He (i.e. Florianus) campaigned against the Persians, and when he was passing through Tarsus, he was assassinated by his own men; he was sixty-five years of age.

(Dodgeon)

4.11.4. The exploits of Odaenathus recalled by Libanius (*c.* 391)

Libanius, *epistulae* 1006 (To Anatolius):[37] Demosthenes was unable to avert the fate of the Olynthians by his many speeches. Nevertheless he is held in high esteem, almost as if he had saved them through setting his mind to save them, and among the paeans raised to him by the sophists, one would see Olynthus (commemorated). Your similarity to him will be obvious to men who recognize zeal rather than achievement and what you wish to achieve rather than what you could achieve. 2. However, in being outspoken on behalf of Eusebius,[38] you seem to me that you would achieve your end. Use every means and do everything in order that he who is innocent should not have to endure in patience. He is upright and temperate and well brought up, being also the son of Odaenathus and a descendant of that Odaenathus, the mention of whose name alone caused the hearts of the Persians to falter. Everywhere victorious, he liberated the cities and the territories belonging to each of them and made the enemies place their salvation in their prayers rather than in the force of arms. 3. This Odaenathus, the father of Eusebius, is among them who, leading a force against them (i.e. the Persians?) and turning them to flight and pursuing them, was heard often in that battle array: 'Comrade, shoot in this wise!' (Hom., *Il.* VIII.282) from the man who Homer said would have sprung out of Zeus himself. The latter could not have performed all this if his parentage was entirely normal.

(Lieu)

4.11.5. Request by Libanius for a copy of the oration on Odaenathus by Longinus (c. 393)

Libanius, *ep.* 1078 (To Eusebius): I am asking for the speech 'Odaenathus', the speech by Longinus. You must give it in fulfilment of your promise.

(Lieu)

5 From Probus to Diocletian

5.1.1. The accession of Bahram II (276-293)

Agathias IV, 24, 6: Varanes' (i.e. Bahram I's) son[1] had the same
name as his father and reigned for seventeen years.

(Cameron, p. 123)

5.1.2. Peace between Probus and the Persians

SHA Prob. 17, 1-6: Having finally established peace in all parts of
Pamphylia and the other provinces adjacent to Isauria, he turned
his course to the East. 2. He also subdued the Blemmyae,[2] and the
captives taken from them he sent back to Rome and thereby created
a wondrous impression upon the amazed Roman people. 3. Besides
this, he rescued from servitude to the barbarians the cities of
Coptos and Ptolemais and restored them to Roman laws. 4. By this
he achieved such fame that the Parthians (*sic*) sent envoys to him,
confessing their fear and arrogance and then went back to their
homes in greater fear than before. 5. The letter, moreover, which he
wrote to Narseus (*sic*),[3] rejecting the gifts which the king had sent,
is said to have been as follows: 'I marvel that you have sent us so
few of the riches, all of which will shortly be ours. For the time
being, keep all those things in which you take such pleasure. If ever
we wish to have them, we know how we ought to get them.' 6. On
the receipt of this letter Narseus was greatly frightened, the more so
because he had learned that Coptos and Ptolemais had been set free
from the Blemmyae, who had previously held them, and that they,
who had once been the terror of nations, had been put to the sword.

(Magie, iii, p. 371)

Moses Khorenats'i, *Hist. Arm.* (II), 77 (Thomson, p. 224): see
Appendix 2, p. 317

5.1.3. Probus' plan to invade Persia and his death (282)

SHA Prob. 20, 1: These spectacles finished, he made ready for war with Persia,[4] but while on the march through Illyricum he was treacherously murdered by his soldiers.

(Magie, iii, p. 377)

5.1.4. Dedication to Probus by Syrian villagers (?282)

IGR III, 1186 (= *PAES* no. 765.12, Greek dedication on a block built into the front wall in a building called Kalybe from the inscription on the northern edge of the village of Um Iz-zetun): Good fortune! For the preservation and victory of our lord Marcus Aurelius Probus Augustus, in (the) seventh year was built the sacred kalybe by the community of the village, successfully.

(Littman-Magie-Stuart, no. 765)

5.1.5. Internal unrest in Persia (*c.* 283)

Pan. Lat. III/11, 17, 2, ed. Galletier, p. 65: Ormias (i.e. Hormizd),[5] with the support of the Sakas and the Rufii[6] and the Geli,[7] attacked the Persians themselves and their king whom he did not respect as sovereign for the sake of majesty nor as a brother for the sake of piety.

(Dodgeon)

5.1.6. The Persian Expedition of Carus, his initial success and his death (283)

Julian, *or.* I, 17D–18A (13.16–18, Bidez): Nor need I (i.e. Julian) recall the second chapter of our misfortunes and the exploits of Carus that followed, when after those failures he was appointed general?

(Wright, i, p. 45)

Chronicon anni 354, p. 148, 17, MGH: Carus: emperor for ten months and five days. He died in Seleucia in Babylonia.

Aurelius Victor, *liber de Caesaribus.* 38, 2–4: Because all the barbarians, informed of Probus' death, had, at this opportune moment, invaded the empire, Carus (having first sent his eldest son to protect Gaul) immediately left for Mesopotamia, accompanied by Numerianus, for that country is exposed, as it were, to perennial invasions by the Persians. 3. There he routed the enemy but while passing immodestly and vaingloriously beyond Ctesiphon, the famous city of Parthia, he was consumed by a thunderbolt. Indeed they report that it deservedly happened to him: for when the oracles had informed him that he could advance in victory as far as the above mentioned city, he had proceeded further and paid the penalty. 5. Accordingly it is difficult to change destiny, and for that reason a knowledge of the future is redundant.

(Dodgeon)

Festus, *brev.* 24, p. 65, 6–11: The victory over the Persians of the emperor Carus seemed to be too mighty in the eyes of divine power. For it undoubtedly incurred divine displeasure and indignation. For when he entered Persia, he devastated it as if no one was defending it, and captured Coche[8] and Ctesiphon, the most distinguished cities of Persia. When in victory he had his camp above the Tigris, he died after being struck by a bolt of lightning.

(Dodgeon)

Eutropius, IX, 18, 1: While he (i.e. Carus) was engaged in a war with the Sarmatians, news was brought of an insurrection among the Persians. He set out for the East, and achieved some noble exploits against that race of people; he routed them in the field, and took Seleucia and Ctesiphon, their noblest cities, but, while he was encamped on the Tigris, he was killed by lightning.

(Watson, p. 522, altered)

Jerome, *Chronicon s.a.* 284,[9] pp. 224, 23–225, 1: Carus of Narbo, after laying waste to the entire territory of the Parthians (*sic*), captured Coche and Ctesiphon, the most famous cities of the enemy. After establishing camp on the Tigris, he was killed by a bolt of lightning.

(Dodgeon)

Ammianus Marcellinus XXIV, 5, 3: (AD 363) This district is rich and well cultivated: not far off is Coche, which is called Seleucia; . . . The emperor (i.e. Julian) himself in the meanwhile proceeded with his advanced guard and reconnoitred a deserted city which had been formerly destroyed by the Emperor Carus, where an ever-flowing spring forms a great pool which joins onto the Tigris.

(Yonge, pp. 364–5, revised.)

SHA Carus 7, 1 and 8, 1–9, 1: And so – not to include what is of little importance or what can be found in other writers – as soon as he (i.e. Carus) received the imperial power by the unanimous wish of all the soldiers, he took up the war against the Persians for which Probus had been preparing. . . .

8 With a vast array and all the forces of Probus, he set out against the Persians after finishing the greater part of the Sarmatian war, in which he had been engaged, and without opposition he conquered Mesopotamia and advanced as far as Ctesiphon; and while the Persians were busied with internal strife he won the name of Conqueror of Persia.[10] 2. But when he advanced still further, desirous himself of glory and urged on most of all by his prefect, who in his wish to rule was seeking the destruction of both Carus and his sons as well, he met his death, according to some, by disease, according to others, through a stroke of lightning. 3. Indeed, it cannot be denied that at the time of his death there suddenly occurred such violent thunder that many, it is said, died of sheer fright. And so, while he was ill and lying in his tent, there came up a mighty storm with terrible lightning, and, as I have said, still more terrible thunder, and during this he expired. 4. Julius Calpurnius, who used to dictate for the imperial memoranda, wrote the following letter about Carus' death to the prefect of the city, saying among other things:

5. 'When Carus, our prince for whom we truly care, was lying ill, there suddenly arose a storm of such violence that all things grew black and none could recognize another; then continuous flashes of lightning and peals of thunder, like bolts from a fiery sky, took from us all the power of knowing what truly befell. 6. For suddenly, after an especially violent peal which had terrified all, it was shouted out that the emperor was dead. 7. It came to pass, in addition, that the chamberlains, grieving for the death of their prince, fired his tent; and the rumour arose, whatever its source, that he had been killed by the lightning, whereas, as far as we can tell, it seems sure that he died of his illness.'

9 This letter I have inserted for the reason that many declare that there is a certain decree of fate that no Roman emperor may advance beyond Ctesiphon, and that Carus was struck by lightning because he desired to pass beyond the bounds which Fate has set up. 2. But let cowardice, on which courage should set its heel, keep its devices for itself.

(Magie, iii, pp. 429–31)

Epitome de Caesaribus 38, 1: Carus, born in Narbo, ruled for two years. He immediately made Carinus and Numerianus Caesars. He was killed near Ctesiphon by a bolt of lightning.

(Dodgeon)

Orosius, *adversus paganos* VII, 24, 4: When he (i.e. Carus) had made his sons, Carinus and Numerianus, colleagues in his rule and after he had captured two very famous cities, Coche and Ctesiphon, in a war against the Parthians (*sic*), in a camp upon the Tigris he was struck by lightning and killed.

(Deferrari, p. 320)

Sidonius Apollinaris, *Carmina* XXIII, 91–6, ed. Loyen, i, p. 147[11]: Who indeed could forget the Persian campaign and the victorious army of the Emperor Carus and Niphates[12] traversed by Roman legions, when the emperor was struck down by lightning, ending a life which was like lightning itself?

(Lieu)

Jordanes, *Historia Romana* 294, p. 38, 6–9: Carus, who reigned with his sons Carinus[13] and Numerianus, was a native of Gallia Narbonensis. In an admirable fashion he occupied Coche and Ctesiphon, the most noble cities of the Persians, after nearly the whole of Persia had been devastated. ... This same Carus, while laying out camp on (the banks of the) Tigris river, was struck down by a bolt of lightning.

(Dodgeon)

Malalas, XII, pp. 302, 20–303, 4: He (i.e. Carus) campaigned against the Persians, and in his invasion he occupied the districts of Persia as far as the city of Ctesiphon, and made his retreat. On the frontier (*limes*) he built a fortress, which he made into a city and granted it the rights of citizenship, which he called Caras (= Carrhae?)[14] after his own name. After returning to Rome, he went out against the Huns in another war,[15] and was slain in the consulship of Maximus and Januarius. He was aged sixty and a half years.

(Dodgeon)

Syncellus, p. 472, 11–12, (p. 724, 11–16, CSHB): And, making war on the Persians, he (i.e. Carus) captured Ctesiphon. While he was encamped by the river Tigris, he was killed in his tent by a sudden bolt of lightning.

(Dodgeon)

Cedrenus, i, p. 464, 6–9: Carus and Carinus and Numerianus reigned for two years. This Carus occupied Persia and Ctesiphon: this is the fourth time that this city had suffered the same fate. (It had been captured before) by Trajan, by Verus, by Severus and by Carus. Carus was killed by plague, . . .

(Dodgeon)

Zonaras, XII, 30, pp. 610, 20–612, 16 (iii, pp. 156, 10–157, 2, Dindorf): When Carus gained the emperorship, he crowned his sons Carinus and Numerianus with the imperial diadem. And presently he campaigned against the Persians with one of his sons, Numerianus, and he gained Ctesiphon and Seleucia. But the Roman army almost came into dire peril; for they encamped in a hollow. The Persians saw this and through a canal led into that hollow the river which at that point flowed nearby. But Carus was successful in attacking the Persians and put them to flight. And he returned to Rome with a multitude of prisoners and much plunder. Then when the Sarmatian nation rose in revolt he joined battle with them and defeated them and brought their nation under his control. By race he was a Gaul, brave and adept in warfare. But there is no agreed version of his death among our records. For some say that he campaigned against the Huns and was killed there, while others say that he was encamped by the river Tigris, and that there his army had formed an entrenched camp. His tent was hit by a thunderbolt and they relate that he perished in it.

(Dodgeon)

5.2.1. Conflicting accounts of the achievements of Numerianus[16] and Carinus, the sons of Carus

Nemesianus, *Cynegetica* 63–75: Soon, bravest sons of the divine Carus, I shall prepare to relate your triumphs to the accompaniment of a better lyre, and I shall sing of the [empire's] shore by the twin limits of the world and the nations subdued by the power of the brother [emperors], which drink the Rhine and Tigris and drink the far-removed first waters of the Saône and the source of the Nile at its earliest point. I would not keep silence at the beginning, Carinus, about the wars which with successful hand you have recently completed in the North – you almost surpass your divine father – and how your brother captured the innermost regions of Persis and the ancient citadels of Babylon, avenging the outraged extremities of Romulus' kingdom. And I shall recount the spiritless flight and fastened quivers of the Parthians and their unstrung bows and lack of arrows.

(Dodgeon)

Aurelius Victor, *liber de Caesaribus* 38, 6–39, 1: Upon the death of his father, Numerianus, thinking that the war was at an end, was returning with the army when he perished through the treachery of Aper, his father-in-law and Praetorian Prefect. 7. In this an opportunity was offered by a disease of the eye which afflicted the young man. 8. For the crime remained undetected for a long time because the corpse was transported in a closed litter, as if the passenger was ill, in order that his vision would not be inconvenienced by the cold draughts.
39 However, after the crime had been revealed by the unpleasant odour of the decomposing corpse, at the advice of the generals and tribunes, Valerius Diocletian who commanded the imperial guards was chosen emperor, for his sagacity: . . .

(Dodgeon)

SHA Carus 12, 1–13, 1: He (i.e. Numerianus) accompanied his father in the Persian war, and after his father's death, when he had begun to suffer from a disease of the eyes – for that kind of ailment is most frequent with those exhausted, as he was, by too much loss of sleep – and was being carried in a litter, he was slain by the treachery of his father-in-law Aper, who was attempting to seize the rule. 2. But the soldiers continued for several days to ask after the emperor's health, and Aper kept haranguing them, saying that he could not appear before them for the reason that he must protect his weakened eyes from the wind and the sun, but at last the stench of his body revealed the facts. They all fell upon Aper, whose treachery could no longer be hidden, and they dragged him before the standards in front of the general's tent. Then a huge assembly was held and a tribunal, too, was constructed. 13 And when the question was asked who would be the most lawful avenger of Numerian and who could be given to the commonwealth as a good emperor, then all, with a heaven-sent unanimity, conferred the title of Augustus on Diocletian, who, it was said, had already received many omens of future rule.

(Magie, iii, p. 435)

Epitome de Caesaribus 38, 4–5: Numerianus, his son, who suffered from an eye ailment and was carried in a litter, was killed in a conspiracy instigated by Aper, his father-in-law. 5. As long as his death was concealed by trickery, Aper was able to seize power but his death was revealed by the stench of the corpse.

(Dodgeon)

Malalas, XII, pp. 303, 5–305, 2: After the reign of Carus, Numerianus Augustus ruled for two years. ... In his reign there occurred a great persecution of Christians; among them were martyred St. George the Cappadocian and St. Babylas. The latter was bishop of Antioch the Great. The same emperor Numerianus arrived [there] when on his way to war against the Persians. Wishing to view the divine mysteries of the Christians, he desired to enter the holy church where the Christians were gathered, to observe what mysteries they were celebrating. For he had heard that the same Galilaeans secretly performed their services. And as he drew near he was suddenly confronted by St. Babylas.[17] And the bishop stopped him, saying to him, 'You are polluted from sacrifice to idols; and I do not assent to your seeing the mysteries of the living God.' The emperor Numerianus was angry with him and immediately executed him. He went out from Antioch and campaigned against the Persians. In the ensuing battle, the Persians launched an attack on him [p. 304] and destroyed the greater part of his forces, and he fled to the city of Carrhae. The Persians put it under siege and took him prisoner, and immediately they executed him. They flayed his skin and made it into a bag. They treated it with myrrh and preserved it for their particular glory. They cut down the remainder of his army. On his death the emperor Numerianus was thirty-six. ... As soon as Carinus became emperor, he campaigned against the Persians to avenge his own brother Numerianus and he overwhelmed them by force.[18]

(Dodgeon)

Chronicon Paschale, p. 510, 2–15: In the year 255 after our Lord's Ascension into heaven, there occurred a persecution of Christians and many were martyred. Among the martyrs were St. George and St. Babylas. This latter was bishop of Antioch the Great, and the emperor Carinus, on his way with his uncle Carus to wage war upon the Persians, arrived there. Carus was struck by a thunderbolt in Mesopotamia. Carinus suffered defeat and fled to the city of Carrhae. The Persians encamped nearby and took him prisoner, and they immediately killed him. They flayed him and made his skin into a sack. And they treated it with myrrh [to preserve it] and kept it as an object of exceptional splendour. This Carinus died at the age of thirty-six. After his death his brother Numerianus campaigned against the Persians to avenge his own brother Carinus and he overcame them in mighty fashion.

(Dodgeon)

Syncellus, p. 472, 14–20 (pp. 724, 16–725, 5, CSHB): After him his son Numerianus reigned for only 30 days. For on his return from Persia he suffered an infection of the eyes and was slain by his own father-in-law, called Aper, being the Praetorian Prefect and zealous to become emperor. But his hopes were frustrated, for the whole army proclaimed as emperor Diocletian, who had campaigned with Carus. Diocletian had then displayed great courage and was a Dalmatian by birth. He had reached senatorial rank and had been honoured with the consulship.

(Dodgeon)

Cedrenus, i, p. 464, 9–12: ... and Numerianus, who had been blinded, was murdered by Aper, his father-in-law, and Numerianus who was *dux* of Moesia became emperor. Saint Babylas suffered martyrdom under him in Antioch. This (other) Numerianus was put to death by Diocletian.

(Dodgeon)

Zonaras, XII, 30, pp. 611, 15–612, 2 (iii, p. 157, 3–17, Dindorf): Whether his life ended in this fashion or otherwise, his son Numerianus was left sole emperor[19] in the camp. He immediately campaigned against the Persians; and when battle was joined, the Persians gained the upper hand and the Romans fell into retreat. Some relate that he was captured while trying to escape and that his skin was flayed from his whole body (like a wineskin) and so he perished; but the other tradition is that on his retreat from Persia he fell ill with eye trouble and was assassinated by his own father-in-law, the Praetorian Prefect. This man cast jealous eyes at the throne but however he did not gain it. For the army selected Diocletian as emperor, who was present there at that time and had displayed many deeds of courage in the war against Persia.

(Dodgeon)

5.2.2. A story associated with the Armenian (Persian?) war of Carus or Carinus

Synesius, *de regno*[20]16, ed. Terzaghi, pp. 36, 16–38, 8 (= ch. 18, *PG* 66. 1082B–1085A): It is therefore worthwhile to make mention of the character and achievements of a certain king, for any particular story will suffice to draw all others along in its wake. It is told of one of no great antiquity but such a one as even the grandfathers of our own elders might have known if they had not begotten their children when young, and had not become grandparents during the youth of their own children. It is said, then, that a certain monarch of those days was leading an expedition against the Parthians, who had behaved towards the Romans in an insulting manner. Now when they had reached the mountain frontiers of Armenia, before entering the enemy country, he was eager to dine, and gave orders to the army to make use of the provisions in the supply column, as they were now in a position to live off the neighbouring country should it be necessary. He was then pointing out to them the land of the Parthians. Now, while they were so engaged, an embassy appeared from the enemy lines, thinking on their arrival to have the first conversation with the influential men who surrounded the king, and after these with some dependants and gentlemen ushers, but supposing that only on a much later day would the king himself give audience to the embassy. However, it turned out somehow that the king was dining at the moment. Such a thing did not exist at that time as the Guards' regiment, a sort of picked force detached from the army itself, of men all young, tall, fair-haired and superb,

'Their heads ever anointed and their faces fair' (*Odyssey*, XV. 332), equipped with golden shields and golden lances. At the sight of these we are made aware beforehand of the king's approach, much as, I imagine, we recognize the sun by the rays that rise above the horizon. Here, in contrast, every phalanx doing its duty, was the guard of the king and the kingdom. And these kings held themselves in simple fashion, for they were kings not in pomp but in spirit, and it was only within that they differed from their people. Externally they appeared in the likeness of the herd, and it was in such guise, they say, that Carinus was seen by the embassy. A tunic dyed with purple was lying on the grass, and for repast he had a soup of yesterday's peas, and in it some bits of salted pork that had grown old in the service.

Now when he saw them, according to the story, he did not spring up, nor did he change anything; but called out to these men from the very spot and said that he knew that they had come to see him, for that he was Carinus;[21] and he bade them tell the young king that very day, that unless he conducted himself wisely, he might expect that the whole of their forest and plain would be in a single month barer than the head of Carinus. And as he spoke, they say that he took off his cap, and showed his head, which was no more hairy than the helmet lying at his side. And he gave them leave if they were hungry to attack the stew-pot with him, but if not in need, he ordered them to depart at once, and to leave the Roman lines, as their mission was at an end. Now it is said that when these messages were reported to the rank and file and to the leader of the enemy, namely, all that had been seen and heard, at once – as might have been expected – shuddering and fear fell upon every one at the thought of fighting men such as these, whose very king was neither ashamed of being a king, nor of being bald, and who, offering them a stew-pot, invited them to share his meal. And their braggart king arrived in a state of terror and was ready to yield in everything, he of the tiara and robes, to one in a simple woollen tunic and cap.

(Fitzgerald, i, pp. 128, 15–130, 8)

5.2.3. Diocletian's truce with the Persians

Panegyrici Latini II/10, 7, 5–6: In my view,[22] the Euphrates in like manner held the rich and fertile land of Syria in a protective embrace before the Persian Kingdom voluntarily surrendered to Diocletian.[23] But he gained this in the fashion of Jupiter his patron through that paternal nod of command which causes everything to tremble, and through the grandeur of your (i.e. Maximianus') name. 6. You, however, invincible Emperor, have tamed those wild and uncontrollable peoples (i.e. German tribes) through devastation, battles, massacres, the sword and the fire.

Pan. Lat. II/9, 1–2: He (i.e. Diocletian) has recently invaded that part of Germany which lies opposite to Rhaetia and with a courage similar to yours he has victoriously advanced the Roman frontier, so much have you in plain and loving fashion attributed to his divinity what measures you had taken for [the defences of] the territories, when you came together from different parts of the globe and joined together your invincible right hands, so full of trust and brotherly feeling was that conference. 2. In it you provided for yourselves reciprocated examples of all the virtues and in turn you increased your stature, something which did not seem possible, Diocletian by showing to you the gifts of the Persians[24] and you by displaying spoils from the Germans.

Pan. Lat. II/10, 6: In this same manner that king of Persia, who had never before deigned to admit that he was a mere man,[25] was a suppliant before your brother (i.e. Diocletian) and laid open his whole kingdom to him, if he thought it right to enter it. In the meantime he offered him varying wonders, he sent wild animals of remarkable beauty; being content to win the name of friend, he earned it through his submission.

(Dodgeon)

5.2.4. Return of Trdat to Armenia with Roman military assistance (?) (c. 287)[26]

Agathangelos, *Hist. Arm.* (I), 46–7 (Thomson, p. 61): See Appendix II, pp. 313–14.
Moses Khorenats'i, *Hist. Arm.* (II), 82 (Thomson, pp. 231–2): See Appendix II, p. 319.

5.2.5. Diocletian fortifies Circesium and reorganizes the eastern frontier (287?)

Ammianus Marcellinus XXIII, 5, 2: The place (i.e. Circesium) had formerly been small and insecure, till Diocletian surrounded it with high towers and walls when he was organizing the frontier defences in depth on the confines of the territories of the barbarians, in order to prevent the Persians from overrunning Syria, as had happened a few years before to the great injury of the province.

(Yonge, p. 325, revised)

Procopius, *de bello Persico* II, 5, 2–3: (AD 540) On the other side of the river stands the last Roman stronghold which is called Circesium, an exceedingly strong place, since the river Aborras (i.e. the Khabur), a large stream, has its mouth at this point and mingles with the Euphrates, and the fortress lies exactly in the angle which is made by the junction of the two rivers. 3. And a long second wall outside the fortress cuts off the land between the two rivers, and completes the form of a triangle around Circesium.

(Dewing, i, p. 295)

See also texts cited in 5.5.5–5.6.1, pp. 136–9.

5.3.1. Diocletian's campaign against the Saracens (? May/June, 290)

Pan. Lat. III/11, 5, 4–5: I[27] pass in silence over the Rhaetian border that was advanced by the sudden defeat of the enemy, I omit to mention the devastation of Sarmatia and the Saracens[28] beset by the bonds of imprisonment, I pass by also those achievements won by the dread of your weapons as though they were feats of arms, the Franks and their king coming to seek peace and the Parthian (*sic*) flattering you with the wonder of his gifts. 5. I set before myself a new condition of rhetoric that, when I seem to be silent upon all which is most important, I shall yet reveal that there are other greater glories present in my praises of you.

Ibid 6, 6: The Rhine, the Danube, and the Nile, and the Tigris with its twin the Euphrates, and the two oceans which receive and return the sun and whatever is between the confines of these lands, rivers and shores, through you are in communion with such affable equanimity as much as the eyes rejoice to be in communion with day(light).

Ibid 7, 1: That laurel crown of victory (won by Diocletian) over the conquered people neighbouring upon Syria and his victories in Rhaetia and Sarmatia made you, Maximianus, triumph in the joy of devotion.

Pan. Lat. IV 8, 3, 3: Indeed, beyond the Tigris, Parthia [*sic*] was reduced; Dacia was restored, the frontiers of Germany and Rhaetia stretch as far as the source of the Danube, the liberation of Britain and Batavia is assured, . . .

Pan. Lat. IV 8, 21, 1: In the same way that a short time ago, Emperor Diocletian, at your order Asia had filled the deserted lands of Thrace with colonists (i.e. Saracen captives), . . .

(Dodgeon)

5.3.2. The accession of Bahram (III) and his brief reign (293)

Agathias IV, 24, 6–8: But Vararanes (i.e. Bahram) III enjoyed the kingdom for only four months. He was called Segansaa; this was for a special reason, in accordance with an old traditional custom. 7. When the Persian kings defeat in war a large tribe among their neighbours and conquer the country, they no longer kill the conquered people but reduce them all to tributary status and let them live in the captured territory and cultivate it, save that they kill the former leaders of the tribe most cruelly, and give their own sons the title of their kingdom, to commemorate and glorify their pride in their victory. 8. So, since the tribe of the Segestani had been enslaved by Vararanes, the father of this King, his son was naturally called Segansaa (*recte* Saganshah),[29] for this means in Greek 'the king of the Segestani'.

(Cameron, p. 123)

5.3.3. The accession of Narses (*c.* 293)

Agathias IV, 25, 1: This king (i.e. Bahram III) soon perished and Narses was the next to hold the throne, for seven years, five months (i.e. 293–302).[30]

(Cameron, p. 123)

5.3.4. Renewal of hostilities by Narses (*c.* 293).

Lactantius, *de mortibus persecutorum* 9, 5: Narses, king of the Persians, emulating the example set him by his grandfather (*recte* father) Shapur, assembled a great army, and aimed at becoming master of the eastern provinces of the Roman Empire.

(Fletcher, p. 304, altered)

Aurelius Victor, *liber de Caesaribus* 39, 22: At that same time, the Persians gravely vexed the East, and Julianus and the Quinquegentianae[31] troubled Africa.

(Dodgeon)

Ammianus Marcellinus XXIII, 5, 11: See below 5.3.5.

Eutropius IX, 22, 1: While disorder thus prevailed throughout the world, while Carausius was taking arms in Britain and Achilleus in Egypt, while the Quinquegentiani were harassing Africa, and Narses was making war upon the east, Diocletian promoted Maximian Herculius from the dignity of Caesar to that of emperor, and created Constantius and Maximian Galerius Caesars, of whom Constantius is said to have been the grand-nephew of Claudius by a daughter and Maximian Galerius to have been born in Dacia not far from Serdica.

(Watson, p. 524)

Jerome, *Chronicon s. aa.* 289–90,[32] p. 225, 18–25: Carausius, having assumed the purple, occupied Britain. Narses made war on the east. The Quinquegentiani laid waste to Africa. Achilleus occupied Egypt. On account of these (setbacks), Constantius (I) and Galerius Maximianus were added to the sovereignty as Caesars, of whom Constantius is said to have been the grand-nephew of Claudius by a daughter and Galerius was born in Dacia not far from Serdica. [= Jordanes, hist. Rom. 297–8.]

(Dodgeon)

Orosius, *adversus paganos* VII, 25, 4: Thus, throughout the confines of the Roman Empire, the roars of sudden strife sounded, Carausius leading a rebellion in the British provinces and Achilleus in Egypt, while the Quinquegentiani disturbed Africa, and Narses also, King of the Persians, pressed the east with war; Diocletian, being disturbed by this danger, made Herculius Maximianus Augustus instead of Caesar, and he appointed Constantius and Galerius Maximianus as Caesars.

(Deferrari, p. 320)

5.3.5. The Persian Campaigns of Diocletian and Galerius (296–298)

PArgent. 480 (= Reitzenstein, 1901: 48, *frag.* 1),[33] recto 1–10: Driven mad by the lashes of Enyo,[34] they all girded on their arrow-holding quivers, and each held bow and spear in his hands and the whole Nisaean[35] cavalry that fights on the plains was gathered together, not a fraction of the cavalry which Nereus had before brought speeding over the ocean on floating rafts. For not such as shrieked under Thermopylae's narrow vale at the hands of the Spartans was the Median host coming to meet my emperor, but much more numerous and stung by the battle cry . . .[36]

PArgent. 480 verso 2–11 (fragmentary): Other leaders also would have hastened from Italy to his aid, had not war in Spain drawn one and the battle-din of the island of Britain encompassed the other.[37] But just as Zeus goes from Crete above Othrys and Apollo (leaves) sea-girt Delos for Pangaeus, and as they don their arms the noisy throng of Giants is set to trembling, in such fashion the elder lord[38] with his army of Ausonians (i.e. Romans) reached the Orient in the company of the younger king. They had the likeness of the blessed gods, one in strength matched Zeus on high and the other the fair-haired Apollo . . .

(Dodgeon)

Lactantius, *de mortibus persecutorum* 9, 6–8: Diocletian, apt to be low-spirited and timorous in every connotation, and fearing a fate like Valerian's, would not in person engage Narses; but he sent Galerius by way of Armenia, while he himself halted on the eastern provinces, and anxiously watched the event. 7. It is a custom among the barbarians to take everything that belongs to them into the field. Having put Narses to flight, and returned with much spoil, his own pride and Diocletian's fears were greatly increased. 8. For after this victory he rose to such a pitch of haughtiness as to reject the appellation of Caesar; and when he heard that appellation in letters addressed to him, he cried out, with a stern look and a terrible voice,'How long am I to be *Caesar*?'

(Fletcher, p. 304, revised)

Julian, *Orationes* I, 18A–B (13.18–27, Bidez): Among those who sat on the throne before your father's time and imposed on the Persians conditions of peace admired and welcomed by all, did not the Caesar (i.e. Galerius) incur a disgraceful defeat when he attacked them on his own account? It was not till the ruler of the whole world turned his attention to them, directing thither all the forces of the empire, occupying all the passes with his troops and levies of hoplites, both veterans and new recruits and employing every sort of military equipment, that fear drove them to accept terms of peace.

(Wright, i, pp. 45–7)

Aurelius Victor, *liber de Caesaribus* 39, 33–6: In the meantime, after Jovius (i.e. Diocletian) had departed for Alexandria, the Caesar Maximianus (i.e. Galerius) received his assignment to cross the borders, and advanced into Mesopotamia in order to stem the tide of the Persian advance. 4. Gravely defeated by them at first, he immediately assembled an army of both veterans and recruits and advanced against the enemy through Armenia; which was almost the only way to victory, or at least the easiest. 35. At length, in that very place he captured the (Persian) king Narses together with his children, his wives and his court. 36. His victory was such that had Valerius (i.e. Diocletian), whose will was law, for whatever reason, not opposed it, the Roman fasces would have been borne into a new province.[39]

(Dodgeon)

Festus, *breviarium* 14, pp. 57, 14–58, 2: In the time of Diocletian, the Romans, vanquished in the first engagement, defeated Narses in the second and captured his wife and his daughters, whom they protected with utmost respect for their honour. After peace had been made, Mesopotamia was restored (to us) and the boundary (*limes*) re-established beyond the Tigris,[40] with the result that we acquired sovereignty of the five states (*gentes*) established across the Tigris. The terms of this treaty were adhered to until the time of the divine Constantius.

Festus, *breviarium* 25, pp. 65, 12–66, 5: Under Emperor Diocletian, a memorable victory was won against the Persians. Maximianus Caesar, in the first engagement, having attacked vigorously an innumerable body of enemies with a handful of men, withdrew defeated, and Diocletian received him with such indignation that he had to run for a few miles before his carriage, garbed in his purple.[41] He gained with difficulty his request that his army should be restored to its full complement from the frontier troops of Dacia and that he should attempt another military engagement. Arriving in Greater Armenia, the commander himself, along with two cavalrymen, reconnoitred the enemy. He suddenly came upon the enemy camp with twenty five thousand troops and, attacking the countless columns of the Persians, he cut them down in a massacre. Narses the Persian king fled, while his wife and daughters were protected with the utmost regard for their chastity. In respect of this admirable behaviour, the Persians admitted the superiority of the Romans not only in warfare but even in character. They restored Mesopotamia with the Transtigritanian regions. The peace that was made endured until our time and was advantageous to Rome.

(Dodgeon)

Eutropius, IX, 24–5, 1: Galerius Maximianus in acting against Narses fought, on the first occasion, a battle far from successful, meeting him between Callinicum and Carrhae,[42] and engaging in the combat rather with rashness than want of courage; for he contended with a small army against a very numerous enemy. Being in consequence defeated, and going to join Diocletian, he was received by him, when he met him on the road, with such extreme haughtiness, that he is said to have run by his chariot for several miles in his scarlet robes.

25 But having soon after collected forces in Illyricum and Moesia, he fought a second time with Narses (the grandfather of Hormisdas and Sapor), in Greater Armenia, with extraordinary success, and with no less caution and spirit, for he undertook, with one or two of the cavalry, the office of a speculator. After putting Narses to flight, he captured his wives, sisters, and children, with a vast number of the Persian nobility besides, and a great quantity of treasure; the king himself he forced to take refuge in the remotest deserts in his dominions. Returning therefore in triumph to Diocletian, who was then encamped with some troops in Mesopotamia, he was welcomed by him with great honour.

(Watson, pp. 525–6)

Jerome, *Chronicon* s. a. 302, p. 227, 12–14: Galerius Maximianus was received with the greatest honour by Diocletian, after he had defeated Narses and captured his wives, children and sisters.

Ibid. s. a. 304, pp. 227, 25–228, 2: The Augustus Diocletian and Maximianus celebrated a triumph at Rome with signal pomp, with the wife and sisters and children of Narses preceding the carriage and all the booty plundered from Persia.

(Dodgeon)

Ammianus Marcellinus XIV, 11, 10: (AD 354) To these exhortations, he (*sc.* Constantius) added by way of precedent an incident from the not too distant past that Diocletian and his colleague (i.e. Maximianus) employed their Caesars as attendants with no fixed abode, dispatching them hither and thither. On one occasion in Syria, (the Caesar) Galerius, clad in purple, had to march on foot for nearly a mile before the carriage of an enraged Augustus (*sc.* Diocletian).

(Yonge)

Ibid. XXII, 4, 8: For it is well known that when, in the time of the Caesar Maximianus, the camp of the king of Persia was plundered, a common soldier, after finding a Parthian jewel-case full of pearls, threw the gems away in ignorance of their value, and went away content with the mere beauty of his bit of leather.

(Yonge, p. 282, revised)

Ibid. XXIII, 5, 11: (AD 363) In truth, they (i.e. Julian's philosopher theurgist friends) brought forward as a plausible argument to secure credit to their knowledge, that in time past, when Caesar Maximianus was about to fight Narses, king of the Persians, a lion and a huge boar which had been slain were at the same time brought to him, and after subduing that nation he returned in safety; forgetting that the destruction which was now portended was to him who invaded the dominions of another, and that Narses had given the offence by being the first to make an inroad into Armenia, a country under Roman jurisdiction.

(Yonge, pp. 326–7)

SHA, Car. 9, 3: For clearly it is granted to us and will always be granted, as our most venerated Caesar Maximianus has shown, to conquer the Persians and advance beyond them, and methinks this will surely come to pass if only our men fail not to live up to the promised favour of Heaven.

(Magie, iii, p. 431)

Synesius, *de regno* 17 (= ch. 13, PG 66.1085A): And another story
more recent than this I think you must have heard, for it is
improbable that anyone has ever heard of a king who assigned
himself the task of getting into the enemy's country for purposes of
espionage by imitating the appearance of an embassy.

(Fitzgerald, i, p. 130,9–13)

Orosius, *adversus paganos* VII, 25, 9–11: Besides, Galerius Maximianus, after he had fought Narses in two battles, in a third battle
somewhere between Callinicum and Carrhae, met Narses and was
conquered, and after losing his troops fled to Diocletian. He was
received by him very arrogantly, so that he is reported, though clad
in purple, to have been made to run before his carriage, but he used
this insult as whetstone to valour, as a result of which, after the rust
of royal pride had rubbed off, he developed a sharpness of mind.
Thus he brought troops together from all sides throughout Illyricum
and Moesia and, hurriedly turning against the enemy, he overcame
Narses by his great strategy and forces. With the Persian troops
annihilated and Narses himself turned to flight, he entered Narses'
camp, captured his wives, sisters, and children, seized an immense
amount of Persian treasure, and led away a great many Persian
noblemen. Returning to Mesopotamia, he was received by Diocletian with the highest honour.

(Deferrari, pp. 321–2)

Chronicon Paschale, p. 512, 18–19: The Persians were utterly
defeated by Constantius and Maximianus Jovius.

Chronicon Paschale. p. 513, 19–20: Under the same consuls, the
Persians were defeated by Maximianus Herculius Augustus.

(Dodgeon)

Jordanes, *Getica*, XXI (110), p. 86, 13–19: After these events (the
sacking of Troy in Asia Minor), the Goths[43] had already returned
home when they were summoned at the request of the Emperor
Maximian to aid the Romans against the Parthians. They fought for
him faithfully, serving as auxiliaries. But after Caesar Maximian by
their aid had routed Narses, king of the Persians, the grandson[44] of
Shapur the Great, taking as spoil all his possessions, together with his
wives and sons, and when Diocletian had conquered Achilles in Alexandria and Maximianus Herculius had broken the Quinquegentiani in Africa, thus winning peace for the Empire, they began rather
to neglect the Goths.

(Mierow, p. 82)

Malalas, XIII, p. 306, 16–21: When the Persians again stirred up trouble, Diocletian took up arms and campaigned against them with Maximianus.[45] When they reached Antioch the Great, the same Diocletian sent Maximianus Caesar against the Persians and waited himself in Antioch.

Malalas, p. 308, 6–15: Maximianus Caesar went away against the Persians, defeated them by force and returned to Antioch. He took prisoner the Persian king's wife, after he had fled with four men to the *limes* of India and their army had been destroyed. Arsane, the queen of the Persians, resided in Daphne for some years and was guarded with honour by command of the Roman emperor Diocletian. After this there was a peace treaty and she was returned to the Persians to her own husband, having endured an honourable captivity. At this time donatives were offered by the emperor to the whole Roman state to celebrate the victory.

(Dodgeon)

Theophanes, *Chronicon*, A. M. 5793, p. 9, 1–15: In this year Maximianus Galerius was dispatched by Diocletian against Narses, the king of Persia, who at that time had overrun Syria and was ravaging it. Meeting him (i.e. Narses) in battle, he (i.e. Galerius) lost the first encounter in the area of Callinicum and Carrhae. While withdrawing from battle, he met Diocletian riding in a chariot. He did not welcome the Caesar (accompanied as he was by his own show of pomp) and left him alone to run along for a considerable distance and precede his chariot. After this the Caesar Maximianus Galerius gathered a great force and was sent again to the war with Narses. He met with success, venturing and achieving what no one else could have done. For he both pursued Narses into the interior of Persia and slaughtered all his camp and his wives, children and sisters, and he took over all that the Persian king had brought with him, a treasure store of money and the nobility of the Persians. When he returned with these, Diocletian, then residing in Mesopotamia, greeted him gladly and honoured him. And each on his own and both together made war on many of the barbarians and won many successes. Diocletian was puffed up with the success of his fortunes and sought to have obeisance made to him by his senators and not be addressed according to the former style. He adorned his footwear with gold, pearls and precious stones.

(Dodgeon)

Eutychius, *Annales* 187, ed. Breydey, p. 66, 1–5: See below, Appendix I, p. 296.

Zonaras, XII, 31, pp. 616, 4–617, 4 (iii, pp. 161, 10–162, 4, Dindorf): When Narses was king of Persia, who is recorded as the seventh (corr.: sixth) King of Persia after Ardashir, whom our historical account mentioned earlier as having restored the kingdom of the Persians – for after this Artaxerxes or Artaxares, there being two forms of the name (i.e. Ardashir,) Shapur became king of Persia, after him came Hormizd, then Varanes (i.e. Bahram I), and after him Vararakh, and again another Varanes (i.e. Bahram II), and besides these came Narses – while this Narses was then ravaging Syria, Diocletian, while passing through Egypt against the Ethiopians, sent his own son-in-law Galerius Maximianus with sufficient strength to fight with him. He clashed with the Persians, was defeated and fled. But Diocletian sent him once more with a larger army. So, fighting with them again, he was so successful that he redeemed his earlier defeat. For he destroyed most of the Persian army and pursued the wounded Narses as far as the interior of Persia. He led away as prisoners his wives, sons and sisters, and he gained possession of all the money that Narses brought with him on the campaign and (possession also) of many of the Persian nobility. When Narses had recovered from his wound, he sent embassies to Diocletian and Galerius, asking that his children and wives be given back to him and that a peace treaty be made. And he gained his request, giving up to the Romans whatever territory they wanted.

(Dodgeon)

5.4.1. Assuristan raided by Armenians(?)

Agathangelos, *Hist. Arm.* (I), 123: (Thomson, pp. 135–6): See Appendix II, p. 314.

5.4.2. Negotiations between Galerius and the envoy of Narses

Petrus Patricius, *frag.* 13, *FGH IV*, pp. 188–9: Apharban, who was particularly dear to Narses, king of Persia, was sent on an embassy and came before Galerius in supplication. When he had received licence to speak, he said, 'It is clear to the race of men that the Roman and Persian Empires are, as it were, two lamps; as with (two) eyes, each one should be adorned by the brightness of the other and not for ever be angry seeking the destruction of each other. For this is not considered virtue but rather levity or weakness. Because men think that later generations cannot help them, they are eager to destroy those who are opposed to them. However, it should not be thought that Narses is weaker than all the other kings; rather that Galerius so surpasses all other kings that to him alone does Narses himself justly yield and yet does not become lower than his forebears' worth'. In addition to this, Apharban said that he had been commanded by Narses to entrust the rights of his Empire to the clemency of the Romans, since they were reasonable. For that reason he did not bring the terms (lit. oaths) on which the treaty would be based, but gave it all to the judgement of the Emperor. He (Narses) only begged that just (his) children and wives be returned to him, saying that through their return he would remain bound by acts of kindness rather than by arms. He could not give adequate thanks that those in captivity had not experienced any outrage there, but had been treated in such a way as if they would soon be returned to their own rank. With this he brought to memory the changeable nature of human affairs.

Galerius seemed to grow angry at this, shaking his body. In reply he said that he did not deem the Persians very worthy to remind others of the variation in human affairs, since they themselves, when they got the opportunity, did not cease to impose misfortunes on men. 'Indeed you observed the rule of victory towards Valerian in a fine way, you who deceived him through stratagems and took him, and did not release him until his extreme old age and dishonourable death. Then, after his death, by some loathsome art you preserved his skin and brought an immortal outrage to the mortal body.' The Emperor went through these things and said that he was not moved by what the Persians suggested through the embassy, that one ought to consider human fortunes; indeed it was more fitting to be moved to anger on this account, if one took notice of what the Persians had done. However, he followed the footsteps of his own forebears, whose custom it was to spare subjects but to wage war against those who opposed them – then he instructed the ambassador to make known to his own king the nobility and goodness of the Romans whose kindness he had put to the test, and that he should hope also that before long, by the resolve of the Emperor, they (i.e. the captives) would return to him.

(J. M. Lieu)

5.4.3. The peace settlement between Diocletian and Narses (298 or 299)

Petrus Patricius, *frag.* 14, *FGH* IV, p. 189: Galerius and Diocletian met at Nisibis, where they took counsel and by common consent sent an ambassador to Persia, Sicorius Probus, an archival clerk. Narses received him cordially because of the hope inspired by the proclamation he made. Narses also contrived some delay. As if he wanted the envoys who came with Sicorius to recover from their weariness, he took Sicorius, who was not ignorant of what was happening, as far as near the Asproudas, a river of Media, until those who had been scattered around because of the war had assembled. Then, in the inner room of the palace, when he had sent out everyone else and required only the presence of Apharban as well as Archapet[46] and Bar(a)sabor, of whom the one was praetorian prefect and the other was chief secretary,[47] he ordered Probus to give an account of his embassy. The principal points of the embassy were these: that in the eastern region the Romans should have Intelene along with Sophene, and Arzanene along with Cordyene and Zabdicene,[48] that the river Tigris should be the boundary between each state,[49] that the fortress Zintha,[50] which lies on the border of Media, should mark the edge of Armenia, that the king of Iberia should pay to the Romans the insignia of his kingdom and that the city of Nisibis, which lies on the Tigris, should be the place for transactions.[51]

Narses heard these things and since the present fortune did not allow him to refuse any of them, he agreed to them all, except, in order not to seem to do everything under constraint, he refused only that Nisibis should be the place of transactions. Sicorius, however, said, 'This point must be yielded. Moreover, the embassy has no power of its own and has received no instructions on this point from the emperors.' Therefore, when these things were agreed on, his wives and children were returned to Narses, for through the emperor's love of honour, pure discretion had been maintained towards them.

(J. M. Lieu)

Johannes Lydus, *de magistratibus* II, 25: And who, then, at first was designated *magister*, I am not able to say because history is silent; for prior to Martinianus, who was *magister* under Licinius, history does not hand down this designation for anyone else. Though he was such under Licinius, when Constantine had gotten possession by himself of the entire power of the imperial office, he appointed

Palladius *magister* of the court, a man who was sagacious and through an embassy had earlier reconciled the Persians with the Romans and Galerius Maximianus.

(Bandy, p. 121)

5.4.4. Participation of Constantine (the Great) in the expedition of Galerius(?)

Constantine, *oratio ad sanctorum coetum* 16, 2, GCS, p. 177, 1–3: Memphis and Babylon [it was declared] shall be wasted and left desolate with their fathers' gods. Now these things I speak not from the report of others, but having myself been present and actually witnessed the pitiful fate of these cities.[52]

(Richardson, p. 573, revised)

5.4.5. The achievements of Verinus in Armenia recalled by Symmachus

Symmachus, *epistulae* I, 2, 7: Should I admire even more your valour in arms, Verinus, you who as commander (*dux*) have tamed the eastern Armenians[53] by the sword or rather your eloquence, the uprightness of your manner of life, and, because, save when in office, for public duty often called on you, you have led your life happily in innocent fields? There is no further need of virtue, for such as there might be, you would have.

5.5.1. The triumph of Diocletian and Galerius at Rome (*c.* 298)

Chronicon a. 354, p. 148, 26–8, MGH: Diocletian and Maximian: (They brought to Rome) a king of the Persians with all his people and placed their garments adorned with pearls to the number of thirty-three about the temples of their lord. Thirteen elephants and six charioteers and two hundred and fifty horses were paraded in the city.

(Lieu)

5.5.2. The victories of Diocletian and Galerius as recalled by Eumenius[54]

Panegyrici Latini V/9, 21, 1–3: May this map, thanks to the indication of the opposing regions, permit them to pass in review the magnificent exploits of our valiant princes, by showing them, as the runners arrive in relay every moment, sweat-covered and announcing victories, the twin rivers of Persia, the Libyan fields devoured by drought, the curve of the branches of the Rhine, the many mouths of the Nile, and inviting them, through the sight of each of these countries, to imagine either Egypt, cured of her madness and calm under your kindly rule, Diocletian Augustus, or else you, invincible Maximianus, hurling a thunderbolt on the crushed Moors, or even, thanks to your strong arm, Emperor Constantius (i.e. Constantine Chlorus), Batavia and Brittany lifting their stained heads above forests and waves, or you, Maximianus Caesar (i.e. Galerius), trampling the bows and quivers of the Persians beneath your feet. For now we are pleased to look upon the map of the world, now that finally we no longer see a foreign country!

(Vince)

5.5.3. Manichaeans accused of being a pro-Persian fifth-column (c. 302)[55]

Collatio Mosaicarum XV, 3: Gregorian, in the Seventh Book, under the title 'Of Sorcerers and Manichaeans':[56]

The Emperors Diocletian and Maximianus [and Constantius] and Maximianus (i.e. Galerius) to Julianus, Proconsul of Africa: Well-beloved Julianus:

1. Excessive leisure sometimes incites ill-conditioned people to transgress the limits of nature, and persuades them to introduce empty and scandalous kinds of superstitious doctrine, so that many others are lured on to acknowledge the authority of their erroneous notions.

2. But the immortal Gods, in their Providence, have thought fit to ordain that the principles of virtue and truth should, by the counsel and deliberations of many good, great and wise men, be approved and established in their integrity. These principles it is not right to oppose or resist, nor ought the ancient religion to be subjected to the censure of a new creed. It is indeed highly criminal to discuss doctrines once and for all settled and defined by our forefathers, and which have their recognized place and course in our system. 3. Wherefore we are resolutely determined to punish the stubborn depravity of these worthless people.

4. As regards the Manichaeans, concerning whom Your Carefulness have reported to Our Serenity, who, in opposition to the older creeds, set up new and unheard-of sects, purposing in their wickedness, to cast out the doctrines vouchsafed to us by Divine favour in

olden times, we have heard that they have but recently advanced or sprung forth, like strange and monstrous portents, from their native homes among the Persians – a nation hostile to us[57] – and have settled in this part of the world, where they are perpetrating many evil deeds, disturbing the tranquillity of the peoples and causing the gravest injuries to the civic communities and there is danger that, in process of time, they will endeavour, as is their usual practice, to infect the innocent, orderly and tranquil Roman people, as well as the whole of our Empire, with the damnable customs and perverse laws of the Persians as with the poison of a malignant serpent. 5. And since all that Your Prudence has set out in detail in your report of their region shows that what our laws regard as their misdeeds are clearly the offspring of a fantastic and lying imagination, we have appointed due and fitting punishments for these people.

6. We order that the authors and leaders[58] of these sects be subjected to severe punishment, and, together with their abominable writings, burnt in the flames. We direct that their followers, if they continue recalcitrant, shall suffer capital punishment, and their goods be forfeited to the Imperial treasury. 7. And if those who have gone over to that hitherto unheard-of, scandalous and wholly infamous creed, or to that of the Persians, are persons who hold public office, or are of any rank or of superior social status, you will see to it that their estates are confiscated and the offenders sent to the (quarry) at Phaeno or the mines at Proconnesus. 8. And in order that this plague of iniquity shall be completely extirpated from this our most happy age, let Your Devotion hasten to carry out our orders and commands. Given at Alexandria, March 31st.

(Hyamson, pp. 131–3, revised)

5.5.4. The accession of Hormizd II (302)

Agathias IV, 25, 1: His (i.e. Narses') son Hormizd succeeded him, and inherited not only his father's kingdom but also the length of his reign. It is a surprising fact that each of them reigned for exactly the same number of years and months (302–309).

(Cameron, p. 123)

5.5.5. General efforts by Diocletian to strengthen the eastern frontier (287ff.)[59]

CIL III *Suppl.* I, 6661 (= *Inv.* VI, 2; Latin inscription found at the so-called Camp of Diocletian at Palmyra):[60] Restorers of the world of whom they are the masters, and leaders of the human race, our lords Diocletian (and Maximianus), Unconquered Emperors, and Constantine and Maximianus, noblest Caesars, have established this entrenchment under favourable auspices, through the care of the most perfect Sossianus Hierocles, governor of the province, devoted to their genius and their majesty.

(Vince)

CIL III, 14397 (= *IGLS* 2675; Latin milestone?, found in a field near Tell Nebi Mindo on the east side of the road to Homs, *c.* 300): To the Emperor, Caesar, Gaius Aurelius Valerius Diocletianus, the Unconquered, Augustus, and to the emperor, Caesar, Marcus Aurelius Valerius Maximianus, the Devout, the Fortunate, the Unconquered, Augustus, and to Flavius Valerius Constantius, and to Galerius Valerius Maximianus, most noble of Caesars . . .

(Prentice, 1908: 274–5, no. 346)

Poidebard, 1934: 75 (Latin milestone found between Palmyra and Hlehle): To our Lord, the most noble Constantine and his family. The Strata Diocletiana.[61] From Palmyra to Aracha, eight (Roman) miles.

(Lieu)

Mouterde, *MUSJ* 15 (1930–31) p. 224 (Latin milestone between Haneybe and Manquoura, *c.* 308/9): Strata. To our lords Galerius Maximianus and Valerius Licinnianus [Licinnius], invincible Augustus and to Galerius Valerius [Maximianus . . .].

(Lieu)

Speidel, Historia 36 (1987), pp. 215–16 (Milestone once on the Roman road to Jawf (Dumata)[62] found at or near Qasr al Azraq (Basiensis), Latin): [Diocletian . . . had built(?). . .] by his very brave soldiers of the legions XI Claudia, and VII Claudia and I Italica and IV Flavia, and I Illyricorum, linked by manned posts (*praetensione colligata*)[63] to his soldiers from the base of legio III Cyrenaica. From Bostra to Basienis (?) sixty-six miles, from Basienis to Amat(a) 70 (?) and from Amata to Dumata two hundred and eight miles.

(Speidel, 1987: 216)

CIL III, 14149 (= Brunnow – v. Domaszewski, 1905: 56, lintel inscription found *in situ* at the Roman *castellum* at Qasr Bshir in the central sector of the *limes Arabicus*, AD 306, Latin): To our best and greatest leaders (*principibus*) Gaius Aurelius Valerius Diocletian, Pious, Fortunate, Unconquered, Augustus and Marcus

Aurelius Valerius Maximianus, Pious, Fortunate, Unconquered, Augustus, and Flavius Valerius Constantius and Galerius Valerius Maximianus, noble caesars. Aurelius Asclepiades, the *praeses* of the Provincia Arabiae commanded the fortress of the headquarters at Mobene(?) (*castra praetorii Mobeni*)[64] to be fully constructed from the foundations.

(Lieu)

Procopius, *de bello Persico* II, 1, 6: (*c.* AD 535) Now this country, which at that time was claimed by both tribes of Saracens,[65] is called Strata, and extends to the south of the city of Palmyra; nowhere does it produce a single tree or any of the useful growth of cornlands, for it is burned exceedingly dry by the sun, but from of old it has been devoted to the pasturage of some few flocks. Now Arethas maintained that the place belonged to the Romans, proving his assertion by the name which has long been applied to it by all (for strata signifies 'a paved road' in the Latin tongue), and he also adduced testimonies of men of the oldest times.

(Dewing, i, p. 263)

Malalas, XII, pp. 307, 20–308, 1: He (i.e. Diocletian) also established three armament factories for the manufacturing of arms for the army. One factory he established at Edessa in order that the arms could be near at hand (for troops on the frontier). Similarly he established a factory at Damascus, bearing in mind the inroads of the Saracens.[66]

Malalas, p. 308,17–22: The same Diocletian also established along the borders from Egypt to the boundaries of Persia (a series of) camps. He stationed *limitanei* in them, and appointed *duces* for the provinces to be stationed to the rear of these camps with a strong force to keep watch. They also raised up boundary posts to the Emperor and to the Caesar on the *limes* of Syria.

Malalas, p. 313, 16–20: In his reign (i.e. Diocletian's) he sent Maxim(ian)us (called also Licinianus) with a great army to guard the districts of the Orient from the Persians and the inroads of the Saracens. For they were lately disturbing the Orient as far as Egypt.

(Dodgeon)

Chronicon Edessenum II, CSCO, 1, pp. 3, 27–4, 2 (Syriac): In the year 614 (AD 303) in the reign of the Emperor Diocletian, the walls of Edessa collapsed for a second time.[67]

5.6.1. A wayfarer's appreciation of the improved provisions for travellers in the frontier regions (late 3rd or early 4th C.)

CIL III 6660 (Inscription found within a Roman camp at Khan Il-Abyad on a road from Damascus to Palmyra, south-west of Qaryatein,[68] Latin):

> A plain that is dry indeed, and hateful enough to wayfarers,
> on account of its long wastes and its chances of death close at
>   hand,
> for those whose lot is hunger, than which there is no graver
>   ill (or: where no graver ill besets)
> thou has made, my lord, a camp, adorned with greatest
>   splendour,
> 5 O Silvinus, warden of a city of the high-road (*limes*), most
>   strong
> in its wall and in the protection of our masters revered in all
> the world: and thou hast contrived that it abound in water
>   celestial,
> so that it may bear the yoke of Ceres and of Bacchus.
> Wherefore, o guest, with joy pursue thy way,
> 10 and for benefit received sing with praise the doings
> of this great-hearted judge who shines in peace and in war.
> I pray the gods above that he, taking a step still higher,
> may continue to found for our masters such camps, arduous
>   though they be,
> and that he may rejoice in children who add honour to their
>   father's deeds.

(Prentice, 1908: 282–3)

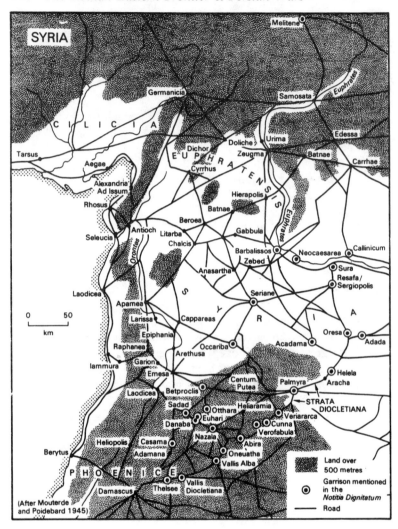

Map 2   Syria

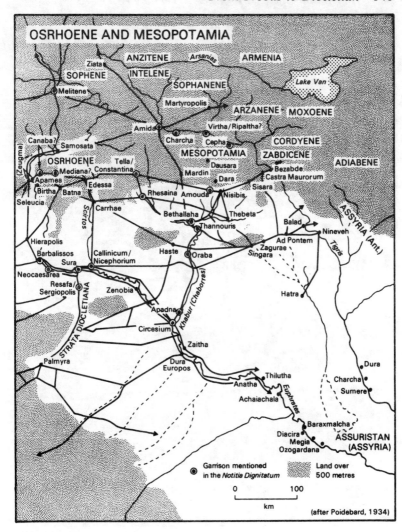

OSRHOENE AND MESOPOTAMIA

Map 3 Osrhoene and Mesopotamia

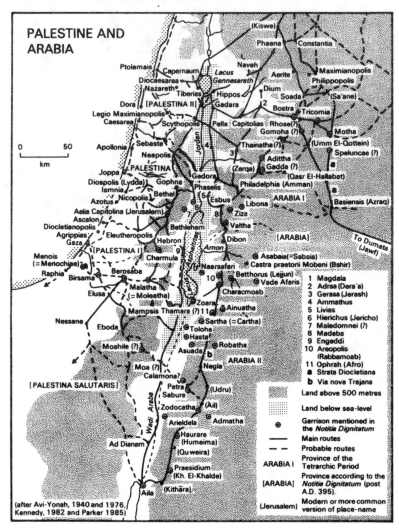

PALESTINE AND ARABIA

0 ___ 50
km

1 Magdala
2 Adraa (Dera'a)
3 Gerasa (Jerash)
4 Ammathus
5 Livias
6 Hиerichus (Jericho)
7 Maledomnei (?)
8 Madeba
9 Engeddi
10 Areopolis
    (Rabbamoab)
11 Ophrah (Afro)
a Strata Diocletiana
b Via nova Trajana

Land above 500 metres

Land below sea-level

⊙ Garrison mentioned in the *Notitia Dignitatum*

── Main routes

─ ─ Probable routes

ARABIA I Province of the Tetrarchic Period

[ARABIA] Province according to the *Notitia Dignitatum* (post A.D. 395).

(Jerusalem) Modern or more common version of place-name

(after Avi-Yonah, 1940 and 1976, Kennedy, 1982 and Parker 1985)

Map 4   Palestine and Arabia

6 Rome and Shapur II
Shapur and Constantine (c. 302–337)

6.1.1. The birth and childhood of Shapur II

Agathias, IV, 25, 2–5: But after them Shapur (II) enjoyed his kingdom for by far the longest time, and his reign was as long as his life. For, while his mother was still carrying him, the royal succession summoned the unborn child to the throne. It was not known whether the child would be a boy or a girl. 3. So all the political leaders offered prizes and gifts to the Magi if they could foretell what would come to pass. So they brought out a mare in foal that was very near her time, and told them to prophesy first about this, as they thought the result would be. In this way they reflected that they could know in a few days how their prophecies turned out and thus judge that whatever they prophesied about the woman would turn out in the same way. What they foretold about the mare I cannot say for sure, for I was not told all the details, except that everything came to pass exactly as they had predicted. 4. The others, judging from this that the Magi were accurate at their craft, urged them to reveal what they thought would happen in the case of the woman too. And when they said that the child would be a boy, they waited no longer but held the crown over her stomach and proclaimed the embryo king, designating by this name a creature just formed and shaped just enough, I suppose, to move about and kick a little inside. 5. And so they changed what is naturally uncertain and unknown by their expectation into revealed certainty, yet even so, their hopes did not fail them; they actually achieved their aim, and even more than they had expected. For not long afterwards Shapur was born, at the same time as his kingdom, and he grew up with it and grew old with it, his life lasting for seventy years.

(Cameron, pp. 123–5)

al-Tabari, p. 836 (Nöldeke, pp. 52–3): see Appendix 1, pp. 289–95.

6.1.2. The cruelty of Adarnases (Shahanshah 309/10)

John of Antioch, *frag.* 178 (*FHG* IV, p. 605): Adarnases,[1] then a child, was asked by his father Narses, the king of the Persians, if the tent which had been procured for him made out of Babylonian skins, was beautiful. But he replied that if he was governing the kingdom, he would make a more beautiful one out of human skins. When he came to power he was duly deprived of his kingship.

(Lieu)

Zonaras XIII, 5, 19–24 (iii, p. 190, 2–17, Dindorf): For Narses had three sons from the foremost of his wives, Adarnases, Hormisdas and a third.[2] Upon the death of Narses, the eldest of these three, Adarnases succeeded to the throne. 20. But he happened to be exceedingly cruel and harsh and for that reason was hated by the Persians and was deprived of his throne.
21. Let me mention a proverbial example of his cruelty. 22. A tent was once brought to his father from Babylon, rather cleverly made from the skins of the native animals. 23. After Narses had seen it stretched out, he asked Adarnases, who happened to be still a child whether he liked the tent. 24. But he answered that if he became king he would make a better one than that from the skins of men. Thus he revealed his cruelty in his childhood.

(Dodgeon)

6.1.3. The problems which beset the Sassanian Empire at the accession of Shapur II and his qualities as a monarch[3]

al-Tabari, pp. 836–7 (Nöldeke, pp. 53–5): see Appendix 1, p. 289.

6.1.4. His early wars against the Arabs

al-Tabari pp. 838–40 (Nöldeke, pp. 55–9): see Appendix 1, p. 291.

6.1.5. The Armenian campaign of Maximinus Daia (c. Nov., 312)

Eusebius, *hist. eccl.* IX, 8, 2–4: In addition to this, (i.e. a painful disease), the tyrant (i.e. Maximinus Daia)[4] had the further trouble of the war against the Armenians,[5] men who from ancient times had been friends and allies of the Romans; but as they were Christians[6] and exceedingly earnest in their piety towards the Deity, this hater of God (i.e. Maximinus Daia), by attempting to compel them to sacrifice to idols and demons, made of them foes instead of friends, and enemies instead of allies. . . . 4. He himself was worn out along with his commanders in the Armenian war; . . .

(Oulton, pp. 285–6)

Malalas, XII, p. 311, 2–14: After Diocletian had abdicated from imperial power, Maximianus, also called Herculi(an)us, reigned for nineteen years. On returning to Rome, he celebrated a triumph for the victory over the Persians and Egyptians. . . . In his reign, the Olympic Festival was celebrated at about the same time when he went to the East to fight the Armenians who had rebelled against the Romans. He triumphed over them and brought them under subjection.

(Dodgeon)

Ibid. pp. 312, 13–313, 2: At the same time the Persians allied themselves to the Armenians who were under attack and came with them against Roman territory and plundered the land. The same Maxentius[7] campaigned against them and made war upon the Persians; and coming against them he destroyed them throughout Armenia, and he detached districts from the Persarmenians and brought them under the Romans. He called that land the Armenia Prima and Secunda of the Romans. While the same Maxentius was in Persarmenia, the Persians broke into Osrhoene and captured a city and burned it and dug up its foundations. And taking great booty they suddenly retired. The city captured by them was called Maximianoupolis. The same emperor Maxentius re-established it and also put up its walls, and lavishing many benefits upon the survivors he relieved them of taxation for three years. And upon his return home he was killed at the age of fifty-three.

(Dodgeon)

al-Tabari, p. 840 (Nöldeke, pp. 58–9): see Appendix 1, pp. 291–2.

6.1.6. Formation of a mobile field army by Constantine (before 325)

Zosimus II, 34, 1–2: Constantine also adopted another measure which allowed the barbarians to penetrate the territories under

Roman domination without encountering any resistance. For, thanks to the forethought of Diocletian, as I have already described, the Roman Empire was protected on all its frontiers by cities, fortresses and signalling towers, in which the entire army was stationed. It was consequently impossible for the barbarians to cross the frontier as there was always sufficient force everywhere to counter and repulse them. 2. Constantine, however, abandoned this security by transferring the greater part of the soldiers from the frontier garrisons and installed them in cities that had no need of defenders,[8] thus depriving those who were exposed to the barbarians of every form of defence, and oppressing the tranquil cities with so great a multitude of soldiers that many of them were totally abandoned by their inhabitants. He likewise lowered the morale of the soldiers through regular shows and comfortable living. In plain terms, he was the original sower of the seeds of decline which afflict us all at present.

(Anon., revised Lieu)

6.2.1. Constantine rebuilt Chalcedon and his defeat by Persians (?) (c. 324)

Cedrenus, i, pp. 496, 5–497, 2: When he (i.e. Constantine) saw that a plague was beginning, he left this city (i.e. Thessalonica) and went to Chalcedon in Bithynia. Finding that it had been desolated by the Persians, he began to rebuild it. Immediately eagles snatched up the bricks of the workmen and hurled them in the direction of Byzantium. When this had happened many times and everyone was perplexed, one of those serving the emperor and by the name of Euphratas[9] explained that it was God's wish that a city be established there for his mother. And so he immediately crossed over and, when he had looked over the site and given it his approval, he left Euphratas with a mighty power and much money to oversee the work. The emperor himself went off against the Persians. There he met with a defeat and by the foresight of God he escaped from their hands and returned back to Byzantium. Euphratas however built the underground water channels and opened up all the springs of water and made a start upon the walls. Again, the Persians moved against Roman territory. The emperor gave instructions to Euphratas concerning the foundation of the temple, and himself took on the peopling of the city. Having received the rings of each of the leading citizens, he built magnificent houses and led their wives, children and all their households into the royal city. The emperor campaigned against the Persians once more, and when he had put them to flight he returned again.

(Dodgeon)

6.2.2. Victory (?) of Constantine over Shapur II and provincial reorganization (date unknown)

Malalas XIII, p. 317, 17–318, 3: And he (i.e. Constantine) campaigned against the Persians and was victorious and made a peace treaty with Sarabarus (i.e. Shapur II), King of the Persians, when the Persian requested to have peace with the Romans. The same emperor, Constantine, made Euphratensis a province (*eparchia*), separating it from Syria and Osrhoene and giving the rank of metropolis to Hierapolis.

(Dodgeon)

6.2.3. The flight of Hormisdas to Rome (324?)[10]

Ammianus Marcellinus XVI, 10, 16 : (AD 357) And the royal prince Hormisdas, whose departure from Persia we have already mentioned (i.e. in an earlier book of Ammianus' history which is now lost), standing by answered (the Emperor Constantius), with the refinement of his nature: . . .

(Yonge, p. 102)

Zosimus II, 27, 1–4: At this time a Persian named Hormisdas, of the royal family, came over to Constantine for asylum under the following circumstances. Once, when his father, then king of Persia, was celebrating his own birthday after the Persian manner, Hormisdas entered the palace, bringing with him a large quantity of game. But as the guests at the table did not make obeisance to him and did not even stand up as was the normal custom, he became furious, and told them he would punish them with the death of Marsyas. 2. This saying most of them did not understand, because it related to a foreign story; but one of them, who had lived in Phrygia, and had heard the story of Marsyas, explained to them the meaning of Hormisdas's menace, while they sat at table. It was so fixed in their recollection that when his father died, they remembered his threat, and chose his younger brother king, though according to law the elder should be preferred above the other children. Not contented with that, they put Hormisdas in chains, and confined him on a hill which lies before their city. 3. But after some time had elapsed, his wife effected his escape in this manner. She procured a large fish, and put a file in its belly, and, sewing it up again, delivered it to the most loyal of her eunuchs, charging him to tell Hormisdas that he must eat the fish when no one was present, and use what he should find in its belly for his escape. When she had contrived this, she sent several camels loaded with wine, and an abundance of meat, to entertain her husband's guards. 4. While they were enjoying the feast she gave them, Hormisdas cut open the fish, and found the file; and with that he filed off the shackles from his legs. He then put on the clothes of the eunuch, and passed through the midst of his keepers, who were by that time completely intoxicated. Taking one of the eunuchs along with him, he fled to the king of Armenia, who was his friend and host. By these means he got safely to Constantine, who showed him all possible kindness and respect.

(Anon., revised Lieu)

John of Antioch, *frag.* 178, *FHG* IV, p. 605: ... he (*sc.* Adarnases) had two brothers; one of them, Shapur, he blinded when he came to power and the other, Hormisdas, he had incarcerated. His (i.e. Hormisdas') mother, however, with his wife as accomplice, prepared by some contrivance iron chains, the inside of which she filled with pearls, and, having procured the favour of the guards, took away his former chains as they were heavy and had them replaced by those (which she had prepared); so that should he be able to flee, he would be carrying riches without the weight. His wife then gave him a file and treated the guards to a meal and caused them to fall asleep. He found a suitable moment and cut the fetters and fled, using a horse at intervals and dressed in the guise of a slave. He was received with honour by Licinius.[11] He was such a good javelin-thrower, however, that he alone was reported to have possessed a spear which was unstained which thereafter he was depicted as holding in his statue.

(Lieu)

Suidas, s. v. 'Marsuas', ed. Adler, ii, p. 331: In the days of the Judges of Judaea (i.e. in Old Testament times) there was a clever man called Marsuas, who invented flutes of reeds and brass through his musical skills. In a fit of depression he threw himself into the river and perished. The river was named after him. The myth concerning him says that he ran away and took his own life. This took place at the same time as the happenings of Jason and the

Argonauts as told by Apollonius of Rhodes. A (related) story is told of Hormisdas the Persian who deserted to Constantine the Great, that after having been out hunting he was not greeted on his return to the palace by those invited to dinner with the usual respect by standing up. He therefore threatened them with the death of Marsyas. Those of the Persians (i.e. the nobles) who learned the meaning of this from someone who had heard (the story) proclaimed the younger son as king after the death of the father. Hormisdas they put into prison and fastened him with chains. His wife brought him out by means of a fish with a (metal) file concealed in it. He escaped and came as a suppliant to Constantine. The story is well known.

(Lieu)

Zonaras XIII, 5, 25–33 (iii, pp. 190, 17–191, 9, Dindorf): For when this man (i.e. Adarnases) was deprived of his kingship in this fashion, Shapur (i.e. Shapur II) was made king in his place. 26. And he immediately blinded one of his brothers and put Hormisdas in chains and kept him under guard. 27. But his (i.e. Hormisdas') wife and mother won over the guards with money and were allowed to go in (the prison) for a visit. 28. And when they entered, they provided him with a file so that with it he might cut through his iron chains. They had also made preliminary plans about what he needed to do after this and had prepared horses for him and men to accompany him on his flight. 29. Then his wife provided the guards with a sumptuous dinner. Filled with an excessive amount of meat and an even more excessive quantity of wine, they were overpowered by a heavy slumber. 30. While they were asleep, Hormisdas cut through his chains with the file and once he left the prison he fled to the Romans and was received with great honour. 31. But it is likely that Shapur rejoiced at his flight inasmuch as he had rid himself of fear from that quarter. For not only did he not request that the fugitive be returned to him, but he also sent his wife to him with great honour. 32. Hormisdas was a man of great strength and a skilful javelin-thrower, such that in casting the javelin at someone he would predict where he would strike the enemy. 33. So this man then campaigned with Constantius against his fellow-countrymen, being appointed to the command of a large troop of cavalrymen.

(Dodgeon)

6.2.4. Construction of a reservoir on the Syrian *limes* (324)

AE 1948, 136 (Latin inscription found about 30 miles east of Mafraq in Transjordan): Vincentius, who was acting as *protector* at

Basia,[12] observing that many of the outlying pickets had been ambushed and killed by the Saracens while fetching water for themselves, laid out and constructed a reservoir for the water. He did this in the consulship of Optatus and Paulinus, both distinguished persons (*vir clarissimus*).

(Iliffe, 1942: 62, revised)

6.2.5. Letter of Constantini the Great to Shapur II (after 324?)

Eusebius, *vita Constantini* IV, 8–13, ed. Winkelmann, GCS: The king of the Persians also made known a desire to form an alliance with Constantine, by sending an embassy and presents as assurances of peace and friendship. The emperor, in negotiating this treaty, far surpassed the monarch who first paid him homage in the magnificence with which he acknowledged his gifts. When he heard, too, that there were many churches of God in Persia,[13] and that large numbers there were gathered into the fold of Christ, he rejoiced at this information and resolved to extend his solicitude for the general welfare to that country also, as one whose aim it was to care for all alike in every nation. He demonstrated this in his own words through the letter which he dispatched to the king of the Persians, putting their (i.e. the Christians') case in the most tactful and sensible manner. This royal missive, which the emperor himself composed, is in circulation among us in the Roman tongue but has been translated into Greek so that it would be more accessible to the readers. The text is as follows:

9   Letter of the Emperor to Shapur, king of the Persians, concerning his care over the people of God.[14]

'By protecting the Divine faith, I am made a partaker of the light of truth: guided by the light of truth, I advance in the knowledge of the Divine faith. Hence it is that, as my actions themselves evince, I profess the most holy religion; and this worship I declare to be that which teaches me deeper acquaintance with the most holy God; allied to whose Divine power, beginning from the very borders of the ocean, I have aroused the whole empire in succession to a well-grounded hope of security; so that all those who, groaning in servitude to the most cruel tyrants, and yielding to the pressure of their daily sufferings, and almost extinct, have shared in the general amnesty and regained new life as if through a healing process. This God I confess I hold in unceasing honour and his symbol is borne on the shoulders by my god-fearing army which is guided wheresoever the word of the righteous one urges, and from them I immediately receive his favour through magnificent victories. This God I confess to honour with undying regard and him I discern clearly with a pure and innocent mind to be clearly in the highest.

10 This God I invoke with bended knees, and recoil with horror from the blood of sacrifices, from their foul and detestable odours, and from every earthly lamp,[15] for the profane and impious superstitions which are defiled by these rites have cast down the whole race of the Gentiles and consigned it to the lowest regions. 2. For the God of all cannot endure that those gifts which, in his own loving-kindness and consideration of the needs of men, he has revealed for the use of all, should be perverted by the lusts of individuals. His only demand from man is purity of mind and an unblemished soul: and by this standard he weighs their deeds of virtue and piety. 3. For he takes pleasure in works of moderation and gentleness: he loves the meek, and hates those who excite contentions; delighting in faith, he chastises unbelief: by him all presumptuous power is broken down, and he punishes overweening pride. While the arrogant and haughty are utterly overthrown, he requites the humble and forgiving with deserved rewards: 4. even so does he highly honour and strengthen with his special help a kingdom justly governed, and preserves the royal counsel in the tranquillity of peace.

11 'I cannot, then, my brother, believe that I err in acknowledging this one God, the ruler and father of all things; whom many of my predecessors in power, led astray by insane madness, have ventured to deny, but who were all visited by such a visible vengeance, that all succeeding generations have held up their calamities as the most effectual warning to any who desire to follow in their steps. 2. Of the number of these I believe him[16] to have been, whom the lightning-stroke of Divine anger drove forth from hence, and banished to your dominions, and leaves among you a notorious legacy of the disgrace that fell upon him.

12 'And it is surely a happy circumstance that the vengeance on such persons as I have described should have so recently been publicly manifested. For I myself have witnessed the end of those who lately harassed the worshippers of God by their impious edicts. And for this abundant thanksgivings are due to God that through his excellent foresight all men who observe his holy laws are gladdened by the renewed enjoyment of peace. Hence I am fully persuaded that everything is in the best and safest arrangement since God deems it worthy, through the influence of their pure and faithful religious service, and their unity of judgement respecting his Divine character, to gather all men to himself.

13 'Imagine, then, with what joy I received information so accordant with my desire, that the finest provinces of Persia are filled with those men on whose behalf alone I am at present speaking, I mean the Christians. For abundant blessing will be to you and to them in equal amounts, for you will find the Lord of the whole world is gentle, merciful and beneficent. And now, because your power is great, I commend these persons to your protection; because your piety is eminent, I commit them to your care. Cherish them with your customary humanity and kindness; for by this proof of faith you will secure an immeasurable benefit both to yourself and us.'

(Richardson, pp. 542–4, revised)

Michael the Syrian, *Chron.* VII, 3, p. 132 (Syriac): The pagans (in Persia) slandered the Christians to Shapur, their king, (accusing them) of sending an embassy to the Roman emperor. Shapur became angry and began to oppress the Christians and destroy their churches. Constantine the Victorious wrote to him saying: 'Considering that I keep the divine faith, I dwell in the light of truth; and conduct myself according to the light of the truth, I profess the true faith, etc.' Shapur not only did not accept his words, but he immediately went up against Nisibis. He withdrew from there covered in confusion, thanks to the prayers of Mar Jacob and Mar Ephrem. In his anger, he took captives from Mesopotamia.[17]

(Vince, revised Brock)

6.2.6. Dedication to Constantine and his family from Arabia (between 326 and 333)

Kennedy, 1982: 90–1 (inscr. 13),[18] (Latin building inscription set up in the entrance of Qasr el-Azraq): To Constantine the Great, Devout, Victorious and Ever Triumphant [Augustus] and Constantine and Constantius, noblest Caesars. Fl(avius) Severinus[19] had commanded [. . .][20] which had collapsed into ruins through incurable old age [to be rebuilt (or repaired) . . .][21]

6.3.1. Unrest in Armenia leading to Persian intervention (?)[22]

Faustus Buzandats'i, *Hist. Arm.* III, 20–1, *FHG* V, pp. 229–31 (Arm.): see below Appendix 2, pp. 303–9.

Moses Khorenats'i, *Hist. Arm.* III, 10 (Thomson, pp. 263–4): see below Appendix 2, pp. 323–4.

6.3.2. The 'lies of Metrodorus' (326/7)

Ammianus Marcellinus, XXV, 4, 23: (AD 363) And since his (i.e. Julian's) detractors have accused him of provoking new wars, to the injury of the commonwealth, let them know the unquestionable truth, that it was not Julian but Constantine who occasioned the hostility of the Parthians (*sic*) by greedily acquiescing in the falsehoods of Metrodorus, as I have explained a while ago.

(Yonge, p. 387, revised)

Cedrenus, i, pp. 516, 12–517, 15: In the twenty-first year of the emperorship of the great Constantine (326/7) they set Shapur the king of the Persians against the Christians, and there arose a persecution so that more than eighteen thousand were destroyed by him. The reason for the breaking of the peace between the Romans and the Persians was the following. A certain Metrodorus, born in Persia, affecting to love wisdom, went away to the Brahmins in India.[23] By exercising great self-control he became venerable among them. He constructed water mills and bathing places, until then unknown among them. He entered into shrines as being a man of piety and stole many precious stones and pearls. He also received (them) from the king of the Indians to take as presents to the emperor. When he returned to Byzantium he gave these to the emperor as though they were his own property. And when the emperor was amazed he said that he had sent others overland, but they had been confiscated by the Persians.[24] Therefore Constantine wrote brusquely to Shapur for them to be sent, and when he (*sc*. Shapur) received (the letter) he did not reply. For this reason the peace was broken.

(Dodgeon)

6.3.3. Caesar Constantius was sent to take command of the Eastern frontier (c. 336)

Julian, *Orationes* I, 13B (= I, 9.46–52, p. 24, Bidez): Accordingly, after you (i.e. Constantius) had gained much valuable experience among (the Celts), you crossed to the other continent and were given sole command against the Parthians and the Medes. There were already signs that a war was smouldering and would soon burst into flame. You therefore quickly learned how to deal with it and, as though you took as model the hardness of your weapons, steeled yourself to bear the heat of the summer season.

(Wright, i, p. 33, revised)

6.3.4. Narses, brother (?) of Shapur II, captured Amida but was killed in battle (at Narasara?) (c. 336?)

Festus, *breviarium* 27, p. 67, 2–3: Nevertheless at the battle of Narasara[25] where Narses was killed, we (i.e. the Romans) were the winners.

Theophanes, *Chronographia*, A.M. 5815, p. 20, 21–6, ed. de Boor: In this same year (336), Narses, the son (*sic*) of the Persian king, overran Mesopotamia and captured the city of Amida. The Caesar Constantius, son of Constantine, made war on him; and suffered minor setbacks. Eventually he inflicted such a defeat on him in battle that Narses himself was killed.

(Dodgeon)

6.3.5. Refortification of the city of Amida by the Caesar Constantius (before 337)

Ammianus Marcellinus XVIII, 9, 1: (AD 359) The city (i.e. Amida) was once a very small one, till Constantius, when he was Caesar, surrounded it with strong towers and stout walls, at the same time that he built another town called Antinopolis, so that the people in the neighbourhood might have a safe place of refuge. And he placed there an arsenal of mural artillery, making it a formidable redoubt, as he had wished it to be called by his own name.

(Yonge, p. 183, revised)

History of Jacob the Recluse,[26] ed. Nau, 1915–1917: 7.1–5 (Syriac): After the Emperor Constantius, son of Constantine the Great, had built Amida, he loved it more than all the cities of his empire and submitted to it many lands, from Reshaina (*sic*) as far as Nisibis and also the land of Maipharqat and of Arzon and as far as the frontiers of Qardou. Because these lands were on the Persian frontier, Persian brigands made continual incursions into these territories and devastated them.

(Vince, revised Brock)

6.4.1. Constantine appointed his nephew Hannibalianus as 'King of Kings and of the Pontic peoples' (335)

Epitome de Caesaribus 41, 20: They (i.e. sons and relatives of Constantine) individually governed these regions: ... Hannibalianus,[27] brother of Delmatius Caesar, Armenia and the surrounding peoples.

(Dodgeon)

Anonymus Valesianus[28] 6, 35: He (Constantine) ... created Dalmatius' brother, Hannibalianus, King of Kings[29] and ruler of the Pontic tribes, after giving him his daughter Constantina in marriage.

(Rolfe)

Chronicon Paschale, p. 532, 1–3: And Hannibalianus he (i.e. Constantine) appointed as king and put on him the purple cloak and sent him to Caesarea in Cappadocia.

(Dodgeon)

6.4.2. Constantine's preparation for war against the Persians and his death (22 May, 337)

Eusebius, *Vita Constantini* IV, 56: It is worthy to record that about the time of which I am at present writing, the emperor (i.e. Constantine), having heard of an insurrection of some barbarians in the East, observed that the conquest of this enemy was still in store for him, and resolved on an expedition against the Persians. 2. Accordingly, he proceeded at once to put his forces in motion, at the same time communicating his intended march to the bishops who happened to be at his court, some of whom he judged it right to take with him as companions, and as needful coadjutors in the service of God. 3. They, on the other hand, cheerfully declared their willingness to follow in his train, disclaiming any desire to leave him, and engaging to battle with and for him by supplication to God on his behalf. Full of joy at this answer to his request, he unfolded to them his projected line of march, ...[30]

(Richardson, pp. 554–5)

Libanius, *Orationes* LIX, 60–75: However, the Persian nation raised its rebellious arm against him (i.e. Constantine), excellent as he was in all aspects and accustomed to victory and experienced in the art of war. And, should any knowledgeable person examine the dates, he will find the beginning of the war preceding Constantine's death, so that, although the war was waged against him, the labour of the war fell on his son. 61. So for what purpose do I say this and what did I want when I introduced the subject? Because if they were at peace when he was alive, but when he quit his life, they rushed into arms, they would not have seemed to themselves to be showing confidence rather than despising their life after Constantine; for if they had made his life the limit of their peace, they would have demonstrated this to everyone. But when they learnt that he was entering the risk of that war, it was clear that they began the war in confidence in their circumstances, but not in the thought that their fear had been utterly destroyed.

62. Accordingly, I wish to relate what induced the Persians to stand such a great hazard. And indeed it does not even seem reasonable to anyone who straightway hears it that those who were content in earlier times, if one did not trouble them, should have wished to go to war when it was possible to live in peace. Therefore I wish to say this in a somewhat concise fashion, as to be clear to all, namely, that they did not come to war for a trifling purpose. 63. What was being done by the Persians was not peace but a delay in war, and they did not even desire peace so they should not fight a war, but they loved peace so as to fight a proper war.[31] They were not even altogether shunning the running of a risk, but, in preparing for the magnitude of the dangers they mixed after a fashion peace with war. They offered a peaceful appearance, but had the disposition of men at war. For when they were caught unprepared and were heavily defeated in earlier times, they did not blame their own good courage but they cited as the reason their deficiency of preparation. They agreed to peace for a preparation of war, and continued indeed to acquit their obligations towards the treaty from that time onwards through embassies and gifts, but arranged everything towards that purpose. 64. They equipped their own forces and brought their preparation to perfection in every form, cavalry, men-at-arms, archers and slingers. They trained to a consummate degree what methods had been their practice from the beginning, but those of which they did not have the understanding they introduced from others. They did not give up their native customs, but added to their existing methods a more remarkable power. 65. But, hearing that his forefathers Darius and Xerxes had measured out their preparation for ten years against the Greeks, he despised them for an inadequate attempt; he himself resolved to prolong the period to four decades. During the occurrence of this interval there was gathered a mass of money and there was collected a multitude of men, and a stock-pile of arms was forged. But

already he had collected a stock of elephants, not just for empty show, but to meet the needs of the future. Everyone was warned to dismiss all other pursuits and practise warfare; and the old were not to depart from arms and the youngest were to be enrolled; they handed the care of the fields to their women and passed their life in arms.

66. It is worthwhile to bring in the open a matter that surpasses many others, which all but escaped my notice. (For) the king of the Persians praised one section of his own land, but found fault with another. For he did not consider it was second to any other as regards the production of manpower, but he found fault with the country because it did not arm the courage of its manpower by revealing a domestic source of iron.[32] The sum of the matter was that he understood how to govern men but that his power was defective through the shortage of equipment (implements). 67. When, therefore, he sat and considered this and fretted over it to a very great extent, he came to the decision to enter upon a deceitful and treacherous path and sent an embassy and became flattering, as was his practice; he made obeisance through his envoys and asked for a great supply of iron, under the pretext that it was for use against another nation of neighbouring barbarians, but in truth he had decided to use the gift against the donors. But the emperor was well aware of the real motive, for the nature of the recipient caused suspicion. But knowing exactly in what direction the benefits of the technology were leading, though it was possible to resist, he gave with eagerness and saw through his reasoning all that would happen as if it had already occurred, but he felt shame at leaving his son enemies who were unarmed. He wanted every excuse of the Persians to be refuted first, but he blocked off his opponents to a nicety, so that although they flourished in all aspects they would be brought low. For the splendour of those defeated contributes to the glory of the conquerors. 68. The emperor readily gave with this magnanimity and hope(s) as wishing to make plain that even if they exhausted the mines of the Chalybes, they would not appear superior through this to the men by whom they were rated as inferior. But thereupon the preparation of the Persian king was complete both from native resources and from external supplies. Some supplies existed in abundance and others had been added surplus to requirements. 69. Indeed, darts, sabres (scimitars?), spears, swords and every warlike implement were forged in a wealth of material. When he examined every possibility and left nothing not investigated, he contrived to make his cavalry invulnerable, so

to speak. For he did not limit their armour to helmet, breastplate and greaves in the ancient manner nor even to place bronze plates before the brow and breast of the horse; but the result was that the man was covered in chain mail from his head to the end of his feet, and the horse from its crown to the tip of its hooves, but a space was left open only for the eyes to see what was happening and for breathing holes to avoid asphyxiation. 70. You would have said that the name of 'bronze men' was more appropriate for these than for the soldiers in Herodotus. These men had to ride a horse which obeyed their voice instead of a bridle, and they carried a lance which needed both hands, and had as their only consideration that they should fall upon their enemies without a thought for their action, and they entrusted their body to the protection of iron mail.[33] 71. When therefore everything was readied and his power was prepared in everything, he could no longer restrain himself. But he saw the multitude of his army and he saw the unbreakable nature of their armour, and he reckoned up the length of their preparation and the period of training; he imagined the hope of successful fortune and sent an embassy to dispute about the borders so that, should we retire from our territory, he might win it without effort, but if we in no way conceded, he might advance this pretext for war.

72. But after the great emperor heard, he hated the Persian for his arrogance and said that he wished to give him his answer in person. And action followed upon words. When he arose, everything was immediately put into action. Having recently undertaken the journey, he came in this city; the Almighty saw that he was inscribed upon many trophies, but that of his two sons the one who had been appointed against the Persians should gain distinction by victories over the barbarians. Having made such a decision, He called the old emperor to Himself, but brought the task and delivered it to the son.

73. And so it is easy to conjecture how what had happened excited the Persians to an act of daring and how they considered they already possessed the cities, but a guardian had been left for them 'far greater', to quote Homer, than any other in reality in anything. However, at that critical time there occurred a need for two very important decisions. For on the one side his father's burial drew his attention, and on the other the din of the Persian onset. His choice was either to meet the enemy and neglect the funeral rites or to observe the rites and open the empire to the enemy. 74. So what did he do? He did not consider advantage more highly than the rites, but rather both duties were successfully combined and the

secondary purpose of the journey was more honourable than any deed. For he himself hastened energetically to the burial, but fear held the Persians back in their own land. Whether they received their fright from heaven and 'drew in their sails' or whether it was through not knowing anything of his retreat but thinking they would feel the emperor's right hand, nevertheless each explanation is sufficient for a eulogy. For the one has proof of God's favour, and the other holds evidence of the efficiency in his government, if indeed the facts of his absence eluded the enemy. 75. However, he accomplished his other duties and met with his brother who is in every way deserving of our admiration; and, hearing that his adversaries as though smitten by God had quit the river bank, he did not suffer this which had long been common talk nor even did he wait for an accident of relief to occur, as the talk wished, and (so) employ the remainder of his time; but considering that such times of crisis needed action, not hope, he again ran and completed the homeward course as if in all truth he was running up and down continually in a stadium rather than traversing the greater part of the world.

(Dodgeon, revised Lieu)

Aurelius Victor, *liber de Caesaribus* 41, 16: In the thirty-second year of his reign, and after thirteen years of sole rule and having completed more than sixty-two years of his life, he marched against the Persians, with whom he would have begun open hostilities, when he died in a region near to Nicomedia called Achyrona, since this catastrophe was portended by the star of the realm which was called a comet.

(Dodgeon)

Festus, *breviarium*, 26, p. 66, 6–13: Constantine, the Lord of the realm, prepared an expedition against the Persians towards the end of his life. For after he had pacified the peoples throughout the world and while enjoying increased renown from his recent victory over the Goths, he marched upon the Persians with every battalion at his disposal. At the news of his coming, the court at Babylonia went into such a panic that a suppliant legation of Persians went to him with all haste, promising to do what he commanded.[34] However they did not even earn a pardon for the incessant incursions which had beset the Orient under Constantius Caesar.

(Dodgeon)

Jerome, *Chronicon*, s. a. 337, p. 234, 8–10: Constantine, while he was preparing for war against the Persians, died in Ancyrona, a public villa near to Nicomedia, in the sixty-sixth year of his life.[35]

(Dodgeon)

Eutropius, *breviarium* X, 8, 2: As he (i.e. Constantine) was preparing for war against the Parthians (*sic*), who were then disturbing Mesopotamia, he died in the Villa Publica, at Nicomedia, in the thirty-first year of his reign, and sixty-sixth year of his age. His death was foretold by a star with a tail, which shone for a long time, of extraordinary size, and which the Greeks called a comet. He was deservedly enrolled among the gods.

(Watson, revised Lieu)

Anonymus Valesianus 6, 35: While Constantine was planning to make war on the Persians, he died in an imperial villa in the suburbs of Constantinople, not far from Nicomedia, leaving the state in good order to his sons. He was buried in Constantinople, after a reign of thirty-one years.

(Rolfe, p. 531)

Orosius, *adversus paganos* VII, 28, 31: And while he was preparing for war against the Persians, he died in his official residence near Nicomedia, leaving the state in very good order for his sons

(Deferrari, p. 331)

Chronicon Paschale, pp. 532, 7–21: (In this year, i.e. 337) the Persians declared war against the Romans and Constantine crossed over (to Asia) in the thirty-second year of his reign, and came to the East to campaign against the Persians. He went as far as Nicomedia and yielded his life gloriously and piously in a suburb of that city on the eleventh day of the month of Artemisia, after having been deemed worthy of salvific baptism by Eusebius, Bishop of Constantinople. He reigned for thirty-one years and ten months. He left behind as Caesars his three sons: Caesar Constantine who held power over the Gallic (parts) for twenty years, Caesar Constantius who reigned after him over the East(ern parts) for eleven years and Caesar Constans who has gone over to the Italian (parts) and is now in the third year of his reign and also Caesar Dalmatius, son of his brother, also in the third year of his reign in Mesopotamia.

(Dodgeon)

Chronicon Paschale p. 533, 5–17: ... Constantius, who was in the East and in Mesopotamia while the Persian war was pending, immediately set off for Constantinople upon receiving the news (of his father's illness). On reaching the city he had (the body of) his famous father carried by the imperial guard in such array and pomp which it is hard to describe properly. The whole garrison turned out fully armed, as during his lifetime, seeing that the whole city was renamed Rome by him and there were just as many splendid (buildings) in her and doles of free corn. Everyone was deep in mourning as no emperor before him had been held in such honour, either living or dead. He was buried in the church of the Apostles, in which lay the relics of the holy apostles Andrew and Luke (the Evangelist) and Timothy, the disciple of Paul the Apostle.

(Dodgeon)

Artemii passio 8 (8.12–19, p. 206, ed. Kotter, see also GCS Philostorgius, pp. 28, 6–29): When the great Constantine ended his life, the Roman Empire was divided into three governing parts and portioned out to his sons, Constantine (II), Constantius (II) and Constans ... Constantius, the second son of Constantine, who was then in charge of the affairs of the East, fighting against the Persians, received the eastern part (of the Empire). He changed the name of Byzantium into Constantinople and made it a new Rome, a capital. Whatever lands from Illyricum to the Propontis which were subject to Rome, Syria, Palestine and Mesopotamia and all the islands were made subject to tribute to his imperial rule and administration.

(Dodgeon)

Theophanes, *Chronographia*, A.M. 5828, p. 33, 15–22: In that same year (337) many of the Assyrians among (or subjected to) the Persians were sold as slaves in Mesopotamia by the Saracens. The Persians declared war against the Romans and the pious Constantine crossed over to Nicomedia to meet the Persians in battle. He became ill and passed away in peace. Some Arian-minded persons say that it was then that he received the holy baptism from Eusebius of Nicomedia, then translated to Constantinople. This is a lie as can be demonstrated, for he was baptized in Rome by the bishop Silvester, as we have already shown.

(Dodgeon)

Zonaras, XIII, 4, 25–8 (iii, pp. 186, 28–187, 9, Dindorf): He (Constantine) set out for war against the Persians and sailed by trireme to Soteriopolis which is now called Pythia, and there partook of the waters of the hot-springs and there he drank a

poisonous drug, mixed for him, it is said, by his half-brothers and
finally he reached Nicomedia. There he died after a long illness. He
was then sixty-five years old and just two months short of having
been emperor for thirty-two of these years. His son Constantius
came to him from Antioch (for he was there to resist the Persians)
and found him still alive, (and, after he died) he buried him with
great magnificence and placed his body in the Church of the Holy
Apostles, in a special vault which he had built over his father's tomb.

(Dodgeon)

Michael the Syrian, *Chronicon* VII, 3, pp. 133–4 (Syriac): Constantine went out to fight the Persians. Having reached Nicomedia, he
fell ill and was baptised in this place, for he had not yet been
baptized because he wanted to be baptized in the Jordan. He made
his will in the hands of a priest who had been recommended to him
by his sister, and who was an Arian. In all he lived sixty-five years
and reigned for thirty-two of them. He died on Whitsunday the
22nd of Iyar (May), the first year of the 279th Olympiad, in the
654th year of the Greeks. His body was taken to Constantinople
and placed in the church of the Apostles.

(Vince, revised Brock)

6.4.3. Hope for Roman victory as expressed by a Christian writer in Persia (*c.* 337)

'Aphrahat',[36] *demonstratio* V, 1; 24 and 25, *PS* 1.184, ff. (Syriac):
Prosperity has come to the people of God, and success awaits the
man through whom the prosperity came (i.e. Constantius). And
disaster threatens the forces which have been marshalled by the
efforts of an evil and arrogant man full of boasting (i.e. Shapur II)
and misery is reserved for him through whom disaster is stored up.
Nevertheless, my beloved, do not complain (in public) of the evil
one who has stirred up evil upon many because the times were
preordained and the time of their fulfilment has come. . . .

24. My beloved, as for what I have written to you about, namely
that the kingdom of the children of Esau is being kept safe for its
Giver, have no doubt about it, as that kingdom (i.e. the Roman
Empire) will not be conquered. For a hero whose name is Jesus shall
come with his power and his armour shall uphold all the forces of
the kingdom. . . .

25. For even if the forces (i.e. the Persian army) shall go up and
triumph, realize that this is the chastisement of God, and if they

win they shall be condemned in a righteous judgement. Yet, be assured of this, that the beast will be killed at its appointed time. But you, my brother, implore earnestly at this time for mercy that there may be peace upon the people of God.

(Gwynn, pp. 352 and 361–2, altered)

6.4.4. The career of a descendant of a Roman prisoner of war in the Persian Empire

Acts of Pusai 2, *AMS* II, pp. 208–9 (Syriac): The heroic Pusai, then, was descended from prisoners [of war], whom Shapur, son of Hormizd brought from Bet Romaye (i.e. the Roman Empire) and settled in Veh-Shapur, a city in the province of Pars. . . . He had lived in this world peacefully as a Christian before his imprisonment.[37] He lived on the command of the king in Veh-Shapur and held the office of superintendent (?). He took a Persian wife from the city, converted her, baptized his children, and brought them up in and taught them Christianity. When Shapur (II) had built the city of Karka de Ladan and settled there captives from various places, he also thought of bringing and settling about thirty families apiece from each of the ethnic groups living in the various cities of his empire among them, so that as a result of inter-marriage, the captives would be bound by family ties and affection, and it would therefore not be easy for them to flee gradually back to their homeland. This was Shapur's clever plan; but God in his mercy used it to the good, so that through this mixing of those deported with the pagans, the latter were caught in the recognition of truth and converted to knowledge of the faith. Like other families from various regions settled in Karka on the order of Shapur, the son of Hormizd, some were brought from Veh-Shapur in Pars. Among these brought from Veh-Shapur and settled in Karka de Ladan were the blessed Pusai, his wife, his children, his brothers and sisters and his whole household. Pusai was an excellent craftsman and was expert in weaving and embroidering gold ornaments. He was also among those craftsmen whom the king gathered from the various ethnic groups, from the deported and from his subjects, and whom he formed into an association with many subdivisions and for whom he fitted out a workshop next to his palace in Karka de Ladan. As the blessed Pusai was skilled in his craft, he was commended before the king, who continually showered him with honours and presents and made him, after a short time, chief craftsman, as he excelled himself daily and increasingly won praise.

(Jordan, revised Brock)

7 Rome and Shapur II

The early wars of Constantius II
(337–350)

7.1.1. Hannibalianus, the king of Pontus and neighbouring regions, was murdered by soldiers loyal to Constantius in a palace coup (337)

Julian, *epistula ad Athenienses* 270C (3.5–8, p. 215, Bidez): Six of my (i.e. Julian's) cousins and his, and my father who was his own uncle and also another uncle of both of us on the father's side (i.e. Dalmatius Caesar) he put to death without a trial[1]. . .

(Wright, ii, p. 249)

Zosimus II, 40, 3: Then, in order to proceed against his relatives, he (Constantius) killed Hannibalianus and commanded his soldiers to cry aloud that they had no other commanders than the sons of Constantine.

(Anon., revised Lieu)

7.1.2. Unrest in Armenia as a consequence of the murder of Hannibalianus (?)

Julian, *or.* I, 18D–19A (14.16–22, pp. 31–2, Bidez):
The Armenians, our ancient allies, revolted, and no small part of them went over to the Persians and overran and raided the country on their borders.[2] In this crisis there seemed to be but one hope of safety, that you (i.e. Constantius) should take charge of affairs and plan the campaign, but at the moment this was impossible, because you were in Paeonia (i.e. Pannonia) making treaties with your brothers . . .[3]

(Wright, i, pp. 47–9)

7.1.3. The first siege of Nisibis (337 or 338)

Jerome, *Chronicon*, s. a. 338, p. 234, 17–18: Shapur, king of the

Persians, besieged Nisibis for two months after laying waste to Mesopotamia.[4]

Jerome *Chronicon*, p. 234, 24–5: Bishop Jacob of Nisibis came to be recognized. The city was frequently delivered from danger through his prayers.

Theodoret, *Historia religiosa* I, 11–12, edd. Canivet and Leroy-Molinghen, pp. 184–8: After the passage of time that great and admirable emperor yielded up his life, with its crowns of piety, and his sons inherited his authority. At this moment the king of the Persians, whose name was Shapur and who despised the sons of Constantine as being less capable than their father, marched against Nisibis at the head of a vast army comprising both cavalry and infantry, and also as many elephants as he could muster. He divided his army as for a siege and completely surrounded the city, setting up machines of war, commissioning towers, erecting palisades, the areas between strewn with branches placed crosswise, then he ordered his troops to raise embankments and build towers against the city towers. Then, while dispatching his archers to ascend the towers and direct their arrows at those defending the walls, at the same time he charged others with undermining the walls from below. Yet all these plans came to nothing, rendered useless by the prayers of Jacob,[5] that inspired man, until finally, by prodigious effort, Shapur stopped up the course of the river which flowed past the city and when as vast an amount as possible of the accumulating water had piled up behind the dam, he released it all at once against the walls, using it like a tremendously powerful battering-ram. The wall could not withstand the force of the water, and indeed, badly shaken by the flood, the whole stretch of that side of the city collapsed.[6] Then there arose a great shout, as though the city were now ready for the taking; for they had overlooked the great wall formed by the city's inhabitants. However, the Persians postponed their assault, since they could see that the water flooding into the city made access impossible. Retreating, then, some distance, as though relaxing their efforts, they rested themselves and tended their horses. The citizens, on the other hand, redoubled their prayers, with the noble Jacob as their intercessor. All those old enough to be of use set to in earnest to rebuild their defences, without regard to appearance or neatness of construction: indeed they threw everything together, pell-mell, stones and bricks, whatever they could carry, and in one night the work progressed and attained a sufficient height to prevent either a cavalry charge or an assault by troops with scaling-ladders. Then everyone begged the man of God to show himself on the ramparts and hurl imprecations down over the enemy. He agreed and mounted the wall, and looking out over the vast multitude of the enemy he prayed to God to send upon them a cloud of gnats and mosquitoes.[7] He spoke, and the Lord, persuaded as he was by Moses, delivered. The men were mortally wounded by the heaven-sent darts, the horses and elephants broke their tethers and escaped, plunging this way and that, unable to bear the stings.

12. The impious king saw now that all his machines had brought him no advantage, that the flooding of the river had been in vain– for the breach in the wall had been repaired –, and that his entire army was exhausted from its labours, suffering badly from exposure and lack of shelter and harassed by this blow from the heavens. When, on top of this, he saw the holy man walking upon the ramparts, he supposed it was the emperor in person who presided over the operations – for he seemed to be wearing the purple robe and the diadem –, and then he turned in anger on those who had deceived him and advised him to undertake this campaign, guaranteeing that the emperor was not present. He condemned them to death, disbanded his army and returned to his royal palace as quickly as possible.

(Dodgeon)

Theodoret, *Historia Ecclesiastica* II, 30, 1–14, GCS: As soon as Shapur, the king of the Persians, had declared war against the Romans, Constantius mustered his forces and marched to Antioch. But the enemy were driven forth, not by the Roman army, but by Him whom the pious in the Roman host worshipped as their God. How the victory was won I shall now proceed to relate. 2. Nisibis, sometimes called Antiochia Mygdonia, lies on the confines of the realms of Persia and of Rome. In Nisibis, Jacob whom I named just now was at once bishop, guardian, and commander in chief. 3. He was a man who shone with the grace of a truly apostolic character. His extraordinary and memorable miracles, which I have fully related in my *Religious History*,[8] I think it superfluous and irrelevant to enumerate again. One, however, I will record because of the subject before us. The city which Jacob ruled was now in the possession of the Romans, and besieged by the Persian army. 4. The blockade was prolonged for seventy days. 'Helepoleis' and many other engines were advanced to the walls. The town was begirt with a palisade and entrenchment, but still held out. 5. The river

Mygdonius flowing through the middle of the town, at last the Persians dammed its flow a considerable distance upriver, and increased the height of its bank on both sides so as to shut the waters in. When they saw that a great mass of water was collected and already beginning to overflow the dam, they suddenly launched it like an engine against the wall. 6. The impact was tremendous; the bulwarks could not sustain it, but gave way and fell down. Just the same fate befell the other side of the circuit, through which the Mygdonius made its exit; it could not withstand the shock, and was carried away. 7. No sooner did Shapur see this than he expected to capture the rest of the city, and for all that day he rested for the mud to dry and the river to become passable. Next day he attacked in full force, and looked to enter the city through the breaches that had been made. But he found the wall built up on both sides, and all his labour vain. 8. For that holy man, through prayer, filled with valour both the troops and the rest of the townsfolk, and both built the walls, withstood the engines, and beat off the advancing foe. And all this he did without approaching the walls, but by beseeching the Lord of all within the church. Shapur, moreover, was not only astounded at the speed of the building of the walls but awed by another spectacle. 9. For he saw standing on the battlements one of kingly mien and all ablaze with purple robe and crown. He supposed that this was the Roman emperor, and threatened his attendants with death for not having announced the imperial presence; 10. but, on their stoutly maintaining that their report had been a true one and that Constantius was at Antioch, he perceived the meaning of the vision and exclaimed 'their God is fighting for the Romans'. Then the wretched man in a rage flung a javelin into the air, though he knew that he could not hit a bodiless being, but unable to curb his passion. 11. Therefore the excellent Ephrem (he is the best writer among the Syrians) besought the divine Jacob to mount the wall to see the barbarians and to let fly at them the darts of his curse. 12. So the divine man consented and climbed up into a tower; but when he saw the innumerable host, he discharged no other curse than to ask that mosquitoes and gnats might be sent forth upon them, so that by means of these tiny animals they might learn the might of the Protector of the Romans. 13. On his prayer followed clouds of mosquitoes and gnats; they filled the hollow trunks of the elephants, and the ears and nostrils of the horses and other animals. 14. Finding the attack of these little creatures past endurance they broke their bridles, unseated their riders and threw the ranks into confusion. The Persians abandoned their camp and fled headlong. So the wretched prince learned by a slight and kindly chastisement the power of the God who protects the pious, and marched his army home again, reaping for all the harvest of the siege not triumph but disgrace.

(Jackson, pp. 91–2, altered)

Philostorgius, *Historia ecclesiastica* III, 23, GCS: Philostorgius says that Shapur, the king of the Persians, waged war against the Romans, and laid siege to the city of Nisibis; but that, contrary to the general expectation, he was obliged to withdraw his forces and to return covered with shame, because Jacob, bishop of that city, had shown the citizens what to do on their own behalf, and had fought wonderfully with a firm hope and confidence in God on behalf of the safety of the city.

(Walford, p. 459, modified)

Historia S. Ephraemi 6–7, ed. Lamy, II, cols 15–19 (Syriac): A little later the great and famous Constantine, the victorious emperor, died; after him his sons took up the dominion. However when a few days had passed, Shapur, king of Persia, despising the youth of Constantine's sons, set forth against Nisibis with a huge army and countless horses and elephants. After dividing up his army, they got ready to prosecute the siege. When the siege had been dragged out for seventy days, some distance away he dammed the flow of the river which entered and divided in the middle of the city; and the wall was unable to withstand the force of the great quantity of water so that it tottered and collapsed. Shapur thought that he could then capture the city without trouble. But the bishop Jacob and the Blessed Ephrem with all the church through the whole time of the siege were interceding with God. Finally the holy bishop raised the strength and morale of the cavalry and of all the inhabitants of the city: he rebuilt the wall and he set up a structure and ballista on it, by means of which he checked and drove back the besiegers. He accomplished these things although in person he was far removed from the wall, being in God's temple and interceding with the Lord of all. However, Shapur was astounded not so much by the ease with which the wall had been raised as by the vision which was afforded to his eyes and had a great effect upon him. For he saw a man standing on the wall who was in an emperor's attire and whose robe reflected the rays of the light. Since he thought that he was the Roman emperor, he poured forth threats against those who had asserted that the Roman emperor was then present in Antioch.[9] Afterwards he understood that the signs were of a vision of the God of the Romans who was fighting on their behalf. Unaware indeed that he was striking the disembodied, the wretched Shapur poured out his threats and hurled his arrows, but soon he was obliged to calm the frenzy of his madness. Then the admirable Ephrem, whom we mentioned earlier, requested of the holy Jacob that he be allowed to climb up on the wall, to look upon the barbarians and to hurl at them his curses' darts. When the glorious (Jacob) heard him, relying on the grace which had accompanied (Ephrem) in the miracle that had once been performed at his hands, he allowed him to climb up. Ephrem climbed up on one of the towers of the wall and, after beholding the great number of their myriads, he raised his gaze to heaven, and requested God to send upon the enemy gnats and midges that by the help of those tiny animals he could so fight the enemy that they should be forced to recognize the power of God. The blessed man had scarcely finished praying when a cloud of gnats and midges went out, which overwhelmed the elephants especially – they have smooth and hairless skin – and filled the noses and ears of the horses and other animals. But those animals, since they could not withstand the might of this punishment, broke their reins, threw their riders, broke rank and quitting the camp hurriedly took flight. But the wretched man (i.e. Shapur), apprised of the power of God the Strengthener of the Christians by (this) small chastisement, departed from there, gathering disgrace instead of victory from his toil. Thus the city was saved by the prayers of the blessed Ephrem.

(Dodgeon, revised Brock)

Jacob of Edessa, *Chronological Canons*, CSCO 9, p. 289 (Syriac): Shapur goes up to make war against Nisibis, and he returns from it ın shame through the prayers of Jacob the bishop; and immediately he goes in wrath and carries off captives from the whole of the land of Meso[potamia], and devastates it in the year [649 (= AD 337)].

(Brooks, p. 310)

Chronicon Paschale (s. a. 337), p. 533, 18–20: Shapur, the king of the Persians, came against Mesopotamia intending to pillage Nisibis and he encamped around it for sixty-three days, and, not being able to prevail over it, he withdrew.

(Dodgeon)

Theophanes, *Chronographia*, A. M. 5829, pp. 34, 33–5, 10: In the same year (337), Shapur, the king of the Persians, came up to Mesopotamia to attack Nisibis and besieged it for sixty-three days, but, not having the power to capture it, he departed. Jacob, the bishop of the Nisibenes, who persevered in the practice of piety, easily accomplished with his prayers the purposes of his resolve. It was he who foiled the hope of the Persians in capturing Nisibis. As soon as they retired from the city, pursued by the blast of his prayer, and returned to their own land, they received famine and plague as wages in payment for the impiety they had committed.

(Dodgeon)

Michael the Syrian, *Chronicon* VII, 3, ed. Chabot, pp. 134–6 (Syriac): When Shapur, king of the Persians, learned that Constantine was dead, he again mounted an attack against Nisibis, which is on the frontiers of the Romans and the Persians. It was called Antioch of the Mygdonia. When Shapur reassembled his army and went up against it (i.e. Nisibis), Constantine's son also gathered an army and came to Antioch. Shapur besieged Nisibis for 70 days: he built ramps against it, he dug ditches and dammed the course of the river which entered and divided itself in the middle of the city. This river was called Mygdonius. Shapur had dykes built on both banks, and had the dam strengthened so that it would resist the raging torrent. The waters flowed over the wall which, unable to withstand the pressure, tottered and fell; he also made a breach in the opposite part, through which the waters escaped. Shapur was confident he could subdue the town without trouble following the collapse of the wall. Having done nothing that day, the next day he saw the wall rebuilt on both sides. The bishop Jacob filled the cavalry and the people with strength by prayer; they built the wall, set up a structure and ballistae above it. He did that while persevering in prayer inside the church. Shapur was astonished, not only at the rebuilding, but also at the vision which appeared to him. He saw a man wrapped in a cloak, who was standing on the wall; his garment and his crown were shedding rays of light. He thought that it was the Roman emperor, and he cursed those who had said to him: 'He is not here.' When he had ascertained that Constantius was at Antioch, he understood and said: 'It is the God of the Romans who is fighting for them.' It is why this wretched man shot an arrow into the air, knowing that he could do no harm. The blessed Ephrem asked the bishop if he could climb up on the wall to curse the barbarians. Seeing their hordes, he prayed to God to send clouds of insects and mosquitoes upon them: they came upon them (immediately); the elephants were particularly bothered by them, because their skin is smooth and hairless. They also entered the nostrils and ears of the horses which, unable to stand the pain, broke their halters, threw off their riders and ran away. And Shapur returned, covered in shame. Ignatius of Melitene says: 'God also sent torrential rain upon the Persians; the plague descended on them and they fled.'

(Vince, revised Brock)

7.1.4. Death of Jacob of Nisibis (after 337/8)

Gennadius, *liber de scriptoribus ecclesiasticis* 1, *PL* 58.1059: Jacob, surnamed the Wise, was bishop of Nisibis, the famous city of the Persians, and one of the confessors under Maximinus the persecutor. ... This man died in the time of Constantius and according to the direction of his father Constantine was buried within the walls of Nisibis, and it turned out as Constantine had expected. For many years after, Julian, having entered Nisibis[10] and grudging either the glory of him who was buried there or the faith of Constantine, whose family he persecuted on account of this envy, ordered the remains of the saint to be carried out of the city, and a few months later (July, 363), as a matter of policy, the Emperor Jovian who succeeded Julian, gave over to the barbarians the city which, with the adjoining territory, is subject unto the Persian rule until this day.

(Richardson, p. 386)

Historia Sancti Ephraemi 7, ed. Lamy, II, col. 21 (Syriac): Not long afterwards (*sc.* the first siege of Nisibis), the holy man of God Jacob, the bishop of Nisibis, ended his life and departed to God, having accomplished famous deeds and replete with every virtue. The Blessed Ephrem, though afflicted with much sorrow, conducted his funeral with great dignity.

(Dodgeon, revised Brock)

Chronicon Edessenum 17, CSCO 1, p. 4, 13–15 (Syriac): In the year 649 (Sel. = AD 338) died Mar Jacob, the bishop of Nisibis.

Jacob of Edessa, *Chronological Canons*, CSCO 5, p. 291: When Jacob, bishop of Nisibis, died, Vologeses succeeded him.

Chronicon Ps. Dionysianum, CSCO 91, p. 174, 1–2 (Syriac): And in the same year (650 Sel. = AD 339), the saintly man Jacob, bishop of Nisibis, departed from this world.

7.1.5. Constantius' return to the East

Zonaras XIII, 5, 5–6 (iii, p. 188, 24–9, Dindorf): As soon as the position of the empire was secure, he (i.e. Constantius) returned to the East and campaigned against the Persians. 6. Shapur, their king, having heard about the death of Constantine, attacked and plundered Roman territory without respite.

(Dodgeon)

7.1.6. The Armenian settlement (*c.* 337/8)

Julian, *or.* I, 20A–21A (15.1–32, pp. 33–4, Bidez): On that subject, however, I shall have a chance later to speak in more detail. This is perhaps the right moment to describe how you controlled the situation, encompassed as you were, after your father's death, by so many perils and difficulties of all sorts – confusion, an unavoidable war, numerous hostile raids, allies in revolt, lack of discipline in the garrisons, and all the other harassing conditions of the hour. You concluded in perfect harmony the negotiations with your brothers, and when the time had arrived that demanded your aid for the dangerous crisis of affairs, you made forced marches, and immediately after leaving Paeonia appeared in Syria. But to relate how you did this would tax my powers of description, and indeed for those who know the facts their own experience is enough. But who in the world could describe adequately how, at the prospect of your arrival, everything was changed and improved all at once, so that we were set free from the fears that hung over us and could entertain brighter hopes than ever for the future? Even before you were actually on the spot the mutiny among the garrisons ceased and order was restored. The Armenians who had gone over to the enemy at once changed sides again, for you ejected from the country and sent to Rome those who were responsible for the governor's exile, and you secured for the exiles a safe return to their own country. You were so merciful to those who now came to Rome as exiles, and so kind in your dealings with those who returned from exile with the governor, that the former did, indeed, bewail their misfortune in having revolted, but still were better pleased with their present condition than with their previous power; while the latter, who were formerly in exile, declared that the experience had been a lesson in prudence, but that now they were receiving a worthy reward for their loyalty. On the returned exiles you lavished such magnificent presents and rewards that they could not even resent the good fortune of their bitterest enemies, nor begrudge their being duly honoured.[11]

(Wright, i, pp. 51–3)

7.2.1. Treaty between Constantius and the Arabs (338?)[12]

Julian, *or.* I, 21B (15.32–5, p. 34, Bidez): All these difficulties (i.e. the Armenian revolt) you quickly settled, and then by means of embassies you turned the marauding Arabs against our enemies.[13]

(Wright, i, p. 53)

7.2.2. Restoration of military discipline by Constantius

Julian, *or.* I, 21B–22A (16, pp. 34–5, Bidez): The previous period of peace had relaxed the labours of the troops, and lightened the burden of those who had to perform public services. But the war called for money, provisions, and supplies on a vast scale, and even more it demanded endurance, energy, and military experience on the part of the troops. In the almost entire absence of all these, you personally provided and organised everything, drilled those who had reached the age for military service, got together a force of cavalry to match the enemy's, and issued orders for the infantry to persevere in their training. Nor did you confine yourself to speeches and giving orders, but yourself trained and drilled with the troops, showed them their duty by actual example, and straightway made them experts in the art of war. Then you discovered ways and means, not by increasing the tribute of the extraordinary contributions, as the Athenians did in their day, when they raised these to double or even more. You were content, I understand, with their original revenues, except in cases where, for a short time, and to meet an emergency, it was necessary that the people should find their services to the state more expensive. The troops under your leadership were abundantly supplied, yet not so as to cause the satiety that leads to insolence, nor, on the other hand, were they driven to insubordination from lack of necessaries.

(Wright, i, p. 55)

7.2.3. Roman cavalry equipment strengthened by Constantius

Julian, *or.* I, 37C–38A (30.15–28, pp. 54–5, Bidez): Your cavalry was almost unlimited in numbers and they all sat on their horses like statues, while their limbs were fitted with armour that followed closely the outline of the human form. It covers the arms from wrist to elbow and thence to the shoulder, while a coat of mail protects the shoulders, back and breast. The head and face are covered by a metal mask which makes its wearer look like a glittering statue, for not even the thighs and legs and the very ends of the feet lack this armour. It is attached to the cuirass by fine chain-armour like a web, so that no part of the body is visible and uncovered, for this woven covering protects the hands as well, and is so flexible that the wearers can bend even their fingers.[14]

(Wright, i, p. 97)

7.2.4. Constantius arrived at the Eastern Frontier but was unable to bring the enemy into open battle (338/9)

Libanius, *or.* LIX, 76–82: Another journey under arms succeeded the journey of speed and he stood upon the borders of Persia and wished to stain his right hand with blood. But there was no one to feel his anger. For those who had promoted the war deferred the war in flight, and not as men who succumbed to fear after encountering the enemy but as men who did not await the encounter because of their fear. Their turning tail was not the result of hand-to-hand fighting but because rumour alone sufficed to cause the rout. 77. What took place deserves special admiration. For the emperor had resolved to undertake neither prolonged sieges nor retreats but, taking advantage of the winter weather, (he resided in) the greatest of the cities in that region; and when the good weather began, he himself was also radiant in arms. He attacked as much Persian territory as his reasoning permitted. While he considered it irksome solely to keep an eye on what was happening there, he nevertheless considered it an act of passivity not to go for an all-out offensive. 78. For that reason he divided his time between campaigning and planning. The sum of his planning was not how to defeat them (i.e. the Persians) when they appeared but how to persuade them to put in an appearance. He had so completely altered their expectations that what they hoped to inflict on others when they started the war was what they were suffering when enveloped by our counter-attacks. 79. Previously it was such a usual practice for them to launch an invasion and a necessity for us to abandon our own territory when they advanced, that you would have found that the cities bordering them were the oldest in date but the most recent in the permanence of their foundation. For these were the cities which the inhabitants had to restore after those who had laid waste to them with fire had departed. But now the situation has been so much reversed that the majority of the Syrians think fit to live in unwalled cities. On the other hand, it seems a sign of victory for the Persians if their concealment can escape our detection.

Let no one think either that I am ignorant of the surprise raids which even now they employed, or that they were able to push forward some force in secrecy, or that they invented a treaty for the cessation of hostilities and employed the period in which our defence had become lax on account of the oaths to further their advantage; or even again that they had clear understanding of this and willingly transgressed (the terms). Far from being embarrassed at these goings on, I think I would have reasonable cause for embarrassment if none of these things had happened. For he who has nothing worth remembering to say of the defeated also takes away the praise due to the victors. Similarly in the games, whenever the crowd despoils the man who is greatly inferior and favours the best, victory may be inevitable for the latter but applause from the spectators would not accompany the victory-crown. So also in warfare the inferiority of the defeated detracts from the value of the victors' glory. 81. I agree that the Persians are experts in robbery and deceit, and they do not lose heart very quickly and would very easily rob us of many things through perjuring their oath. Nevertheless, those who have discovered such paths to war did not bear to gaze steadily upon the emperor's helmet. The surest proof of both of these statements is that if they heard he was approaching, they vanished into thin air; but when they received notice of his absence, they would attack those arrayed against them. In the first instance they admitted their fear, but in the second they demonstrated their stealth. It was in this way that they acquired their military experience, but when the emperor made his appearance they were so frightened that they lost all memory of their experience. That they did not unreasonably squander their opportunities but used them in a sensible manner is demonstrated by experience. When they were not able to hide their true nature, no sooner had they made their swift appearance before the emperor than, being caught in the net, they transferred their allegiance to us. There were not some who surrendered and others who were taken captive in the course of battle, but simply all of them in the same manner of crouching down and extending their hands in supplication.

(Dodgeon, revised Lieu)

7.2.5. The Persian war used as an excuse by Arian leaders for not appearing before Pope Julius who had summoned them (c. 338)

Athanasius, *apologia contra Arianos* 25, ed. Bright, p. 36: (Letter of Julius) But perhaps they (i.e. the Arians) did not come on account of the aspect of the times, for again you (the bishop Eusebius) declare in your letter, that we ought to have considered the present circumstances of the East, and not to have urged you to come.

Idem, *Historia Arianorum* 11, ed. Bright, p. 190: Athanasius, however, before these things happened, at the first report of their proceedings, sailed to Rome, knowing the rage of the heretics, and for the purpose of having the Council held as had been determined. And Julius wrote letters to them, and sent the Presbyters Elpidius and Philoxenus, appointing a day, that they might either come, or consider themselves as altogether suspected persons. But as soon as Eusebius and his fellows heard that the trial was to be an Ecclesiastical one, ... they were so alarmed that they detained the Presbyters till after the appointed time, and pretended an unseemly excuse, that they were not able to come now on account of the war which was begun by the Persians. But this was not the true cause of their delay, but the fears of their own consciences.

(Atkinson *ap.* Robertson, p. 273)

7.3.1. Dedication to Constantius who was on the point of embarking on his Persian campaign by a contemporary epitomator of the campaigns of Alexander and Trajan (before 340)

Anon.[15], *Itinerarium Alexandri* 1–11, ed. Volkmann, pp. 1–2: Lord Constantius, Emperor better than good, knowing full well that it would be an auspicious omen both for you and your command, if, now that you have begun successfully and have undertaken your Persian campaign, I were to compose (by you) an itinerary of those emperors who won fame in the same task, namely Alexander the Great and Trajan, I have applied myself to it gladly indeed and with pleasure in the work both because my own wish to do it requires it and is a matter for concern and because the successes of rulers summon their subjects to take part (as well). And if by this I afford some help or lead the way, I shall know that some reward will fall to me also since every mortal man by the law of nature values himself more in that activity by which he himself is protected.

2. But although my inadequate tongue is an unworthy witness of remarkable deeds, nevertheless I boldly undertake the task, relying not on my own powers but on those of a foreign intellect, and not using inferior sources from the number of worthy ones that exist, but those whom opinion of old declares most supportive of good faith and those whom I collected for you here wherever I could with some curtailment of my own research interests, and allowing indeed some refinement of language in a rather constrained way, since service to our shared desire was looked for, not the glory of personal ostentation.

3. Finally, I wrote over the top 'itinerary', in place of 'summary' seeking even by the name of that work to set aright the opportunity, that is to say a kind of central point for your virtues (to revolve around). Indeed, for a mind thirsty for glory it acts as an incentive to know that in a once similar cause fortune submitted to reason; especially since you enter upon the campaigns from that position where each leader of greater fearlessness has been raised higher by his deserved emperorship. Then you are imbued with your services of triumph, where every leader enjoying superior fortune has set the summit to his exploits. Of course, while you bring your youthful undertakings to match the mature deeds of your father, you surpass the merits of the most renowned emperors. From the outset in all this equality may you feel no dissatisfaction for them nor for your judgment, nor indeed be embarrassed over your fortune.

4. And yet I am aware of the far greater and more successful precedents which you in fact possess from the great Constantines, your father and your brother. Certainly (although by your services you made successful the earlier times) I think that, if perception remains in the dead, they will through prayer themselves attend upon them.

5. You have a hereditary duty towards the Persians, inasmuch as they have trembled for so long at Roman arms; through you at length they have been admitted to our name, and among your provinces they have been granted Roman citizenship. Through the kindness of the conquerors may all those who are counted as soldiers there in times of war on the imperial registers and as slaves in peacetime learn to be free.

6. Therefore if Terentius Varro once worked upon that book, under the name of a 'Diary', for Pompey who was *** (text corrupt) *** to campaign in Spain, so that the same man, when he was going to enter upon his proper tasks, might know with ease the change in level of the ocean and with the assurance of foreknowledge might

seek all the remaining heavenly movements, so that he might avoid (them); why should I not bear before you, when you have set out upon the task of our salvation, this torch from the noble flame of virtues? Since through this prayer I am as much superior to Varro as I am inferior to him in talent: so that even from that viewpoint, though physically unimpeded, I may nevertheless campaign for you in strength of intellect.

7. Only may I indicate what path to bravery they have laid, which you must now take up for everyone's wellbeing. For I am not here aiming at elegance of expression upon which toil is expended for the reward of its very exercise: since for the man who engages upon such a task it is a greater source of good fortune to have been the first to dictate what is advantageous than to have written what pleases (the reader); the result is that the less fluid the simple style of the diction is, the more credibility and clearness the account has, since indeed in such matters truth has snatched up the palm of eloquence; when it is covered with artistry, the author rather than the performer of the deeds receives the praise.

8. But here I enjoy an agreeable similarity of subject-matter and a like kind of hope when I am about to write in your regard accounts of greater significance than the glories of Alexander and those of Trajan, with whom you share, of course, the task of encroaching on this fateful barrier of war; whereas you now also are of the (same) age as one of them, but you have the wisdom of the other with which you overcome (the shortcomings of) your age.

9. In truth you will in the meantime equal the famous Alexander: he was great by name, but you are the son of the greatest (Constantine), you were born in almost the same part of the earth, and you are leading in the same direction as he an army equal in number of soldiers but better in the balance. You intend to avenge the same injury, but for a different insult.

10. In consequence of this binding duty you must of course anticipate that campaigning under a similar omen you win a like success. To this extent you are his associate by precedent, but more fortunate in terms of merit; if indeed prayers conceived by right and sobriety are more acceptable to God our Protector than those which inconsiderate arrogance seizes upon in its savage style.

11. Alexander boasted of his victory to himself only and became quite merciless to his friends, and as his success grew with the advantage of victory, he became hardened for that reason against those who caused disturbance. But you are campaigning for the

salvation of Rome, soon striving for that empire at an age whose immortal glory will go with you. And here indeed I shall begin lest I any longer interrupt you, engaged as you are upon such important tasks.

(Dodgeon)

7.3.2. Roman raids across the Tigris (340ff.?)[16]

Julian, *or.* I, 22 A–B (16.20–17.8, p. 35, Bidez): I shall say nothing about your great array of arms, horses and river-boats, engines of war and the like. But when all was ready and the time had come to make appropriate use of all that I have mentioned, the Tigris was bridged by rafts at many points and forts were built to guard the river.[17] Meanwhile the enemy never once ventured to defend their country from plunder, and every useful thing that they possessed was brought in to us. This was partly because they were afraid to offer battle, partly because those who were rash enough to do so were punished on the spot. This is a mere summary of your invasions of the enemy's country.

(Wright, i, pp. 55–7)

7.3.3. A Persian city was captured by Constantius on one of his forays into enemy territory (*c.* 343)

Libanius, *or.* LIX, 83–7: By a shouted command (i.e. of Constantius), the complement of a not unimportant city among the Persians[18] was transferred with all its households as if caught in a net. They cursed those who had sown the seed of war, and lamented the desolation of their native land, but had not altogether despaired of better hopes from the mild disposition of their conqueror. And they were not deceived. I mean now that in my judgement his policy after the capture was even more admirable than the capture. For when he captured them, he did not kill them as the Corcyreans slew the Corinthian settlers from Epidamnus, nor even did he sell the prizes of war, as Philip did with the prisoners of the Olynthians; but he had the notion to make use of the captives in the place of a victory monument and trophy. He transported them to Thrace and settled them (as colonists) to act as reminders to later generations of their misfortune. 84. And these facts should not be disbelieved. For we are not recounting an action which has been blotted out by time, as antiquity fights on the side of falsehood, but I think that everyone bears before his eyes the procession of prisoners that took place yesterday and the day before. 85. This is what I mean is finer and more statesmanlike than the winning of a victory. Many men, indeed, on many occasions, have brought cities to terms, but it has not been the act of many to arrange the results of the capture to fit in with necessary policy. For let us consider how much he combined in this one deed. Firstly, he civilized a very considerable wild region of Thrace by providing colonists to bring it under cultivation. Then he transmitted the memory of his virtuous successes to accompany for all time the succession of their generations, and did not allow forgetfulness to thrive at the expense of his accomplishments. Thirdly, he exhibited the same mark of kindliness and generosity by being moved to pity by their tears and shedding his anger at their change of fortune. 86. Furthermore, he did not overlook us who were settled further away on the enemy's land and feasted on the hearsay alone of what had happened, for he made us eye-witnesses of the whole and filled us with much joy and good hope. We rejoiced at his successes and perceived the future from his achievements. 87. But if I must say a word of what gratified me, at long last justice had been done for the Greeks carried off from Euboea by his taking these prisoners away from their native land in return for the Eretrian generations.[19]

(Dodgeon, revised Lieu)

Athanasius, *Historia Arianorum* 16, pp. 193–4, ed. Bright: When they (i.e. the Arian bishops at the Council of Serdica) heard this, being still more alarmed, they had recourse to an excuse even more unseemly than that they pretended at Antioch, namely, that they betook themselves to flight because the Emperor (i.e. Constantius II) had written to them the news of his victory over the Persians.

(Atkinson *ap.* Robertson, p. 275)

Julian, *or.* I, 22B–D (17.7–21, pp. 35–6, Bidez): Who, indeed, in a short speech could do justice to every event, or reckon up the enemy's disasters and our successes? But this at least I have space to tell. You often crossed the Tigris with your army and spent a long time in the enemy's country, but you always returned crowned with the laurels of victory. Then you visited the cities you had freed, and bestowed on them peace and plenty, all possible blessings and all at once. Thus at your hands they received what they had so long desired, the defeat of the barbarians and the erection of trophies of victory over the treachery and cowardice of the Parthians. Treachery they had displayed when they violated the treaties and broke the peace, cowardice when they lacked the courage to fight for their country and all that they held dear.

(Wright, i, p. 57)

7.3.4. The battle of Singara (343 or 344)[20]

Libanius, *or.* LIX, 99–120: Come, let us also mention the last battle. We can call the same both the last and great (battle) and much more deserving of the title of great than the celebrated battle at Corinth. I promise to demonstrate here that the emperor defeated the Persians together with their allied forces. And let no one distrust the hyperbole before he hears anything, but let him await the arguments and then express his judgement. For in this way his observation of the whole would be more accurate.

100. When the Persians grew tired of the emperor's inroads and were distressed by the length of the war, they assumed the necessity of their fortune as an inspiration for their risk-taking; for death is not irksome to men who do not spend life in pleasure. Indeed, being willing even to endure a degree of suffering through their actions, they raised their levies amongst the men from youth upwards and did not even grant an exemption without penalty to those who were very young. They conscripted their womenfolk to act as sutlers in the army. There were various nations of barbarians on their borders and some they persuaded by entreaty to share their dangers, others they compelled by force to enter military service. To these they offered a quantity of gold, a hoard preserved since ancient times and then for the first time expended in payment to mercenary soldiers. 101. When they had scrutinized all the land in this way, they left their cities empty and herded the whole populace together in a crowd on foot. They practised their training on the march and set off for the river. The emperor had got wind of what was afoot. How could so massive a cloud of dust have gone unnoticed, rising up as it did to fill the centre of the sky? Not to mention that the confused din of horses, men and arms, made it impossible even for those very far away to snatch any sleep, and that our scouts who personally watched the manoeuvre brought back news which was based on observation and not on guesswork using other sources.[21] 102. When an accurate report of this had reached the emperor, his expression did not change like a man whose heart is struck with terror, but he sought a strategy that was advantageous to meet the needs of the present emergency. His orders to those established on guard duty along the frontiers were to retreat with utmost speed and

neither to harass them when they bridged the river, nor to prevent their landing nor to hinder their fortification (of a camp); but even to allow them to dig trenches, if they wished, to put up a palisade, to fence themselves in, to lay in a supply of water and to seize beforehand the advantages of the terrain. For if they crossed over and encamped, this did not cause him to panic; but if they were beaten off from the start, they would take it as an excuse for flight. The strategy required that the enemy be beguiled by ease of the landing.

103. When these apparent concessions had been made and no one from our side opposed them, they bridged the river at three points and crossed over in closed ranks everywhere. At first, running day into night, they continually poured across the river. Afterwards, when the necessity arose to fortify their position, they raised a circuit wall on the same day more quickly than the Greeks at Troy. Already the entire position was full of those who had crossed over the river bank, the breadth of the plain and the mountain peaks. But there was no type of military equipment which did not complement their army, archers, mounted archers, slingers, heavy infantry, cavalry and armed men from every part. While they were still deliberating as to where they should muster, their king made his appearance in truly Homeric image; outstanding in brilliance and fitly armed, he supervised the whole operation.[22] 104. Then the Persians developed a strategy somewhat along the following lines. They drew up their archers and javelin men on the peaks and on the wall, and they pushed forward their heavily armoured troops in front of the wall. The remainder took up arms and advanced against their enemies to rouse them to action. When they saw the Romans go into action, they immediately broke off the engagement and fled and led them to within missile range so that they might be shot at from above. 105. And so the pursuit continued for some time and indeed for the greater part of the day, until those who had fled had retreated within the wall. Thereafter the archers and those before the wall who had not been engaged were called up to take advantage of the situation. Then the emperor won a victory, not in the style of the usual conquests nor even such as have occurred frequently both in the present age and in the past, nor even one whose result lay in skill at arms and military equipment, nor even a victory for which there was need of association with others, without which it might not otherwise have been accomplished. But it was a victory which we are permitted to class as rightly belonging to the victor. 106. What is the nature of

this? He alone discovered the intention behind what was happening, and not only was he not deceived by the battle array but he alone shouted out and ordered our troops not to pursue nor to be forced into obvious danger. Now indeed I admire all the more the concept of the poet who says that a reflection that has a share of wisdom is more effective than the work of many hands. By following this maxim, the emperor immediately grasped the entire situation and saw that the future outcome would be no worse than the present circumstances as they unfolded. 107. This was indeed a most natural assumption. For between the camps there was an interval of one hundred and fifty stades, and they began the pursuit in the forenoon and were already drawing near the wall by late afternoon. In fact, in considering the entire position, the burden of their arms, the length of the pursuit, the burning heat of the sun, their critical state of thirst, the onset of night and the archers on the hilltops, he thought it right to disregard the Persians and to rely on the opportunity. 108. If they (i.e. the Roman troops) had been more receptive to reasoning and their temper had not overborne his advice, nothing would have prevented both the enemy from being laid low, as at the present time and the victors from being kept safe. However, the more one finds fault with them, the more one increases the emperor's reputation. For as they blundered by not obeying orders they have enhanced the counsel of their adviser. 109. Indeed, I invoke the victories of the emperors which they achieve in partnership, but I understand that much more honourable are those where it is not possible to name more than one participant. As a result, if one should strive the hardest not to yield everything to the soldiers in what one judges to be right, nothing would have prevented them from completely restoring the position, and the emperor from winning total victory, first and foremost, over the very men amongst whom his judgment had proved to be superior to their own.

110. It is appropriate to examine the merits of those who fought and make obvious to all from what small beginnings they started out to fulfil such a role. First of all, when they clashed with the cavalry (cataphracts) before the wall, they discovered a tactic superior to their armour. For the infantry soldier stepped aside from the charging horseman and rendered the attack useless, while he himself struck the rider on the temple with his club as he passed by and knocked him off, and the rest of the business was finished off quite easily. Whereupon, since those who arrived at the wall did not restrain their hands, everything from the battlements was pulled

down to the lowest foundation and there was no one to stop them. 111. I would have considered it valuable also to tell who was the first to break through the encircling wall and to spend my time on their act of courage – for perhaps this would be no less pleasing to hear than the fire which spread over the ship of the Thessalians (*Iliad*, XV.704ff.). But since time does not allow this, I think one should not be side-tracked anywhere. 112. The encircling wall therefore lay flattened to a nicety, while they poured in, thinking that what was accomplished was all too insignificant. They plundered the tents and carried off the produce of those who had been labouring in the neighbourhood and they slew all they caught. Only those who took to flight were spared. When the rout had become manifest, their action only required a brighter day, if somehow it were possible, for the completion of their achievements; but when it drifted on into a night battle, they were shot at from the hills and showered by darts from all sides, and already arrows were broken off and clung to their bodies. They were prevented by the night from using their weapons in the manner they knew; nonetheless the heavy infantry advanced in the darkness against the lighter-armed troops whose effectiveness lay in fighting at a distance. Thoroughly exhausted, they lost some good soldiers against fresh men but they drove their enemies off the field. 113. Who would have withstood their courage, aided and abetted by reasoning? Faced with such great obstacles they were prevented by nothing from settling the issue with a nobler bearing. For who would not believe that the Persians who crossed over to conquer others were clearly worsted and, though enjoying such great advantages, abandoned their hopes and departed? 114. Whether, therefore, his superiority in good counselling is acknowledged by someone and the emperor has been demonstrated to be superior to friends and opponents alike in what he determined, or whether it is more pleasurable for one to approve by scrutiny the bare facts; at all events, the Persians quit the camp and started for the pontoon-bridge, whereas there were those of our men who conquered with their spirits but renounced their bodies. Our men who returned did not make the homeward march before they cleaned our land of the enemy. Nor do I need to add the point that the nature of the terrain caused more damage than the prowess of the enemy, nor even that the Persians enlisted the help of their women in the danger, whereas the flower of our army did not participate in the battle.

115. So let us define three phases of the battle and so consider our judgement: firstly, the period before the battle, secondly, the

engagement itself and thirdly, the period of the rout. 116. So, then, the enemy accomplished their landing and bridged the river, not by forcing back those who were pressing against them, but borrowing their freedom of action from those who did not wish to hinder them. When they had landed (on our side) and scouted around, they seized what in their judgement were the strongpoints, but as though suffering a dearth of arms they did not launch an offensive against those who appeared. 117. Up to now they had enjoyed good fortune, but when the armies clashed, instead of standing up to the attackers and fighting it out hand to hand, they began to flee. When they had barricaded themselves within their defensive perimeter, they did not maintain outer defences but they gave up their fortification, and in addition they lost the treasure stored in their tents. Those who were left behind there fell in no order and looked on as the king's son, the successor to the throne, was taken prisoner, flogged, pierced and, a little later, executed.[23] Indeed if they managed any effective fighting anywhere, what happened was a trick of war, not an act of courage.

118. These were the events in the battle and the others took place in that country. They did not recover their slain but rushed into flight, broke down the bridges and did not even hope in their dreams to counteract the (stunning) blow. But their king of brilliant potential, and of noble reputation (until his threats), tore out and rent that head of hair which he would earlier adorn; he struck his head frequently and lamented the slaughter of his son, lamented the destruction of his conscripts and wept over this land bereft of its farmers. He resolved to cut off the heads of those who failed to win for him the success of the Romans. 119. It is not my speech, composed to gratify, which proves this, but their deserters who surrendered themselves and clearly announced the news. We must accept their word: for they do not delight in the false tales of their difficulties. It is not, therefore, a matter of dispute that he won a victory like the one at Tanagra and, by Heaven, the victory at Oresthis by the Tegeans and Mantineans. (Cf. Thuc. IV, 134)

120. However, I can say much more than this, which I think not even the king of the Persians himself would contradict. For it has been admitted by both sides that in the night battle those who were the survivors returned home again. In the circumstances, one of two possibilities must have occurred, either that they were defeated and fled or that they won, but nevertheless were wary over the next development. If therefore we suppose the first possibility, the victory lay clearly with us. But if in the night battle, although they

held the advantage, their confidence did not allow them to follow up the attack thereafter, the emperor's victory becomes much greater. For they defeated their opponents, but did not stand against his right hand and, presumably, made it clear to all that the emperor's strength lies not in the outcome but in his nature.

(Dodgeon, revised Lieu)

Julian, *or.* I, 22D–25B (18–20.17, pp. 36–9, Bidez): But lest anyone should suppose that, while I delight in recalling exploits like these, I avoid mentioning occasions when luck gave the enemy the advantage – or rather it was the nature of the ground combined with opportunity that turned the scale – and that I do so because they brought us no honour or glory but only disgrace, I will try to give a brief account of those incidents also, not adapting my narrative with an eye to my own interests, but preferring the truth in every case. For when a man deliberately sins against the truth he cannot escape the reproach of flattery, and moreover he inflicts on the object of his panegyric the appearance of not deserving the praise that he receives on other accounts. This is a mistake of which I shall beware. Indeed my speech will make it clear that in no case has fiction been preferred to the truth. Now I am well aware that all would say that the battle we fought before Singara was a most important victory for the barbarians. But I should answer, and with justice, that this battle inflicted equal loss on both armies, but proved also that your valour could accomplish more than their luck; and that although the legions under you were violent and reckless men, and were not accustomed, like the enemy, to the climate and the stifling heat. I will relate exactly what took place.

(19) It was still the height of summer, and the legions mustered long before noon. Since the enemy were awestruck by the discipline, accoutrements and calm bearing of our troops, while to us they seemed amazing in numbers, neither side began the battle; for they shrank from coming to close quarters with forces so well equipped, while we waited for them to begin, so that in all respects we might seem to be acting rather in self-defence, and not to be responsible for beginning hostilities after the peace. But at last the leader of the barbarian army, raised high on their shields, perceived the magnitude of our forces drawn up in line. What a change came over him! What exclamations he uttered! He cried out that he had been betrayed, that it was the fault of those who had persuaded him to go to war, and decided that the only thing to be done was to flee with all speed and that one course alone would secure his safety,

namely, to cross, before we could reach it, the river, which is the ancient boundary-line between that country and ours. With this purpose, he first gave the signal for a retreat in good order, then gradually increasing his pace he finally took to headlong flight, with only a small following of cavalry, and left his whole army to the leadership of his son and the friend in whom he had most confidence. When our men saw this, they were enraged that the barbarians should escape all punishment for their audacious conduct, and clamoured to be led in pursuit, chafed at your order to halt and ran after the enemy in full armour with their utmost energy and speed. For of your generalship they had had no experience so far, and they could not believe that you were a better judge than they of what was expedient. Moreover, under your father they had fought many battles and had always been victorious, a fact that tended to make them think themselves invincible. But they were most of all elated by the terror that the Parthians now showed, when they thought how they had fought, not only against the enemy, but against the very nature of the ground, and if any greater obstacle met them from some fresh quarter, they felt that they would overcome it as well. Accordingly they ran at full speed for about one hundred stades,[24] and only halted when they came up with the Parthians, who had fled for shelter into a fort that they had lately built to serve as a camp. It was, by this time, evening, and they engaged battle forthwith. Our men at once took the fort and slew its defenders. Once inside the fortifications they displayed great bravery for a long time, but they were by this time fainting with thirst, and when they found cisterns of water inside, they spoiled a glorious victory and gave the enemy a chance to retrieve their defeat.

(20) This then was the issue of that battle, which caused us the loss of only three or four of our men, whilst the Parthians lost the heir to the throne who had previously been taken prisoner, together with all his escort. While all this was going on, of the leader of the barbarians not even the ghost was to be seen, nor did he stay his flight till he had put the river behind him. You, on the other hand, did not take off your armour for a whole day and all the night, now sharing the struggles of those who were getting the upper hand, now giving prompt and efficient aid to those who were hard-pressed. And by your bravery and fortitude you so changed the face of the battle that at break of day the enemy were glad to beat a safe retreat to their own territory, and even the wounded, escorted by you, could retire from the battle. Thus did you relieve them all from the risks of flight. Now what fort was taken by the enemy? What city

did they besiege? What military supplies did they capture that should give them something to boast about after the war?

(Wright, i, pp. 59–65)

Julian, *or.* 26B (21.6–13, pp. 40–1, Bidez): About six years had passed since the war I have just described, and the winter was nearly over (Jan. 350) when a messenger arrived with the news that Galatia (i.e. Gaul) had gone over to the usurper (i.e. Magnentius), that a plot had been made to assassinate your brother and had been carried out, also that Italy and Sicily had been occupied, lastly that the Illyrian garrisons were in revolt and had proclaimed their general (i.e. Vetranio) emperor, though for a time he had been inclined to resist what seemed to be the irresistible onset of the usurpers.

(Wright, i, p. 67)

Libanius, *or.* XVIII, 208 (written in 365): See below, Ch. 8, p. 227

Festus, *brev.* 27, pp. 66, 14–67, 13: Constantius fought against the Persians with varying and more indifferent outcome. In addition to the skirmishes of those on guard duty along the 'limes', there were nine pitched battles; on seven occasions these were conducted by his generals, and he was personally present twice. However, in the battles at Sisara, at Singara and at Singara a second time[25] (in which Constantius was present), and at Sicgara (*sic*), also at Constantia (*sic* = Constantina?) and when Amida was captured, the state suffered a severe loss under that emperor. Nisibis was besieged three times, but the enemy suffered the greater loss while maintaining the siege. However at the battle of Narasara, where Narses was killed,[26] we were the winners. But in the night battle at Eleia[27] near Singara, the outcome of all the expeditions would have been counterbalanced if, though terrain and night were adverse, the emperor himself by addressing them had been able to recall his soldiers, excited with their aggression, away from an inopportune time for a battle. They however with undefeated strength, an unexpected help against thirst when evening was now pressing on, attacked the Persian camp. They smashed down the defences and seized it and put the king to flight. When they recovered their breath from the battle and gazed in amazement at the water which was discovered with the lights held high, they were overwhelmed by a cloud of arrows since they provided illumination in the darkness to direct the arrow hits with more effect upon themselves.

(Dodgeon)

Eutropius, *breviarium*, X, 10, 1: The fortune of Constantius was different; for he suffered many grievous calamities at the hands of the Persians, his towns being often taken, his walled cities besieged, and his troops cut off. Nor had he a single successful engagement with Shapur, except that, at Singara, when victory might certainly have been his, he lost it, through the irrepressible eagerness of his men, who, contrary to the practice of war, mutinously and foolishly called for battle when the day was declining.

(Watson, pp. 531–2)

Jerome, *chronicon, s. a.* 348, p. 236, 3–237, 2: Nocturnal battle against the Persians near Singara in which we lost a highly dubious victory through the stolidity of our forces. Indeed, of the nine very heavy battles against the Persians, none was more severe. To pass over the others, Nisibis was besieged (346 and 350) and Bezabde and Amida were captured (AD 359).

(Dodgeon)

Ammianus Marcellinus XVIII, 5, 7: (AD 359) ... while he (i.e. the traitor Antoninus) recounted the events of the forty years; urging that, after all these continual wars, and especially the battles of Hileia and Singara, where that fierce combat by night took place, in which we lost a vast number of our men, as if some herald had interposed to stop them, the Persians, though victorious, had never advanced as far as Edessa on the bridges over the Euphrates.

(Yonge, p. 170)

Socrates, *Historia ecclesiastica* II, 25, 5, ed. Hussey, i, pp. 263–4: After his (*sc.* Constantine's) death, the Persian war was raised against the Romans, in which Constantius did nothing prosperously: for in a battle fought by night on the frontiers of both parties, the Persians had to some slight extent the advantage.

(Zenos, p. 53)

Consularia Constantinopolitana (Fasti Hydatiani),[28] p. 236, MGH (*Auct. Ant.* IX): (AD 348) (Flavius) Philippus and (Flavius) Salia. Under these consuls, a nocturnal battle was fought against the Persians.

(Lieu)

Jacob of Edessa, *Chronological Canons*, CSCO 5, p. 293 (Syriac): The year 660 of the Greeks (= AD 348). This year Constantius built the city of Amida between the rivers; and the same year the Romans fought a battle with the Persians by night

(Brooks, p. 311)

Zonaras XIII, 5, 33 (iii, pp. 191, 10–13, Dindorf): The emperor Constantius often clashed with the Persians and had the worse of it and lost many of his own men. And very many of the Persians fell and Shapur himself was wounded.

(Dodgeon)

7.3.5. Defeat and flight of Constantius (date uncertain)

Ammianus Marcellinus XXV, 9, 3: (AD 363): Then a man by the name of Sabinianus, eminent among his fellow citizens (i.e. of Nisibis) both for his fortune and birth, replied with great fluency that Constantius too was at one time defeated by the Persians in the terrible strife of fierce war, that afterwards he fled with a small body of companions to the unguarded frontier post of Hibiuta, where he lived on a scanty and uncertain supply of bread which was brought him by an old woman from the country; and yet that to the end of his life he lost no territory; . . .

(Yonge, p. 399, revised)

7.4.1. Capture of Singara by the Persians (date uncertain)

Ammianus Marcellinus XIX, 2, 8: (Siege of Amida, 359) Nor was there less grief or less slaughter in the city where the cloud of arrows obscured the air, and the vast engines, of which the Persians had got possession when they took Singara, scattered wounds everywhere.

(Yonge, p. 188)

Ammianus Marcellinus XX, 6, 5: (Siege of Singara, 360) . . . one day on the approach of evening a very heavy battering-ram was brought forward among other engines, which battered a round tower with repeated blows, at a point where we mentioned that the city had been laid open in a former siege.

(Yonge, p. 224)

7.4.2. Constantius in Nisibis (May, 345)[29]

Ephrem Syrus, *Carmina Nisibena* XIII, 4–6, CSCO 218, p. 35, 7–15 (Syriac):

4. In the first (i.e. Jacob), He opened the door,* for the chastisement which came over us;
in the second (i.e. Babu), He opened the door,* for the imperial majesty[30] that came down on us;
in the last (i.e. Vologeses), He opened the door,* for the good tidings that came up for us.

5. In the first, (He opened the door,* for the battle between the two armies;
in the second, He opened the door,* for the kings from both (directions of) wind;
in the last, He opened the door,* for the envoys from both sides.

6. In the first, He opened the door,* for battle because of sins;
in the second, He opened the door,* for the kings because of strife;
in the last, He opened the door,* for envoys because of mercy.

(Stopford, p. 180, revised)

7.4.3. The foundation of Tella/Constantia (346 ?)

Jacob of Edessa, *Chronological Canons*, CSCO 5, p. 293 (Syriac): [The city of] Tella in Mesopotamia was built and was called [Cons]tant[ia], which was formerly called [Antipolis]

(trans. Brooks, p. 311)

7.4.4. The foundation of other fortresses in Mesopotamia (date unknown)

History of Jacob the Recluse, ed. Nau, p. 7.5-13 (Syriac): The Tur Abdin was in the midst of these lands (i. e. Mesopotamia) and (Constantius) built two great castles there to protect these countries against Persian bandits: he built one of them at the frontier of Bet Arabaie, on the top of the mountain, and the other on the Tigris, and he named it the Castle of the Stone (Hesn-Kef) and he made it the chief city of the land of Arzon.

(Vince, revised Brock)

7.4.5. The second siege of Nisibis (346)

Firmicus Maternus, *de errore profanarum religionum* 3, p. 127, 18-20, Heuten: The battalions of your adversaries had been turned back, and the rebellious armies had fallen down before your gaze.

The most arrogant people had been yoked and the Persian hopes had foundered.

(Lieu)

Jerome, *chronicon, s. a.* 346, p. 236, 19: Shapur again besieged Nisibis for three months.

Theophanes, *chronographia*, A.M. 5837, p. 38, 9–11: (346) But Shapur, the king of the Persians, returned to Mesopotamia and besieged Nisibis for seventy-eight days. Again frustrated, he withdrew.

(Dodgeon)

7.5.1. Redemption of prisoners by bishop Babu[31] of Nisibis (after 346)

Ephrem Syrus, *Carmina Nisibena* XIV, 4 and 23 and XIX, 16, CSCO 218, p. 37, 22–4, p.40, 1–3 and 53, 11–15 (Syriac):

> XIV, 4. The first priest (i.e. Mar Jacob) by means of a fast* closed up the doors (of men's) mouths.
> The second priest (i.e. Babu) for the captives* opened the mouths of the purse.
> But the last (i.e. Vologeses) pierced through the ears* and fastened in them the ornaments of life.
> 23. When she (i.e. the church at Nisibis) comes before the Rich One* she will show the treasures of the first;
> When she comes before the Saviour* she will show the liberated ones of the second;
> when she goes forth to meet the Bridegroom* she will show the oil of her lamps.
> XIX, 16. Along with the priest Jacob the resplendent,* with him she (i.e. the church) was made victorious as he was.
> Because he joined his love to zeal,* with fear and love he was clothed.
> With Babu, a lover of alms-giving,* she (i.e. the church) redeemed the captives with silver.
> With Vologeses, a scribe of the law,* her heart she opened to the Scriptures.
> With Thee then may her benefits be manifold!* Blessed be He who has magnified His merchantmen.

(Stopford, pp. 182ff., revised)

7.5.2. Constantius in Edessa (*c.* 346)

Athanasius, *apologia contra Arianos* 51, ed. Bright, p. 65: (From a letter of Constantius to Athanasius) Our pleasure was, while we abided at Edessa, and your Presbyters were there, that, on one of them being sent to you, you should make haste to come to our Court, in order that you might see our face, and straightway proceed to Alexandria.

(Atkinson *ap.* Robertson, p. 128)

7.5.3. Nocturnal Sally by two Roman units based at Singara (348?)

Ammianus Marcellinus XVIII, 9, 3: (AD 359) In the garrison of this town (i.e. Amida) the fifth or Parthian legion was already located with a considerable squadron of native cavalry. But at that time six legions, by forced marches, had outstripped the Persian host in its advance and greatly strengthened the garrison: they were the Magnentian and Decentian legions ... and two legions of light infantry called *praeventores* and *superventores*, under the command of Aelianus, a count. With these latter, when only recruits, we have already spoken as sallying out from Singara at the instigation of this same Aelianus, then only one of the guard, and slaying a great number of Persians whom they surprised in their sleep.

(Yonge, pp. 182–3, revised)

7.5.4. Rebuilding of a tower by the *dux* Silvinianus (348)

Littmann – Magie – Stuart, III. A., no. 225, (Greek inscription found at 'Inak, originally from Der il-Khaf, Syria): Under my lord Silvinianus,[32] most eminent *dux*, the tower was built, by provision and effort of Priscus, prefect. In the year 243 (of the era of Bostra = AD 348).

(Littmann – Magie – Stuart, III. A.: 125)

7.5.5. The third siege of Nisibis (350)[33]

Ephrem Syrus, *Carmina Nisibena* I, 3 and 8, II, 9 and 17–19, III, 6, XI, 15–17, XIII, 17–18, CSCO 218, p. 1 ff. (Syriac):

I, 3. Lo! all kinds of billows trouble me;
and I have called the Ark blessed:
for only waves encompassed it,

whereas mounds and arrows as well as waves encompass me.
It was unto thee a storehouse of treasures,
but I have been a store house of debts (or sins):
It in Thy love subdued the waves;
I in Thy wrath am left blinded among the arrows;
the flood bore it, the river threatens me.
O Helmsman of the Ark,
be my pilot on dry land!
To it Thou gavest rest in the haven of a mountain;
To me give Thou rest also in the haven of my walls.
8. The flood assails, and dashes against our walls:
May the all-sustaining might uphold them!
Let them not fall as the building of the sand,
for I have not built my doctrine upon the sand:
a rock shall be for me the foundation,
for on Thy rock have I built my faith;
the secret foundation of my trust shall support my walls.
For the walls of Jericho fell,
because on the sand she had built her trust.
Moses built a wall in the sea,
for on a rock his understanding built it.
The foundation of Noah was on a rock;
the dwelling place of wood it bore up in the sea.
II, 9. He afflicted us by the breaches* that He might punish our crimes:
He raised the mounds that thereby,* He might humble our boasting.
He made a breach for the seas that thereby,* He might wash away our pollution.
He shut us in that we might gather together* in His Temple.
He shut us in and we were quenched;* He set us free and we went astray.
We are like unto wool,* which passes into cvery colour.
17. Who has ever seen, that a breach became as a mirror?
Two parties looked thereinto;* it served for those without and those within.
They saw therein as with eyes,* the Power that breaks down and builds up:
they saw Him who made the breach* and again repaired it.
Those without saw His might;* they departed and tarried not till evening:
those within saw His help;* they gave thanks yet sufficed not.

18. Let the day of thy deliverance,* arouse thee from sloth!
When the wall was broken through,* when the elephants pressed
in,
when the arrows showered,* when men did valiantly,
then was there a sight for the heavenly ones.
Iniquity fought there;* mercy triumphed there;
loving kindness prevailed below;* the watchers shouted on high.
19. And thine enemy wearied himself,* striving to smite by his
wiles,
the wall that encompassed thee,* a bulwark to thine inhabitants.
He wearied himself and availed not;* and in order that he might
not hope,
that if He broke through He should also enter* and take us
captive,
he broke it through and not once only;* and was put to shame,
nor was that enough,
even unto three times,* that he might be shamed thrice in the
three.
III, 6. The day of thy deliverance* is king of all days.
A Sabbath overthrew thy walls,* overthrew the ungrateful;
the day of the Resurrection of the Son,* raised again thy ruins;
the day of Resurrection raised thee* according to its name,
it glorified its title.* The Sabbath relaxed its watch;
for the making of the breaches,* it took blame to itself.
XI, 15. A sea has broken through,* and cast down, the watch
tower wherein I had triumphed.
Iniquity has dared to set up,* a temple wherein I am shamed:
its drink offering chokes me.
16. My prayers on my walls,* my persecutors have heard the sun
and his worshippers,* are ashamed of their Magis,
for I have triumphed by Thy cross.
17. All creatures cried out,* when they saw the struggle,
while Truth with falsehood,* on my battered walls,
fought and was crowned conqueror.
XIII, 17. For the first siege was opposed* by the first and
illustrious priest (i.e. Mar Jacob).
The second siege was opposed* by the second and merciful priest
(i.e. Babu).
But the prayers of the last (i.e. Vologeses)* repaired our breaches
secretly.
18. Nisibis is planted by the waters,[34]* waters secret and open.
Living streams are within her;* a noble river without her.

The river without deceived her;* the fountain [i.e. Baptism]
within has preserved her.

(Stopford, pp. 167ff., revised)

Ephrem Syrus, *Sermones de Nicomedia* XV, 97–120 and 145–70,
ed. Renoux, *PO* 37 (1975), pp. 316–20 (Armenian):

> The sack-cloth of Zion could insult the Assyrian.
> The Persians' contempt could not offend our city.
> It put on worthy sack-cloth;

100 thanks to which it became most honourable.
    If you honour such things,
    who will not take refuge in you?
    The captors did not insult
    chaste women, because of (their) sack-cloth.
105 Oh! more than any other, our city knows
    what sack-cloth is.
    Thanks to it our ramparts were honoured
    which the outsiders had offended.
    The impure insulted (them) and were insulted,
110 while this city was honoured through sack-cloth.
    The seas invaded and were conquered by the sack-cloths;
    hills were raised and they humbled them.
    Elephants arrived and were defeated
    by sack-cloth, ashes and prayer.
115 Archers came and were wounded,
    for those who were clothed in sack-cloth defeated them.
    Cuirass-clad warriors came without,
    and were defeated by sack-cloth within.
    The bow which was outside the ramp
120 was defeated by prayer from within.
    [***]
145 Yesterday you (*sc.* Vologeses) went out on the plain
    and, against them, you waged war.
    The square in this city was cramped
    for marshalling your troops in battle.
    You emerged on to a spacious battlefield,
150 and there you won a magnificent crown.
    At the head of your battle-lines
    marched a priest who was the general.
    The old age of our pastor
    marches to these combats (better) than his youth.

155 For in this secret combat,
   youth is vanquished.
   For its struggle is against concupiscence;
   because of the latter, its dissipation increases.
   That is why old age is necessary,
160 its weakness can conquer.
   O wonderful combat,
   for weakness is necessary to it.
   In all battles strength is appropriate;
   but in this one the weakness of strength.
165 However, O aged man, your youth
   gains the crown through (its) modesty.
   And your old age, O chaste one,
   acquires great virtue.
   Both rejoiced at each other,
   your youth and your old age.

(Vince, revised Russell)

Idem, *Hymni contra Julianum*, II, 23–6: (see below after Julian)

Themistius, *orationes* I, ed. Schenkl and Downey, p. 17, 12–13 (I, 12a Harduin and I,13, Dindorf): What destroyed him (*sc.* the Persian King) then was not Mesopotamia[35] but the emperor's virtue shining near him.

(Dodgeon)

Julian, *or.* I, 27A–29A (22.1–60, pp. 41–4, Bidez): But the Persians ever since the last campaign had been watching for just such an opportunity, and had planned to conquer Syria by a single invasion. So they mustered all forces, every age, sex, and condition, and marched against us, men and mere boys, old men and crowds of women and slaves, who followed not merely to assist in the war, but in vast numbers beyond what was needed. For it was their intention to reduce the cities and, once masters of the country, to bring in colonists in spite of us. But the magnitude of your preparations made it manifest that their expectations were but vanity. They began the siege and completely surrounded the city with dykes, and then the river Mygdonius flowed in and flooded the ground about the walls, as they say the Nile floods Egypt. The siege-engines were brought up against the ramparts on boats, and their plan was that one force should sail to attack the walls while the other kept shooting on the city's defenders from the mounds. But the garrison made a stout defence of the city from the walls. The whole place was filled with corpses, wreckage, armour, and missiles, of which some were just sinking, while others, after sinking from the violence of the first shock, floated on the waters. A vast number of barbarian shields and also ship's benches, as a result of the collisions of the siege-engines on the ships, drifted on the surface. The mass of floating weapons almost covered the whole surface between the wall and the mounds. The lake was turned to gore, and all about the walls echoed the groans of the barbarians, slaying not, but being slain in manifold ways and by all manner of wounds.

Who could find suitable words to describe all that was done there? They hurled fire down on to the shields, and many of the hoplites fell half-burned, while others who fled from the flames could not escape the danger from the missiles. But some while still swimming were wounded in the back and sank to the bottom, while others who jumped from the siege-engines were hit before they touched the water, and so found not safety indeed but an easier death. As for those who knew not how to swim, and perished more obscurely than those just mentioned, who would attempt to name or number them? Time would fail me did I desire to recount all this in detail. It is enough that you should hear the sum of the matter. On that day the sun beheld a battle the like of which no man had ever known before ... (28D) So after spending four months, he (i.e. Shapur) with an army that had lost many thousands, and he who had always seemed to be irresistible was glad to keep the peace, and to use as a bulwark for his own safety the fact that you (i.e. Constantius) had no time to spare and that our own affairs were in confusion.

(Wright, i, p. 73)

Julian, *or.* II, 62B–67A (III, 11–13.30, pp. 132–8, Bidez): And now, with regard to the battle, if there be anyone who declines to heed either the opinion expressed in my narrative or those admirably written verses, but prefers to consider the actual facts, let him judge from those. Accordingly, we will next, if you please, compare the fighting of Ajax in defence of the ships and of the Achaeans at the wall with the Emperor's achievements at that famous city. I mean the city to which the Mygdonius, fairest of rivers, gives its name, though it has also been named after King Antiochus. Then, too, it has another, a barbarian, name which is familiar to many of you from your intercourse with the barbarians of those parts. This city was besieged by an overwhelming number of Parthians with their Indian allies, at the very time when the Emperor was prepared to march against the usurper. And like the sea crab which they say engaged Heracles in battle when he sallied forth to attack the Lernean monster, the king of the Parthians, crossing the Tigris from the mainland, encircled the city with dykes. Then he let the Mygdonius flow into these, and transformed all the space about the city into a lake, and completely hemmed it in as though it were an island, so that only the ramparts stood out and showed a little above the water.[36] Then he besieged it by bringing up ships with siege-engines on board. This was not the work of a day, but I believe of almost four months. But the defenders within the wall continually repulsed the barbarians by burning the siege-engines with their fire-darts. And from the wall they hauled up many of the ships, while others were shattered by the force of the engines when discharged and the weight of the missiles. For some of the stones that were hurled on to them weighed as much as seven Attic talents. When this had been going on for many days in succession, part of the dyke gave way and the water flowed in in full tide, carrying with it a portion of the wall as much as a hundred cubits long.

Thereupon he arrayed the besieging army in the Persian fashion. For they keep up and imitate Persian customs, I suppose, because they do not wish to be considered Parthians, and so pretend to be Persians. That is surely the reason why they prefer the Persian manner of dress. And when they march to battle they look like them, and take pride in wearing the same armour, and raiment adorned with gold and purple. By this means they try to evade the truth and to make it appear that they have not revolted from Macedon, but are merely resuming the empire that was theirs of old. Their king, therefore, imitating Xerxes, sat on a sort of hill that had been artificially made, and his army advanced accompanied by their beasts. These came from India and carried iron towers full of archers. First came the cavalry who wore cuirasses, and the archers, and then the rest of the cavalry in huge numbers. For infantry they find useless for their sort of fighting and it is not highly regarded by them. Nor, in fact, is it necessary to them, since the whole of the country that they inhabit is flat and bare. For a military force is naturally valued or slighted in proportion to its actual usefulness in war. Accordingly, since infantry is, from the nature of the country, of little use to them, it is granted no great consideration in their laws. This happened in the case of Crete and Caria as well and countless nations have a military equipment like theirs. For instance, the plains of Thessaly have proved suitable for cavalry engagements and drill. Our state, on the other hand, since it has had to encounter adversaries of all sorts, and has won its pre-eminence by good judgment combined with good luck, has naturally adapted itself to every kind of armour, and to a varying equipment.

But perhaps those who watch over the rules for writing a panegyric as though they were laws, may say that all this is irrelevant to my speech. Now whether what I have been saying partly concerns you I shall consider at the proper time. But, at any rate, I can easily clear myself from the accusation of such persons. For I declare that I make no claim to be an expert in their art, and one who has not agreed to abide by certain rules has the right to neglect them. And it may be that I shall prove to have other convincing excuses besides. But it is not worthwhile to interrupt my speech and digress from my theme any longer when there is no need. Let me, then, retrace my steps to the point at which I digressed.

(12) Now when the Parthians advanced to attack the wall in their splendid accoutrements, men and horses, supported by the Indian elephants, it was with the utmost confidence that they would at once take it by assault. And at the signal to charge they all pressed forward, since every man of them was eager to be the first to scale the wall and win the glory of that exploit. They did not imagine that there was anything to fear, nor did they believe that the besieged would resist their assault. Such was the exaggerated confidence of the Parthians. The besieged, however, kept their phalanx unbroken at the gap in the wall, and on the portion of the wall that was still intact they posted all the non-combatants in the city and distributed among them an equal number of soldiers. But when the enemy rode up and not a single missile was hurled at them from the wall, their confidence that they would completely reduce the city was strengthened, and they whipped and spurred on their horses, so that their flanks were covered with blood, until they had left the dykes behind them. These dykes they had made earlier to dam the mouth of the Mygdonius, and the mud thereabouts was very deep. In fact, there was hardly any ground at all because of the wood, and because the soil was so rich, and of the sort that conceals springs under its surface. Moreover, there was in that place a wide moat that had been made long ago to protect the town, and had become filled up with a bog of considerable depth. Now when the enemy had already reached this moat and were trying to cross it, a large force of the besieged made a sally, while many others hurled stones from the walls. Then many of the besiegers were slain, and all with one accord turned their horses in flight, though only from their gestures could it be seen that

flight was what they desired and intended. For, as they were in the act of wheeling them about, their horses fell and bore down the riders with them. Weighed down as they were by their armour, they floundered still deeper in the bog, and the carnage that ensued has never yet been paralleled in any siege of the same kind.

Since this fate had overtaken the cavalry, they tried the elephants, thinking that they would be more likely to overawe us by that novel sort of fighting. For surely they had not been stricken so blind as not to see that an elephant is heavier than a horse, since it carries the load, not of two horses or several, but what would, I suppose, require many wagons, I mean archers and javelin-men and the iron tower besides. All this was a serious hindrance, considering that the ground was artificially made and had been converted into a bog. And this the event made plain. Hence it is probable that they were not advancing to give battle, but rather were arrayed to overawe the besieged. They came on in battle line at equal distances from one another. In fact, the phalanx of the Parthians resembled a wall, with the elephants carrying the towers, and hoplites filling up the spaces between. But drawn up as these were, they were of no great use to the barbarian. It was, however, a spectacle which gave the defenders on the wall great pleasure and entertainment, and when they gazed their fill at what resembled a splendid and costly pageant in procession, they hurled stones from their engines, and, shooting their arrows, challenged the barbarians to fight for the wall. Now the Parthians are naturally quick-tempered, and they could not endure to incur ridicule and lead back this imposing force without striking a blow; so by the king's express command they charged at the wall and received a continuous fire of stones and arrows, while some of the elephants were wounded and perished by sinking into the mud. Thereupon, in fear for the others also, they led them back to the camp.

(13) Having failed in this second attempt as well, the Parthian king divided his archers into companies and ordered them to relieve one another and to keep shooting at the breach in the wall, so that the besieged could not rebuild it and thus ensure the safety of the town. For he hoped by this means either to take it by surprise, or by mere numbers to overwhelm the garrison. But the preparations that had been made by the Emperor made it clear that the barbarian's plan was futile. For in the rear of the hoplites a second wall was being built, and while he thought they were using the old line of the wall for the foundations and that the work was

not yet in hand, they had laboured continuously for a whole day and night till the wall had risen to a height of four cubits. And at daybreak it became visible, a new and conspicuous piece of work. Moreover the besieged did not for a moment yield their ground, but kept relieving one another and shooting their javelins at those who were attacking the fallen wall, and all this terribly dismayed the barbarian. Nevertheless he did not at once lead off his army but employed the same efforts over again. But when he had done as before, and as before suffered repulse, he did lead his army back, having lost many whole tribes through famine, and squandered many lives over the dykes and in the siege. He had also put to death many satraps one after another, on various charges, blaming one of them because the dykes had not been made strong enough, but gave way and were flooded by the waters of the river, another because when fighting under the walls he had not distinguished himself; and others he executed for one offence or another. This is, in fact, the regular custom among the barbarians in Asia, to shift the blame of their ill-success on their subjects. Thus, then, the king acted on that occasion, and afterwards took himself off. And from that time he has kept the peace with us and has never asked for any covenant or treaty, but he stays at home and is thankful if only the Emperor does not march against him and exact vengeance for his audacity and folly.

(Wright, i, pp. 165–79)

Ephrem Syrus, *Hymni contra Julianum* II, 23–6, CSCO 175, pp. 82, 15–83, 10 (Syriac, written after 363):

23. How much has truth shown its face in our city!
In our breaches it revealed itself to all regions,
until even the blind saw it in our preservation.
The (Persian) king discerned it in our deliverance
and because he had seen it outside our city in the victory,
when he entered the city he honoured it with gifts.
24. The battle was the refining fire and the king saw within it
How beautiful was truth, how shameful deceit;
he came to know through experience the Lord of that house,
that he is good and also just in all things,
for (when) he wearied him, he [God] did not give him the city
because it believed in him,
but when the sacrifices provoked him to anger he delivered it
without trouble.
25. That city which was the head of the area between the rivers

was preserved by the sack-cloth of the blessed one and was exalted.

The tyrant by his blasphemy had abased it and it was humbled.
Who has weighed its shame, how great it was!
For the city which was head of all that West
they have made the last heels of all that East.
26. Let not the city be thought of like (i.e. other) cities,
for so many times has the Good One delivered it from Sheol, –
the battle under the earth and the battle above it,
and because it rejected its Saviour, he deserted it.
The Just One, whose wrath is powerful, mixed with anger his compassion in that he did not send us into captivity or expel us, he made us to dwell in our land.

(J. M. Lieu, *ap.* Lieu, 1986a: 128)

Libanius, *or.* XVIII, 208 (written in 365): (See below, Ch. 8, p. 227)

Ammianus Marcellinus, XXV, 1, 15: (AD 363, the Roman withdrawal after the death of Julian): Their (i.e. the elephants') drivers (i.e. mahouts) rode on them, and bore knives with handles fastened to their right hands, remembering the disaster which befell them at Nisibis: in case the animal ran berserk and could not be controlled by its driver, he would sever with all his strength the vertebra where the head is joined to the neck so that the beast might not turn upon their own side, as had happened on that occasion.

(Yonge, p. 376, revised)

Zosimus, III, 8, 2: While Constantius was thus engaged, the Persians, with Shapur as their king, ravaged the regions between the two rivers (i.e. Mesopotamia). Overrunning the territory round Nisibis, they besieged the city with all their might. However, Lucillianus the commander (*strategos*) was a worthwhile opponent of the siege, making the fullest use of good fortune and sometimes resorting to stratagems. As a result, the city survived the pressing situation, though it was in very great peril.

(Anon., revised Lieu)

Chronicon Paschale, pp. 536, 18–539, 3: Shapur, the king of the Persians, came against Mesopotamia and besieged Nisibis for one hundred days; he prosecuted the war against the city in various ways and made use of many engines, and brought also a mass of elephants adapted to his service and mercenary kings and all kinds of equipment with which, if they did not wish to cede the city, the Persians threatened to destroy it down to its foundations.

When the Nisibenes held out against surrender, then Shapur determined to flood the city with the river next to it.

The Nisibenes through their prayer prevailed over their enemies, and God was well-disposed to them. For when the waters were about to bring down the lie of the walls in a collapse, a section of the wall was damaged (in conformity to God's assent) to suit their advantage, as will be revealed in what comes next. For it happened both that the city was kept safe and that the enemy were fended off by the waters in such manner that many of them were destroyed.

The Persians having suffered even this threatened to enter through the collapsed section of the wall, and disposed their armoured elephants, and urged on their host to prosecute the war more violently and made use of all kinds of engines.

The soldiers who were garrisoning the city obtained their victory from the foresight of God. For they packed the whole place with every kind of armament and slew large numbers of elephants with catapults; but the remainder fell into the muddy water of the ditches while others were hit and turned back; and they slew above ten thousand of their troops. And a lightning bolt from heaven fell on the rest, and with the onset of dark clouds and violent rain and the crashing of thunder they filled them all with panic so that the majority of them perished through fear.

Shapur, the new Pharaoh, being encompassed on every side, was defeated and floundered fearfully in the waves of terror.

When he was on the point of destroying the city, and the wall had undergone a very great breach and the city was finally on the verge of being surrendered, a vision was revealed during the day to Shapur around the time when he was pressing his attack: a certain man running onto the walls of Nisibis. And the man who appeared was in image Constantius Augustus; as a result Shapur was more enraged at the inhabitants of Nisibis, saying that 'Your king has no strength. Let him come out and make war; or hand over the city.'

When they said: 'It is not right for us to hand over the city when our emperor Constantius Augustus is absent,' as a result of this Shapur was more enraged. They were lying according to the vision he had seen and he said, 'Why are you lying? With my own eyes I behold your emperor Constantius running onto the walls of your city.' In the meantime, Shapur, being engaged in war by God in various ways, failed in his purpose and retreated, having threatened his Magi with death. When the Magi learnt of the reason they discerned the power of the angel who had appeared with Constantius, and they gave Shapur their interpretation. And when Shapur discovered the source of the danger, in a panic he ordered the siege machines to be burnt and all the things which he had prepared in readiness for war to be broken up. He himself with his own followers fled and reached his native country at high speed. But first large numbers were destroyed by a plague. This is recorded in a letter of Vologeses, bishop of Nisibis, which reveals the story stage by stage.

(Dodgeon)

Theophanes, *chronographia*, A.M. 5841, pp. 39, 13–40, 13: In this year once more Shapur, king of the Persians, encamped by Nisibis and caused quite enough damage to it, inasmuch as he brought a troop of elephants adapted for helping in the war and kings hired in his service and all kinds of ballistas; so that they threatened to destroy the city utterly if they would not give way. But the Nisibenes held out against surrender; then finally he determined to flood it with the river nearby. But the citizens defeated the enemy with their prayers, having God well-disposed to them. For when the waters were about to level the site of the walls through a collapse, a section of the wall gave way, and this was with the assent of God, as will be revealed in the subsequent passage. For it immediately happened that the city was protected and the enemy swamped by the waters, and many were destroyed by the water. But, although they suffered this loss, they threatened to enter via the collapsed wall. They placed armoured elephants at the ready and prepared the mass of men and more vehemently turned every kind of engine to their war effort. But the soldiers guarding the city thenceforth gained the victory through the forethought of God, and they filled the spot with every kind of armament. They slew the majority of the elephants with catapults, while others fell in the muddy water of the ditches. And others were hit and turned to flight. More than ten thousand of their infantry perished. And on the rest a thunderbolt fell from heaven, and the rattlings of storm-clouds, violent rainstorms and thunder frightened the remainder, so that the majority died of fright. Shapur the New Pharaoh was beset on all sides and defeated by the waves of fear; gazing at the fallen wall, he saw an angel standing on the summit splendidly clad, and by his hand the victorious emperor Constantius. He was immediately thrown into confusion and threatened his Magi with death. When they learnt the reason they decided to interpret to the king the power of the phenomenon, namely, that it was greater than they possessed. Then when he learnt the reason for the danger he became fearful and ordered the engines to be burnt and that all he had prepared for the prosecution of the war be broken up. He himself with his own retinue sought his native land in flight – but first [many] were destroyed by plague.

In this year Constantius Augustus became sole emperor;[37] he proclaimed his own cousin Gallus as associate Caesar of his own throne. Giving him the name Constantius,[38] he sent him to Antioch in the Orient since the Persians were still pressing their attack.

(Dodgeon)

Zonaras, XIII, 7, 1–14 (iii, pp. 193, 24–195, 7, Dindorf): While Constantius was considering this and delaying, Shapur, who had come to know of the events concerning Constans, took advantage of the opportunity and with a powerful army came against the lands and cities subject to the Romans. 2. He plundered much of the territory and took some fortresses and finally besieged Nisibis which once belonged to the kingdom of Armenia; but in the time of Mithridates, who was the son-in-law of the then ruler of Armenia, Tigranes, and had taken the city from him, it was captured by the Romans in a siege. 3. When Shapur arrived there, he moved up every kind of engine so that the city might be taken by him; for he brought rams against the walls and had underground passages dug, but the besieged nobly resisted every form of attack. 4. He diverted the river which flowed through the middle of the city so that the people in the city would be oppressed by thirst and hand the city over to him. 5. But they had an ample supply of water both from wells and from springs. 6. When his designs produced nothing effective, he devised something else. Moving upstream of the river which, as was said, flowed through the city, he came to a chasm where the area through which the river flowed was reduced in width. He blocked the place up and checked the flow of the river. 8. When the water backed up in flood, all at once he took away the barrier blocking the exit of the water and let the flood down on the city. The mass of flood water struck the wall with excessive force and brought down part of it. 9. However, the barbarian (king) did not immediately enter the city, thinking that it was already captured. Since dusk was approaching, he deferred capturing the city till the following day as there was no sign of resistance. 10. The people in the city were thrown into confusion by the breach in the wall, but when they saw the Persians delaying their entry, they passed the night without sleep and, with many hands helping, they fortified their position with a second wall on the inside. 11. When Shapur saw this in the early morning, he ascribed his ill-fortune to his own negligence. 12. However, after he devised many other stratagems towards the city and lost very many of his own men (for during the siege of Nisibis he is said to have lost more than twenty thousand men from the Persian army), he retired in ignominy. 13. For already the Massagetae had invaded Persia and were causing damage there. 14. The emperor Constantius strengthened Nisibis and recovered its citizens. Since there was now a truce in the Orient with the Persians, he set off for the West.

(Dodgeon)

7.5.6. Constantius at Edessa (after Jan. 350)

Philostorgius, *historia ecclesiastica* III, 22, p. 49, 2–6: He (i.e. Philostorgius) says that Constans was put to death by the tyrant Magnentius, on account of his zeal for Athanasius. After his death, Constantius stayed for some time at Edessa on account of the Persian war.

(Walford, p. 458)

7.6.1. Strengthening of the Syrian frontier by Constantius prior to his departure to the West (350)

Julian, *or.* I, 26D–27A (21.20–5, p. 41, Bidez): On learning these facts you thought you (i.e. Constantius) ought not to waste your time in idleness to no purpose. The cities of Syria you stocked with engines of war, garrisons, food supplies, and equipment of other kinds, considering that, by these measures, you would, though absent, sufficiently protect the inhabitants, while you were planning to set out in person against the usurpers.

(Wright, i, p. 69)

7.6.2. Building inscriptions from the Syrian-Arabian frontier (350–353)

Littmann – Magie – Stuart, III. A, Pt. 2, p. 104, no. 177 (Greek inscription found built into the eastern wall of the town of El-Meshkuk): Good Fortune! The tower was successfully built. Bassus, veteran in the rank of *ordinarius*,[39] having served in Mesopotamia (erected it). Uranius (was) the builder. There were expended 15,000(?) denarii. In the year 245 (of the era of Bostra = AD 350).[40]

IGLS 9062 (= Sartre, *Syria* 50 (1973), p. 230, Latin inscription found in the court of citadel at Bostra): [To our Lord, Flavius, Claudius Constantius] (i.e. Gallus), most brave and most victorious Caesar, Aurelius Valerianus, *v(ir) p(erfectissimus), dux,*[41] devoted to his divine quality and his majesty. (352–3)

7.6.3. Importance of Antioch to the Persian Campaigns of Constantius

Libanius, *or.* XI, 177–9: When this last Persian war was unchained, for which the Persian government had been preparing for a long time, and when the emergency called for adequate counter preparation to match the threat, and, even more than for preparations, called for a place capable of receiving all those things that such a war requires, this land of ours is the one that rose above the emergency with its abundance and collected the forces to its bosom and sent forth the entire army, when the time called. 178. For there flowed to it, like rivers to the sea, all the soldiers, all the bowmen and horsemen and the horses, both those of the fighting men and those carrying burdens, and every camel and every band of soldiers, so that the ground was covered with men standing and men sitting; the walls were covered with shields hung up and spears and helmets were to be seen everywhere; everything resounded with hammering and noise and whinnying, and there were so many units stationed here that their officers alone would have added no small population to the city, or rather such a great army was gathered that in other places the drinking water would have been exhausted; but everyone received the soldiers as pleasantly as though they were caring for a kinsman who came for a visit after a long interval; and each one fared as well from the land as though behind each dwelling the area had been transformed automatically into the semblance of a cavern filled with provisions; and it was possible in this way for men to be nourished to satiety, so that it seemed that it was not human intention or labour which provided the foresight or the service, but as though the gods, as the power of gods is, prepared everything in unseen fashion. 179. Wherefore the Persians blame us especially among their enemies because we provide this city as a base of operations which rivals the warlike prowess of the emperor, and we have nowhere diminished his eager courage by any deficiency of the help which we supply.'

(Downey, 1959: 671)

7.6.4. The Persian mailed cavalry (cataphracts) as described in contemporary fiction

Heliodorus,[42] *Aethiopica*, IX, 14, 3–15, ed. Rattenbury and Lumb, iii, pp. 56–8: For in fact it is this brigade of Persians (i.e. the cataphracts) which is always the most formidable in action; placed in the front line of battle, it serves as an unbreakable bulwark.

15 Their fighting equipment is furnished in this way: a picked man, chosen for his bodily strength, is capped with a helmet which has been compacted and forged in one piece and skilfully fashioned like a mask into the exact shape of a man's face; this protects him entirely from the top of the head to the neck, except where eye-holes allow him to see through it. His right hand is armed with a pike of greater length than the spear, while his left is at liberty to hold the reins. He has a sabre slung at his side, and his corselet extends, not merely over his breast, but also over the rest of his body. 2. This corselet is constructed thus: plates of bronze and of iron are forged into a square shape measuring a span each way, and are fitted one to another at the edges on each side, so that the plate above overlaps the next one to it, all forming a continuous surface; and they are held together by means of hooks and loops under the flaps. Thus is produced a kind of scaly tunic which sits close to the body without causing discomfort, and clings all round each limb with its individual casing and allows unhindered movement to each by its contraction and extension. 3. It has sleeves, and descends from neck to knee, with an opening only for the thighs so far as is required for mounting a horse's back. Such a corselet is proof against any missiles, and is a sure defence against all wounds. The greaves reach from above the flat of the foot to the knee, and are joined on to the corselet. 4. The horse is protected by a similar equipment: round his feet greaves are fastened, and his head is tightly bound all about with frontlets. From his back to his belly hangs on either side a housing of plaited strips of iron, serving as armour, but at the same time so pliable as not to impede his more rapid paces. 5. The horse being thus equipped and, as it were, encased, the rider bestrides him, not vaulting of himself into the saddle, but lifted up by others because of his weight. When the moment comes to engage in battle, he gives his horse the rein, applies his spurs, and in full career charges the enemy, to all appearance some man made of iron, or a mobile statue wrought with the hammer. 6. His pike projects with its point thrust far ahead: it is supported by a loop attached to the horse's neck, and has its butt-end suspended by a strap alongside

the horse's haunches; so that it does not recede in the clashes of conflict, but lightens the task of the rider's hand, which only directs the blow. He braces himself and, firmly set so as to increase the gravity of the wound, by his mere impetus transfixes anyone who comes in his way, and may often impale two persons at a single stroke.

(Lamb, pp. 231–2)

8 Rome and Shapur II
The later wars of Constantius II
(353-360)

(A) CHRONOLOGY AND ANALYSIS OF THE SOURCES

The years of comparative peace (353-356)

Gallus, a cousin of Constantius, was made Caesar and placed in charge of the defence of the East in 351. Cf. Philostorgius, III, 25. His alleged success in keeping the Persians at bay: idem,[1] III, 28 and *Artemii Passio*[2] 12. See also Zosimus III, 1, 1. Inroads of Saracens:[3] Amm. XIV, 4, 1-7. Shapur meanwhile was preoccupied with campaigns against nomadic invaders from Central Asia: Amm. XIV, 3, 1 and XVI, 9, 3; general reduction in the scale of fighting (353 ff.): Amm. XVI, 9, 1. (354) Abortive Persian raid on Batna[4] in Osrhoene by a Nohodares. Cf. Amm. XIV, 3, 1-4. Ursicinus[5] was summoned from Nisibis by Gallus to investigate treason charges. Cf. Amm. XIV, 9, 1. Marriage between Olympias, daughter of the late Caesar Ablabius, to Arsaces, king of Armenia (c. 354): Athanasius, *hist. Arian.* 69, Amm. XX, 11, 3, see also XIV, 11, 4 and Faustus Buzandats'i, *Hist. Arm.* IV, 15 and Moses Khorenats'i, *Hist. Arm.* III, 21. (356) Sporadic Persian raids into Mesopotamia: Amm. XV, 13, 4 and Zos. III, 1, 1.

The prelude to war (357-359)

(357) Negotiations for a localized cease-fire between Musonianus and Tamsapor: Amm. XVI, 9, 2-3 (see also XVI, 10, 21 and XVII, 10, 12). Shapur II wintered in the land of the Chionitae[6] (357). Cf. Amm. XVI, 9, 4. Meanwhile Ursicinus resumed his command in the East: Amm. XVI, 10, 21.

(357/8) A Persian embassy to Constantius at Antioch. Cf. Themistius, *or.* IV, ed. Schenkel and Downey, pp. 81, 20-82, 12

(= Harduin 57B), Petrus Patricius, *frag*. 17, *FHG* IV, p. 190 and Zos. III, 27, 4. Shapur demanded the return of territory ceded by Narses:[7] Amm. XVII, 5, 3–8 and Zonaras XII, 9, 25–7. The demands of Shapur were rejected by Constantius. Cf. Amm. XVII, 5, 9–14 and Zonaras, XIII, 9, 28–9.

(357/8) The defection of the *protector* Antoninus[8] to the Persians: Libanius, *or*. XII, 74 and Amm. XVIII, 5, 1–3.

(358) An embassy was sent by Constantius to Shapur to avert war. Cf. Libanius, *ep*. 331, Basil, *ep*. 1, Eunapius, *vit. soph*. VI, 5, 1–10 and Amm. XVII, 14, 1–2. Another embassy, led by Procopius and Lucillianus,[9] was sent to Shapur: Amm. XVII, 14, 3 and XVIII, 6, 17–18.

(*c.* 359) Description of the frontier regions (especially of the prosperity of the Mesopotamian cities) by an anonymous author: *Expositio totius mundi et gentium*[10] 19–20 and 22.

The outbreak of hostilities (359)

Ursicinus was summoned away from the Eastern Frontier to replace Barbatio. Cf. Amm. XVIII, 5, 5. Antoninus' advice to Shapur to avoid repeating his past errors in the choice of invasion routes: Amm. XVIII, 5, 6–8 and XVIII, 6, 3–4. Ursicinus was recalled to the East as second-in-command under Sabinianus: Amm. XVIII, 6, 5. Domitius Modestus,[11] an experienced commander, was sent to Euphratensis and Mesopotamia to take measures against the Persian invasion. Cf. Libanius, *epp*. 46, 367, 383 and 388.

Ursicinus and his staff narrowly escaped capture by advance elements of the Persian army at Nisibis.[12] Cf. Amm. XVIII, 6, 8–16. Ursicinus established his command at Amida and received a secret message[13] from Procopius of Persian troop movements. Cf. Amm. XVIII, 6, 17–19. Ammianus was sent on a secret mission to Jovinianus, the satrap of Cordyene:[14] Amm. XVIII, 6, 20–3 and 7, 1–2.

Military preparations for the Persian invasion (esp. along the Euphrates): Amm. XVIII, 7, 3–6. The 'inaction' of Sabinianus, the *Magister Equitum* (East):[15] Amm. XVIII, 7, 7. The Persian army by-passed Nisibis but, finding its way into Syria blocked by the Euphrates which was then in flood, it headed north.[16] Cf. Amm. XVIII, 7, 8–11 and Zonaras, XIII, 9, 30–1. Roman fear of Persian attempts to cross the Euphrates: Libanius, *ep*. 49. Ambushed en route to Samosata and separated from Ursicinus, Ammianus escaped to Amida: Amm. XVIII, 8, 1–14.

The siege and fall of Amida (359)

Description of Amida and its defences:[17] Amm. XVIII, 9. Surrender of two Roman forts (Reman and Busan) to Shapur and the capture of the wife of Craugasius, an important citizen of Nisibis: Amm. XVIII, 10.

The citizens of Amida refused Shapur's terms for surrender: Amm. XIX, 1, 1–6. Death of the son of Grumbates, the king of the Chionitae: ibid., 1, 7–11.[18] The Persians made two major assaults against the defences within two days but were repelled. Cf. ibid. XIX, 2. Ursicinus' plan to relieve the siege by a diversionary attack was overruled by Sabinianus. Cf. ibid. XIX, 3. Plague broke out in Amida because of the insanitary conditions and lasted for ten days. Cf. ibid., XIX, 4, 1 and 8. The Persians installed siege-engines and artillery against one side of the city while gaining entry through a passage on the side facing the Tigris; but were repelled after heavy fighting. Cf. ibid. XIX, 5. Capture of Ziata by the Persians and the parade of Roman prisoners before Amida: ibid. XIX, 6, 1. Incensed by the suffering of the captives, elements of Gallic legions in Amida made a night attack on the Persian camp and were stopped just short of the royal tent. They withdrew after inflicting heavy casualties on the Persians. Cf. ibid. XIX, 6, 3–13. Towers and other siege engines were brought up to the walls of the city but were set on fire by the Romans. Cf. ibid., XIX, 7. The city was stormed by the Persians who erected high mounds against the walls. Cf. ibid. XIX, 8, 1–4. Escape of Ammianus from Amida: ibid. XIX, 8, 5–12.

Execution of captured Roman commanders at Amida: Amm. XIX, 9, 1–2. Defection of Craugasius of Nisibis: ibid. XIX, 9, 3–8.

The aftermath of the fall of Amida (359–360)

Shapur's concern over the extent of Persian casualties: Amm. XIX, 9, 9. (360) Constantius demanded the transfer of certain units under Julian's command in Gaul to the East. Cf. Julian, *ep. ad Ath.* 282D (10.12–17, Bidez), Libanius, *or.* XII, 58 and XVIII, 90–1 Eutropius, X, 15, 1 and Amm. XX, 4, 1–2. Relief of Ursicinus from his command: Amm. XX, 2. Constantius hastened to reinforce the East: Amm. XX, 4, 1.

Singara was taken and destroyed by Shapur. Cf. Amm. XX, 6. Bezabde[19] was stormed and garrisoned by Shapur. Cf. Amm. XX, 7, 1–16 and Theophanes, *chron.*, A. M. 5852, p. 46, 9–10. On the fate of the Roman captives taken at Bezabde, see *Acts of the Martyrs of Bezabde (The Martyrdom of the Prisoners of War)*, ed. Bedjan, *AMS* II, pp. 316–24 (Syriac). Shapur failed, however, to capture Virtha, a well-defended city on the frontier of Mesopotamia which was an Alexandrian foundation.[20] Cf. Amm. XX, 7, 17.

Constantius sent for Arsaces, the king of Armenia, and did his utmost to retain his loyalty. Cf. Amm. XX, 11, 1–3. See also *CT* XI, 1, 1 (Law granting exemption from taxes in kind to the royal family of Armenia). (23 April) Constantius set off for Mesopotamia via Melitene, Lacotena and Samosata and arrived at Edessa on 21 Sept. Cf. Amm. XX, 11, 4. He inspected the ruins of Amida (ibid. XX, 11, 4–5) and laid siege to Bezabde (XX, 11, 6–25). On failing to recapture the city, he withdrew to Antioch via Hierapolis (17 Dec., cf. *CT* VII, 4, 6): Amm., XX, 11, 31–2 and Theophanes, *chron.*, A. M. 5852, p. 46, 10–14. (After 29 May) Constantius crossed the Euphrates at Capersana and headed for Edessa where he planned for a second assault on Bezabde and reorganized the defences in Mesopotamia. Cf. Amm. XXI, 7, 7 and 13, 1–5. Shapur withdrew from the Tigris because of unfavourable omens and Constantius returned to Hierapolis (some mss. give Nikopolis). Cf. ibid. XXI, 13, 8. On receiving news of the refusal of Julian to renounce the title of Augustus, Constantius departed from Antioch amidst general panic in the city. Cf. Libanius, *or.* XII, 71 and Zonaras, XIII, 11, 10. (3 Nov.) Death of Constantius at Mopsucrenae: Amm. XXI, 15, 2 and Soc., II, 47, 4 and III, 1, 1.

For later views of Constantius' conduct of the Persian Wars, see esp. Libanius, *or.* XVIII, 205–11.

(B) THE SOURCES (IN ALPHABETICAL ORDER OF THEIR AUTHORS)

Ammianus Marcellinus, see Introduction, *supra.* p. 7.

Artemii Passio 12 (12.16–22, p. 208, ed. Kotter) And Gallus having then been sent by Constantius kept a tight rein on the affairs of the East. The Persians, once they learnt of him, took fright when they ascertained that he was a young man and hot-blooded for action.

They no longer made their expedition against the Romans. And while Gallus was in Antioch in Syria, Constantius settled affairs in the West. And then especially the Roman Empire enjoyed a genuine peace. [See also Zosimus III, 1, 1, cited below.]

Athanasius, *hist. Arian.* 69, ed. Bright, p. 232: So likewise he (i.e. Constantius) treated his brother (i.e. Constans) in an unholy manner; and now he pretends to build his sepulchre, although he delivered up to the barbarians his betrothed wife Olympias, whom his brother had protected till his death, and had brought up as his intended consort.

(Atkinson *ap.* Robertson, p. 296)

Basil, *ep.* 1 (To Eustathius): Nay, so love-sick was I that I was compelled either to take the road to Persia and go with you as you advanced to the uttermost limits of the land of the barbarians – for indeed you went even thither, so obstinate was the demon who kept us apart – or else take up my abode here at Alexandria.

(Deferrari, i, p. 5)

Bezabde, The Acts of the Martyrs of, *(The Martyrdom of the Prisoners of War)*, ed. Bedjan, *AMS* II, pp. 316–24 (Syriac): Shapur, king of the Persians, advanced in his fifty-third year of rule against the borders and citadels of the Romans, besieged the fort (*castra*) of Bet Zabdai, captured it, destroyed its walls, delivered many of its warriors to the mouth of the sword and took prisoners roughly nine thousand souls, men and women, among them the Bishop Heliodorus, the old priests Dausa and Maryahb who were with him, (other) priests, deacons and the community (*qyama*) of (holy) men and women. And, as they were led to Bet Huzaje, the king and his army marched along the road with them.

2 At one stop called Daskarta, Bishop Heliodorus fell ill; he consecrated Dausa as bishop and made him the head of them all. He also handed over to him the altar he had taken with him, that he might serve conscientiously at it. He fell to sleep and was buried there with honours.

3 As they made their way from there, they began to come together as one congregation and to recite psalms in choirs. And, as they gave praise to God daily thus, the evil Magi felt themselves to be pierced to their hearts; their conscience was upset and they accused them before Adarfarr, the Chief Mobed, on whose advice much blood of the martyrs of God was spilt in the Orient.[21] This accursed one went before the king and said: 'Good King, among these

prisoners is a head of the Christians, called Dausa, who gathers around him many prisoners of like mind, men and women, who rise up and with one voice curse and vilify your majesty; and they do this daily. I sent and scolded them once and then twice, but they cursed you even more and vilified the gods of the Persians.'

4 The king had made a halt at Dursak, in the area of Daraye, and he ordered this Mobed and a high ranking official, called Hazaraft (= *Chiliarch*): 'Go, and bring together by cunning the head of these Christians and of all those of like mind, and say to them: 'It pleases the king to do good things for you, and he commanded that you settle here on this mountain; the land is fat, its villages are beautiful, the ground is well watered; that will give you constant peace all the days of your lives.' Watch for when all those collect together, who gather every day, vilify our majesty and scorn our gods; take them up on to this mountain and question them on some spot. Those who do my will, who worship the sun and the moon and who deny the god whom the Caesar (i.e. the Roman emperor) prays to, may settle according to their wish in these villages. But whoever disobeys this order shall be delivered to the sword.'

5 At this, these two important officials went with one hundred horsemen and two hundred foot soldiers, called before them the Bishop Dausa, Maryahb, the Chorepiscopos, the priests, deacons, the community (*qyama*) and the lay believers who were attached to them, and they talked treacherously to them. Together there were about three hundred people. They took them up on to the mountain, called Masabadan, to a village called Gefta and arranged them outside the village. There, all of a sudden that bitter man, the Mobed Adarfarr, that spiller of blood, revealed his treachery, showed his deceit and said: 'You must know that the king commanded that you should all be killed here, because every day you scorn him and vilify the gods of the Persians. But if you now listen to our advice, you can live and be saved. Henceforth, do the will of the king, worship the sun and the moon, abandon the religion of the Caesar, accept the religion of Shapur, the King of Kings. For you are his servants, and he has authority over you. If you obey in this, I am empowered by him to leave you in these rich and fertile villages and in this region which, as your eyes can see, is planted with vines, olives and palms. He will also give you all the gifts and presents which you ask of me. But if you do not obey the command of the king, then you must know that you will die today by the sword and that, in accordance with the decree we have received from him, none of you shall remain alive.'

6 The courageous Dausa said out loud: 'O people, which swims in the blood of its own land and which revels in blood of other lands, see, your own people and foreigners are being killed; natives and immigrants are being slain. What advantage have you, and how can you defend yourselves? See, your punishment has been written by justice; judgement has been made on you and will not be forgotten. Since you have been covered with blood of the martyrs of the East, are you going to sprinkle yourselves with the blood of the martyrs of the West, with the holy blood sealing in martyrdom your written document; to join the victorious blood of the holy martyrs which you have (already) slain? The secret of the treachery which you reveal to us is a covert joy for us, and the command of the evil one, which you showed us, is for us an open rejoicing. With this, we are no longer taken captive and made aliens to our homeland, nor have we died in foreign parts, nor do we die as prisoners. Who will kill us? Let him neither stand still nor hesitate. Who will murder us? Let him not delay or dally. The God of us all is one, who, for our sins, has put us in your hands. Now he has taken pity on us and is reconciled with us; so that for his sake we die today by your hand. Far be it from us to worship the sun and the moon, the work of His hands, and to do the will of your king; who devours human flesh. We will be strong in our faith; we worship our true God, whom the Emperor (i.e Constantius) worships as well, and believe in Him. We shall go to the place destined for us, singing his praises. But woe to you, you impure and depraved people, who have misled the Orient by your godless teaching. God will quickly destroy it in you, He will ruin you in it, destroy your deception and cull your lie from the whole land of the Orient. You must know that we will all persist in this firm view which I have given you. Do now what you have been commanded, without delay.' So he (i.e. Mobed Adarfarr) ordered his soldiers and they began to lead away and kill fifty men and women at a time, until the number rose to two hundred and seventy-five. Now twenty-five men and women became weak to the shame of their souls and worshipped the Sun. They settled them there until this day.

7 A deacon called Abdisho remained alive, because the sword did not strike him squarely. After the sun had gone down, he rose, went into the village and met a poor man, who led him into his house and washed and dressed his wounds. When day came, Abdisho led that man and his two sons to the dead and showed them the corpse of Dausa, of Maryahb and of the other old priests. The three of

them took them, climbed a little higher, found a small cave, laid them down in it and closed them in with huge stones. Then they went back to Abdisho and found him kneeling and crying in prayer at the place of execution.

8 Pagan Karmanian shepherds, who had led their sheep to grass, saw there over three nights hosts of angels, who were hovering up and down over the execution place of the saints and praising God. They were frightened and announced it in the whole region, and because of this vision they were converted to the faith.

9 Abdisho, who despite the stroke of the sword remained alive, began to lead to life the souls which had died through sin. He had decided, because of the bones of the just people who had fallen there, to remain there all his days. For thirty days he did not stop teaching piety through actions and good works. But when an evil man, the lord of the village, saw that he was converting people from error to a knowledge of the truth, Satan enviously entered him and the Evil one taught him murderous jealousy. He seized Abdisho, hit him, held him in chains for four days and said: 'If you go forth from here and no longer teach in this village, then I will set you free: go where you will.' The blessed Abdisho said: 'I have decided to remain here and not to stop giving this teaching to the ears of all who hear, obey and turn to life.' At this the evil man flared up, led him out of the village to the place where his friends had been killed and gave a Karmanian fifty silver pieces. The latter struck him with a sword and so he died. Then the poor man came out again with his sons; they took the body of that hero Abdisho, hid it and erected over it a large mound of stones, which until today is called the Grave of Abdisho. But heaven's anger struck the godless murderer and his house. His four sons were handed over to a demon, who quickly killed them. He himself became dropsical; he sat for thirty days on the dungheap in unspeakable torment and when he died there, he was eaten by his dogs. He lost his fortune suddenly; his servants fled and dispersed; his wife begged for her bread and died with a mental breakdown. As the river of that village had been dug by man, God let mice breed in it, and they filled it with earth by their burrowing. And when the inhabitants of the village came together and took out the earth, the mice dug again and filled it up. This happened repeatedly, and as the village suffered drought and its plantation withered, it remained desert for twenty-two years and became as though accursed in the whole region.

10 After this came a son of the man who had taken in Abdisho and buried him and had hidden the martyrs of God, and he prayed

at the mouth of the cave and made a vow to come every year to commemorate the martyrdom. After this, he dug out the village's river, built houses and settled in peace. God blessed him, he came to own it, and it was called after him. Each time he celebrated the memory, miracles of healing occurred through the bones of the saints.

11 A head of a monastery, zealous with the wonderful zeal of God, built a martyrium there, took their bones from the cave, laid them to rest in the house he had built, and until today gatherings (for worship) are held there.

(Jordan, revised Brock)

Codex Theodosianus, XI, 1, 1: Emperor Constantine (*sic*) Augustus to Proclianus. With the exception of the property of Our private domain and the Catholic churches and the household of Eusebius, of Most Noble memory, Ex-Consul and Ex-Master of the Horse and Foot, and the household of Arsaces, King of Armenia, no person in accordance with Our order shall be assisted by special advantages for his family property. ... Given on the fifteenth day before the kalends of July at Constantinople in the year of the fourth consulship of Constantine and of Licinius. June 17, 315 (*sic*). (January 18, 360, Mommsen).

(Pharr, p. 291)

Eunapius, *vitae sophistarum* VI, 5, 1–10: With regard to Eustathius, it would be sacrilegious to leave out what would convey the truth. All men were agreed that he was not only observed to be a most noble character, but also most gifted with eloquence when put to the test, while the charm that sat on his tongue and lips seemed to be nothing less than witchcraft. His mildness and amiability so blossomed out in what he said and gushed forth with his words, that those who heard his voice and speeches surrendered themselves like men who had tasted the lotus, and they hung on that voice and those speeches. 2. So closely did he resemble the musical Sirens, that the emperor, for all that he was wrapped up in the books of the Christians, sent for him at the time when he was alarmed by the state of affairs, and was hard pressed by impending danger from the king of the Persians, who had once already laid siege to Antioch and raided it with his bowmen. For unexpectedly and on a sudden he seized the height that commanded the theatre, and with his arrows shot and massacred that great crowd of spectators. 3. In this similar crisis all men were so held captive and enchanted by Eustathius, that they did not hesitate to commend a man of the Hellenic faith to the ears of the emperor; although the earlier emperors had been accustomed to elect for embassies men who had won distinction in the army, or military prefects, or men who were next in rank to these and had been selected for office. 4. But at that time, at the imperious call of necessity, Eustathius was sought out and admitted by general consent to be the most prudent of all men. Accordingly he was summoned by the emperor, and came forthwith, and so potent was the charm on his lips that those who had advised that the embassy should be dispatched in the charge of Eustathius won greater consideration than before from the emperor, and he inclined more favourably towards them. 5. Moreover, some of these men set out of their own accord to accompany the embassy, because they wished to employ a still greater test, whether in his encounter with the barbarians Eustathius should prove to possess the same power to enchant and persuade. 6. When they arrived in Persia, Sapor was reported to be and actually was tyrannical and savage towards those who approached him; nevertheless, when Eustathius, for the embassy in general, was allowed access to the king, the latter could not but admire the expression of his eyes which was at once amiable and proudly indifferent, in spite of the many preparations that the king had devised in order to dazzle and overawe the man. 7. And when he heard his voice conversing so equably and with no effort, when he heard him run over his arguments so modestly and good-naturedly, he bade him withdraw; and Eustathius went out, leaving the tyrant a captive to his eloquence. Presently he sent a message by his household officials to invite him to his table, and when he obeyed the summons, since the king seemed to him to have a natural bent for virtue, Sapor joined him at the banquet. 8. Thus Eustathius became his companion at table, and by his eloquence won such influence over him that the king of Persia came within an ace of renouncing his upright tiara, laying aside his purple and bejewelled attire, and putting on instead the philosopher's cloak of Eustathius; so successfully did the latter run down the life of luxury and the pomps and vanities of the flesh, to such depths of misery did he seem to bring down those who loved their bodies. 9. But this was prevented by certain Magi who happened to be at the court, and kept asserting that the man was nothing but a mere conjuror; and they persuaded the king to reply to the Roman emperor (10.) by asking him why, when Fortune had bestowed on them so many distinguished men, they sent persons no better than slaves who had enriched themselves. And the whole result of the embassy was contrary to men's expectations.

(Wright, pp. 393–9)

Eutropius, *breviarium* X, 15, 1: Not long after, when the German armies were being transferred from the defence of Gaul, Julian was made emperor by the unanimous consent of the army, and after the lapse of a year, went to take the government of Illyricum, while Constantius was engaged in war with Parthia (*sic*).

(Watson, p. 533, revised)

Expositio totius mundi et gentium 19–20 and 22, ed. Rougé, pp. 152–5: After them (*sc.* Indians) are the Persians, the neighbours of the Romans, who are recorded to be exceedingly [. . .] in all evils and brave in wars. It is said that great impieties are committed by them, who are ignorant of the dignity of nature; acting like dumb animals, they sleep with their mothers and sisters. They behave impiously towards the God who created them. On the other hand, they are said to abound in all things. For since the permission to trade is given (by them) to all the neighbouring peoples, they appear to be well in all things.

20 Not far from them dwells the race of the Saracens who intend to spend their lives in archery and pillage. They resemble the Persians in being impious and deceitful, incapable of keeping their promises either in war or in any other business. Women are said to rule among them. . . .

22 After them are our lands, for Mesopotamia and Osrhoene are next. Mesopotamia has many different cities, two of which, as I shall describe, are outstanding. They are Nisibis and Edessa which have the most remarkable people of all: astute in business and skilled in the chase. In particular they are rich and adorned with all good things. For what they receive from Persia, they sell to all Roman territory, and purchase (goods) for exporting to them in return, besides iron and bronze, because it is not permitted to give iron and bronze to the enemy. They have famous walls which always break down the courage of the Persians in time of war. Buoyant with trade, they enjoy a high standard of living together with the rest of the province. Edessa is a specially splendid city.

(J. C. Morgan)

Faustus Buzandats'i, *Hist. Arm.* IV, 15 (Armenian): When the king (i.e. Arsak) was persuaded that it would be impossible for him to be loved by this princess (Pharandzem), he sent messengers to Greece, from where a certain Olympia, of imperial blood, was brought to him as a wife.

(Considine)

Julian, *ep. ad Ath*. 282D (10.12–17, Bidez): For he (Constantius) gave orders for the withdrawal from Gaul of, I might almost say, the whole of the most efficient troops without exception, and assigned this commission to Lupicinus and Gintonius, while to me he wrote that I (Julian) must oppose them in nothing.

(Wright, ii, p. 279)

Libanius, *ep.* 46: (To Modestus) I rejoice at such chicanery, and I shall rejoice all the more if you once again say that you have nothing, even though you have more letters. For it is the deceit of a lover who through his desire to receive letters denies that they have come. 2. So just as, if you received one letter and commended a wealth of correspondence, you would be making it clear that there was no need of letters, so now in inveighing against the many that have arrived on the grounds that none had come, you make it plain that no weight of letters would have ended this thirst of yours. I can say therefore that our swallows are more numerous than yours unless you make this point, that the man who has sent three in the midst of his activities has surpassed the five of the correspondent whose only occupation is writing. 3. Even formerly I hated the Persians for trying to cause damage and loving evil deeds after they had themselves suffered; now all the more I consider them hostile for encircling you with difficulties and depriving us for such a long time of your most pleasant society. But even though you are absent, you gladden us to whom you give hope by frightening the enemy with your simple preparations. 4. And even if you are somewhat delayed, yet I shall see you more honoured in winning a reward of acclamation for these many marches. Then indeed, then you will remember with pleasure the present disagreeable position.

(Dodgeon)

Libanius, *ep.* 49: (To Modestus) I hear that the fears have reached crisis point, that bridges have been completed by the Persians and that the crossing is open to them. But may this ensure that your foresight is greater, but let there be absent disturbance to your foresight. For this very fact will ensure the possibility of foreknowledge, since reasoning is necessarily clouded in confusion. But firstly let it encourage you that this is not the first invasion that the Persians have dared, but they are always trying to cross over since the war began; but in always suffering heavy casualties they have condemned themselves for their expectations. Then the victory does not altogether follow the greater numbers but generally it happens that the multitude is defeated by prudence. But if the larger host were stronger, I suppose that this king's ancestor should have gained possession of Greece. But you know now that he campaigned from desire for her, but during his flight from there his desire was to return alive. For the same men were not able to dig through mountains and overcome courageous warriors. And indeed this king will meet with the strategy of generals who will teach him that it would have been better for him to fight with deer. Should he in fact cross the Tigris, he will be defeated by the city walls and will be able neither to ravage the land nor harvest it; for it has been ravaged. He will be seeking all along to capture the cities by the Euphrates, but will not appear to have been successful. For the emperor's fortune fortifies them. You must expect such a turn of events; I have not neglected your affairs which stood in need of a letter of Hermogenes, but we the mice are trying to help you the lions, rather than you the lions helping us.

(Dodgeon)

Libanius, *ep.* 331: (To Aristaenetus) Spectatus,[22] on his return from the embassy, seemed fortunate in the eyes of many, to some because he had seen so much of the land and the mountains and the rivers (of that country); to others because he had observed the Persian way of life and the customs and laws by which they live. Yet others made much of his seeing the king himself and the precious stones which he wore; while others considered it a fine thing to have exchanged gifts and departed. 2. This gave me also a certain measure of delight, but it seemed to me that the fairest thing was that he returned having shown in Susa the power of his oratory. Indeed I thought he had lost this power, transferred elsewhere, after so long now away from his books. But his personality had retained the skill. 3. For when the Persian (king) was giving audience and the talk centred on their differences, there was much pressure in his demand for the restoration of the borders held by his grandfather Narses. There were frequent questions whether it was unjust that the misfortunes of ancestors descended to their children, and thereupon Spectatus intended to answer the tricks of the other side, if he should be able to defeat their laughter. He employed some arguments which were very noble, and indeed confounded the specious talk of the Persian. 4. For he said, 'Your Majesty, if Constantius appropriates your land, remain in arms while he maintains an imperialistic policy. But if you accuse the dead of a long time ago with whom Narses went to war, and now Constantius, retaining the advantage, wishes to end the fighting, take care lest, in making your charge of imperialism, you be accused of similar behaviour.'

5. In such a way they say he put on a brave show, so that the king examined his youth and scrutinized his argument and shook his head not a few times. Because of your friend's questioning, the king, he who sought to catch us in verbal traps was reduced to silence. So he spoke clearly to another, 'Whatever would a legate from us to you state more clearly on his own behalf, or one to us from Persia?'

(Dodgeon)

Libanius, *ep*, 367: (To Modestus) Were you yourself also held back by what I too suffered? When evening approaches, a time when I am accustomed to visit you, I demand of my feet the journey, but am pained when I cannot see you. 2. Perhaps the same thing happens to you also at sunset. I am instructed in this both by your different temper and by the charges through which you censured me when I accompanied you. 3. You said, then, that you had been ill-treated for two days when I abandoned your company, and the accusations were sweeter than honey to me. Since I blamed the sickness which troubled my head and stated that I had stayed at home on account of that necessity, you discovered a second charge of not informing you of this. 4. This indeed is the converse of private citizens among themselves – the governor to the governed. But that a man who is loved should know how to love (in return) is no less a demonstration of virtue than passing judgment in the way that you do. You act well in imitating Heracles in your labour and the Persians in your swiftness. But we need your wings not only to bring you quickly over the Euphrates but to restore you speedily also to our river, the Orontes.

(Dodgeon)

Libanius, *ep*. 383: (To the same) I did both things in fair degree; I both wrote and abstained from writing. For, on the one hand, I desired to receive a letter from you, on the other, through not receiving one, I was hesitant to set my hand to it once again. Now therefore since it has come to pass that I am in receipt of a letter, you will clearly see me as an archer dispatching a rain of letters. 2. But in wishing to learn of my present circumstances, you seem likely to be yearning for sorrow. For from those times until this day my heart has not been able to be at peace. 3. There was in addition to this a greater evil, the fact that I could not even visit you, which for one so distressed would have been a better medicine than anything. As you well know, even if I should be healthier than

Croton, yet being parted from you I place myself among the unwell.
4. Daphne, beloved of Apollo – I do not now mean the nymph, but
the place into which the maiden was transformed – I considered
even before was beautiful, and I consider it all the more beautiful
now since it seems so to you. Yet I do not share in the place when
I have become a prisoner of my art. For what governing is to you,
teaching is to me.

(Dodgeon)

Libanius, *ep.* 388: (To the same) There are many who announce
that you will come, but I do not yet see it put into effect.
Therefore turn the shadow of our joy into a true gladness. For
if there was need for reflection on affairs pertaining to the
Euphrates, sufficient provision has been made; if men needed to
know what kind of man you are beneath the blazing sun, you
seem not to have fallen short of Heracles' endurance. 2. Therefore why do you deprive of hope a great and fair city that loves
you, to which you owe a debt of gratitude for its affection, and
cannot find fault with? 3. But, excellent friend, compose your
defence and come and visit those you have wronged. For should
you appear immediately, yet the interval of time demands an
orator's skill. But you must by no means hire another to speak
for you when you have already in person saved many by your
voice.

(Dodgeon)

Libanius, *or.* XII, 58: Then he (Constantius) stripped him of a large
part of his forces, to weaken him (i.e. Julian); but he remained no
less strong. Then he called for his whole force, putting forward the
pretext of operations against Persia and under these most specious
terms betraying both the emperor and the cities.

(Norman, i, p.71.)

Libanius, *or.* XII, 71: Constantius had stripped the eastern empire
of its picked troops when he began his march. He entrusted the
cities to the weakest of his forces who, protectors to all appearances,
themselves needed protection. Thus both flock and watch-dog alike
were in fear and trembling. We thus felt that we had before our eyes
the sack of our cities, though it had not yet occurred, and that our
safety lay in flight.

(Norman, i, pp. 79–81)

Libanius, *or.* XII, 74: That doubly damned rogue (i.e. Antoninus),
that second Demaratus who filled the ears of the Persian king with

the tale of our wealth and who promised to betray to him during the winter our city in thrall . . .

(Norman, i, p. 81)

Libanius, *or.* XVIII, 90–1: . . . As a consequence, he (Julian) became the victim of the envy of the man who owed him his crowns of victory, for he began to recall the pick of the army and those ready for any emergency, allowing only those past their prime, whose contribution was numbers instead of deeds, to stay with him. 91. The ostensible reason was the Persian war, and the fact that a now peaceful Gaul required no troops, as though it were not a simple matter for the treacherous barbarians to ride roughshod over their agreements and as if it were unnecessary for military backing to support the articles of peace. He clearly had no need of an army bigger than the one he had already to deal with Persia, for a section of that was enough for the job, and however many times he raised a force like it, he would never have gone into battle, for he was bent on procrastination.

(Norman, i, pp. 338–9)

Libanius, *or.* XVIII, 205–11 (composed in 365): What makes you so eager for the story (of Julian's expedition) is the thought of the might of the Persians, and how great was the power of Constantius whom they used to vanquish, and against what pride and audacity the hero of my speech did so fearlessly advance. The fact is that Constantius, besides the possession of the islands and the regions lying upon the Atlantic, was master of the land from the very shores up to the streams of the Euphrates – a region producing other things of all sorts, and tall men and courageous souls, wherewith to form an army invincible. 206. Nevertheless this prince, so abounding in resources, the possessor of innumerable and splendid cities, in receipt of those vast tributes, he that was drawing that immense amount of gold from his mines, he who clad the bodies of his cavalry in steel with greater care than the Persians themselves, who protected from wounds the very horses by means of armour – this prince, having inherited a war from his father that called for courage befitting an emperor, and a soul knowing how to employ his forces to the best advantage, he, just as though he had determined to assist his adversaries, never took thought how he might wrest anything from them, or defend his own from falling into their hands, but leading an army, year by year, at the beginning of summer, whilst they were laying siege to places with the opening of spring, crossing the Euphrates and halting his mighty armament in its vicinity, with the intention of beating a retreat if the enemy should show themselves, almost within hearing of the lamentations of his besieged subjects, he thought it better generalship to avoid fighting and not to succour his own people! 207. What, therefore, was the result of his camping there? The one monarch battered down walls, demolished towns, and returned home carrying away goods and captives; the other sent out persons to view the desolation, and was grateful to Fortune that no greater mischief had been done, and made his return through the middle of the cities in broad daylight, welcomed by the population and with the cries that are appropriate to victory! And this was the programme of each successive year. The Persian king crossed the frontier, the other intended so doing; he attacked the fortifications, the other began to move; he was on the point of taking them, the other made inquiries about the matter; he took them, the other was well satisfied at not having come to blows; the one exulted in the multitudes of his captives, the other in his horse-races; the one received crowns from the cities, the other was giving them to charioteers. Is not such a man rightly to be styled an ally of the Persians? For when it is in one's power to hinder mischief, to permit it is next door to assisting in it with your own hands. 208. And let not anyone suppose me ignorant of that nocturnal battle (of Singara), in which both sides with mutual gall and loss separated; nor yet that sea-fight upon dry land (at Nisibis), in which they with difficulty saved the town that had endured so much; for this is the very hardship of the case, that he who had received by inheritance spirits knowing how to strike fear into the enemy, trained them into feeling fear, and by a bad education unnerved courageous dispositions. 209. What the force of training is in all matters philosophers point out, and the fable too declares; for it can change the better and the worse into the opposite of their former selves, if given to the former of a worse kind than his natural disposition, and to the latter, superior to the same. It (practice) has made women ride on horseback and rendered them more than a match for men in arms; and if it has forced the man endued by nature with virtue to live in the midst of revelling and drunkenness, his virtue forsakes him, and when he has learned this way of living instead of an honourable one, his former course grows hateful to him, and habit has distorted his natural character. 210. Something of this sort do I say that prince's soldiers experienced through his fault, when they took up arms but were forbidden to come to blows, and were taught to slumber under their tents whilst their countrymen were taken captive, and not to dread disgrace, but to fear death; at which lessons they were at first impatient, as was natural for courageous men; then, less so; next they assented to, and finally they approved of them. 211. Consequently, a cloud of dust rising in the distance, such as would be made by cavalry, did not stir them up to the conflict, but made them turn to flee. But when a squadron, and that only a small one, showed itself, they prayed earth to swallow them up, preferring to suffer any fate rather than look a Persian in the face. And when their manhood had been thus extirpated, their confidence was equally destroyed, to such a degree that in the houses where they were billeted, whenever they demanded to be served by their hosts, the word 'Persian' put a stop to their being troublesome; and everyone used to say, jeering at them, 'Here comes a Persian soldier!' and they forthwith turned red in the face and jumped away. Nevertheless, when led against their own countrymen, they knew how to strike and to suffer blows, but the Persian terror, growing in the course of long years, had become so fixed in them that somebody said they even would have trembled at the Persians in a picture.

(King, pp. 186–9, altered)

Petrus Patricius, *fragmenta* 17, *FHG* IV, p. 190: When envoys of the Persians came to Constantius, Narses, the leader of the embassy, blending the harshness of the letter he was bearing with the gentleness of his own manner, handed it over to be read.

(Dodgeon)

Philostorgius, *hist. eccl.* III, 25, GCS: While Constantius was preparing his expedition against the tyrant Magnentius, intelligence was brought to him that the Persians had already set their forces in motion against the provinces of the East. On this account he deemed it necessary to nominate Gallus as Caesar, and to send him into the East against the Persians. . . .

28. Gallus having shown considerable valour in the war against the Persians, certain calumniators endeavoured to stir up against him.

(Walford, pp. 459–60)

Themistius, *or.* IV, ed. Schenkel and Downey, pp. 81, 20–82, 12 (= Harduin 57B): And thus I (i.e. Themistius) am asserting the truth, and he is not only emperor there when he is seen, but indeed, when he is in camp among the Gauls, he compels the Persians to desire peace. And just recently in the city of Antioch I saw in person men who had arrived from Susa and Ecbatana with heralds' wands and an ancient letter wrapped in white linen. And the letter earnestly entreated the prefect to make a truce with the Achaemenids (*sic*) and give friendly assurances from the emperor. I, therefore, am of the view that this victory is more powerful than if they had just been overwhelmed in battle and their land had been divided and we had taken garrisons and prisoners. For then they blamed fortune and threatened to fight back, but now they have willingly cowered and show by their very attitude that they are vanquished. And Darius reluctantly at a late date made his request of Alexander, having been smashed at the Granicus and afterwards at Issus in Cilicia; but when our emperor has turned his arms from the stream of the Tigris to the Western Ocean, those in Babylon did not withstand his threat from so far away.

(Dodgeon)

Theophanes, *chronographia*, A.M. 5852, p. 46, 9–14: In this year the Persians captured the stronghold called Bezabde, and Constantius, hearing that Julian in Gaul had won a reputation in war and had been declared emperor by the army, as he was residing in Antioch because of the Persian war, set out against the usurper Julian. Coming to Mopsucrena at the first stopping place from Tarsus, he died on the third day of the month of Dius, having made many charges against his own folly.

(Dodgeon)

Zonaras, XIII, 9, 25–31 and XIII, 11, 10 (iii, pp. 202, 19–203, 5 and 207, 14–16, Dindorf): When, however, Constantius was marching from the West and returned to Byzantium, envoys from the Persians met him around Sirmium. They were sent by Shapur, who demanded that Mesopotamia and Armenia should be returned to Persia, that they might put an end to the war with Rome; 26. for these territories had been a source of problems to them since the time of their ancestors; 27 but if he (i.e. Constantius) did not comply, he made it clear to the emperor that he would appeal to Ares to judge the outcome of the matter.

On this matter, Constantius sent back the reply that he was amazed that Shapur seemed to have forgotten that the Persians were once enslaved to the Macedonians. When the Macedonians became subject to Rome, those who were in servitude to them became subject to the Romans. Shapur, angered by this, decided upon war.

Again (Shapur) laid siege to Nisibis.[23] When his attempt on it failed, he left and tried other cities. 31. However, when he was also beaten off from them, he came to Amida and captured it.

(XIII, 11), 10. ... at the time of his death Constantius was returning from the war against the Persians (and the king of Persia returned at the same time to his country) to march against the usurper (i.e. Julian).

(Dodgeon)

Zosimus, III, 1, 1 and 27, 4:... besides which (i.e. the invasion of the Franks, the Alamanni, etc.), the Persians were perpetually harassing the eastern provinces, though they had till then been peaceful, fearing an attack from Gallus Caesar; ...

(27) (A.D. 363) 4. For in this battle a satrap of distinction called Daces was killed. In former time he happened to have been sent on an embassy to Constantius, to discuss peace and the cessation of war.

(Anon., revised Lieu)

9 Rome and Shapur II

The Persian Expedition of Julian
(March–June, 363)

(A) CHRONOLOGY AND ANALYSIS OF THE SOURCES

The preliminaries

Julian's desire to avenge the frontier regions which had suffered from the recent Persian incursions and his refusal to discuss peace with an embassy from Persia: Libanius *or.* XVII, 19 and XVIII, 164. His boast that he would restore Singara: Ephrem, *Hymni Contra Julianum* II, 15. (On his refusal to defend Nisibis on account of its citizens' loyalty to the Christian faith, see Sozomen, V, 3, 5 = *ELF* 91). He commanded Arsak (Arsaces), the king of Armenia, to muster a large army and to join him later at a place to be designated: Amm. XXIII, 2, 2, Lib., *or.* XVIII, 215 and Soz., VI, 1, 2.[1] He ordered ships to be built in Samosata: Malalas, XIII, pp. 328, 21–329, 2 (= Magnus of Carrhae, *FGrH* 225, F 1). His enquiries at various famous oracles: Theodoret, *Historia Ecclesiastica* III, 21, 1–4. His intention to establish Hormisdas as ruler of Persia: Libanius, *ep.* 1402, 3. See also Libanius, *ep.* 737, 1–3 for an example of Roman optimism concerning the campaign.

From Antioch to Callinicum (5–27 March)

Upon leaving Antioch, Julian headed for Hierapolis via Litarbae[2] (**5 March**),[3] Beroea (**6 March**) and Batnae (**8 March**). Cf. *ELF* 98 (= *ep.* 58, Wright). He was met by a delegation from the Antiochene *curia* at Litarbae and rejected their requests: *ELF* 98. See also Libanius, *or.* I, 132 and XVI, 1. (Malalas, XIII, p. 328, 6–19 suggests that he passed through Cyrrhus, but this is unlikely as Cyrrhus was not on the direct route from Antioch to Litarbae.) A colonnade collapsed at Hierapolis[4] and killed fifty soldiers: Amm.

XXIII, 2, 6. He remained there for three days and, after crossing the Euphrates, he reached Batnae (i.e. Sarug in Osrhoene) on **12 March**: Zos. III, 12, 2. There another fifty soldiers were killed while foraging: Amm. XXIII, 2, 7–8. He came to Carrhae on **18 March** after a forced march. Cf. Amm. XXIII, 3, 1 and Zos. III, 12, 2, Malalas, XIII, p. 329, 4 (= Magnus, F 2). He avoided Edessa because of its strong Christian connections: Theodoret, *Historia Ecclesiastica* III, 26, 1. At Carrhae he divided his forces: Amm. XXIII, 3, 4–5, Zos. III, 12, 3–5 and Sozomen, VI, 1, 2.[5] He feigned a march across the Tigris and at some point between Carrhae and Nisibis he turned south towards Callinicum which he reached on **27 March**.[6] Cf. Amm. XXIII, 3, 6–7 and Zos. III, 13, 1. The next day he received a delegation of Saracen chieftains who presented him with a gold crown: Amm. XXIII, 3, 8. See also *ELF* 98, 401D (= *ep.* 58, Wright). On his refusal to pay them their usual bribe, see Amm. XXV, 6, 10. He was joined by the fleet under the command of Lucillianus:[7] Amm. XXIII, 3, 9. See also Zos., III, 13, 2–3.

From Callinicum to Maiozamalcha (April–mid-June)

Julian set off from Callinicum for Circesium where he crossed the river Abora (the Chabur) on a bridge of boats: Amm. XXIII, 5, 1 and Zos. III, 14, 2. At Circesium he received a letter from Sallustius beseeching him to call off the campaign: Amm. XXIII, 5, 4. Leaving Circesium, the army marched southwards along the right bank of the Euphrates and passed Zaitha[8] on **4 April** (Amm. XXIII, 5, 7 and Zos. III, 14, 2). Julian was urged on by his theurgist/philosopher friends in his retinue to continue the campaign despite adverse omens: Amm. XXIII, 5, 10. Cf. Soc., III, 21, 6. His speech to the troops: Amm. XXIII, 5, 16–23. See also Malalas, XIII, p. 329, 18–23 (= Magnus F 2–5). The army entered Assyria and the arrangement of the units for the march is given in Amm. XXIV, 1, 2 and Zos. III, 14, 1. The army passed the deserted city of Dura (Europos) on the opposite bank on 6 April: Amm. XXIII, 5, 8 and 12 and XXIV, 1, 5 and Zos. III, 14, 2. Anatha[9] was captured on 11 April after a show of strength. Cf. Amm. XXIV, 1, 6–10, Zos. III, 14, 2–3 and Lib., *or.* XVIII, 218. On the fate of the prisoners, see Amm. XXIV, 1, 9, Lib., *ep.* 1367, 6 and *Chron. Ps. Dionys.*, s. a. 674, CSCO 91, pp. 179, 24–180, 2. On **12 April**, the force was struck by a hurricane and some grain-ships were sunk because sluice-gates were breached (through enemy action?) Cf. Amm.

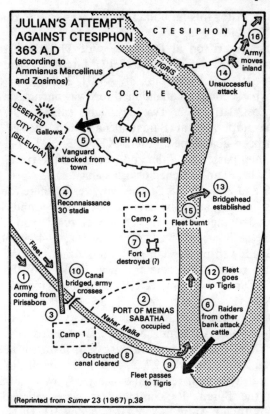

JULIAN'S ATTEMPT AGAINST CTESIPHON 363 A.D
(according to Ammianus Marcellinus and Zosimos)

CTESIPHON

TIGRIS

⑯ Army moves inland

⑭ Unsuccessful attack

C O C H E

(VEH ARDASHIR)

DESERTED CITY (SELEUCIA) Gallows

⑤ Vanguard attacked from town

④ Reconnaissance 30 stadia

⑪

Camp 2

⑬ Bridgehead established

⑮ Fleet burnt

⑦ Fort destroyed (?)

Fleet

① Army coming from Pirisabora

⑩ Canal bridged, army crosses

③

Camp 1

② PORT OF MEINAS SABATHA occupied

Nahar Malka

⑫ Fleet goes up Tigris

⑥ Raiders from other bank attack cattle

⑧ Obstructed canal cleared

⑨ Fleet passes to Tigris

(Reprinted from *Sumer* 23 (1967) p.38)

Map 5   Julian's attempt against Ctesiphon

XXIV, 1, 11. After this an unnamed city was captured and burnt: ibid. XXIV, 1, 12.

The Persian garrison at the fortress of Thilutha[10] decided to remain neutral and was bypassed (? 13 March). Cf. Amm. XXIV, 2, 1–2, Zos. III, 15, 1 and Lib., *or.* XVIII, 219. Achaiacala[11] was similarly bypassed and an abandoned fort was burnt: Amm. XXIV, 2, 2. Cf. Zos., III, 15, 2. Two days later (mid-April), the army crossed the Euphrates at Baraxmalcha[12] and entered Diacira[13] which had been abandoned: Amm. XXIV, 2, 3 (? 17–19 March). The army then passed by Sitha and (recrossed the river? at) Megia (cf. Zos. III, 15, 3) and reached Ozogardana[14] *c.* 22 April. Cf. Amm. XXIV, 2, 3 and Zos. III, 15, 3. The army rested there for two days. Hormisdas, leading a reconnaissance party, was ambushed by the Persians under the command of the Suren[15] and Podosaces, Phylarch of the Saracens.[16] Cf. Amm. XXIV, 2, 4–5 and Zos. III, 15, 4–6. Shadowed by Persian forces (cf. Amm. XXIV, 2, 5), the Roman army reached Macepracta[17] near the start of the Naarmal-cha (Royal Canal)[18]: Amm. XXIV, 2, 6 and crossed the canal: Amm. XXIV, 2, 7–8 and Zos. III, 16–17. Pirisabora,[19] a key fortress guarding the canal approach to Ctesiphon, was taken after siege (? 27–9 April). Cf. Amm. XXIV, 2, 9–22, Zos., III, 17, 3–18, 6, Lib., *or.* XVIII, 227–8 and *Suidas , s. v. 'ἀνασχοῦσα'*. See also Eunap., *frag.* 21 (= Blockley 27, 2, p. 39). On the day after the fall of Pirisabora, a Roman reconnaissance party was ambushed and routed by the Suren. Its commanders were relieved of their command by Julian: Amm. XXIV, 3, 1–2, Zos. III, 19,1–2 and Lib., *or.* XVIII, 229. The army marched along the canal past Phissenia[20] but the advance was slowed by the Persians breaching the dams and turning the low ground into marsh-land. Cf. Amm. XXIV, 3, 10–11, Zos. III, 19, 3–4[21] and Lib., *or.* XVIII, 222–6 and 232–4. At this point the Euphrates was divided into many small streams: Amm. XXIV, 3, 14. In this district they found an abandoned Jewish setlement:[22] Amm. XXIV, 4, 1. Julian headed the bridging operation and led his army to Bithra[23] where they found the ruins of a palace: Zos. III, 19, 4. Maiozamalcha,[24] a well-fortified city, was taken after a laborious siege (? 10–13, May). Cf. Amm. XXIV, 4, 2–30, Zos. III, 20, 2–22, 7 and Lib., *or.* XVIII, 235–42. The Romans then passed over a series of canals, and an attempt to stop them by the Persians was foiled: Amm. XXIV, 4, 31.

The relative ease with which the Roman army reached the outskirts of Ctesiphon is briefly mentioned in many other sources. See e.g., Lib., *ep.* 1402, 2–3, Eutrop., X, 16, 1, Festus, *brev.*, 28,

p. 67. 18–19, Gregory Nazianzenus, *or.* V, 9, Socrates, III, 21, 3, Soz., VI, 1, 4, Malalas, XIII, pp. 329, 23–330, 2 (= Magnus, F 3–6) and Zonaras, XIII, 13, 1.

The Roman army at Seleucia/Coche/Ctesiphon

The Romans came upon a palace built in Roman style and left it untouched (? 15 May). They also found the King's Chase well stocked with game: Amm. XXIV, 5, 1–2, Zos. III, 23, 1–2 and Lib., *or.* XVII, 20 and XVIII, 243. At the site of the former Hellenistic city of Seleucia,[25] Julian saw the impaled bodies of the relatives of the Persian commander who surrendered Pirisabora: Amm. XXIV, 5, 4. Here Nabdates, former Persian commander of Maiozamalcha, who had surrendered to the Romans but had grown insolent, was burnt with 80 men: Amm. XXIV, 5, 4. A strong fortress was captured (? 16 May): ibid. XXIV, 5, 6–11. This could be the Meinas Sabath[26] mentioned in Zos. III, 23, 3. The fleet then sailed down the Naarmalcha and the army pushed on to Coche.[27] Cf. Amm. XXIV, 6, 1–2, Zos. III, 24, 2, Lib., *or.* XVIII, 245–7 and Malalas, XII, p. 330, 10–16 (= Magnus F 7).

Coche and Ctesiphon were both strongly defended: Greg. Naz., *or.* V, 10. Julian partially unloaded the fleet and used the boats to ferry soldiers across the Tigris: Amm. XXIV, 6, 4–6, Zos., III, 25–6, Lib., *or.* XVIII, 248–55, Greg. Naz., *loc. cit.* and Soc., VI, 1, 5–18. See also Eunap., *frag.* 22, 2 (= Blockley 27, 3, p. 39), Lib., *or.* I, 133 and XXIV, 37 Festus, *brev.* 28, pp. 67, 19–68, 3 and Malalas XIII, p. 330,16–19 (= Magnus, F 8). The Romans were victorious at a battle before the gates of Ctesiphon but were unable to exploit the victory because of ill-discipline. Cf. Amm. XXIV, 6, 8–16, Zos., III, 25, 5–7, Lib., *or.* XVII, 21 and XVIII, 248–55, Festus, *brev.* 28, p. 68, 3–7, Greg. Naz., *loc. cit.* and Sozomen, VI, 1, 7–8. Julian rejected the peace overtures from Shapur II: Lib., *or.* XVIII, 257–9 and Soc., III, 21, 4–8 (compressed chronology). See also *Art. Pass.* 69.

A council of war was held (at Abuzatha?)[28] and a decision to march inland was made (? 5 June). Cf. Amm. XXIV, 7, 1–3, Zos. III, 26, 1, Lib., *or.* XVIII, 261. See also Eunap., *frag.* 22, 3 (= Blockley, 27, 5, p. 41) and 27 (= Blockley, 27, 6, p. 41) and Zon., XIII, 13, 10. The transport fleet was burnt (11–15 June): Amm. XXIV, 7, 3–5, Zos., III, 26, 2–3, Lib., *or.* XVIII, 262–3, Ephr., *HcJul.* III, 15, Greg. Naz., *or.* V, 11–12, Soz., VI, 1, 9, Thdt., *h.e.* III, 25, 1, Festus, *brev.* 28, p. 68, 9, Zon., XIII, 13, 2–9. On the theory that Julian was led astray by one or more Persian double-agents, see Greg. Naz., *or.* V, 11, Ephr., *HcJul.* II, 18, Festus, *brev.* 28, p. 68, 9–10, Soc., III, 22, 9, Soz., VI, 1, 9–12, Philostorgius, VII, 15, Malalas, XIII, pp. 330, 20–332, 21 (= Magnus, F 9–11) and *Art. Pass.* 69.

A second council of war was held (at Noorda?)[29] and the decision to head for Cordyene rather than to return via Assyria was confirmed (? 16 June). Cf. Amm. XXIV, 8, 2–5 and Zos. III, 26, 3. The army struck camp on 16 June: Amm. XXIV, 8, 5. The army marched due north towards the river Douros (Diayala?).[30]

The Roman withdrawal

The Persians were encountered on the Douros and were defeated: Amm. XXV, 1, 1–3, Zos., III, 26, 4–5 and Lib. *or.* XVIII, 264. After crossing the Douros, the army marched east (?) towards Barsaphtas: Zos. III, 27, 1. Hucumbra (or Symbra)[31] was reached *c.* 17 June: Amm. XXV, 1, 4 and Zos. III, 27, 2. [The account of Libanius (*or.* XVIII, 264–7) becomes very vague after the battle on the Douros and mentions only frequent skirmishes, giving no specific details.] The Romans began to suffer from shortage of supplies as the effects of the scorched-earth policy of the Persians were becoming apparent. Cf. Amm. XXV, 1, 10, Zos. III, 26, 4, John Chrys., *de S. Babyla* XXII/122, Thdt., *h.e.* III, 25, 4 and Zon. XIII, 13, 13–14. See, however, the denial by Libanius (*or.* XVIII, 264). The army continued its march up the right bank of the Tigris, passing Danabe,[32] Synce and Accete. In between Danabe and Synce the Persians raided the Roman column and lost Adaces, a distinguished satrap, in the skirmish. Cf. Amm. XXV, 1, 5–6 and Zos. III, 27, 4. Accete was reached around 20 June and the Romans again found the crops burnt: Zos. III, 28, 1. The Persians attacked the Roman column as it passed through a district called Maranga (Zos.: Maronsa)[33] but were repelled with heavy losses (? 22 May). Cf. Amm. XXV, 1, 11–19 and Zos. III, 28, 2. The Romans however lost some ships because they lagged too far behind: Zos., *loc. cit.* A truce of three days was agreed upon after the battle: Amm. XXV, 2, 1. Toummara[34] on the Tigris was reached probably on 25 June after an exhausting march, during which the Romans regretted the earlier decision to burn the fleet: Zos. III, 28, 3. Another Persian attack was repelled: Zos., *loc. cit.*

Death of Julian (26 June)

Amm. XXV, 3, Zos. III, 28, 4–29, 1, Lib., *or.* XVIII, 268–74, Eunap., *frag.* 20 (= Blockley, 27, 8, p. 41) and 26 (= Blockley 28, 6, p. 45), Festus, *brev.* 28, p. 68.11–16, Ephr., *HcJul.* III, 16, Greg. Naz., *or.* V, 13–14, John Chrys., *de S. Babyla* XXII/123, Soc., III, 21, 9–18, Soz., VI, 1, 13–16, Thdt., *h.e.* III, 25, 5–7, Philost., VII, 15, Malalas, XIII, pp. 331, 21–333, 6 (= Magnus, F 12–15), *Art. Pass.* 69.

Election of Jovian (27 June)

Amm. XXV, 51–7, Zos. III, 30, 1, Eunap., *frag.* 23 (= Blockley, 28, 1, pp. 41–2), Greg. Naz., *or.* V, 15, Soc., III, 22, 1–5, Soz., VI, 3, 1–6, Thdt., *h.e.* IV, 1, 1–6, Philost., VIII, 1 and Malalas, XIII, p. 333, 7–17. The withdrawal resumed: Amm. XXV, 6, 1. A Persian attack was repelled: ibid. XXV, 6, 2–3 and Zos. III, 30, 2–4. The body of Anatolius,[35] killed in the same battle as Julian, was recovered at Sumere and buried. Cf. ibid. XXV, 6, 4 and Zos., III, 30, 4. A few days later the army found refuge at Charcha[36] (? 29–30 June) and on 1 July it reached Dura[37] (not Europos), where they were delayed for four days by Persian attacks. Cf. Amm. XXV, 6, 9–11. The Romans seized a bridge-head on the opposite bank of the Tigris by a daring raid, but the raging current prevented the Tigris from being successfully bridged. Cf. Amm. XXV, 6, 11–7, 4 and Zos. III, 30, 4–5.

The peace negotiations (? 8–11 July)

Amm. XXV, 7, 5–14, Zos. III, 31, 1–2, Soc., III, 23, 7–8 and Ps.-Joshua the Stylite, *Chronicle* 7, trans. W. Wright, pp. 6–7, Malalas, XIII, pp. 335, 1–336, 10 and Zon. XIII, 14, 4, 6. See also Lib., *or.* XXIV, 9. After the terms were settled, the Roman army continued its withdrawal via Hatra, Ur, (Singara) and Thilsaphata: Amm. XXV, 8, 4–12. At Thilsaphata,[38] the expeditionary force met up with the diversionary force under Procopius and Sebastianus: Amm. XXV, 8, 16. The surrender of Nisibis (? 25 Aug.): Amm. XXV, 8, 13–15 and 9, 1–3, Zos., III, 33, 1–34, 1, Eunap., *frag.* 29, ed. and trans. Blockley, pp. 45–7 (= John of Antioch, frag. 181), Ephr., *HcJul.* II, 16–III, 8, John Chrys., *de S. Babyla* XXII/123, Philost., VIII and Malalas, XIII, pp. 336, 11–337, 2.

(B) THE SOURCES (IN ALPHABETICAL ORDER OF THEIR AUTHORS)

Agathias, *historiae* IV, 25, 6–7: In the twenty-fourth year of his (i.e. Shapur II's) reign the city of Nisibis fell to the Persians. It had long been subject to the Romans, but Jovian their own emperor yielded it and gave it up. For Julian the previous Roman emperor had suddenly been killed while actually in the interior of the Persian kingdom, and Jovian was proclaimed by the generals and the armies and the rest of the throng there. 7. And since he had only just come to the throne, and affairs were naturally disturbed – and all this in the middle of enemy country too – he could not under these circumstances devote much time to settling the present situation. So, in order to rid himself of the need to stay in a strange and hostile country and wanting nothing so much as to return home quickly, he made a shameful and disgraceful truce, so bad that it is even now harmful to the Roman state, by which he made the empire contract into new boundaries and cut off the outer parts of his own territory.

(Cameron, p. 125)

Ammianus Marcellinus,   XXIII, 2–XXV, 8. See Introduction, p. 7.

Artemii passio   69–70 (69.1–70.5, pp. 243–4, Kotter): Julian set out from Antioch with all his forces and marched against Persia. When he had arrived at Ctesiphon, he thought after accomplishing this great feat he would go on to other mightier deeds. The accursed emperor did not realize that he had been tricked. For having acquired a devilish devotion to idolatry and hoping through his godless deities to hold his emperorship for a long time and to become a new Alexander, and to overcome the Persians and to obliterate the name of the Christians for all time, he fell victim to his overweening purpose. For he met an aged Persian and was led astray by him (on the promise) that he would without trouble succeed to the kingdoms of the Persians and all their wealth; he drew him into the Carmanian desert, into trackless regions, ravines and desert-like and waterless areas with all his army. And when he had exhausted them with thirst and hunger and killed off all their cavalry, the Persian willingly confessed that he had led them astray so that they might be destroyed by him and he might not see his own native land laid waste by its worst enemies. Therefore they straightway cut this man up limb from limb and dispatched him to his death. But immediately, in this state of distress, they encountered against their will the army of the Persians. A battle occurred and while Julian himself was rushing here and there and organizing his men, he fell to the spear, so it is said, of a soldier; but, as others record, to the spear of a Saracen serving with the Persians. But in the true Christian version which is ours, the spear belonged to the Lord Christ who was ranged against him. For suddenly a bow from the skies stretched taut and launched a missile at him as at a target and it pierced through his side, and wounded him in the abdomen. And he wailed deeply and woefully and thought that our Lord Jesus Christ was standing before him and exulting over him. But he, filled with darkness and madness, received his own blood in his hands and sprinkled it into the air, and when he became breathless shouted out, saying: 'You have won, Christ. Take your fill, Galilaean!' Thus he ended his life in a most fearful and hateful manner after many reproaches had been heaped upon his own gods. 70. When the transgressor fell in the no-man's land around the army, Jovian was proclaimed emperor by the army. He made a peace treaty with the Persians by which he handed over Nisibis without its inhabitants to the Persians. He then departed from there for the army was being destroyed by hunger and disease.

(Dodgeon)

Cedrenus, i, pp. 538, 16–23 and 539, 16–21: Having marched into Persia, he (Julian) was tricked by certain deserters into burning his ships. Afterwards he marched to his satisfaction through desert and rough country, and began to run out of all the necessities and provisions. The men with him began to suffer great distress. When the time for war arrived, while he went around the camp and drew up his men, he was struck with a lance from an unknown direction in the lower abdomen and as a result moaned aloud. He took the blood into his hand and sprinkled it into the air, saying, 'You have won, Christ! Be satisfied, Nazarene.' . . .

He (Jovian) was proclaimed emperor by the whole army in the place in which the Transgressor was destroyed. He was tall in stature, so that not even one of the imperial robes fitted him. After one encounter in battle, peace was declared in unison (as at God's command) both by the Romans and the Persians, and it was specified to last for thirty years.

(Dodgeon)

Chronicon ad AD **724** *(Liber Calipharum),* CSCO 6, pp. 133, 14ff. (Syriac): In the year 674 (Sel. = AD 363), the defiled Julian descended into the land of the Chaldaeans, to Bet Aramaye, where his ruin came about at the hand of the Romans (*sic*) . . . (and Julian was slain) on the twenty-seventh day of the month Iyyar (= May) of the year 674.

In the month of Haziran (= June) in the year 674 on a Friday by the bank of the great river Tigris, on the north side of Kaukaba (= Coche?) and Ctesiphon, in the region called Bet Aramaye[39] Jobininus (i.e. Jovian) assumed the great crown of the Roman Empire, and he made peace and concord, and put an end to the hostilities between both the mighty empires of the Romans and the Persians. However, in order that there should be peace between them and that he should free the Romans from the straits in which they were, he gave to the Persians all the area of the east belonging to Nisibis, certain of the villages which surround the city and the whole of Armenia together with the regions subject to Armenia(?)[40] itself. ⟨The inhabitants of⟩ Nisibis went into exile in the territory of the Edessenes in the month of Ab (August) in the year 674 and Nisibis was handed over to the Persians devoid of its inhabitants.

(Lieu, revised Brock)

Chronicon Ps.-Dionysianum,   CSCO 91, p. 179, 23–180, 8 (Syriac): In the year 674 (Sel. = AD 363), the emperor Julian descended into Persia and devastated the entire region from Nisibis as far as Ctesiphon in Bet Aramaye. He took a large number of captives from there and settled them at Mt. Snsw. In the same year he died in Persia, struck by a dart thrown through the air. Jovian, commander of his army, then reigned in his place. He made peace between the two empires and ceded Nisibis to the Persians. The persecution came to an end in Persia because of the peace he made and all the churches were (re)opened. All the inhabitants of Nisibis went into exile to Amida in Mesopotamia and he constructed walls for them west of the city.

(Lieu, revised Brock)

Ephrem Syrus,   *Hymni contra Julianum* II, 15–22 and 27 and III, CSCO 174, pp. 78, 23–82, 14 and 83, 11–85, 8:[41]

II

According to the tune '*Rely on Truth*'

15   But he (i.e. Julian) gave omens and promises and wrote and (sent) to us

that he was setting out and subduing and would lay bare

Persia,
that he would rebuild Singara – the threat of his letter.[42]
Nisibis [was taken] through his descent (into battle),
and by his diviners [he brought low] the host who believed in
him;
like a (sacrificial) lamb the city saved his camp.
RESPONSE: Blessed be he who blotted him out and saddened
all the sons of error.

16 (God) had appointed Nisibis, which was taken, as a mirror
so that we might see in it how the pagan, who had set out (i.e.
for Persia)
because he took what was not his, lost what was his –
that city which proclaimed to the world
the disgrace of his diviners[43] and that [his] shame was
unending;
(God) had delivered it to a steadfast, untiring herald.

17 This is the herald who, with four mouths, cried out in the earth
the shame of his diviners,
and the gates, that during the siege were opened, also unlocked
our mouth to the praise of our redeemer.
Today the gates of that city are shut fast
so that through them the mouth of the pagans and the erring
is closed.

18 Let us seek the reason how and wherefore
they yielded that city, the shield of all cities.
The insane one (i.e. Julian) raved and set on fire his ships near
the Tigris.
The bearded ones deceived him,[44] and he did not perceive it,
he the goat who avowed that he knew the secrets;
he was deceived in visible things so he was put to shame in the
non-visible.

19 It is the city which had proclaimed the truth of its saviour;
the waters suddenly burst out and smote against it,
earthworks were brought low and elephants were drowned.
The (Christian) king by his sackcloth had preserved it,
the tyrant by his paganism debased the victory
of the city which prayer had crowned with triumph.

20 Truth was its wall and fasting its bulwark.
The Magians came threatening and Persia was put to shame
through them,
Babel through the Chaldaeans and India through the
enchanters.

For thirty years truth had crowned it
(but) in the summer in which he established an idol within the city
mercy fled from it and wrath pursued and entered it.

21   For empty sacrifices rendered void its fullness;
demons of the waste laid it waste with libations;
the (pagan) altar which was built uprooted and cast out
that sanctuary whose sackcloth had delivered us (i.e the city).
Festivals of frenzy reduced to silence its feast,
because the sons of error ministered, they made void its ministrations.

22   The Magian who entered our place, kept it holy, to our shame,
he neglected his temple of fire and honoured the sanctuary,
he cast down the altars which were built through our laxity,
he abolished the enclosures, to our shame,
for he knew that from that one temple alone had gone out
the mercy which had saved us from him three times. . . .

27   While the (our) king was a (pagan) priest and dishonoured our churches,
the Magian king honoured the sanctuary.
He doubled our consolation because he honoured our sanctuary,
he grieved and gladdened us and did not banish us.
(God) reproved that erring one through his companion in error,
What the priest abundantly defrauded, the Magian made abundant restitution.

III
According to the same tune

1   A fortuitous wonder! There met me near the city
the corpse of that accursed one which passed by the wall;
the banner which was sent from the East wind
the Magian took and fastened on the tower[45]
so that a flag might point out for spectators
that the city was the slave of the lords of that banner.
RESPONSE: Praise to him who clothed his corpse in shame.

2   I was amazed as to how it was that there met and were present
the body and the standard, both at the same time.
And I knew that it was a wonderful preparation of justice
that while the corpse of the fallen one was passing,
there went up and was placed that fearsome banner so that it

might proclaim that
the injustice of his diviners had delivered that city.

3 For thirty years Persia made war in every way
and was not able to cross the boundary of that city.
Even when it was breached and lying low, the Cross went down
and saved it.
There I saw a foul sight,
the banner of the captor, which was fixed on the tower,
the body of the persecutor, which was lying on the bier.

4 Believe in 'Yes and No', the word that is true,
I went and came, my brethren, to the bier of the defiled one
and I stood over it and I derided his paganism,
I said: Is this he who exalted himself
against the living name and who forgot that he is dust?
(God) has returned him to within his dust that he might know
that he is dust.

5 I stood and was amazed at him whose humiliation I earnestly
observed.
For this is his magnificence, and this his pride,
this is his majesty, and this his chariot,
this is earth which is decayed.
And I debated with myself why, during his prime,
I did not see in anticipation his end, that it was this.

6 I was amazed at the many who, in order to try to please
the crown of a mortal, had denied him who gives life to all.
I looked above and below and marvelled, my brethren,
at our Lord in that glorious height,
and the accursed one in low estate, and I said: Who will be
afraid
of that corpse and deny the True One?

7 That the Cross when it had set out had not conquered
everything
was not because it was not able to conquer, for it is victorious,
but so that a pit might be dug for the wicked man,
who set out with his diviners to the East;
when he set out and was wounded, it was seen by the
discerning
that the war had waited for him so that through it he might be
put to shame.

8 Know that for this reason the war had lasted and delayed –
so that the pure one might complete the years of his reign
and that the accursed one might also complete the measure of

his paganism.
So when he completed his course and came to ruin,
then (both) sides were glad, then there was peace
through the believing King, the associate of the glorious ones.

9   The Just One was able to finish him off with every way of dying
but he kept him for that fearsome and bitter humiliation
so that on the day of his death there was arrayed before his
eyes everything –
where is that divination which gave him assurance,
and the goddess of weapons who did not come to help him,
and the companies of his gods who did not come to save him?

10   The Cross of him who knows all went down before the army,
it endured and was mocked, 'He does not save them!'
The king it kept in safety, the army it gave to destruction
because it knew that paganism was within them.
Therefore let the cross of him who searches all be praised
for fools without discrimination reproached him at that time.

11   For they did not hold fast to the banner of him who redeems
all;
indeed, that paganism which they exhibited at the end
was evident to our Lord from the beginning.
Although he knew well that they were turning to paganism,
his cross saved them; and when they rejected him,
there they ate corpses, there they became a proverb.

12   When the (Jewish) people were defeated near Ai of the
faint-hearted,
Joshua tore his clothes before the ark of the covenant
and uttered dreadful words before the Most High;
there was a curse among the people and he did not know –
just as there was paganism hidden in the force
while, instead of the ark of the covenant, they were carrying
the Cross.

13   So justice herself had in wisdom summoned him,
not indeed by force did it guide his free will;
through enticement he set out towards that spear to be
wounded.
He saw the fortifications which he subdued and he was proud;
but adversity did not incite him to turn back
until he had gone down and fallen into the abyss.

14   Because he dishonoured him who had removed the spear of
Paradise,
the spear of justice passed through his belly.

They tore open that which was pregnant with the oracle of the diviners,
and (God) scourged (him) and he groaned and remembered
what he wrote and published that he would do to the churches.
The finger of justice had blotted out his memory.

15 The king saw that the sons of the East had come and deceived him,
the unlearned (had deceived) the wise man, the simple the soothsayer.
They whom he had called, wrapped up in his robe,
had, through unlearned men, mastered his wisdom.
He commanded and burned his victorious ships,
and his idols and diviners were bound through the one deceit.

16 When he saw that his gods were refuted and exposed,
and that he was unable to conquer and unable to escape,
he was prostrated and torn between fear and shame.
Death he chose so that he might escape in Sheol
and cunningly he took off his armour in order to be wounded
so that he might die without the Galilaeans seeing his shame.

17 When he mocked and nicknamed the brethren 'Galilaeans':
behold in the air the wheels of the Galilaean King!
He thundered in his chariot, cherubim were carrying him.
The Galilaean made known and handed over
the flock of the diviner to the wolves in the wilderness
but the Galilaean flock increased and filled the earth.

(J. M. Lieu, *ap.* Lieu, 1986a: 112–20)

Epitome de Caesaribus 43: After the administration of the Roman world had been brought under his control, Julian, being excessively eager for fame, set out against the Persians. 2. There he was led by a certain deserter into an ambush and when the Parthians (*sic*) were pressing him hard on this side and that, he rushed forth from his camp which had just been set up, having snatched up merely a shield. 3. And when he strove with ill-advised eagerness to rally his ranks for the battle, he was struck by one of the fleeing enemy with a lance. 4. He was brought back to his tent and again went out to encourage his men; he suffered a gradual loss of blood and expired around midnight, having stated earlier that he was deliberately giving no instructions concerning the succession, lest, as usually happens in a crowd with competing interests, he would bring hazard to a friend through jealousy, and danger upon the army through political disagreement. . . . 7. He had an inordinate desire for praise;

his worship of the gods was full of superstition. He was more daring than is fitting for an emperor, whose personal safety should be preserved to the utmost for the security of all, and especially in time of war. 8. Thus his rather passionate desire for fame had won him over with the result that neither by earthquake nor by numerous presentiments, by which he was forbidden to attack Persia, was he induced to put an end to his eagerness, and not even the sight of a huge sphere falling at night from the heavens before the day of the war made him cautious.

(Dodgeon)

Eunapius, *Fragmenta historica* 20–2 and 26–7:

20. (= B 27, 8, p. 41) When the troop of mounted cataphracts over and above four hundred rushed down upon the rear-guard.

21. (= B 27, 2, p. 39) Some of the Parthians had wickerwork shields and wickerwork helmets woven in a traditional manner.

22. (= B 27, 1, p. 39) [He says] that the war against the Persians reached its peak under Julian and that either by invoking the gods or by calculation he comprehended from afar the disturbances of the Scythians, like waves on a smooth sea. Thereupon he says to someone in a letter, 'The Scythians are now lying quiet, equally, they will not do so in the future'. His forethought for the future extended over such a period that he knew in advance that they would remain quiet only for his own time.

(= B 27, 3, pp. 39–40) [He says] that Julian, having previously revealed the plain before Ctesiphon as an orchestra for war, as Epaminondas said, now paraded it as a stage for Dionysus, providing relaxation and amusement for the troops.

(= B 27, 5, p. 41) [He says] that there was such an abundance of the provisions in the suburbs of Ctesiphon that the overriding danger faced by the troops was that of being destroyed by luxury.

(= B 27, 6, p. 41) [He says] that mankind, besides, seems generally inclined towards and readily given over to envy. And since the troops have no means of taking sides fairly about what is done, 'From the tower', they say, 'they judged the Achaeans', each one of them desirous of being versed in military matters and possessed of more than usual good sense. To some, then, any matter was the subject of foolishness, but he who followed the arguments right from the beginning went back to his own domain.

26. (= B 28, 6, p. 45) [Concerning the end of Julian the Apostate and Soldier, the reply of the oracle was as follows]

But when that time comes when you shall tame the Persian blood with your sceptre and bring them beneath your rule, driven back as far as Seleucia by your sword, then indeed a chariot bright as fire leads you to Olympus, a chariot swallowed up in the turmoil of whirlwinds and lightning, leaving behind the wretched distress of human limbs. And you shall come to the ancestral halls of the ethereal light, whence you came, led astray to take the form of a human body.

Inspired by such eloquent words as these, and even more by prophecies, they say he was most agreeably exalted above mortal destruction. . . .

There is an oracle which was given to him while he was waiting at Ctesiphon:

(= B 27, 6, p. 41) Zeus, the all-wise, once destroyed a race of Earth-born giants most hateful to the blessed ones who dwell in the Olympian halls. Julian the god-like, Emperor of the Romans, contending for the cities and long walls of the Persians, fighting hand-to-hand, destroyed them with fire and the valiant sword, subdued without pause their cities and many races. Seizing also, with heavy fighting, the German soil of those people of the west he laid waste their land.

(M. Morgan)

B 29, 1 (= John of Antioch, *frag.* 181, *FGH* IV, pp. 606–7) He (i.e. Jovian) reigned after Julian. . . . Coming to Nisibis, a populous city, he spent only two days there. He exhausted all its resources and had neither a kindly word nor an act of philanthropy for the inhabitants. . . . As I have said, when he became Emperor of the Romans after Julian, he was so eager to enjoy his rank which had befallen him that he ignored everything else. He fled from Persia and hurried to get within (the boundaries of) the Roman provinces in order to proclaim his new found fortune. He ceded to the Persians the city of Nisibis, which had long been subject to the Romans. Therefore they mocked him in ditties, parodies and in the so-called *famosi* (lampoons) because of his surrender of Nisibis.

(Lieu)

Eutropius, X, 16, 1–2: Julian then became sole emperor, and made war, with a vast force, upon the Parthians; in which expedition I was also present. Several towns and fortresses of the Persians he induced to surrender, and some he took by storm. After laying waste to Assyria, he fixed his camp for some time at Ctesiphon. 2. As he was returning victorious, and mingling rashly in the thick of a battle, he was killed by the hand of an enemy, on the 26th of June, in the seventh year of his reign, and the thirty-second of his life, and was enrolled among the gods.

(Watson, pp. 533–4, altered)

Festus, *breviarium* 28–9 (pp. 67, 14–69, 6): Julian, who was of proven good fortune against the external enemies of the empire, lacked moderation in the war against the Persians. With great magnificence, as befitting the ruler of the whole world, he raised his menacing standards against the Parthians (*sic*), and advanced his fleet, stocked with provisions, along the Euphrates. In the course of his intrepid advance, a great many Persian towns and strongholds either surrendered to him or were captured by force of arms. Having pitched his camp opposite to Ctesiphon on the bank where the Tigris joins the Euphrates, he spent the day in athletic contests to relieve the enemy of their watchfulness. In the middle of the night he embarked his soldiers and suddenly carried them across to the far bank. They struggled over the escarpment, where the ascent would have been difficult even in daytime when no one was trying to stop them. They threw the Persians into confusion by the unexpected terror and the armies of their entire nation were turned to flight. The soldiers would have victoriously entered the open gates of Ctesiphon if the opportunity for booty had not been greater than their concern for victory. After winning such great glory, when he received a warning from his retinue concerning the return, he put greater trust in his own purpose and burnt his fleet. He was misled by a deserter who had surrendered for the purpose of leading him astray, and was induced to follow a direct route to Madaeana (Media ?). Retracing his route upstream along the Tigris (with the river on his right), he exposed the flank of his troops. When he wandered along the column too incautiously, after the dust was stirred up and he lost sight of his own men, he was pierced through the abdomen as far as the groin by the lance of an enemy horseman. Amidst the excessive loss of blood, when in spite of having been wounded he had restored the ranks of his army, and after a long address to his companions, he breathed forth his lingering life.
29   Jovian took over an army that was victorious in battle but confused at the sudden death of their departed emperor. There was a lack of supplies and a very extensive march ahead of them on their return. The Persians also delayed the progress of the column by frequent sallies, at one moment upon the vanguard, then the rear, also upon the flanks of the centre. After several days were

spent, so great was the respect for the name of Rome that the first talk of peace came from the Persians, and the army, consumed by famine, was allowed to be brought back on imposed terms prejudicial to the interests of the Roman state (something which had never happened before): namely, that Nisibis and part of Mesopotamia should be handed over, and in this Jovian acquiesced, being inexperienced in government and more desirous of the emperorship than of good renown.

(Dodgeon)

Gregory Nazianzenus,[46] *orationes* V, 8–13, ed. Bernardi, pp. 306–20: Having levied in these parts a double force, one military, the other of the demons who led him on (in which he placed the more confidence of the two), he marched against the Persians, placing his trust rather in his senseless daring than in the strength of his armed forces, not being able to discern, very wise as he was, that courage and rashness however similar they may be in sound,[47] are yet widely different from each other in reality as much as what we call manliness and unmanliness ...

9. Now, the first steps in his enterprise, excessively audacious and much celebrated by those of his own party, were as follows. The entire region of Assyria that the Euphrates flows through, and skirting Persia, there unites itself with the Tigris; all this he took and ravaged, and captured some of the fortified towns, in the total absence of anyone to hinder him, whether he had taken the Persians unawares by the rapidity of his advance, or whether he was out-generalled by them and drawn on by degrees further and further into the snare (for both stories are told); at any rate, advancing in this way, with his army marching along the river's bank and his flotilla upon the river supplying provisions and carrying the baggage, after a considerable interval he reached Ctesiphon, a place which, even to be near, was thought by him half the victory, by reason of his longing for it.

10. From this point, however, like sand slipping from beneath the feet, or a great storm bursting upon a ship, things began to go black for him; for Ctesiphon is a strongly fortified town, hard to take, and very well secured by a wall of burnt brick, a deep ditch, and the swamps coming from the river. It is rendered yet more secure by another strong place, the name of which is Coche, furnished with equal defences as far as regards garrison and artificial protection, so closely united with it that they appeared to be one city, the river separating both between them. For it was neither possible to take

the place by general assault, nor to reduce it by siege, nor even to force a way through by means of the fleet principally, for he would run the risk of destruction; being exposed to missiles from higher ground on both sides, he left the place in his rear, and did so in this manner. He diverted a not inconsiderable part of the river Euphrates, the greatest of rivers, and rendered it navigable for vessels, by means of a canal, of which ancient vestiges are said to be visible; and thus joining the Tigris a little in front of Ctesiphon, he saved his boats from one river by means of the other river, in all security; in this way he escaped the danger that menaced him from the two garrisons. But, as he advanced, a Persian army suddenly started up, and continually received fresh reinforcements, but did not think it advisable to stand in front and fight it out, without the greatest necessity (although it was in their power to conquer, from their superior numbers); but from the tops of the hills and narrow passes they shot arrows and threw darts, whenever opportunity served, and thus readily prevented his further progress. Hence he is reduced to great perplexity, and, not knowing to what side to turn, he finds out an unlucky solution for the difficulty.

11. A Persian of considerable standing, following the example of that Zopyrus employed by Cyrus in the case of Babylon, then pretended that he had had some quarrel, or rather a very great one and for a very great cause, with his king, and was on that account very hostile to the Persian cause, and well-disposed towards the Romans. He gained the emperor's confidence through his pretence as follows: 'Your Highness, what means all this, why are there so many shortcomings in so important an enterprise? What need is there of this provision-fleet, this superfluous burden – a mere incentive to cowardice; for nothing is so unfit for fighting, and fond of laziness, as a full belly, and the having the means of saving oneself in one's own hands? But if you will listen to me, you will burn this flotilla: what a relief to this fine army will be the result! You yourself will take another route, better supplied and safer than this; along which I will be your guide (being acquainted with the country as well as any man living), and will cause you to enter into the heart of the enemy's country, where you can obtain whatever you please, and so make your way home; and me you shall then recompense, when you have actually ascertained my good will and sound advice.'

12. And when he had said this, and gained credence to his story (for rashness is credulous, especially when God goads it on), everything went wrong at once. The boats became the prey of the

flames. They were low on victuals. Everywhere there was ridicule, and the whole venture resembled a suicide attempt. Hope vanished when the guide disappeared along with his promises. They were surrounded by the enemy and battle waged on all sides. It was difficult to advance and provisions were not easy to procure. In despair, the army became disenchanted with their commander. There was no hope for safety left, but one wish alone, as was natural under the circumstances, the ridding themselves of bad government and bad generalship.

13. Up to this point, such is the universal account; but thenceforward, one and the same story is not told by all, but different accounts are reported and made up by different people, both those present at the battle, and those not present; for some say that he was hit by a dart from the Persians, when engaged in a disorderly skirmish, as he was running hither and thither in his consternation; and the same fate befell him as it did to Cyrus, son of Parysatis, who went up with the Ten Thousand against his brother Artaxerxes, and by fighting inconsiderately threw away the victory through his rashness. Others, however, tell some such story as this respecting his end: that he had gone up upon a lofty hill to take a view of his army and ascertain how much was left him for carrying on the war; and that, when he saw the number considerable and superior to his expectation, he exclaimed, 'What a dreadful thing if we shall bring back all these fellows to the land of the Romans!' as though he begrudged them a safe return. Whereupon one of his officers, being indignant and not able to repress his rage, ran him through the bowels, without caring for his own life. Others tell that the deed was done by a barbarian jester, such as follow the camp, 'for the purpose of driving away ill humour and for amusing the men when they are drinking.'[48] Some give this honour to one of the Saracens. At any rate, he received a wound truly seasonable (or mortal) and salutary for the whole world, and by a single cut from his executioner he pays the penalty for the many entrails of victims to which he has trusted (to his own destruction); but what surprises me, is how the vain man, that fancied he learned the future from that means, knew nothing of the wound about to be inflicted on his own entrails! The concluding reflection is for once very appropriate: the liver of the victim was the approved means for reading the future, and it was precisely in that organ that the arch-diviner received the fatal thrust.

(King, pp. 91–7, revised.)

Jerome, *chronicon, s. aa.* 363–4, p. 243, 6–20, GCS (revised according to the text of Schoene): Julian, on setting out against Persia, promised our blood to the gods after his victory. Whereupon the Apostate was led by a certain bogus traitor into the desert and lost his army through hunger and thirst. When he incautiously wandered off his ranks, it so happened that he was pierced by a lance from an enemy cavalryman whom he met, and died at the age of thirty-two. Jovian who was *primicerius* from the (corps of) the *domestici* was made emperor. Jovian reigned for eight months.

(*s.a.* 364) Jovian was compelled by the necessity of the events to cede Nisibis and a large part of Mesopotamia to the king of the Persians.

(Dodgeon)

John Chrysostom,[49] de *S. Babyla contra Julianum et Gentiles* XXII (122–4, Shatkin, cf. *PG* 50.569–70): ... For in fact Julian, at the head of an army whose numbers had never been surpassed under any previous emperor, was fully expecting to overrun the whole of Persia on the spur of the moment, as it were, and without any effort. However, he fared as wretchedly and pitiably as if he was accompanied by an army of women and young children rather than men. For one thing, he brought them to such a pitch of desperation through shortage of provisions that they were reduced to consuming some of their cavalry horses and slaughtering others as they wasted away of hunger and thirst. You would have thought Julian was in league with the Persians, anxious not to defeat them but to surrender his own forces, for he had led them into such a barren and inhospitable region that he in fact surrendered without being defeated.

123. Even those who were eye-witnesses or forced to experience the many disasters which befell the campaign could hardly begin to describe the full picture, for it defies description. To come to the gist of the matter, Julian died disgracefully and without honour – for some say that he was mortally wounded by one of his own baggage-bearers, out of resentment at the appalling predicament of the army. Another version says that he died at the hands of an unknown assassin, recounting only that he was struck down and that he requested that he should be buried in Cilicia, where his body remains to this day.

124. When he had perished thus ignominiously, the soldiers, realizing that they were in dire straits, prostrated themselves before the enemies and gave pledges to surrender the most secure of all our

fortresses (i.e. Nisibis) which acted as an unbreachable circuit wall
to our empire. They were humanely treated by the barbarians and
thus a few of them were able to escape and returned home utterly
exhausted physically. Though ashamed of what they had agreed
upon in the treaty, they were constrained by the pledges to abandon
their ancestral captivity. For the inhabitants of that city were
treated with hostility by those from whom they would expect to
receive favours inasmuch as they, like a bulwark, had placed
everyone within a safe haven, always putting themselves forward on
behalf of everyone else in the face of all dangers. Yet they were
moved to alien territory, abandoning their own houses and fields,
and wrenched from their ancestral possessions and suffering all this
at the hands of their own kinsmen. Such are the blessings we have
enjoyed from this noble prince.

(M. Morgan)

John Lydus,   *de mensibus* IV, 118, p. 155, 23–157, 9: Julian is said
by Libanius and the many other augurs to have uttered the Homeric
phrase concerning his return from the War against the Persians:
'I stand in awe of the Trojans and the long-robed Trojan women.'
(*Iliad*, VI, 442)

After he had crossed the Tigris, he took control of many cities
and garrisons of the Persians and in every other respect proved
irresistible before the Persians. Nonetheless, he was destroyed by
guile and all his army with him. For two Persians cut off their
own ears and noses and came and deceived Julian, complaining
that they had suffered the indignities at the hands of the Persian
king. Nevertheless they were able, if Julian followed them, to
bring him to victory over Gorgo herself, queen of Persia. Julian
forgot his pressing destiny and at the same time the story of
Zopyrus in Herodotus and Sinon in Vergil; he fired his ships by
which he was carried along the Euphrates, for the purpose
supposedly was not to give the Persians the licence of using
them. His army carried some modest supplies and he followed
behind his treacherous guides. They led him into an arid and
waterless wilderness and revealed their trickery: they themselves
– for what else was to be expected? – were destroyed, but the
emperor discovered he could neither advance in that same direction nor turn back and he perished in a pitiable manner. When
a large part of the army had fallen, the Persians launched an
attack upon him as he was sick, but they were worsted and then
attacked a second time. Now he did not even have twenty

thousand men, when before he had led one hundred and seventy thousand. However, Julian fought most valiantly. One man from the Persian division of the so-called Saracens guessed the identity of the emperor from his purple robe, and cried out in his own language 'malchan' (meaning 'the king'). And he let loose with a swish his scimitar (Gk.: ῥομφαία) and pierced Julian's abdomen. Oribasius brought him back to the camp and advised him to make his final settlement, and, after Julian had nominated Jovian as emperor, he died.

(Dodgeon)

Ps. Joshua the Stylite, *Chronicle 7* (Syriac): In the year 609 (AD 297–298) the Greeks got possession of the city of Nisibis, and it remained under their sway for sixty-five years. After the death of Julian in Persia which took place in the year 674 (AD 362–363), Jovian, who reigned over the Greeks after him, preferred peace above everything, and for the sake of this he allowed the Persians to take possession of Nisibis for one hundred and twenty years, after which they were to restore it to its (former) masters.

(Wright, pp. 6–7)

Julian (Imperator), *ELF* 98: (To Libanius) I travelled as far as Litarbae, – it is a village of Chalcis, – and came upon a road that still had the remains of a winter camp of Antioch. The road, I may say, was partly swamp, partly hill, but the whole of it was rough, and in the swamp lay stones which looked as though they had been thrown there purposely, as they lay together without any art, after the fashion followed also by those who build public highways in cities and instead of cement make a deep layer of soil and then lay the stones close together as though they were making a boundary-wall.[50] When I passed over this with some difficulty and arrived at my first halting-place, it was about the ninth hour, and then I received at my headquarters the greater part of your (i.e. the Antiochene) senate. You have perhaps learned already what we said to one another and, if it be the will of heaven, you shall know it from my lips.

From Litarbae I proceeded to Beroea, and there Zeus, by showing a manifest sign from heaven, declared all things to be auspicious. I stayed there for a day and saw the Acropolis and sacrificed to Zeus in imperial fashion a white bull. . . .

Next, Batnae entertained me, a place like nothing that I have ever seen in your country, except Daphne; though not long ago, while the temple and statue were still unharmed, I should not have hesitated to compare Daphne with Ossa and Pelion or the peaks of Olympus, or Thessalian Tempe, or even to have preferred it to all of them put together. ...

Thus much, then, I was able to write to you from Hierapolis about my own affairs. But as regards the military or political arrangements, you ought, I think, to have been present to observe and pay attention to them yourself. For, as you well know, the matter is too long for a letter even three times as long as this. But I will tell you of these matters also, summarily, and in a very few words. I sent an embassy to the Saracens and suggested that they could come if they wished. That is one affair of the sort I have mentioned. For another, I dispatched men as wide-awake as I could obtain, that they might guard against anyone's leaving here secretly to go to the enemy and inform them that we are on the move. After that I held a court martial and, I am convinced, showed in my decision the utmost clemency and justice. I have procured excellent horses and mules and have mustered all my forces together. The boats to be used on the river are laden with corn, or rather with baked bread and sour wine. You can understand at what length I should have to write in order to describe how every detail of this business was worked out and what discussions arose over every one of them.

(Wright, iii, pp. 201–9)

Libanius, *ep.* 737: (To Pappos) I rejoice in receiving your letter, not only because the letter from a friend is most welcome, but also because there are signs that your country (i.e. Mesopotamia) is being freed from the enemies. This is exactly what Julian is hoping to achieve. Those who had appeared before (i.e. Constantius and his generals) in the past had made the enemies more audacious. 2. Most worthy Pappos, to rejoice in the present security is justified, so that the smile would not desert the face of him who is accustomed to good cheer. 3. The Persians will act as men who are accustomed to war against the gods customarily do. Every one of them (i.e. the gods) will pick up their arms and attack them (i.e. the Persians) and instruct them to flee. 4. Your son wishes to be a rhetor and his talents are not inferior to his desires. He should therefore learn to be more modest. When one of the young shows this, he draws me and receives more from me than any other. 5. Write to him, therefore, (and tell him) to guard his morals and you would not need to beseech me. (June, 362).

(Dodgeon)

Libanius, *ep.* 1220: (To Scylacius) Although I had not yet ceased from my tears, you cast me into a state of greater lamentation with your letter, so precisely did you discuss both the good things we once enjoyed and the ones we might have had, if one of the gods had given back to us the man who won the victories. 2. For those whom he smote praise him (Julian) more now than those on whose behalf he stood in line of battle. But of these peoples two cities (Caesarea and Antioch) danced for joy, and for one of them I feel ashamed. 3. Yet they can be forgiven. For the man who wishes to be mischievous considers his enemy to be the fellow who does not allow him to be mischievous, and, should it happen that his teacher of morality dies, the man who is unable to be moral rejoices at his freedom now to work mischief. We live in the company of such a crowd that is hostile both to gods and to Julian, about whom you entertain the right opinion when you enrol him among the chorus of the gods. 4. I myself have also come to this conclusion and at the same time I groan when I reckon what hopes were held and what was the outcome. Indeed if he (Julian) is with the Higher Powers, my affairs at any rate are worse. For with regard to my affairs let them be stated as follows. 5. For what would it have been like if he had arrived from Persia and you from Phoenicia, he leading prisoners and you on your way to see the prizes of his labours, and I to speak something about his achievements, a small contribution for his great efforts, and that he should relate his own story! A swarm of jackdaws would have come, food for laughter to you and me, that did not know how to speak but tried to strike others to counter their own ignorance. 6. Such an assembled audience an evil day took from us. Many attacked me with arms and I might never have held out, if he (Mercury) had not hurried me away who also stole away Mars in chains. Now someone in hiding has launched an arrow, and I have been indicted for committing awful crimes, but again one of the gods blunted the missile and I remain at my post and hope to be undisturbed. 7. It would have pleased the archers like these to relax their bowstrings (at Julian) but the land of the Persians has been sufficiently wasted. However, I have been requesting an account of what was done from friends among those who returned and those who it was likely would not neglect a written account of such events. Each said that he had an account and would give it but none did, and not even orally did he inform me, for he who has passed on his way is disregarded, but each man's zeal is entirely upon his own affairs. 8. Certain soldiers who did not formerly know me, gave me the list of some days and route distances and names of places; but nowhere an account of his achievements that can fully explain, but obscurity and shadow that will be insufficient for (the talk of) the compiler. 9. If indeed you also are eager for this knowledge, apprise me of it and the talk of the soldiers will reach you; for these have written their accounts, but I hoped for others. (AD 363)

(Dodgeon)

Libanius, *ep.* 1367: (To Modestus) 1. Do you see how far conscientiousness can get you? Previously you had high offices and now you enjoy the same confidence, and in no way did your public responsibility end with the old regime. 2. The reason for this is that at that time you did not belong to those who bought their offices or those who used their offices for purposes of personal gain, even though that would have been possible and those who wanted to be just were laughed at. Clearly, the divine one (i.e. Julian) whom the Persians so hate discovered this and thus accorded to you as a reward for your voluntary poverty the highest office next to that of the Emperor, though to Julian (not the emperor) he gave a task requiring the greatest degree of righteousness, such as Rhadamanthys had. 3. Bithynia may be the limit of his district, but his love carries him over to you; for as such a good friend was close by, he was drawn irresistibly to him. Thus he will enjoy the most pleasant society, but the courier freed me from a great fear into which I had been driven by the tidings which had previously reached here: that in the capital city there was much suffering and many ill deeds. 4. What he did report was that some of those thoroughly despicable people without any home were right out of control, while the larger and better part of the population remained calm. You yourself [he said] had acted impeccably, but had bent before the storm and quickly arranged an understanding. Your return to the town was glorious and marvelled at everywhere, for you were surrounded by masses of people and your praise was in every mouth. Your team of horses could not be seen, it was surrounded by the rejoicing crowd. 5. The (military) courier reported this, but I let it be known, driving out one set of tidings with another, the false with the true. But your letter has crossed the Euphrates, no wonder then that it only arrived late in the Emperor's hands. 6. The latter is advancing, overrunning the Persian Empire. Where he is at the moment, he alone would know best. The prisoners of war tell us what he is achieving, and they tell that he is making quick progress and that the towns are in ruins. But we do not know what to do with all the prisoners. 7. I have said this to excuse the delay of the (military) courier and to give you joy and myself pleasure. (AD 363)

(Dodgeon)

Libanius, *ep.* 1402, 1–3: (To Aristophanes) I think that rumour even now has done as of old and has instructed the Greeks in the sufferings of the barbarians; for you know how such a thing was accomplished by it in earlier times, when it announced the victory of the conquering army to an army on the point of battle and gave it heart – if therefore a report has not yet come to you, then let the Greeks know that the descendants of Darius and Xerxes are being punished by them as they see their own cities destroyed by fire – these were the men who two years ago were razing ours to the ground. 2. For when the emperor launched his offensive in the spring in an area which they did not consider, the Assyrians were immediately taken, (also) many villages and a few cities; for there were not many. Then the Persian woke up and was dismayed and fled, but he (Julian) pursued and captured everything without a battle; or rather the majority without a battle; he killed six thousand who came on a reconnaissance and at the same time for a fight, if the chance arose. 3. This is the news from the men who spend their lives on the flying camels – for may their speed be honoured by the title of 'wings' – and there is a hope that the emperor will come leading (in captivity) the present ruler and handing over the (Persian) government to the fugitive (i.e. Hormisdas). ... (AD 363)

(Dodgeon)

Libanius, *ep.* 1508: (To Seleucus) I wept over the letter and I said to the gods, 'What is the meaning of this, o gods?' And I gave the letter to those among the others whom I particularly trust and I saw the letter having the same effect on them also. For each man calculated the circumstances in which you have been compelled to live, compared with what you deserved to meet with. 2. But I shall tell you with what (thoughts) I reassured both them and myself; and indeed I think this will please you. I was reminded of the famous Odysseus, who, when he had pulled down Troy, was crossing the sea, as you know, but we neither require tree branches before our 'naked manhood' nor even would we need them, nor are we berated by the household servants and your household is free of all drunken behaviour. 3. But if you are excluded from cities and their baths, just think how many men, when they can spend their time in the city, choose their pleasures in the countryside and judge them more agreeable than the uproar in town. But if you were Achilles and you had to accompany the Centaur on Pelion, what would you have done? Would you have run off to the city and considered the mountain a misfortune? 4. Do not, by Zeus, beat yourself, Seleucus, nor forget those famous generals who had no sooner put up their trophies than one was in chains, and the others were fleeing into exile. For we learnt those stories (in school) not so we might suffer but so that in a crisis we might gain relief from them. 5. You have now an opportunity to show off your courage and you lament, and although you did not fear the Persians you consider the trees a dread terror; and when you endured the sun along the Tigris but have the shade of foliage in Pontus, you desire the market-places in the towns and say that you are lonely. This should be the last thing to happen to a literary man. For how would you be abandoned by Plato, Demosthenes and that famous band who must stay wherever you wish? 6. Therefore converse with these and compile the history of the war which you promised, and as you regard a prize so great you will be unaffected by your present circumstances. This also made Thucydides' exile easy to bear, and I would have explained it entirely if you did not well understand it. 7. Be assured that by your writing you will gratify everyone. For in company with many you saw what was done, but of those who saw only you have a voice worthy to record the events.

(Dodgeon)

Libanius, *or.* I, 132–4: When our city council escorted him on his way with prayers that they might be forgiven the charges against them, he replied that, if heaven preserved him, he would favour with his presence Tarsus in Cilicia. 'Though I have no doubt that you will react to this', he went on, 'by pinning your hopes upon him who will be your envoy, yet he too will have to go there with me.' Then without a tear he embraced me in my tears, with his gaze now fixed on the ruin of Persia. He sent me a first letter from the frontier of the Empire, and marched on, ravaging the countryside, plundering villages, taking fortresses, crossing rivers, mining fortifications and capturing cities. 133. There was no messenger to tell us of any of these achievements, but we rejoiced just as if we saw them, confident that events would happen as they did, as we looked to him. But here Fortune played her usual trick. The army had revelled in the slaughter and rout of the Persians and in the athletic competitions and horse races, on which the inhabitants of Ctesiphon had gazed from their battlements with no grounds to trust even their thickness of wall: the Persians had decided to come as suppliants with prayers and gifts, knowing that it was against common sense for a man to oppose heaven's will. Then, as their envoys remounted their horses, a spear pierced the side of our wise Emperor, and with the victor's blood it drenched the land of the vanquished, and the pursuers it delivered into the hand of the fugitive. 134. It was by means of a deserter that the Persians found their good fortune, but we in Antioch discovered it through no human agency: earthquakes were the harbingers of woe, destroying the cities of Palestine–Syria either wholly or in part. We were sure that by these afflictions heaven gave us a sign of some great disaster, and, as we prayed that our guess should be right, the bitter news reached our ears that our great Julian was dead, that some nonentity held the throne, and that Armenia, and as much of the rest of the Empire as they liked, was in Persian hands.

(Norman, pp. 78–9)

Libanius, *or.* XVII, 19–22: You should not, then, my dear friend, have rejected the Persian embassy, when it asked for peace and was submissive to your will. But the sufferings of the lands near the Tigris, ravaged and derelict, the victim of many incursions, every one of which caused the transfer of our wealth into Persian hands, diverted your attention. You thought it tantamount to treason to desire peace and to refrain from exacting punishment. 20. But there! Heaven opposed you, or, rather, you tried to exact a punishment disproportionate to the crime. There was the land of Assyria, queen of the Persian domains, shaded with tall palms and other trees of all kinds, their strongest storehouse of gold and silver, with magnificent palaces built therein, with herds of boars, deer and all the animals of the chase contained within their enclosures, with forts towering aloft into mid-air beyond the strength of hostile hand, with villages comparable to cities and with unparalleled prosperity. 21. Here he directed his attack, and he so harried and overwhelmed them, himself all smiles and allowing his troops to make merry amongst it, that the Persians would need to colonize it and a man's lifetime would not be enough to repair the disaster. Moreover, the incredible ascent of the bank, the night battle that slew a vast number of Persians, the trembling that seized their limbs and, in their cowardice, the vision from afar of the ravaging of their lands – all this was part of the punishment he inflicted upon them. 22. Restore to us then, supreme consul of the gods, your namesake who invoked you so often at the year's beginning. His colleague, despite his advanced years, you have allowed to complete his year – but he was overcome in its mid-course. And while he lay slain, we at Daphne were worshipping the Nymphs with choric dance and other delights, ignorant of the disaster that had befallen us.

(Norman, i, pp. 263–5)

Libanius, *or.* XVIII, 212–75: See Introduction, p. 7.

Libanius, *or.* XXIV, 9: I feel that the gods were angered against that emperor (i.e. Jovian) and so he was compelled to make peace on terms such that the enemy gained more than they could ever have dreamed of, the whole of Armenia, the acquisition of the important frontier city (of Nisibis) and many strong fortresses.

(Norman, i, p. 497)

Magnus of Carrhae: see under Malalas.

Malalas,   XIII, pp. 328, 5–337, 11: Then he left and went through the city of Cyrrhus against the Persians. . . .
(= Magnus of Carrhae, *FGrH* 225 F) 1. Marching against Sabbourarsakios (i.e. Shapur II), king of the Persians, the Emperor Julian reached Hierapolis. There he sent [p. 329] for ships to be built in Samosata, a city of Euphratensis, some from wood and others from skins, as the extremely wise Magnus of Carrhae, the historian who was with the Emperor Julian, has noted. 2. He left Hierapolis and came to the city of Carrhae where he found two routes, one leading to the city of Nisibis which once belonged to the Romans, and the other going to the Roman fortress called Circesium which lies between the two rivers, the Euphrates and the Aborras, which the Roman Emperor Diocletian established. Julian then divided his army and sent Nisibis sixteen thousand armed men with two commanders, Sebastianus and Procopius. 3. Julian himself reached the fortress of Circesium and left in that fortress six thousand soldiers whom he found stationed there, together with four thousand additional armed men with two commanders, Accameus and Maurus. 4. He left there and crossed the river Aborras by a bridge while the ships, the number of which was one thousand two

hundred and fifty, reached the river Euphrates. 5. He assembled his army, taking with him the *magister* Anatolius and Salustius the Praetorian Prefect and his *magistri militum*, and climbed up to a high platform from which he addressed the army, commending them and urging them to fight keenly and in a disciplined manner against the Persians. 6. The Emperor then [p. 330] ordered them to board the ships while he himself went on board the ship which had been prepared for him. He commanded 1,500 brave men from the unit of lancers (*lanciarii*) and javelin-throwers (*mattiarii*) to go ahead as advance scouts and gave orders that his standards be carried and that Count Lucianus, a man highly skilled in war, should be with him. This man sacked many Persian fortresses lying along the Euphrates and on islands in the middle of the water and killed the Persians in them. He stationed Victor and Dagalaiphus behind the rest of the boats to guard the host. 7. Then the Emperor set out with all the army through the great canal which joins the Euphrates to the Tigris. He reached the Tigris itself, where the two rivers join and form a great lake and crossed into Persia in the region of those who are called the Mauzanites, near the city of Ctesiphon where the Persian king lived. 8. Then the Emperor Julian, having gained the upper hand, encamped in the plain of that city, Ctesiphon, intending to go on with his own Senate as far as Babylon and take the area there.

9. King Sabbourarsakios, thinking that Julian, the Roman Emperor, was coming via Nisibis, hastened against him with his whole force. Then he was informed [p. 331] that Julian, the Roman Emperor, was behind him, taking Persian regions and that the Roman generals with a large force were coming against him from the front, and, realizing that he was in the middle, he fled to Persarmenia. Then, to avoid being overtaken, he secretly sent two of his councillors with their noses cut off with their consent, to Julian the Roman Emperor, to deceive him. These two Persians, with their noses cut off, came to the Roman Emperor wanting, as they said, to betray the Persian king because he had punished them. 10. The Emperor Julian was deceived by their oaths and followed them with all his army, and they diverted him for one hundred and fifty miles, deceiving him, to a waterless desert until the twenty-fifth day of the month of Desius or of Junius. 11. He found there ancient, fallen walls of a city called Bubion, and another place whose buildings were standing but which was deserted, and this was called Asia. The Emperor Julian entered it with all the Roman army and encamped there. While in this area, they were without food and there was not even any fodder for the animals, for it was a

wilderness. When all the Roman army realised that the Emperor had been deceived and had led them astray and brought them to desert areas, they turned to utter disorderliness. 12. On the next day, the twenty-sixth of June, he brought out the Persians who had misled him and examined them. They confessed with the words 'For the sake of our country and our king, that [p. 332] he might be saved, we gave ourselves to death and deceived you. Now, as your slaves, we die.' He believed them and did not kill them but gave them his promise if they would lead the army out of the desert area.

13. About the second hour of the same day, the Emperor Julian was walking among the army and urging them not to behave in an undisciplined manner when he was wounded by someone unknown. He went into his tent and died during the night as Magnus, whom we referred to earlier, relates. 14. However, Eutychianus, the historian from Cappadocia, who was a soldier and a *vicarius* of his unit of the *Primoarmeniaci* (Legio I Armeniaca ?), and who was himself present in the war, wrote that the Emperor Julian entered Persian territory by way of the Euphrates for fifteen days' marching. There he was victorious and conquered and took everything as far as the city called Ctesiphon which was the seat of the Persian king. The latter fled to the territory of the Persarmenians, while Julian decided with his Council and his army to set out for Babylon on the next day and to take it by night. 15. While he slept he saw in a dream an adult man, wearing a cuirass, approaching him in his tent near the city of Ctesiphon, in a city called Asia, and smiting him with a spear. Distraught, he awoke and cried out. The eunuchs of the bed-chamber and the body-guard and the unit who guarded the tent arose and came to him with royal torches. When [p. 333] the Emperor Julian realised that he had been fatally wounded in the armpit, he asked them, 'What is the name of the village where my tent is?', and they told him that it was called Asia. Then he immediately cried out, 'O Sun, you have slain Julian', and having lost blood, he died at the fifth hour of the night in the year 411 of the era of Antiochus the Great.

Then the army, before the Persian enemy should learn of this, went to the tent of Jovian, a count among the officials of the bodyguard (*comes domesticorum*), who had the rank of a stratelates. They led him – not knowing what had happened – to the royal tent, as if the Emperor Julian wanted him. When they had entered the tent, they held him there and hailed him as Emperor on the twenty-seventh of the month of Desius or Junius before the dawn. The rest of the army, some of which was encamped at Ctesiphon and some at a great distance, did not know what had happened until dawn, because they were some way away. Thus the Emperor Julian died when he was thirty-three years old.

After the rule of Julian the Apostate, Jovian the son of Varronianus became emperor; he was crowned by the army (there) in Persia during the consulship of Sallustius. He was a strong Christian and reigned for seven months.

Scarcely had he become emperor when he addressed the entire army and the senators [p. 335] in his company, shouting out in person, 'If you wish me to be your emperor, you must all be Christians.' And all the army and the senators shouted their approval. Jovian himself and his army left the desert for the fertile land of Persia and he pondered anxiously how he might leave Persia. When Sabbourarsakios, the Persian king, learnt of the death of the emperor Julian, he was distressed by a great anxiety. From the country of Persarmenia he dispatched as envoy one of his highest nobility called Suren to the Roman emperor, with a request and plea for peace. The holy Emperor Jovian gladly received him and consented to receive his embassy for peace, stating that he was also sending an ambassador to the Persian king. When Suren, the Persian ambassador, heard this, he asked the Emperor Jovian to sign a peace treaty immediately and forthwith. And Jovian gave the appointment to a senator of his, the patrician Arintheus, and entrusted the entire negotiations to him. He agreed to stick to what was sanctioned by him or was signed. The emperor disdained in person to make a peace treaty with a man of senatorial rank, albeit a Persian envoy. A relaxation of hostilities for three days was granted for the deliberations about peace. An agreement was struck [p. 336] between the Roman patrician Arintheus and Suren, the Persian senator and ambassador; the Romans would give to the Persians all the so-called province of Mygdonia and its chief city called Nisibis, empty and with only its walls, without its inhabitants. And when this was settled and a peace was put into writing, the Emperor Jovian took with him one of the satraps, a Persian in the company of the ambassador and called Junius. The purpose of this was to safeguard him and his expedition out of Persian territory and (for the Persians) to take over the province and its main city. When the Emperor Jovian reached the city of Nisibis, he did not enter it, but encamped outside its walls. But Junius the Persian satrap entered the city in accordance with the emperor's command and raised the Persian standard on one of the towers. The Roman emperor ordered all the citizens, down to the last man, to depart with all their possessions. Silvanus, who was a count by rank and a governor of the same city, went out to him and fell at the emperor's feet, begging him not to betray the city to the Persians. He did not persuade him. For the emperor said that he had sworn an oath and did not wish to have a reputation for perjury in everyone's estimation. Outside the city wall of Amida he encircled another city and called it Nisibis, and there he made a settlement of all the people [p. 337] from the territory of Mygdonia, and including their governor Silvanus.

Then, crossing into Mesopotamia, he immediately raised all the aspirations of the Christians, gave the control of affairs to Christians and dispatched Christian governors and commanders over the whole Orient. And quitting the Orient the same emperor Jovian, after the completion of his peace treaty with Persia for a brief period, speedily set out for Constantinople with his army on account of the winter; for the weather was severe. And during his return he reached the territory of Galatia; and he died a natural death in the village called Dadastana at the age of sixty.

(Dodgeon)

Orosius, *adversus paganos* VII, 30, 4–31, 2: Moreover, Julian, when he was preparing war against the Parthians (*sic*) and was taking with him to destined destruction Roman forces brought together from all sides, vowed the blood of Christians to his gods, intending to persecute the churches openly if he should be able to win a victory. 5. Indeed, he ordered an amphitheatre to be constructed at Jerusalem, in which on his return from the Parthians he might offer the bishops, monks, and all the saints of the locality to beasts deliberately made more ferocious and might view them being torn apart. 6. Thus, after he moved his camp from Ctesiphon, being led into the desert by a treacherous traitor, when his army began to perish from the force of thirst, the heat of the sun, and especially when affected by the difficulty of marching through the sands, the emperor, anxious because of the danger of the situation as he wandered rather carelessly over the wastes of the desert, was struck by a lance of a cavalryman of the enemy whom he met, and died. Thus, the merciful God ended these evil plans by the death of their evil author.

31   In the one thousand one hundred and seventeenth year after the founding of the City, Jovian, in a very critical state of affairs, was made the thirty-seventh emperor by the army, and when, being caught in an unfavourable locality and being surrounded by the

enemy, he possessed no chance to escape, he made a treaty with Shapur, the king of the Persians, although, as some think, little worthy yet quite necessary. 2. For, that he might free the Roman army, safe and sound, not only from an attack of the enemy, but also from the dangers of the locality, he conceded the town of Nisibis and part of upper Mesopotamia to the Persians.

(Deferrari, pp. 334–5)

Philostorgius, *historia ecclesiastica* VII, 15: The apostate Julian undertook an expedition against the Persians, relying upon the prophecies of the heathen oracles in different quarters, that his might would prove irresistible. But a certain old man, one of those who had long since been discharged from the Persian service, approached the Apostate as he was making war in Persia. And when he had brought the Romans into the greatest straits by leading them into a pathless desert, in which a very great portion of the army perished, he gave the enemy, like the prey of a hunter, into the hands of his countrymen. For the Persians rushed upon the Romans, having joined to their forces as allies some Saracen horsemen who were armed with spears. One of them thrust a spear at Julian, which struck him forcefully on the thigh near the groin; and when the spear was drawn out, it was followed by a quantity of bile and blood also. Subsequently, one of the body-guard of the emperor immediately attacked the Saracen who had wounded the king, and cut off his head: while the Romans immediately placed the mortally wounded Julian on a shield, and carried him off into a tent. Many even thought that the fatal blow was struck by Julian's own friends, so sudden and unexpected was it, and so much at a loss were they to know where it came from. But the wretched Julian took up in his hands the blood which flowed from his wound, and cast it up towards the sun, exclaiming in a clear voice, 'Take thy fill!' and he added curses upon the other gods as villains and destroyers. In his train was a most distinguished physician, one Oribasius, a native of the Lydian city, Sardis. But the wound was far beyond all medical art, and carried Julian off after three days of suffering, after he had enjoyed the dignity of Caesar for five years, and the imperial throne two years and a half from the death of Constantius. Philostorgius in this passage writes that Julian sprinkled his blood towards the sun and cursed his gods. But most historians write that he used this act as an expression of hatred against our Lord and only true God, Jesus Christ.'

(Walford, pp. 483–4, revised)

Socrates, *historia ecclesiastica* III, 21: The emperor meanwhile invaded the country of the Persians a little before spring, having learnt that the races of Persia were greatly enfeebled and totally spiritless in winter. 2. For from their inability to endure cold, they abstain from military service in that season, and it has become a proverb that 'a Mede will not draw his hand from underneath his cloak.' And well knowing that the Romans were inured to brave all the rigours of the atmosphere, he let them loose on the country. 3. After devastating a considerable tract of country, including numerous villages and fortresses, they next assailed the cities; 4. and having invested the great city of Ctesiphon, he reduced the king of the Persians to such straits that the latter sent repeated embassies to the emperor, offering to surrender a portion of his dominions, on condition of his quitting the country, and putting an end to the war. 5. But Julian was unaffected by these submissions, and showed no compassion to a suppliant foe: nor did he think of the adage, 'To conquer is honourable, but to be more than conqueror gives occasion for envy.' 6. Giving credit to the divinations of the philosopher Maximus, with whom he continually discoursed, he was deluded into the belief that his exploits would not only equal, but exceed those of Alexander of Macedon; so that he spurned with contempt the entreaties of the Persian monarch. 7. He even supposed, in accordance with the teachings of Pythagoras and Plato on 'the transmigration of souls,' that he was possessed of Alexander's soul, or rather that he himself was Alexander in another body. 8. This ridiculous fancy deluded him and caused him to reject the negotiations for peace proposed by the king of the Persians. 9. Wherefore the latter, convinced of the uselessness of them, was constrained to prepare for conflict, and therefore on the next day after the rejection of his embassy, he drew out in order of battle all the forces he had. 10. The Romans indeed censured their prince for not avoiding an engagement when he might have done so with advantage: nevertheless they attacked those who opposed them, and again put the enemy to flight. 11. The emperor was present on horseback, and encouraged his soldiers in battle; but confiding simply in his hope of success, he wore no armour. 12. In this defenceless state, a javelin was thrown at him unexpectedly and pierced his arm and entered his side. 13. In consequence of this wound he died, and the identity of the killer was unknown. Some say that a certain Persian deserter hurled the javelin; others assert that one of his own men was the author of the deed, which indeed is the best corroborated report. 14. But Callistus, one of his body-guards, who celebrated this emperor's deeds in heroic verse, says, in narrating the particulars of this war, that the wound of which he died was inflicted by a demon. 15. This is possibly a mere poetical fiction, or perhaps it was really the fact; for vengeful furies have indeed destroyed many persons. 16. Be the case however as it may, this is certain, that the ardour of his natural temperament rendered him incautious, his learning made him vain, and his affectation of clemency exposed him to contempt. 17. Thus Julian ended his life in Persia, as we have said, in his fourth consulate, which he bore with Sallust his colleague. 18. This event occurred on the 26th of June, in the third year of his reign, and the seventh from his having been created Caesar by Constantius, he being at that time in the thirty-first year of his age.

(Zenos, p. 90, revised)

Sozomen, *historia ecclesiastica* V, 3, 5 and VI, 1, 1–14 and 3, 1–2: When the inhabitants of Nisibis sent to implore his (i.e. Julian's) aid against the Persians, who were on the point of invading the Roman territories, he refused to assist them because they were wholly Christianized, and would neither reopen their temples nor resort to the sacred places; he threatened that he would not help them, nor receive their embassy, nor approach to enter the city before he should hear that they had returned to paganism.

(Hartranft, p. 328)

VI, 1   I have narrated in the preceding book the occurrences which took place in the Church, during the reign of Julian. This emperor, having determined to carry on the war with Persia, made a rapid transit across the Euphrates in the beginning of spring, and, passing by Edessa from hatred to the inhabitants, who had long professed Christianity, he went on to Carrhae, where there was a temple of Jupiter, in which he offered up sacrifice and prayer. 2. He then selected twenty thousand armed men from among his troops, and sent them towards the Tigris, in order that they might guard those regions, and also be ready to join him, in case he should require their assistance. He then wrote to Arsacius, king of Armenia, one of the Roman allies, to join him in the war. 3. In this letter Julian manifested the most unbounded arrogance; he boasted of the high qualities which had, he said, rendered him worthy of the empire, and acceptable to the gods for whom he cared; he reviled Constantius, his predecessor, as an effeminate and impious emperor, and threatened Arsacius in a grossly insulting way; and since he understood that he was a Christian, he intensified his insults, or eagerly and largely uttered unlawful blasphemies against Christ, for he was accustomed to dare this in every case. He told Arsacius that unless he acted according to his directions, the God in whom he trusted would not be able to defend him from his vengeance. 4. When he considered that all his arrangements had been duly made, he led his army through Assyria.

He took a great many towns and fortresses, either through treachery or by battle, and thoughtlessly proceeded onwards, without reflecting that he would have to return by the same route. He pillaged every place he approached, and pulled down or burnt the granaries and storehouses. 5. As he was journeying up the Euphrates, he arrived at Ctesiphon, a very large city, whither the Persian monarchs had now transferred their residence from Babylon. The Tigris flows near this spot. As he was prevented from reaching the city with his ships, by a part of the land which separated it from the river, he judged that either he must pursue his journey by water, or quit his ships and go to Ctesiphon by land; and he interrogated the prisoners on the subject. Having ascertained from them that there was a canal which had been blocked up in the course of time, he caused it to be cleared out, and, having thus effected a communication between the Euphrates and the Tigris, he proceeded towards the city, his ships floating along by the side of his army. 6. But the Persians appeared on the banks of the Tigris with a formidable display of horse and many armed troops, of elephants, and of horses; and Julian became conscious that his army was besieged between two great rivers, and was in danger of perishing, either by remaining in its present position, or by retreating through the cities and villages which he had so utterly devastated that no provisions were obtainable; therefore he summoned the soldiers to see horse-races, and proposed rewards to the fleetest racers. 7. In the meantime he commanded the officers of the ships to throw over the provisions and baggage of the army, so that the soldiers, I suppose, seeing themselves in danger by the lack of necessary provisions, might turn about boldly and fight their enemies more desperately. After supper he sent for the generals and tribunes and commanded the embarkation of the troops. They sailed along the Tigris during the night and came at once to the opposite banks and disembarked; 8. but their departure was perceived by some of the Persians, who defended themselves and encouraged one another, but those still asleep the Romans readily overcame. At daybreak, the two armies engaged in battle; and after much bloodshed on both sides, the Romans returned by the river, and encamped near Ctesiphon.

9. The emperor, being no longer desirous of proceeding further but wishing only to return to the (Roman) empire, burnt his vessels, as he considered that they required too many soldiers to guard them; and he then commenced his retreat along the Tigris, which was to his left. The prisoners, who acted as guides to the Romans, led them to a fertile country where at first they found an abundance of provisions. 10. Soon after, an old man who had resolved to die for the liberty of Persia, allowed himself to be taken prisoner, and was brought before the emperor. On being questioned as to the route, and seeming to speak the truth, he persuaded them to follow him as capable of transporting the army very speedily to the Roman frontiers. 11. He observed that for the space of three or four days' journey this road would be difficult, and that it would be necessary to carry provisions during that time, as the surrounding country was sterile. The emperor was deceived by the discourse of this wise old man, and approved the march by this route. 12. On advancing further, after the lapse of three days, they rushed headlong into an uncultivated region. The old prisoner was put to torture. He confessed that he had exposed himself voluntarily to death for the sake of his country, and was therefore prepared willingly to endure any sufferings that could be inflicted on him.

The Roman troops were now worn out by the length of the journey and the scarcity of provisions, and the Persians chose this moment to attack them.

13. In the heat of the conflict which ensued, a violent wind arose; and the sky and the sun were totally concealed by the clouds, while the air was at the same time mixed with dust. During the darkness which was thus produced, a horseman, riding at full gallop, directed his lance against the emperor, and wounded him mortally. After throwing Julian from his horse, the unknown assailant secretly went away. Some conjectured that he was a Persian; others, that he was a Saracen. 14. There are those who insist that he who struck the blow was a Roman soldier, who was indignant at the imprudence and temerity which the emperor had manifested in exposing his army to such peril. . . .[51]

3   After the decease of Julian, the government of the empire was, by the unanimous consent of the troops, tendered to Jovian. When the army was about to proclaim him emperor, he announced himself to be a Christian and refused the sovereignty, nor would he

receive the symbols of empire; but when the soldiers discovered the cause of his refusal, they loudly proclaimed that they were themselves Christians.

2. The dangerous and disturbed condition in which affairs had been left by Julian's strategy, and the sufferings of the army from famine in an enemy's country, compelled Jovian to conclude a peace with the Persians, and to cede to them some territories which had been formerly tributary to the Romans.

(Hartranft, pp. 345–7, revised.)

Suidas, *s. v.* ʼἀνασχοῦσα' (A2094), ed. Adler, i, p. 190, 6–8: For the first person to emerge (ἀνασχὼν) out of the tunnel was Magnus, a manly and exceptionally daring person.[52]

(Lieu)

Theodoret, *historia ecclesiastica* III, 21 and 25, 1–6, GCS: No sooner had the Persians heard of the death of Constantius than they took heart, proclaimed war, and marched over the frontier of the Roman empire. Julian therefore determined to muster his forces, though they were a host without a God to guard them. 2. First he sent to Delphi, to Delos and to Dodona, and to the other oracles and enquired of the seers if he should march. They bade him march and promised him victory. One of these oracles I subjoin in proof of their falsehood. It was as follows: 'Now we gods all started to get trophies of victory by the river beast and of them I, Ares, bold raiser of the din of war, will be leader.' 3. Let them that style the Pythian a God wise in word and prince of the muses ridicule the absurdity of the utterance. I who have found out its falsehood will rather pity him who was cheated by it. The oracle called the Tigris 'beast' because the river and the animal bear the same name. 4. Rising in the mountains of Armenia, and flowing through Assyria, it discharges itself into the Persian gulf. Beguiled by these oracles, the unhappy man indulged in dreams of victory, and after fighting with the Persians had visions of a campaign against the Galileans. . . .

25 Julian's folly was yet more clearly manifested by his death. He crossed the river that separates the Roman Empire from the Persian, brought over his army, and then forthwith burnt his boats, so making his men fight not in willing, but in forced obedience. 2. The best generals are wont to fill their troops with enthusiasm, and, if they see them growing discouraged, to cheer them and raise their hopes; but Julian, by burning the bridge of retreat, cut off all good hope. A further proof of his incompetence was his failure to fulfil

the duty of foraging in all directions and providing his troops with supplies. 3. Julian had neither ordered supplies to be brought from Rome, nor did he make any bountiful provision by ravaging the enemy's country. He left the inhabited world behind him, and persisted in marching through the wilderness. 4. His soldiers had not enough to eat and drink; they were without guides; they were marching astray in a desert land. Thus they saw the folly of their most wise emperor. 5. In the midst of their murmuring and grumbling, they suddenly found him who had struggled in mad rage against his Maker wounded to death. Ares who raises the war-din had never come to help him as he promised; Loxias had given lying divination; he who rejoices in the thunderbolts had hurled no bolt on the man who dealt the fatal blow; the boasting of his threats was dashed to the ground. 6. The name of the man who dealt that righteous stroke no one knows to this day. Some say that he was wounded by an invisible being, others by one of the Nomads who were called Ishmaelites; others by a trooper who could not endure the pains of famine in the wilderness.

(Jackson, pp. 104–6)

Theophanes, *chronographia,* A.M. 5855, pp. 52, 19–53, 4: Julian dispatched many men in different places to both oracles and places of divination so that he might seem to be undertaking war against Persia under the guardianship of demons. Many different oracular responses were brought to him, and one I shall mention says: 'Now all we gods have set off to carry the trophies of victory by the bestial river; I, Ares, raising the din of war, am leading them.' Assured by these words, he prepared for the war against Persia and levied a heavy fine on the Christians. ... He worked much great harm against the Christians and announced that he would do more after the Persian war, but he wretchedly came to the end of his cursed life in it. For while on foreign territory he was killed by divine justice. He was emperor for two years and nine months, and he died in Persia on the twenty-sixth day of the month of January (*sic*) in the sixth indiction. He was then thirty-one years of age.

(Dodgeon)

Zonaras, XIII, 13, 1–14, 6 (iii, pp. 213, 18–217, 13, Dindorf):[53] He (i.e. Julian) advanced against the Persians and at first was successful; he took some cities, killed many people, acquired a lot of booty and prisoners, and besieged Ctesiphon. 2. Then suddenly affairs turned to the worse for him and he and the majority of his army perished. 3. For the Persians in despair decided to rush headlong into destruction in order to do something really terrible to the Romans. 4. Therefore two men in the guise of deserters hurried to the Emperor and promised him victory over the Persians if he followed them. 5. They advised him to leave the river and burn the galleys he had brought along with the other cargo vessels, 6. so that the enemy could not use them; while they would lead his army to safety through a different way. It would quickly and safely reach the inner parts of Persia and conquer it with ease. 7. The wicked man in his derangement believed them although many told him, and even Hormisdas himself, that it was a trap. But he set fire to his ships and burnt them all except twelve. 8. There were seven hundred galleys and four hundred cargo vessels. 9. After they had been completely burnt, when many of the tribunes objected that what was said by the deserters was a trap and a trick, he reluctantly agreed to examine the false deserters. Questioned under torture, they disclosed their conspiracy.

10. Some, therefore, say that Julian was deceived in this way. Others say he gave up the siege of Ctesiphon because of its strength and, since the army was running out of necessities, he considered returning; 11. as they were leaving, the Persians came into view behind them and harried the rear. 12. The Gauls who were guarding the rear resisted the enemy bravely and killed many of them, not only ordinary men but even some nobles amongst them. 13. However, the Romans were hard-pressed by lack of necessities, 14. so Julian, uncertain as to what he should do and from where he ought to return, chose to make the journey through the mountains. 15. The Persians discovered this, mustered there and attacked the Romans. On the left wing the Romans were victorious but on the right they were defeated. 16. When Julian realized this, he hastened to aid those who were being worsted. 17. Because of the weight, and the heat of the sun, – for the season was warm – he took off his helmet. 18. And so, when he was in the midst of the enemy, he was hit in the side by a spear. 19. It is said that a violent wind blew then and thick gloom covered the air there and, because the great number of soldiers were stirring up a lot of dust, they did not know where they (the enemy) were or what they were doing. 20. So it was not clear from where the spear which wounded him was thrown, whether it was by an enemy or by one of his own men or from some divine power: for even that is said in songs. 21. Therefore they say he took some blood from the flowing wound in the hollow of his hand and scattered it in the air, saying 'Take your fill, Nazarene!' . . .

14   The tribune Jovian was chosen to occupy the throne which was vacated by the death of Julian. He was a pious man. He was the son of Count Varronianus. 2. At first he refused the authority which had deferred to him; and when he was asked the reason, he cried: 'It is because I am Christian, and I do not want to rule over pagans.' 3. The soldiers cried with one voice, as if in unison, that they were Christians as well as he. 4. He accepted the title of emperor, and made a treaty with the Persians which was hardly honourable, but necessary at the time. 5. He conceded two famous cities to them, Nisibis and Singara, and transferred the inhabitants of them elsewhere, who, stressed by the violence of grief, spoke to him in terms far removed from the respect which they owed him. 6. He abandoned to them (i.e. the Persians) some provinces and rights which had belonged to the Romans for a long time. When the hostages had been handed over from one side to the other, the Romans left to return to their country; but they suffered great discomfort throughout their whole journey, and were extremely hard pressed by hunger and thirst.

(Dodgeon)

Zosimus,   *historia nova*, III, 12–34. See Introduction, p. 7.

Appendix 1 Select passages from sources in Arabic and New Persian

(1) **al-Tabari**,[1] *Annales*, pp. 813–45, edd. Barth – Nöldeke (German trans. Nöldeke, pp. 1–68) (Arabic)

Since Alexander's capture of Babylon five hundred and twenty-three years had passed, according to the reckonings of Christians and adherents of the older revelations, two hundred and sixty-six years, according to the reckonings of the magi, when Ardashir rose up, the son of Pabak Shah, king of Chir, son of the younger Sasan, son of Sasan, son of Pabak, son of Mihrmas (?), son of Sasan, son of king Bahman, son of Spendijar, [N., p. 2] son of Bistasp, son of Lohrasp, son of Kai Ogi (?), son of Kai Manus. According to other information however his family tree is: Ardashir – Pabak – Sasan – Pabak – Zarar – Behafridh – the older Sasan – Bahman – Spendijar – Bistasp – Lohrasp. Well, [N., p. 3] he arose, as he maintained, [p. 814] to avenge the blood of his cousin Dara (i.e. Darius) – son of Dara, grandson of Spendijar – who made war against Alexander and who was murdered by his two servants. As he explained, he wished to restore power to the legitimate family, to establish authority as it had been in the days of his ancestors, who had lived before the Diadoche, and to unite the empire under one head and one king again. It is said that he was born in a village called Tirudih, which belongs to the region of Chir and to the administrative area of Istakhr. His grandfather, Sasan, was such a brave and courageous man, [N., p. 4] that he once fought single-handed against eighty strong and vigorous men of Istakhr and put them to flight. His wife came from the house of Bazrangi, a king's family in Pars; she was called Rambehist and was a beautiful, excellent woman. Sasan was overseer of a fire-temple in Istakhr, called 'the fire temple of Anahedh', and at the same time a zealous huntsman and horseman. To him Rambehist bore Pabak; when he was born his hair was already longer than a hand's span. When he was grown up he followed his father in the government of men. Then his son Ardashir was born to him. At that time the king of Istakhr was a man of the Bazrangi, who was called Gozihr, according to others. This same man had a eunuch [p. 815] called Tire, whom he had made commandant [N., p. 5] of Darabgerd. When now Ardashir was seven years old, his father went with him to Gozihr, who was living in Baida, introduced his son to him and asked that he (the boy) should be handed over to Tire, to be educated so that he should become commandant after him. The king agreed to this and wrote out for him an official appointment. Thereupon the father took him to Tire, who received him kindly and took him for his son. And so, after Tire's death Ardashir took over his office and held it well. Then some of the astrologers and sooth-sayers told him that he had been born under lucky signs and that he would rule the lands. Then, it is said, Ardashir became very humble and daily increased in goodness. Once in a dream [N., p. 6] he saw an angel sitting at his head and this angel told him that God gave him dominion over the lands; and that he should set about getting it. When he awoke he rejoiced about this and felt in himself a strength and boldness such as he had never known before. His first act was to march to a place called Gopanan, in the area around Darabgerd, where he killed the king Pasin. Thereupon he went to a place called Konus (?) and killed the king there, one Manocihr, then he went to another place called Lurwir (?) and killed the king Dara. In all these places he installed his own people as regents. Then he wrote to his father, telling him what he [N., p. 7] had done and urged him to rise up against [p. 816] Gozihr, who was in Baida; he did that, killed Gozihr and took his crown. Then he (Pabak) wrote to Ardawan the Pahlawi, king of the mountain-land (i.e. Media) and of the neighbouring lands and humbly begged permission to crown his son Shapur with the crown of Gozihr. But Ardawan [N., p. 8] wrote him an ungracious letter and declared, that he and his son Ardashir had behaved as rebels by killing the men. Pabak did not care about that however. When he lay dying in those days, his son Shapur had himself crowned and became king in place of his father. As such he wrote to Ardashir, telling him to come to him (Shapur); Ardashir however refused. Then Shapur became very angry, collected an army and marched to fight against him. When he had departed from Istakhr (and had settled in the building of the

Chumai on the road to Darabgerd, a piece of the building fell on him and killed him. As soon as Ardashir heard the news, he went to Istakhr); there he met a great many of his brothers who, although some of them were older than him, altogether offered him the throne and crown, so that everything would be his. When he was crowned and had ascended the throne, he immediately manifested strength and zeal, installed some people in certain ranks, made [N., p. 9] a man called Abarsam the Buzurgframadhar and clothed him with great power, and he made another called Pahr (?) the Chief Mobedh. Then he realized that his brothers and some other people close to him were making [N., p. 10] a plot against him; so then he killed a great many of them. Then he heard that the inhabitants of Darabgerd had rebelled against him; so he went there again and took the town, after [p. 817] killing many of the inhabitants. After that he went to Kerman, where there was a king called Balas. After a violent battle, in which he personally took part, he took him captive, seized control of the (capital)-city and made one of his sons, also called Ardashir, governor of Kerman. There was however at the Persian Sea coast a king called Astawadh (?), to whom was paid divine honour; Ardashir marched against him also, killed him, cut him [N., p. 11] in two with his sword, killed his entourage as well and brought out from their treasuries many treasures heaped up there. Then he wrote to Mihrak, king of Abarsas (?) in the district round Ardashir-Churra, and some of his peers, and told them to submit to him; when they did not do that he marched out against them and killed Mihrak. Thereupon he went to Gor, founded the town and began to erect the palace, called Tarbal, as well as a temple to fire. While he was occupied with this, an ambassador from king Ardawan suddenly came to him with a letter. Ardashir summoned the people together and read the letter aloud in the presence of everybody; it said: 'You have overstepped your limit and brought your fate upon yourself, you Kurd, who was brought up in the tents [N., p. 12] of the Kurds. Who has permitted you to put on a crown, to take possession of lands, to subject their kings and inhabitants, who has ordered you to erect the town' – that is, Gor – 'on the plain of . . . . . .? If we allow you to go on building like this in peace, then build yourself a town with an area of ten Parasangs and call it Ram-Ardashir.' At the same time he informed him that he had sent the king of Ahwaz, to bring him [p. 818] before him in chains. Ardashir answered the letter thus: 'God gave me the crown, which I put on, made me the king of the lands which I captured and helped me against the governors and kings, whom I killed. As far as the town is concerned, which you say I should build and call Ram-Ardashir, I hope that I shall get you in my power and send your head with all your possessions to the fire-temple which I have built in Ardashir-Churra.' Then Ardashir went to Istakhr; when he had been there a short time, a letter came from Abarsam, whom he had left behind in Ardashir-Churra, saying that the king of Ahwaz had truly appeared but had already retreated, [N., p. 13] defeated (by him). Then Ardashir went to Ispahan, took captive its king Sadh-Shapur and killed him. Then having returned home to Pars, he set out to do battle against Nirofarr (?), the prince of Ahwaz. He marched via Aragan, Sambil and Tasan, which belong to (the area round about) Ram-Hormizd, as far as Surrak. When he had got that far, he rode with some of his men to the little Tigris, took the town (situated there) and built (in its place as a new foundation) the town Suq al Ahwaz. Then he returned with the booty to Pars. A second time he went from Pars to Ahwaz by way of Gireh and Kazerun, and from there further to Maisan, where he killed king Bandu (?) and built the town Karak-Maisan. Once again he returned [N., p. 14] to Pars, then however sent a challenge to Ardawan, that he should determine for them both a place for a battle. This letter answered: 'I will meet you on a plain called Hormizdagan on the last day of the Mihr-month.' Now Ardashir arrived there before the appointed time, occupied a suitable place on the plain, made a ditch around himself and his army and took possession of [p. 819] a spring there. Then when Ardawan arrived the army got into battle order. But Shapur, Ardashir's son, had already advanced to protect him; it came to a fight, and Shapur killed with his own hand the Dadhbundadh, Ardawan's scribe. Then Ardashir himself came out from his position and killed him; a great many of his companions fell and [N., p. 15] the rest fled. It is said that Ardashir got off his horse and trampled Ardawan's head underfoot. On that day he received the title Shahan-Shah. Then he went from there to Hamadhan and took it by force, as well as the rest of the mountain-land, Azarbaijan, Armenia and (the region of) Mosul. Following that he went from Mosul to Suristan, i.e. the Sawad, took possession of it and on the west bank of the Tigris, opposite the town of Ctesiphon, which [N., p. 16] forms the eastern side of Madain, he built another place, which he named Veh-Ardashir, assigned to it an administrative area, consisting of the offices of Behrasir, Rumakan, Nahar Darqit, Kutha and Nahar Gaubar, and appointed [N., p. 17] local administrators for them. – Then he went from Sawad back to Istakhr, from there first of all to

Sagistan, then to Gurgan, then to Abrasahr, Marw, Balch and Chwarizm as far as the outer limits of the lands of Chorasan, whereupon he returned to Marw. After he had killed many people and sent their heads to the fire-temple of Anahita, he returned from Marw back to Pars and settled in Gor. There came to him ambassadors of the king of the Kushan [p. 820], of the king of Turan and the king of Mokran (Makuran), with the declaration of their submission. Hereafter Ardashir proceeded from Gor to Bahrain and besieged the king there –Sanatruk – until he [N., p. 18] in extreme need fell from the fortress wall and died. Then he went back to Madain, remained there some time and in his own lifetime crowned his son Shapur. – It is said that there was in Alar, a village in the region of Kucaran (part of the coast-land of Ardashir-Churra), a queen who enjoyed divine veneration and had much wealth and many soldiers; Ardashir made war on her priests, killed the queen and took as booty much money and treasures which she had. – He is supposed also to have built 8 towns – to be precise in Pars Ardashir-Churra, i.e. Gor (I), Ram-Ardashir (II) and Rew-Ardashir (III); in Ahwaz Hormizd-Ardashir, i.e. 'the market of Ahwaz (IV)'; in Sawad Veh-Ardashir, the western town [N., p. 20] of Madain (V) and Astarabadh-Ardashir, i.e. Karak Maisan (VI); in Bahrain Pasa (?)-Ardashir, i.e. the town of Chatt (VII) and in (the region of) Mosul Budh-Ardashir, i.e. Hazza (VIII). – It is also said that on his first appearance Ardashir wrote compelling letters to the diadoche, urging them to obey him. [N., p. 21] – Towards the end of his life he wrote his testament for his successor. – He was always glorious and victorious; never [p. 821] was his army defeated nor his banner driven back; he conquered and subjected all kings, surrounding his territory, and in all lands he appeared as lord. He formed administrative regions and founded cities, established the various ranks and saw to it that the land flourished. – His rule lasted, calculated from the fall [N., p. 22] of Ardawan until his death, fourteen years, according to some others however, fourteen years and ten months.

A report which goes back to Hisam b. Muhammed tells the following story: When Ardashir was advancing with the Persians to achieve dominion over 'Iraq, he there met Papa as king of the Ardawanians; according to Hisam's own explanation the former are the Nabataeans of Sawad, the latter the Nabataeans of Syria. They were both fighting each other for supremacy, but united however against Ardashir, by agreeing to fight him on alternate days. When it was Papa's day, Ardashir could not hold out against him, but when it was Ardawan's turn it was the other way round. When Ardashir saw this he made a treaty with Papa, whereby he would surrender Ardawan to him, but keep his lands and all that was in them. So then he only had Ardawan to deal with, he killed him quickly and took over all his possessions. Then (of necessity) Papa also became subject to him. Ardashir seized 'Iraq, forced its princes to obedience and overpowered the obstinate inhabitants, forcing them to do what they did not wish to, but what he desired. [N., p. 23] . . .[2]

After Ardashir, son of Pabak, had died, his son Shapur became king of Persia. [p. 823] – When Ardashir [N., p. 26] son of Pabak, attained supremacy, he shed in rivers the blood of the Asakanians, of whom the diadoche were a part, until he exterminated them all, and all this because of an oath which Sasan the Elder, son of Ardashir, son of Bahman, son of Spendijar, the ancestor of Ardashir, son of Pabak had sworn, that, if he became king, he would not leave alive a single member of the family of Asak, son of Churra, binding also his successors and holding them to it in his last will and testament, that they also, if they came to rule, would leave none of them alive. Since Ardashir was the first of his children's children to achieve this, he killed them all and left none alive because of this decree made by his ancestor Sasan. It is said that not one of them was left over except a girl; he found her in the royal palace and, taken by her perfect beauty, he asked her, the daughter of the murdered king, about her origins [N., p. 27], and she said she was the maid-servant of one of the wives of the king. To his question, whether she was a virgin or a widow, she answered: 'a virgin', and then he slept with her, took her for himself, and she became pregnant by him. After she was no longer afraid of him, because of her condition, she finally told him that she was of Asak's family: immediately he left her however, called the Hargand (?), son of Sam, an aged man, informed him that she had admitted being of Asak's family and said: 'Above all it is our duty to carry out completely the oath of our father Sasan, as dear to our heart as she is, as you well know; [p. 824] so take her away and kill her.' When the old man was going away to kill her, she told him that she was pregnant, which was confirmed by the midwives, to whom he took her. Then he kept her in a cellar, cut off his own male member, put it in a box and sealed it. Having returned to the king, he answered his question about what he had done by saying she was safely in the bosom of the earth, and at the same time he handed over the box, asking the king to put a seal on it as well and keep it safely in one of his treasuries; and that the king did. The girl however stayed with the old man and was eventually safely delivered of a boy. The old man did not like to give the king's son a more humble name (than his rank required), but neither did he wish to let him know of the matter before he was grown-up and completely educated; [N., p. 28] moreover at the hour of the boy's birth he had investigated his fate by reading his horoscope and had recognized that he would come to rule: for these reasons he gave him a name which would serve to describe him and as a name with this in mind, that when he knew about it, he would have the choice (that is, whether he wished to keep it as his own name); so he called him Sahpuhr, i.e. son of a king, and he is the first, so to be called. This is the son of Ardashir, who is called in Arabic 'Shapur of the hosts'. – Some, however, maintain that he called the boy Ashapur, i.e. descendant of Asak, of whose tribe his mother was. – So now Ardashir lived for a while childless; then one day the old man, at whose house the boy was, went into his room and found him downcast. 'What makes you sad, o king?' he asked. The latter replied, 'How should I not be sad? Admittedly between rising and going down I have defeated everything with my sword, I have achieved what I wanted and won completely for myself the empire, the empire of my fathers, but now I shall die without any heir to follow my rule and without having any part of it myself (after my death).' Then the old man said to him: 'God give you joy, o king, and let you live long! At my house there is a noble, splendid son of yours. But first of all send for the box [N., p. 29] which I gave you for safe keeping and which you sealed, so that I may give you the proof.' Then Ardashir sent for the box, tested the seal, broke it then [p. 825] and found therein the old man's member with a piece of writing as follows: 'After we had discovered that Asak's daughter was pregnant by Ardashir king of kings, we did not consider it right, despite the order, to kill her and destroy the noble seed of the king, but we kept it safe in the bosom of the earth, as the king ordered us, but we tried also to prove clearly our innocence so that no-one could slander it; we endeavoured to protect the right which had been sown, until it should finally come to the one entitled to it. These things happened at such and such a time in such and such a year.' Then Ardashir ordered that the boy be put with one hundred – according to others with one thousand – boys of his own age, similar to him in appearance and size and had them all brought in to him together, avoiding any differentiation in dress, size and behaviour. The old man did that, and as soon as Ardashir looked at them, he recognized his son immediately in spirit, and knew who he was, without being given any hint or indication. Then on his command they were all taken into the palace courtyard, were given bats and played ball, while he sat in his palace on the throne. While they were playing the ball flew into the palace where the king was. All the boys were too afraid to go into the castle; only Shapur stepped out of the throng and went in. Ardashir, who of course at first sight had recognized him in spirit and felt a tenderness for him as for none of his comrades, now could tell clearly from his bold entry that this was his son. So he asked him in Persian: 'What is your name?', whereupon he answered, 'Sahpur'; [N., p. 30] then Ardashir repeated: 'Sahpur' (son of a king!). When he was convinced by this, that it was his son, he acknowledged him publicly and declared him crown-prince.

Already before he came to rule and while his father was still alive the Persians experienced many examples of Shapur's [p. 826] understanding, greatness of spirit, knowledge, furthermore his great courage, his eloquence, his graciousness to his subjects and his tender sensitivity. When now the crown was put on his head, the great ones assembled around him, called out their wishes that he should live long and spoke most generously about his father and his excellent qualities. Then he gave them to know that what they had said about his father had made him most happy and he made them fair promises. Thereupon he sent for money which was in the treasuries, gave rich presents to the people there and distributed it among the respected ones, the troops and the needy ones, whom he considered deserving of it. He also wrote to his governors in the various regions and lands, that they should do the same with the money. So his goodness and beneficence extended near and far, to noble and insignificant, high and low and for all of them life was made easier. Then he chose governors for them, but he excelled mightily above them and all his subjects. So his splendid way of life became well-known, his fame spread and he stood high above all kings. – It is said that after ruling for eleven years he marched to the town of Nesibin (i.e. Nisibis), where there were Roman troops and [N., p. 32] he besieged it for a time; then he heard of circumstances in Chorasan, which required his personal attention; he went there, arranged matters and then went back to Nesibin. It is said that the wall split (by itself) causing a breach, through which he could penetrate. He killed the soldiers, made women and children slaves and seized as booty great sums of money, deposited there for the Emperor. Then he continued to Syria and the Roman lands and occupied many cities there. It is said that Ciliciia and Cappadocia were among his conquests, and that he besieged a Roman Emperor, Valerianus, in the town of Antiochia, took him captive, led him [p. 827] and a great many others away and settled them in Gundeshapur. [N., p. 33] He is supposed to have forced Valerianus to build the dam of Sostar 1000 Ells across. The Roman is said to have had this carried out by people drawn from his Empire; after the completion of the dam Shapur is supposed to have agreed to his being freed. According to some he took a lot of money from him and cut off his nose, before letting him go; according to others he finally killed him.

In the mountains of Tekrit between Euphrates and Tigris there was a town called Hadr (i.e. Hatra); there lived [N., p. 34] a man of the Garamaeans called Satirun. It is he of whom Abu Duad der Ijadit says:

> And I see how death hangs down from Hadr over
> the lord of its inhabitants Satirun.

The Arabs however call him Daizan; he is supposed to have been [N., p. 35] a man of Ba-Garma, but according to Hisam b. (Muhammed) Kelbi he was an Arab of the Qoda's tribe, to be precise Daizan b. Mu'awija b. 'Abid b. Agram (?) b. 'Amr b. Nacha' b. Salih b. Holwan b. 'Imran b. Hafi b. Qoda'a, while his mother was Gaihala of the tribe Tazid b. Holwan; he is said to be called after her name. As Hisam maintains, he was king of Mesopotamia and had around him countless number of the Banu 'Abid b. Agram and the other Qoda'a tribes; his rule extended as far as Syria. When now [N., p. 36] Shapur, son of Ardashir, was once absent in [p. 828] Chorasan, he made a raid in Sawad, this was reported to the king when he returned home. Of Daizan's deed 'Amr b. Ila b. Gudai b. Daha b. Gusam b. Holwan b. 'Imran b. Hafi b. Qoda'a says:

> We came upon them with a host of (the tribe)
> Ilaf and with the hard-shot, male horses.
> Then our chastisement fell upon the Persians and we murdered
> the priests of Sahrzur.
> From a great distance we drew near the
> foreigners with hosts from Mesopotamia like the glow of fire.

So when Shapur heard of Daizan's behaviour, he marched out against him and camped outside his fortress; he however fortified himself therein. According to Ibn Kelbi's statement Shapur lay for four years outside his fortress, without destroying it or being able to reach Daizan. [N., p. 37] But A'sa Maimum b. Aais mentioned in his poem that he only camped there for two years; he says:

Have you not looked at Hadr, whose inhabitants
always lived well? – but is any man, who lives well, immortal?
Sahpur the man of the armies camped there
for two years and hewed his axes in there.
But God gave him (the king of Hadr) no more
strength, and an axe like his could not remain still.
When God saw his action, he suddenly descended
upon him, and he could not defend himself.
But he had called out to his people: Rise up
for your cause, which is already decided!
[p. 829] So die then in honour by your own
swords; I consider that a true man will take his own death upon him.

Now however one of Daizan's daughters called Nadira was menstruating and according to the local custom was therefore taken to the outskirts of the town. She was one of the most beautiful women of her time, as Shapur was supposed to be one of the most handsome men [N., p. 38] of his time. When they caught sight of each other they fell in love immediately. She sent a message to him: 'What will you give me if I show you how to destroy the walls of this town and kill my father?' To which he answered: 'Whatever you will; and I will raise you up above all my wives and put you closer to me than them.' Then she told him the following: 'Take a greenish dove with a ring around its neck and with the menstrual blood of a blue-eyed virgin write something on its foot; then let it go, and it will sit on the wall around the town, and this will collapse.' For this was the talisman of the town, that it could only be destroyed in this way. When he was doing that and preparing for battle she said further: 'I will give the troops wine and then when they lie (drunk), kill them and enter the town.' The king did all of this, the town collapsed, he stormed it and killed Daizan immediately. The Qoda'a tribes, which he had around him, were destroyed also, so that there are no known remnants of them. The same kind of extermination befell some tribes of Banu Holwan also. So 'Amr b. Ila, who had been with Daizan, says:

Are you not downcast as the news arrives about
what happened to the heads of Banu 'Abid,
[N., p. 39] And about the fall of Daizan and

his fleshly brothers and of the men of Tazid,
who always rode in the armies?
Shapur, the man of the armies, rode out against
them with elephants covered with blankets and
with heroic fighters.
And he destroyed the rocky blocks of the pillars
of that fortress, whose foundations were like iron sheets.

Then Shapur destroyed the town and took with him Daizan's daughter Nadira. The wedding took place in 'Ain-attamar. It is said that she complained all night long about the roughness of the couch, which was however stuffed with finest silk and raw silk. As they tried to find out what was causing her discomfort they found a myrtle leaf [p. 830] in one of the folds of her belly, where it had lodged itself. Because her skin was so delicate, you could see right through to the marrow of her bones. Then Shapur said to her: 'Tell me, what did your father give you to eat?' She answered: 'Cream, bone-marrow and the honey of virgin bees together with the finest wine.' 'By your father!' he exclaimed, 'truly you have only known me a short time and yet you love me more than your father, who gave you such food!' Then, at his command, a man mounted a wild horse, she was tied by her hair to its tail and the horse was made to gallop until she fell to pieces. Of this the poet says:

[N., p. 40] Deserted is Hadr of Nadira, as well
as Mirba' and the shore of the Tharthar.

In general the poets write a lot about this Daizan; he is referred to by 'Adi b. Zaid in the words:

And (where is now) the man of Hadr, who once
built it and taxed the land by the Tigris and Chaboras?
He built a marble castle, covered with plaster
and the birds nested in its summits.
He did not fear an unhappy fate, and yet he
lost the dominion and his gate was lonely.

It is also said that Shapur built in Maisan (the town) Sadh-Shapur, called Dima (?) in Nabataean. – In Shapur's time Mani the Zandik appeared. – It is told that Shapur came to the place where he wanted to build the town Gunde-Shapur and there he met an old man, called Bel, whom he asked, whether [N., p. 41] it was permitted to build a town on this spot. Bel answered; 'If I can still learn to write, at my age, then it is permitted to build a town in this place.' But Shapur answered: 'Now [p. 831] both things, which you consider impossible, shall take place.' Therewith he had the plan of the town marked out and at the same time handed Bel over to a teacher, in order to teach him to write and do arithmetic within a year. The teacher kept him at his house and began by shaving his hair and beard, so that they would not distract him; then he taught him continuously and, when he brought him to Shapur, he had made such progress in learning that the former handed over to him the book-keeping for the expenses of the town. There the king instituted an administrative area; and gave (the town and this area) the name Beh-az-Andew-i-Shapur', i.e. 'better than Antiochia of Shapur'; that is the place which is generally known as Gunde-Shapur but which the inhabitants of Ahwaz call Bel, after the man, who guided its construction. – Now, when he was near to death [N., p. 42] he declared his son Hormizd to be king and gave him testamentary instructions, according to which he was to conduct himself. – There are various views about the length of his rule: according to some he reigned thirty years and fifteen days, according to others it was thirty-one years six months and nineteen days.

Shapur, son of Ardashir, grandson of Pabak [N., p. 43], was succeeded by his son Hormizd, known also as 'the Bold'. In his whole appearance he was similar to Ardashir, but did not equal him in insight and skill; yet he is supposed to have excelled himself in boldness, courage and physical size. It is said that his mother was one of the daughters of king Mihrak, whom Ardashir had killed in Ardashir-Churra. For the astrologers had foretold to Ardashir that one of Mihrak's descendants would come to reign, so Ardashir had all the family sought out and executed. But Hormizd's mother, a clever, beautiful and strong woman fled and came to a desert place, where she took refuge among shepherds. [p. 832] One day while Shapur was hunting he followed the game too far and became very thirsty: then he spotted the tents, where Hormizd's mother had taken refuge. He approached them but found the shepherds were not there; [N., p. 44] but on his request the woman gave him water. It was then that he noticed her outstanding beauty, her splendid form and her noble face. When, shortly after, the shepherds returned, Shapur asked them about the woman and one of them gave her out to be a member of his family, so Shapur asked him for her to be his wife. He agreed to it, and so he took her home, had her cleaned up, dressed and adorned and wished to sleep with her. But when he was alone with her and demanded what a man demands from a woman she resisted and overcame him in wrestling in a way that was by no means tender, so that he was astonished by her strength. But when this had gone on for some time he became annoyed and asked her what the reason was. Then she told him that she was the daughter of Mihrak and had only behaved thus, in order to protect him from Ardashir. He, however, vowed not to speak of her circumstances; then he lay with her and she gave birth to Hormizd. But he kept the child hidden. When he was a few years old, however, Ardashir was out riding and went by Shapur's home, because he wanted to say something to him, entered unannounced and sat down: just at that time Hormizd came out, a grown boy, carrying a bat to play ball and ran shouting after a ball which had shot off. When Ardashir saw him, he was annoyed about it, but immediately he was struck by the likeness to his own family; for the royal nature of Ardashir's descendants could not be concealed and could not be mistaken by anyone because of certain signs: facial beauty, fullness of limbs and other special physical characteristics. So Ardashir called the boy up to him and asked Shapur who he was. [N., p. 45] Then Shapur fell on his knees, begging for mercy, admitted his offence and told his father what had really happened. [p. 833] But his father was pleased about it and told him that only now did he understand what the astrologers had meant with Mihrak's descendant coming to royal power in future, that they had meant Hormizd, who was of course of Mihrak's tribe; so now at last he was free of all his worry. – When Shapur came to rule after Ardashir's death he made Hormizd governor of Chorasan. There he made independent appearances, subjected the kings of the neighbouring peoples and showed the proud strength of a ruler. For this reason people slandered him to Shapur and instilled the suspicion that he would not come if he (Shapur) summoned him, and that he wished to rob him of the crown. When Hormizd heard that, it is said that he, quite alone and secretly, cut off his own hand, put medicine on it to preserve it, wrapped it in a precious piece of cloth, put it in a box and sent it to Shapur; at the same time he wrote saying what he had heard and that he had done this thing in order to dispel any suspicion, for according to the ordering of their state, no mutilated man could become king. When Shapur received the letter he was ready to die of grief, and he wrote back saying how very grieved he was about what he had done, he apologized and declared that even if he should mutilate his whole body, limb by limb, yet the succession would go to no other; thus he appointed him to be king. – When the crown was put on his head, it is said that all the great ones came in and hailed him; but he gave them fair answer and they [N., p. 46] recognized from that that the story (just told) was true. He behaved very well to them, was just to his subjects and walked in the ways of his fathers. He set up the administrative area of Ram-Hormizd. His reign lasted one year and ten days.

Then came the reign of his son Bahram, that is Bahram, son of Hormizd, son of Shapur, son of Ardashir, son of Pabak. He (Bahram) was one of the (provincial) governors of Shapur, son of Ardashir, and Hormizd, son of Shapur and Bahram son of Shapur.

. . .

It is said that Bahram, son of Hormizd, was a gentle and good man, so the people rejoiced when he came to the throne. He behaved well to them and followed as king in the steps of his fathers in his treatment of people. – It is said that Mani the Zandik tried to convert him to his religion, but he had the matter scrutinized and found him to be an apostle of Satan; so he ordered that he should be killed, then skinned and his skin to be stuffed with chaff and to be hung up at one of the gates of Gunde-Shapur, which gate (since that) is called the Mani-gate; he also executed his companions and adherents. His [N., p. 48] reign lasted, it is said, three years, three months and three days.

Then came the reign of his son Bahram, son of Bahram, son of Hormizd, etc. and he was said to be an efficient ruler. When the crown had been put on his head the great ones called out similar blessings as they had done for his fathers; he gave them a fair [p. 835] answer and treated them well. He said (then): 'If fate is good to us [N., p. 49] we accept it with gratitude; if not, we will be satisfied with what is our portion.' There are differing opinions on his years of rule: according to some he reigned eighteen, according to others seventeen years.

Then Bahram, with the surname Shahan Shah, son of Bahram [N., p. 50] son of Bahram, son of Hormizd etc. became king. When the crown had been put on his head, the great ones assembled around him and called to him their wishes for a blessed reign and long life, and he gave them a fair answer. Before he came to reign he had been the king of Sagistan. He reigned four years.

Then came the reign of Narse (i.e. Narses), son of Bahram [N., p. 51] a brother of the third Bahram. When he had been crowned, the nobles and great ones came in and called out their blessings; but he promised them good things and commanded them to help him in his office. He behaved very justly to them. On the day he took over the governing he said: 'We shall never cease thanking God for the grace shown to us.' He reigned nine years.

Then the king was Hormizd, son of Narse, son of Bahram, etc. The people were afraid of this man, as they had got to know him to be hard and stern; but he gave them to know, that he was well aware how much they feared a harsh reign by him, but that he had exchanged the hardness and inflexibility of his nature for softness and leniency. So he ruled them then very kindly and treated them very justly. [p. 836] He strove to support the weak, to make the land flourish and to get justice for his subjects, then he died without leaving a son. The people were sad about this and in their affection for him they asked after his women; then they heard that one was pregnant. Others do say that Hormizd himself had bequeathed the crown to the unborn child in its mother's womb. Then the woman gave birth to Shapur, [N., p. 52] the Man of Shoulders. According to one source Hormizd ruled six years and five months, according to another seven years and five months.

After him Shapur, the Man of Shoulders, son of Hormizd etc. was born king, since his father had bequeathed the title to him. The people rejoiced at his birth, spread the news of it in all directions and sent letters about it by messengers [N., p. 53] to all corners of the earth. The viziers and scribes, however, kept the posts they had occupied in his father's reign. So things remained, until the news spread outside the boundaries of the Empire, that the Persians had no king, but were waiting for a boy in the cradle and no-one knew how he would turn out. Then the Turks and Romans desired their Empire. Now, however, the lands of the Arabs were nearest to Persia and in addition these people were more dependent than others on getting provisions and places to live elsewhere, for their circumstances were miserable and their food scarce. So they came in hordes out of the region of 'Abdalqais, out of Bahrain and Kiazma over the sea to Resahr, the coastal area of Ardashir-Churra and the other coastal lands of Persia, they took cattle, corn and [N., p. 54] other provisions from the inhabitants and made serious trouble [p. 837] in the land. They did this for some considerable time, without a single Persian attacking them, for they had of course crowned a child, of whom the people had little fear. This went on until Shapur stirred himself and grew up. When this happened, it is said that his practical sense and fine intellect were manifest on the following occasion. When he was once sleeping at night in the royal palace at Ctesiphon he was woken up towards morning by the noise of the people. When he asked what it was, he was told that the noise came from the throng of people crossing to and fro over the Tigris bridge. Then he ordered that another bridge be built, so that people would go one way on one bridge and the other way on the other and there would be no need for pushing people going in the opposite direction on the bridge. When the people saw what a good solution he had found, despite his tender years, they were very glad. He had the order carried out immediately and even before sunset on the same day a second bridge is supposed to have been erected near the first one. The people now no longer needed to endanger their lives, when they crossed the bridge. Now, in a single day the boy made such progress as others in a long time. Regularly the scribes and viziers brought one matter after another before him; among these was the affair of the troops, who were on the borders facing the enemy, for there came news, that most of them were in a sorry frame of mind. They painted a black picture to him, but he said to them: 'Don't be so worried about it, there's an easy solution to it.' So he ordered all these armies to be written to, telling them he had heard how long they had been at their posts and what exertions they had taken up [p. 838] for their brothers and those whom they were protecting; [N., p. 55] if anyone wished to return to his family he was welcome to do so and got leave to do so; but if any wished to complete his service by remaining at his post, this would not be forgotten. Furthermore he ordered that those who wanted to return home could stay with their families at home, until they were needed. When the viziers heard such words from him they were amazed at them and said: 'If he had already had long experience in affairs of state and leadership of the army he could not have shown greater insight nor spoken more appropriately than we have just heard from him.' Then came tidings upon tidings into the provinces and frontier areas about directions he had given to raise up his own people and cast down the enemies. When he was at last 16 years old, could bear arms and ride a horse and had gained great strength, he summoned the highest ones of his people and troops together and spoke to them. He spoke of the grace which God had shown him and them all through his fathers, how the latter had taught them right dealings and had driven away their enemies and how, in contrast, things had slipped backwards in the recent times of his childhood. Now, however, he added, he was going to act to defend the dearest possession, now he was determined to wage war against an enemy; only one thousand warriors should accompany him. Then the people came up to him with words of gratitude and blessing, but begged him, however, to stay where he was, and send the leaders of the army and troops out instead of him on the campaign he was determined on. He, however, was not willing to stay and equally unwilling to accede to their next request, to raise the number he mentioned. Rather he selected one thousand riders from the bravest and most warlike warriors, ordered them to advance at his command, forbade them, however, to spare any Arab that they came across, [N., p. 56] and to be concerned with taking booty. So he set off with them and attacked the Arabs, who regarded Pars as their own private territory, [and] before they knew what had happened, he wrought appalling havoc amongst them, took them into harsh captivity and chased away any who were left. Then he crossed the sea [p. 839] with his people, came to Chatt and, murdering, he marched through the land of Bahrain, refusing to be bought off or to bother with booty. Then he went further and came to Hagar, where there were Bedouins of the tribes of Tamim, Bekr b. Wail and 'Abdalqais; amongst these also he brought great carnage and shed so much blood, that it ran like a river filled by rain. Even those who fled could not believe that any cave in the mountains nor any island in the sea would be safe from him. Then he turned upon the land of the 'Abdalqais and exterminated everything apart from those who managed to escape into the sandy deserts. Then he advanced to Jamama, where he murdered in a similar fashion. He stopped up every one of the Arabs' watering-places that he passed, every spring he blocked up. Then he approached Medina; there also he killed all the Arabs he came across or made them prisoner. Straight away he turned aside to the land of the Bekr and Taghlib, which lies between the Persian Empire and the line of Roman frontier fortresses in Syria; there he killed all the Arabs he could find or took them prisoner and stopped up all their watering-places. [N., p. 57] He did, by the way, settle some of the Taghlib in Bahrain, i.e. in Darin, which is also called Haig, and in Chatt, he settled people of the 'Abdalqais and some sections of the Tamim in Hagar, people from the Bekr b. Wail in Kerman – the ones called 'Bekr of Aban' – and people of the Hanzala in Ramalija he settled in Ahwaz. – At his command a town was built in Sawad, which he called Buzurg-Shapur, i.e. 'Ukbara, and another which he called Peroz-Shapur, i.e. Ambar; furthermore in Ahwaz [N., p. 58] he had two towns built [p. 840] Eran-Churra-Shapur, i.e. 'Shapur and his land', called Karch in Syrian, and Sus, a town which he built near the fortress, where lies the coffin with the body of the Prophet Daniel. When he had marched against the Romans and had there made many prisoners [N., p. 59] he settled these in Eran-Churra-

Shapur, out of which the Arabs made the abbreviation Sus. Moreover at his command a town was built in Ba Garma, which he called Giba-Shapur (?) and to which he granted an administrative area, and in Chorasan he built a town, which he called Neshapur, and to this also he gave an administrative area.

Shapur had made a truce with the Roman Emperor Constantine, the builder of the city of Constantinople and the first Christian ruler of the Romans. Then Constantine died and after him [N., p. 60] his three sons, among whom he had divided the Empire; then the Romans made a man of his house, Lulianus (i.e. Julian), Emperor and he was an adherent of the Roman religion, which had prevailed before Christianity. Previously he had of course kept this secret and had given himself out to be a Christian, but when he came to power, he confessed openly the Roman religion, re-established it, ordered that it should be called to life again, that the churches be destroyed and bishops and Christian priests should be killed. Then he assembled great hosts of Romans, Chazars and Arabs, who were in his Empire, in order to fight Shapur and his Persian troops. The Arabs, however, were very happy to take this opportunity [p. 841] to have vengeance on Shapur, who had of course killed Arabs. So one hundred and seventy thousand Arabs assembled in Lulianus' army. Lulianus sent these ahead with a Roman patrician, Jovinianus as commander of the vanguard. He advanced himself until he had penetrated Persian territory. When Shapur heard how many Roman, Arab and Chazar troops he had, he was very afraid and sent out spies [N., p. 61] to bring him news and tell him how many they were, how brave and how much damage they were doing. But the reports of the spies about Lulianus and his army did not agree, so Shapur disguised himself and, accompanied by a few close companions, he went to spy out the army himself. When he came near to the army of Jovinianus, the leader of the vanguard, he sent some of his companions into the army to gather information and to bring it to him, telling the truth. But the Romans spotted them, took them captive and brought them before Jovinianus. Not one of them admitted why they had been sent into the army, except one single man, who told him how things were, said where Shapur was and asked him to give him a section of troops and he would hand the king over to them. But no sooner had Jovinianus heard these words, than he sent one of his closest companions to Shapur to tell them what happened and to warn him. So Shapur rode quickly away from that place to his army. But the Arabs in Lulianus' army asked him for permission to attack Shapur [p. 842], and when he granted their request they attacked him, scattered his hosts and brought great slaughter among them. Shapur fled with the remnant of his army and Lulianus was able to take possession of Shapur's residence, Ctesiphon, and the treasuries there with all the king's wealth. The latter then wrote to the troops in distant regions and told them what had happened to him at the hands of Lulianus and his Arab accomplices, and he ordered all commanders to come to his aid quickly with all their troops. When now in a short time the hosts had assembled [N., p. 62] from all directions, he turned about, attacked Lulianus and snatched back from him the town of Ctesiphon. Lulianus then quartered his army and himself in Veh-Ardashir and the surrounding area. Then Lulianus and Shapur negotiated zealously with each other through messengers going to and fro. But one day when Lulianus was sitting in his room an arrow, shot by an invisible hand, hit him fatally in the heart. Thereupon the army lost all its composure; they were appalled at his fate and despaired of ever getting out of Persia. They were now a consultative body without king and without a leader; so they asked Jovinianus to take over the reins of government. He, however, refused, and when they pushed him, he explained to them, that he was a Christian and did not wish to rule over people who were of a different faith from himself. But now the Romans also declared that they shared his faith and that they had only kept it secret for fear of Lulianus. So then he acceded to their request: they made him Emperor and openly confessed Christianity again. When Shapur heard of the end of Lulianus he sent the following message to the Roman leader: 'God has now put you in our power and granted us recompense for the wrong you did us and for your coming into our land. We [p. 843] hope now that you will die of hunger there, without us having to draw a single sword or lance in battle against you. So send us your leader (for negotiations) if you have chosen one.' While Jovinianus was quite willing to go to Shapur, none of his commanders favoured this intention. He, however, insisted and came to Shapur, with eighty of the most respected men in the camp and in the whole army, and wearing the crown. [N., p. 63] When Shapur heard that he was coming he went out to meet him. They both fell on the ground (in obeisance) before each other; then Shapur embraced him in gratitude for what he had done for him. He ate a meal with Shapur and was of good cheer. Shapur meanwhile, however, gave the Roman leaders and governors to understand that if they had made any other than Jovinianus to be Emperor, they would all have perished in

Persia; it was only because of his nomination that he did not let them feel his power. So through his efforts Jovinianus' position became very strong. Then he said: 'The Romans attacked our land, killed many people, chopped down date-palms and other trees in Sawad and devastated agriculture; now, they shall either pay us the full price for what they destroyed and laid waste to, or give up the town Nesibin with its territory as compensation.' Jovinianus and his military leaders agreed to give Shapur compensation and yielded Nesibin to him. When the inhabitants of this town heard of it, they emigrated to other places in the Roman Empire because they feared the reign of a king who was of a different religion. When Shapur heard this, he had twelve thousand people of good family from Istakhr, Ispahan and other regions of his lands sent to Nesibin and settled them there. [N., p. 64] Jovinianus, however, returned with his troops to the Roman land, where he died after a brief reign.

Until his own death Shapur was busily engaged in slaughtering the Arabs [p. 844] and tearing out the shoulder-bones of their chiefs; for this reason they called him the 'man of shoulders'. Some reporters say that after Shapur had overcome the Arabs and driven them out of the nearby territories, into which they had come i.e. Pars, Bahrain and Jamama, he invaded Syria and came to the Roman frontier; then he declared to his companions that he wanted to get into the Roman Empire in order to find out their secrets and to gather information about [N., p. 65] their towns and the number of their troops. This he did and for a time he roamed around in the Roman Empire. Then he heard that the Emperor was giving a banquet and had summoned the people together to share his meal. Shapur also, disguised as a beggar, went along to join in the company, to see the Emperor, to find out what he looked like and what happened at his feast. But he was recognized, taken prisoner and on the Emperor's command he was put in the skin of a bull. Then the Emperor marched with his troops to Persia, taking Shapur along like this. On the way he provoked much murdering, devastation of towns and villages, chopping down of date-palms and other fruit-trees. Finally he came to Gunde-Shapur. The inhabitants defended themselves behind their fortifications, but he erected the catapults and with them destroyed a part of the town. While matters stood like this the Romans, who were supposed to be guarding Shapur, were inattentive one night; the latter ordered some prisoners from Ahwaz, who happened to be nearby, that they should pour oil from pipes there onto his chains. They did that and his skin became supple; he slipped out and crawled further and further to the gate of the town. There [N., p. 66] he told the garrison his name. So after he had been let in, the inhabitants were very joyful [p. 845] and praised God so loud, that the Emperor's men were woken up. But Shapur assembled all who were in the town, armed them and in the same night, towards morning, he made an attack on the Romans. He slaughtered them, made the Emperor himself a prisoner and took as booty his treasures and his women. Then he had him put in heavy chains and gave him the task of making good everything which he had laid waste. He is supposed to have forced the Emperor to bring earth from the Roman land to Madain and Gunde-Shapur to restore what had been destroyed there, and to plant olives instead of the date-palms and other trees which had been destroyed. Then he cut off his heels, shod him and sent him on a donkey back to the Romans with the words: 'That is your punishment for the outrage committed against us.' That is why the Romans no longer put boots on their horses, but shoe them with iron.

[N., p. 67] Thereafter Shapur stayed a long time in his Empire, but then he marched against the Romans, killed many, took many prisoners and settled these in a town, which he built near Sus and called Eransahr-Shapur. – Then he made peace with the Arabs and settled a few tribes from the Taghlib, 'Abdalqais and Bekr b. Wail in Kerman, Tawag and Ahwaz. – He also built the town Nishapur and other towns in Sind and Sagistan. – He sent for a doctor from India, whom he settled in Kark near Sus; after this man's death the people of Sus inherited his skill and this is why the inhabitants of that region [N., p. 68] are the most skilful in medicine of all Persians. – He bequeathed the royal title to his brother Ardashir. His reign lasted seventy-two years.

(2) **Eutychius,**[3] *Annales*, ed. Cheikho, CSCO 50, pp. 109, 10–110, 5:

However, Shapur, the son of Ardashir, the king of the Persians returned to Nisibis. When he saw what they had accomplished in defensive preparation, he blamed them for their treachery and said, 'You have acted in a deceitful and cunning manner.' And [again] he put them under siege, yet when he had been unable to storm the city after expending a great deal of time there, he found this very fact a cause of vexation. Therefore he said to his companions, 'Can you not find anyone in our army who is not distressed by what we are suffering?' And so after holding an investigation they found two men given over to wine and song. The king said to them, 'It is clear that our situation pleases you since you so conduct yourselves as if what we are doing were of no concern to you.' They replied, 'O king, if the situation of this city upsets you, we hope we shall capture it with that strategy which we are going to disclose to you.' When he said 'Then what is it?', they answered that he should advance with his forces. 'Joining your hands together you should (all) utter your prayers to the Lord that he allow you to storm the city.' When Shapur did this and saw that it was of no use, he said to them: 'We followed your plan and see that it is by no means close to accomplishment. So what do you say now?' They replied: 'We are afraid that men will belittle our plan; but if you take care that all as one man utter their prayers in a genuine frame of mind, you will obtain your wish.' Therefore Shapur summoned his retinue and asked them to act with genuine feelings and with a sincere attitude. They (later) asserted that they had not repeated two short prayers before the city wall was split from top to bottom and a gap opened up through which men could enter. The inhabitants of the city were very frightened by this. They said, 'This is the end of our deception.' Therefore Shapur entered the city and slew whatever men suitable for war came into his hands; the remaining inhabitants of it he led away as prisoners, and he found a great quantity of wealth in that [place]. However, he ordered the site which became the split in the wall to be left as it was, so that men might see it and take warning. Afterwards he captured various cities in Syria and slew many and took many prisoners. He also invaded the land of the Greeks, causing great slaughter among them and captured Kalonia (? = Lycaonia?) and Cappadocia.

Eutychius, *Annales* 186, ed. Breydey, CSCO 471, p. 66, 1–5:
Maximianus (i. e. Galerius) marched into Persia, laid waste most of the country, massacred the inhabitants, burnt down trees and laid siege to Gundeshapur for days. Shapur entered the town through a ruse. He and his supporters attacked the Byzantines, defeated them, killing a large number and took their money and possessions. They then marched into their country and destroyed many towns. The Byzantine territory was stricken by epidemic, famine and plague to the extent that the people were always pressed for time to bury their dead.

(3) *Chronicle of Se'ert*[4] 2, ed. Scher, PO 4, pp. 220–1 (Arabic):

In the eleventh year of his reign, Shapur, the son of Ardashir invaded the territories of the Romans; he remained there a long time, destroying several towns. He defeated the Emperor Valèrian and carried him off into imprisonment in the land of the Nabataeans. Once there, Valerian fell victim to depression and died. The Fathers (i.e. Christian bishops) whom the cursed Valerian had exiled therefore returned to their episcopal towns. Shapur left the territories of the Romans, taking with him prisoners whom he settled in the countries of Iraq, Susiana, Persia and in the towns his father had founded. He also built three towns and gave them names derived from his own name. One was in the land of Maisan and was called Sod Shapur (i.e. Deir Mahraq). The second, in Persia, is still called Shapur today. He rebuilt Gunde-Shapur which had fallen into disrepair and named it Anti-Shapur, a word half Greek and half Persian, meaning: 'You are Shapur's equal (?).' He constructed a third town on the banks of the Tigris called Marw Habor (which is 'Ukbara and its environs). These towns were populated by his prisoners who were provided with homes and land to till.

The Christians also multiplied in Persia, building churches and monasteries.[5] Their number included priests who had been taken prisoner at Antioch. They colonised Gundeshapur and elected Azdaq (= Hierax?) of Antioch as their bishop, owing to Demetri-(an)us, the patriarch of Antioch, having fallen ill and died of sorrow. Before this second period of exile (?),[6] and after Demetri-(an)us' first period of exile, Paul of Samosata had become Patriarch of Antioch. His biography has been set down by Daniel Ibn Mariam.

(4) **Firdawsi**, *Shahnamah* (Epic of the Kings)[7] 25, (New Persian):
The Reign of Shapur, Son of Ardashir. His War with the Romans.

The time came when the news was divulged that the royal throne was vacant. Ardashir, that wise king, had left the throne and diadem to Shapur.[8] Revolt broke out in every land and region from Cappadocia to Rum, and when tidings of this came to Shapur the Shah he paraded his drums and banners and troops. As far as Paluina he dispatched a light-armed force without full supplies or impedimenta. Out of Cappadocia there marched an army from whose dust the sun itself grew dark, and another army marched out of Paluina, in command of which was a prince named Bazanush

[Valerian]. He was a proud knight of illumined spirit and much valued by the Caesars, a lasso-thrower, great in fame and lofty of dignity.

As the clamour of the drums arose on either side, that noble warrior stepped forth from the heart of his army, while from the foe there came out a gallant nobleman whose name was Garshasp the Lion. He was a brave knight who, on the day of the combat, feared nothing, whether it was a raging elephant or a man that stood opposed to him. The two warriors wrestled together in their struggle and their dust dropped onto the stars. Many were the devices by which they attempted to satisfy their rage but neither man could be overcome by the other. At last the entire armies on either side clashed together like mountain against mountain. From the great clamour caused by trumpets and Indian gongs you would have thought the sky dislodged from its place. In the midst of his army the warrior Bazanush was taken captive with bleeding heart, and of the Rumis in Paluina ten thousand were killed among the battle ranks, a thousand and twice three hundred were made prisoners and panic seized the hearts of the remaining warriors.

To Shapur, son of Ardashir, the Caesar sent a man of intelligence to inquire how long he would continue to shed blood for the sake of money. What would his answer be to God the All-wise when on the day of reckoning he was asked what excuse he could make? He, the Caesar, would send all that he possessed if no further pain was inflicted. He would obey any command concerning tribute and send numbers of his kinsmen as hostages. As for the Shah, it would be a just act on his part to retire from Paluina. Shapur stayed till the Caesar had sent him as tribute and tax ten oxhides filled with gold and Caesarian dinars, to which he added many valuables more.

For the sake of the captives of Rum, Shapur built a citadel in a prosperous territory. That region now holds the gate to the Khuzis and every traveller must pass through it. In Fars he raised a lofty citadel, magnificent and rich, and he built the fortress in the city of Nishapur which is rightly named Shapur-kard. Wherever he went the Shah carried Bazanush with him and listened to his discourse on all matters. At Shustar there was a river so wide that even fish could not traverse it, and to Bazanush Shapur said,.

'If you are an engineer, you will build me a bridge as continuous as a cable, such a one as will remain everlastingly in position as a pattern to the wise when we have turned to dust. The length of this bridge, reckoned in cubits, shall be one thousand; you may demand from my treasury all that is required. In this land and region apply all the science of the philosophers of Rum, and when the bridge is completed, you may depart to your home or else remain as my guest for as long as you live.'

In gallant fashion Bazanush undertook the task and brought the bridge to completion within three years. When it was done he departed from Shustar and speedily set his face towards his own home.

(Levy, 1967: 283–4)

Appendix 2   Select passages from Armenian historians

(1) **Faustus Buzandats'i,**[1] *History of the Armenians*, III, 8–9, and 20–1, pp. 16–17 and 110–16 (tr. P. Considine, © 1989):

8. The planting of the forests; war with Persia; the line of the noble house of the Bznuni family is cut off.

When peace had been established for a time in the land of Armenia, Xosrov (Khosrov), king of Armenia, issued orders that gifts should be given to all the brave men who for the sake of Greater Armenia had served him and risked their lives in so many confrontations on the field of battle. To his commander Vač'ē he gave the mines of Janjanak, Jrabašxik' and C'luglux (Bull's Head), together with all their territories, and to the other nobles too he gave great gifts.

The king ordered his commander to collect plenty of saplings from the country-side – to bring the wild oak of the forest and to plant it in the district of Ararat. And so they planted oak trees from the fortified royal castle, which they call Garni, as far as the plain Mecamawr up to the hill which is called by the name of Duin and stands on the North side of the great city of Artašat, and along the river below as far as the palace of Tikuni. He named it Tačar Mairi [Forest Palace]. To the south of the reed beds here they created another forest by filling the plain with a plantation of oak trees. They named it Xosrovakert, and built the royal palace there. They did not join the two forests together; instead they surrounded them with separate enclosures so as to leave a broad highway between them. The trees established themselves and grew; and the king ordered that every kind of wild animal and game should be collected to stock the enclosures and turn them into parks for field sports, for his royal pleasure. The commander Vač'e immediately carried out the king's instructions.

While Xosrov was seeing to the planting of the forests, information was suddenly brought to him in the district of Hēr and Zarawand that the Persian army was ready to march and wage war on him. Then King Xosrov gave orders to Databē, head of the Bznuni family, to raise a special task force from the country, and with its entire strength to take the field against the Immortal Band [Persian crack cavalry], to advance on them, engage them head on, and overwhelm the enemy. So Databē, with the massed Armenian forces, marched against the Persian army. When he came up with it, he proposed a pact to the commander of the Persian army, offering to deliver into their hands the king of Armenia, his master. He urged the enemy to lay an ambush for his own army, and to put his own army to the sword. All at once, without warning, as by a bolt from the blue, 40,000 men of the Armenian army perished together; the rest of the army took to flight. The wicked Databē took over the Persian army and was all set to fall upon the king of Armenia. But the fugitives from the army soon reached the camp of the king of Armenia, with tidings of the catastrophic overthrow of his fortunes and their wicked betrayal by the outlaw Databē.

Then Xosrov the Armenian king, together with the chief priest Vert'anes, cast himself prostrate before God and besought his aid with fervent prayers and flowing tears. And after this he hastened to gather to himself an army of about 30,000, with Vač'e as commander. He marched against them with all his noblest and greatest princes, and they met on the shores of the Sea of Bznunik' at the village of Aṙest by the royal fishery on a stream. They saw the forces of the Persians and their numberless hosts; they were as the stars of the heavens and the sand on the shores of the sea, for they had come with numberless elephants and measureless forces. The Armenians put their trust in God and fell upon the camp; they smote, slew and massacred and left not a single one of them. They possessed themselves of much booty and of the elephants and of all the resources of their army. The commander Vač'ē and the valiant Vahan Amatuni took Databē prisoner and brought him before the great king Xosrov, and they stoned him with stones as a man who had betrayed his country, his comrades and his master's army.

And he (Vač'ē) found his family, wife and children, in a fortress of the prince (*naxarar*) of Rštunik' on an island called Aɫtamar. And the commander Vač'ē took ship and came to the island and left not a single person on it, neither man nor woman. And so the ruling line of this province came to an end; and their house was forfeit to the king. Even after this the Persians did not cease to make war on

King Xosrov. And he enacted a law that the greatest nobles and princes, provincial governors and overlords, who commanded 10,000 or even 1,000 men should stay with the king as part of his entourage, and that none of them should go and enlist in the King's Own Army. For he was afraid that perhaps their attitude to him was somewhat equivocal, and that they might do what Databē had done and defect from him. But he still had confidence in old Vačʿē, the tried and trusted Commander of the forces of Greater Armenia, and in the valiant Vahan Amatuni; so he combined the troops of all the noble houses with the royal troops and gave the joint command into their hands. They were in constant readiness for deeds of valour in war in Persian territory, and they gave the enemy no opportunity to invade and lay waste the land of Armenia – or even to get within sight of it. And the king was untroubled and the country prospered and was at peace all the days of his life.

9. The Viceroy Bakur rebels against the king of Armenia; he is crushed by the Armenian army, and is replaced as Viceroy by Vałinak Siwni.

At that time one of the servants of the king of Armenia, the great lord of Ałjnikʿ, who was called by the title of Viceroy (*bdeašx*), rebelled against the king. He was one of four men who occupied the highest seats of honour at the king's court; but he threw in his lot with the king of Persia, and betrayed the royal house which trusted him. He brought in the Persian king's troops to support him, broke away from the land of Armenia and his allegiance to it, and waged war on the king of Armenia with help from the Persian Empire. The war was waged with great bitterness. Then the king of Armenia sent his faithful servants Jon, the regent (*išxan*) of Korduk', Mar, the regent of Great Cop'k', Nerseh, the regent of Šahē-Cop'k', Vałinak, the regent of Siwnik', Dat, the regent of Hašteank', Manak, the regent of Basean, together with a large army. They marched against the Persian army and vanquished it, and put all alike to the sword. They killed the viceroy, together with his brothers and sons, and bore the head of the viceroy Bakur to the king. But his little daughter they brought before the king, and since no-one else of the family had survived, he gave the girl in marriage to his beloved Vałinak, king of Siwnik', together with the house of Ałjnik'; and he made him viceroy and heir of that house. He prospered in his inheritance, and together with his country and with all his might, the viceroy Vałinak remained loyal in the service of the king. But of the sons of the viceroy Bakur, one lad escaped and fled to the Armenian commander (*zawravar*) Vač'ē, and survived by being hidden in his house. Afterwards he became heir to his house, and at a later time returned and claimed his inheritance. His name was Xeša.

20. King Tiran is betrayed by his chamberlain P'isak of Siwnik', deceived and taken prisoner by the Persian regent Varaz. The whole of Armenia is taken with him.[2]

Relations between the two kings, the kings of Armenia and Persia, were now friendly. In the land of Atrpatakan (i.e. Atropatene) dwelt a man of the highest rank called Šapuh Varaz. Now while there was perfect peace between the two kings, Providence decreed that it should be interrupted, for the most trifling of causes, by a single worthless man, who was a very devil in depravity. His name was P'isak, and he was chamberlain to King Tiran; he came from Siwnik' He had been sent as a messenger to Varaz Šapuh, whom the Persian king had left as Governor in the land Atrpatakan.

Now King Tiran had a horse which was greatly admired. It had a coat of dapple-grey, and was widely known as a magnificent, mettlesome animal, bigger, taller and broader than any other horse, and more handsome in appearance. It was in a class of its own; its equal was not to be found. When P'isak the king's chamberlain went on his mission, he told Varaz about the horse, because he was already on friendly terms with him. He was given a letter by Varaz, which he took and gave to the king of Armenia. The king was not persuaded to part with the horse, and did not welcome the proposal. But since he suspected that this man Varaz would be making trouble between the two kings, he started a search for a horse of the same colour, the same markings and the same build (except for size; nothing so big could be found). When he had found a similar-looking dapple-grey, he sent it, with letters of authority and gifts, by the hand of the depraved P'isak, to the regent Varaz in Atrpatakan. Having given the matter some thought, this is what he decided to do: he told P'isak to say: 'This is the horse for which you asked; as a mark of friendship he does not begrudge him to you.'

But when P'isak came to Varaz he made it clear that actually the horse had been 'begrudged', and in fact he did all he could to provoke a quarrel. He was not at all disposed to mitigate his treachery; in fact he revelled in his malicious talk. 'Tiran, king of Armenia', he said, 'feels such spite, envy and jealousy towards the king of Persia and the whole Persian army – such hostility, hatred and ill-will – such distrust and arrogance – that he has actually refused you a single beast. He has tricked you and made fun of you. He has substituted one horse for another, and it is the substitute which he has handed over to me to bring here. That is the one he has sent you. And this is not all. He has hopes of the Emperor and his army and he thinks to deprive the Sassanians of the Persian monarchy. You should hear him talk: "This dominion was ours and our forefathers".' I shall not rest until the honour of our forefathers is restored. I shall restore their former kingship to their son and to their posterity, to my line, to my house, to myself.' With talk like this the impious P'isak proved himself against his rightful overlord, and plotted the death of his own king.

When Varaz Šapuh, Governor of Atrpatakan, heard all this rabid talk from the unbridled tongue of P'isak, Varaz at once wrote a letter of complaint about the king of Armenia and sent it to Nerseh, king of Persia. To such an extent did he upset, incense and provoke the king of Persia against the king of Armenia, he so thoroughly angered and enraged him, that he promptly received orders from him to find any way, devise any means, set any trap, to hunt down and seize the king of Armenia. And so it came about that while there was peace between these two kings, the anger of the Lord was provoked and roused to vengeance and the impious Tiran called to account for the sacred blood of the deaths of two great and eminent priests.

Thereupon Varaz sent a messenger to the king of Armenia on the pretext of discussing peace and reconciliation with him. Pretending that he desired friendship, he asked for permission to come to him. When Tiran, king of Armenia, heard this, he readily, promptly and indeed joyfully ordered that he should be invited. Before Varaz arrived, the king took into his confidence his closest servants, his personal attendants. He said to them: 'It is fitting for us to entertain the man who is coming to us, and to make him glad with hunting and banquets and every kind of pleasure. But the Persian people are so envious, jealous, ill-natured and treacherous, that it is not really fitting that he should see the great hunting grounds here in our own country. Instead of that, you are to prepare sparser hunting grounds to look like them – that will be quite enough for us to entertain him with. We will not hunt on the better stocked grounds and have a great show piece of a hunt with killing and slaughter. No, let us have quite a modest hunt, since these people are such a bad, disagreeable lot. Prepare the area at the foot of the great mountain of Masik' in the land of Apahunik" – the area of which the chief city is called Ałiorsk'.

Šapuh Varaz arrived with 3,000 men and met the king in the land of Apahunik', and received a warm welcome from him. What the king had said about the hunt quickly came to the ears of the Persian commander through the mouth of the crazed informer P'isak, that false, lying, treacherous servant and murderer of his lord and destroyer of his country. For a few days they enjoyed themselves together. The Persian regent, with cunning diplomacy, skilfully disguised the hostility he felt in his heart, and prepared a feast to complete the deception. And this is how it all turned out:

At that time the commanders were not on hand but were stationed elsewhere, and so were the greatest princes and chief heads of noble houses, while the king's troops were in their respective quarters or camps or at the the posts to which they had been posted. There was no-one left with the king, no troops, no cavalry; he was alone with a few servants, net-layers for the hunt, road-makers, and others of the common people who performed menial tasks, together with his queen and the young prince Aršak. Although so few of his people happened to be with him at that time, and he saw that the Persian commander had arrived with a strong force of 3,000 men, fully armed and equipped, he was totally unsuspicious and felt quite safe, because he saw him arrive with apparently the most peaceful intentions, with fine gifts, precious offerings, and an extravagant show of respect.

Not many days had passed before the king was asked to a meal; they invited him to dinner. There was plenty of wine to drink, and the king and his companions got thoroughly drunk. A company of soldiers who were standing by surprised and seized every one of them as they were at table; they were unprepared, unsuspecting, expecting anything but this. King Tiran was surrounded by a ring of spearmen. They seized and bound him hand and foot with bonds of iron, and despoiled his camp of all they found in it: the treasures and possessions, the wife and children of the king, whom they found in the camp, they removed from the land of Apahunik'.

When they arrived at a place called Dalarika', and when the Persian commander arrived and made his entry into this village of Dalarika', he brought King Tiran in with him in chains. And Varaz said: 'Now, see about a charcoal fire in which we can heat the iron to burn out the eyes of the king of Armenia.' And they brought in charcoal, with which they burnt out the eyes of Tiran. Then Tiran himself began to speak, and said: 'Since my two eyes have been burnt out and I have lost my sight in this place, instead of the name Dalarika', from now on its name is to be Acuł [charcoal]. Let it continue to be a warning sign in memory of me. It has come home to me now – now I realize that what has been exacted from me is in revenge for my wicked crimes: I brought darkness to the land of which I was king in place of the light of two learned Teachers (*vardapet*), and I thought to extinguish the light of the truth which they both faithfully preached. It is because of this that my eyes which beheld the light are now in darkness.'

Thereupon the Persian king's regent immediately and in haste set off from the village of Acuł and came by forced marches to the land of Persia, together with Tiran the king and all the prisoners. He then went on to Assyria, to his master, the king of Persia.

The full tragic story of these terrible events became known with all the sudden shock of an unexpected disaster. There was a gathering of the princes and regents, administrators, senior army officers and the chief men from all over the country: they came and met together in a great assembly. Although troops were also assembled and equipped, and were prepared and anxious to pursue Varaz, they were unable to catch up with him. However, they did reach and take an area of the land of Persia. They killed everyone in it indiscriminately, and burnt and plundered the land. They themselves returned and gathered in a certain place where they put on mourning and wept with grief for their rightful lord the king of Armenia. And so they showed their distress at the overthrow of their country and their own masterless condition, attended as it was by such dreadful affliction.

21. The Armenian princes meet in united assembly; they go to the Greek king and bring him to Armenia to support and help them; the Persian king comes with a great army and escapes with a single horse to flee back to Persia.

Then again the Armenian people gathered together in a great united assembly from all over the country – their princes, great men and elders, local and regional governors, nobles and army officers, judges, rulers and regents – and, as well as the commanders, some people from the lower peasant class. People began talking to each other and saying: 'What is the point of this mourning of ours? The enemy are just taking advantage of it. But it won't be long before the enemy are on the march and away from here. So come on, we must cheer each other up, and see to the defence of our country and ourselves, and avenge our rightful lord.' Then the whole population of the country assembled together with one accord to form an alliance and find support for their cause.

It was then that they sent some of the great princes of the Armenian court with gifts to the king of the Greeks; they were to offer him their hand and become his obedient servants, while he gave them his support as an ally in exacting vengeance from their enemies. They sent Andovk, ruler of Siwnikʻ, and Aršavir Kamsarakan, ruler of Aršarunikʻ: they went to the land of Greece and entered the Imperial Palace of the kings. They handed over the letter and presented the gifts which they had brought, and delivered to the king their country's plea for help. The king listened to their story, and showed himself perfectly prepared and even anxious to find out what had been happening. He allied himself with the land of Armenia in support – the more readily in that he remembered the treaty of alliance which had been struck with binding oaths and ratified by negotiation between the Emperor Kostandianos and King Trdat.

But before the messengers who had come from the land of Armenia to the Imperial Court had returned to their own country, Nerseh, king of Persia, himself left the Eastern territories and came to take, burn, plunder, lay waste and annex to himself the provinces of the land of Armenia. He mustered his whole army with all its own equipment and great train of camp followers, together with a herd of elephants, no end of provisions, his own documents of state, and all the womenfolk, together with the queen of queens, and then he came and crossed into Armenian territory. He filled every part of the land chock-full. Thereupon the noble born regiments of the Armenian princes took their families and became refugees, escaping to Greek soil, where they gave the Emperor the bad news that the satraps' camp contained a great host of men.

When the king of the Greeks[3] heard all this, he too mustered his army and marched off to the land of Armenia to confront the Persian king. He left his own camp near the town of Satał, personally selected two of the best, most level-headed, men from the Armenian camp (they were actually Aršavir and Andovk, the very men mentioned above as the original messengers who had come to him), and together with them he, the Emperor, entered the Persian camp disguised as a village greengrocer. This camp was pitched in the district of Basean, at a place called Oxsa. And so they came and entered the camp of the Persian king; they spied out the lie of the land and took measure of the strength of their forces.[4] Then they returned to their own camp and made ready. They made for the camp of the Persian king and when they reached it (it was still in the same position) they took it off-guard and unawares, relaxed and unsuspecting. They came by daylight, fell upon the king of Persia and put the whole camp to the sword, sparing not a single one of them. They despoiled the camp and drove into captivity the king's wives and the princess and all that they possessed, their wives and treasures, their provisions and equipment. The king alone escaped by a hair's breadth, a mounted courier ahead of him; he got clear, took to flight and just managed to reach his own country.

The Emperor appeared in the midst of the camp in all his pomp and glory and majesty. Every male who had come of age they killed, and all the rest they drove into captivity in the land of Greece. The Emperor made much of Andovk and Aršavir, conferred great honours and gifts on them and left them as lord-protectors of the country. He made them responsible for all the princes and their country, and he himself marched off and came to his own land, the land of Greece.

The king of Persia came as a fugitive to his own land. And when he reached it, he gathered together all who remained of his allegiance, and initiated a full-scale enquiry. He was determined to have a thorough investigation, and he gave fresh orders that the original causes of the dispute and the war should be investigated and clarified. In due course they came up with the answer, and the whole story was made clear to him: they concluded that it had all started with a trivial incident and for the worst of reasons – that the reason for all the trouble was that that demented man Šapuh Varaz had been suspicious about a horse. Then the king gave orders that he should be deprived of his office and stripped of his official robes. He found him deserving of the supreme penalty: in accordance with Persian custom he ordered that he should be flayed and his skin stuffed with straw and exhibited as a laughing-stock in the public square.

He himself was sorry about what had happened, and he sent noble lords humbly to sue for peace, to arrange that the prisoners should be sent back again by the Emperor – and in particular to send suppliants with overtures of peace to ask the Emperor at least to return his wives from captivity and so spare him any further embarrassment, public criticism and loss of face. Then Valēs, king of the Greeks, wrote a letter to the king of the Persians. 'First you', he said, 'must return the prisoners taken in the land of Armenia, and the king Tiran himself unharmed, and everything which was taken. When you have done this, I for my part will return what I took. If you do not return the booty taken from them, I will ⟨not⟩ return yours. And when the king of Persia received this order, he promptly carried it out. He brought the king Tiran out of the prison where he was held, courteously assured him that he would send him back to his own country and make him king, and that he would go back in honour. Then Tiran gave his reply: 'It is inappropriate and futile of me – in fact it is quite impossible for me in my blindness – to reign as king. Make my son Aršak king instead of me.

Thereupon he made Aršak his son king over the country of Armenia. He then returned the wives of the king and all the others who had been captured, together with the treasures, offerings and possessions; he made full restitution of all that had been taken. Tiran himself the Persian king robed and arrayed in the finest array, and sent from his own country to the land of Armenia, and so faithfully carried out the orders of the Greek king. After accompanying them to Armenia, he sent messengers who had come to him from the Greek king back to the Greek king to report how well he had carried out his orders, so that the Greek king in turn should return the prisoners which he had taken from the Persian king. And so it came about that when the Greek king heard all about how the Persian king had carried out to the letter the orders he had given him, and had had the Armenian prisoners and King Tiran returned, he was satisfied. Thereupon the Greek king arranged the return of the prisoners captured from the Persian king. And the Greek king robed and adorned the wives of the Persian king with great honour, and returned all their prisoners with them from the land of Greece to the land of Persia, and had them escorted safely to the king.

(2) **Agathangelos**,[5] *History of the Armenians*, (I), 18–37 and 46–7 and 123 (tr. R. W. Thomson, 1976 State University of New York, reproduced by agreement)

18. The period of the Parthian kingdom came to an end when sovereignty was taken away from Artavan son of Valarsh on his murder by Artashir son of Sasan. The latter was a prince from the province of Stahr who had come and united the forces of the Persians; they then abandoned and rejected and disdained the sovereignty of the Parthians and happily chose the sovereignty of

Artashir son of Sasan. So after the sad news of his death reached Khosrov king of the Armenians – who was second in the kingdom of the Persians, for whoever was king of Armenia had second rank in the Persian kingdom – although he was quickly informed of the sad news, he had no time to complete preparations for war. Then he returned in great sadness at the course of events, for he had been unable to accomplish anything. And he returned to his own country greatly distressed.

19. But at the start of the next year Khosrov king of Armenia began to raise forces and assemble an army. He gathered the armies of the Albanians and the Georgians, opened the gates of the Alans and the stronghold of the Chor; he brought through the army of the Huns in order to attack Persian territory and invade Asorestan as far as the gates of Ctesiphon. He ravaged the whole country, ruining the populous cities and prosperous towns. He left all the inhabited land devastated and plundered. He attempted to eradicate, destroy completely, extirpate, and overthrow the Persian kingdom and aimed at abolishing its civilization. At the same time he made an oath to seek vengeance with great rancor for their (the Parthians') loss of sovereignty; ruthlessly he attempted to exact thorough vengeance [cf. I Macc. 9.42]. He was greatly puffed up [cf. II Macc. 9.4], trusting in the number of his forces and hoping in the valor of his army. There quickly arrived in support great numbers of strong and brave cavalry detachments, Albanians, Lp'ink', Chilpk', Kaspk' and others from those regions, in order to seek vengeance from the blood of Artavan.

20. For because of his family relationship to that dynasty he was very grieved that they (the Persians) had submitted and accepted the rule of the Stahrian and had united with him. And although Khosrov sent an embassy so that his relatives would support him and with his own kingdom oppose (the Persians), and that there would also come to his aid (contingents) from the regions of the Kushans, brave and valiant armies both from that area and their own land, yet his relatives, the chiefs and princes and leaders of the Parthians paid no heed. For they had attached themselves in obedience and subjection to the rule of Artashir, rather than to the rule of their relative and brother.

21. Nonetheless Khosrov took the vast numbers of his army, plus whatever lancers had arrived to support him in the war. And when the Persian king saw the great size of this force bearing down upon him with enormous strength, he advanced against them in battle array. However, he was unable to resist them, and fled before

them. In pursuit they cut down the whole army of the Persians, scattering corpses over the plains and roads, and inflicting cruel and unbearable suffering. After this great slaughter the Armenian king joyfully and victoriously returned with much booty to the land of Armenia, to the province of Ayrarat and the city of Valarshapat, with great rejoicing, with good renown, and with much plunder.

22. Then he commanded that ambassadors be sent throughout the land, that edicts be composed and vows be made to the seven altars of the temples of the cult of the images of the idols. He honored the sites of the ancestral worship of his Arsacid family with white oxen and white rams, white horses and white mules, gold and silver ornaments, fringed and tasseled silks, gold crowns and silver altars, beautiful vases with precious gems, gold and silver, shining raiment and lovely decoration. Similarly he took a fifth of all the enormous booty he had collected and gave splendid gifts to the priests. And to the soldiers who had followed him he gave gifts before dismissing them.

23. Then at the beginning of the next year he gathered a great army [cf. I Macc. 4.27–8], summoning the same troops; and with even more than these, because the forces of the Tachiks had come to his support, he spread his invasion over the regions of Asorestan. They plundered the whole land and victoriously returned to their own countries. And for ten years they made continual incursions in this manner, plundering all the lands which were under the suzerainty and authority of the Persians.

24. But when the Persian king saw all these misfortunes which had befallen him, he was oppressed, afflicted, tormented, and plunged into hesitation and doubt [cf. I Macc.3.29–31]. He summoned all the kings and governors and princes and generals and leaders and nobles of his kingdom and they held council. He begged them all to seek and find a solution, promising all sorts of rewards. 'If only someone be found,' he said, 'who will be able to exact vengeance,' he promised to elevate him to second rank in his kingdom, if only someone would undertake to avenge him. 'Only I and my throne will be above him, be he of very humble or of honorable origin.' He promised to grant him all sorts of honors and gifts and rewards.

25. Now there was in the council a leading chieftain of the Parthian kingdom, called Anak. He rose, and coming forward promised to exact vengeance from his own king as if from an enemy.

26. He (the king) began to address him and said: 'If only you settle this account loyally, I shall return to you (your) native Parthian (land), your own Pahlav, and I shall honor you with a crown and make you famous and honored in my kingdom and call you second to me.'

27. The Parthian replied and said: 'Do you succor the rest of my family, while my brother and I today take our leave from you.'

28. Then the Parthian made his preparations and arrangements, and with his brother, his household, their wives and children, and all his retinue, took his departure; he journeyed, spying out the roads, and came to Armenia on the pretext of emigrating, as if he had revolted against the Persian king. He came before king Khosrov in the province of Uti, at the city of Khalkhal, in the winter quarters of the Armenian king.

29. When the Armenian king saw him, he gladly went to meet him and welcomed him with great joy – especially when he began to speak deceitfully and fraudulently with him and to show the sincerity of his coming: 'I came to you,' he said, 'in order that we might be able to make common cause in seeking vengeance.'

30. Now when the king saw this man arriving with all his household, he sincerely believed in him. Then he honored him in royal fashion and established him in the second rank of his kingdom. And for the whole duration of that winter they passed the days of chilling winds and ice in cheerfulness.

31. But when the warmer days of the southerly winds arrived to open the gates of spring, the king departed from those regions. They descended to the province of Ayrarat, to the city of Valarshapat. And while they happily relaxed there the king decided to gather an army and invade Persian territory [cf. I Macc. 4.35].

32. When the Parthian heard of this he remembered the oath of his compact with the Persian king. He also remembered the promises of rewards, and had a yearning for his own country which was called Pahlav. So he decided on an evil plan. He and his brother took the king aside, as if for recreation and to consult with him [cf. II Macc. 4.46]. They had half-drawn their steel swords, and suddenly raised their weapons and struck the king dead to the ground. As soon as the news of this event was divulged, the lamentation of the crowd waxed strong; meanwhile they had mounted their horses and had fled.

33. But when the princes of the Armenian army learned of this they split into groups and made pursuit. Some hastened by land to reach the head of the bridge at the gate of the city of Artashat. For

the river Araxes had risen and was flowing full to both banks [cf. Jos. 3.15] with swollen masses of icy water from melting snow at the time of its flooding. The others passed over the bridge of the city of Valarshapat which is called the bridge of Metsamawr and hastened to precede them to the head of the bridge of Valarshapat. In a narrow passage of the road they arrested them and from the bridge of Tap'er they cast them into the river. They themselves then returned with cries of woe and lamentation, and the whole land gathered to mourn the king.

34. Before the warm spirit had left his breast and he had breathed his last [cf. II Macc. 7.14], (the king) ordered the extermination of their family. Then they began to massacre and slaughter them. From among the children they left not even those too young to know their right hand from their left [cf. Jonah 4.11]. Likewise they exterminated the female side of the family by the sword. Only two infant sons of the Parthian did someone save and rescue through their nurses, who took them and fled, the one to Persian territory and the other to Greek territory.

35. And it happened that when the Persian king heard of all this he greatly rejoiced, and he made that day a great and joyous festival and carried out many vows to the fire-temples. He assembled an army and hastened to make incursions throughout the regions of Armenia. He brought into captivity men and beasts, old men and infants, youths and children alike.

36. But there escaped from the raid one of the sons of Khosrov king of Armenia, an infant called Trdat; his tutors took him and fled to the emperor's court in Greek territory. Then the Persian king came and imposed his own name on Armenia, and set the Greek army to flight, pursuing it to the borders of Greece. He had ditches dug to fix the frontier, and called the place 'the gate of ditches' instead of the earlier title 'the Pit.'

* * *

46. Then the emperor greatly honoured Trdat and bestowed handsome gifts on him. He crowned his head with a diadem, and decorated him with the purple and the imperial insignia. And he entrusted to him a great army for his support, and sent him to his own land of Armenia.

47. So after his victorious show of strength, Trdat, king of Greater Armenia, returned from Greek territory. The king hastened to Armenia; when he arrived he found there a great army of Persians, because they had subdued the country for themselves. Many he slaughtered and many he threw back in flight to Persia.

And he brought under his own sway his ancestral kingdom and ruled over its borders [cf. I Macc. 2.46].

* * *

123. King Trdat spent the whole period of his reign devastating the land of the Persian kingdom and the land of Asorestan. He plundered and caused terrible distress. Therefore this saying was adopted among the proverbial sayings: 'Like the haughty Trdat, who in his pride devastated the dykes of rivers and in his arrogance dried up the currents of seas.' For truly he was haughty in dress and endowed with great strength and vigor; he had solid bones and an enormous body, he was incredibly brave and warlike, tall and broad of stature. He spent his whole life in war and gained triumphs in combat. He acquired a great renown for bravery and extended throughout the whole world the glorious splendor of his victories. He threw his enemies into disarray and revenged his ancestors. He devastated many of the regions of Syria and took a great amount of booty from them. He put to the sword the armies of the Persians and acquired enormous booty. He became commander of the cavalry of the Greek army, and handed over to them the camps (of the enemy). He expelled the armies of the Huns by force and subjected the regions of Persia.

(3) **Moses Khorenats'i**,[6] *History of the Armenians* (II), 71–83 and (III), 4–8 and 10–15 (tr. R. W. Thomson, © 1978 by the President and Fellows of Harvard College, reproduced by agreement)

(II) *The intermediate Period*

71. The first invasion of Khosrov into Assyria in which he intended to aid Artavan

After Artashir, son of Sasan, had killed Artavan and gained the throne, two branches of the Pahlav family called Aspahapet and Surēn Pahlav were jealous at the rule of the branch of their own kin, that is, of Artashēs, and willingly accepted the rule of Artashir, son of Sasan. But the house of Karēn Pahlav, remaining friendly toward their brother and kin, opposed in war Artashir, son of Sasan. As soon as Khosrov, king of Armenia, heard of the troubles he set out to aid Artavan, if possible to arrive in time to rescue at least Artavan. When he entered Assyria, he heard the sad news of Artavan's death and of the alliance of all the Persian troops and nobles – both of his own family the Parthians and of the Pahlavik', except for the branch of Karēn. To the latter he sent messengers and then returned to our country in great sadness and regret. And immediately he made haste to inform Philip, the Roman emperor, seeking help from him.

72. Khosrov receives aid from Philip and attacks Artashir in war

Because there were troubles in Philip's empire, he was unable to spare any Roman forces to give military assistance to Khosrov. But he helped him by means of a letter ordering that he be given assistance from every region. When they received this command they came to his support from Egypt and the desert, from as far away as the shores of the Pontic Sea. Having acquired such a multitude [of troops] he marched against Artashir, and giving battle put him to flight; he took from him Assyria and the other lands where he had a royal residence.

Again he sent through messengers to his own kin the Parthian and the Pahlav families, and to all the forces of the land of the Kushans, that they should come to him and exact vengeance from Artashir; and [he said] that he would make the most worthy among them king so that the throne would not pass from them. But the aforementioned branches named Aspahapet and Surenean did not agree, so Khosrov returned to our land, not so much happy at his victory as upset at the falling away of his kin. Then there came to him some of his own messengers who had gone to the more illustrious nation far inland as far as Bahl. They brought him word that 'your kinsman Vehsachan with his branch of the Karēn Pahlav has not given obeisance to Artashir, but is coming to you in answer to your summons.'

73. The renewed attack of Khosrov against Artashir without Roman help

Although Khosrov was greatly delighted at the news of the coming of his kinsmen, yet his joy was short-lived; for the sad news quickly arrived that Artashir himself with his united forces had caught up with them and slaughtered all the branch of the Karenean Pahlav, killing all the males from young men to sucklings, save for one youth whom a friend of his house, Burz by name, had taken in flight to the land of the Kushans and brought to some of his powerful relatives. Artashir made great efforts to seize the child but was unable [to obtain him] from his kin who had rallied together, even when he swore against his will that there would be no danger for the child. For this reason the Persians have composed myriad fables about him, to the effect that animals served the child. The latter was Perozamat, the ancestor of our great family of Kamsarakan, of whom we shall speak in his place.

But now we [shall tell] of what happened after the slaughter of the family of the Karenean Pahlav, vengeance for which the Armenian king Khosrov was not slow in seeking. Although Philip had died and the Roman empire was in confusion – many men seeking power from each other in a brief period: the emperors Decius and Gallus and Valerian, who did not aid him – nonetheless Khosrov with his army and other friends who had rallied to him and with the nations of the north was victorious over Artashir and pursued him as far as India.

* * *

76. Artashir's attack against us, and his victory over the Emperor Tacitus

This same man (i.e. Firmilian) says that after the murder of Khosrov the Armenian princes united and brought to their own assistance the Greek army, which was in Phrygia, to oppose the Persians and save the country. And straightway they informed the Emperor Valerian. But because the Goths, crossing the River Danube, had taken many provinces captive and had plundered the Cyclades Islands, for that reason Valerian was not in time to protect our land. Nor did he live much longer; Claudius gained the throne from him, and after him Aurelian, following each other in quick succession. Within a few months there reigned the brothers Quintus and Tacitus and Florian. Therefore Artashir freely invaded us and, putting the Greek army to flight, took captive the major part of the country and turned it into a wilderness. Fleeing from him, the Armenian nobles, with the Arsacid family, took refuge in Greece. Among them was Artavazd Mandakuni, who took Trdat, son of Khosrov, and brought him to the imperial court. Therefore Tacitus was obliged to come to oppose Artashir in the regions of Pontus, and he sent his brother Florian with another army to Cilicia. But Artashir overtook Tacitus and put him to flight. The latter was killed by his own [troopš] in Chaniukʻ in Pontus, that is, Khałṭikʻ; likewise his brother Florian [was killed] eighty-eight days later in Tarsus.

77. Concerning the peace between the Persians and the Greeks, and Artashir's accomplishments in Armenia during the years of anarchy

Probus became emperor of the Greeks, and, making peace with Artashir, he divided our land and dug ditches to mark the frontiers. Artashir subjected the nobility, brought back those who had emigrated, and destroyed their fortified places – except for a certain noble called Awtay from the family of the Amatunik', who was related by marriage to that of the Slkunik' and was the foster father of Khosrovidukht, the daughter of Khosrov. He had ensconced himself in the fortress of Ani, as if hidden in a tranquil lair.

Artashir organized Armenia in a splendid fashion and re-established its former order. Likewise the Arsacids, who had been deprived of the crown and of their residence in Ayrarat, he re-established in the same place with their former revenues and emoluments. He increased the cults of the temples and ordered the fire of Ormizd, which was on the altar at Bagavan, to be kept perpetually burning. But the statues that Valarshak had set up as the images of his ancestors with those of the sun and moon at Armavir, and which had been transferred from Armavir to Bagaran and then brought to Artashat, these Artashir broke up. He subjected the land to tribute by an edict and completely consolidated his own authority.

Furthermore he renewed the frontiers established by Artashēs by setting stones in the ground, and he changed their names to his own, 'Artashirakan.' He governed our land like one of his own territories with Persian governors for twenty-six years and after him, for one year until the reign of Trdat, his son Shapuh – which means 'child of the king.'

78. The slaughter of the Mandakuni family by Artashir

Artashir had heard that one of the Armenian princes had fled with one of Khosrov's sons and had saved him by bringing him to the imperial court. Having investigated who that might be, he had discovered that it was Artavazd of the Mandakuni family. He ordered that entire family to be exterminated. When the Armenians had fled from Artashir, these too had fled with the families of the other princes. And when Artashir had subjected the rest, they returned and were all put to the sword. But a certain

Tachat, who was from the family of Ashots' and descended from Gushar Haykazn, abducted a beautiful maiden from among Artavazd's sisters; and having rescued her by fleeing to the city of Caesarea, he married her because of her wonderful beauty.

79. Concerning the prowess of Trdat during the years of anarchy in Armenia

He speaks of the prowess of Trdat: first of all, in his youth he delighted in horse riding; he was an expert horseman, dexterous in the use of arms, and a willing pupil of other military exercises. And then according to the oracle of the Peloponnesian temple of Hephaistos, in the boxing match he outdid Clitostratos of Rhodes who used to win by a neck grip, and also Cerasos of Argos; for the latter pulled out the hoof of an ox, whereas he [Trdat] with one hand held two wild bulls by the horn, twisted, and threw them with a crash. And wishing to drive a chariot in the races of the hippodrome, he was thrown by the skill of his opponent and fell to the ground. But he seized the chariot and stopped it, at which all were amazed. And in the war of Probus against the Goths there was a great famine. Finding no stores, the soldiers revolted and killed him; similarly they rose up against all the nobles. But Trdat alone resisted them, preventing anyone from entering the palace of Licinius, with whom Trdat was living.

Carus then reigned with his sons, Carinus and Numerian. Gathering an army, he gave battle to the Persian king, and after gaining the victory he returned to Rome. Therefore Artashir, bringing many nations to his support and having the desert [peoples] of Tachikastan on his side, gave battle a second time to the Roman army on both sides of the Euphrates. In the battle Carus was killed at Ṙinon. Similarly Carinus, who had marched into the desert against Koṙnak in the company of Trdat, was slaughtered with his army; those who survived turned in flight. At this point Trdat's horse was wounded so he did not gallop away with the fugitives. But he picked up his arms and the horse's accoutrements and swam across the wide and deep Euphrates to his own army, where Licinius was. In those days Numerian was killed in Thrace, and Diocletian succeeded to the throne. But Agathangelos informs you of Trdat's various deeds in his time.

* * *

82. The prowess of Trdat during his reign before his conversion

Because there is no true history without chronology, therefore we made a detailed investigation and found that Trdat gained the throne in the third year of Diocletian and that he came here with a large army. When he arrived at Caesarea, most of the princes went to meet him. And arriving in this country he found that Awtay had raised his sister Khosrovidukht and had guarded the treasures in his fortress with great constancy. He was a just and persevering man, reliable and very wise; for although he did not know the truth about God, yet he realized the falsity of the idols. Similarly his protégée Khosrovidukht was a modest maiden, like a nun, and did not at all have an open mouth like other women.

Trdat made Awtay commander-in-chief of Armenia and honored him in gratitude, and even more his own foster brother, Artavazd Mandakuni, because he had been the cause of his escape and of his attaining the glory of his fathers. Therefore he entrusted him with the command of the Armenian army. For the same reason he appointed Tachat, his brother-in-law, prince over the province of Ashots'. It was the latter who in future was to warn his father-in-law Artavazd and he to warn the king first that Gregory was Anak's son, and later about the sons of Gregory, as he had learned [about them] when living in the city of Caesarea.

The valiant Trdat quickly engaged in many battles, first in Armenia and then in Persia, gaining the victory himself in person. On one occasion, surpassing that Elianan in the Old Testament [cf. 2 Kings 23; Chron. 11:11], he raised his spear over an equally large number of wounded. And on another occasion, the powerful Persians felt the strength of the giant and the force of his arms. They had inflicted many wounds on his horse and killed it with their arrows; struck down, it threw the king to the ground. But he rose up and attacked on foot, in turn overthrowing many of the enemy. Seizing the horse of one of them, he boldly mounted. On the second occasion furthermore, willingly being on foot, with his sword he scattered the ranks of elephants. Such were his heroic deeds while he remained in Persia and Assyria, even making an attack beyond Ctesiphon.

83. Concerning Trdat's marriage to Ashkhēn and Constantine's to Maximina, and how he was converted

When Trdat arrived in our land he sent General Smbat, the father of Bagarat, to bring the maiden Ashkhēn, the daughter of Ashkhadar, to be his wife. This maiden was no less tall than the king. He ordered her to be inscribed as an Arsacid, to be vested with purple, and to be crowned in order to become the king's bride. From her was born a son Khosrov, who did not attain the stature of his parents.

In those same days occurred also the marriage of Maximina, the daughter of Diocletian, in Nicomedia; her husband was the Emperor Constantine, son of Constantius, the Roman emperor, who had not been born from Maximian's daughter but from a prostitute, Helen. This Constantine at [the time of] his marriage became friendly with our King Trdat. And when Constantius died not many years later, Diocletian sent his son and his own son-in-law Constantine as his successor.

* * *

87. The defeat of Shapuh and his unwilling submission to Constantine the Great, Trdat's capture of Ecbatana and the arrival of his relatives, and the discovery of the saving wood at that time

But Trdat, although he had gained the victory, nonetheless because his army had been mauled and many princes had fallen, hesitated to challenge Shapuh alone before being joined by the mass of the Roman army, which had attacked Assyria, put Shapuh to flight, and plundered the whole land. Then Trdat, with all his men and the troops under them, invaded the northern regions of the Persian empire in a year-long expedition.

* * *

(III) *The Conclusion*

4. The withdrawal of the bdeashkh Bakur from alliance with the Armenians, and the princes' plan to make Khosrov king

As we find it said in the divine histories, the Hebrew nation, after the Judges and in the time of anarchy and unrest, had no king and each man acted according to his own pleasure [cf. Judges 21: 24]. One could also see the same thing in our own country. For on the death of the blessed Trdat, the great prince Bakur, who was entitled the *bdeashkh* of Aḷdznik', seeing Sanatruk reigning in P'aytakaran, conceived the same plan for himself. Although he did not wish to reign because he was not an Arsacid, nonetheless he wished to be independent. Abandoning his alliance with the Armenians, he assisted Ormizd, king of Persia. When the Armenian princes became aware of this and reflected on it, they gathered together in the presence of Vrt'anēs the Great and sent two of the honourable lords – Mar, lord of Tsop'k', and Gag, lord of Hashteank' – to the capital city to the Emperor Constantius, son of Constantine, with presents and a letter, which ran as follows:

5. A copy of the Armenians' letter

'Archbishop Vrt'anēs and the bishops under him and all the princes of Greater Armenia, to our lord the emperor Caesar Constantius, greetings.

'Remember the sworn covenant of your father Constantine with our King Trdat and do not give this country over to the godless Persians, but help us with an army to make Khosrov, Trdat's son, king. For God has made you lord not only of Europe but also of all the Mediterranean, and the awe of your power has reached the ends of the earth. And we desire that you rule over an ever-greater empire. Be well.'

Agreeing to this, Constantius sent Antiochus, his palace prefect, with a strong army, and purple robes, and a crown, and a letter, which ran as follows:

The Letter of Constantius

'The emperor Augustus Caesar Constantius, to Vrt'anēs the Great and all your fellow countrymen, greetings.

'I have sent an army to your support with the command to make Khosrov, son of your King Trdat, king over you, in order that having established good order you may serve us loyally. Be well.'

6. The arrival of Antiochus and his actions

When Antiochus arrived, he made Khosrov king and appointed to the same command over the army the four generals whom Trdat had established in his own lifetime, after the death of his tutor Artavazd Mandakuni who had been the single supreme commander and general of all Armenia. The first was Bagarat the *aspet*, as general of the western force; the second was Mihran, prince of Georgia and *bdeashkh* of Gugark', as general of the northern army; the third was Vahan, prince of the Amatunik', as general of the eastern force; the fourth was Manachihr, prince of the Ṙshtunik, as general of the southern army. And he divided the troops and gave each one [his portion]. He sent Manachihr with the southern army and that of Cilicia to the regions of Assyria and Mesopotamia; and Vahan, prince of the Amatunik‘, with the eastern force and the army of Galatia he sent to the regions of Azerbaijan to keep them secure from the Persian king.

He himself, leaving behind King Khosrov, – for he was small of person and weak boned and did not approximate to the stature of a warrior – took with him Mihran and Bagarat with their armies, and in unison with all the Greek [forces] marched against Sanatruk. But the latter, having filled the city of P‘aytakaran with Persian troops, fled with the princes of the Aluank to King Shapuh for refuge. When Antiochus saw that they had not submitted to peaceful obedience, he ordered the lands of the rebels to be subjected to pillage. He himself collected the tribute and returned to the emperor.

7. The crime of Manachihr against Jacob the Great, and his death

When Manachihr arrived in the regions of Assyria with the Armenian southern force and the Cilician army, he offered battle to Bakur the *bdeashkh* and slew him, putting to flight his army and the Persians who had come to his aid. He captured Bakur's son Heshay and sent him in iron bonds to Khosrov. He unmercifully condemned to the sword all the provinces of his state, not only the warriors but also the common peasants. He took many captives from the regions of Nisibis, including eight deacons of the great Bishop Jacob. After this Jacob came and urged Manachihr to free the common captives as being in no way culpable. But Manachihr did not agree, adducing the king in excuse.

When Jacob addressed himself to the king, Manachihr was even more vexed and at the instigation of the inhabitants of the province he ordered the eight deacons, who were in bonds, to be thrown into the sea. When Jacob the Great heard of this he returned to his own see full of anger, like Moses leaving the presence of Pharaoh [cf. Exod. 11:9]. Climbing a certain mountain from which the whole province was visible, he cursed Manachihr and his province. And God's judgment was not slow to overtake him. Like Herod, Manachihr died of various sufferings; the fertility of the irrigated province turned into a salt march [cf. Ps. 106:34], the sky overhead became bronze according to Scripture [cf. Deut. 28:23], and the sea, contrary [to its nature], covered the fields. When Vrt'anēs the Great and King Khosrov heard of this, in anger they ordered the captives to be freed and that the same man [Jacob] should be implored with penitence that the wrath of the Lord might be averted. After the depature of Jacob from this world, through his intercession Manachihr's son and heir obtained healing for the province by sincere repentance, copious tears, and lamentation.

8. Concerning the reign of Khosrov the Small, the transfer of the court, and the planting of the forest

In the second year of Ormizd, king of Persia, and the eighth year of reign of the Emperor Constantius, with the latter's help Khosrov became king. Not only did he give no evidence of prowess like his father's, but he did not even make any opposition to the regions that had rebelled, after the single occasion when they had been taken by the Greek armies. Leaving the Persian king to his wishes, he made peace with him, considering it sufficient to rule over the territories that he retained and having absolutely no desire for noble projects. Although he was small in body, yet he was not so small as Alexander of Macedon who was only three cubits high, though this did not impair the vigor of his spirit. But Khosrov was unconcerned for valor and good repute; he occupied himself with pleasure and hunting birds and other game. It was for this reason that he planted the forest beside the Azat River, which is called by his name to this day.

He also transferred the court to a spot above the forest and built a shady palace. The place is called Duin in Persian; in translation it means 'hill.' Because at that time the sun was in Ares, and there were blowing hot, fetid, and pestilential winds, which those who dwelt at Artashat could not endure, they willingly agreed to the change.

* * *

10. The death of Khosrov and the war of the Armenians with the Persians

After this, when Khosrov realized that Shapuh, the Persian king, was assisting his enemies, he broke the peace he had with him and withheld from him the special tribute, giving it [instead] to the emperor. And bringing up the Greek army he opposed the Persian king. But he lived not much longer before dying, having reigned for nine years. He was taken and buried in Ani beside his fathers. Vrt'anēs gathered all the Armenian princes with the army and the generals and entrusted the land of Armenia to Arshavir Kamsarakan, as the pre-eminent and most honorable man after the king. Then he took Tiran, Khosrov's son, and went to the emperor [to ask] that he might make him king of Armenia in his father's stead.

But the Persian king Shapuh, when he heard of Khosrov's death and that his son Tiran had gone to the emperor, gathered a great army under his brother Nerseh, as if he intended to make him king of Armenia. And he sent them to our country since he considered it to be leaderless. But they were opposed by the valiant Arshavir Kamsarakan with all the Armenian forces, who gave battles on the plain called Mṛul. And although many of the greatest nobles fell in the war, nonetheless the Armenian army, gaining the victory, put the Persian army to flight and guarded the land until Tiran's arrival.

11. Concerning the reign of Tiran, and the departure from this world of Vrt'anēs the Great, and the succession of Saint Yusik to the [patriarchal] throne

In the seventeenth year of his reign Augustus Constantius, son of Constantine, made Tiran, Khosrov's son, king and sent him to Armenia with Vrt'anēs the Great. After his arrival he peacefully gained control of our land, making a treaty with the Persians and not war. Paying tribute to the Greeks and a special tribute to the Persians, he lived in tranquility like his father and evinced no deed of bravery or valor. Nor did he follow his father's virtue, but in secret he abandoned all piety, although he was unable to serve vice openly because of Vrt'anēs the Great. After Vrt'anēs the Great had completed fifteen years of his episcopate, he departed from this world in the third year of Tiran. And at the latter's orders he was taken and buried in the village of T'ordan, as if he had seen with a prophetic eye that after a long time his father's relics would also be laid to rest in that spot. To the [patriarchal] throne succeeded Yusik his son in the fourth year of Tiran; he was a true follower of the virtues of his fathers.

12. The war of Shapuh against Constantius

But Shapuh, son of Ormizd, established greater friendship toward our King Tiran, even supporting and assisting him: he saved him from an attack of the northern nations who, having united, penetrated the pass of Chor and encamped on the borders of Albania for four years. Shapuh also subdued many barbarian nations into alliance, and then he attacked the Mediterranean lands and Palestine. But Constantius, after making Julian Caesar, took up arms against the Persians. And when they gave battle, both sides were defeated, for many fell from both sides. But neither turned their back to the other, so they came to terms and made peace for a few years. When Constantius returned from Persia, after a long illness he died in the city of Mospuestia in Cilicia, having reigned for twenty-three years. In his days appeared the luminous cross in the time of the blessed Cyril.

13. How Tiran[7] met Julian and gave hostages

At that time the impious Julian became emperor of the Greeks. He denied God, worshipped idols, raised persecutions and trouble against the church, and tried in many ways to extinguish the Christian faith. However, he did not induce belief by force but attempted by deceitful means to have the cult of Christ abolished and demons worshipped. When justice armed him against the Persians, he crossed Cilicia and reached Mesopotamia. The Persian army defending that area cut the cords of the bridge of boats across the Euphrates and barred the crossing. Then our King Tiran came down to meet Julian, attacked the Persian army, and dispersed it. Offering his services, he brought the impious Julian across with a host of cavalry, and he was very greatly honoured by him.

He [Tiran] requested that he [Julian] not take him with him to Persia on the grounds that he was unable to ride. Julian agreed but asked for troops and hostages. Tiran, to spare his second son Arshak, gave him his third son Trdat with his wife and sons, and also his grandson Tirit, son of the dead Artashes, his eldest son. These Julian accepted, and he immediately sent them to Byzantium. Tiran he dispatched to his own country, and he gave him his own image painted on tablets on which were also [the imageš] of various demons with him. He ordered it to be set up in church, at the eastern end, saying that whoever were tributary to the Roman empire acted thus. Tiran agreed and brought it back, unaware that by deceit the images of the demons would be worshipped.

14. The martyrdom of Saint Yusik and Daniel

Now when Tiran reached the province of Tsop'k', he wished to set up the image in his own royal church. But Saint Yusik snatched it from the king's hands, and throwing it to the ground, trampled on it and broke it to pieces, warning the king about the deceitfulness of the matter. Tiran paid no heed because he feared Julian and thought that he would be put to death for trampling on the emperor's image. And even more inflamed at the vexation he suffered from Saint Yusik by his continual reprimands at his transgressions, he ordered him to be beaten for a long time with thongs of ox hide, until he gave up the ghost under the whipping.

After his death Tiran was cursed by the old priest Daniel, who had been a disciple and servant of Saint Gregory's. So Tiran ordered him to be strangled. His disciples took him and buried him in his hermitage called 'the garden of ash trees.' The body of Saint Yusik they placed beside his father in the village of T'ordan. He had been in the episcopate for six years.

15. How Zawray took the Armenian army, seceded from Julian, and was slaughtered with his family

News of the murder of Saint Yusik and the murmuring of all the nobles reached the prince of the Řshtunik', Zawray, who was the general of the Armenian southern force in place of Manachihr and who had followed Julian with his army at Tiran's command. When he heard these reports, he said to his troops: 'Let us not heed the orders of the man who casts a stumbling block in the way of the worship of Christ and murders his saints. Let us not accompany this impious king.' Having persuaded his troops, he returned and fortified himself in Tmorik' until he could see what the other nobles would do. But Julian's couriers preceded his arrival, bringing to Tiran a letter, which ran as follows:

Julian's letter to Tiran

'The emperor Julian, offspring of Inak', son of Aramazd and destined for immortality, to Tiran our governor, greetings.

'The army that you sent to us has been taken off by its general and has deserted. We would have been able with our innumerable forces to send after them and halt them, but we allowed them to go for two reasons. First, lest the Persians say of us that it was by force and not of their free will that he led the army. And second, to test your sincerity. Now, if he has not done this at your wish, massacre him and his family so that no successor is left for him. Otherwise I swear by Ares, who granted us the throne, and by Athena, who gave us the victory, that on our return with our invincible might we shall destroy you and your country.'

When Tiran saw this he was very frightened, and he sent his mardpet, who was called Hayr, and with an oath summoned Zawray to his presence. But when his army saw that all the nobles remained silent, according to the usual lack of perseverance of our nation, they dispersed each one to his house. Zawray, being left alone, unwillingly went to the king. And the king seized him, took also their fortress of Alt'amar, and massacred them all. Only one child, the son of his brother Mehendak, escaped and was saved by his tutors. The king put in his place Salamut', the lord of Antsit.

Appendix 3   Select documents from Dura Europos

(1) FROM THE FILES OF THE XX COHORS PALMYRENORUM

Among the many documents on papyri recovered through excavation at Dura Europos (mod. Salihye) are those from the files of the *Cohors Vicesima Palmyrenorum*. It was formed probably from a contingent of Palmyrene archers who were known to be in the city in 170/1 and the oldest document which names the cohors is dated to AD 208. The unit was the main garrison of Dura until the fall of the city to the Persians in 256. It was a cohors miliaria divided with a maximum of six centuries of infantry, augmented by cavalry and dromedarii. The following three texts are chosen because of their uniqueness, their relatively good state of preservation and the fact that they fall chronologically into the period covered by this collection.
(For translation of military terms, see Glossary, pp. 401–402.)

(A) Morning reports

Unit journals had been in existence for the Roman Army since the Late Republic and the specimens from Dura are among the fullest preserved anywhere. Besides giving the total of the available manpower with separate statements of their NCOs for the infantry, the dromedarii and the cavalry, they also include such material of interest as the name(s) of the tribune, the full title of the unit (which changes with each new emperor) and departures and returns of detachments or individuals on specific tasks. For full discussion, see Fink, 1971: 179–82.

(i) *PDura* 82 (Inv. D. P. 3 R, Latin) (*c.* AD 233)

Col. i

March 27: net number of milites caligati 914,[1] including 9 centurions, 8 duplicarii, 1 sesquiplicarius, 34 dromedarii (including 1 sesquiplicarius), 223 equites, (including 5 decurions, 7 duplicarii, 4 sesquiplicarii), (total strength) of the Twentieth Palmyrene Cohort, Severiana Alexandriana.

Iulius Rufianus tribune: watch-word [   ] from the *septizonia*.[2]

Sent out [   ] 5 soldiers including [2?] dromedarii: from the century of Marianus, Aurelius Licinnius; from the century of Pudens, Aurelius Demetrius; from the century of Nigrinus, Aurelius Romanus and Aurelius Rufus; from the turma of Antoninus, Iarhaboles son of Odeatus.

Returned: Those previously dispatched with [   ] from the turma of Tiberinus [   ]. Timinius Paulinus, decurion, proclaimed the orders which had been sent [. . . We will do what is ordered,] and at every command we will be ready. There are standing watch at the signa of our lord Alexander Augustus: decurion Timinius Paulinus, aedituus Aurelius Silvanus, [   ] son of Vabalathus, curator Aurelius Rubathis, (title)[3] Iarhaeus son of Malchus, curator II Claudius Agrippas, eques [   ].

March 28: net number of milites caligati 914, including 9 centurions, 8 duplicarii, 1 sesquiplicarius, 34 dromedarii (including 1 sesquiplicarius), 223 equites (including 5 decurions, 7 duplicarii, 4 sesquiplicarii), (total strength) of the Twentieth Palmyrene Cohort, Severiana Alexandriana.

Iulius Rufianus tribune: [   ] from the *septizonia*.

[   ] Antoninus; from the century of Antoninus, Aurelius Marinus and (cancelled) Aurelius Heliodorus; from the century of Gaianus, Iarhaboles son of Iarhaeus; from the century of Nigrinus, Aurelius Apollinarius.

[   ] Gaianus son of Iarhaboles. [   ] Becchuf(rayn?) [   ] one soldier, from the century of Gaianus [   ].

[   ], from the century of Antoninus [   ].

Timinius Paulinus, decurion, proclaimed the orders which had been sent [. . . Because . . .] will be discharged (?) on March 29, supplicatio and animal sacrifice; and at every command we will be ready. There are standing watch at the signa of our lord Alexander Augustus: decurion Timinius Paulinus, [   ] Aurelius [   ], aedituus Aurelius Silvanus, signifer Claudius Natalius, librarius Aurelius Capiton, (title) Antonius Valentinus, optio II Ogelus son of

Malchus, eques [   ] Malchus son of Zebidas, eques Aelius Heliodorus [   ] Claudius Iulius Menander [   ].'

Col. ii

March 29: net number of milites caligati 914 [   ], (total strength) of the Twentieth Palmyrene cohort, Severiana Alexandriana.
Iulius Rufianus tribune [   ]. Sent to procure barley [   ] soldiers, including [   ] equites [   ].
Sent to arrange for transportation (or as escort) for the barley-collectors [   ] soldiers, from the century of Marianus [   ].
Returned: those previously dispatched to Atha: two soldiers, from the century of Nigrinus, Iulius Zabdibolus [   ].
Returned: those previously dispatched to the governor's headquarters with letters [   ] soldiers [   ].
Returned from among those previously dispatched with them to the governor's headquarters from the *cohors II eq* [   ]
Sent to procure wood for the bath 1 soldier, from the century of Nigrinus, Zebidas son of Barneus.
Sent (cancelled).
Timinius Paulinus, decurion, proclaimed the orders which had been sent [. . . There are standing watch . . .]: decurion Timinius Paulinus, aedituus Aurelius Silvanus [   ] III Aurelius Bassus, IIII Aurelius Heliodorus [   ].
March 30: number of milites caligati 914 [   ], (total strength) of the Twentieth
Palmyrene Cohort, Severiana Alexandriana.
Iulius Rufianus tribune: [   ].
[   ]
Absent without leave: four soldiers, from the century of [   ] from the century of Marianus [   ] son of Themarsas, from the century of [   ].
Missing (?): one eques [   ].
Transferred (?) [   ] from among those previously dispatched [   ].
Transferred (?) [   ] from [   ].'

(ii) *PDura* 89 (Inv. D. P. 9 R, Latin) (AD 239)

Aurelius Germanus, first centurion, proclaimed the orders which had been sent [   ] We will do what is ordered, and at every command we will be ready. There are standing watch at the signa of our lord the Emperor Marcus Antonius Gordianus Pius Felix

Invictus Augustus: centurion Aurelius Germanus, [   ] signifer Ulpius Marianus, bucinator Aurelius Priscus, sacerdos Themes son of Mocimus, tesserarius Aurelius Mocimus, (title) Ulpius Silvanus, signifer II Flavius Demetrius (the second of that name?), signifer III Aurelius Malchus, discens mensorem [   ] Aurelius Iarhaboles [   ] and [   ] four [   ] are ready.

May 27: there are in the winter quarters of the Twentieth Palmyrene Cohort, Gordiana, the net figure of (?) [   ], 781,[4] including 6 centurions, 8 duplicarii, 1 sesquiplicarius, 36 (?) dromedarii including [   ] sesquiplicarii, 233 (?) equites, including 4 decurions, 6 duplicarii, 2 sesquiplicarii: the total strength (?) of the Twentieth Palmyrene Cohort, Gordiana. [All (?)] were present.

'[   ] Avitus, legionary centurion, praepositus [   ]; sent as watch-word *Security.*

'Aurelius Germanus, first centurion, proclaimed the orders which had been sent [   ] We will do what is ordered, and at every command we will be ready. There are standing watch at the signa of our lord the Emperor Marcus Antonius Gordianus Pius Felix Invictus Augustus: centurion Aurelius Germanus, signifer Ulpius Marianus, bucinator Aurelius Priscus, sacerdos Themes son of Mocimus, tesserarius Aurelius Mocimus, (title) Ulpius Silvanus, signifer II Flavius Demetrius, signifer III Aurelius Malchus, discens mensorem [   ] Aurelius Iarhaboles [   ] and [   ].

May 28: there are in the winter quarters of the Twentieth Palmyrene Cohort, Gordiana, a net figure (?), 781, including 6 centurions, 8 duplicarii, 2 sesquiplicarii: [the total strength (?)] of the Twentieth Palmyrene Cohort, Gordiana. [All (?)] were present.

'[   ] Avitus, legionary centurion, praepositius [   ]; sent as watchword *Iuppiter Dolichenus sanctus* (?).

Recruits approved by [. . . . .]nius, vir clarissimus, our consularis, two in number, [   ], Aurelius Germanus, effective from May 10, AD 239.

[   ] Two recruits whose names [   ] also heights I have ordered appended [   ] approved [   ] in the Twentieth Palmyrene Cohort, Gordiana [   ].

(B) List of men and mounts

This unique document lists in detail cavalrymen of the cohort who had lost their mount and establishes the identity of each man's horse and the authority by which it had been approved or assigned.

The names of those listed probably came from the same turma. As six men out of nineteen had recently lost horses, the unit might well have been in action. The prospects of the unit could not have been very bright, with a quarter of its horses having to be replaced in a period of four months and a third of the equites still lacking mounts. Cf. Welles *et al.* 1959: 296–302 and Fink, 1971: 340–4.

PDura 97 (Inv. D. P. 3 V, Latin) (AD 251, after 31 August): . .].lus son of Malchus: lost his horse effective from the day before [date]. (The original entry, cancelled after 'son of Malchus,' ran as follows: '. .].lus son of Malchus: a horse, four years old [   ], white [fore or hind feet?], brands on right thigh and shoulder, approved by the then prefects, October 20, AD 246[5]: 125 denarii.')
Malchus son of Goras: lost his horse [date].
Aurelius Alexander: a horse, *aequatus* (with smooth teeth?, i.e. seven or more years old), [   ], approved by Atilius Cosminus then consularis, March 16, AD 251: 125 denarii.
[Name: a horse, etc.], two years old, black brands on right thigh and shoulder, approved by then prefects, December 29, AD 251: 125 denarii.
[Name]: lost [his horse, date].
[Name]: a horse, [   ], protruding muzzle, white hind feet, without brand, approved by Atilius Cosminus then consularis, March 16, AD 251: 125 denarii.
[Name]: a horse, [   ], mouse-coloured, brands on right thigh and left shoulder, approved by the then prefects, December 29, AD 245: 125 denarii.
[Name]: a horse, [   ], approved by the then prefects, same day and year: 125 denarii.
[Name] son of Vhabalathus: a horse, [   ], approved by the then prefects, September 10, AD 249: 125 denarii.
Aurelius Bar[. . . . .]s: lost his horse [date].
[Name]: a horse, [   ], white hind feet, without brand, approved by Atilius Cosminus then consularis, January 22, AD251: 125 denarii.
[Name: a horse, etc.], reddish-bay, brand on right shoulder, appraised (?) by Pomponius Laetianus, vir egregius, procurator of our two Augusti, April 13, AD 251: 45 denarii[   ] 55 denarii.
Aurelius Mambogeus: [a horse], four years old, [etc., appraised?] by Pomponius Laetianus, vir egregius, procurator of our two Augusti, May [8–14] AD 251: 125 denarii.
Also SAL[   ].

Barhathes son of Maesum: a mare, *aequata* (with smooth teeth?),
[   ], without brand, approved by the then prefects, September 21,
AD 249.

[Name]: a mare, four years old, [   ], whitish fore feet, without
brand, 'sealed' by Licinius Pacatianus then dux, August 10, AD 245.

[Name: lost] his horse August 31, AD 251.

[Name: a mare], *aequata* (with smooth teeth?), reddish-sooty? (or
dirty red?), brand on left [   ], 'sealed' by Licinius Pacatianus then
dux, August 11, AD 245.

[Name]: a horse, *aequatus* (with smooth teeth?), [   ], bluish-
gray?, [brand on] left thigh, approved by Ulpius Tertius then dux,
[day and month], AD 248.

(2) DOCUMENTS IN MIDDLE IRANIAN

(A) Letter of a Persian official to Shapur

The discovery from a house inside Dura of a letter in Middle
Persian sent by an important official in charge of transportation
who appears to be on familiar terms with Shapur seems to give
support of Rostovtzeff's hypothesis that the city was briefly held by
the Persians in 253. Rostovtzeff (1943: 52–60) adduced this from
an incomplete wall painting of horsemen in a Sassanian style of a
Persian (?) victory from a private house and a drawing found in the
office of the *actuarius* of the XX Palmyrene Cohort. depicting a
Roman officer sacrificing to the Palmyrene god Jarhibol in the
presence of a mounted dignitary apparently in Palmyrene dress
whom Rostovtzeff identified as Odaenathus and to whom he
credited the restoration of the city to Roman rule during his first
expedition against the Persians. Bellinger (1943: 64–5 and 1949:
209) has shown that such a view appears to be supported by the
provenance and the apparent date of burial of at least six
coin-hoards in the city and its vicinity as these contain no coins
issued later than 253. MacDonald (1986: 56–60) has recently
challenged Rostovtzeff's interpretation of the paintings on the
grounds that the mounted figure in the first lacked a number of
Sassanian attributes and that the second represents the scene of an
oft-repeated ceremony rather than a celebration of a Palmyrene
victory. Although there is little doubt that the city finally fell in 256
(see above, Ch. 3, note 23), the fact the hoards only contain coins
issued in 253 or earlier only points to a *terminus post quem* of the
event. They might have been buried in 253 by citizens in panic

when Shapur's army advanced from Pirisabora to Anatha at the beginning of his 'Second' Campaign. Cf. Kettenhofen, 1982: 78. The following letter, found behind Blocks L7 and L8 in Wall Street, therefore, could have been composed, *mutatis mutandis*, during or after the fall of the city.

PDura 154 (Inv. D. Pg. 37, Middle Persian):
  (Recto)
    . . . . greetings, homage, much sent (to) all. And now:–
    . . . . so servants and slaves (?) did . . . .
    . . . . then further you said that . . . .
    . . . . whereas a rescript from Shapur . . . .
5   . . . . Shapur to M . . . .
    . . . . gave [instructions?]that I. . . .
    . . . . apart from. . . ., that . . . .
    . . . . I and you (?) . . . .

  (Verso)
  Bring the load towards the Tigris . . . .
  there is not. Now send me something that . . . .
  where there be something of mine, as extra-load (?) . . . .
  apart from [that which is] herein required, ...
5   [blank]
    . . . . the chief(?) army-corps (?) . . . .
  [blank]

                              (Henning, *ap.* Welles, 1959: 416)

(B) Inscriptions from the Synagogue

Among other sources possibly related to the history of the fall of the city are a number of dipinti and graffiti in Middle Iranian from the Jewish Synagogue at Dura in one of the buildings which were dismantled in the building of the embankment to counter Persian efforts at mining. The dipinti record the visit to the synagogue and the viewing of its famous wall-paintings by important persons, some accompanied by their scribes. Several of the dipinti are dated to the fourteenth or fifteenth years (presumably of the reign of Shapur, i.e. between 253 and 254).
A typical specimen reads:

In the month Miθr, in the year
fourteen, and on the day Saθrevar,
when Yazdānpēsē, the scribe,

and the scribe of the radak
to this house
came
[and by them] this picture [was looked at]
[and] by them praise was made.

(No. 43, p. 302, trans. Geiger)

Geiger (*ap.* Kraeling, 1956: 297–300) argues against the visitors being Jews from Babylonia on grounds of their unmistakably Iranian names, some even being theophoric of Zoroastrian deities. Some might have been Persian envoys sent to Dura before its fall who visited the synagogue as part of their sight-seeing. One, according to Geiger, even left a warning of the impending doom of the city by referring to the Jewish religious leader who accompanied him as *zndky* – a term which Geiger equates with mp. *zndyky* (heretic, esp. used of the Manichaeans):

In the month Miθr, in [the year] fourteen, and
    on the day *[Fravar]ṭin*
When Hormazd, the scribe, and Kantak, the *zandak*,
    and the scribe of the building,
and this *zandak* of the Jews to his edifice of the
    God [of] the Gods
of the Jews came and by them [. . .] this picture was
    beheld,
and by them it was looked at and beheld [. . .],
    it was looked at,
[. . .] the picture [. . .]'

(No. 44, p. 344, trans. Geiger)

Geiger's interpretation of *zndky* has not won universal acceptance. (See e.g. Gignoux, 1972: 38 who defines it as '(?) titulature juive'.) Moreover, as MacDonald (1986: 62) has pointed out, 'repetitive inspection of this small facility within a short time is hardly likely', if we are to assume that the majority of these visits took place while the city was briefly held by the Sassanians. Some Jews in Babylonia were known to have become so Iranized that they had adopted Iranian names (cf. Neusner, 1966: 100–3). The majority of these visitors were probably Jews from Babylonia where there were stronger Jewish communities than anywhere in the cities along the Eastern Roman frontier. The relevance of these texts to the political history of the city has been unjustifiably exaggerated.

Appendix 4 Eastern victories in imperial titulature. From Alexander Severus to Constantius II (222–361)[1]

Alexander Severus (Aug. 222–235)
PARTICO MAX. [PERSICO] MAX.(?)[2]

Philip (Aug. 224–229)
PERSICUS MAXIMUS (*CIL* VI, 1097 [after 244])
PARTHICUS MAXIMUS (*CIL* III, 4634, ibid. 10619, ibid. 143546)

Gallienus (Aug. 253–268)
GERM. PERSICUS MAX. (*CIL* III, 22765 [262 or 263])
PARTH. MAX. GERM. (*IRT* 956 [262])
GERM. MAX. PARTH. MAX. (*CIL* X, 4784 [265] and XI, 3089)
GERM. MAX. PERS. MAX. (*EE* IX, 582 [264 or 265])
GERM. MAX. DAC. MAX. PERS. MAX. (*IRT* 927 [264])

Claudius II (Aug. 268–270)
GOTH. MAX. PARTH. MAX. (*CIL* VIII, 4876 [?269])

Aurelian (Aug. 270–275)
ARABICUS MAX. CARP. MAX. PERS. MAX. (*CIL* II, 4506 [10 Dec. 271/ 9 Dec. 272])
ARABICUS MAX. PERSICUS MAX. (*AE* 1936, 129 [271/2])
[GERMANICO GOTHIC]O PARTHICO (*CIL* VIII, 9040 [10 Dec. 271/ 9 Dec. 272])
PARTH. MAX. GOTH. MAX. GERM. MAX. CARP. MAX. (*CIL* III, 7586 [end of 272, before 10 Dec.])
GERM. MAX. GOTH. MAX. PARTH. MAX. (*CIL* XII, 2673 [274] and 5456 [before 10 Dec., 273]) GERM. MAX. GOTH. MAX. PAR]TH. MAX. CARP. MAX. (*CIL* XII, 5549, [after 273])
GERM. MAX. GOTH. MAX. PARTH. MAX. PERS. MAX. (*CIL* XII, 5561 [after 273])

GOTH. MAX. PALMYRENICUS MAX. GERM. MAX. (*CIL* V, 4319 [Dec. 274])
GOTH. MAX. GERM. MAX. PARTH. MAX. CARP. MAX. (*CIL* VI, 1112 [end of 274])
GERM. MAX. GOTH. MAX. PARTH. MAX. DAC. MAX. CARP. MAX. (*CIL* XIII, 8973 [275])

Vaballathus (Aug. 272)
PERS. MAX. ARAB. MAX. ADIAB. MAX. (*AE* 1904, 60 [270/1])

Probus (Aug. 276–282)
Γωθ. μέγ, Περσ. μέγ. Γερμ, μέγ. (*POxy.* 164, 35 [280])
Παρθ. μέγ. Γωθ. μέγ. (*POxy.* 168, 32 [282])
Γωθ. μέγ, Παρθ. μέγ. Γερμ, μέγ. (*POxy.* 1256, 20–21 [282])
Γερμ. μέγ, Μηδ. μέγ. Παρθ. μέγ. (*PAmh.* 106, 4 [282])

Carus (Aug. 282–283)
Περσικός (*IGR* I, 1144 [282/3])
PERS. MAX. GERM. MAX. (*CIL* VIII, 12522 [282/3])

Carinus (Aug. 283–285) and Numerianus (Aug. 283–285)
GERM. MAX. BRIT. MAX. PERS. MAX. (*CIL* XIV, 126 [284] and 127)

Diocletian (Aug. 284–305)
GERM. MAX. PERS. MAX. (*CIL* III, 5810 [290])
GERM. MAX. II SARM. MAX. PERS. MAX. (*CIL* XIII, 5249 [294])
GERM. MAX. V SARM. MAX. IIII PERS. MAX. II BRIT. MAX. (*CIL* III, 6151 [before 300])
Ἰβηρικὸς μέγ. Περσ. Βρετ. Γερμ. μέγ. Σαρμ. μέγ. (*IGR* I, 1291, 21–22 [between 298 and 305])
GERM. MAX. VI SARM. MAX. IIII PERS. MAX. II BRIT. MAX. CARP. MAX. ARAM.[3] MAX. MED. MAX. ADIAB. MAX. (*AE* 1973, 526a [301, before 1 Sept.])
GERM. MAX. VI SARM. MAX. IIII PERS. MAX. II BRIT. MAX. CARP. MAX. ARMEN. MAX. MED. MAX. ADIAB. MAX. (*CIL* III, p. 824 [301, between 20 Nov. and 9 Dec., cf. Barnes, 1982: 23])
[SARM. MAX. V PERS. MAX. II BRIT. MAX. CARP. MAX. V] ARMEN. MAX. II MED. MAX. [ADIAB. MAX.] (*AE* 1958, 190 [7 January 304 or 305, cf. Barnes, 1982: 19–20])
Γερμ. μέγ. Σαρμ. μέγ. [Παρ]θ. μέγ. Περσ. μέγ. Βρετ. μέγ. Καρπ. μέγ. Ἀδιαβ. μέγ. Μηδ. μέγ. (*PThead.* 2, 2–3 [11 Mar. 305])

Maximianus Herculius (Aug. 286–305)
GERM. MAX. SARM. MAX. PERS. MAX. (*CIL* XIII, 5249 [294])

'Αρμενικὸς Μηδ. 'Αδιαβ. (*IGR* I, 1291, 25 [between 298 and 305])

GERM. MAX. V SARM. MAX. IIII PERS. MAX. II BRIT. MAX. (*CIL* III, 6151 [before 300])

GERM. MAX. V SARM. MAX. III PERS. MAX. II BRIT. MAX. PART. MAX. ARAB.[4] MAX. MED. MAX. ADIAB. MAX. (*AE* 1973, 526a [301, before 1 Sept.])

GERM. MAX. V SARM. MAX. IIII PERS. MAX. II BRIT. MAX. CARP. MAX. MED. MAX. ADIAB. MAX. (*CIL* III, p. 824 [301, between 20 Nov. and 9 Dec.])

GERM. [MAX. VIII SARM. MAX. IV PERS. MAX. II BRIT.] MAX. CARP. MAX. V ARMEN. MAX. II MED. MAX. ADIAB. MAX. (*AE* 1958, 190 [7 January 304 or 305])

Γερμ. μέγ. Σαρμ. μέγ. [Παρ]θ. μέγ. Περσ. μέγ. Βρετ. μέγ. Καρπ. μέγ. Ἀδιαβ. μέγ. Μηδ. μέγ. (*PThead.* 2, 2–3 [11 Mar. 305])

Constantius Chlorus (Caes. 293–305, Aug. 305–306)

GERM. MAX. V SARM. MAX. IIII PERS. MAX. BRIT. MAX. (*CIL* III, 6151 [before 300])

Γερμ. Περσ. Βριτ. Παρθ. 'Αρμενικὸς 'Αδιαβ. (*IGR* I, 1291,30 [between 298 and 305])

GERM. SARM. PERS. BRIT. CARP. ARAM.[5] MED. ADIAB. (*AE* 1973: 526a [301, before 1 Sept.])

GERM. MAX. II SARM. MAX. II PERS. MAX. II BRIT. MAX. CARP. MAX. ARMEN. MAX. MED. MAX. ADIAB. MAX. (*CIL* III, p. 824 [301, between 20 Nov. and 9 Dec.])

[GERM. MAX. V SARM. MAX. III PE]RS. MAX. BRIT. MAX. CARP. MAX. V ARMEN. MAX. MED. MAX. (*AE* 1958, 190 [7 January 304 or 305])

Γερμ. μέγ. Σαρμ. μέγ. Περσ. μέγ. (*PThead.* 2, 3 [11 Mar. 305])

GERM. MAX. V SARM. MAX. III PERS. MAX. II BRIT. MAX. II CARP. MAX. V ARMEN. MAX. MED. MAX. ADIAB. MAX. (*AE* 1961, 240 [7 Jan., 306])

Galerius (Caes. 293–305, Aug. 305–311)

PERS. MAX. SARM. MAX. BRIT. MAX. (*CIL* VI, 1137)

GERM. MAX. V SARM. MAX. IIII PERS. MAX. BRIT. MAX. (*CIL* III, 6151 [before 300])

GERM. SARM. PERS. BRIT. CARP. ARAM.[6] MED. ADIAB. (*AE* 1973: 526a [301, before 1 Sept.])

GERM. MAX. II SARM. MAX. II PERS. MAX. II BRIT. MAX. CARP. MAX. ARMEN. MAX. MED. MAX. ADIAB. MAX. (*CIL* III, p. 824 [301, between 20 Nov. and 9 Dec.])

[GERM. MAX. V SARM. MAX. III PE]RS. MAX. BRIT. MAX. CARP. MAX. V ARMEN. MAX. MED. MAX. (*AE* 1958, 190 [7 Jan. 304 or 305])
Γερμ. μέγ. Σαρμ. μέγ. Περσ. μέγ. (*PThead.* 2, 3 [11 Mar. 305])
GERM. MAX. V SARM. MAX. III PERS. MAX. II BRIT. MAX. II CARP. MAX. V ARMEN. MAX. MED. MAX. ADIAB. MAX. (*AE* 1961, 240 [7 Jan., 306])
GERM. MAX. VII AEGYPT. MAX. THEB. MAX. SARM. MAX. V PERS. MAX. III BRIT.
MAX. II CARP. MAX. VI ARM. MAX. MED. MAX. ADIAB. MAX. (*CIL* III, 12133, [late 310, cf. Barnes, 1982: 21])
PERS. MAX. III BRIT. MED. MAX. ADIAB. MAX. (*CIL* III, 6979 [late 310, cf. Barnes, 1982: 21])
Γερμ. μέγ. <VII>, 'Αιγυπ. μέγ. Θηβαΐ. μέγ. Σαρμ. μέγ. V Περσ. μέγ. <III Βρετ. μέγ.> II Κάρπ. μέγ. VI 'Αρμεν. μέγ. Μηδ. μέγ. 'Αδιαβ. μέγ. (Eusebius, *hist. eccl.* VIII, 17, 3 [311, cf. Barnes, 1982: 22])

Maximinus Daia (Aug. *c.* 309–313)
SARM. GERM. PERS. (*ILAl* I, 3956 [312/3])

Constantine (Caes. and Aug. 306–337)
GERM. SARM. PERS. (*ILAl* I, 3956 [312/3])
PERS. MAX. ADIAB. MAX. MED. MAX. GOTH. MAX. (*CIL* VIII, 23116 [315])
GERM. MAX. III SARM. MAX. BRIT. MAX. CARP. MAX. ARAB. MAX. MED. MAX. ARMEN. MAX. GOTH. MAX. (*CIL* VIII, 8412 [318 or 319])

Constantius II (Caes. 324–337, Aug. 337–361)
SARMATICUS [PER]SIC[US] MAX.[7] (*CIL* III, 12483 [before 340])
GOTH. MAX. ADIAB. MAX. (*CIL* III, 3705 [354])

Appendix 5 The frontier units according to the *notitia dignitatum*

'The List (*notitia*) of all high offices (*dignitatum*), both civil and military, in the Eastern (*Oriens*) and Western (*Occidens*) parts' of the Empire, preserved only in the form of a copy made in 1551, of an original manuscript, now lost, which existed in Speir, is a document of unique importance to the study of the distribution of army units along the Eastern Frontier. The list contains the titles of high officials, those of their staff officers, illustrations of military and civil insignia as well as an enumeration of military units and their garrisons. The work is divided into two parts, covering the Eastern and Western halves of the Empire as it was divided in 395. It is generally accepted that the Eastern half of the work was finished before 413 and probably not much later than 395. The disposition of the frontier units in the East reflects the frontier changes after Jovian's treaty with Shapur in 363 as no units are assigned to fortresses ceded to the Persians in the treaty such as Nisibis, Singara, Bezabde and Castra Maurorum. Nevertheless, many of the units listed in the Notitia would have been in their given bases in the period between Diocletian and Jovian. Epithets such as 'Diocletiana', 'Iovia', 'Herculia', 'Valeria', 'Flavia' and 'Constantina' suggest Tetrarchic or Constantinian origins to their bearers. Similarly, 'Valentiana', 'Valentiniana', 'Honoriana' or 'Gratiana' presuppose post-Jovianic dates for the units' formation. Therefore, despite its Theodosian date of composition, the Notitia is a frequently cited document in any serious study of the military reforms and frontier reorganization from the Tetrarchy onwards and of the historical geography of the frontier regions. Cf. Jones, 1964 (iii): 347–80 and Hoffmann, 1969: 516–19.

[In the MS. each of the following lists is preceded by a diagram enclosing names of the principal forts in each ducate.]
(For translation of military terms, see Glossary on p. 401)

Or. XXXII, 17–44: (Phoenice)

(17) Under the control of the *vir spectabilis* the *dux Foenicis:*
(18) Equites Mauri Illyriciani, at Otthara (Ghounthour, cf. Dussaud, 1927: 268)
(19) Equites scutarii Illyriciani, at Euhari (Euhara in diagram; Hauwarin, ibid.)
(20) Equites promoti indigenae, at Saltatha[1]
(21) Equites Dalmatiae Illyriciani, at Lataui[2]
(22) Equites promoti indigenae, at Avatha[3] Site not securely identified.
(23) Equites promoti indigenae, at Nazala (mod. Qaryatein)
(24) Equites sagittarii indigenae, at Abina (Abira in diagram, = Abira[ca], mod. Khan. al-Basiri, castellum on the Strata Diocletiana, cf. Poidebard, 1932: 47 and Van Berchem, 1952: 13)
(25) Equites sagittarii indigenae, at Casama[4]
(26) Equites sagittarii indigenae, at Calamona[5]
(27) Equites Saraceni indigenae, at Betproclis (mod. Bir el-Fourqlos on the main road between Emesa and Palmyra)
(28) Equites Saraceni, at Thelsee (mod. Dmeir, a major Roman camp dating back to the Antonine period can be found to the east of the city, cf. Dussaud, 1927: 270)
(29) Equites sagittarii indigenae, at Adatha[6]
(30) (Headquarters of the) Prefect of Legio I Illyricorum,[7] at Palmyra
(31) (Headquarters of the) Prefect of Legio III Gallica, at Danaba[8]
(32) And these which are assigned from the lesser register (*de minore laterculo*):
(33) Ala prima Damascena, at Mons Iovis (not identified)
(34) Ala nova Diocletiana, at Veriaraca (or Beriaraca, mod. Khan el-Hallabat, castellum on the Strata Diocletiana)
(35) Ala prima Francorum, at Cunna (not identified)
(36) Ala prima Alamannorum, at Neia (probably [Car]neia, Khan el-Qattar)
(37) Ala prima Saxonum, at Verofabula[9]
(38) Ala prima Foenicum, at Rene[10]
(39) Ala secunda Salutis, at Arefa (= Arpha in Jos., *Bell. Jud.*

III,57, unidentified, probably east of Trachonitis)

(40) Cohors tertia Herculia, at Veranoca (not identified)

(41) Cohors quinta pacata Alamannorum, at Onevatha (= Anab[atha], Khan Aneybe)

(42) Cohors prima Iulia lectorum, at Vallis Alba (Khan el-Manqoura)

(43) Cohors secunda Aegyptiorum, at Vallis Diocletiana (Khan at-Trab)

(44) Cohors prima Orientalis, at Thama (Khan as-Samat).

Or. XXXIII, 15–35: (Syria and Euphratensis)

(15) Under the command of the *vir spectabilis*, the *dux Syriae et Euphratensis*:

(16) Equites scutarii Illyriciani, at Seriane (Isriye. Cf. Dussaud, 1927: 273 and Mouterde–Poidebard, 1945: 90–1)

(17) Equites promoti Illyriciani, at Occariba ('Agerbat. Cf. ibid. p. 49)

(18) Equites sagittarii indigenae, at Matthana (not identified)

(19) Equites promoti indigenae, at Adada (Qasr el-Hûr. Cf. Mouterde–Poidebard, 1945: 103–4 and 115)

(20) Equites sagittarii indigenae, at Anatha (Ana, see above, Ch. 3, n. 8)

(21) Equites sagittarii, at Acadama (Qdeym. Cf. Mouterde–Poidebard, 1945: 103–6)

(22) Equites sagittarii, at Acauatha

(23) (Headquarters of the) Prefect of Legio IV Scythica, at Oresa (?Oriza, at-Tayibe, about 90 km. N.E. of Palmyra)

(24) In Augusta Euphratensis:

(25) Equites Dalmatae Illyriciani, at Barbalissos (Balis)

(26) Equites Mauri Illyriciani, at Neocaesarea (Dibsi Faraj)[11]

(27) Equites promoti indigenae, at Rosafa (= Resapha-Sergiopolis)

(28) (Headquarters of the) Prefect of Legio XVI Falvia firma, at Sura (Suriya)

(29) And these which are assigned from the lesser register:

(30) Ala prima nova Herculia, at Ammuda ('Amouda. Cf. Poidebard, 1932: 158)

(31) Ala prima Iuthungorum, at Salutaria (not identified)

(32) Cohors prima Gotthorum, at Helela (Hlehle. Cf. Poidebard, 1932: 76)

(33) Cohors prima Ulpia Dacorum, at Claudiana (not identified)

(34) Cohors tertia Valeria, at Marmantarum (not identified)
(35) Cohors prima victorum, at Ammattha (confusion for Admatha? See below Or. XXXIV, 33.)

Or. XXXIV, 17–48: (Palestina)

(17) Under the control of the *vir spectabilis*, the *dux Palestinae*:
(18) Equites Dalmatae Illyriciani, at Benosaba (Beersheba. Cf. *GRP*, pp. 35–6)
(19) Equites promoti Illyriciani, at Menochia (or Maon, Khan Ma' in. Cf. *GRP*, p. 78)
(20) Equites scutarii Illyriciani, at Chermula (el Kamil. Cf. *GRP*, p. 78)
(21) Equites Mauri Illyriciani, at Aelia (i.e. Aelia Capitolina, Jerusalem. Cf. *GRP*, pp. 69–70)
(22) Equites Thamudeni Illyriciani, at Birsama (Khan el Fâr. Cf. *GRP*, p. 43)
(23) Equites promoti indigenae, at Sabaia (or Asabaia, Qsar Supa'ia. Cf. *GRP*, p. 32)
(24) Equites promoti indigenae, at Zodocatha (es Sadaqa. Cf. *GRP*, p. 104)
(25) Equites sagittarii indigenae, at Hauana (or Hauare,? Khan el Khaldi cf. *GRP*, p. 64)
(26) Equites sagittarii indigenae, at Zoara (Ghôr es Sâfi. Cf. *GRP*, p. 104)
(27) Equites sagittarii indigenae, at Robatha (Khan er Ruwat. Cf. *GRP*, p. 91)
(28) Equites primi felices [sagittarii indigenae] Palestini, at Sabure (Sobora, es Sabre. Cf. *GRP*, p. 97) or Veterocaria
(29) Equites sagittarii indigenae, at Moahile (?Qasr Mahalle. Cf. *GRP*, p. 81)
(30) (Headquarters of the) Prefect of Legio X Fretensis, at Aila ('Aqaba. Cf. *GRP*, p. 27)
(31) And these which are assigned from the lesser register:
(32) Ala prima miliaria Sebestana, at Asuada (Khan es Samra. Cf. *GRP*, p. 33)
(33) Ala Antana dromedariorum, at Admatha (or Ammatha, Humeima. cf. *GRP*, p. 28)
(34) Ala Constantiana, at Toloha (Qasr et Tlâh. Cf. *GRP*, p. 102)
(35) Ala secunda felix Valentiana, near Praesidium (Ghôr el Feife. Cf. *GRP*, p. 89)

(36)   Ala prima miliaria, at Hasta (Wâdi el Khusaiya. Cf. *GRP*, p. 64)

(37)   Ala Idiota constituted (?)[12]

(38)   Cohors duodecima Valeria, at Afro (Ophrah, Seil 'Afra near et Taiyibe. Cf. *GRP*, p. 85)

(39)   Cohors decima Carthaginensis, at Cartha (var. Sartha, Sari. Cf. *GRP*, p. 93)

(40)   Cohors prima agentenaria (?), at Tarba[13]

(41)   Cohors quarta Frygum, at Praesidium (el Kitara in Wâdi 'Itm. Cf *GRP*, p. 88)

(42)   Cohors secunda Gratiana, at Iehibo[14]

(43)   Cohors prima equitata, at Calamona (Bîr Madhkûr? Cf. *GRP*, p. 45)

(44)   Cohors secunda Galatarum, at Arieldela (Gharandal. Cf. *GRP*, p. 31)

(45)   Cohors prima Flavia, at Moleatha (Malatha, Tell el Milh. Cf. *GRP*, p. 78)

(46)   Cohors quarta Palaestinorum, at Thamana (Tamara, 'Ain el Hûsb. Cf. *GRP*, p. 99)

(47)   Cohors secunda Cretensis, near to the River Jordan

(48)   Cohors prima salutaria, between Aelia and Hiericius (Jericho. Cf. *GRP*, p. 78)[15]

Or. XXXV, 14–34: (Osrhoene)

(14)   Under the control of the *vir spectabilis*, the *dux Osrhoenae*.

(15)   Equites Dalmatae Illyriciani, at Ganaba (Gallaba in diagram)[16]

(16)   Equites promoti Illyriciani, at Callinicum (mod. Raqqa)

(17)   Equites Mauri Illyriciani, at Dabana ('Aïn el 'Arous on the Balikh, south of Carrhae)

(18)   Equites promoti indigenae, at Banasa[17]

(19)   Equites promoti indigenae, at Sina Iudaeorum (Fafa, 45 km. N.N.W. of Nisibis)

(20)   Equites sagittarii indigenae, at Oraba (Tell Adjadje West or Arban, on the Khabur, about 40 km. S. of Thannuris, cf. Röllig–Kuhne, 1977: 125)

(21)   Equites sagittarii indigenae, at Thillaamana[18]

(22)   Equites sagittarii indigenae Medianenses, at Mediana[19]

(23)   Equites [sagittarii indigenae] primi Osrhoeni, at Rasis (*sic*)[20]

(24)   Prefect of the Legio IV Parthica, at Circesium (al-Buseir)

(25)   [. . .],[21] at Apatna[22]

(26) And these which are assigned from the lesser register:
(27) Ala septima Valeria praelectorum, at Thillacama[23]
(28) Ala prima Victoriae, at Touia (Seeck: Iovia?) opposite to Bintha (*contra Bintha*)[24]
(29) Ala secunda Paflagonum, at Thillafica[25]
(30) Ala prima Parthorum, at Resaia (*sic*) (i.e. Rhesaina)[26]
(31) Ala prima nova Diocletiana, between Thannuris (Tell Touneynir) and Horaba (perhaps = Oraba in line 20)[27]
(32) Cohors prima Gaetulorum, at Thillaamana
(33) Cohors prima Eufratensis, at Maratha[28]
(34) Ala prima salutaria, formed (constituta) at Duodecimus (not identified)

Or. XXXVI, 18–36: (Mesopotamia)

(18) Under the command of the *vir spectabilis*, the *dux Mesopotamiae*:
(19) Equites scutarii Illyriciani, at Amida (Diyarbakir)
(20) Equites promoti Illyriciani, at Rhesaina-Theodosiopolis (Ras al 'Ain)
(21) Equites ducatores Illyriciani, at Amida
(22) Equites felices Honoriani Illyriciani, at Constantina (Viransehir)
(23) Equites promoti indigenae, at Constantina
(24) Equites promoti indigenae, at Apadna[29]
(25) Equites sagittarii indigenae Arabanenses, at Mefana-Cartha (= Maiferqat?)[30]
(26) Equites scutarii indigenae Pafenses,[31] at Assara[32]
(27) Equites sagittarii indigenae Thibithenses,[33] at Thilbisme[34]
(28) Equites sagittarii indigenae, at Thannuri.
(29) Prefect of the Legio I Parthica Nisibena,[35] at Constantina
(30) Prefect of the Legio II Parthica,[36] at Cefa.
(31) And these which are assigned from the lesser register:
(32) Ala secunda nova Aegyptiorum, at Cartha[37]
(33) Ala octava Flavia Francorum, at Ripaltha (= Ripalthas in Procop., *aed.* II, iv, 14, on the right bank of the Tigris, upstream from Cefa. Cf. Dillemann, 1962: 231–2.)
(34) Ala quintadecima Flavia Carduenorum,[38] at Caini[39]
(35) Cohors quinquagenaria Arabum, at Bethallaha[40]
(36) Cohors quartadecima Valeria Zabdenorum,[41]
at Maiocariri (= Meicarire in Amm. XVII, 10, 1 and Maïacariri in Theophylactus Simocatta I, 13, 4. Mod. Khan Cheikhan, in the Tur

Abdin on the route from Monocarton to the Tigris. Cf. Dillemann, 1962: 157)

Or. XXXVII, 14–35: (Arabia)[42]

(13)   Under the control of the *vir spectabilis*, the *dux Arabiae*:

(14)   Equites scutarii Illyriciani, at Motha (Imtan. Cf. *GRP*, p. 81)

(15)   Equites promoti Illyriciani, at Tricomia (Qasr el Bâghiq, near Salkhad. Cf. *GRP*, p. 102)

(16)   Equites Dalmatae Illyriciani, at Ziza (Jiza, 5 km. S. of el-Qastal, near Zuweiza. Cf. Parker, 1986: 41)

(17)   Equites Mauri Illyriciani, at Areopolis (or Raggath Moab, mod. Rabba. Cf. *GRP*, p. 90)

(18)   Equites promoti indigenae, at Speluncis[43]

(19)   Equites promoti indigenae, at Mefa (Na'afa. cf. *GRP*. p. 80)

(20)   Equites sagittarii indigenae, at Gadda (Khan Samra. Cf. *GRP*, p. 58)

(21)   (Headquarters of the) Prefect of the Legio III Cyrenaica, at Bostra (Busra eski Sham. Cf. *GRP*, p. 43)

(22)   (Headquarters of the) Prefect of the Legio IV Martia,[44] at Betthorus (el-Lejjûn, the site of a legionary fortress east of the Dead Sea. Cf. Brünnow, 1909: 71 and Parker, 1986: 10 and 59–74)

(23)   Equites sagittarii indigenae, at Dia-Fenis (?)45

(24)   And these which are assigned from the lesser register:

(25)   Ala nona miliaria, Auatha (see above Or. XXXII, 7)

(26)   Ala sexta Hispanorum, at Gomoha (Jumha. Cf. *GRP*, p. 63)

(27)   Ala secunda Constantiana, at Libona (el Lubbân. Cf. *GRP*, p. 75)

(28)   Ala secunda Miliarensis, at Naarsafari (Naar Sarari, Khan Qasr el Buleida in Wadi Zafri. Cf. *GRP*, p. 82)

(29)   Ala prima Valentiana, at Thainatha (Umm el Jîmal. Cf. *GRP*, p. 100)

(30)   Ala secunda felix Valentiniana, near (*apud*) Adittha[46]

(31)   Cohors prima miliaria Thracum, at Adtitha (*sic*)[47]

(32)   Cohors prima Thracum, at Asabaia (Qasr Supa'ia. Cf. *GRP*, p. 32)

(33)   Cohors octava voluntaria, at Valtha (Khan Ishkandar in Wâdi el Wâlî. Cf. *GRP*, p. 103)

(34)   Cohors tertia felix Arabum, at the Arnona Camp on the bank of the river Vade Afaris (Wadi Hafir. Cf. *GRP*, p. 103)

(35) Cohors tertia Alpinorum, near Arnona (Wadi Mojib. Cf. *GRP*, p. 31)[48]

Or. XXXVIII, 10–30: (Armenia and Pontus)

(10) Under the command of the *vir spectabilis*, the *dux Armeniae*:
(11) Equites sagittarii at Sabbu[49]
(12) Equites sagittarii at Domana
(13) (Headquarters of the) Prefect of the Legio XV Apollinaris at Satala (see below, p. 363, n. 19)
(14) (Headquarters of the) Prefect of the Legio XII Fulminata at Melitene (mod. Malatya)
(15) In Pontus
(16) (Headquarters of the) Prefect of the Legio I Pontica at Trapezus (mod. Trebizond, cf. *PECS*, p. 932a, Wilson)
(17) Ala Rizena, at Aladaleariza (not identified, probably the same as Olotoaelariza in *Itin. Anton.* 183, 2, p. 24 and Ole- | -obdera (?) in *Tab. Peut.* X, 5 and XI, 1.)
(18) Ala Theodosiana near Avaxa (Avaza or Avsa, standing at the foot of the Kolat dağlari. Cf. Adontz, 1970: 81)
(19) Ala felix Theodosiana at Silvana[50]
(20) And these which are assigned from the lesser register:
(21) Ala prima Augusta colonorum at Chiaca (Hadzana, a village on the Değqir-mendere. Cf. Adontz, 1970: 81)
(22) Ala Auriana at Dascusa (Ağqin. Cf. *PECS*, pp. 258b–259a, Harper)
(23) Ala prima Ulpia Dacorum at Suissa (see above p. 363, n. 19)
(24) Ala secunda Gallorum at Aeliana (not identified)
(25) Ala constituted at castellum Tablariensis (not identified)
(26) Ala prima praetoria recently constituted
(27) Cohors tertia Ulpia miliaria Petraeorum at Metita (Butan. Cf. Miller, 1916: col. 684)
(28) Cohors quarta Raetorum at Analiba (near Divir. Cf. Miller, 1916: col. 676)
(29) Cohors miliaria Bosporiana at Arauraca (near Choschbürük. Cf. Miller, ibid.)
(30) Cohors miliaria Germanorum at Sisila (Melishan. Cf. Miller, ibid.)
(31) Ala prima Iovia felix at Chaszanenica (= Gizenenica of the *Itin. Anton.*, mod. Hadzana, a village on the Değir-mendere. Cf. Adontz, 1970: 81)
(32) Ala prima felix Theodosiana at Pithia[51]

(33)   Cohors prima Theodosiana at Valentia (not identified)

(34)   Cohors Apuleia of Roman Citizens at Ysiporto (= ῞Υσσον λιμήν of Arrian, mod. Surmene, a port on the Black Sea east of Trebizond. Cf. Adontz, 1970: 81)

(35)   Cohors prima Lepidiana at Caene-Parembole (Καινή- παρεμβολή = new camp, probably not a proper place name. Cf. Adontz, 1970: 81)

(36)   Cohors secunda Valentiana at Ziganne (mod. Zigana, at the entrance of the Zigana Pass. Cf. Adontz, 1970: 81)

(37)   Cohors prima Claudia equitata, at Sebastopolis[52]

(38)   Cohors, at Mochora (= Mogaro of the *Itin. Anton.* (205, 1, p. 28), east of Zigana. Cf. Adontz, 1970: 81)

Notes

1 THE RISE OF THE SASSANIANS

1 The Cadusaei were originally a proto-Median tribe who dwelt on the south-west coast of the Caspian Sea. See also pp. 368, n. 54.

2 The genealogy of Ardashir presented by Agathias is different from that given by Shapur I for his father on his Great Inscription. According to the latter, Ardashir was the son of King Papak (*ŠKZ*, Gk line 1, see p. 35), a certain Denak was mother of King Papak and a Radak was mother of Ardashir, King of Kings (line 55). Sasan was simply honoured as a lord, his name coming before that of Papak (line 46) but specifying no relation. Frye (1983: 116–17) suggests that Sasan might have been the natural father of Ardashir, but the latter was adopted by Papak either after the death of Sasan or that of his own son Shapur. The version of Agathias appears to have been derived from a tradition which is also found in the *Kārnāmak i Artaxšēr i Papakan* (Book of Deeds of Ardashir, son of Papak) and is transmitted to later writers like Tabari and Firdawsi through the *Khwaday-namagh* (Book of Lords) – a fairly official historical work (now lost) which covered Persian history from its beginnings to the end of Khusrau II's reign (AD 628) and compiled under Yazdgird III (631–57). Cf. Cameron, 1969–70: 112–17 and 136–7; Widengren, 1971: 714–25; Frye, 1984a: 266–7; and Felix, 1985: 25.

3 The most decisive of the engagements was fought at Hormizdagān (near mod. Gulgayagan, between Isfahan and Nihawand, cf. Widengren 1971: 743) where Artabanus was killed. According to the chronology established by Nöldeke, the battle took place some time in September, AD 224. A more precise date, and one which is often encountered, is given by the so-called *Chronicle of Arbela (Chronicon Ecclesiae Arbelae)* attributed to Msiha-Zkha. First published by Mingana in 1907, the relevant part of this Syriac work says (ed. Kawerau, *CSCO* 467, pp. 29–30 = Mingana, pp. 28–9):

> The Parthians showed themselves to be strong and powerful and proud that they sought only murder, but God who has said through his prophet: 'Though you soar aloft like the eagle, though your nest is set among the stars, thence I will bring you down ...' (Obadiah

4), restrained them and brought about their overthrow. In former times, the Persians had desired to overthrow the Parthians and many times they had put their power to test in battle; but they were repulsed and proved unable to get the better of the Parthians. However, the Parthians were weakened by the great number of their wars and battles (i.e. against the Romans). The Persians and the Medes perceived this and they joined forces with Shahrat, King of Adiabene and with Domitianus, King of Karka de Bet Selok; and in spring they engaged the Parthians in a mighty struggle. The Parthians were defeated and their kingdom ceased to exist. Beginning from this, they hurled themselves against Mesopotamia, then Bet-Aramaye, then Bet-Zabdai (i.e. Zabdicene) and then Arzon (i.e. Arzanene). Within a year, they took all the regions. All the Parthian effort at resistance was useless – for their day had come and the hour had arrived. In the end, they all fled to the high mountains, leaving to the Persians all their land and all the treasures stored in the Cities (i.e. Seleucia and Ctesiphon). The young son of Artaban (i.e. Artabanus), called Arshak (i.e. Arsaces), was killed in cold blood by the Persians at Ctesiphon, and they took up residence there and made it their capital. The day which saw the end of the kingdom of the Parthians, children of the mighty Arshak (i.e. the Arsacids), was a Wednesday, the 27th of Nisan, the year of 535 of the Greek kingdom (*recte* 28 April, 224).

In recent years, however, considerable doubt has been cast by modern scholars on the authenticity of this Syriac work as major discrepancies have been found between the only surviving manuscript and Mingana's printed version. The historical information it provides must, therefore, be treated with extreme caution. Cf. Brock, 1979–80: 23–4; and Bivar, 1983: 92.

4   Artabanus V was not the sole Parthian ruler. He only had control of the eastern part of the Parthian Empire. His brother Vologeses (Valagas) V had been ruler of Mesopotamia and Babylonia since 207/8. Cf. Widengren, 1971: 741.

5   This excursus on the origins of Ardashir is not preserved in the Armenian original of Agathangelos. It is a later interpolation and shows clear influence of Karnamak material (see Note 2). The sympathetic and romantic depiction of Ardashir in this excursus is not typical of the manner in which he is portrayed in the main part of the history. Cf. Felix, 1985: 29–30.

6   By Assyria the interpolator means the area coinciding roughly with the later Nestorian ecclesiastical province of Bet Aramaye (= Sassanian Assuristan) so as to distinguish the magnates from Parthian noblemen.

7   This might well have been based on a historical person as among the names of the Sassanian court listed on *ŠKZ* (Gk line 54) is a certain Zig (*sic*) with the title of δ(ε)ιπνοκλήτωρ (lit.: 'the meal announcer', i.e. 'chief of ceremonies'. Cf. Back 1978: 348; Felix 1985: 30.

8   George was the author of several poems on the reign of Heraclius (AD 610–41). His *Heraclias*, composed after 628, is a survey of the achievements of the emperor at home and abroad.

9   This should not be taken to mean that Ardashir moved against Media and Armenia after his initial failure to capture Hatra. Parthia and Media were already in his hands and he was attacking Hatra from Media Atropatene. Cf. Widengren, 1971: 757.

10   The correlation of the events in Armenia between classical and Armenian sources reveals major discrepancies in chronology and genealogy. The main Armenian tradition, as represented by Agathangelos and (Ps.) Moses Khorenats'i, gives the Armenian king Khosrov (Chosroes) (I) as the hero of the hour. Also known as Trdat (Tiridates) (II), he was a relative of the defeated Artabanus (referred to as 'brother' of the Parthian king in the Greek version of Agathangelos, 9a.32, ed. Lafontaine), and it was he who thwarted Ardashir's design by his skills in battle and he even raided Assuristan, the heartland of the new Sassanian Empire. Some time after Shapur I had come to power, this Khosrov was murdered by agents of the Persian king. Armenia was then successfully invaded by the Sassanians but his son Trdat (i.e. the future Trdat III or Tiridates the Great) managed to flee to the Roman Empire. Cf. Chaumont, 1969: 25–57; Chaumont, 1976: 158–71. However, this traditional interpretation of the sources has been called into doubt by Toumanoff who, in an influential article (1969: 237ff.), draws attention to the claim by the Armenian historian Elishe (Eliseus) (tr. Thomson, 1982: 123) that the father of Trdat (i.e. Tiridates the Great) was murdered by his uncles and that according to the chronological synchronism of the Armenian historian Sebeos (Eusebius) this event took place in 287. To this we may add that one of the Persian agents who instigated the murder had the unlikely name of 'Anak' which is nothing more than the Parthian word for 'evil', the implication being that Khosrov/Trdat could not have been defeated in battle. Cf. Russell, 1982: 167. Toumanoff (1969: 250) argues that this Khosrov (I) was a composite figure, 'a hyperbolic memory preserved by the Armenian tradition'. At the time of the coming to power of Ardashir in Iran and Iraq, the ruling Armenian king was Trdat II who was a relative of Artabanus V. It was he who resisted Ardashir with the help of first some unsubdued Medes and later the Roman forces sent by Alexander Severus. He was succeeded by Khosrov II who was murdered by his kinsmen and the throne was then passed on to Trdat (III) who ruled Armenia as a Persian vassal. The son of Khosrov II, Trdat (IV) fled to Rome and was restored by Diocletian after 298/9. Khosrov I was a much earlier ruler who died in captivity in Rome between 216 and 217. See further pp. 374–5, n. 26.

11   The emendation from 'fourteen' to 'ten' is generally accepted even though it has no manuscriptal support. Herodian states elsewhere (e.g. VI, 9, 8) that Alexander Severus ruled for fourteen years – though most modern scholars would subscribe to thirteen (i.e. 222–35). It is difficult to imagine that both the Persian and German campaigns could have been undertaken in the space of one year, especially when the former clearly spanned at least one winter. The date of 231/2 for the Persian campaign is also suggested by the numismatic and epigraphic evidence. Cf. Cassola, 1968: 284n.; Whittaker, 1970: 88–9, n. 1; and Felix, 1985: 32–3.

12   It is questionable whether Ardashir had intended so early in his reign to restore the Persian Empire to its Achaemenid frontiers. Herodian was likely to have tried to explain present Persian intentions in the light of traditional Graeco-Roman (especially Greek) historiography. The desire of Ardashir to establish Sassanian control over the frontier client kingdoms like Hatra and Armenia would have inevitably embroiled him in conflict with Rome, which saw them as an essential buffer zone for its defences in the east. Cf. Potter 1990: 371–80.

13   Ensslin (1939: 128–9) has suggested on the basis of this inscription that the southern and central columns (see 1.3.3.) probably advanced as far south as Palmyra in order for Alexander to disguise the main direction of his attack. Alexander might have personally led the southern column as far as Palmyra before leaving it to join the main force which was following the Euphrates route.

14   The northern column or 'wing' of the expedition under the command of Julius Palmatus probably took the road from Zela (modern Sille) to Sebastopolis (modern Sulusaray), as evidenced by the inscriptions translated on p. 352. The route links the Pontic port of Amisos and the metropolis of Amasia with the main thoroughfare to Armenia passing through Sebastopolis.

15   The route of this southern column appears to be designed to bypass the Sassanian capital-complex of Seleucia-Ctesiphon and to ravage Mesene and Elymias. It would later reunite with the main force under the emperor. The difficulty of ascertaining the precise route of this column is intrinsic to Herodian's weak grasp of geography of the more outlying areas of his known world. Cf. Cassola, 1968: 298.

16   The most natural route for the central column, the main thrust of Alexander Severus' attack, would have been to cross the Euphrates at Zeugma and then march across Mesopotamia via Carrhae to the Tigris. Cf. Dillemann, 1962: 209. However, the mention of a visit by Alexander to Palmyra (see p. 23) suggests a more southerly route, perhaps a feint march to convince Ardashir that the main attack would come in the south. The latter appeared to have swallowed the bait as it was against the southern column that he directed his main counterattack. The central column may have sailed down the Euphrates past Dura Europos where the holder of the recently created post of *dux ripae* may have been in charge of transit arrangements. The army then marched across the Syrian desert to Singara.

17   The presence of substantial numbers of women in Persian expeditionary forces is often noted by Roman writers. See, e.g., Zonaras XII, 23 (ii, p. 596, 1–4), Libanius, *or.* LIX, 100 and Julian, *or.* I, 27A. Cf. Lieu, 1986b: 480.

18   The hostility of the Arsacid royal house in Armenia to the Sassanians would have undoubtedly assisted the passage of this column through the kingdom. The close connection between Rome and Armenia in this period is also attested by the appearance of 'Arta[xata]', an important Armenian city, in a list of satrapies inscribed on a Roman shield found under the 'Tower of the Archers' at Dura Europos. Cf. Cumont, 1926: 331 (Les Parchemins IX, line 12).

19   This blaming of the domination of Alexander by his mother Mamaea

for the disaster is typical of Herodian's understanding of the last year of the emperor's reign. Cf. Whittaker, 1970: 114, n. 1.

20 The tradition of the annihilation of the southern column appears to have come from a source hostile to Alexander Severus and is inconsistent with Herodian's own statement that the Persians failed to exploit their victory and agreed to a truce. Cf. VI, 6, 5–6. It is possible that the battle was bitter but indecisive, causing serious losses to both sides. Cf. Welles, 1941: 100–1.

21 This brief but heroic depiction of Alexander's achievements by the author of the *SHA* differs considerably from the more detailed one by Herodian. For a comparative study of the main sources on the Persian campaign of Alexander Severus, see Roesger, 1978: 172–4.

22 Maricq, op. cit., 1957, suggests that Singara was Alexander Severus' advance headquarters. It would have given him easy access to the Tigris route.

23 Modern Salihye, former Macedonian colony and Parthian administrative centre for the region of Parapotamia, it became a Roman frontier outpost on the Euphrates under the Antonines. Cf. Watzinger 1940: 149.7–169.31; *PECS*, pp. 286a–287a (Hopkins).

24 The Greek word used here, θρεπτός, often found in inscriptions in Asia Minor, 'denotes a child reared from infancy, and probably, though evidence here is lacking, was applied to the purchased as well as to the slave-born in the household or rescued from exposure' (Cameron, 1939: 53).

25 As commander of a frontier garrison watching over a certain district (the *ripa*), the office of *dux ripae* at Dura Europos seems to presage the *dux limitis* of the fourth century. However, unlike the latter, he was certainly subordinate to the legate of Syria Coele. In this period both Syrian legions were stationed in the north of the province, mainly for the defence of Antioch and the Cyrrhestica; the garrison at Dura played a major 'tripwire' role in frontier defence. Cf. Gilliam, 1941: 169–71. See also Lieu, 1985: 65–6.

26 i.e. to be remembered by a deity. Cf. Rostovtzeff *et al.* 1952: 33.

27 Probus was probably his comic 'side-kick'.

28 The last line presents considerable difficulty in interpretation. Cf. Rostovtzeff *et al.* 1952: 35, where other epigraphical parallels from Dura are cited.

29 The Osrhoenean archers later plotted against Maximinus after the murder of Alexander Severus. The plot fizzled out after the execution of the *praepositus* (?) of the Osrhoeneans, a certain Macedo, by Maximinus. Cf. Herodian VII, 1, 9–11. The Roman camp at Zagurae (Ain Sinu, on the main route between Singara and the Tigris) might have been the recruiting and training ground for these mounted archers. Cf. Oates 1968b: 91–2.

30 Jardé (1925: 81–2) has drawn attention to an African milestone, part of which reads: '[I]mp. Caes. Aurelio [Ale]x[andro] invicto pio [f]elice Aug. Divi Magni Severi [nep.] Partico (*sic*) max. [Persico] max.', which appears to confirm in part the salutations listed here. See also Whittaker, 1970: 124–5. However, it must be remembered that after the death of Elagabalus in March 222, his memory was condemned

and his name was erased from some of his monuments to be replaced by that of his successor, Alexander Severus (e.g. *ILAl* I, 3892), with the latter assuming his titulature. Elagabalus himself had assumed his titles from Caracalla, his alleged father. Alexander's salutation of 'Part(h)ico [max.]' might have originally belonged to Caracalla whom Julia Mamaea claimed to have been the father of both Elagabalus and Alexander Severus. The restoration '[Persico] max.' is also questionable as the salutation was not generally used before Philip the Arab. Cf. Gricourt, 1961: 319; Kneissl, 1969: 167–8; Kerler, 1970: 131.

31   Loriot (1975a: 763) suggests that the fall of Hatra was part of a general invasion of Roman Mesopotamia which resulted in the capture of Rhesaina, Singara and possibly also the garrison camp of Zagurae (Ain Sinu, cf. Oates 1968b: 91–2) as the first two cities were later restored to Roman rule by Timesitheus. It is just as likely that these cities were lost under Maximinus Thrax during whose brief reign (235–8) there was a complete suspension of minting in Mesopotamia. Cf. Kettenhofen, 1983: 155.

32   The source is a small papyrus codex containing sections of biographical accounts of Mani, the founder of the gnostic evangelical religion of Manichaeism. Cf. Henrichs and Koenen, 1970: 97–216; Lieu, 1985: 30–1.

33   This form of Ardashir's name is unique and, if genuine, must be related to the Sassanian claim that the dynasty was linked to the Achaemenids. Cf. Henrichs and Koenen, 1975: 20, n. 40. See also Henrichs and Koenen 1970: 121, n. 53. The absence of a Greek nominal ending suggests the form *rdkšr in Aramaic script. The Greek is probably a shortened version of the mp. Daryaw-Ardaxsahr. Cf. Sundermann, 1986: 293, 390–1. Such combined name forms are not unusual as Shapur's son Hormizd appears as Hormizd-Ardashir in his father's inscription (*ŠKZ*, line 40). Cf. Back, 1978: 190.

34   The garrison was probably starved into surrendering to the besiegers as archaeology has not so far yielded any clear evidence of a violent end to the city. Cf. Milik, 1972: 355; and Drijvers, 1977: 827.

2   THE PERSIAN EXPEDITION OF GORDIAN III

1   This was the revolt led by a certain Sabinianus (perhaps governor of the province of Africa) against Gordian III. Cf. Pflaum, 1960: 829–30.

2   On Timesitheus, see 2.2.1.

3   According to the *CMC* (18.1–10, see above 1.5.1), Shapur received the diadem as co-regent on the eighth day of Pharmuthi in the year in which he captured Hatra (i.e. 17/18th April, 240). The exact date of his accession to sole rule is not known, but a date in 242 is commonly held to be the most likely. The length of his reign varies in our sources between thirty-one years, six months and nineteen days (cf. Nöldeke, p. 42) and thirty years (Elias of Nisibis, *opus chron.* CSCO 62, p. 92). Cf. Felix, 1985: 43–4, Cameron, 1969–70; 138 and Mosig-Walburg, 1980: 122–4. However, according to a recently published inscription on a column capital found near Shiraz (cf. Tavoosi and Frye, 1990: 30–8), the Roman invasion of Parthia and Persis took place in the

third year of the reign of Shapur I. This would confirm the year of accession of Shapur as 240/1 and not later as most scholars have thought. Many problems surround the interpretation of this important new text and readers are advised to consult the publication by Tavoosi and Frye (op. cit.)

4 On the provinces of the Sassanian Empire see Map 1, p. xiii. For description and identification, see especially Honigmann amd Maricq, 1953: 39–110. See also Morony, 1982: *passim*; Morony, 1984: 125–68; Gignoux: 1971 *passim*; Sundermann, 1979: 144–5; Sundermann, 1986: 281–4.

5 Edessa (modern Urfa), the chief city of Roman Osrhoene, was recaptured from the Parthians by Avidius Cassius in 165. On the status of the city under the Severans, see especially Wagner, 1983: 103–15.

6 Edessa ceased to be the capital of the Abgar dynasty under Caracalla and became a Roman colony. It still possessed the title of 'the renowned Antoniniana Edessa, Colonia Metropolis Aurelia Alexandria' in the Syriac Deed of Sale from Dura Europos (*PDura* 28, cf. Welles *et al.*, 1959: 146) which is dated to May 243. The restoration of Edessa as an independent kingdom must have taken place shortly afterwards. Cf. Drijvers, 1978: 878–82; Kettenhofen, 1982: 28–9. The presence of Gordian at Edessa and the restoration of the Abgar dynasty are both well attested to in local coinage. Cf. *BMC Mesopotamia*, pp. 113–18. Furthermore, Carrhae, Nisibis, and Singara all resumed the minting of Roman coins under Gordian. Cf. ibid., pp. 89–90, 121, 135–6.

7 The battle was fought between 13 January 244 (date of the last extant imperial legislation of Gordian, cf. *CJ* VI, 10, 1) and 14 March 244 (date of the first edict of Philip, cf. *CJ* III, 42, 6). Cf. Loriot, 1975b: 789, *contra* Honigmann and Maricq, 1953: 122, n. 1. On Meshike, see Note on Peros-Sabour below. The fact that this major defeat was not mentioned in any Late Roman source attests to the tight control over 'media coverage' of this event.

8 The word 'ἀ]νήρη' is presumably a rare passive form of 'ἀναιρέω' or a mason's mistake for 'anerethe'. It may also be an impersonal form of the passive, leaving open deliberately the precise cause of Gordian's death. Cf. Kettenhofen, 1983: 165; Felix, 1985: 49. Sassanian imperial reliefs depict a dead Roman emperor (identified by the wreath around the brows) under the charger of Shapur I. Cf. MacDermot, 1954: 76–80 and plate IV.

9 The extant Roman and Byzantine sources on the death of Gordian can be divided into four categories according to their different emphases: (1) the tradition which mentions the opening of the gate of the temple of Janus by Gordian, his initial success against the Persians and his subsequent murder by Philip, cf. Aurelius Victor, Eutropius, Jordanes, and John of Antioch; (2) the success of the Roman arms under Timesitheus, the change of fortunes after his death and the death of Gordian in a mutiny incited by Philip and the burial at Zaitha, cf. Festus, Jerome, Ammianus, *SHA*, *Epitome de Caesaribus*, Orosius, Zosimus, Syncellus, and Zonaras; (3) Gordian died in battle after

falling from a horse and crushing his thigh, cf. Malalas (ap. Sathas), Georgius Monachus, Cedrenus, and Zonaras (on Gordian II); (4) Gordian fell in 'the ranks' as a direct result of a colleague's jealousy, cf. *Oracula Sibyllina*. None of the sources, with the possible exception of the *Oracula*, hints at the Roman defeat at Meshike. Cf. Loriot, 1975a: 770–3; Potter, 1990: 204–8.

10   Lines 19–20 of this oracle have long been a source of perplexity to the editors of the text as the first word of line 19: *ιδετεωσ* is clearly corrupt and the translation here follows Willamowitz's suggestion of 'νεμέσεως'. Still this is not entirely suitable to the context, nor will it scan. Among the various suggestions in Geffcken's apparatus, 'ζηλοσύνης' makes the best historical sense. Potter (1990: 166, 199–200) suggests an inversion of the two lines and gives as translation (ibid. 140): 'he will fall in the ranks, smitten by burning iron because of jealousy and betrayed by a companion'. These two lines have been used by Honigmann and Maricq (1953: 119) to prove that Gordian fell in battle against the Persians and was not victim to the conspiracy of Philip. However, as they stand, they imply that Philip deliberately brought about the death of Gordian in battle, which is not supported by other sources. Loriot (1975a: 773) surmises that the *fraus Philippi* might have been a tactical error committed by the prefect, such as allowing the Roman army to fall into a position in which the redoubtable Sassanian cavalry could be deployed against it with the most devastating effect. The words 'ἐν τάξει' here translated as 'in the ranks' can mean either 'in battle' or 'in the camp'.

11   A *votum* 'pro salute a[tque incolumitat]e et victor[ia]' of Gordian (*CIL* III, 6763) dedicated by a legate of the XXII Legion at Mainz on 1 July 242, gives one of the earliest dates for the start of Gordian's expedition. Cf. Townsend, 1934: 128; Loriot, 1975a: 759–60.

12   Zaitha is probably the name of a region and not merely of a place. According to the evidence of Ammianus and Zosimus (see p. 232), the monument would have been situated about twenty miles south of Circesium. The location of this monument in Persian-held territory may be significant as it might well have marked the actual place of his death and argues against the Persian claim that Gordian died in battle at Meshike. This was not the actual grave of Gordian, as his remains were taken to Rome (cf. Eutropius and Festus, *trans. supra*). Cf. Potter, 1985: 174. For a more precise attempt to locate Zaitha, see Musil 1927: 237–8.

13   Philip did not suffer *damnatio memoriae* in the reign of his successor, an alleged adversary (cf. Eutropius, IX, 2–3). This may imply that Gordian was the victim of a general uprising of the defeated Roman troops who were angry at the young and inexperienced emperor. Philip was not the most important man in imperial service at the time. His brother Julius Priscus would have preceded him in seniority in the praetorian prefecture. Philip's elevation, as Potter (1990: 204–12) has suggested, may have been due to the reluctance of those who held most power to select one of their members to rule when none of them was pre-eminent – witness the elevation of Diocles (later Diocletian) after the death of Numerianus and that of Jovian after Julian. The guilt of

the murder was later shifted to Philip, the one who had apparently derived the greatest benefit from Gordian's death. This 'deformation' of the facts in the sources probably took place during the reign of Decius, who was hostile to the memory of Philip, and was the work of the senatorial aristocracy who regarded the young Gordian as their creature. Cf. MacDonald 1981: 507–8. See also Mazzarino, 1971a: 69–76; Kettenhofen, 1983: 165–6, n. 67.

14 Reading 'ac Sapore Persarum rege (post Artaxerxen) summoto [et post Artaxansen] . . .'. Cf. Soverini 1983, ii: 828. See also Zos. I, 18, 1.

15 The important role played by Timesitheus in the initial Roman victory at Rhesaina and the restoration of Carrhae (and Nisibis?) may also be commemorated in the Jewish Apocalypse of Elijah, which says in the second great Roman campaign against the Persians – the first being that of Alexander Severus – the prefects Philippus (reading 'nphīlipus for 'phlīphu) and Timesitheus (reading mistus bn priphqtus for dmitrus bn puriphus) will lead a force of 100,000 cavalry, 100,000 foot, and 30,000 men from ships. Cf. Krauss, 1902: 363, 371; Krauss, 1903: 627–33; Potter, 1990: 194, n. 21. For a more cautionary note on Krauss' emendations, see Honigmann and Maricq, 1953: 119, n. 2. On the career of C. Furius Sabinius Aquila Timesitheus, see PIR^2 III, 581; Howe, 1942: 78–9; Pflaum, 1960: 811–21; and Sartre, 1982: 89.

16 A play on the words, *reges* and *leges*. Cf. Hohl, 1985, ii: 319. The Persians might well have attempted to impose fire-worship on inhabitants of conquered Roman territories. See below, 3.3.3.

17 Carrhae and Nisibis were restored to Roman rule in 242 by Timesitheus before Gordian arrived in the main theatre of war.

18 The fact that the decisive battle was fought at Meshike/Pirisabora – later a key to the defence of Ctesiphon – bears out the claim of a deep penetration into Assuristan.

19 M. Julius Philippus (PIR^2 III, 462) was probably vice-prefect with his brother C. Julius Priscus (see 2.3.2; cf. Howe, 1942: 79, no. 46). The latter was already Praetorian Prefect while Timesitheus was still alive. Cf. *CISem.* II, 3932 (*supra* 1.3.1), and Prentice 1908: 312, no. 399. He may well have played a significant role in the elevation of this brother after the death of Gordian.

20 The retreating Persians probably carried out a scorched earth policy, as they would against Julian in 363. This would have accentuated the problems of supplies for the advancing Roman army which had begun its march much earlier than the normal campaigning season.

21 Reading 'λιμός' for 'λοιμός'.

22 This is almost certainly an error. The battle of Rhesaina was fought on the approaches to the Khabur, the main tributary of the Euphrates.

23 This fragment of Malalas (?) has been adduced as additional evidence by Honigmann and Maricq (1953: 120, n. 1) for the death of Gordian in battle. However, one must bear in mind its similarity to accounts of the death of Gordian II in battle in Africa and of the death of Philip. MacDonald (1981: 507) suggests that the topos of falling from the horse and fracturing the thigh may ultimately have its origin in the official report of the death of Gordian III submitted to the Senate by Philip. Cf. *SHA Gordian* 31, 2 and Zos. I, 19, 1. See also Mazzarino,

1971b: 655–78 which traces the story back to the *Anonymous Continuator of Dio Cassius*. For a critical evaluation of the Byzantine chronographical sources on the reign of the three Gordians, see Patzig, 1896: 41–2. Most of the relevant material is translated in Jeffreys, 1986: 159–60.

24   He may have had to make his escape for fear of the mutinous troops. Cf. Oost, 1958: 106–7; De Blois, 1978–9: 13.

25   Philip probably paid a regular tribute to Shapur in addition to the 500,000 aurei mentioned by the ŠKZ. The burden of this expense would have been borne by the inhabitants of the eastern provinces. Cf. Potter, 1990: 246. For the identification of the denarii of the ŠKZ with the aurei, see Guey, 1961: 261–74.

26   Modern al-Anbar. It appears as Pirisabora in Roman sources. Cf. Ammianus Marcellinus XXIV, 2, 9; Zos. III, 16, 3 (Versabora). Its importance as a military depot is reflected in its Arabic name Anbar – 'the granary'. Cf. Morony, 1982: 24; Morony, 1984: 144–5. Known as Pumbedita in the *Babylonian Talmud*, it possessed an important Jewish community. Cf. Oppenheimer, 1983: 351–68.

27   This must be distinguished from Lesser Armenia which had been part of Cappadocia since the first century AD and had as its provincial capital Sebasteia after the reforms of Diocletian. The division of the Kingdom of Armenia into Greater (or Pers-)Armenia and Lesser Armenia was consequent to the treaty between Theodosius I and Shapur III (*c.* 384). Besides imprecision of geographical terminology, Evagrius' statement contradicts the assertion by Zosimus (III, 32, 4, *trans. supra*) that no Roman territory was lost by Philip. Cf. Chaumont, 1969: 46; Kettenhofen, 1982: 34–5, n. 72.

28   This appears to imply that Philip did not concede any territory to the Persians. Zosimus stressed this to underscore the loss of Nisibis by the Christian Jovian in 363.

29   The part of the treaty between Philip and Shapur regarding the position of Mesopotamia is also uncertain. The Roman colony of Rhesaina, liberated by Timesitheus, minted Roman coins throughout the reign of Decius (cf. *BMC Mesopotamia*, 'Resaina', pp. 127 (no. 10)–133 (no. 41). The appointment of Julius Priscus, his brother and Praetorian Prefect, as Prefect of Mesopotamia would indicate that the province was not entirely ceded to the Persians. Furthermore, the fact that Shapur had to precede his 'second' campaign in 253 with the capture by force of Nisibis and the first objectives of the campaign being Roman garrisons like Anatha on the Euphrates argues against the possibility of total abandonment. Cf. Kettenhofen, 1982: 36, n. 72. On the other hand, withdrawal of Roman support for Armenia and Hatra might have been seen by some as significant contraction of the sphere of Roman influence. Cf. Wirth, 1980–1: 334–5, n. 75. Diocletian's acceptance of the Singara–Nisibis line as the boundary between the two empires even after Galerius' great victory in 297/8 may indicate a partial abandonment by Philip of some outlying areas which were not regained by Timesitheus. Cf. Oates, 1968: 89.

30   These two lines (28–9) are rendered here as traditionally interpreted by most scholars. Potter (1990: 225–7), however, asserts that these

lines only make sense in terms of events during the 240s if ποίμνη in line 28 is understood as a dative of advantage and the passage rendered, 'but when the wolf should make oaths to the white-toothed dogs with respect to the flock' (or, less prosaically, 'with an eye to the flock').

31 Lines 21–34 refer to events before the mid-summer of 247. Cf. Potter, 1990: 229.

32 Pacatianus was an officer of the Danubian army; hence the 'German Ares'. He rebelled against Philip in 247 but was murdered two years later. His rebellion was both disastrous to Philip and opportune to the Persians. Cf. Felix 1985: 53.

33 The date of his appointment to the prefecture (or governorship) of Mesopotamia is hard to pin-point despite the evidence of Zosimus. An acephalous inscription found at Rome (*CIL*, VI 1638 = Dessau 1331) gives the *cursus* of an equestrian official which completes a distinguished career in imperial service in both the prefecture of Mesopotamia and the praetorian prefecture. This unknown official had also performed the duties of *praepositus* of a legionary vexillation at the behest of one of the Gordians. The identification of him with C. Julius Priscus is a tempting one. Cf. Domaszewski, 1899: 159–60; Howe, 1942: 79, no. 46. Pflaum (1960: 833–6; cf. *PIR*² III, 488), however, has earlier argued against this and given a post-249 date to the praetorian prefecture of this unknown official on the grounds that some of the many posts held by him, especially the *iuridicus Alexandriae vice praefecti Aegypti*, could not be attributed with confidence to Priscus. More recently, Potter (1990: 214) has drawn our attention to the fact that the province of Mesopotamia was ordinarily described as *provincia Mesopotamiae et Osrhoenae* after the abolition of the dynasty of Abgar at Edessa in 214 by Caracalla; this official would have been *praefectus Mesopotamiae* during the period (240–2) when the kingdom was temporarily restored by Gordian. See above, 2.1.4. See also Duncan-Jones, 1969: 229–33; Duncan-Jones, 1970: 107–9. This may imply that if the official of the acephalous *cursus* was indeed Priscus, he would already have held the prefecture of Mesopotamia during the early part of the Persian campaign of Gordian, either prior to or concurrent with the praetorian prefecture.

34 The lines refer to the harsh administration of Julius Priscus who remained in charge of the east after the departure of Philip. According to Zosimus (I, 20, 2), the eastern provinces declared (M. F. R. (u.)) Iotapianus as emperor in 248 or 249. The revolt was dated to the reign of Decius (249–51) by Aurelius Victor (29, 1), and placed by Polemius Sylvius (*Laterculus* I, p. 521, 37–8, *MGH*) in Cappadocia but under Philip.

35 The precise powers of this office are unknown but the title certainly resembles that of '*restitutor* (or *corrector*) *totius orientis*' granted later to Vaballathus (and Odaenathus?) by Gallienus. (See below, 4.5.5.) Cf. Pflaum, 1960: 835; Paschoud, 1971: 145, n. 46.

36 An official rating 200,000 sesterces.

37 *Miliariae*, indicated by a numerical symbol on the inscription.

38 The unit was originally recruited in the Near East and had spells of

garrison duty in Germany and Pannonia. Cf. *CIL* XIII, 7323 = Dessau, 9148. It was part of the growing field army when it returned to the east under Gordian III and retreated to Bostra after his death. Cf. Speidel, 1977: 705.

39   The Legio VIII 'Augusta', or at least a detachment of it, was stationed at Syria at various times since Augustus. At first it was stationed mainly near Beirut and, under Philip, moved to Baalbek. Cf. Prentice, 1908: 129.

3   THE SECOND AND THIRD CAMPAIGNS OF SHAPUR I AGAINST THE ROMAN EMPIRE

1   The date adopted here is that given by al-Tabari (eleventh year of the reign of Shapur: i.e. 251/2), but Nisibis is not among any of the lists of captured cities in the *ŠKZ*, nor is its capture stated unequivocally in Roman sources. Its recapture by Odaenathus for the Romans, however, is well known. Cf. SHA Gallieni Duo 10, 3 and 12, 1 and *triginta tyranni* 15, 3. The occupation of Nisibis would have been a logical preliminary step to the invasion of Armenia in 252, but a later date cannot be ruled out as the same consideration would have applied to Shapur's 'third' campaign in 260, which began in Mesopotamia and was probably launched from Nisibis. Cf. Kettenhofen, 1982: 44–6; Potter, 1985: 329–30.

2   This passage is not found in the more recent edition of Eutychius by Breydey. 1985. See below, p. 394, n. 3

3   I.e. the reign of Trebonianus Gallus (251–3). This late date for the murder of Khosrov and the flight of Tiridates (*c.* 252) is accepted by Hewsen (1978–9b: 99) on the basis of the traditional length of the reign of Khosrov (thirty-five years, i.e. 216/7–252). See also Kettenhofen, 1982: 38–43.

4   The original manuscript gives 'children' (παίδων). The emendation to 'πατρῶων' follows the suggestion of Markwart on the evidence of a letter from a group of Armenian priests and nobles to Theodosius the Great, which mentions the education on Roman soil of the young Tiridates after his escape from the hands of 'cruel uncles and parricides', preserved in the Armenian history of Elishe (trans. Thomson 1982: 23). Cf. Chaumont, 1969: 54; Felix, 1985: 54.

5   The asylum given by the Romans to Tiridates probably constituted a breach of some form of 'non-intervention' clause in the treaty between Philip and Shapur and was therefore used as a pretext for launching an invasion which would pre-empt any Roman attempt to interfere in Armenia. Cf. Chaumont, 1969: 58–60. For other suggestions, see Olmstead, 1942: 257; Sprengling, 1953: 84–5 and Ensslin, 1949: 98.

6   **Barbalissos** (modern Qal'at Balis) is listed among the Roman garrisons on the Euphrates in the *Not. Dig* (Or. XXXIII, 25). This defeat, like that of Meshike under Gordian III, finds no echo in Roman sources. The Roman army was probably the permanent garrison of Syria commanded by the legate of the province. Cf. Ensslin, 1949: 100; Gracey, 1981: 87.

7   The list gives the cities in groups, which suggests that after Barbalissos

the main Persian army was divided into detachments for the purpose of raiding. It describes therefore a number of simultaneous rather than continuous actions.

8 **Anatha**, modern 'Āna, fortified island on the Euphrates. Cf. Musil, 1927: 6–7; Kettenhofen, 1982: 50–1; Kennedy, 1986b; Kennedy and Northedge, 1989. **(Birth)-Arupan**, modern Qreiye, a fortress in Syria. Cf. Poidebard, 1934: 87; Honigmann and Maricq, 1953: 162; Back 1978. **(Birth-) Asporakan**, modern Halebiye, a fortress in Syria, later the site of Zenobia on the Euphrates. Cf. Honigmann and Maricq, 1953: 162–3. Gignoux, 1972: 47; Back, 1978: 191; Kettenhofen, 1982: 52. **Sura** or **Soura**, modern Suriya, near al-Hammam, city on the west bank of the Euphrates, important for its situation at the head of the *Strata Diocletiana*. Cf. *RE* IV A/1, cols 953–60 (Honigmann); Poidebard, 1934: 71–88. These cities were clearly captured by the main Persian force on its march up the Euphrates before encountering the main Roman army at Barbalissos.

9 After its victory at Barbalissos, the Persian army probably advanced as far as **Hierapolis** (modern Menbij), an important route centre in Syria between Beroea and the Euphrates. Cf. *RE Suppl.* IV, cols 733–42 (Honigmann); and Cumont, 1917: 20. Using Hierapolis as a base, a Persian army group turned south and ravaged cities in the vicinity of Chalcis: **Beroea,** or **Ber(rh)oia**, modern Halab or Aleppo, cf. *PECS*, p. 150b (Rey-Coquais); **Chalcis** (ad Belum), ruins at Qennisrin, near modern 'Is, important city in the Syrian *limes*, cf. Mouterde and Poidebard, 1945: 17, 21–3; Apamea, modern Qal'at el-Mudig, later metropolis of Syria II, cf. *PECS*, pp. 66b–67b (Rey-Coquais); and **Rephanea**, modern Rafniye, in Syria, former legionary headquarters of III Gallica, cf. Mouterde and Poidebard, 1945: 29–31. All these cities lie along the same main road from Hierapolis and the main objective of this group might have been the neutralization of the threat posed by the military base at Rephanea.

10 From Hierapolis another army group moved north towards **Zeugma** (Seleucia on the Euphrates), modern Balqiz, an important river crossing and legionary headquarters of IV Scythica (cf. Wagner, 1976: *passim*, especially pp. 165–288; *PECS* p. 1000 (Rey-Coquais); Mouterde and Poidebard, 1945: 212–13), where it joined the main road from Edessa to Antioch, capturing also **Ourima** (?), modern Horum Huyuk, between Belkis and Rum Kale on the Euphrates (cf. Hellenkemper, 1977: 467; Frézouls, 1977: 167). This northern army group, consisting mainly of cavalry under Hormizd, then headed towards Antioch, capturing *en route*: **Gindaros**, modern Gindaris, a large village in Syria administered from Antioch, **(L)armenaza**, modern Armenaz, and Seleucia. One would expect the last mentioned place-name to be that of Seleucia Pieria, modern el-Kabusaye, port of Antioch on the Orontes, cf. *PECS* p. 822 (Rey-Coquais), indicating an attempt by the Persians to cut off Antioch from the sea. However, it is difficult to envisage how the Persians could have accomplished their drive to the sea without first capturing Antioch. The first Seleucia could therefore be **Seleucia (ad Belum?** = Seleukobelos?, modern Seluqiye on the Orontes, cf. Ensslin, 1949: 101; Kettenhofen, 1982:

67) which was captured by the Persian force advancing on Antioch from Apamea. Cf. Potter, 1985: 298–9, n. 2.

11 **Cyrrhus**, modern Qal'at Nebi Huru, chief city of the region known as the Cyrrhestica, NE of Antioch, was an important Roman military base. Cf. Frézouls 1977: *passim*. It was probably bypassed by the Persian column advancing on Antioch from the Euphrates and was not captured till later.

12 Either Seleucia Pieria, the port of Antioch, or Seleukobelos. See above, Note 10.

13 After the fall of Antioch, an army group moved into northern Syria via **Alexandria (ad Issum)**, modern Iskenderun, a city on the Syrian coast founded by Alexander near the site of his famous battle, cf. *PECS* p. 38 (MacKay) and raided **Nikopolis**, modern Islahiya, in Cilicia Campestris, while another army group marched from Antioch up the Orontes, capturing **Sinzara (?)** (identified by Henning 1939: 827 as Larissa on the Orontes in Syria, modern Saizar), **Chamath** (modern Hama, an ancient city in Syria on the Orontes, refounded as Epiphaneia by the Greeks, cf. Honigmann 1923: 184 (no. 170); Sauvaget, 1941, i: 36–53; Kettenhofen, 1982: 70, **Ariste** (modern ar-Rastan, also known as Arethousa, cf. Honigmann, 1923: 163 (no. 65); Kettenhofen, 1982: 70). This particular expedition probably withdrew after its defeat by a local militia at Emesa. See below, Note 30.

14 **Dichor**, city or settlement of uncertain location probably south of Doliche in Euphratensis (modern Zevkir?) (cf. Honigmann and Maricq, 1953: 154–5), and **Doliche**, modern Duluk, north of Gaziantep (cf. Kettenhofen, 1982: 76–7), were probably raided by another Persian contingent pushing out from Antioch.

15 The listing of two place-names on the Euphrates in a south to north order: **Dura Europos**, see Chapter 1, Note 23, and **Circesium**, modern el-Busaira, situated at the junction of the Euphrates and the Khabur, suggests that they were captured by a special invasion force from Pirisabora. Cf. Kettenhofen, 1982: 83.

16 The appearance of **Germanicia**, modern Mar'aš, city and important communication centre in Cilicia Campestris, linking routes from Armenia to Syria and Cappadocia (cf. *RE Suppl.* IX, col. 70 (Treidler)), after Circesium returns the reader's attention to the north. As the northernmost city listed on the ŠKZ for this campaign, it probably marks the point from which the Persians made their withdrawal. This seems to be confirmed by the immediately following mention of two place-names on the Euphrates route south.

17 There are at least two places with the name of **Batna(e)** which could have been captured by the Persians on their southward retreat. One is in Osrhoene, modern Sarug, an ancient city renamed Anthemusis by the Greeks which was capital of an eponymous region (i.e. Anthemusia), cf. Segal, 1970: 34, 137. The other is in Syria, modern Tell Batnan, which was visited by Julian on his march from Antioch to the Euphrates in 363. Cf. Cumont, 1917: 20. The first seems more likely to be the Batna mentioned here because we know that its walls were repaired by the prefect Aurelius Dasius some time after 256. The

Batna in Syria was a only a large village and would not have merited mention as a city 'with its surrounding territory' in the *ŠKZ*. Cf. Petersen, 1977: 277–8.

18 **Chanar** has been identified with caution by some scholars as Ichnai in Osrhoene. Cf. Honigmann and Maricq, 1953: 155–6; Kettenhofen, 1982: 77. This, together with the identification of Batnae with Sarug, points to the Persians withdrawing along the eastern bank of the Euphrates.

19 Most scholars are agreed that the following Cappadocian cities were raided by a Persian force which operated out of Armenia, commanded perhaps by the crown prince Hormizd (cf. Ensslin, 1949: 104; Chaumont, 1969: 63): **Satala**, modern Sadak, an important military base on the Cappadocian *limes* (cf. *PECS* p. 810 (Harper); Crow, 1986: 84); **Doman(a)**, city, probably in Armenia Minor and situated in the locality of Kose, (cf. Honigmann and Maricq, 1953: 155–6); **Artangil**, city (?) of uncertain location (in Armenia Minor?) which must not be confused with Artaxanses in Armenia (cf. Honigmann and Maricq, 1953: 156); **Souisa**, out-post(?) located near modern Kelkit/Ciftlik, probably to be identified with Suissa, a *statio* in Cappadocia on the road between Satala and Nicopolis (cf. *RE* IV A 1, *s. v.* 'Suissa', col. 722 (Rugé); Kettenhofen, 1982: 87); **Souid(a)**, city(?) of unknown location (in Cappadocia?) (cf. Kettenhofen, 1982: 87); **Phreata**, city(?) of unknown location, perhaps the Phreata placed by Ptolemy (*Geog.* V, 6, 13, ed Müller, p. 878) in Garsauritis (cf. Honigmann and Maricq, 1953: 156).

20 Shapur's invasion of Syria is firmly placed by Zosimus in the reign of Trebonianus Gallus, i.e. 253, as the passage earlier mentions events which took place towards the end of the reign of Decius. Cf. Felix, 1985: 56.

21 See Note 2 above.

22 The name Mariades is probably a slightly Graecized form of the Syriac: Maryad'a, which means 'my Lord knows'. Cyriades is a partial Greek translation of the name. Cf. Felix, 1985: 59.

23 The metropolis of Antioch was probably the main Persian objective in the 'second' campaign of Shapur as it would have provided the most plunder and numbers of captives. The way to it was opened by the Persian victory at Barbalissos, and the fact that its capture is celebrated in the *ŠKZ* means that the exact date of the event is central to any attempt to date the whole campaign. Mentioned in the same campaign is Doura (Europos), the final capture of which could not have taken place earlier than 256 because of the presence on the corpses of Roman soldiers of *Antoniniani* of the second emission of Antioch for Valerian and of coins of the next-to-last issue from the same mint (both dated to 256) found in the grave of a hastily buried victim of the siege. Ammianus dates the capture of Antioch through the treachery of Mariades to the time of Gallienus. Though he was Augustus from 253 to 268, his sole rule did not begin till after the capture of Valerian in 260. The date of 253 for the 'first' capture of Antioch is, however, unequivocally stated by Zosimus and suggested by a break in the emission of its coins between the second issue of

Trebonianus Gallus and Volusianus and the first issue of Valerian (spring 254). The second campaign (agoge) of Shapur as outlined on the ŠKZ could have covered more than one year of campaigning. Cf. Alföldi 1937: 56; Kettenhofen 1982: 65.

24   Rzach reads ἐπίκλητος for ἐπὶ κλίνης, i.e. someone who was summoned, an ally.

25   Most probably a corruption of Oromastes, the Graecized form of the Persian name Hormizd. The commander mentioned here might well have been the crown prince Hormizd-Ardashir. Cf. Felix, 1985: 60.

26   The phrase 'through the *limes* of Chalcis' does not necessarily imply the existence of an inner defensive zone in the region of Chalcis for the protection of Antioch as interpreted by Mouterde and Poidebard, 1945, i: 1–7. It may simply mean 'by the Chalcis-route'. Cf. Liebeschuetz 1977: 487–9.

27   The date of 314 (Gk δτ´) Antiochene Era (= AD 265/6) given in the Bonn text of Malalas is an emendation from the impossible τιδ´. The altered date is nevertheless still too late for the Mariades episode. Müller (*FGH* IV, p. 192) has proposed emending the figure to 304 (Gk δτ´ = AD 255/6). Cf. Stauffenberg, 1931: 366. For a detailed discussion of this passage, see Felix, 1985: 56–8.

28   Cf. Downey, 1961: 589–90, Nock, 1962: 306–9; Lieu, 1986a: 44.

29   I.e. the siege of Bezabde in the reign of Constantius. See Chapter 8.

30   Emesa (modern Homs) was the capital of a local sheikdom which enjoyed a considerable measure of independence until the Flavians. However, the dethroned dynasts, the Sampsigerami, continued to be mentioned in inscriptions as members of a local aristocracy. Cf. Sullivan, 1977: 219. The Sampsigeramus mentioned here is almost certainly the Emesene usurper, L. Iunius Aurelius Sulpicius Uranius Antoninus. His activities are attested mainly on the coins which were issued after his victory over the Persians. Though he adopted the titles of 'imperator' and 'Augustus', he at first struck coinage with local reverses and as his ambition grew he regarded himself as the junior colleague of Valerian and Gallienus. After Valerian's victory over Aemilianus in 253, a compromise appears to have been reached between him and Uranius who renounced the imperial title, but, in exchange, 'adopted a long legend, expressing his illustrious descent, and he retained the imperial bust with the laurel wreath.' (Delbrueck, 1948–9: 28). His subsequent fate is unknown. Whether the name Uranius is a Hellenized form of Sampsigeramus (= Syr.: Sismosgram (?) which means 'the sun has decided') is disputable. Domninus, Malalas' source, might well have tried to conceal the identity of the usurper behind the more acceptable figure of the heroic priest of Aphrodite. Cf. Felix, 1985: 61–3. On Uranius Antoninus, see especially Delbrueck, 1948; Baldus, 1971: 236–55.

31   Domninus' claim that Shapur met his death at Emesa is not supported by any other evidence. It may be that the commander of the southern Persian army group was killed in the manner described at Emesa. Emesa is conspicuous by its absence from the ŠKZ. Cf. Baldus, 1971: 240.

32   Malalas/Domninus is referring probably to the main Sassanian

invasion of Armenia in 252/3.

33 Olmstead (1942: 408) has interpreted these hardly legible and enigmatic graffiti as commemoration for the victory of a local hero over a major enemy. The stated date of 252/3 is certainly suggestive of the events described by Malalas. Cf. Baldus, 1971: 250–1.

34 For this interpretation of the phrase 'tute[lae] gratia' see Speidel, 1977: 725.

35 Aelius Aurelius Theon was imperial legate in Arabia from 253 to 259 as attested by inscriptions from Bostra (*IGLS* 9078–80). Cf. Sartre, 1982: 92. The transfer of troops to Arabia might have been a direct reponse to the impending Persian threat.

36 **Carrhae**, modern Harran, ancient city and Macedonian colony in Osrhoene. Cf. *PECS* pp. 200b–201a (Segal); *RAC* XIII, 634–50 (Cramer).

37 This was almost certainly Successianus, who had earlier (*c.* 254) repelled an attack of the Borani against Pityus on the Black Sea and on account of this was made Praetorian Prefect and assisted Valerian in the restoration of Antioch (*c.* 256–7) after the earthquake. His complete disappearance from Roman sources after the capture of Valerian strongly suggests that he was taken prisoner along with his emperor. Cf. Howe, 1942: 80–1.

38 **Samosata**, modern Samsat, former chief city of Commagene, then of Euphratensis, was an important route centre. Cf. *PECS* pp. 803b–804a (Serdarogu); *RE* IA/2, cols. 2220–4 (Weissbach). The decision of Shapur to make straight for Samosata is completely understandable as it was there that Valerian had stationed his reserves. See 3.3.4. The main Persian army might then have moved on to Antioch-on-the-Orontes. Its capture is not listed in the *ŠKZ* but it is difficult to imagine how the Persians could have penetrated as deeply into Asia Minor as they did on this campaign with Antioch in Roman hands; unless the capture of Valerian and the destruction of the field army had such a demoralizing effect on the metropolis that its garrison refrained from interfering with the Persian raids.

39 **Alexandria** = Alexandria ad Issum, see above, Note 13. Like nearby Rhossos, modern Arsuz, the capture of which is known to us from Philostratus (ap. Malalas) but is not recorded on the *ŠKZ*, Alexandria probably fell to a Persian raiding party from Antioch. Cf. Kettenhofen, 1982: 102–3.

40 After the capture of Samosata, the main Persian army under the command of Shapur headed for the Cilician coast at **Katabolos** (Kartarayya), city(?) of unknown location (in Cilicia, near modern Burnaz?) and made for the important city and route centre of Tarsus, modern Tarsus, cf. *PECS* pp. 883b–884a (Gough) and capturing *en route* in Cilicia Campestris: **Aig(e)ai**, modern Ayas, a port and naval base, **Mopsuestia**, modern Misis (cf. *PECS* pp. 593b–594a (Gough)), Mallos, a Roman colony in Cilicia Campestris of uncertain locality (probably Bebeli near Karatas), (cf. *PECS* p. 547b (Gough); Honigmann and Maricq, 1953: 159), and the inland cities of **Adana**, later Antioch ad Sarum, modern Adana (cf. *PECS*, p. 8a (Gough)), and **A(u)gusta** or Augustina, colony (?) in Cilicia(?). The latter is

mentioned only in the Middle Persian version (line 17) of the ŠKZ: 'gns(t)yn' y, and is difficult to locate. Honigmann (1939: 37) has suggested that it might have been a translation of the Persian for Sebastia. See also Maricq, 1958: 341; Back, 1978: 180.

41   After capturing **Zephyrion**, modern Mersin, city in Cilicia Campestris (cf. *PECS* pp. 999b–1000a (Gough)), this particular Persian army group probably continued westwards and added to their tally of cities: **Sebaste**, modern Ayas, a Roman colony and important naval station in Cilicia Campestris (cf. *PECS*, *s.v.* 'Elaeusa', pp. 294a–295a (Gough); Kettenhofen, 1982: 111), and **Korykos**, modern Korgos, ruins near Kizaklesi, a city in Cilicia Aspera (cf. *PECS*, pp. 464b–465a (MacKay)). It fell victim to a seaborne attack led by Callistus (cf. Zonaras XII, 23, *trans. infra* 3.3.1.) at Pompeiopolis (Soloi), a coastal settlement immediately to the west of Zephyrion. Sebaste and Korykos were then possibly abandoned by the Persians as a consequence of their defeat by the Romans at Pompeiopolis.

42   After the unexpected turn of events at Pompeiopolis, the main army group, commanded probably by Shapur himself, withdrew through eastern Cilicia capturing the following six cities in the eastern part of the province: **Agrippiada**, modern Anavarza, Roman colony, also known as Anazarbos (cf. *PECS*, pp. 53b–54a, *s.v.* 'Anazarbos' (Gough)) and **Kastabala**, modern Bodrum (cf. *PECS* p. 392, *s.v.* 'Hierapolis Castabala' (Gough)); **Neronias** (later Irenopolis ?), a city in eastern Cilicia in the region of modern Yarpuz, east of Anazarbus (cf. Maricq, 1958: 356; Kettenhofen, 1982:112); **Flavias**, modern Kadirli, a Roman colony (cf. *PECS*, p. 330, *s.v.* 'Flaviopolis' (Gough)); **Nikopolis**, modern Islahiya, (see above, Note 13) and **Epiphaneia/** Oiniandos, modern Gozene near Erzin (cf. *PECS* p. 315 (Gough)).

43   The next series of six cities in the ŠKZ, all situated on the coast of Cilicia Aspera (later Isauria), poses considerable problems to the historical reconstruction of the events. Its position on the list after the cities captured by the main Persian force in Cilicia suggests that the cities were captured by an army group, probably a vanguard which had advanced beyond Sebaste before the Roman counterattack or a rearguard which had remained at Sebaste after Shapur had withdrawn his main force. From Sebaste the group proceeded to capture **Kelenderis**, modern Gilindire (cf. *PECS*, p. 445 (Mitford)) and **Anemurium**, modern Anamur (cf. *PECS*, p. 58 (Russell)), and reached the westernmost point of penetration by any Persian force in Shapur's campaigns at **Selinos**, modern Selinti (cf. *PECS*, p. 823 (Bean)). It then divided itself into two groups to attack on their return the cities which had been bypassed along the coast. One group took **Myonpolis**, city of uncertain location, perhaps near modern Iskele (cf. Kettenhofen, 1982: 116), while another went for Antioch (ad Cragum), modern Endiseguney (cf. *PECS*, p. 63 (Bean)), before returning east via **Seleucia (ad Calycadnum)**, modern Silifke (cf. *PECS*, pp. 821–2 (MacKay)). There is no support for the suggestion of Downey (1961: 589, n. 7) that the Antioch and Seleucia mentioned here signify the second capture of the two cities with the same names on the Orontes in Syria.

44 **Dometioupolis**, modern Dinbebol(?), city in Cilicia Aspera. The Parthian version (line 14) reads: miustynprws. Cf. Honigmann and Maricq, 1953: 160; Gignoux 1972: 58, *s.v.* 'mzdnprws'. This city could have been captured by a splinter-force which advanced upon it from Selinus, as suggested by Sprengling (1953: 105) – a route which would have involved travelling over difficult terrain, or by a force using the more natural route from Seleucia (ad Calycadnum).

45 After sending out a column to invest Pompeiopolis, the main Persian force withdrawing from Selinus then headed north for the important Roman colony of **Tyana**, modern Kemerhisar and later metropolis of Cappadocia II (cf. *PECS*, p. 942 (Harper)). There it split into two groups, one advancing deeper into Cappadocia towards Armenia Minor and the other westwards into Lykaonia. The first group captured the metropolis of **Caesarea**, formerly Mazaka, modern Kayseri, (cf. *PECS*, p. 182 (Harper)), probably after heavy fighting. From Caesarea, a minor force raided **Comana**, modern Sar (cf. *PECS*, pp. 233–4 (Harper)), and advanced as far north as **Sebastia**, modern Sivas, on the River Halys and later capital of Armenia Minor, (cf. *PECS*, p. 816 (Firatti)). The second group headed southwest from Tyana for **Kybistra**, modern Eregli (we have no option here but to abandon the *ŠKZ* order of Comana – Kybistra – Sebasteia), thence **Birtha** (= Barata? in modern Madensehir) (cf. Honigmann and Maricq 1953: 152) and **Rhakoundia**, a city or settlement of uncertain identification but located probably near Barata (cf. Honigmann and Maricq, 1953: 157–8). A subsidiary force might have advanced from Kybistra to **Laranda**, modern Karaman, while the main battle group advanced on their main objective of **Iconium**, modern Konya. Cf. Kettenhofen, 1982: 117–22.

46 The Roman sources on the capture of Valerian give three contradictory versions: (1) he was captured after defeat in open battle, thus agreeing with the Persian account (cf. Eutropius and the *Epitome de Caesaribus*); (2) he was treacherously seized while he was trying to negotiate with Shapur (cf. Zosimus and Petrus Patricius); and (3) he sought protection from the Persian king from his mutinous troops at Edessa (cf. Zonaras). A major Roman defeat is the most likely as Valerian, like Crassus before him, had unwisely chosen to fight on the open plain between Edessa and Carrhae, which would have given the Sassanian cavalry considerable advantage. Cf. Potter, 1985: 336.

47 It is unlikely that Lactantius here has in mind the scene of the captured Valerian kneeling in supplication before a mounted Shapur as depicted on the Sassanian rock reliefs at Naqs-i-Rustam. The main inspiration behind this alleged comment of Shapur must have been Psalm CX, 1, chosen here as the fulfilment of a prophecy against an emperor who was a persecutor of Christians. The paintings referred to by Lactantius may be official wall-paintings depicting scenes from imperial campaigns. Cf. *SHA Max. Thrax* 12, 10, *Tac.* 16, 2 and 25, 4 and *Aur.* 10, 2. For a full discussion of this passage, see Schwartz, 1978: 99–101; Felix, 1985: 69. One cannot, however, rule out completely the fact that returned Roman captives who might have helped with the sculpturing of the Sassanian rock reliefs could have

contributed their knowledge to the Roman official paintings.

48   'Gallienus could very effectively plead that the acute problems of central defence during his reign precluded any possibility of considering vengeance on Persia; but he may have wished to dissociate himself from the demoralizing effects of his father's capture' (Creed, 1984: 86.)

49   Lactantius' account of the treatment of Valerian at the hands of Shapur agrees in general with that of Tabari (pp. 826–7, Nöldeke, pp. 32–3, see Appendix 1, pp. 282–3.)

50   Coins of Valerian continued to be struck in Egypt until Aug./Sept. 260 but the earliest official documents of the usurpers Macrianus and Quietus appeared in late Sept. (*PFlor.* II 195: 26 Sept. and *POxy.* XII 1476: 29 Sept.). The last dated document of Valerian (with Salonina and Gallienus) on papyrus was issued on 28 Aug. 260 (*POxy* 2186). Cf. Felix, 1985: 66. The capture could have taken place as early as late spring. Cf. Christol, 1975: 819–20.

51   The main part of the *vita* of Valerian in the *SHA* has not survived but the extant portion gives the impression that it was positive and even laudatory, very different from the Christian accounts of his reign.

52   Reading: '. . . Sapori[s] rex regum Velsolus:' (ed Hohl) for '. . . Sapori regi regum vel soli:' (ed. Magie). Velsolus is otherwise unknown. The title of King of Kings was normally the preserve of the King of Iran and Non-Iran but it had earlier been allowed (with the right to exhibit it on coinage) to the kings of Pontus and of Armenia. Cf. Alföldi, 1939: 175–6.

53   This letter which appears to be the reply from an otherwise unknown vassal king to Shapur's message of victory is almost certainly apocryphal. The purpose of this falsification may have been a pagan riposte to the Christian accounts of Valerian's capture, as exemplified by that of Lactantius, and underscores the fact that Romans were no less formidable and respected even in defeat. Cf. Alföldi, 1963: 1–3.

54   The Cadusii or Cadusaei were mentioned in Xenophon (*inst. Cyr.* V, 2, 25 etc.) as a warlike people living on the south-west coast of the Caspian Sea. We are grateful to Sir Ronald Syme for drawing our attention to the fact that, in this period, this ethnic term features mainly in works of fiction such as the *Life of Apollonius of Tyana* by Philostratus (I, 19).

55   'Artavasdes rex Armeniorum' should not be seen as a 'classicization' of Hormizd-Ardashir, the son of Shapur and the Sassanian king of Armenia.

56   The Great Inscription of Kirder the Mobed (*KKZ* lines 12–13, see 3.3.3.) speaks of the Sassanian invasion of Iberia, Albania, and other Caucasian and Caspian lands, which seems to imply that these territories had not yet been fully brought into the Sassanian politicial sphere. Cf. Toumanoff, 1969: 255.

57   Shapur I had a reputation for cruelty and harshness to his enemies which even someone as devoted to his cause as the prophet Mani could not readily brush aside. Cf. Sundermann, 1981: 107 (11.2, lines 1660–7).

58   The heavy fighting round the city gave currency to the rumour that

Shapur slew 12,000 Jews in Caesarea-Mazaka. Cf. Neusner, 1966: 45–8.

59 On Mani's service in the entourage of Shapur and his travels in the frontier regions, see Lieu 1985: 58–9, 63; Sundermann, 1981: 95; Sundermann, 1987: 64–5.

60 Alexander was a Neo-Platonist philosopher writing at the beginning of the fourth century.

4 THE RISE AND FALL OF PALMYRA

1 Septimius Odaenathus, the architect of the meteoric rise of Palmyra in the years after Valerian's capture, was born *c.* 220 and was elevated to senatorial rank probably under Philip the Arab. His ancestry and early history are far from clear. Cf. *PLRE* I, pp. 638–9, Gawlikowski, 1985: 261 and Potter 1990: 381–94. On the history of Palmyra under the High Empire, see esp. Drijvers, 1977: 837–46 and Matthews, 1984: 158–73.

2 This inscription has been given an early date in this collection because of the absence from it of the more grandiose titles which Odaenathus enjoyed after his victory over the Persians and the Roman usurpers.

3 The safeguarding of the trans-continental trade, so vital to the prosperity of Palmyra, might have lain at the heart of this attempt at a treaty by Odaenathus with Shapur. Earlier, Palmyra's trade had greatly benefited from her close connection with the Romans. The city became a *civitas libera* under Hadrian and a *colonia* under Septimius Severus. Archaeological evidence has shown that Palmyrene troops were stationed on the island of Ana on the Euphrates under the Parthians and continued to do so after the island had passed into Roman hands *c.* 208 and their presence is recorded as late as 252. Cf. Kennedy, 1986b: 103–4 and Invernizzi, 1986: 359. A date after the defeat of Valerian is commonly suggested for Odaenathus' attempt at a treaty with Shapur, but he could have come to realize the precarious position of Rome after the fall of Ana in 253 and of Dura in 256.

4 The vagueness of this title probably reflects the confused state of the Roman East after the death of Gordian III. Cf. Gawkilowski, 1985: 261.

5 Prior to the discovery of this inscription, it was generally assumed that Odaenathus the Great was the son or nephew of another Odaenathus – the Odaenathus Senior mentioned by the Anonymous Continuator of Dio Cassius (*trans. infra* 4.5.1.). Upon the murder of this Odaenathus 'Senior', power was briefly held by his son Septimius Haeranes (*c.* 251) who was the grandson of Vaballathus Nasor. He was soon succeeded by Odaenathus 'Junior', i. e. Odaenathus the Great and husband of Zenobia. The late date of this new inscription dedicated to an Odaenathus who was the son of Vaballathus Nasor effectively rules out the existence of an Odaenathus 'Senior' who held power in Palmyra till 251. Odaenathus the Great was the same Odaenathus who was the son of Haeranes and grandson of Vaballathus Nasor. Septimius Haeranes was his son and not his brother or uncle. Cf. Gawkilowski, 1985: 257–61.

6　Sherira Ben Hanina (*c.* 906–1006) was *gaon* of Pumbedita from 968 to 1006. His famous epistle, *Iggereth Rav Sherira Ga'on*, which chronicles the origins of the *Mishnah* and of the *Talmud*, was composed in 987.

7　Neusner (1966: 48–9) believes that the date should be altered to 262 or 263. On Odaenathus and the Jews of Babylonia, see De Blois, 1975: 12–16 and the documents translated in Neusner, 1966: 43–52.

8　On the identification see Neusner, 1966: 50 and De Blois, 1975: 12.

9　Nehardea (modern Tall Nihar, cf. Oppenheimer, 1983: 287) was an important Jewish settlement in the Middle Euphrates and the destruction of its famous academy is well documented in Rabbinic sources. The incident provides clear indication of the southward penetration of Palmyrene forces under Odaenathus. For a more cautious view, see Neusner, 1966: 49–52.

10　The location of Sekansiv is unknown.

11　Mahoza was a suburb of Veh-Ardashir on the east bank of the Tigris and an important centre of Jewish life in the Sassanian period. See map in Oppenheimer, 1983: 233. The name Mahoza is also applied to the area covered by a large conurbation comprising: (1) Mahoza (= Maizomalcha i.e. the 'Royal Fort' or 'Royal Port' mentioned by Ammianus), (2) Aksak (= ancient Opis), (3) Veh-Ardashir (= Coche) and (4) (the ruins of) Seleucia. Cf. Oppenheimer, 1983: 179–93.

12　Pumbedita is the Jewish name for Pirisabora (al-Anbar).

13　T. Fulvius Junius Quietus (Aug. 260–261) was the younger son of Macrianus and brother of T. Fulvius Iunius Macrianus. He was a tribune under Valerian. Cf. *PLRE* I, pp. 757–8.

14　The allegation that Ballista murdered Quietus and seized the throne for himself is not supported by other evidence. Cf. *PLRE* I, p. 146.

15　The imperial title granted to (or assumed by) Odaenathus is reflected in Manichaean missionary texts. Cf. Sundermann, 1981: 42 (3.3, lines 451–2).

16　The person is otherwise unknown; the reading of Quintus (= Quietus) by Müller and the suggestion of Mai for Carinus (= Macrianus) are both rejected by Boissevain.

17　He was almost certainly the same person as Herodes, the son of Odaenathus by an earlier marriage. His victory over the Persians on the Orontes might have caused them to withdraw from Antioch.

18　He is likely to have been the same person as Aurelius Vorodes who had been honoured as early as 258/9. See above 4.2.4. The large number of dedications to him shows that he probably held the reins of power in Palmyra during Odaenathus' periodic absences from the city.

19　A certain Vorod 'the *agoranomos*' is listed on the *ŠKZ* (Gk, line 67) among those who had submitted to Shapur's authority. If this was the same person as Septimius Vorodes, then it would suggest that he was the leader of a pro-Persian party in Palmyra. Or he might have been the leader of the Palmyrene delegation which had unsuccessfully negotiated with Shapur. Cf. Schlumberger, 1972: 339–41. Such an act of homage demonstrates the need for a trading city like Palmyra to keep her channels of communication open with both super-powers on which her trade depended.

20 We know from a Palmyrene inscription (*CISem* II, 3971, *trans. infra* 4.5.5.) that Zenobia is called Septimia Bath Zabbai and Bath Antiochus. The latter might have been Antiochus IV Epiphanes (175–64 BC) whose wife Cleopatra Thea was the daughter of Ptolemy VI Philometer (181–145 BC) or Antiochus VII Sidetes, the third husband of Cleopatra Thea. Cf. Ingholt, 1976: 137.

21 Herodianus had already shared some of his father's more important titles since 251 and was clearly groomed as his successor. This might well have angered Zenobia, who had designs for her son Vaballathus Athenodorus.

22 By 'the younger Odaenathus', the anonymous author must have meant Vaballathus Athenodorus. Cf. Mommsen, 1894: 436, n. 2.

23 The allegation rests solely on her possible favour to Judaism and the Judaizing character of Paul of Samosata's teaching. Cf. Millar, 1971: 13.

24 Iuppiter Hammon was the tutelary god of Bostra. Legio III Cyrenaica was then stationed at Bostra and it is highly probable that it was the standard bearer and the hornblowers (i.e. those responsible for the religious life of the legion) of this legion which took an active part in the plundering of the Temple of Bel at Palmyra (see below 4.9.4.) in revenge for this earlier act of sacrilege.

25 Commercial interests, rather than dynastic claims, lay behind the Palmyrene invasion of Egypt. The Blemmyae in S. Egypt had revolted and come from below the Second Cataract of the Nile (i.e. between Semna and Buhen) to occupy much of the Thebaid, thus threatening the caravan trade which used the Red Sea ports. Furthermore, L. Mussius Aemilianus, the prefect of Egypt from 258, had supported the usurpers Macrianus and Quietus and minted their coins at Alexandria. He was defeated and captured by Aurelius Theodotus, who then commanded the troops who had remained loyal to Gallienus and succeeded as prefect *c.* 262. Aemilianus might have been opposed to Odaenathus because of their destruction by the Palmyrene prince at Emesa. Cf. Schwartz, 1976: 145–6.

26 Aurelius Timagenes probably belonged to a party in Alexandria which supported Odaenathus out of commercial interests and because he was acting on behalf of Gallienus when he suppressed the rebels. Cf. Schwartz, 1976: 148–9.

27 Babylon (modern Kasr-Ash-Shama) was a major Roman fortress on the Nile Delta and the base of the Legio XIII Gemina (*Not. Dig.*, Or. XXVIII, 15). It was the scene of a famous siege during the Arab Conquest. Cf. Butler and Fraser, 1978: 238–48.

28 Some Roman units, especially those of the cavalry, might have been pressed into service alongside the Palmyrenes in Egypt. Cf. Speidel, 1977: 724.

29 This title has been translated by some scholars (e.g. Gawlikowski, 1985: 256 as '*corrector orientis*'. However, a more exact equivalent of '*corrector*' in Palmyrene is its transliterated form as held by Vaballathus. See below 4.5.5. Cf. Millar, 1971: 10.

30 The main text of the document, which is an application by the citizens of Oxyrhynchus to the keepers of the archives for the formal entry into

their registers of a right of inviolability, is here omitted.

31   The author of the *HA* appears to be using the term '*Saraceni*' here in the same way as Ammianus to mean the Scenitae Arabes. He was probably embroidering his third century source, the lost (so-called) 'Kaisergeschichte', with anachronistic material. Cf. Bowersock, 1987: 78–9.

32   This arrogant letter, allegedly translated by Nicomachus, but in fact the work of Longinus, demonstrates the eagerness of the author of the *HA* to exonerate Zenobia. Cf. Bowersock, 1987: 78.

33   The titles 'Sarmaticus', 'Armeniacus' and 'Adiabenicus' have not yet been discovered on inscriptions of Aurelian. Cf. Kneissl, 1969: 177. 'Adiabenicus', however, was part of the titulature of Vaballathus. See above, 4.7.3.

34   The 'Third Legion' was the Legio III Cyrenaica stationed at Bostra. See above, note 23.

35   Cf. Rey-Coquais, 1978: 60.

36   Knowledge of the properties and villas in the suburbs of Rome is a characteristic of the author of the *HA*. Cf. Bowersock, 1987: 78–9.

37   Anatolius was a native of Cilicia and was senator of Constantinople *c.* 390–393. Cf. Seeck, 1906: 69, 'Anatolius VI' and *PLRE* I, pp. 61–2, 'Anatolius 9'.

38   Cf. Seeck, 1906: 146, 'Eusebius XXXIV' and *PLRE* I, p. 306, 'Eusebius 27'.

5   FROM PROBUS TO DIOCLETIAN

1   According to Elias of Nisibis (CSCO 62, p. 46, 21–2), Bahram II came to the throne in 588 Sel. which begins on 1 Oct. 276, and was succeeded by Bahram III in 605 Sel. which begins on 1 Oct. 293 (CSCO 62 p. 96, 18–19) after a reign of seventeen years as stated by Agathias. Cf. Cameron, 1969–1970: 142 and Felix, 1985: 96–7.

2   On the revolt of the Blemmyae in Upper Egypt under Gallienus, see above Ch. 4, n. 25.

3   Bahram II is the only Persian king whose reign paralleled that of Probus (Jul. 276–Oct. 282). Narses was the fourth son of Shapur I and was the king of the Sakas under Shapur I. Bahram I, who succeeded his brother Hormizd after his short reign of one year, may have been the son of a minor queen or even of a concubine, and Narses objected to his being succeeded by his son Bahram II. However, there is no sign that he actually rebelled during the relatively long reign of Bahram II. He became king of Persian-held Armenia some time before 293 and therefore enjoyed the title of 'King of Kings'. Cf. Frye, 1983: 127–8 and Skjaervø 1983(ii): 10–11. Narses' subsequent accession to Shahanshah of Persia was the outcome of a power struggle between two political factions, one supporting him and the other supporting Bahram III. Still, it is difficult to see how Bahram II could have entrusted the negotiations with the Romans to him, unless of course the negotiations had to do with Armenia. (On this, see below, note 26). The author of the *SHA* might have confused an embassy from Narses to Diocletian

(*infra* 5.4.2.) with one from Bahram II to Probus. Cf. Felix, 1985: 97–8.

4 There is no numismatic evidence to support such a proposed campaign, but Probus' peace treaty with the Persians might have been a precursor to military action with the restoration of Tiridates to the throne of Armenia as the possible aim. See below *SHA Car.* 7, 1, in 5.1.5. Cf. Chaumont, 1969: 98–9 and Felix, 1985: 98.

5 Hormizd, the brother of Bahram II, was the governor of Khorasan. With the aid of Kushans and the Gelani, he established an independent state in the East. This insurrection was suppressed and Bahram II crowned his son the future Bahram III as 'King of the Sakas'. Cf. Agathias IV, 24, 7–8, *trans. infra* 5.3.2. The need to undertake such a major military campaign in Central Asia might have weakened the defences of Iran's western frontiers, thus enabling Carus to capture Ctesiphon in 283. Cf. Christensen, 1944: 227–30.

6 'Rufii' is probably a misspelling or copyist's error for 'Cussi' – the people of the Central Asian kingdom of Kushan. Cf. Markwart, 1901: 36, n. 1.

7 The Gelani were inhabitants of a region on the S. W. coast of the Caspian Sea.

8 Coche is the name of a hillock around which Ardashir founded the city of Veh-Ardashir to replace the nearby city of Seleucia which had fallen into ruins after two important changes in the course of the Tigris towards the end of the first century had deprived the former Seleucid capital of its important river frontage. Veh-Ardashir is generally referred to as Seleucia in western sources. It was also the seat of the Catholicos of the Christians in Persia. Cf. Fiey, 1970b: 44 and Oppenheimer, 1983: 223–5. See above, Ch. 4, note 11.

9 Jerome's dating is incorrect as nearly all our sources place the death of Carus in 283.

10 Carus bears the title of 'Persicus maximus' in his inscriptions and coins. See below Appendix 4, p. 337.

11 Gaius Sollius Apollinaris Sidonius (*c.* 430–479) was a Gallo-Roman of noble birth. After holding a number of minor offices at Rome and in Gaul, he was consecrated bishop of Auvergne. He was both famous for his skills as a poet and panegyrist and for his heroic leadership of his people in resisting the Goths.

12 Niphates is the name of a mountain in Armenia which is situated to the south of the headwaters of the Euphrates and to the north of Lake Van. Cf. Chaumont, 1976: 184. It is far too out of the way of the normal itinerary of an invasion directed against Ctesiphon, unless, like Trajan, Carus first marched into Armenia. See also the reference to Armenia in a story concerning Carinus (*trans. infra* 5.2.2.).

13 M. Aurelius Carinus was appointed emperor by his father Carus in 282 and placed in command of the western provinces. He was killed in battle against Diocletian at Margum in Moesia in 285. Cf. Felix, 1985: 103.

14 Carrhae (ancient Harran) did not receive its name from Carus nor was it turned into a major fortress. It was abandoned by the Romans in 359 because of the weakness of its fortifications. Cf. Amm. XVIII, 7, 3.

15   Malalas' source for the claim that Carus died fighting the Huns might have been the *Anonymous Barbari* (*Chron. Min.* I, p. 388, 15, MGH). Cf. Stauffenberg, 1931: 394–5.

16   Numerianus, the son of Carus, was allegedly a highly reputable poet and was said to have competed for literary honours against Olympius Nemesianus, the author of this poetic treatise. Nemesianus's poem on the art of hunting is the only partially surviving one of three poems which were known to have been well received in the provincial cities. Cf. *SHA Car.* 11, 2. It was composed after the death of Carus but before that of his sons. Cf. Clinton, 1845: 323. His praises for the deeds of the sons of Carus in the East are more literary than historical, but they may also reflect contemporary uncertainty over the precise nature of Carus' death and the prosecution of the war. Cf. Felix, 1985: 103–4.

17   In the majority of the traditions concerning the martyrdom of Babylas, Philip the Arab, rather than Numerianus, was the emperor who ordered his execution. Cf. Lieu, 1986a: 52–3.

18   This is followed in the account of Malalas by the story of the Saints Cosmas and Damian (pp. 304, 13–306, 6) which was set in Cyrrhestica in the winter period of truce after Carinus' victory in a bitterly contested battle and prior to Carinus' departure for Persia.

19   Numerianus was made Augustus two months before the death of his father. Cf. *PLRE* I, p. 634.

20   Synesius (*c.* 370–*c.* 414) was a native of Cyrene and was chosen bishop of Ptolemais *c.* 410. His speech *de regno*, which depicts the ideal Roman emperor, was delivered before the emperor Arcadius in 399.

21   Carinus could not possibly have taken part in the Persian expedition of 283. Chaumont (1976: 101) proposes taking 'Carinus' as a confusion for 'Carus' and that this episode, fictional though it may first appear, suggests Carus' intention to restore Trdat to Armenia – a suggestion which is supported by the Armenian historian Moses Khorenats'i (II, 79, Thomson, p. 227, see Appendix II, p. 318) who says that Tiridates served in the army of Carinus and, when the latter was defeated and killed by the Persian general Kornak, he fled across the Euphrates to Licinius.

22   The panegyrist is Mamertinus (cf. *PLRE* I, 'Mamertinus 1', pp. 539–40) and the panegyric was delivered on 21st April, 289, in honour of the emperor Maximianus.

23   This does not imply, as suggested by Christensen (1944: 227), that the Romans withdrew in 283 after a peace had been concluded with the Persians. The reasons for Bahram II's desire to negotiate must be found in the internal history of Persia. Cf. Ensslin, 1942: 9 and Barnes, 1982: 50–1.

24   These were not likely to have included territorial concessions. Shapur II would later name only Narses as the Shahanshah who had conceded territory to the Romans (Amm. XVII, 5, 6.). Cf. Ensslin, 1942: 13–14 and Felix, 1985: 105.

25   A literary topos which would be repeated almost verbatim by Pacatus in his panegyric to the Emperor Theodosius (*Pan. Lat.* XII/2, 22, 5).

26   The date of 287 ('the third year of the reign of Diocletian') is given by

Moses Khorenats'i for the restoration of Trdat. This was carried out, according to Agathangelos (46, trans. Thomson, p. 61) with the aid of a large Roman army. Such a view, Toumanoff (1969: 153–265) argues, may be over-simplistic. The negotiations between Probus and 'Narses' (see above Note 3) might have been over the recognition of the *de facto* division of the Kingdom of Armenia into a Roman (western and smaller) and a Persian (eastern and larger) zone. This would explain why, on his inscription at Paikuli (section 89, ed. Skjaervø, 1983: 71), a monument raised between 293 and 296, Narses was congratulated by a 'Trdat the king'. As Narses himself was the Sassanian king of Armenia until 293, Trdat could not have ruled over the whole kingdom from 287 onwards. The discrepancy has led Toumanoff (1969: 253–9) to suggest that the Trdat of the inscription might have been one of the murderers of Khosrov II, the Armenian king who succeeded Trdat II and who was restored to suzerainty over western Armenia under the treaty negotiated between Narses and Probus in 279/80. Upon the accession of Narses as Shahanshah, Trdat (III) became king over the whole of Armenia, but ruling as a vassal of Persia, and it was in this capacity that he was listed among the congratulants on the Paikuli inscription. This state of affairs lasted until the defeat of Narses in 298 when the Romans restored Trdat (IV), the exiled son of Khosrov, as king of the whole of Armenia. Trdat II vanished from the records to be confused sometimes with Khosrov. The accounts of the latter's death had subsequently been whitewashed by Armenian historians to make Khosrov the victim of a Persian-instigated plot. The restoration of Trdat (IV) the Great was virtually unattested in classical sources and 'Armeni(a)cus Maximus' did not become part of the imperial titulature till after 298.

27   The panegyrist is again Mamertinus and the panegyric, also in honour of Maximianus, was delivered in 291 (probably on 21 July).

28   This particular campaign can be dated with reasonable accuracy. Diocletian was in Emesa on 10 May, 290 (*CJ* IX, 41, 9) and the first extant legislation of his after his return to Sirmium (discounting *CJ* VI, 30, 6) issued from 'Sirmi' (*sic*) is dated 21 Sept. 290. Cf. Ensslin 1942: 15. His motives for such a campaign are harder to discern. The destruction of Palmyra by Aurelian had led to a realignment of Arab tribes and Diocletian's campaign may have been directed against those who were potential allies of the Persians and posed a threat to his plans for the reorganization of the frontier by raiding new foundations such as Diocletianopolis in S. Palestine. Cf. Felix, 1985: 108. Diocletian took the title of 'Persicus Maximus' rather than 'Arabicus Maximus' in the same year (*CIL* III, 5810 = Dessau 618), probably for reasons of prestige and propaganda. On the use of the word 'Saraceni' in the Latin Panegyrics, see Bowersock, 1987: 73.

29   This attempt by Agathias to explain the origins of Bahram's title is erroneous. The Saganshah was the Sassanian governor (with royal rank) of Sistan – a title which Narses also held. See the important discussion in Sundermann, 1987: 60 and n. 141.

30   Agathias seems to have confused the length of Narses' reign with that

of Hormizd II. Narses reigned for nine years (293–302). Cf. Felix, 1985: 110.

31   The Quinquegentianae were tribal inhabitants of the Atlas Mountains with modern Setif as their main centre.

32   Jerome's dating is at least two years too early for the renewal of the war by Narses.

33   The fragment, probably from an epic composed in the reign of Diocletian, was discovered by Reitzenstein in the papyri collection of the University of Strasburg.

34   Enyo-Bellona was the Roman god of war.

35   The region of Nisaya in Media was famous for its horses and was therefore the traditional recruiting ground for Persian cavalry.

36   The more legible fragments of what must have been an epic poem on the achievements of the Tetrarchs appear to refer to the defeat of Diocletian and Galerius in Mesopotamia in 296. Cf. Barnes, 1976a: 182–3.

37   Constantius I (Chlorus) was the ruler who was occupied in Britain. The other ruler who was detained in Spain would have almost certainly been Maximianus. This Spanish campaign is otherwise unattested. The poet follows the Latin panegyrists in comparing the military exploits of Diocletian and his associates with those of their celestial patrons. Cf. Cumont, 1902: 39.

38   A clear reference to Diocletian who was accompanied on his campaign by Galerius, his Caesar in the Tetrarchy.

39   The traditional order of events, viz. Diocletian left Alexandria for the eastern frontier in March 297 after the suppression of the revolt of Achilleus, has been revised by Barnes (1982: 54) on new papyrological evidence. Diocletian went to Egypt *after* and *not* before the initial defeat of Galerius.

40   Though control of Arzanene and Gordyene would have given the Romans considerable territory east of the Tigris, the latter, especially its middle course, remained the *de facto* boundary between the two empires till 363. Cf. Amm. XVIII, 5, 3 and XXV, 6, 10 and 7, 8–9.

41   Galerius' running before Diocletian's carriage might have been a form of Tetrarchic court ceremonial rather than a sign of humiliation. Cf. Eadie, 1967: 147–8. Barnes (1981: 17) suggests that Diocletian and Galerius took the field together and the junior colleague was made to shoulder the blame after the defeat.

42   The route of Narses' advance is hard to discern. The venue of the battle gives the impression that the Persians were taking the Tigris-route with the intention of invading Osrhoene or that Narses was invading Mesopotamia from Armenia. Galerius was probably attacked (or tricked into attacking) before the arrival of the main force under Diocletian.

43   The Goths were pacified by Galerius before 297. Cf. *Pan. Lat.* IV, 10, 4.

44   Shapur I was the father, not the grandfather, of Narses.

45   Malalas has confused Maximianus 'Herculius', the then Augustus of the West, with Galerius, whose full name was C. Galerius Valerius Maximianus.

46 Archapet, i.e. Hargbed (mp. *hlgwpt*, pth. *hrkpty*) a very high ranking Sassanian official. In Sassanian inscriptions, his position comes before even that of the royal princes. Cf. Skjaervø, 1983 (ii): 39.

47 The original manuscript reads 'had the command of Sumia' (τὴν τοῦ Συμίου εἶχεν ἀρχήν). The translation follows Peeter's (1931: 27) emendation from 'Συμίου' to 'σημείου'. Cf. Ensslin 1942: 51.

48 The five 'provinces' or satrapies ceded by Narses gave the Romans strategic control of the Upper Tigris, but this does not altogether seal off Armenia from Sassanian interference as it might have appeared at first sight. **Intelene**: region centred on Karkathiokerta (mod. Egil), 40 km. north of Amida, and later (Roman) Armenia IV after the partition of Armenia at the end of the fourth century, cf. Dillemann, 1962: 120–1; **Sophene**: region on the river Arsanias and centred on Asmosaton, cf. Dillemann, 1962: 121–6; **Arzanene**: region east of the river Nymphios (mod. Batman Suyu) with capital at Cefa since the time of Constantius, cf. Whitby, 1983: 205–7; **Cordyene**: region south of Arzanene and north of the Tur Abdin. Cf. Dillemann, 1962: 110–12; **Zabdicene**: is the region surrounding the city of Bezabde. See below pp. 389–90, n. 19. For a detailed study of the territorial implication of this treaty to both sides, see esp. Blockley, 1984: 29–36 and Winter, 1988: 171–84.

49 The frontier agreed upon between Narses and Sicorius ran roughly along the Tigris in the north-east down to Bezabde (Amm. XX, 7, 1) and a number of regions beyond the Tigris (the Transtigritanian regions) came under Roman influence. From the Tigris the frontier ran south-east to include Singara and westwards to the Euphrates, following the river until Circesium where it met the Khabur. Cf. Gracey, 1981: 96.

50 Some scholars have suggested that Zintha is a miscopying of Ziatha (cf. Amm. XIX, 6, 1), a fortress in Intelene, 156 km. north of Amida, probably to be identified with Kharput which according to Arab sources was earlier called Hisn Ziyad. Cf. Bivar, 1986: 11. See also Ioannes Scylitzes, *synop. hist.* p. 316, 18–22, CFHB. Such an identification, however, would place the boundary too far to the west. Zintha as stated by Petrus must have been situated in Media (i. e. Media Atropatene). Cf. Chaumont, 1969: 106–7. On the other hand, Winter (1988: 181–2) argues for Zintha = Ziatha on the grounds that the place marked the boundary between Armenia and Rome and not between Armenia and Persia.

51 The designation of Nisibis as the sole venue for transaction between the two empires was clearly an attempt to limit the scope of espionage by cross-frontier traders. Cf. Felix, 1985: 127 and Lieu, 1986b: 491–2.

52 Constantine served on the staff of Galerius until his return to his father's court under controversial circumstances in 305. If this statement was not an empty boast, then one may infer from it that Galerius undertook an invasion of Sassanian Mesopotamia on one of his two campaigns against Narses. Cf. Barnes, 1981: 18 and Barnes 1982: 63.

53 This has traditionally been assigned to the Armenian campaign of Maximinus Daia (*infra* pp. 145–6). Castritius (1968–1969: 102) has conjectured that Verinus (Lucer)'s service should go back to the

Persian War of Galerius and that his friendship with Constantine, therefore, goes back to 298. Cf. Barnes, 1982: 118–19.

54   The oration was composed in the spring of 298.

55   The edict was issued in 302 and not in 297 as had previously been suggested by scholars. Cf. Barnes, 1982: 169.

56   The *Collatio legum Mosaicarum et Romanarum* is an anonymous compilation composed between AD 390 and 428 with the explicit aim of comparing selected Roman legal norms with the Laws of Moses. It preserved the texts of a number of important imperial edicts from the Tetrarchic period.

57   War-psychology and political propaganda as well as religious conservatism were undoubtedly the main motives behind this edict. However, there is little to support the theory that Narses had hoped to use the Manichaeans as a fifth-column. The Manichaeans were a persecuted sect under Bahram II and most of the Manichaean missionaries in the Roman Empire would have been refugees from Sassanian Mesopotamia. Cf. Lieu, 1985: 91–5.

58   I.e. the Elect members of the sect who were roving ascetics and missionaries.

59   The following is no more than a representative selection of the large number of inscriptions found in the frontier regions which are dated to the Tetrarchy. For other examples see *IGLS* 59, 499, 9058, 9060–9061 and Littmann, Magie, and Stuart, III.A, nos. 114, 205–207 and III.A. 2, Appendix V,A and B, VI,B, VIII,A and IX,A.

60   Palmyra became the base of the Legio I Illyricorum (cf. *Not. Dig.*, Or. XXXII, 30) after its occupation by the Romans.

61   The Strata Diocletiana was a military road, constructed, or largely rebuilt, by Diocletian to act as the main line of defence for Syria Phoenice. The principal line ran south-east from Sura on the Euphrates to Palmyra and then along the Jebel Rawaq to Khan abu khamat, near Dmeir (Thelsee). It continued from there to the Hauran and joined a similar road along the Arabian frontier. The Strata made use wherever possible of low hills both partly to enable the defenders to see better and partly because the higher ground helped to attract precipitation. Forts were built at regular intervals (about 30 Roman miles from each other) with intermediate signalling stations and watch-towers. Heavier units were stationed at key road-junctions to the rear of the Strata. The idea of basing a system of defence on a main road is not new, and in its Arabian section, the Strata Diocletiana ran for some distance parallel to the Via Nova Trajana. Cf. Poidebard, 1932: 73–84 and Gracey, 1981: 100.

62   The road which follows the depression of the Wadi Sirhan linked Damascus and Bostra with the Persian Gulf and its protection from raiding Saracens and Persians would have been the essential task of the Roman army in Arabia. Cf. Bowersock, 1983: 95–109 and Speidel, 1987: 213. On the threat of attacks from Saracens, see below 6.2.4.

63   The word '*praetensio*' is a *hapax* and Speidel (1987: 219–20) believes it is derived from the verb *praetendere*, 'to be stationed out in front, beyond the main line of defense'. The *praetensio* at Basiensis was

probably one of a chain of outposts responsible for patrolling and intelligence gathering.

64 This may indicate that an earlier structure, a *praetorium*, was replaced in 306 by a fort. Cf. Parker, 1986: 54.

65 The dispute was between the Arab tribes allied to Rome and those under the leadership of al-Mundhir (Alamoundaras) allied to Persia.

66 The third factory was at Antioch. Cf. *Not. Dig.*, Or. XI, 22–3.

67 We may presume that the walls of Edessa were restrengthened or rebuilt by Diocletian.

68 Qaryatein was Roman Nazala which was the base of a legionary cavalry unit (*Equites promoti indigenae*) according to the *Not. Dig.* (Or. XXXII, 23).

6 ROME AND SHAPUR II: SHAPUR AND CONSTANTINE

1 Adarnases (Adurnarseh) was the son of Hormisdas (Hormizd) II and not of Narses. His reign lasted for only 40 days. Cf. Felix, 1985: 128.

2 This third son might have been the Shapur who was called the king of the Sakas in two inscriptions. Cf. Frye, 1983: 133.

3 Cf. Christensen, 1944: 234–5 and Frye, 1983: 131–2.

4 Galerius Valerius Maximinus Daia was Augustus from *c.* 309 to 313. Cf. *PLRE* I, p. 579.

5 The origins of this particular campaign in Armenia are completely obscure. It might have been undertaken to assist Trdat in suppressing rival claimant(s) to the throne who might have had the support of the Christians. It was about this time (312–13) that the titles of 'Persicus Maximus', of 'Medicus' and 'Armenicus Maximus' were recorded for Constantine and Licinius. See Appendix 4, p. 339.

6 The importance of Christianity in Armenia prior to the conversion of Constantine has recently found additional attestation in the Manichaean account in Sogdian (TM 389d R 1 – V 40) of the visit of Gabryab, one of the more important early disciples of Mani, to (E)revan where he debated with Christian leaders at the court of the local king. Cf. Sundermann, 1981: 45–9 and Lieu, 1985: 77–8. Trdat IV then was not a Christian and later tradition attributed to him the authorship of a letter to Diocletian in support of the latter's religious policy. Text in Garitte, 1946: 37, trans. Thomson, 1976: 441, n. 82.

7 M. Aur. Val. Maxentius was the son of Maximianus 'Herculius' and was Augustus from 306 to 312. He never had a major command in the East. Cf. *PLRE* I, p. 571. Malalas appears to have confused him with Maximinus Daia.

8 The creation of a sizeable field army by Constantine was an important change in military policy. The central striking force was placed under the command of two newly-created officers, the *magister peditum* and *magister equitum*. Units of this field army (the *comitatenses*) were given privileges superior to those of the *ripenses*, i.e. the soldiers of the frontier legions, in a law of 325 (*CT* VII, 20, 4). The formation of the *comitatenses* probably dates back to Constantine's campaigns against Maxentius in 312. Cf. Jones, 1964 (i): 97 and Hoffmann, 1969(i): 186–93 and 226–36.

9   An official by this unusual name is recorded as quaestor and praetor at Rome before 287/8. Cf. *PLRE* I, p. 299 and Barnes, 1982: 187. The details of these early 'Persian' (or probably Armenian) campaigns of Constantine are unknown.

10 On the career of Hormisdas (Hormizd), see esp. *PLRE* I, p. 443 (Hormisdas 2). His potential as a rival (and pro-Roman) candidate to the Sassanian throne was not exploited by the Romans until Julian's invasion in 363.

11 Licinius was Augustus in the east until his defeat by Constantine in 324.

12 Basia is probably the same place as 'Basiensa' found on an inscription recorded by Stein at Qasr al-Azraq (cf. Kennedy, 1982: 179–85) or 'Basiensis' of the praetensio inscription (*supra* 5.5.5.)

13 There had been sporadic persecutions of Christians in Persia since the reign of Bahram II, but widespread persecution did not begin until after 337 when Simeon bar Sabba'e, the ninth Catholicos, refused to collect a double tax from the Christian community in aid of Shapur's war effort (Narratio de Simeone 4–5, *PS* 2.789–98). Cf. Decret, 1979: 125–35, Brock, 1978: 167–8 and Brock, 1982: 3–8.

14 The letter should probably be dated very shortly after October, 324. Cf. Barnes, 1985: 131–2. The reason for their visit may have been related to the asylum given to Hormisdas by Licinius or Constantine.

15 I.e. lamps used in pagan rites. Cf. Lampe, p. 791.

16 I.e. the emperor Valerian. See above 3.3.1.

17 Michael has clearly telescoped the main events in Romano-Persian relations in the last decade of Constantine's reign. The first siege of Nisibis in which Jacob played a heroic part began in 337, shortly after the death of Constantine. See below 7.1.3.

18 For earlier publications of this inscription, see Bowersock, 1971: 241 and *AE* 1974, 661.

19 Fl. Severinus is otherwise unknown. He may have been either the garrison commander or the provincial governor. Cf. Kennedy, 1982: 91.

20 What sort of building had collapsed and therefore needed repair work is not clear from the inscription. Bowersock (1971: 241) suggests reading: aedem (?) inc]uria vetustate / parietu]m ruina conlapsam/ refici (?) iu]ssit et [. . .].

21 I.e. the future Constantine II and Constantius II.

22 The reconstruction of the events in Armenia in the last years of Constantine is beset with problems and uncertainties. Until recently, most scholars have accepted the hypothesis of Baynes (1955: 187–9, first published in 1910) that the account of the abduction of Tiran (Tigranes) – an event which is placed in the reign of Valens by Faustus Buzandats'i (III, 21–2) – actually took place in *c.* 335. Baynes' redating rests on his belief that Faustus had wrongly placed the consecration of Nerses, the first Catholicos of Armenia, in the reign of Valens – an event which in fact took place under Constantius, thereby post-dating the events of the latter's reign. In Bayne's schema, Trdat the Great died *c.* 318 and his successor Khosrov II reigned probably until 327. He was succeeded by Tiran who was deposed after being

betrayed to the Persians by one of his satraps and was blinded (*c.* 335). This was followed by a Persian invasion of the kingdom which was repelled by a group of Armenian nobles with Roman assistance. It was at this stage that Constantine made Hannibalianus king of Armenia and of the Pontic regions. Shapur II, realizing the reluctance of the Armenians to accept a non-Arsacid as king, released Tiran's son Arsak (Arsaces II) who returned as king of Armenia and a Persian ally. See below p. 309. The comprehensive redating of the history of the third century Arsacids by Toumanoff (1969) has inevitable effects on their fourth century successors. Accepting Toumanoff's dating of the reign of Khosrov II to *c.* 278–287 (i.e. before rather than after the reign of Trdat IV), Hewsen (1978–79b: 99–108) dates the death of Trdat IV (the Great) to *c.* 330 instead of *c.* 317, and argues that events attributed to the reign of Tiran in fact took place under Trdat III. Faustus' (III, 20) naming of the Persian king who ordered the blinding of Tiran as Nerseh (i.e. Narses) is indicative of a chronological error. The murder of Trdat in 330 was followed by a period of unrest until the accession of Arsak (Arsaces II) who ruled from 337/8 to 367. 'Tiran' was not a personal name but a kind of title, referring to the Armenian sun-god Tir (Helios) which an Armenian king might have prefaced to his name. 'Tiran' and 'Trdat' (Tiridates), both being theophoric names, are virtually synonymous and could have been confused in the Armenian sources. Cf. Hewsen, ibid. pp. 104–5.

23 The historicity of his peregrinations cannot be doubted as, according to Rufinus (*Historia Ecclesiastica* I, 9, PL 21.478–80), they inspired those of a certain Meropius. Cf. *PLRE* I, p. 601, Lightfoot, 1981: 17–18 and Lieu, 1986b: 492–3.

24 The Persians had always regarded the re-exportation of silk and luxuries from India and China as an important source of wealth to their state. Cf. Pigulewskaja, 1969: 152.

25 Ensslin (1936: 106, n. 1) believes that Narasara may be identified with the station Nararra (Nehar Harre) on the road from Amida to Tigranocerta, about 13 Roman miles east of Amida. Peeters (1931: 44–5), on the other hand, believes that the 'pugna Narasarensi', where Narses was killed, was part of the battle of Singara.

26 Jacob the Recluse was a monk who began his ascetic calling in Egypt in the reign of Julian. After a period of wandering, he came with some companions to Hesn-Kef via Amida. At Hesn-Kef they were later captured by Shamir, the Persian general, and one of Jacob's companions suffered martyrdom with ten of his disciples. According to the *vita* (unpublished Syriac manuscript, Add. 12,174, fol. 417a–419a in the British Library), the Persian army was immediately afterwards dispersed and destroyed by a hailstorm and earthquake. Jacob built a small convent at Shilloh or Salah called the Convent of the Recluse. He died in 421. Cf. Wright, 1872 (3): pp. 1135–6, DCCCCCLX, and Bell and Mango, 1982: 10–13 and 147.

27 He was the son of Dalmatius and a nephew of Constantine. Cf. *PLRE* I, p. 407, 'Hannibalianus 2'.

28 The anonymous *Excerpta Valesiana* are preserved on one manuscript in Berlin. They were first published by the great classical scholar

Henricus Valesius in 1636. The first part, composed about 390, an incomplete biography of Constantine the Great from 305 to 337 which is based on reliable sources.

29   Barnes (1985: 132) theorizes that Constantine was planning to install Hannibalianus as Christian Shahanshah upon his successful invasion of Persia. This may explain why the exiled Hormisdas, who presumably was a Zoroastrian, was not put forward as a rival claimant to Shapur II. However, our sources are too scanty for us to discern clearly Constantine's motives behind his appointment. The fact that he was positioned in Caesarea, often the first port-of-call of Armenian exiles, may indicate that he was appointed to represent the interests of the exiled Armenian royal family and to gather valuable information. His title 'King of Kings' was appropriate for one who had to defend Roman interests in Armenia, Iberia and the Pontic region in general as the epithet had historically been part of the titulature of the kings of Pontus and of Armenia. See above Ch. 3, n. 52.

30   The next verse and the whole of the next chapter (i.e. 57), with the exception of the chapter heading, are missing from most manuscripts because of a lacuna in the text. The translation given by Richardson of the linking material (here omitted) is based on an interpolation found in a seventeenth-century edition of the *Vita*.

31   Libanius had clearly minimized the events in Armenia to exaggerate the Persian build-up in 337. Nevertheless, it is odd that he made no mention of Constantius' achievements in Armenia in a panegyric which was partly dedicated to this particular emperor.

32   The shortage of high-grade iron ore on the Iranian Plateau is a known geological feature. There is also a lack of wood to treat the mineral when extracted Cf. Lightfoot, 1981: 37, n. 116. The Roman ban on the export of weapon-grade iron to Persia is well attested. Cf. *Expositio totius mundi et gentium* 22, trans. *infra* p. 221, and Procopius, *de bello Persico* I, 19, 25–6.

33   For a detailed but albeit fictionalized description of the Persian cataphracts, see below 7.6.4.

34   This last-minute effort by the Persians to avoid war is also recorded by Eusebius in the now lost portion of his *vita Constantini* (IV, 57) but the extant heading reads: 'How he (i.e. Constantine) received an embassy from the Persians and how he kept the vigil (lit. spent the night) with the others at the Feast of Pascha.' If Shapur was sole aggressor in 337, then his efforts to make peace would hardly have been sincere. Constantine might well have broken the peace by his desire to invade Persia, using the plight of the Christians there as his pretext. Cf. Seeck, 1911: 24–5 and Barnes, 1985: 32.

35   Constantine died on 22 May, 337. Cf. Barnes, 1982: 80.

36   The name Aphrahat is Persian and he was probably the son of a Roman Christian captive. To him is attributed the authorship of twenty-three treatises (or demonstrations) in Syriac. The first ten demonstrations can be dated to 336–337. Cf. Murray, 1975: 29, Barnes, 1985: 126–8 and Brock, 1982: 7–8.

37   Pusai was martyred along with the Catholicos, Simeon Bar Sabba'e in 339. On his career in general, see esp. Brock, 1982: 4.

7 ROME AND SHAPUR: THE EARLY WARS OF CONSTANTIUS II

1   Constantine the Great had a large number of male relatives, mainly
    half-brothers who were sons of his father's second marriage to
    Theodora. These were the main victims of the massacre, which took
    place not long after the funeral of Constantine (?Aug., 337) when most
    of his relatives were still in residence at Constantinople. The massacre
    left the three sons of Constantine, i.e. Constantine II, Constantius II
    and Constans, as the only claimants to the throne. Cf. Seeck, 1911:
    6–9. The future emperor Julian and his half brother Gallus, sons of
    Julius Constantius who perished in the massacre, were spared because
    of their young age, and, in the case of Gallus, also his apparent frailty.

2   Julian is our sole witness in classical sources of an anti-Roman revolt
    in Armenia *c*. 337. For this reason, his statement has been variously
    interpreted, especially in the light of Baynes' redating of the abduction
    of Tiran by Shapur II to the reign of Constantine. See above Ch. 6,
    n. 22. Peeters (1931: 14–20) has proposed that with the murder of
    Hannibalianus disappeared the only realistic hope of some form of a
    Pontic confederation headed by a Roman prince. Roman victory in
    Armenia while Constantius was Caesar (see above 6.3.4) might have
    given rise to a pro-Roman faction in Armenia, led by the nobles who
    had appealed to Rome for help after the abduction of Tiran. In the
    meantime Shapur, realizing the difficulty of controlling Armenia
    without an Arsacid on the throne, had raised Arsak (Arsaces) as
    vassal-king and returned him to Armenia. His return, coming so soon
    after the murder of Hannibalianus, might have occasioned the
    desertion of Rome's allies in Armenia, who naturally preferred an
    Arsacid as their monarch, as described here by Julian. Cf. Dodgeon,
    1967: 51–3. Warmington (1977: 512), however, believes that Julian
    might have exaggerated in a flattering manner the difficulties in
    Armenia. Under the new chronological scheme of Hewsen, however,
    the events of these years are virtually left blank. Lightfoot (1981:
    327–8) suggests that the unrest referred to by Julian might have been
    the revolts of Sanatruk and Bacour (Faustus Buzandats'i III, 9, see
    below pp. 302–3).

3   The three royal brothers met in Pannonia during the late summer or
    early autumn of 337 and partitioned the empire. Cf. Barnes, 1980:
    160–1.

4   The sources give the impression that the siege began in 337, soon after
    the death of Constantine and before the end of August, as the Persian
    army would have been in a high state of alert anticipating Constan-
    tine's expedition. Cf. Barnes, 1985: 133. However, a date of 338
    cannot be ruled out as August was well into the campaigning season.

5   Jacob was the first recorded bishop of Nisibis and was one of the few
    bishops from sees east of the Euphrates who attended the first
    Ecumenical Council of Nicaea in 325. Most of the surviving stories
    concerning his early life found in Theodoret and Faustus Buzandats'i
    are of a legendary nature. Cf. Peeters, 1920: 286–95 and Drijvers,
    1981: 28–30.

6   For the river to be used as a battering ram, the dam constructed by the Persians would have to be of enormous height in order for the water to acquire sufficient pressure prior to its release onto the plains and thereby to lose momentum. The historicity of the account has therefore been much questioned, partly on grounds of scientific improbability and partly because it reads like an embroidered account of the third siege in which the Mygdonius was also utilized for siege purposes by the Persians. However, though there is little comparable evidence in Roman sources, the diversion of rivers for the undermining of defences was used by the Chin Shih Huang-ti (259–210 BC), the 'First' Emperor of China in his campaigns to unify Northern China. Cf. *Tzu-chih t'ung-chien* 7.228 (CHSC edn.). The effect of water against foundations of battlements in a dry climate could be devastating.

7   Nisibis (Nusaybin) had a reputation among Arab travellers in the Middle Ages for the fierceness of its gnats. Cf. Le Strange, 1905: 95.

8   For a comparison of the two accounts of the siege by Theodoret, see esp. Peeters, 1920: 297–300. Both are probably derived from Syriac sources. In the Syriac version of the vita of Jacob by Theodoret, the description of the siege is closer to that of the *Historia religiosa* rather than the *Historia ecclesiastica*. Cf. Schiwietz, 1938: 80–3.

9   Constantius arrived at Antioch at the end of 337, too late to play any significant part in the siege. Cf. Barnes, 1980: 162.

10   This is incorrect as Julian never visited Nisibis. However, he did deny the Nisibenes the special protection which they had demanded from him. See above pp. 231 and 268.

11   Shapur had obliged Arsak to give military assistance against the Romans and Armenian forces took part in the siege of Nisibis as allies of the Persians. Cf. Faustus Buzandats'i, *Hist. Arm.* IV, 20 and the more abbreviated version in Procopius, *Pers.* I, 5, 10–15, where the common enemy were some unspecified barbarians rather than 'Greeks'. After Shapur's apparent defeat before the ramparts of Nisibis, a pro-Roman and anti-Persian faction emerged around Vardan the Mamikonian. When Constantius arrived at Caesarea in early 338, he had the choice of supporting either this pro-Roman faction or the more popular Arsak. His sound political sense led him to give an amnesty to Arsak for the support he gave to the Persians in return for Armenian friendship and neutrality. This was gained at the expense of the pro-Roman faction, viz. those who, in Julian's words (21A), 'were better pleased with their present condition than with their previous power.' Cf. Peeters, 1931: 39–41 and Dodgeon, 1967: 52–4.

12   Constantius was at Emesa in 338 as he issued an edict from there on 28 October. Cf. *CT* XII, 1, 25. It is quite likely that both the Armenian Settlement and the treaty with the Arabs were negotiated during his sojourn at Emesa.

13   Imru 'al-qais, Rome's most significant ally among the Arab chieftains, had died in 328. This, together with the death of Constantine in 337, appears to have led to the dissolution of the pro-Roman alliance (foedus) among the Arab tribes. Shahid (1984: 76–9) believes that their Christianization and their subscription to the anti-Arian creed of

the Council of Nicaea led to disenchantment with the Roman alliance in the last years of Constantine when the pro-Arian party was in the ascendant. They might have even transferred their alliance to Persia with the renewal of the conflict in 337. The Arabs referred to here were located to the east of the province of Syria, beyond the Roman frontiers. The statement that Constantius received a series of embasies suggests that he was dealing with an organized federation and not with individual tribes. See also Barcelo, 1981: 84–5 and Lightfoot, 1981: 263–71.

14 On the development of the Roman heavy cavalry under Constantius and Julian, see the important discussion in Hoffmann, 1969(i): 265–77.

15 The *Itinerarium Alexandri* is an anonymous brief history of Alexander (the Great)'s expedition against Persia based mainly on the *Anabasis Alexandri* of Arrian and the *Res Gestae Alexandri Macedonis* – a Latin version of the Greek Ps.-Callisthenes (*Romance of Alexander*). The fact that the *Codex Ambrosianus P 49* (9th–11th C.) contains both a Latin version of Ps.-Callisthenes by Julius Valerius and the text of the *Itinerarium* has given rise to the hypothesis that the author of the latter might have been Iulius Valerius Alexander Polemius (consul of 338, cf. *PLRE* 1, 709–10, 'Polemius 3 and 4') whose name is in fact given (almost) in full (Iuli Valeri Alexandri Polemi v(iri) c(larissimi)') in one manuscript version of the *Res Gestae Alexandri Macedonis*. It would have been highly appropriate for a politician of the prominence of Polemius to be the author of a contemporary dedication to Constantius who was then about to launch his campaign. However, although most modern scholars accept the consul Polemius as the translator of Ps.-Callisthenes, they are on the whole more sceptical in attributing the authorship of the *Itinerarium* to Polemius. Cf. Herzog, 1989: 212–15, esp. 215. On the importance of the *Itinerarium* for Romano-Persian relations, see esp. Barnes (1985: 135–6) who argues that the comparison of Constantius to Alexander and Trajan reflects the mood of the times which expected him to undertake an offensive war against the Persians – i.e. the continuation of a war which he had inherited from his father Constantine.

16 Constantius was at Edessa in August 340, as indicated by an edict issued from there on 12 August (*CT* XII, 1, 30, reading 'Edessae' for 'Bessae', cf. Seeck, 1919: 188).

17 On these raids in the early years of the reign of Constantius, see also Libanius, *or.* XVIII, 206, *trans. infra.* p. 226. Hierapolis, about one hundred miles to the north-east of Antioch, was probably Constantius' base for this campaign. Cf. Bowen, 1982: 75–6.

18 There were no major Persian cities within easy reach of the Romans across the Tigris with the exceptions of Arbela and Karka de Bet Selok. More likely was the ancient city of Nineveh which was still inhabited under the Seleucids and even enjoyed the status of a Greek polis. Cf. Oates, 1968: 61–2. It was mentioned by Ammianus (XVIII, 7, 1) as 'an important city of Adiabene'. This would also explain the title of 'Adiabenicus Maximus' which Constantius had included in his titulature by 354 (*CIL* III, 3705 = Dessau 732).

19　A reference to the enslavement of the Eretrians by Darius I who settled them near Susa. Cf. Herodotus VI, 101 and 119.

20　The date of the battle has long been a source of dispute because of a conflict in the ancient sources. While Jerome and other chroniclers who follow his lead place it under 348, Julian says that it took place 'about six years' prior to the revolt of Magnentius (Jan., 350). For a full survey of the arguments on the date, see esp. Stein and Palanque, 1959: 138; Barnes, 1980: 163, n. 13. See also below note 25.

21　The Persian objective was most likely the capture of Singara rather than a full scale invasion of Mesopotamia in the manner of the campaigns of Shapur I. Singara (mod. Beled Sinjar) lies at the southern foot of Jebel Sinjar and was well positioned to observe Persian military activities on the Middle Tigris, and therefore changed hands regularly between the two sides (Amm. XX, 6, 9). On Singara, see esp. Oates, 1968: 97–106.

22　For a detailed comparison of the sources on the battle, see esp. Seeck, 1920: 2337.24–2338.52, Peeters, 1931: 43–5 and Dodgeon, 1967: 72–6. Libanius' account of the battle follows closely the rules of rhetoric for describing the military achievements of the Roman emperors as recommended by Menander the Rhetor (II, 373.15–25, ed. and trans. Russell and Wilson, pp. 84–6). Libanius' panegyric on the achievements of Constantius and Constans was composed *c.* 348/9. Cf. Gladis, 1907: 4–5.

23　The death of the Persian crown-prince at the battle may explain why Shapur II was eventually succeeded by his 'brother' (more likely his nephew, cf. Frye, 1983: 140–1) after his death in 379.

24　Libanius (*or.* LIX, 107) gives 150 stades, i.e. about 30 kilometres.

25　Barnes (1980: 163, n. 13) proposes *two* battles at Singara, as a solution to the problem of dating one in summer/autumn 343, and a nocturnal one at Eleia in 348. However, Libanius' description of the battle makes it clear that the fighting at Singara began at mid-day and drifted into dusk and it was in the night engagement that the Romans threw away through indiscipline what could have been a major victory. Nevertheless, there must have been a number of engagements at or near Singara because of its strategic importance to both sides, and it is entirely possible that the chroniclers had combined two battles into one; the nocturnal battle mentioned here by Festus may be the same engagement in which the Romans, under the leadership of the *comes* Aelianus, made a successful nocturnal raid on the Persian camp. See below 7.5.3.

26　Festus is the only source to name the Persian prince killed at the battle of Narasarensi. Theophanes (supra 6.3.4) mentions the death of a Narses, brother of Shapur, in Armenia in the reign of Constantine. The Byzantine chronicler might have transferred the name in error to the earlier event.

27　Peeters (1931: 44) has shown that the 'Eliensi prope Singaram' in Festus is Eleia which was situated in a gorge at the foot of the Jebel Sinjar, on a water-course which still bears the name of Nahr Ghiran, which may be the 'Narasarensi' or 'Nararensi' in Festus.

28　The *Fasti Hydatiani* is a composite consular chronicle (284 BC–AD 468) mistakenly attributed to the fifth century Spanish bishop Hydatius. It falls into three parts and the second part, covering the period from 330 to 389, was compiled in Constantinople. Cf. Bagnall *et al.*, 1987: 54.

29 Constantius issued an edict from Nisibis on 12 May, 345 (*CT* XI, 7, 5).

30 This does not necessarily mean that Constantius personally directed the siege or led the relief-force. All it means is that Babu was bishop of Nisibis at the time of Constantius' visit shortly after the end of the second siege. Cf. Barnes, 1980: 163, n. 14.

31 On the role of the bishops in the redemption of captives in the frontier zone, see Lieu, 1986b: 487–90.

32 Silvinianus was *dux Arabiae* from 348 to 351. Cf. *PLRE* I, p. 842 and Sartre, 1982: 103.

33 For a detailed analysis of the sources of this, the most important and best documented of the three sieges of Nisibis, see Sturm, 1936: 742.60–746.59, Dimaio, 1977: 285–90 and Lightfoot, 1981: 94–103.

34 Syr.: nsybt, a play on the name Nisibis (Syr.: Nsybyn).

35 Bidez-Cumont (1932: 36–7, n. 2) believes that this brief mention of a Roman victory in Mesopotamia refers to the battle of Singara while Sturm (1936: 743.43) suggests the third siege of Nisibis. As the panegyric was composed in 350, the latter seems more likely.

36 The Mygdonius (Dschaghschagh) flowed past (not through) the city. Its course is still marked by a bridge of Roman date. The historicity of Julian's description of the siege has been called into question as a sea-battle on land taxes one's credulity, and the account itself shares a number of stylistic and topological similarities with the fictional account of the siege of Syene in the *Aethiopica* of Heliodorus, a work which was published in the second half of the fourth century. For the towers of Nisibis to be 'just visible above the waters', the earthen mound needed to hold the moat would have to be of enormous strength and height. The Persian use of the Mygdonius against the defences cannot be denied because of the innumerable references to flood-water and its effects in the poems of Ephrem who was a witness to the events of the third siege.

37 Flavius Julius Constans, the Augustus of the western half of the Empire, was murdered by the usurper Magnentius in 350.

38 Flavius Claudius Constantius Gallus was proclaimed Caesar on 15 March, 351. Cf. *PLRE* I, p. 225.

39 This means he was a centurion of the *primi ordines*, probably in the wars of Constantius against Shapur II. Cf. Speidel, 1977: 722.

40 Speidel (1977: 722) gives AD 351 for the conversion of the date.

41 On this equestrian *dux Arabiae*, see esp. Sartre, 1982: 103.

42 Heliodorus was a Phoenician from Emesa and wrote his novel, the *Aethiopica*, towards the end of the fourth century. Cf. *PLRE* I, p. 411, 'Heliodorus 3'.

8 ROME AND SHAPUR II: THE LATER WARS OF CONSTANTIUS II

1 Philostorgius was an Arian church-historian and was favourable to

Gallus because, like Constantius, Gallus was an ardent Arian. Nevertheless, based at Hierapolis, Gallus probably made 'what was at least a highly successful demonstration against him (i.e. the Persian commander)'. Cf. Thompson, 1947: 57.

2 The *Artemii Passio* draws its historical material heavily from the now very imperfectly preserved ecclesiastical history of Philostorgius and therefore shows the same pro-Arian bias towards Gallus. However, it was not blind to the faults of Gallus as an administrator. Cf. ch. 6, pp. 204–5, ed. Kotter. On the relationship between the Passio and the lost work of Philostorgius, see esp. Bidez's introduction to his GCS edition of Philostorgius (pp. XLIV–LXI).

3 On Ammianus as a source for the Saracens, see esp. Shahid: 1984: 83–5 and Lightfoot, 1981: 269–75.

4 The continuing importance of the September Fair at Batna (mod. Sarug) shows that the stipulation of Nisibis as the sole venue of exchange between Rome and Persia in the treaty between Diocletian and Narses (supra 5.4.3.) was not strictly enforced.

5 On the career of Ursicinus (*Mag. Equ.* 349–59 and *Mag. Ped.* 359–60), a key figure in the defence of the Eastern Frontier in the later years of Constantius, see esp. *PLRE* I, pp. 985–6 ('Vrsicinus 2'). See also Thompson 1947: 42–55.

6 The Chionitae were a Hunnic tribe who had occupied Transoxania in Central Asia. The most detailed study on them, drawing from both classical and oriental sources, remains Enoki Kazuo, 1955: 757–80.

7 Ammianus has almost certainly preserved the original text of the letter. The titulature of the Shapur corresponds in part to that of his father in his inscription at Hajjiabad. Cf. Christensen, 1944, 237–8. Ammianus probably obtained a copy of it through his friendship with Libanius. The latter was a close friend of Spectatus (see below) who took part in the negotiations. Cf. Sabbah, 1970: 173, n. 49.

8 Cf. *PLRE* I, pp. 74–5, 'Antoninus 4' and Sabbah, 1970: p. 196, n. 165. The latter's identification of this Antoninus with a decurion who ran into financial problems at Antioch (cf. Libanius, *ep.* 210, 1) is by no means certain. Antoninus' defection was a major boon to Shapur because as a *protector* he would have taken part in recruitment and his former role as accountant (or quarter-master) to the *dux* of Mesopotamia meant that he would have known the exact troop-strength of the Roman garrisons on the frontier as well as their disposition. The lengthy negotiations were needed to establish his credentials and the value of his information. Cf. Lieu, 1986b: 494–5 and Matthews, 1986: 556–7 and 1989: 39–47.

9 Cf. *PLRE* I, pp. 517–18, 'Lucillianus 3' and pp. 742–3, 'Procopius 4'. The former defended Nisibis successfully against Shapur in 350.

10 The *Expositio* is a geographical handbook for commercial travellers composed by someone with first-hand knowledge of the Roman East. The fact that it mentions Nisibis as a Roman city which had heroically withstood sieges by the Persians suggests that it was composed in the 350's, before the city was ceded to the Persians in 363.

11 On the distinguished career of this important official, see *PLRE* I, pp. 605–8, 'Modestus 2'.

12 A new and distinctive feature of this campaign is the successful use by the Persians of mobile cavalry units advancing ahead of the main army for the purpose of disrupting the Roman preparations for defence and confusing the defenders as to the exact direction of the main attack. Cf. Lightfoot, 1981: 142 and Matthews, 1986: 551–2.

13 Ostensibly a description of the ambitions of Shapur, the message was coded to give the Roman commanders on the frontier some idea of Shapur's intended invasion route. By the rivers 'Granicus' (site of Alexander's first victory over Darius in 334 BC) and 'Rhyndaces' (site of Lucullus' victory over Mithridates in 74/73 BC) was meant the rivers Tigris and Anzaba (the Greater Zab) which Shapur was about to bridge. The 'successor of Hadrian' was, of course, a reference to the deserter Antoninus. Cf. Matthews, 1986: 558 and esp. 1989: 48–56.

14 Though some elements of this episode may seem fantastic, there is little doubt that the reconnaissance visit by the future historian did take place. Cf. Lightfoot, 1981: 142–3 and Matthews, 1986: 559–61.

15 Sabinianus (*PLRE* I, p. 789, 'Sabinianus 3') was consistently portrayed in an unfavourable manner by Ammianus, who considered him as an unworthy successor of his patron Ursicinus. However, Sabinianus' decision to remain at Edessa was a sound one as the main field force under his command would have blocked off Shapur's most direct route to the Euphrates. Cf. Lightfoot, 1981: 143 and Matthews, 1986: 555–6.

16 Warmington (1977: 515) has adduced from Antoninus' admonition and the subsequent events that the Persian plan of attack in 359 was to cross the Tigris north of Singara then head straight for the Euphrates, bypassing Nisibis. This was foiled by the flooding of the Euphrates. However, Ammianus himself probably deduced the Persian change of plan from the actual events of the campaign. It seems odd that the Persians who were experts in hydrodynamic engineering could not bridge a flooded river. The presence of the main Roman field army at Edessa could have been an equally strong factor in Shapur's decision to head north towards the Taurus Mountains.

17 The classic study of Amida and its Byzantine and medieval defences remains Gabriel 1940(i): 85–205. See esp. 90–2 (topography) and 175–82 (estimated size of the city at the time of Constantius). Ammianus' description of Amida needs to be reordered for it to agree with basic topographical factors. The Tigris washes the eastern (and not the southern) side of the city and the plains of Mesopotamia lay to the south (not to the east). However, Ammianus is partly correct in his alignment of the city in that there was a tower on the south-eastern side of the city which overlooked the Tigris. Cf. Lightfoot, 1981: 82 and Matthews, 1989: 57–66.

18 On the Chionitae at the siege of Amida, see esp. Bivar, 1955: 200–6. However, Bivar's identification of the royal figure described in Amm. XIX, 1, 3, with the Kushano-Sassanian ruler Bahram II on the similarity between the crown of Bahram as shown on his coins and the helmet won by the Persian commander as described by Ammianus (p. 202), is almost certainly groundless. Cf. Lightfoot, 1981: 161–3.

19 Most modern scholars have assumed that Bezabde stood on the same

site as Jazirat Ibn-Omar (mod. Cizre) originally founded on the eastern bank of the Tigris, but not on the western bank because the river took a more direct route through an artificial channel to the east of the city. A recent archaeological survey in the region directed by Algaze (1989: 249–52 and 265, fig. 9 and 267, fig. 11) has located a major late Roman site at Eski Hendek, 13 km north of Cizre, and south-west of Fenik on the opposite bank of the Tigris, which fits in well with our knowledge of Bezabde from literary sources. For an earlier attempt to identify the site south of Cizre, see Lightfoot, 1981: 85–92; 1983: 189–204.

20   Virtha (Birtha)-Makedonopolis has been identified by Cumont (1917: 144–50) as Biredjik on the Euphrates on the basis of local inscriptions and lists of bishops at the Council of Chalcedon (451) in which Daniel of Makedonopolis appears in the Syriac list as Daniel of Birtha. However, Shapur's route across Mesopotamia after the fall of Bezabde is hard to retrace. His failure at Virtha may in part be due to his having over-extended his supply lines. Cf. Dillemann, 1962: 299.

21   The fate of the Christian prisoners taken from Bezabde was in stark contrast to that of the nuns who were well treated by Shapur after their capture at Reman and Busan in the campaign of 359 (Amm. XVIII, 10, 4). The ability of the Christian clergy to organize and raise the morale of the prisoners was clearly the main cause for their execution rather than mere religious intolerance. Cf. Lieu, 1986b: 496–7.

22   On the use by the Roman authorities of philosophers as envoys, see Lieu, 1986b: 492–3. On the journey of Spectatus, see esp. Sievers, 1868: 239–40 and the other sources, mainly the letters of Libanius, cited in *PLRE* I, p. 850.

23   In this campaign, Nisibis was picketed by the Persians rather than besieged. Cf. Amm. XVIII, 6, 8–16.

9   ROME AND SHAPUR II: THE PERSIAN EXPEDITION OF JULIAN

1   The extant text of Julian's letter to Arsaces (*ELF* 202 = *ep.* 57, Wight), composed in a haughty tone and intimating major loss of Roman territory, is generally acknowledged to be a forgery.

2   Mod. Elterib, a site of great antiquity in the region of Chalcis on the road from Antioch to Beroea. Cf. Cumont, 1917: 2.

3   The dates in bold type are those given by ancient authorities, those in plain are suggested by Brok, 1959: 257–8.

4   Mod. Menbij, about 30 km. west of the Euphrates. The infantry was assembled here so as not to alert the Persians of Julian's intention to use the Euphrates as his main invasion route.

5   Cf. *PLRE* I, 'Procopius 6', pp. 742–3 and 'Sebastianus 2', pp. 812–13.

6   Deception was the key to Julian's plan, as his false march towards Nisibis was to mislead the Persians into thinking that his main force was to use the Tigris route, thereby drawing the main Persian army under Shapur up the Royal Road and away from Assuristan. The use of a large transport fleet was to allow the Roman infantry to make a swift and unencumbered descent down the Euphrates towards Seleucia

(Veh-Ardashir) and Ctesiphon. Cf. Ridley, 1973: 318–19, Bowersock, 1978: 119–20 and Lieu 1986a: 92–3.

7 Cf. *PLRE*, I, p. 517, 'Lucillianus 2', not to be confused with 'Lucillianus 3'.

8 On Zaitha, see above, Ch. 2, note 12.

9 See above Ch. 3, note 8. The island was linked by a stretch of sand with the river-bank at low-water. Cf. Musil, 1927: 345 and Fontaine, 1977, ii: 137–8, n. 300.

10 Almost certainly to be identified with modern Telbes, a rocky islet 14 km. south of Ana. Cf. Fontaine, 1977, ii: 141.

11 Probably situated somewhere in the vicinity of modern Haditha, about 75 km. down river from Ana (or 45 km. as a crow flies). Cf. Musil, 1927: 239.

12 According to Musil (1927: 239), 'Barax' may be a corruption of the Arabic root farad 'ford' and Baraxmalcha, 'The Royal Crossing'.

13 Identified as mod. Hit by Musil (1927: 239) on the grounds that Diacira means 'bitumen-giving', as a place called Is on the Euphrates is mentioned by Herodotus (I, 179) as the source of bitumen for the walls of ancient Babylon. Cf. Fontaine, 1977, ii: pp. 142–3, n. 317 and Brok, 1959: 111. Is, however, appears more likely to be the modern name of Sitha, a place in this region mentioned by Zosimus (III, 15, 2).

14 Ozogardana ('Zaragardia' in Zos, III, 15, 3) is identified by Musil (1927: 239) with mod. Sari-al-Hadd.

15 'Suren' is the hereditary title of one of the seven Persian families, charged with the second-in-command of the Persian armed forces. Cf. Fontaine, 1977, ii: 143, n. 319.

16 Podosaces was emir of the Assanite Saracens who were allied to the Persians. Though Julian requested the envoys of the Arab federates to join him after initially refusing to pay them their usual bribe, Arab irregulars, essential for scouting and raiding, feature far more often in the accounts of the campaign fighting on the Persian rather than the Roman side. Cf. Fontaine, 1977, ii: 143–4, n. 320 and Shahid, 1984: 132–5. On Julian's lack of accurate military intelligence, see further, Lieu, 1986a: 93–4.

17 The mention by Ammianus (XXIV, 2, 6) of the remains of a rampart at Macepracta has helped Musil (1927: 240) to locate it near the beginning of an ancient rampart at Ummu-r-Rus, which stretches from the north bank of the Euphrates northward as far as the Tigris.

18 By Naarmalcha (the Royal Canal) Ammianus means a water-way beginning at Pirisabora on the Euphrates which was divided into two branches; the upper branch passed through the Hellenistic metropolis of Seleucia which no longer joined the Tigris at the time of Julian, while the Parthian port-city of Vologesias was situated on the northern bank of the lower branch which was called Maarsares by Ptolemy (*Geog.* V, 20) and was probably dug by the Parthian King Vologeses. The latter was probably the one Julian found to be blocked by the Persians and the same waterway was used previously by Trajan and Septimius Severus for conveying their fleets to the Tigris. On the Royal Canal, the Arabic geographer Ibn Serapion (c. AD 900) wrote:

'From the Euphrates also is taken a canal called the Nahr-al-Malik. Its point of origin is five leagues below the head of the Nahr Sarsar. It is a canal that has along it numerous domains and fertile lands. There is also a Bridge-of-Boats over it: and further many villages and fields (along its banks). From it branch numerous other canals, and its lands form a District of the Sawad. Finally it flows out into the Tigris on its western bank, three leagues below al-Madain (trans. Le Strange, 1895: 70).' Cf. Fiey, 1967: 13–14 see also Musil, 1927: 272–4 and Dillemann, 1961: 153–8.

19 On Pirisabora (mod. Al-Anbar), see above, p. 358, note 26.

20 Identified by Musil (1927: 240–1) with modern 'Akar an-Na Jeli, lying about two kilometres from the Euphrates on the left bank of the canal.

21 Ridley's translation of the first phrase of III,19,3 (p. 60) as 'Advancing further and crossing the river, he came to . . .' may be misleading as an equally plausible translation is: 'While advancing along the course of the river, he arrived at . . .'. Cf. Paschoud, 1979: 36 and 139, n. 50.

22 Probably Nehardea, the great centre of Jewish learning in Babylonia. See above 4.3.1. Cf. Oppenheimer, 1983: 276–93, esp. p. 290.

23 The location of Bithra or Birtha (= fort, a common name in this region) is not entirely certain. Musil (1927: 241) has tentatively identified it with Ibrahim al-Halil, about 25 km. south-east of Phissenia. The mention by Zosimus of a palace there suggests that it was not the same place as the abandoned Jewish settlement mentioned in Amm. XXIV, 4, 1. Cf, Musil, 1927: 241.

24 The name in Aramaic means 'royal fort (or port)', so called because of its position on the Naarmalcha. Musil (1927: 241) noticed a ruin mound (present Han az-Zad) about ninety stades (i.e. 18 km.) west of Ctesiphon. The "ma'oz" part of the name is probably derived from Mahoza, the name given by Jews and Christians to a suburb of Veh-Ardashir. Cf. Oppenheimer, 1983: 179–93.

25 The ruins of the Hellenistic metropolis of Seleucia were now used as a place of execution of criminals (including Christian martyrs) by the Sassanian kings. Cf. Fiey, 1967: 8.

26 Meinas Sabath was identified by Maricq (1959: 264–76) as the site of the Parthian river port of Vologesias (Walasapat). However, Oppenheimer (1983: 390–3) believes it should be identified with a suburb of Veh-Ardashir.

27 On Coche (Zokhase in Zos. III, 23, 3), see above, Ch. 5, note 8.

28 Modern site unknown. Seen from the context of the narrative, it must have been east of Ctesiphon. Cf. Sarre and Herzfeld, 1911: 86, n. 2 and Paschoud, 1979: 180, n. 72.

29 Sarre and Herzfeld (1911: 86) suggests identifying it with Djsir Nahrawan near the river Tamarra.

30 On identifying the Diyala, an important tributary of the Tigris, with the Douros of Zosimus, see Dillemann, 1961: 146 and Paschoud, 1979: 188.

31 Identified by Herzfeld (1948: 65) with 'Ukbara, about 50 km. north of Baghdad. Founded by Shapur II, its Syriac name was Buzurg Sabur. See also Brok, 1959: 172. It is vitally important to remember that the Tigris in this period followed a more direct north-south course below

Samarra than it does now. Cf. Le Strange 1905: 37 and map facing p. 25, Adams, 1965: 90–1 and Oppenheimer, 1983: 452–6.

32 Regarded by Dillemann (1961: 145–6) as a confusion by Zosimus for Mischanabe – the latter itself a corruption of Meschana.

33 Identified by Herzfeld (1948: 65) with Tell-Hir, about 54 km. from the modern city and former Abbasid capital of Samarra.

34 Site unknown, probably situated not far south of Samarra. Cf. Paschoud, 1979: 200, n. 83.

35 Cf. *PLRE* I, p. 61 'Anatolius 5'.

36 Identified by Herzfeld (1948: 67) with Karkh Fairuz, about 11 km. north of Samarra.

37 Probably Dur Arabaya, about 5 km. further north of Charcha. Cf. Herzfeld, 1948: 67.

38 Almost certainly the same place as Thebeta of the *Tab. Peut.* in the desert regions of Mesopotamia between Singara and Nisibis. Cf. Dillemann, 1962: 312 and Fontaine, 1977: 269, n. 678. 39. The words in brackets are supplied by the editor.

39 The CSCO edition has 'RMNY', clearly an error for 'RMY'. (S. P. Brock).

40 The ms. reading is HRMN. Brooks takes it as 'RMN (i.e. Armenia, but this would normally be 'RMNY') with note suggesting Rehimene.

41 Cf. Malalas, XIII, pp. 336, 21–2.

42 For fuller commentary on these verses, see esp. Lieu, 1986a: 127–33 and Griffith, 1987: 247–58.

43 See below Soz. V, 3, 5: p. 268.

44 One of the earliest references to Julian being tricked by the Persian 'traitors' into setting fire to his transport fleet.

45 Cf. Amm. XXV, 9, 1.

46 One of the Cappadocian Fathers, Gregory met Julian at Athens where they both studied. His two orations against Julian, published within a few years of the death of the apostate emperor were the earliest surviving Christian polemical works of the reign.

47 Greek: θάρσος (courage) and θρασύς (overconfidence).

48 The motif of the barbarian guard being responsible for the death of an emperor is also found in *SHA Sev. Alex.* 62, 4–5. Cf. Straub, 1980: 242.

49 A student of Libanius, John Chrysostom ('the golden-mouthed') was consecrated deacon in his native city of Antioch in 381. He became Patriarch of Constantinople in 398 against his wishes and at the time of his death in 407, he was one of the most outspoken critics of the Empress Eudoxia. On his works against Julian the Apostate, see Lieu, 1986a: 59–63.

50 Julian may have encountered a geological phenomenon, common in that part of Syria, where linear outcrops of lava had been weathered down by the natural processes of erosion into something resembling a badly paved road. Cf. Cumont, 1917: 8.

51 The passages here omitted include Sozomen's refutation of a section of Libanius' panegyric on Julian (*or.* XVIII, 268) and the intimation of the emperor's death received by Didymus the Blind. The latter is a common theme in hagiographical literature. See similar accounts in

[Pachomius] *Epistula Ammonis* 32–4 (trans. A. Veilleux, *Pachomian Koinonia* II, Kalamazoo, 1981, pp. 102–4), Palladius, *historia Lausiaca* 4, 4 (trans. R. T. Meyer, Washington, 1964) p. 36, Theodoret, *historia religiosa* 14 (trans. Russell, Kalamazoo, 1985, pp. 29–30) and Theodoret, *hist. eccl.* III, 24, GCS (trans. Jackson, p. 105). A later tradition names Mercurius as the 'Christian' executioner of Julian. Cf. Frend, 1986: 69–70. See also Malalas, XIII, pp. 333, 18–334, 12.

52　This Magnus is very probably the Magnus of Carrhae who wrote an account of Julian's campaign. (See above, Malalas). The incident referred to here is the capture of Pirisabora.

53　For a detailed historical commentary on this section of Zonaras, see esp. Dimaio, 1977: 420–47.

APPENDIX 1

1　Abu Dja 'far Muhammad b. D̲jarir, al-Tabari, was born *c.* 839 C.E. at Amul in Tabaristan where he devoted himself to serious study at a precociously young age. His later travels took him first to Baghdad, then to Syria and Egypt. He returned to Baghdad in 872 C.E. where he remained as a celebrated scholar until his death in 923 C.E. His most important work is the history of the world (*Ta'rikh al-Rusul wa'l-Muluk*) which begins with the history of the Patriarchs and ends in July, 915 C.E. It was afterwards continued by other historians. The translation of this extract on the section on the Sassanians is the joint work of Ahmad al-Issa and Doris Dance, with generous acknowledgement to the outstanding German translation of Th. Nöldeke.

2　The sections on the history of the desert kingdom of Hira are here omitted.

3　Sa'id b. al-Bitrik (Eutychius) was born at Fustat in 876 C.E. and was Patriarch of Alexandria from 933 to 939 C.E. He was the author of several medical and historical works. The best known is his Arabic chronicle, Nazm al-D̲jawhar (String of Pearls), which records main events from the time of Christ to 938 C.E. The work was first published in the West by Pocoke in 1658/9 and a critical edition was prepared for CSCO by Cheikho in 1906. However, Breydey published in 1985 a new CSCO edition based on a shorter version preserved in the Sinaiticus Arab. 582 which the editor believes to be the author's autographed manuscript.

4　Compiled shortly after 1036 C.E., the Nestorian *Chronicle of Se'ert*, which draws on early Syriac material, is a source of primary importance for the study of Christianity in Persia.

5　On the importance of these exiles to the diffusion of Christianity in Persia, see Peeters, 1924: 294–8 and 308–14, Decret, 1979: 110–11 and Lieu, 1986b: 481–2.

6　This is a problematic section and Sher's French translation (p. 224): 'Avant ce second exil, et après le premier exil de Démétrius, Paul de Samosate était devenu patriarche d'Antioche', has been used by scholars to support the view that Antioch was twice captured by Shapur I (256 and 260). Peeters (1924: 296) gives: 'Hic (*sc.* Demetrius) enim iam ante secundam hanc captivitatem (Antiochia) excesserat. Et

Antiochiae patriarcha, postquam captivus abductus est Demetrius patriarcha, factus Paulus Samosatenus, ...'; and Felix (1985: 57) suggests: '... er war schon vor diese 2. Gefangennahme fortgeschafft worden, und Patriarch von Antiochia nach der Gefangennahme seines Patriarchen wurde Paulos von Samosata.' A more radical departure has been suggested to us by Prof. Ze'ev Rubin (unpublished): 'He (*sc.* Demetrius) had already been taken out of [the city] before this second captive (*sc.* Azdaq, i.e. the second to be taken out according to the chronological order of events). And Paul of Samosata became Patriarch over Antioch after Demetrius, its Patriarch, had been taken prisoner.'

7   Firdawsi (Abu 'l-Kāsim), the famous Persian poet, was born in 932 C.E. at Tabaran in Khorasan. He lived on a small estate left to him by his father. A *dihkān* (i.e. landed proprietor) whom he knew gave him a Book of Kings (see above, Ch. 1, note 2) to put into verse and it was this that inspired him to compose the *Shāhnāmah* (Book of Kings), an epic of about 60,000 lines – a task which took him thirty-five years to complete, by which time he was already in his 80's.

8   Shapur I, son of Ardashir, is here confused with Shapur II, son of Hormizd, and the wars of the two Shahanshahs are also confused.

APPENDIX 2

1   The *History* of Faustus of Buzanda traces the fortunes of the Kingdom of Armenia from 327 to 387 (the year in which Armenia was partitioned between the Romans and Persians). Earlier suggestions that he was a contemporary of the Catholicos Nerses the Great (353–373) rest on a misidentification. The work, as it stands, was compiled in the second half of the fifth century. The author, whose identity is unknown (Buzanda is probably Podandus in the Taurus), uses as his sources the Life of Mashtots' by Koriun, the Life of St. Basil and the Anaphora of the same saint as well as popular epics recounting the deeds of Armenian kings.

2   See above Ch. 6, n. 22.

3   The 'Greek emperor' is commonly identified as Caesar Constantius. However, Libanius' silence on any military achievement by the Caesar in Armenia prior to the death of Constantine in his long panegyric on Constantius and Constans (*or.* 59) is significant. Perhaps the Roman intervention in Armenia was brought about by the revolt of Bacour (cf. Faustus, III, 8 and Moses Khor. (III), 4). The Roman commander may have been Flavius Eusebius who was *Magister Equitum et Peditum* under Constantius and was Consul in 347. His household, together with that of Arsaces, king of Armenia, was granted special exemption from taxation by Constantius in 360. See above Ch. 8, p. 219. This was probably a belated token of respect for Eusebius' unpublicized services in Armenia. Cf. Lightfoot, 1981: 30–1, n. 80.

4   Faustus' account of the Persians' defeat in Armenia by the 'Greek King' is clearly influenced by Roman accounts of Galerius' victory against Narses in 298. The topos is of the Roman commander spying on the disposition of the Persian encampment and the capture of the Shahanshah's harem. Cf. Ensslin, 1936: 104–5.

5 The *History* of Agathangelos has as its main theme the reign of Trdat (Tiridates the Great) and the life and mission of Gregory the Illuminator. It exists in Armenian, Greek and (in part) Arabic versions and many recensions, not all of which are derived from the extant text of the Armenian. The author purports to be an eye-witness of the events of the reign of Trdat, but the work is almost certainly a tendentious fifth-century compilation. Cf. Thomson, 1976: xi–xvii and Winkler, 1980: *passim*.

6 Moses of Khorene, the name given to the author of an Armenian chronicle which covers the history of Armenia from the Biblical Age of the Patriarchs to the death of the Armenian Patriarch Sahak (early 5th C.), is regarded in the Armenian literary tradition as the 'Father of History'. However, his birthplace of Khorene is unknown and his claim to have been a contemporary of Mesrop (the inventor of the Armenian alphabet) and Sahak is unsupportable because the chronicle utilizes material later than the fifth century. Thomson (1978: 60–1) believes that the work fits most appropriately into the first decades of Abbasid control over Armenia. For the Early Sassanian period it cites Agathangelos and Faustus among its authorities but there are considerable differences between 'Moses' version of the events and those of his alleged sources. See esp. Thomson, 1978: 40–9.

7 There is little doubt that Arsak (Arsaces II) was King of Armenia during the short reign of Julian. The root of the error in synchronism lies in the confusion by 'Moses' (or some intermediate source) of the date of the year when Constantius became Caesar (AD 323) with that of his accession to the imperial title (337), thereby advancing events of the fourth century by fourteen years and in doing so making Julian a contemporary of Tiran (–Trdat IV). Cf. Hewsen, 1978–79b: 113–15.

APPENDIX 3

1 This figure is most probably that of the total for the infantry and excludes the cavalry and *dromedarii*.

2   Fink, 1971: 187: 'Iulius Rufianus, tribune, sent the password (chosen) from the Seven Planets: Mercury s(anctus ?)'.

3 His title was perhaps *circitor* (an inspector of the watch) abbreviated as *ci*. Cf. Fink, 1971: 185, n. 7.

4 This lower total figure compared with that of the earlier document may indicate the participation of the unit in the skirmishes against the Persians in which its tribune Julius Terentius was killed. (See above 1.4.4.) Cf. Welles, 1959: 30.

5 In the original document the year is given by the names of the consuls in office.

APPENDIX 4

1 Cf. Kneissl, 1969: 232–48, Homo, 1904: 352–61, Barnes, 1976a: 182–6 and 191–3, idem, 1976b: 149–55, idem, 1980: 162–6 and idem, 1982: 254–8.

2 See above Ch. 1, note 30.

3 'ARAM. M.' is almost certainly an error for 'ARM(ENICUS) M.'. Cf. Barnes, 1982: 18.
4 'ARAB. M.' may also be an error for 'ARM(ENICUS) M.'. Cf. Barnes, 1982: 18.
5 See above, note 3.
6 See above, note 3.
7 For an attempt to date the inscription to the last months of 336 and the first part of 337 and therefore linking the title of Persicus to the early campaigns of Constantius, see Arce, 1982: 247–9.

APPENDIX 5

1 Site not securely identified. Dussaud (1927: 268–9) suggests Sadad, on the route between Damascus and Salamiye.
2 Site not securely identified. Dussaud (1927: 269) tentatively suggests Deir 'Atiye, south of Sadad.
3 Dussaud (1927: 269) suggests 'Atni, north east of Damascus which appears to have been the site of a Roman camp.
4 Placed in the *Tab. Peut.* on the route between Palmyra and Damascus, probably mod. Nebek. Cf. Van Berchem, 1952: 16.
5 Site not securely identified but most likely to be located in the region of Jebel Qalamoun, north of Damascus. Cf. Van Berchem, 1952: 16.
6 Site not securely located. Honigmann (1923: 153) suggests Hadata in the neighbourhood of Hauwarin.
7 This implies that the Legio I Illyricorum was stationed at Palmyra.
8 The *Tab. Peut.* gives Danoua as one of the stops between Damascus and Palmyra, perhaps at Méhin. Cf. Poidebard, 1932: 41. The presence of the Legio III Gallicorum at 'Danavae Damasco' is also confirmed by an inscription from Sistov (Nicopolis, Moesia): *CIL* III, 755.
   Dussaud (1927: 271) conjectured Jebel Seis and Musil, 1928: 43ff. suggests Abu Sindâh, between Homs and Palmyra.
9 Perhaps 'Ayn Wou'ôul or Harbaqa, both beyond the Jebel Rawaq. Cf. Poidebard, 1932: 49.
10 Dillemann places Rene (1962: 239) in Mesopotamia, south of Dara, and argues that the unit has been listed in error under the ducate of Phoenice.
11 Many scholars believe that the ancient name of Dibsi Faraj was Athis. Harper (1977: 457) believes that, though founded as Athis, its name was changed to Neocaesarea under Diocletian in honour of Caesar Galerius.
12 Seeck suggests: Ala prima Iota constituta. Böcking: (perhaps) Ala prima quingenaria Iota constituta.
13 Thomsen (1906: 125) suggests identifying Tarba with Jebel umm Tarfa between el-Mesadd and el-Kwera.
14 Location uncertain. Thomsen (1906: 125) proposes identifying it with Joppa, Flavia Joppe, mod. Jaffa, if situated in the north, and Wadi Guweibe, west of el-Busera, if in the south.
15 Avi-Yonah (1976: 78) believes that the cohort was stationed at Maledomnei.

16   May have been the same place as Canaba in the *Itin. Anton.* 189, 3, p. 25, ed. Cuntz, situated between Mediana (see below) and Zeugma.

17   Identified by Dillemann (1962: 229) with Banasymeon in Procop. *de aed.* II, 4; mod. Qartemin, S.S.E. of Midyat. See, however, Honigmann, 1961: 13, n. 4.

18   Probably the Monithilla of George of Cyprus (ed. Honigmann, 1939: 25, no. 900) and the Thiolla of Procop., *de aed.*, II, vi, 14.; perhaps mod. Tell Taouil. Cf. Dillemann, 1962: 108.

19   Perhaps the same as the 'In Medio' – the halfway point on the main road from Edessa to Zeugma as given in the *Itin. Anton.* (189, 4, p. 25, ed. Cuntz). Cf. Lightfoot, 1981: 302, n. 15.

20   Identified by Dillemann (1962: 232) as Redje (or Radjil), about 5 km. S.S.E. of Hisn Kef beside the Tigris.

21   Most scholars accept Seeck's suggestion that the missing unit is Legio III Parthica.

22   Located by Poidebard (1932: 134) to Tel Fedein (= Apphadna in Ptolemy). See also Fink, 1971: 15 and Röllig and Kuhne, 1977: 120–1 and 133..

23   Probably the Thilaticomum of the *Itin. Anton.* (192, 1, p. 26) on the main road between Batna (Serug) and Hierapolis (Membij). Located by Miller (1916: col. 776) at mod. Tell el Ghara.

24   Bintha is most likely a copyist's error for Birtha/Macedonopolis (mod. Birecik). The unit was probably stationed on the western bank of the Euphrates. Cf. *Diz. Epig.* IV, p. 1343.

25   Probably the Phichas in Procop., *de aed.* II, iv, 14, mod. 'Aïn el Beida. Cf. Dillemann, 1962: 187.

26   Rhesaina appears to be the base of two units, one from the Mesopotamian and the other from the Osrhoenean command. Cf. Gracey, 1981: 106.

27   The unit would have been stationed on the Lower Khabur where numerous sites have yielded evidence of Late Roman occupation. Cf. Röllig and Kuhne, 1977: 121–5 and 128.

28   Identified by Dillemann (1962: 108 and 225) with the fortress of Zamarthas and the monastery of Samarthê in Procop., *de aed.*, II, vi, 14 and V, ix, 32, both restored by Justinian.

29   Probably the same as Apatna above (Or. XXXV, 25).

30   Dillemann (1962: 239) prefers identifying it with the Monocarton in Theophylactus Simocatta I, 13, 3, and locates it at Tell Armen near Constantina. See, however, Honigmann, 1939, no. 903.

31   The Equites Pafenses may have derived their name from Tell Fafan (Til) at the confluence of the Tigris and the Bohtan-su between Cepha and Bezabde. Cf. Sarre and Herzfeld, 1911 (i): 148 and Lightfoot, 1981: 298.

32   Assara may perhaps be amended to Massara, placed by Dillemann (1962: 230) at the village of Maserte (perhaps the Matzaron of Theoph Sim. II, 18, 17) about 10 km. W. of Fafa in the Tur Abdin to the north of Dara. For other identifications see *Diz. Epig.* IV, p. 1332.

33   The unit appears to have been raised in the region of Thebeta (Amm. XXV, 9, 3) on the road between Singara and Nisibis (Miller, 1916: col.

771) and located by Dillemann (1962: 212) at El Qoinet in the valley of the Radd.

34 Identified by Dussaud (1927: 491, n. 5) as Tell Bisme, W. of Mardin and 50 km. N.E. of Viransehir at the confluence of the Khabour and the Djurdjub, perhaps the same place as the Bimisdeon in Procop., *de aed.* II, iv, 14.

35 Established by Septimius Severus, the Legio I Parthica was originally stationed at Singara. Its epithet 'Nisibena' in the Notitia suggests a long association with the city of Nisibis where it was probably based to counter the repeated attacks of Shapur II. The legion, or some of its elements, also took part in the defence of Singara in 360. Cf. Amm. XX, 6, 8.

36 The legion, or elements from it, also took part in the defence of Bezabde in 360. Cf. Amm. XX, 7, 1.

37 Perhaps a copyist's error for Carcha (Syriac word for 'fort') and therefore alternative name for the. Birtha (which also means 'fort') on the Tigris, between Bezabde and Amida. Cf. Dillemann, 1962: 235 and 238, map.

38 The title of the unit implies that it was recruited in the early part of the fourth century in Cordyene, one of the five regiones, ceded to Rome by Narses.

39 Site unknown; Dillemann (1962: 239, n. 3) believes it was listed in error under the ducate of Mesopotamia.

40 Dillemann (1962: 226) identifies Bethallaha with Thallaba on the *Tab. Peut.* (Miller, 1909: col. 781) and locates it at Tell Brak, site of Byzantine remains on the Dschaghschagh between Nisibis and Thannouris.

41 The title of the unit implies that it was raised during the Tetrarchy in Zabdicene, one of the five new Transtigritanian *regiones*. Those who served in this and similar units (see e.g. line 34) were treated as traitors by the Persians. After the fall of Amida in 359, survivors of these units were rounded up and executed without distinction. Cf. Amm. XIX, 9, 2.

42 For a detailed study of the history of the Roman army in Arabia, see Speidel, 1977: passim.

43 Deir el-Khaf (Khaf = 'cavern') is commonly sugested as the site of Speluncis. Cf. *GRP*, p. 98. However, Kennedy (1982: 299) expresses caution on the grounds that the Deir el-Khaf is more suitable as a base for an infantry rather than a cavalry unit.

43a *GRP*, p. 80 suggests Na'afa but Kennedy and Riley (*Rome's Desert Frontier from the Air*, in press, London, commentary to Fig. 135) think the large rectangular fort at Umm er-Resas, Al-Asimah, Jordan, 31° 30′ N and 35° 54′ E is a more likely location as one of the four later churches built against its walls has yielded a mosaic of AD 785 (first published by Piccirillo) identifying the site as 'Kastron Mephaa'. We are extremely grateful to Dr Kennedy for allowing us to draw on this yet unpublished information.

44 The name of the legion may reflect Galerius' special relation with Mars, his protective deity. This suggests a date shortly after 293 for the creation of this legion – a suggestion which is now supported by

numismatic evidence from the site. El-Lejjūn is also close to Areopolis, the 'City of Mars'. Cf. Parker, 1986: 62–3.

45   Brünnow (1909: 71) believes that Dia-Fenis should be sought in the S. Hauran, probably at Qasr el-Azraq but pottery from el-Azraq seems to stop in mid-fourth century and epigraphical evidence from the site suggests that its Roman name was Basienis. Cf. Kennedy and MacAdam, 1985: 100–2 and Speidel, 1987: 215–19.
     GRP, p. 100 conjectures Umm el Jîmal but Kennedy (1982: 152) suggests locating it at or near the XXIII mile-station on the *Via Nova Trajana*.

46   Brünnow (1909: 73) locates the unit to Qal'at ez-Zerqā – where there is an Islamic fort which may have Roman foundations as it was the site of the discovery of a Latin inscription *c.* 260. See above 3.2.5.

47   Aditta is commonly identified with mod. el-Hadid. Cf. *GRP*, p. 63. Kennedy (1982: 149), however, points out that such an identification would involve inverting Gadda and Hatita (*sic*) on the itinerary as given in the *Tab. Peut.* (X, 1, col. 818) and that Gadda is an equally suitable candidate for el-Hadid. Cf. Miller, 1916: col. 818.

48   On the remains of Roman military buildings in this region, see esp. Parker, 1986: 48ff.

49   Located by Wagner (1977: 678, map) to the west bank of the Euphrates between Zimara and Dascusa.

50   Perhaps to be identified with Sule at the source of Harmut-su near Kalecik. Cf. Adontz, 1970: 81.

51   Better known as Pithyus , probably the Thia of the *Itin. Anton.* (217, p. 31) – a Black Sea port between Trachea and Sebastopolis. Cf. Wagner, 1977: 673, map.

52   Pre-Roman Dioscurias in Colchis, mod. Sukhumi. Cf. *PECS*, p. 277, Bernhard.

Glossary of Roman military terms

aedituus, temple guard, shrine keeper (the *aedituus* must have had charge of the *aedicula* where the *signa* (*v. infra*) were kept (cf. Fink, 1971: 185, n. 7).

ala, cavalry regiment.

beneficiarius, seconded for special duty by the officer who is cited; if *consularis*, by the provincial governor.

bucinator, trumpeter.

caligati (milites), common soldiers, rank and file.

cataphracti, general term for armoured cavalry (see also *clibanarii*).

clarissimi, grade of senatorial order.

clibanarii, heavy mailed cavalry (*clibanus*: oven – a reference to the discomfort of their armour).

cohors, an infantry regiment consisting of about 500 men.

comitatenses, soldiers of the mobile field army.

curator, caretaker.

decurion, (military) commander of a troop of cavalry.

discens mensorem, apprentice surveyor.

dromedarius, camel rider.

duplicarius (lit. received double pay), as a reward either for valour or responsibility.

dux (pl. *duces*), military commanders of frontier districts.

egregius, grade of equestrian order.

eminentissimus, grade of equestrian order.

equites, cavalry.

equites promoti, legionary cavalry.

Illyricianus, of or composed of Illyrians.

immolatio, sacrifice.

indigena, a native, an original inhabitant of a place.

laterculum minus, register of minor military commissions.

limitanei, frontier troops, also called *ripenses, riparienses.*

optio, second-in-command, lieutenant, to a centurion awaiting promotion.

praeses, governor of a province.

(legiones) pseudocomitatenses, units made redundant by the surrender of frontier territory to the Persians by Jovian and added to the mobile army of the East.

sacerdos, priest.

sesquiplicarius, received an extra half rate of pay as a reward either for valour or for responsibility.

signa, standards.

signifer, standard-bearer.

spectabilis, grade of senatorial order.

tesserarius, keeper of the watch-word.

turmae, cavalry squadrons (acc. to Hyginus, an *ala milliaria* is divided into twenty-four turmae).

vexillatio, cavalry regiment.

Bibliography of secondary works

Adams, R. McC. 1965. *Land Behind Baghdad, A history of settlement on the Diyala Plains*, Chicago.

Adontz, N. 1970. *Armenia in the Period of Justinian*, trans. N. Garsoïan, Lisbon.

Alföldi, A. 1937. 'Die Hauptereignisse der Jahre 253–61 n. Chr. im Spiegel der Münzprägung', *Berytus* 4: 41–68.

Alföldi, A. 1939. 'The Crisis of the Empire (AD 249–270)', *CAH* XII: 165–231.

Alföldi, A. 1963. 'Zwei Bemerkungen zur *Historia Augusta*', in *Bonner Historia-Augusta-Colloquium* 2, Antiquitas, Reihe IV, 2: 1–8.

Algaze, G. 1989. 'A New Frontier. First Results of the Tigris-Euphrates Archaeological Reconnaissance Project'. *Journal of Near Eastern Studies*, 48/3: 240–81.

Arce, J. J. 1974. 'On Festus' sources for Julian's Persian Expedition', *Athenaeum* 52: 340–3.

Arce, J. J. 1982, 'The Inscription of Troesmis (ILS 724) and the first victories of Constantius II as Caesar', *ZPE* 48: 245–9

Asdourian, P. 1911. *Die politischen Beziehungen zwischen Armenien und Rom von 190 v. C. bis 428 n. C.*, Venice.

Asmussen, J. P. 1975. *Manichaean Literature*, Delmar, New York.

Austin, N. H. 1972. 'Julian at Ctesiphon: a fresh look at Ammianus' account', *Athenaeum* 50: 301–9.

Avi-yonah, M. 1976. *Gazetteer of Roman Palestine*, QEDEM 5, Jerusalem.

Back, M. 1978. *Die sassanidischen Staatsinschriften*, Acta Iranica III/8 (18), Leiden.

Bagnall, R. S. *et al.* 1987. *Consuls of the Later Roman Empire*, Atlanta.

Baldus, H. R. 1971. *Uranius Antonius. Münzprägung und Geschichte*, Antiquitas, Reihe III, 11, Bonn.

Balty, J. Ch., 1987. 'Apamée (1986): nouvelles données sur l'armée romaine d'Orient et les raids sassanides du milieu du IIIe siécle', *CRAI*: 213–41.

Balty, J. Ch., 1988. 'Apamea in Syria in the Second and Third Centuries AD', *JRS*, 78: 91–104.

Barcelo, P. A. 1981. *Roms auswärtige Beziehungen unter der Constantinischen Dynastie (306–363)*, Eichstatter Beiträge 3, Regensberg.

Barnes, T. D. 1976a. 'Imperial Campaigns, AD 285-311', *Phoenix* 30: 174-93.

Barnes, T. D. 1976b. 'The Victories of Constantine', *ZPE* 20: 149-55.

Barnes, T. D. 1980. 'Imperial Chronology', *Phoenix* 34: 160-6.

Barnes, T. D. 1981. *Constantine and Eusebius*, Camb., Mass.

Barnes, T. D. 1982. *The New Empire of Diocletian and Constantine*, Cambridge, Mass.

Barnes, T. D. 1985. 'Constantine and the Christians of Persia', *JRS* 75: 126-36.

Bauzou, T. 1986. 'Deux milliaires inédits de Vaballath en Jordanie du Nord'; in Freeman-Kennedy (eds) 1986: 1-8.

Baynes, N. H. 1910. 'Rome and Armenia in the Fourth Century', *English Historical Review* 25: 625-43. Reprinted in *Byzantium and Other Essays*, London, 1955: 186-208.

Beck, E. 1953. 'Das Bild vom Spiegel bei Ephräm', *Orientalia Christiana Periodica* 19: 5-24.

Bell, G. I. 1913. 'Churches and Monasteries of the Tûr 'Abdîn and Neighbouring Districts', *Zeitschrift für Geschichte der Architektur* 9: 61-112.

Bell, G. I. and Mango, M. 1982. *The Churches and Monasteries of the Tur 'Abdin*, London (The sections by Bell were originally published in Van Berchem and Strzygowski, 1910: 224-62 and Bell, 1913.)

Bellinger, A. R. 1943-1944. 'The Numismatic Evidence from Dura', *Berytus* 8: 61-71.

Bellinger, A. R. 1949. *The Excavations at Dura-Europos. Final Report VI. The Coins*, New Haven.

Bellinger, A. R. and Welles, C. B. 1935. 'A Third-Century contract of sale from Edessa in Osrhoene', *Yale Classical Studies* 5: 95-154.

Bertinelli, M. G. A. 1976. 'I Romani oltre l'Eufrate nel II secolo d. C.', *ANRW* IX/1: 3-45.

Bidez, J. and F. Cumont, 1932. *L'Empereur Julien, I, Discours de Julien César*, Paris.

Bivar, A. D. H. 1955. 'The Kushano-Sassanian Episode, Cultural Crosscurrents in Bactria AD 225-375', DPhil. Diss., Oxford Univ., unpublished.

Bivar, A. D. H. 1972, 'Cavalry equipment and tactics on the Euphrates frontier', *Dumbarton Oaks Papers*, 26; 271-91, pls 1-30.

Bivar, A. D. H. 1983. 'The Political History of Iran under the Arsacids', in Yarshater, 1983: 21-99.

Bivar, A. D. H. 1986. 'Bandes Skleros, the Buwayhids, and the Marwanids at Hizn Ziyad in the light of an unnoticed Arabic inscription', in Freeman and Kennedy, 1986: 9-21.

Blockley, R. C. 1972. 'Constantius Gallus and Julian as Caesars of Constantius II', *Latomus* 31: 433-68.

Blockley, R. C. 1973. 'Festus' source on Julian's Persian expedition', *Classical Philology* 68: 54-5.

Blockley, R. C. 1981 and 1983. *The Fragmentary Classicising Historians of the Later Roman Empire*, 2 vols, Liverpool.

Blockley, R. C. 1984. 'The Romano-Persian treaties of AD 299 and 363', *Florilegium* 6: 28-49.

Blockley, R. C. 1987. 'The Division of Armenia between the Romans and Persians at the end of the Fourth Century AD', *Historia* 36: 222–34.

Böcking, G. E. (ed.),1839. *Notitia Dignitatum*, I, Bonn.

Borries, E. v. 1918. 'Julianos (Apostata)', *RE* X/1: 26. 57–91. 63.

Bowen, R. F. 1982. 'The Emperor Constantius II (AD 317-361): a critical study', Ph.D. Diss., Leeds Univ., unpublished.

Bowersock, G. W. 1971. 'A report on Arabia Provincia', *JRS* 61: 219–29.

Bowersock, G. W. 1976. 'Limes Arabicus', *Harvard Studies in Classical Philology*, 80: 219–29.

Bowersock, G. W. 1978. *Julian the Apostate*, London.

Bowersock, G. W. 1983. *Roman Arabia*, Cambridge, Mass.

Bowersock, G. W. 1987. 'Arabs and Saracens in the *Historia Augusta*', *Bonner Historia-Augusta-Colloquium 1984-1985*, Antiquitas IV, 19 Bonn: 71–80

Boyce, M. 1984. *Zoroastrianism*, 'Textual Sources for the Study of Religion', Manchester.

Braund, D. 1983. *Rome and the Friendly King*, London.

Brock, S. P. 1978. 'A martyr at the Sasanid Court under Vahran II: Candida', *Analecta Bollandiana* 96: 167–81.

Brock, S. P. 1979/80. 'Syriac Historical Writing: A Survey of the Main Sources', *Journal of the Iraqi Academy (Syriac Corporation)*, 5: 1–30.

Brock, S. P. 1982. 'Christians in the Sasanian Empire: A case of divided loyalties', in S. Mews (ed.), *Religion and National Identity, Studies in Church History* 18, Oxford: 1–19.

Brok, M. F. A. 1959. *De perzische expeditië van Keizer Julianus volgens Ammianus Marcellinus*, Groningen.

Brünnow, R. 1909. 'Die Kastelle des arabischen Limes', in *Florilegium Melchoir de Vogüé*, Paris: 65–77.

Brünnow R. and A. von Domaszewski, 1904-1909. *Die Provincia Arabia*, 3 vols, Strassburg.

Bureth, P. 1964. *Les Titulatures impériales dans les papyrus, les ostraca et les inscriptions d'Égypte, (30 a.C.-284 a.C.)*, Brussels.

Butler, A. J. 1978. *The Arab Conquest of Egypt*, revised by P. M. Fraser, Oxford.

Cameron, A. 1939. 'ΘΡΕΠΤΟΣ and related terms in the inscriptions of Asia Minor', in *Anatolian Studies Presented to William Hepburn Buckler*, eds W. M. Calder and J. Keil, Manchester.

Cameron, A. M. 1963. 'Agathias and Cedrenus on Julian', *JRS* 53: 91–4.

Cameron, A. M. 1969/70. 'Agathias on the Sassanians', *Dumbarton Oaks Papers*, 23/24: 69–183.

Carson, R. A. G. 1968. 'The Hama Hoard and the Eastern Mints of Valerian and Gallienus', *Berytus* 17: 123–42.

Cassola, F. (ed. and trans.) 1968. *Erodiano, Storia dell'impero Romano dopo Marco Aurelio* (Florence).

Castritius, H. 1968. 'Der Armenienkrieg des Maximinus Daia', *Jahrbuch für Antike und Christentum*, 11: 94–103.

Chabot, J.-B. 1902. *Synodicon orientale ou recueil de Synodes nestoriens* (= Notices et Extraits de la Bibliothèque Nationale et autres bibliothèques publiés par l'Académie des Inscriptions et Belles-Lettres, 37) Paris.

Chapot, V. 1907. *La Frontière de l'Euphrate de Pompée à la conquête arabe*, Paris.

Chaumont, M. L. 1964. 'Les Sassanides et la christianisation de l'Empire iranien au IIIe siècle de notre ère', *Revue de l'Histoire des Religions* 165: 165–202.

Chaumont, M. L. 1969. *Recherches sur l'histoire d'Arménie*, Paris.

Chaumont, M. L. 1974. 'Corégence et avènement de Shahpuhr Ier', in *Mémorial Jean de Menasce*, eds P. Gignoux and A. Tafazzoli, Louvain: 133–46.

Chaumont, M. L. 1976. 'L'Arménie entre Rome et l'Iran, *ANRW* IX/1: 71–193.

Chaumont, M. L. 1979. 'A propos de la chute de Hatra et du couronnement de Shapur Ier', *Acta Antiqua ... Hungaricae* 27: 207–37.

Christensen, A. (and Ensslin, W.) 1939. 'Sassanid Persia', *CAH* XIII, Cambridge: 105–37.

Christensen, A. 1944. *L'Iran sous les Sassanides*, 2nd edn, Copenhagen.

Christol, M. 1975. 'Les règnes de Valérien et de Gallien (258–268)', *ANRW* II/2: 803–27.

Clermont-Genneau, M. 1920. 'Odeinat et Vaballat, rois de Palmyre et leur titre romain de Corrector', *Revue Biblique* 29: 382–419.

Clinton, H. F. 1845. *Fasti Romani*, 2 vols, Oxford.

Coulston, J. C. 1986. 'Roman, Parthian and Sassanid Tactical Developments', in Freeman and Kennedy, 1986: 59–75.

Cramer, W. 1985. 'Harran', *RAC* XIII, cols. 634–50.

Creed, J. L. (ed. and trans.) 1984. *Lactantius, De Mortibus Persecutorum*, Oxford.

Crow, J. 1986. 'A review of the physical remains of the frontiers of Cappadocia', in Freeman and Kennedy 1986: 77–91.

Crow, J. and French, D. 1980, 'New research on the Euphrates frontier in Turkey', in W. S. Hanson and L. J. F. Keppie eds, *Roman Frontier Studies*, Pt. 3, BAR, S 71: 903–12.

Cumont, F. 1902. 'Note sur deux fragments épiques relatifs aux guerres de Dioclétien', *Revue des études anciennes* 4: 36–40.

Cumont, F. 1905. 'Deux pierres milliaires du Pont', *CRAI* 1905: 347–51.

Cumont, F. 1907. 'Inscriptions latines des armées de l'Euphrate', *Bulletin de l'Académie royale de Belgique*: 55–78.

Cumont, F. 1917. *Études syriennes*, I, Paris: 1–33.

Cumont, F. 1926. *Fouilles de Doura-Europos (1922-23)*, 2 vols, Paris.

Debevoisse, N. C. 1938, *A Political History of Parthia*, Chicago.

De Blois, L. 1975, 'Odaenathus and the Roman-Persian War of 252–64 AD', *Talanta* 6: 7–23.

De Blois, L., 1978–1979. 'The reign of the Emperor Philip the Arabian', *Talanta* 10–11: 11–43.

Decret, F. 1979. 'Les Conséquences sur le christianisme en Perse de l'affrontement des empires romain et Sassanide de Shapur Ier à Yazdgard Ier', *Recherches Augustiniennes* 14: 91–152.

Delbrueck, R. 1948. 'Uranius of Emesa', *Numismatic Chronicle*, Sixth Series, 8: 10–29.

Delehaye, H. 1905. 'Les Versions grecques des actes des martyrs Persans', *Patrologia Orientalis* 2: 405–560.

De Vries, B. 1987. 'The Fortification of el-Lejjūn', in Parker, 1987a: 311–51.

Dillemann, L. 1961. 'Ammien Marcellin et les pays de l'Euphrate et du Tigre', *Syria*, 38: 87–157.

Dillemann, L. 1962. *Haute Mésopotamie orientale et pays adjacents*, Paris.

Dimaio, M. 1977. *Zonaras' Account of the Neo-Flavian Emperors*, Ph.D. Diss., Missouri Univ. 1977 (Ann Arbor, University Microfilms, 78–914112).

Dodgeon, M. H. 1967. 'Relations between the Roman and Persian Empires from the death of Constantine (337) to the death of Theodosius (395)', M. Litt. Diss., Bristol Univ., unpublished.

Domaszewski, A. von 1899. 'Uber Julius Priscus, Bruder des Philippus', *Rheinisches Museum für Philologie* 54: 159–60.

Domaszewski, A. von 1967. *Die Rangordnung des römischen Heeres*, 2nd edn revised by B. Dobson, Cologne.

Downey, G. 1950. 'Aurelian's victory over Zenobia at Immae', *Transactions of the American Philological Association* 81: 57–68.

Downey, G. (trans.)1959. 'Libanius' Oration on Antioch', *Proceedings of the American Philosophical Society* 103: 652–86.

Downey, G. 1961. *A History of Antioch in Syria from Seleucus to the Arab Conquest*, Princeton, New Jersey.

Drijvers, H. J. W. 1977. 'Hatra, Palmyra und Edessa', *ANRW* II/8, Berlin: 799–906.

Drijvers, H. J. W. 1981. 'Hellenistic and Oriental Origins', in S. Hackel ed., *The Byzantine Saint*, Supplement to Sobornost: 25–33.

Drijvers, H. J. W. 1985. 'Jews and Christians at Edessa', *Journal of Jewish Studies* 36: 88–102.

Dufraigne, P. (ed. and trans.) 1975. *Aurelius Victor, Livre des Césars*, Paris.

Dunand, M. 1931a. 'La Strata Diocletiana', *Revue biblique*, 40: 227–48.

Dunand, M. 1931b. 'A propos de la Strata Diocletiana', ibid.: 579–84.

Duncan-Jones, R. 1969. 'Praefectus Mesopotamiae et Osrhoeniae, *Classical Philology* 64: 229–33.

Duncan-Jones, R. 1970. 'Praefectus Mesopotamiae et Osrhoeniae – A Postscript', *Classical* Philology 65: 107–9.

Dussaud, R. 1927. *Topographie historique de la Syrie antique et médiévale*, Paris.

Eadie, J. W. (ed.) 1967. *The Breviarium of Festus, A Critical Edition with Historical Commentary*, London.

Eadie, J. W. 1967. 'The development of Roman Mailed Cavalry', *JRS* 57: 161–73.

Eadie, J. W. 1986. 'The Evolution of the Roman Frontier in Arabia', in Freeman and Kennedy, 1986: 243–52.

Echols, E. C. (trans.) 1961. *Herodian of Antioch's History of the Roman Empire*, Berkeley and Los Angeles.

El-'Ali, S. 1968–1969. 'Al-Mada'in and its surrounding area in Arabic literary sources', *Mesopotamia* 3–4: 417–39.

Enoki Kazuo, 1955. 'Sogudeiana to Kyodo (Sogdiana and the Huns)', *Shigaku Zasshi* 64: 757–80 (in Japanese).

Ensslin, W. 1936. 'Zu dem vermuteten Perserfeldzug des rex Hannibalianus', *Klio* 29: 102–10.

Ensslin, W. 1939. 'Sassanid Persia: (VI) The Wars with Rome', *CAH* XII: 126–37.

Ensslin, W. 1942. *Zur Ostpolitik des Kaisers Diokletian, Sb.* (Bayr.) 1942/1, Munich.

Ensslin, W. 1949. *Zu den Kriegen des Sassaniden Schapur I, Sb.* (Bayr.) 1947/5, Munich.

Felix, W. 1985. *Antike literarische Quellen zur Aussenpolitik des Sasanidenstaates, Sb.* (Wien) 456, Vienna.

Fiey, J. M. 1967a. 'Topographie chrétienne de Mahozé', *L'Orient Syrien* 12: 397–420.

Fiey, J. M. 1967b. 'The Topography of al-Mada'in', *Sumer* 23: 3–38.

Fiey, J. M. 1967c. 'Auteur et date de la *Chronique d'Arbèle*', *L'Orient Syrien* 12: 265–302.

Fiey, J. M. 1969. 'L'Elam, la première des métropoles ecclésiastiques syriennes orientales', *Melto V. Kaslik (Liban)*: 221–67.

Fiey, J. M. 1970a. 'L'Elam, la première des métropoles ecclésiastiques syriennes orientales (suite)', *Parole de l'Orient* 1, Kaslik (Liban): 123–53.

Fiey, J. M. 1970b. *Jalons pour une histoire de l'église en Iraq*, CSCO 310, Subs. 36, Louvain.

Fiey, J. M. 1974. 'Les communautés syriaques en Iran des premiers siècles à 1552', *Hommages universels* III, *Acta Iranica* 3: 279–97.

Fiey, J. M. 1977. *Nisibe métropole syriaque orientale et ses suffragants des origines à nos jours*, CSCO 388, Subs. 54, Louvain.

Fink, R. O. 1971. *Roman Military Records on Papyri*, Philological Monographs of the American Philological Association 26, Cleveland.

Fitz, J. ed. 1977. *Limes. Acts of the XI Limes Congress, 1976*, Budapest.

Fontaine, J. (ed. and trans.) 1977. *Ammien Marcellin, Histoire, IV (Livres XXIII–XXV)*, 2 vols, Paris.

Freeman, P. and D. Kennedy, (eds) 1986. *The Defence of the Roman and Byzantine East*, BAR, S297, Oxford.

Frend, W. H. C. 1986. 'Fragments of an Acta Martyrium from Q'sar Ibrim', *Jahrbuch für Antike und Christentum*, 29: 66–70.

Frézouls, E. 1977. 'Cyrrhus et la Cyrrhestique jusqu'à la fin du Haut-Empire', *ANRW* II/8: 164–97.

Frézouls, E. 1981. 'Les Fluctuations de la frontière orientale de l'empire romain', in *La Géographie administrative et politique d'Alexandre à Mahomet*, Actes du Colloque de Strasbourg 14–16 Juin, 1979, Leiden: 177–225.

Frye, R. N. 1971. 'History and the Sasanian Inscriptions', in *Persia 1971*: 215–23.

Frye, R. N. 1977. 'The Sassanian System of Walls for Defense', in *Studies in Memory of Gaston Wiet*, Jerusalem: 7–15.

Frye, R. N. 1976. *The Heritage of Persia*, 2nd edn, London.

Frye, R. N. 1983. 'The political history of Iran under the Sasanians', in Yarshater (ed.) 1983: 116–80.

Frye, R. N. 1984a. 'Historical Problems in Middle Iranian Sources', in S. Skalmowski and A. van Tongerloo eds, *Middle Iranian Studies*, Orientalia Lovaniensia Analecta 16, Leuven: 263–8.

Frye, R. N. 1984b. *The History of Ancient Iran*, Handbuch der Altertums wissenschaft III/7, Munich.

Gabriel, A. 1940. *Voyages archéologiques en Turquie orientale*, 2 vols, Paris.

Gagé, J. 1953. 'Les Perses à Antioche et les courses de l'hippodrome au milieu du IIIe siècle', *Bulletin de la Faculté des Lettres de Strasbourg*, 31: 301–12.

Gagé, J. 1964. La Montée des Sassanides et l'heure de Palmyre, Le Mémorial des Siècles, Paris.

Gagé, J. 1965. 'Comment Sapor a-t-il "triomphé" de Valerian?', *Syria* 42: 343–88.

Garitte, G. 1946. *Documents pour l'étude de livre d'Agathange*, Studi e Testi 127, Vatican.

Garsoïan, N. 1967. 'Politique ou Orthodoxie? L'Arménie au Quatrième siècle', *RÉA*, N. S. 4: 297–320.

Garsoïan, N. 1971. 'Armenia in the Fourth Century, an attempt to redefine the concepts of "Armenia" and "Loyalty"', *RÉA*, N. S. 8: 341–52.

Garsoïan, N. 1984. Introduction to the reprint of the St Petersburg edition of the Armenian text of the *Epic Histories of P'awstos Buzandats'i*, New York: v–xiii.

Gawlikowski, M. 1971. 'Inscriptions de Palmyre', *Syria* 48: 407–26.

Gawlikowski, M. 1984. *Palmyre VIII, Les Principia de Dioclétien*, Warsaw.

Gawlikowski, M. 1985. 'Les Princes de Palmyre', *Syria* 52: 251–61.

Gesche, H. 1969. 'Kaiser Gordian mit dem Pfeil in Edessa', *Jahrbuch für Numismatik und Geldgeschichte*, 19: 47–77.

Ghirshman, R. 1962. *Iran, Parthians and Sassanians*, London.

Ghirshman, R. 1975. 'Chapour Ier, "Roi des Rois" sans couronne', *Monumentum H. S. Nyberg*, I, Acta Iranica 4: 257–67.

Gignoux, P. 1971. 'La Liste des provinces de l'Eran dans les inscriptions de Sabuhr et Kirdir', *Acta Antiqua . . . Hungaricae* 19: 83–93.

Gignoux, P. 1972. *Glossaire des Inscriptions Pehlevies et Parthes*, Corpus Inscriptionum Iranicarum, Suppl. Ser. I, London.

Gilliam, J. F. 1941: 'The *Dux Ripae* at Dura', *Transactions of the American Philological Association* 72: 157–75.

Gilliam, J. F. 1958. 'The Governors of Syria Coele from Severus to Diocletian', *American Journal of Philology* 79: 225–42.

Gilliam, J. F. 1986. *Roman Army Papers*, MAVORS, Roman Army Researches 2, ed. M. P. Speidel, Amsterdam.

Gladis, C. 1907. *De Themistii Libanii Iuliani in Constantium Orationibus*, Bratislava.

Goldman, B. and A. M. G. Little, 1980. 'The beginning of Sasanian Painting and Dura-Europos', *Iranica Antiqua*, 15: 283–98.

Gracey, M. H. 1981, 'The Roman Army in Syria, Palestine and Arabia', D.Phil. Thesis, Oxford Univ., unpublished.

Graf, D. 1978. 'Saracens and the defence of the Arabian frontier', *Bulletin of the American School of Oriental Research* 229, 1–26.

Gray, E. W., 1973. 'The Roman Eastern *Limes* from Constantine to Justinian', *Proceedings of the African Classical Association*, 12: 24–40.

Gregory, S. and Kennedy, D. L. (eds) 1985, *Sir Aurel Stein's Limes Report*, BAR, S272, Oxford.

Gricourt, J. 1961. 'Alexandre Sévère "Parthicus Maximus"?', *Congresso internazionale Numismatica*, *Atti*, Vol. 2, Rome: 319–26.

Griffith, S. H. 1987. 'Ephraem the Syrian's Hymns "Against Julian" – Meditations on history and imperial power', *Vigiliae Christianae* 41: 238–66.

Guey, J. 1961. 'Autour des *Res Gestae Divi Saporis*. 1. Deniers (d'or) et (de compte) anciens', *Syria* 1961: 261–74.

Haeckl, A. E. 1987. 'The Principia of el-Lejjūn', in Parker, 1987a: 203–309.

Halkin, F. 1960. 'L'Empereur Constantin converti par Euphratas', *Analecta Bollandiana*, 78: 5–17.

Harper, R. 1977. 'Two Excavations on the Euphrates Frontier 1968–1974', *Vorträge des 10. Internationalen Limes-kongresses in der Germania Inferior*, Beihefte der Bonner Jahrbücher 38, Köln/Bonn: 453–60.

Hellenkemper, H. 1977, 'Der limes am nordsyrischen Euphrat. Bericht zu einer archäologischen Landesaufnahm', ibid.: 461–71.

Henning, W. B. 1939. 'The Great Inscription of Sapur I', *BSOAS* 9: 823–49.

Henrichs, A. and Koenen, L. 1970. 'Ein griechischer Mani-Codex', *Zeitschrift für Papyrologie und Epigraphik* 5: 97–216.

Henrichs, A. and Koenen, L. 1975. 'Der Kölner Mani-Codex (P. Colon. inv. nr. 4780) Edition der Seiten 1–72', ibid. 19: 1–85.

Herzfeld, E. 1948. *Geschichte der Stadt Samarra*, Munich.

Herzog, R. (ed.) 1989. *Handbuch der lateinischen Literatur der Antike, Bd. 5, Restauration und Erneuerung*, Handbuch der Altertumswissenschaft VIII. 5, Munich.

Hewsen, R. H. 1978–79a. 'Introduction to Armenian Historical Geography', I, *RÉA*, N. S. 13: 77–97.

Hewsen, R. H. 1978–79b. 'The Successors of Tiridates the Great: A Contribution to the History of Armenia in the Fourth Century', *RÉA* N. S. 13: 99–126.

Hewsen, R. H. 1983. 'Introduction to Armenian Historical Geography', II, *RÉA* N. S. 17: 123–43.

Hill, G. F. 1922. *Catalogue of Greek Coins in the British Museum*, Vol. 28, Nabataea, Arabia, etc., London.

Hoffmann, D. 1969. *Das spätrömische Bewegungsheer und die Notitia Dignitatum*, Epigraphische Studien VII/1 and 2, Düsseldorf.

Hohl, E. *et al.* (trans.) 1985. *Historia Augusta. Römische Herrschergestalten*, 2 vols, Zurich and Munich.

Homo, L. 1904. *Essai sur le règne de l'empereur Aurélien (270–275)*, Paris.

Honigmann, E. 1923 and 1924. 'Historische Topographie von Nordsyrien in Altertum', *Zeitschrift des Deutschen Palästina-Vereins*, 46: 149–93 and 47: 1–64.

Honigmann, E. 1939. *Le Synekdémos d'Hierocles*, Brussels.

Honigmann, E. 1961. *Die Ostgrenze des byzantinischen Reiches*, Brussels.

Honigmann, E. and Maricq, A. 1953. *Recherches sur les Res Gestae Divi Saporis*, Mem. de l'Acad. royale de Belg., Classe des lettres, 47/4, Brussels.

Howe, L. L. 1942. *The Praetorian Prefect from Commodus to Diocletian* (AD 180–305), Chicago.

Ingholt, H. 1976. Varia Tadmoria, in *Palmyre 1976*: 101–37.

Invernizzi, A. 1986. Kifrin and the Euphrates Limes, in Freeman and Kennedy, 1986: 357–81.

Jardé, A. 1925. *Études critiques sur la vie et le règne de Sévère Alexandre*, Paris.

Jeffreys, E. *et al.* (trans.) 1986. *The Chronicle of John Malalas*, Byzantina Australiensia 4, Melbourne.

Jones, A. H. M. 1964. *The Later Roman Empire*, 3 vols, Oxford.

Jones, G. D. B. 1978–1979. 'Concept and Development in Roman Frontiers', *Bulletin of the John Rylands University Library of Manchester* · 61: 115–44.

Justi, F., 1895. *Iranisches Namenbuch*, Marburg.

Kawerau, P. 1983. *Ostkirchengeschichte I, Das Christentum in Asien und Afrika bis zum Auftreten der Portugiesen im Indischen Ozean*, CSCO 451, Subs. 70, Louvain.

Kennedy, D. L. 1982. *Archaeological Explorations on the Roman Frontier in North East Jordan*, BAR, S 134, Oxford.

Kennedy, D. L. 1986a. *The Frontiers: The East*, in Wacher, 1986: 266–308.

Kennedy, D. L. 1986b. 'Āna on the Euphrates in the Roman Period', *Iraq* 48: 103–4.

Kennedy, D. L. and Macadam, H. I. 1985. 'Latin inscriptions from the Azraq Oasis', *ZPE* 60: 97–108.

Kennedy, D. L. and Northedge, A. 1989. 'Āna in the Classical sources', in A. Northedge *et al.* (eds), 'Excavations at 'Āna, Qal'a Island', *Iraq Archaeological Reports* – 1, London: 6–8.

Kerler, G. 1970. *Die Aussenpolitik in der Historia Augusta*, Habelts Diss. Drucke 10, Bonn.

Kettenhofen, E. 1982. *Die römisch-persischen Kriege des 3. Jahrhunderts n. Chr.*, Beihefte zum TAVO, Reihe B, Nr. 55, Wiesbaden.

Kettenhofen, E., 1983, 'The Inscription of Sapuhr I at the Ka'be-ye Zartost', in Mitchell (ed.) 1983: 151–71.

Kirsten, E. 1963. 'Edessa. Eine römische Grenzstaadt des 4 bis 6 Jahrhunderts im Orient', *Jahrbuch für Antike und Christentum* 6: 144–72.

Kirsten, E. 1966. 'Edessa', *RAC* VI: cols. 552–97.

Kneissl, P. 1969. *Die Siegestitulatur der römischen Kaiser*, Hypomnemata 23, Göttingen.

Kraeling, C. H. *et al.* 1956. 'The Synagogue'. Yale University & Académie des Inscriptions et Belles-Lettres. The excavations at Dura-Europos. Final Report Vol. 8, part 1.

Kraft, K. 1958. 'Die Taten der Kaiser Constans und Constantius II', *Jahrbuch für Numismatik und Geldgeschichte*, 9: 144–86.

Krauss, S. 1902. 'Der römischen-persischen Krieg in der judischen Elia-Apokalypse', *Jewish Quarterly Review* 14: 359–72.

Krauss, S. 1903. 'Neue Aufschlusse über Timesitheus und der Perse-rkriege', *Rheinisches Museum für Philologie* 58: 627–33.

Labourt, J. 1904. *Le Christianisme dans l'Empire Perse* (Paris).

Lampe, G. W. H. (ed.) 1961 *A Patristic Greek Lexicon*, Oxford.

Langlois, V. 1869. *Collections des historiens anciens et modernes de l'Arménie*, II, Paris. (Vol. I = FHG V).

Le Strange, G. 1895. 'Description of Mesopotamia and Baghdad written about AD 900 by Ibn Serapion', *Journal of the Royal Asiatic Society*, Jan. & April, 1895: 1–76 and 255–315.

Le Strange, G. 1905. *The Lands of the Eastern Caliphate*, Cambridge.

Levy, R. (trans.) 1967. *Firdausi, Shah-nama (Epic of the Kings)*, rev. by A. Banani, London.

Liebeschuetz, J. H. W. G. 1972. *Antioch, City and Administration in the Later Roman Empire*, Oxford

Liebeschuetz, J. H. W. G. 1977. 'The Defence of Syria in the Sixth Century', *Limes Congress* 10: 487–99.

Lieu, S. N. C., 1985. *Manichaeism in the Later Roman Empire and Medieval China, A Historical Survey*, Manchester.

Lieu, S. N. C. 1986a. *The Emperor Julian: Panegyric and Polemic* (with · contributions by M. Morgan and J. M. Lieu), Translated Texts for Historians 2, Liverpool.

Lieu, S. N. C. 1986b. 'Captives, Refugees and Exiles: A Study of cross-frontier civilian movements and contacts between Rome and Persia from Valerian to Jovian', in Freeman and Kennedy, 1986: 475–505.

Lightfoot, C. S. 1981. 'The Eastern Frontier of the Roman Empire with Special Reference to the Reign of Constantius II', D.Phil. Diss. Oxford Univ., unpublished.

Lightfoot, C. S. 1983: 'The Site of Roman Bezabde', in Mitchell, 1983: 189–204.

Lightfoot, C. S. 1986. 'Tilli – A Late Roman Equites fort on the Tigris?', in Freeman and Kennedy 1986: 509–29.

Lightfoot, C. S. 1988. Facts and fiction – The Third Siege of Nisibis AD 350), *Historia* 37: 105–25.

Littmann, E., Magie, D. and Stuart, D. R. 1921–1922. *Syria, Publications of the Princeton University Archaeological Expeditions to Syria in 1904–5 and 1909, Div. III, Greek and Latin Inscriptions: (A) S. Syria; (B) N. Syria*, Leiden.

Loriot, X. 1975a. 'Les Premières Années de la grande crise du IIIe siècle: De l'avènement de Maximin le Thrace (235) à la mort de Gordien III (244)', *ANRW* II/2: 657–787.

Loriot, X. 1975b. 'Chronologie du règne de Philippe l'Arabe', ibid.: 788–802.

Macadam, H. I. 1986. *Studies in the History of the Roman Province of Arabia, The Northern Sector*, BAR S295, Oxford.

Macdermot, B. C. 1954. 'Roman Emperors in the Sassanian Reliefs', *JRS* 44: 76–80.

Macdonald, D. J. 1979. 'The Genesis of the "Res Gestae Divi Saporis"', *Berytus* 27: 77–83.

Macdonald, D. J. 1981. 'The Death of Gordian III – Another Tradition', *Historia* 30: 502–8.

Macdonald, D. J. 1986. 'Dating the fall of Dura Europos', *Historia* 35: 45–68.

Mann, J. C. 1974. 'The Frontiers of the Principate', *ANRW* II/1: 521–5.

Maricq, A. 1957. 'Classica et Orientalia 2. Les dernières années de Hatra: L'alliance romaine', *Syria* 34: 288–96.

Maricq, A. 1958. 'Classica et Orientalia 5'. *Res Gestae Divi Saporis, Syria* 35: 295–360.

Maricq, A. 1959. Vologésias, l'emporium de Ctésiphon, *Syria* 36: 264–76.

Markwart, J. 1901. *Eransahr nach der Geographie des Ps. Moses Xorenac'i, Abh.* (Gött.), 3/2.

Maróth, M. 1979, 'Le Siège de Nisibe en 350 Ap. J.-Chr. d'après des sources syriennes', *AAS* 27: 239–43.

Matthews, J. F. 1984. 'The Tax Law of Palmyra: Evidence for economic history in a city of the Roman East', *JRS* 74: 157–80.

Matthews, J. F. 1986. 'Ammianus and the Eastern Frontier in the Fourth Century', in Freeman and Kennedy, 1986: 549–64.

Matthews, J. F. 1989. *The Roman Empire of Ammianus*, London.

Mazzarino, S. 1971a. 'La tradizione sulle guerre tra Shabuhr I e l'Impero Romano: "Prospettiva" e "deformazione storica", *Acta Antiqua . . . Hungaricae* 19: 59–82.

Mazzarino, S. 1971b. 'L'Anonymus post Dionem e la "topica" delle guerre romano-persiane 242/4 d. C. – 283/(4?) d. C.', in *Persia 1971*: 655–78.

Milik, J. T. 1972. *Recherches d'épigraphie proche-orientale, I, Dédicaces faites par des dieux (Palmyre, Hatra, Tyr) et des thiases sémitiques à l'époque romaine*, Paris.

Millar, F. G. B. 1971. 'Paul of Samosata, Zenobia and Aurelian: The Church, local culture and political allegiance in Third-Century Syria', *JRS* 61: 52–83.

Miller, K. 1916. *Itineraria Romana. Römische Reisewege an der Hand in Tabula Peutingeriana dargestellt*, Stuttgart.

Mitchell, S. (ed.) 1983. *Armies and Frontiers in Roman and Byzantine Anatolia*, BAR, S156, Oxford.

Mitford, T. B. 1974. 'Some inscriptions from the Cappadocian Limes', *JRS* 64: 160–75.

Mommsen, T. 1894. *Römische Geschichte, Vol. 5: Die Provinzen von Caesar bis Diokletian*, Berlin.

Morony, M. G. 1982. 'Continuity and Change in the Administrative Geography of Late Sasanian and Early Islamic Al-'Iraq', *Iran* 20: 10–49.

Morony, M. G. 1984. *Iraq after the Muslim Conquest*, Princeton, New Jersey.

Mosig-Walburg, K. 1980. 'Bisher nicht beachtete Münzen Sapurs I', *Boreas* 3: 117–26.

Mouterde, R. 1930–31. 'La Strata Diocletiana et ses bornes milliares', *MUSJ* 15: 219–33.

Mouterde, R. and Poidebard, A. 1945. *Le Limes de Chalcis*, 2 vols, Paris.

Murray, R. 1975. *Symbols of Church and Kingdom, – A Study in Early Syriac Tradition*, Cambridge.

Musil, A. 1927. *The Middle Euphrates – a topographical itinerary*. New York.

Musil, A. 1928. *Palmyrena*, New York.

Nau, F. 1915–1917, 'Résumé de monographies syriaques', *Revue de l'Orient Chrétien*, 2nd ser. 10: 3–12.

Neusner, J. 1966. *A History of the Jews in Babylonia*, Vol. 2, Leiden.

Nischer, E. C. 1923. 'The army reform of Diocletian and Constantine', *JRS* 23: 175–89.

Nock, A. D. 1962. 'Sapor I and the Apollo of Bryaxis', *American Journal of Archaeology*, 66: 307–10.

Nöldeke, T. 1879. *Geschichte der Perser und Araber zur Zeit der Sasaniden. Aus der arabischen Chronik des Tabari übersetzt und mit ausführlichen Erläuterungen und Ergänzungen verversehen.* Leiden.

Nyberg, H. S., 1959. 'Die sassanidische Westgrenze und ihre Verteidigung', in *Studia Bernhardo Karlgren dedicata*, Stockholm: 316–26.

Oates, D. 1955. 'A Note on Three Latin Inscriptions from Hatra', *Sumer* 11: 39–43.

Oates, D. 1968a. 'The Roman Frontier in N. Iraq', *Geographical Journal* 113: 189–99.

Oates, D. 1968b. *Studies in the Ancient History of Northern Iraq*, Oxford.

Oates, D. and Oates, J. 1959. 'A Roman frontier post in Northern Iraq', *Iraq*, 21: 207–42.

Olmstead, A. T. 1942. 'The Mid-Third Century of the Christian Era', *Classical Philology*, 37: 241–62 and 398–420.

Oost, S. I. 1958. 'The Death of the Emperor Gordian III', *Classical Philology*, 53: 106–7.

Oppenheimer, A. 1983. *Babylonia Judaica in the Talmudic Period*, Beihefte, zum TAVO, Nr. 47, Wiesbaden.

Palmyre 1976. Palmyre bilan et perspectives. Colloque de Strasbourg (18–20 Oct. 1973), Strasbourg.

Parker, H. M. D., 1933. 'The Legions of Diocletian and Constantine', *JRS* 23: 175–89.

Parker, S. T. 1986. *Romans and Saracens: A History of the Arabian Frontier*, American School of Oriental Research Dissertation Series 6, Winona Lake.

Parker, S. T. (ed.) 1987a. *The Roman Frontier in Central Jordan*, (Interim Report on the Limes Arabicus Project) BAR S340, Oxford.

Parker, S. T. 1987b. 'History of the Late Roman Frontier East of the Dead Sea', in *idem* ed., 1987a: 793–823.

Paschoud, F. 1971 and 1979. *Zosime, Histoire Nouvelle*, I (Livres I et II) and II/1 (Livre III), Paris.

Patzig, E. 1896. 'Über einige Quellen des Zonaras', *Byzantinische Zeitschrift* 5: 24–53.

Peeters, P. 1920a. 'La Légende de S. Jacques de Nisibe', *Analecta Bollandiana* 38: 285–346.

Peeters, P. 1920b. 'Le Début de la persécution de Sapor d'après Fauste de Byzance', *RÉA* 1: 15–33.

Peeters, P. 1924. 'S. Demetrianus évêque d'Antioch?', *Analecta Bollandiana* 42: 288–314.

Peeters, P. 1931: 'L'Intervention politique de Constance II dans la Grande Arménie en 338', *Académie royale de Belgique, Bulletins de la Classe des lettres et des sciences morales et politiques*, V/17: 10–47.

Peeters, P. 1935. 'Le "Passionaire d'Adiabène"', *Analecta Bollandiana* 43: 261–304.

Peka'ry, T. 1961. 'Autour des *Res Gestae Divi Saporis*. 2. Le "tribut" aux Perses et les finances de Philippe l'Arabe', *Syria* 1961: 275–83.

Persia 1971. La Persia nel Medioevo (Roma, 31 Marzo–5 Aprile, 1970), Accademia Nazionale dei Lincei anno 368, Quaderno n. 160, Roma.

Petersen, H. 1977. 'A Roman Prefect in Osrhoene', *TAPA*, 107: 265–82.

Pflaum, H.-G. 1952. 'La fortification de la ville d'Adraha d'Arabie

(259/260 à 274/275)', *Syria* 25: 307–30.

Pflaum, H.-G. 1957. 'Les Gouverneurs de la province romaine d'Arabie de 193 à 305', *Syria* 34 (1957) 138–44.

Pflaum, H.-G. 1960. *Les carrières procuratoriennes équestres sous le Haute-Empire romaine*, Vol. 2, Paris.

Pigulevskaja, N. 1963. *Les villes de l'état iranien aux époques Parthe et Sassanide*, Paris.

Pigulevskaja, N. 1960, 'Les Arabes à la frontière de Byzance au IVe siècle', *Actes du XXVe Congrès Internationale des Orientalistes*, Moscow, 1960, I: 443–5.

Pigulewskaja, N. 1969. *Byzanz auf den Wegen nach Indien. Aus der Geschichte des byzantinischen Handels mit dem Orient vom 4.–6. Jahrhundert*, Berlin.

Poidebard, A. 1932. *La Trace de Rome dans le désert de Syrie*, 2 vols

Potter, D. S. 1985. 'An Historical Commentary on the Thirteenth Sibylline Oracle', D.Phil. Diss., Oxford Univ., unpublished.

Potter, D. S. 1990. *Prophecy and History in the Crisis of the Roman Empire. A Historical Commentary on the Thirteenth Sibylline Oracle*, Oxford.

Prentice, W. K. 1908. *Greek and Latin inscriptions*, Part III of the Publications of an American Archaeological Expedition to Syria, New York.

Reitzenstein, R. 1901. *Zwei religionsgeschichtliche Fragen nach ungedruckten griechischen Texten der Strassburger Bibliothek*, Strassburg.

Rey-Coquais, J.-P. 1978. 'Syrie romaine de Pompée à Dioclétien', *JRS* 68: 44–73

Ridley, R. T. 1973. 'Three Notes on Julian's Persian Expedition', *Historia* 22: 317–30.

Riley, D. N. 1986: 'Archaeological Air Photography and the Eastern Limes', in Freeman and Kennedy, 1986: 661–76.

Roesger, A. 1978. 'Die Darstellung des Perserfeldzugs des Severus Alexander in der *Historia Augusta*', in *Bonner Historia Augusta Colloquium 1975–1976*, Antiquitas IV, 13 Bonn: 167–74.

Röllig, W. and Kuhne, H. 1977. 'The Lower Habur, a preliminary report on a survey conducted by the *Tübinger Atlas des Vorderen Orients* in 1975', *AAS* 27: 115–40.

Rostovtzeff, M. 1943. '*Res gestae divi Saporis* and Dura', *Berytus* 8: 17–60.

Rostovtzeff, M. *et al.* 1952. *The Excavations at Dura-Europos, Ninth Session, 1935–36*, New Haven.

Russell, J. R. 1982. 'Zoroastrianism in Armenia', Ph.D. Diss., London Univ. (SOAS), unpublished.

Sabbah, G. (ed. and trans.) 1970. *Ammien Marcellin, Histoire II (Livres XVII–XIX)*, Paris.

Sarre, F. and Herzfeld, E. 1911–1920. *Archaeologische Reise im Euphrat- und Tigrisgebiet*, 4 vols, Berlin.

Sartre, M. 1982. *Trois études sur l'Arabie romaine et byzantine*, Collection Latomus 178, Brussels.

Sauvaget, J. 1941. *Alep. Essai sur le développement d'une grande ville syrienne des origines au milieu du XIXe siècle*, 2 vols, Paris.

Schachermeyr, F. 1931: 'Mesopotamien', *RE* XV/1: 1105.36–1163.47.

Schiwietz, S. 1938. *Das morgenländische Mönchtum, III, Das Mönchtum in*

Syrien und Mesopotamien und Aszetentum in Persien, Mödling bei Wien.

Schlumberger, D. 1972. 'Voród l'agoranome', *Syria* 49: 339–41.

Schwartz, J. 1966. 'L'Histoire Auguste et Palmyre', in *Bonner Historia-Augusta-Colloquium, 1964–1965*: 185–95.

Schwartz, J. 1973: 'Le *limes* selon l'*Histoire Auguste*', in *Bonner Historia-Augusta-Colloquium 1968–1969*, Antiquitas IV, 7, Bonn: 233–8.

Schwartz, J. 1976. 'Palmyre et l'opposition à Rome en Égypte', in *Palmyre 1976*: 139–51.

Schwartz, J. 1978. 'A propos des ch. 4 à 6 du *De Mortibus Persecutorum*', in J. Fontaine et M. Perrin eds, *Lactance et son temps*, Paris: 91–102.

Seeck, O. 1900. 'Constantius II', *RE* IV/1: 1044.57–1094.38.

Seeck, O. 1906. *Die Briefe des Libanius zeitlich geordnet*, Leipzig.

Seeck, O. 1911. *Geschichte des Untergangs der antiken Welt*, IV, Stuttgart.

Seeck, O. 1919. *Regesten der Kaiser und Papste für die Jahre 311 bis 476 n. Chr.*, Stuttgart.

Seeck, O. 1920. Sapor (II), *RE* IA/2: 2334.1–2354.41.

Segal, J. B. 1955. 'Mesopotamian Communities from Julian to the Rise of Islam', *Proceedings of the British Academy* 31: 109–29.

Segal, J. B. 1964. 'The Jews of N. Mesopotamia', in *Sepher Segal*, eds J. M. Grintz and J. Liver, Jerusalem: 31*–63*

Segal, J. B. 1970. *Edessa the Blessed City*, Oxford.

Seyrig, H. 1954. 'Antiquités Syriennes', *Syria* 31: 212–24.

Seyrig, H. 1963. 'Les fils du roi Odainat', *AAS* 13: 159–72.

Seyrig, H. 1966. 'Vhaballathus Augustus', *Mélanges Michalowski*, Warsaw: 659–62.

Shahid, I. 1984. *Byzantium and the Arabs in the Fourth Century*, Washington.

Sievers, R. 1868. *Das Leben des Libanius*, Berlin.

Skjaervø, P. O. (ed. and trans.) 1983 *The Sassanian Inscription of Paikuli*, Pt 3.1 (Restored text and translation), Pt 3.2. (Commentary), Wiesbaden.

Soverini, P. (ed. and trans.) 1983. *Scrittori della Storia Augusta*, 2 vols, Turin.

Speidel, M. P. 1975. 'Ethnic units in the Imperial Army', *ANRW* II/3: 202–31.

Speidel, M. P. 1977. 'The Roman Army in Arabia', *ANRW* II/8: 687–730.

Speidel, M. P. 1984. '"Europeans" – Syrian élite troops at Dura Europos and Hatra', in idem ed., *Roman Army Studies*, MAVORS 1, Amsterdam: 301–9.

Speidel. M. P. 1987. 'The Roman Road to Dumata (Jawf in Saudi Arabia) and the Frontier Strategy of *praetensione colligare*', *Historia* 36: 213–21.

Sprengling, M. 1953. *Third Century Iran. Sapor and Kartir*, Chicago.

Stark, J. K. 1971. *Personal Names in Palmyrene Inscriptions*, Oxford.

Starcky, J. and Gawlikowski, M. 1987. *Palmyre*, Paris.

Stauffenberg, A. Schenk von, 1931. *Die römische Kaisergeschichte bei Malalas, griechischer Text der Bücher IX–XII und Untersuchungen*, Stuttgart.

Stein, A. 1936. 'The Roman Limes in Syria', *Geographical Journal* 87: 66–76 (= review of Poidebard, 1932).

Stein, A. 1938. 'Note on the remains of the Roman *Limes* in North

Western Iraq', ibid. 92: 62-6.

Stein, A. 1941a. 'Surveys on the Roman Frontier in Iraq and Transjordan', ibid. 96: 299-316.

Stein, A. 1941b. 'The Ancient Trade Routes past Hatra and its Roman posts', *Journal of the Royal Asiatic Society*, 1941: 299-316. [See also under Gregory and Kennedy (eds), 1985.]

Stein, E. 1959. *Histoire du Bas-Empire I: De l'État Romain à l'État Byzantin (284-476)*, Edition française par J. R. Palanque, Paris.

Straub, J. 1980. '*Scurra barbarus*. Zum Bericht der *Historia Augusta* über das Ende des Severus Alexander', in *Bonner Historia-Augusta-Colloquium 1977-78*, Bonn: 233-53.

Sturm, J. 1936. 'Nisibis', *RE* XVII/1: 714.16-757.18.

Sullivan, R. D. 1977. 'The Dynasty of Emesa', *ANRW* 8: 197-219.

Sundermann, W. 1979. 'Die mittelpersischen und parthischen Turfantexte als Quellen zur Geschichte des vorislamischen Zentralasien', in J. Harmatta ed., *Prolegomena to the Sources on the History of Pre-Islamic Central Asia*, Budapest: 143-9.

Sundermann, W. 1981. *Mitteliranische manichäische Texte Kirchengeschichtlichen Inhalts*, Berliner Turfantexte XI, Berlin.

Sundermann, W. 1986 and 1987. 'Studien zur kirchengeschichtlichen Literatur der iranischen Manichäer II', *Altorientalische Forschungen*, 13: 239-317; III, ibid., 14: 41-107.

Suolahti, J. 1947. *On the Persian sources used by the Byzantine historian Agathias*, Studia Orientalia (Societas Orientalis Fennica) XII/9, Helsinki.

Szidat, J. 1977 and 1981. *Historischer Kommentar zu Ammianus Marcellinus Buch XX-XXI, Teil I: Die Erhebung Julians; Teil II: Die Verhandlungsphase*, Historia Einzelschriften 31 and 38, Wiesbaden.

Tavoosi, M. and Frye, R. 1990. 'An Inscribed Capital Dating from the time of Shapur I', *Bulletin of the Asia Institute* 3: 25-8.

Thompson, E. A. 1947. *The Historical Work of Ammianus Marcellinus*, Cambridge.

Thomsen, P. 1906. 'Untersuchungen zur altern Palästinaliteratur', *Zeitschrift des Deutschen Palästina-Vereins* 29: 101-28

Thomson, R. W. (ed. and trans.) 1976. *Agathangelos, History of the Armenians*, Albany, New York.

Thomson, R. W. (trans.) 1978, *Moses Khorenats'i, History of the Armenians*, Cambridge, Mass.

Thomson, R. W. (trans.) 1982. *Elishe, History of Vardan and the Armenian War*, Cambridge, Mass.

Toumanoff, C. 1969. 'The Third Century Armenian Arsacids – A chronological and genealogical commentary', *RÉA*, N.S. 6: 233-81.

Townsend, P. W. 1934. 'The administration of Gordian III', *Yale Classical Studies* 3: 59-132.

Turcan, R. 1966. 'L'Abandon de Nisibe et l'opinion publique (363 ap. J. C.)', in *Mélanges d'archéologie et d'histoire offerts à André Piganiol*, ed. R. Chevalier, Vol. 2, Paris: 875-90.

Tyler, P. 1975. *The Persian War of the Third Century AD and Roman Imperial Monetary Policy AD 253-263*, Historia Einzelschriften 23, Wiesbaden.

Van Berchem, D. 1952. *L'Armée de Dioclétien et la réforme Constantinienne*, Paris.

Van Berchem, D. 1954. 'Recherches sur la chronologie des enceintes de Syrie et de Mésopotamie', *Syria* 31: 254–70.

Van Berchem, M. and J. Strzygowski, 1910. *Amida*, Heidelberg.

Van Esbroeck, M. 1971. 'Un nouveau témoin du Livre d'Agathange', *RÉA*, n. s. 8: 13–96.

Vattioni, F. 1981, *Le inscrizioni di Hatra*, Supplemento n. 28 agli Annali, Vol. 41, fasc. 3, Naples.

Von Gerkan, A. 1935. Die Stadtmauer von Palmyra, *Berytus* 2: 25–33.

Vööbus, A. 1958a *Literary Critical and Historical Studies in Ephrem the Syrian*, Papers of the Estonian Theological Society in Exile 10, Stockholm.

Vööbus, A. 1958b. *A History of Asceticism in the Syrian Orient*, Vol. 1, CSCO 184, Subsidia 14, Louvain.

Wacher, J. (ed.) 1986. *The Roman World*, 2 vols, London.

Wagner, J. 1976. *Seleukeia am Euphrat/Zeugma*, Beihefte zum TAVO, Reihe B, Nr 10, Wiesbaden.

Wagner, J. 1977. 'Vorarbeiten zur Karte "Ostgrenze des römischen Reiches" in Tübinger Atlas des Vorderens Orients', in Fitz 1977: 669–93.

Wagner, J. 1983. 'Provincia Osrhoenae'. New archaeological finds illustrating the military organization under the Severan Dynasty, in Mitchell 1983: 103–30.

Warmington, B. H. 1976. 'Objectives and Strategy in the Persian War of Constantius II', in Fitz, 1977: 509–20.

Watzinger, C. 1940. 'Dura (Europos)', RE Suppl. VII: 149.7–169.31.

Welles, C. B. 1941. 'The Epitaph of Julius Terentius', *Harvard Theological Review* 34: 79–102.

Welles, C. B. 1951. 'The Roman population of Dura', in *Studies in Honour of A. C. Johnson*, Princeton, New Jersey.

Welles, C. B. *et al.* 1959. *The Excavations at Dura-Europos, Final Report V, The Parchments and Papyri*, New Haven.

Wheeler, R. E. 1952. 'The Roman Frontier in Mesopotamia', *The Congress of Roman Frontier Studies* (= *Limes Congress 1*), Durham: 112–28.

Whitby, L. M. 1983. 'Arzanene in the Late Sixth Century', in Mitchell, 1983: 205–18.

Whittaker, C. H. (ed. and trans.) 1970. *Herodian, II* (*Bks. V–VIII*), LCL, London and Cambridge, Mass.

Widengren, G. 1971. 'The Establishment of the Sassanian Dynasty in the Light of New Evidence', in *Persia 1971*: 711–82.

Will, E. 1966. 'Le sac de Palmyre', *Festschrift A. Piganiol*, Paris: 1409–16.

Wilson, D. R. 1960. 'Two Milestones from Pontus', *Anatolian Studies*, 10: 133–40.

Winkler, G. 1980. 'Our present knowledge of the History of Agat'angelos', *RÉA*, N. S. 14: 125–41.

Winter, E. 1988. *Die sasanidisch-römischen Friedensverträge des 3. Jahrhunderts n. Chr. – ein Beitrag zum Verständnis der aussenpolitischen Beziehungen zwischen den beiden Grossmachten*, Frankfurt am Main.

Wirth, G. 1978, 'Julians Perserkrieg. Kriterien einer Katastrophe', in R.

Klein ed, *Julian Apostata*, Wege der Forschung 509, Darmstadt: 455–507.

Wirth, G. 1980–1981. 'Rom, Parther und Sassaniden, Erwägungen zu den Hintergründen eines historischen Wechselverhältnisses', *Ancient Society* 11–12: 305–47.

Wright, W. 1872. *Catalogue of the Syriac Manuscripts in the British Museum*, Part 3, London.

Yarshater, E. 1971. 'Were the Sassanians heirs to the Achaemenids?', in *Persia 1971*: 517–31.

Yarshater, E. (ed.) 1983. *The Cambridge History of Iran*, Vol. 3, 2 pts, Cambridge.

Ziegler, K. H. 1964. *Die Beziehungen zwischen Rom und dem Partherreich*, Wiesbaden.

POSTSCRIPT

The following articles which contain new sources relevant to Chapter 2 of this book appeared too late to be fully utilized in this collection which was completed in early 1989:

Feissel D. and Gascou, J. 1989. 'Documents d'archives romains inédits du Moyen Euphrate (IIIe siècle après J.-C.)', *CRAI* 1989 (July-Dec.): 531–61.

Tavoosi, M. and Frye, R. 1990. 'An inscribed capital dating from the time of Shapur I', *Bulletin of the Asia Institute (of Wayne State University)*, 3: 25–8.

Teixidor, J. 1989. 'Les derniers rois d'Edesse d'après deux nouveaux documents syriaques', *ZPE* 76: 219–22.

The following important monographs on the Eastern Frontier also appeared too late to be used for our work:

French, D.H. and Lightfoot, C.S. (ed.) 1989. *The Eastern Frontier of the Roman Empire. Proceedings of a colloquium held at Ankara in September 1988.*

Isaac, B. 1989, 2nd edn 1992. *The Limits of Empire. The Roman Army in the East*, Oxford.

Kennedy, D. and Riley, J. 1991. *Rome's Desert Frontier from the Air*, London.

Particularly important among the many books and articles on Romano-Persian relations and the Eastern Frontier published since 1991 is:

Blockley, R.C. 1992. *East Roman Foreign Policy, Formation and Conduct from Diocletian to Anastasius*, Leeds.

Important note on 6.2.1 (p. 146)

Cedrenus has based his account of Constantine's Persian campaign and the construction work of Euphratas almost entirely from Byzantine hagiographical material on the Emperor. (For examples of his possible sources see Guidi, I. 1907. 'Un *BIOS* di Constantino', *Rendiconti della Reale accademia dei Lincei, Classe di Scienze Morali, Storiche e Filologiche*, 5th Ser. 16: 316–19. Halkin, F. 1959, 'Une nouvelle vie de Constantin dans un legendier de Patmos', *Analecta Bollandiana* 77: 84–91 and Devos, P. 1982, 'Une recension nouvelle de la passion grecque BHG 639 de Saint Eusignios', *Analecta Bollandiana* 100: 225–7. For a critical discussion of these later sources on Constantine see esp. Kazhdan, A. 1987. 'Constantine "imaginaire"'. Byzantine legends of the ninth century about Constantine the Great, *Byzantion* 57: 234–40.) Cedrenus' account, which is not corroborated by more contemporary sources, therefore has no historical value except as an example of the popular desire among Byzantine hagiographers to portray Constantine as a victor over oriental foes.

(Lieu)

Index of translated passages

General index